BEHAVIORAL, SOCIAL, AND EMOTIONAL ASSESSMENT OF CHILDREN AND ADOLESCENTS

Behavioral, Social, and Emotional Assessment of Children and Adolescents

Kenneth W. Merrell
THE UNIVERSITY OF IOWA

LEA LAWRENCE ERLBAUM ASSOCIATES, PUBLISHERS

1999 Mahwah, New Jersey   London

Lawrence Erlbaum Associates, Inc., Publishers
10 Industrial Avenue
Mahwah, NJ 07430

Cover design by Kathryn Houghtaling Lacey

Library of Congress Cataloging-in-Publication Data

Merrell, Kenneth W.
Behavioral, social, and emotional assessment of children and adolescents / Kenneth W. Merrell.
p. cm
Includes bibliographical references and index.
ISBN 0-8058-2886-9 (hardcover : alk. paper).
1. Psychological tests for children. 2. Child development—Testing.
3. Behavioral assessment of children. 4. Teenagers—Psychological
testing. 5. Behavioral assessment of teenagers. I. Title.
BF722.M45 1998
155.4'028'7—dc21   98-8363
                                                            CIP

Printed in the United States of America

10   9   8   7   6   5   4   3

Contents in Brief

CONTENTS

PREFACE

During the past two or three decades, the enterprise of psychological and educational assessment of children and adolescents has witnessed some incredible advancements in research and applications. New and innovative developments have occurred rapidly, sometimes outstripping the ability of the field to keep pace with them. At the same time, psychological and educational assessment practices with youth have continued to be mired in some of the same traps and impasses that have existed for years. One only needs to briefly consider the continuing failure to effectively link assessment to valid systems of classification and treatment, a reliance on assessment methods and techniques that are substantially lacking in empirical support, a lack of sensitivity of many current assessment practices to important group and individual differences, and the gross misuse of assessment technology to understand that the field still has a long way to go.

This book attempts to help elevate the practice of psychological and educational assessment of children and adolescents—specifically, the domain of behavioral social and emotional assessment—to the increasingly higher standards that we as professionals are setting for ourselves. In my view, this type of assessment has been particularly vulnerable to some of the continuing problems associated with misuse and poor assessment practice. Thus, this book was developed to provide a foundation or road map for conducting comprehensive assessments of child and adolescent social-emotional behavior in a practical, defensible, empirically sound, and culturally appropriate manner. It was written as both a graduate level training textbook and a practical professional reference book. It is specifically relevant to the fields of school psychology and clinical child psychology. However, professionals in related fields who work with children and youth with behavioral social and emotional problems (e.g., special education, counseling, social work, and child psychiatry) may also find it useful.

The chapters within are roughly divided into two major sections. Part I, *Foundations and Methods of Assessment*, includes eight chapters that provide a general foundation for assessment practice. These chapters include coverage of basic professional and ethical issues, classification and diagnostic problems, and comprehensive introductions to six primary assessment methods: behavioral observation, behavior rating scales, clinical interviewing, sociometric techniques, self-report instruments, and projective-expressive techniques. Part II, *Assessment of Specific Problems, Competencies, and Populations,* includes six chapters regarding applications for assessing specific social-emotional behavior domains, including externalizing problems, internalizing problems, other problems, social skills and peer relationships, young children, and diverse cultural groups. Together, these two sections provide a framework for a model of assessment that is practical, flexible, sensitive to specific needs, and empirically sound. To the greatest extent possible, this book weaves together the most recent research evidence and common application issues in a scholarly yet practical manner. It is intended to complement professional training, and not to act as a substitute for it.

Technically speaking, this book is a revision of a previous work, *Assessment of Behavioral, Social, and Emotional Problems: Direct and Objective Methods for Use With Children and Adolescents* (Merrell, 1994a). However, the changes implemented are substantial, and in many respects it is a new work, reflecting a new title, a new publisher, a broadened emphasis, and a significant amount of new material. Each of the chapters that were retained from the 1994 work were *substantially* updated and enlarged. New chapters on projective-expressive techniques, assessment of "other" problems, assessment of young children, and assessment and cultural diversity have been added. The strong empirical model that was proposed in the 1994 work has been retained but modified to be more flexible, encompassing, and inclusive. These changes reflect the continuing evolution and refinement of psychological and educational assessment. It is assumed that further changes will be needed to keep pace with future developments in this dynamic field.

ACKNOWLEDGMENTS

I would like to acknowledge the editorial staff at Lawrence Erlbaum Associates, particularly Lane Akers, for their confidence in my work, and for their willingness and commitment to make this book the best that it could be. I would also like to acknowledge the LEA production staff for their high quality, timely, and careful work with this book.

My family has been a continual source of support and encouragement during the preparation of this book during the past 5 years. Thanks Susan, Emily, Daniel, Ben, and Joanna. You provide the grounding that has made possible the constructive expression of my creativity.

My thinking and practice regarding behavioral social and emotional assessment of children and adolescents, and the general direction of my work in this area, have been influenced greatly by several academic colleagues with whom I have worked closely thus far in my career. In this regard, I would especially like to acknowledge Hill Walker, Stephanie Stein, Susan Crowley, Grayson Osborne, and Gretchen Gimpel.

Finally, I wish to acknowledge all the graduate students with whom I worked at Utah State University and The University of Iowa between 1994 and 1998, the time period in which this book was either being contemplated or under active construction. Their enthusiastic involvement in clinical assessment of children has helped me to advance my thinking in this area in a major way. I especially would like to acknowledge Clarice Jentzsch, Amy Walters, Paul Caldarella, Lisa McClun, Deanna Sanders, Mike Williams, Kurt Michael, and Melissa Holland for taking an active part in my research and for challenging me to take my work to higher levels. Their suggestions, insights, and applications have made this a better book. Their struggles, triumphs, and trust have made me a better person.

PART

I

FOUNDATIONS AND METHODS
OF ASSESSMENT

1

FOUNDATIONS OF ASSESSMENT

This chapter introduces some important issues in social-emotional assessment, provides a foundation for understanding the design and flow of subsequent chapters, and overviews the current state of the art in best assessment practices. It begins with an orientation to the referral process, and discusses how it should shape the approach to assessment, which is conceptualized and proposed as a comprehensive problem-solving process. A discussion of pertinent legal and ethical issues in assessment follows, and specific recommendations for legal and ethical assessment practices are provided. The focus then turns to how theory guides practice and provides a detailed outline of social cognitive theory, which is emphasized in this book. The last sections serve to map out what is referred to as direct and objective assessment, and to illustrate the preferred way for conducting assessments of behavioral, social, and emotional problems through the use of a multimethod, multisource, multisetting design. The chapter ends with a brief discussion of what criteria were used for including specific assessment techniques and instruments within the book. Essentially, this chapter serves as an introduction and guide for understanding the overall goals of the entire text.

THEORETICAL FOUNDATIONS OF SOCIAL AND EMOTIONAL BEHAVIOR

Think about this for a moment: Can practitioners conduct reliable and valid assessments of youngsters with behavioral, social, and emotional problems without being firmly grounded in a theoretical orientation as to how these problems develop, progress, and change? Well, they might administer some tests and interpret the results under this scenario. But is this type of approach the most desirable? It is probably not. Without a solid theoretical background and orientation, the assessor is relegated to the role of a technician or tester, and no matter how skilled, may never integrate the assessment findings to the subject's past and future with an adequate degree of continuity or unity. Additionally, developing a solid theoretical understanding of the origins of

theory + assessment

this book adheres to a social learning / social cognitive theory

behavioral, social, and emotional problems may have important implications when it is time to link assessment results to a workable intervention plan.

Without attempting to be dogmatic, this book was designed with a specific theoretical foundation in mind, namely, social learning or social cognitive theory. Before delving into an exploration of social learning theory, this section first briefly discusses some other approaches to conceptualizing human behavior, and then explores social cognitive theory and its related approach to explaining the influences of human behavior, namely, triadic reciprocality.

no one unitary force of Ψ thought

To say there is a traditional theory of human behavior, or even a small handful of these theories, in modern psychology is misleading. Whereas psychodynamic theory and behaviorism were strong unitary forces in the early days of psychology, neither one of these schools of thought, like most other ways of conceptualizing human behavior, is currently considered a unitary force; as they have matured, to some extent they have split into factions or differing schools of thought that go back to the same lineage.

Consider behaviorism as an example. In the modern world of behaviorism, there are divergent schools of thought that take significantly different approaches and yet still fall under the umbrella of behaviorism. The "true believers" in behaviorism are probably those who claim the strongest legacy to Skinner, Watson, and Raynor, and ultimately to Thorndike. This contingent of behaviorism is perhaps best exemplified by those who are active practitioners of applied behavior analysis, which can be traced directly to B. F. Skinner's brilliant and voluminous work spanning from 1930 to 1990. To summarize applied behavior analysis or the work of Skinner within a few short sentences is both simplistic and presumptuous to say the least, but there is a point to be made here: This school of thought within behaviorism contends that behavior is shaped by controlling and consequential forces within the environment, which is the key to understanding, predicting, and changing behavior. On the other hand, a more recent school of thought within the behavioral world is a diverse group of individuals and ideas for changing behavior that center around the term *cognitive behavioral therapy.* This loose-knit faction does indeed claim some legacy to Skinner's work, as emitted behaviors, consequences, and the environment are important. However, the emphasis on internal cognitive processes and mediating events that links most theories in cognitive behavioral therapy is a clear departure from the framework advocated by Skinner and his colleagues. In fact, shortly before his death in 1990, Skinner presented a keynote address at the meeting of the American Psychological Association in which he thoroughly lambasted "cognitive science," portraying it as a misguided attempt to explain human behavior through studying underlying mental processes that is a throwback to turn-of-the-century introspectionism.

Many small branches of diff schools in Ψ

The point to be made by this brief analysis of the evolution of modern behaviorism is that the traditional theoretical schools of thought that are discussed in general psychology textbooks have evolved tremendously, over the years, often branching into smaller groups that share common backgrounds. This same process is also true for other traditional theoretical schools of thought, such as psychodynamic theory, the neurobiological model, and the humanistic movement. The philosophical base of each of these areas has evolved tremendously, and there are no longer just a small and powerful handful of theoretical schools with which a practitioner may be aligned. In fact, present-day clinicians and researchers are much more likely to consider themselves "eclectic" in their theoretical approach to human behavior than to rigidly align themselves with a particular school of thought. These present circumstances have

Today = Eclectic

[handwritten: dual effect = ① less dogmatism ② Lack of theoretical foundation 5]

had a <u>dual effect</u>: On the one hand, the decreasing amount of dogmatism has paved the way for acceptance of new and influential theories such as social cognitive theory, but on the other hand, the current generation of clinicians are perhaps less likely to place a great deal of thought on their theoretical orientation, which could lead to an unanchored approach to assessment and treatment.

Social Cognitive Theory: An Integrated Orientation

[handwritten: Cog theory = cause ←→ effect]

Social cognitive theory, a primary underlying orientation within this book, is a sophisticated and complex theory that takes into account not only the multiple causes of behavioral, social, and emotional problems, but the reciprocal nature of the relation between causes and effects. This theory is not overviewed in order to proselytize the nonbeliever—it is not a philosophy of life and does not have to carry any metaphysical implications. Social cognitive theory is proposed as a solid foundation for assessment of children and adolescents because it takes into account many potential factors contributing to the assessment problems, it is flexible, and in its fullest form, has strong implications for linking assessment data to intervention planning.

[handwritten: BANDURA]

Components of Social Cognitive Theory. Social cognitive theory, and the related concepts of triadic reciprocality and observational learning, are based on the work of Bandura (1977, 1978, 1986). Most persons who have studied psychology and related fields at the graduate level are familiar with Bandura's work on social learning processes in aggression. These processes were demonstrated in the famous "Bobo Doll" experiments, wherein the effects of models and perceived consequences were found to have a tremendous impact on both aggressive and prosocial behavior in school-age and preschool-age children. These particular demonstrations of social cognitive theory do not tell the full story, nor account for the entire complexity of the process. Although it is impossible to completely detail social cognitive theory within a portion of one book chapter (for a comprehensive account, see Bandura, 1986), it is useful to at least review its major components.

[handwritten: People are shaped from internal + external forces]

As stated by Bandura (1986), social cognitive theory holds that people "are neither driven by inner forces nor automatically shaped and controlled by external stimuli. Rather, human functioning is explained in terms of a model of triadic reciprocality in which behavior, cognitive and other personal factors, and environmental events all operate as determinants of each other" (p. 18). The nature of persons is explained in terms of five basic human capabilities: *symbolizing capability, forethought capability, vicarious capability, self-regulatory capability,* and *self-reflective capability.*

<u>Symbolizing capability</u> is said to involve the use of various symbols, including language, as a means of altering and adapting to different environments. The use of symbols <u>allows communication</u> with others, even at distant times or places. <u>Forethought capability</u> consists of the <u>anticipation</u> of likely consequences of behavior, and is demonstrated by intentional and purposive actions that are future-oriented. <u>Vicarious capability</u> is illustrated by the fact that <u>not all learning must result from direct</u> experience, but can occur through the observation of other persons' behaviors and the consequences that follow them. <u>Self-regulatory capability</u> affects the development of individuals' <u>internal standards and self-evaluative reactions</u> to their behavior—discrepancies between people's internal standards and their actual behaviors serve to govern their future behavior. <u>Self-reflective capability</u> involves <u>self-consciousness</u>, or the uniquely human ability that enables people to think about and evaluate their own

thought processes. Put together, these five fundamental human capabilities are the basis for individuals' vast human potential, and help explain the inner workings that result in their behavioral output.

Triadic Reciprocality: Understanding the Determinants of Behavior. The social cognitive viewpoint supports a conception of the causes of human behavior being due to *reciprocal determinism*. The idea behind reciprocal determinism is that the causes behind an individual's behavior become influenced and shaped by the behavior itself. Specifically, the type of reciprocal determinism favored by social cognitive theory is known as *triadic reciprocality* (Bandura, 1977, 1978). This view contends that behavior, environmental influences, and various personal factors (such as cognition, temperament, biology) all work together in an interactive manner, and have the effect of acting as determinants of each other. Bandura's theory of triadic reciprocality is illustrated in Fig. 1.1.

Triadic reciprocality in social cognitive theory can be exemplified in practical terms through an example of the interaction process between parents and a newborn child. For example, take a scenario where the infant happens to have a very "high-strung," or irritable, temperament, which is present at birth and is probably biological in nature. The infant's irritable temperament is an example of a personal factor. Because this particular infant tends to cry almost constantly, is highly demanding, and sleeps only for short periods of time (behavioral factors), an environment is created where constant demands, noise, and limited opportunities for sleep interact with the personal factors of the parents, to help shape their own behavior and characteristics in the direction of them being constantly tired, more irritable than normal, anxious, and perhaps somewhat depressed. The behavior of the parents continues to shape the environment of the child, and the child's behavior continues to shape the environment of the parents, which in turn affect their personal characteristics. If the infant persists in being highly irritable and demanding, and the parents tend to reinforce these demands with immediate attention, the child's irritable-demanding personal characteristics will probably become strengthened and persist. If the parents learn to deal with their child in a quiet and relaxed manner, the child's demanding irritability may be reduced, and the behavioral demands in the environment may change.

In expanding on Bandura's social cognitive model/triadic reciprocality models, Kauffman (1989) related it to what he referred to as an *interactional-transactional model* of influence. Whereas triadic reciprocality and the interactional-transactional model are much too complex to cover in one chapter section, they can be reduced into two

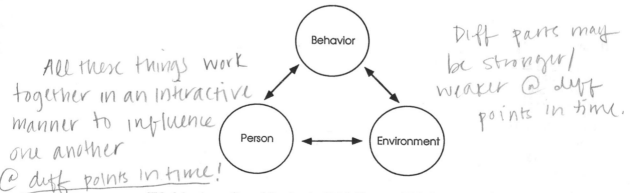

All these things work together in an interactive manner to influence one another @ diff points in time!

Diff parts may be stronger/ weaker @ diff points in time.

FIG. 1.1. An outline of Bandura's (1986) Theory of Triadic Reciprocality.

[handwritten margin note at top: Two points of triadic reciprocality + inter/trans = ① child + adult have = effects on each other ② understand family interact. by taking reciprocity into account.]

[handwritten page number: 7]

points on family influences that are highly salient for conducting assessments of behavioral, social, and emotional problems: "(1) children have effects on adults that are equal to adults' effects on children, and (2) family interactions are understandable only when reciprocal influences of parent and children on each other are taken into account" (Kauffman, 1989, p. 165). Patterson and his associates at the Oregon Social Learning Center (e.g., Patterson, 1982; Patterson, Reid, & Dishion, 1992) also wrote extensively on the phenomena of reciprocal influences in developmental psychopathology, particularly antisocial behavior. Their numerous investigations into the topic have linked the development and maintenance of child behavioral and emotional problems to coercive, reciprocal interactions within families. It takes only a small leap from these examples of parent–child interactions to understand that human behavior is shaped through complex, mutually influential interactions, whether it is in the home, school, workplace, or community. *[handwritten: Behav. shaped by mutual interactions]*

In completing this discussion of triadic reciprocality, it is useful to understand that the three parts of the triad (personal, behavioral, and environmental factors) are thought to make differing contributions at various points in time. Bandura (1986) noted that "reciprocality does not mean symmetry in the strength of the bidirectional influences . . . [and] the triadic factors do not operate in the manner of a simultaneous holistic interaction" (pp. 24–25). In other words, there are times when an environmental factor may become the strongest influence in the reciprocal interaction, and at other times, personal factors of behavior may become preeminent. The important thing is to consider *[handwritten: ✱]* that each factor may influence and shape the other two in some way.

[handwritten: modelling = rule learning a behav]

Observational Learning: A Multiprocess Analysis. To conclude this brief excursion into social cognitive theory, it is worthwhile to take a brief look at the process of *observational learning.* As outlined by Bandura (1977, 1986), observational learning is a model for understanding the learning process in a social context, fully compatible with social cognitive theory and triadic reciprocality. Individuals who have only a superficial knowledge of observational learning might consider it to be equivalent to simple modeling or mimicking of behavior, but it is far more comprehensive than such comparisons would suggest. As Bandura (1986) stated, "Most human behavior is learned by observation through modeling . . . [but] in skill acquisition, modeling is more accurately represented as rule learning rather than mimicry" (pp. 47–48).

What then are the elements that guide the process of rule learning? Bandura (1986) *[handwritten: 5 diff effects that guide modelling]* outlined five different types of *effects* that are said to guide the process of modeling. *Observational learning effects* include new behaviors, cognitive skills, and standards of judgment that are acquired through directly observing others. These effects are thought to be stronger when the behavior observed is novel or unique. *Inhibitory and disinhibitory effects* determine how likely it is that a newly learned behavior will be demonstrated. It is more likely that a newly learned behavior will be performed if a person believes that a positive outcome will result, and less likely if it is perceived that a negative outcome will result. Individuals' perception of what is likely or not likely to happen following their behaviors will either inhibit or disinhibit them from performing those behaviors. *Response facilitation effects* involve the actions of others that serve as social prompts for people to engage in behaviors they have learned. Peer pressure or encouragement is an example of how a child is prompted to engage in certain social behaviors. *Environmental enhancement effects* encompass the physical circumstances of the environment individuals have observed in that it will result in their performing a behavior in a certain way. For example, a child who has observed two other children fighting on the playground where one child "wins" the fight by throwing a handful of dirt and gravel might engage in the same behavior if confronted with a conflict situation in the same spot. Finally, *arousal effects* involve the level of emotional intensity, or arousal, that are elicited in observers. When emotional arousal is heightened, the form or intensity of ongoing behaviors can be altered; interactions that might normally result in an argument might result in a fistfight in an environment of intense emotional arousal. In sum, these five modeling effects can serve to instruct, inhibit or disinhibit, facilitate, and enhance the behaviors people engage in, whether they are prosocial, neutral, or antisocial in nature.

Observational learning also involves four related cognitive processes that help determine how effectively individuals are able to learn through observation. According to Bandura (1986), these four processes work as follows:

1. *Attentional processes.* Learning will only occur through the observational process if adequate attention is focused on the event. It is interesting to note that humans do not give their attention equally to all stimuli—people are more focused and attentive if the behavior is novel, or if they consider the model to have high status.

2. *Retention processes.* Retention processes involve the encoding of the event or behavior individuals have observed into their memory. There is some evidence that two major memory systems are involved in retention processes: imaginal and verbal (Barnett & Zucker, 1990).

3. *Production processes.* This subprocess pertains to people's ability to actually perform the behaviors they have observed and retained. In this sense, motor abilities are often involved, and may limit people's ability to enact the behavior they have learned. Although virtually all basketball aficionados would pay careful attention to and be able to retain a memory representation of a star athlete's trademark slam-dunks, very few could actually produce the behavior.

4. *Motivational processes.* In social cognitive theory, there is a differentiation between learning and performance, as people tend not to enact everything they learn. Whether or not individuals are motivated to enact a newly learned behavior depends mainly on the incentives they believe are involved. Incentives can be either internal or external, and can be direct, vicarious, or self-produced.

In sum, although there are many competing theories on the development of human behavioral, social, and emotional problems, social cognitive theory has many advantages for conceptualizing and assessing child and adolescent behavioral and emotional problems, and is emphasized in this text. Social cognitive theory and its related processes and components offer a highly sophisticated and relevant framework for conceptualizing the referral problems and treatment issues in assessing children and adolescents. Although it is not necessary to adopt social cognitive theory (or any other theoretical approach) in order to conduct technically adequate assessments, using it as a basis for understanding will allow for better conceptualization of referral problems, and for a framework to deal with the assessment-intervention process in a cohesive manner.

Finding a Theoretical Foundation That Works for You

This section illustrates the importance of having a theoretical foundation for assessment. The integrated development of theory and philosophy as a foundation for assessing and treating human behavior is increasingly being ignored or minimized in graduate training programs in professional psychology and related mental health fields. It seems as though the generic umbrella of eclecticism in selecting treatment techniques is being used as a substitute for putting any serious thought into the development of a personal framework for conceptualizing child and adolescent social and emotional behavior. What many graduate students and professionals do not fully comprehend is that the move toward pragmatic eclecticism in selecting appropriate treatment modalities does not replace a solid theoretical foundation for conceptualizing how problems begin in the first place. Without an underpinning theoretical framework for conceptualizing behavior, professionals conducting assessments move out of the scientist-practitioner mode, and relegate their conduct to the role of technician.

Social-cognitive theory has been outlined in this chapter and is emphasized to some extent throughout the book. Despite the value and appeal of this theory for professionals conducting child and adolescent assessments, it is understood that it will not fit equally well with all professionals. Therefore, readers are strongly encouraged to put some serious thought into their own views on the human condition, and to adopt and develop an appropriate and congruent underlying theoretical framework to guide their practice. There are many benefits to taking such a step.

UNDERSTANDING AND CLARIFYING ASSESSMENT REFERRALS

Any professional with experience in assessing children would agree that referrals for assessment come in a wide variety of dimensions. Sometimes, the pervasive nature of the problems leading to the referral make professionals contemplate why the referral did not happen earlier. And, at other times, the character of the referral problem seems so benign as to make them consider if there was truly a need for it in the first place. What these disparate examples serve to illustrate is that in order to conduct a sound assessment, the reasons for referral and circumstances leading up to the point of referral must first be carefully analyzed and explored. Practically every child will at some time exhibit behavioral, social, or emotional problems serious enough to cause some concern for their parents or teachers, but a relatively small percentage of these problems will ever result in a referral for assessment or treatment. What, then, are the factors that result in behavioral, social, or emotional problems being taken to the point of referral? Investigate the reasons for referral!

It is important to consider that, unlike adult mental health clients, who are typically self-referred, children and adolescents are usually referred for assessment by someone else (such as a parent or teacher), and very often do not even recognize or admit that their perceived problems exist, or understand why the assessment is happening. Knoff (1986) suggested that referrals are often "the result of a perceived discrepancy between the referred child's behaviors, attitudes, or interpersonal interactions . . . and some more optimal level desired and defined by the referral source" (p. 4). The basis of these discrepancies is thought to stem from different perspectives that define the referral sources' idea of what constitutes acceptable and unacceptable social-emotional behavior.

Three specific perspectives that influence referral decisions have been postulated by Knoff (1986), including the *sociocultural perspective*, the *community subgroup perspective*, and the *setting-specific perspective*. The sociocultural perspective involves the broad environment within a community: generalized precepts about what constitutes acceptable and unacceptable ways of behaving that are pervasive at most levels within a given community or society. A child or adolescent who is referred because of a discrepancy related to this perspective would likely be exhibiting behaviors that are in opposition to overall societal standards. Community subgroup perspectives are shaped by smaller groups within a community—religious organizations, neighborhoods, and specific cultural or ethnic groups, for example. Referrals related to discrepancies from this perspective may involve behaviors or attitudes that are unacceptable within one subgroup but may be acceptable within another. For example, adolescents who listen to rap or rock music and adopt attitudes based on this form of artistic expression may cause considerable concern within some community subgroups, but go almost unnoticed within others. The setting-specific perspective involves social-behavioral norms that are very distinctive to individual settings, such as specific families and classrooms; what is tolerated as normal by some parents or teachers may be totally unacceptable to others.

The essential point to consider in analyzing referrals from these perspectives is that all three are interdependent. One cannot focus singly on a given perspective without taking into account the others. Children who come from a family background where there is open disrespect for a general societal standard, such as law enforcement, may reject typically acceptable standards of behavior in the school or community while still maintaining solidarity with the standards set within their family. In contrast, children with families who have recently immigrated from another part of the world might adopt typical values of their new culture that create dissension within the family but are hardly cause for notice within the school or larger community. So, it becomes the job of the clinician to carefully examine the reasons for referral, and how these reasons relate to the three basic perspectives. In some cases, referrals may need to be refused as being improper, and in other cases, the referral may require a complete assessment to determine to what extent behavioral, social, or emotional problems are present.

Clinician must examine the referral in reference to the perspective it comes from.

ASSESSMENT AS A PROBLEM-SOLVING PROCESS

Given that assessment is one of the primary activities of many psychologists and other education/mental health practitioners, it is surprising that so little attention has been paid to identifying and clarifying the purposes of assessment. There are many specific potential purposes for assessment, such as problem clarification, diagnosis, classification, intervention planning, and intervention evaluation. And yet, some practitioners continue to view assessment as being synonymous with *testing*. In reality, these two activities are related, but not equal. Testing is the process of administering and scoring tests, whether they be simple or complex. Within the most narrow interpretation of the process, testing can become both a means and an end, a nearly self-contained activity. Assessment, on the other hand, is clearly superordinate to testing. Assessment, in the broad view, is a process whereby information is gathered regarding a specific problem or issue. This information-gathering process may also involve testing, but not out of necessity. A critical aspect of the broad view of assessment is that it is a means to an end, rather than an end in and of itself. Ideally, the end result of assessment will be to gather information that may be used to help solve specific problems.

"Testing" vs. Assessment

There have been a few attempts to develop models of assessment as a problem-solving process. For example, Sloves, Docherty, and Schneider (1979) proposed a scientific problem-solving model of psychological assessment that consisted of three

Problem-Solving Model of Assess. differs greatly from "testing"

basic elements: a six-step problem-solving process, levels of organizational action, and methods. The purpose of this model was to help differentiate the practice of psychological assessment as a process of problem solving from testing as one set of methods for problem solving. In a similar vein, Nezu (1993) delineated a conceptual model of assessment based on a problem-solving framework, whereby the clinician is considered the problem-solver, and the problem to be solved is the discrepancy between the client's current state and desired state. Both of these model-building attempts are laudable, as are other attempts to promote assessment as a broad problem-solving process. And yet, the reality of the situation is that none of these models fully integrates the assessing social and emotional behavior of children and adolescents into a comprehensive problem-solving process. *Neither model integrates the assess. of soc/emo behav into a prob-solving process!*

A Proposed Model for Assessment as a Problem-Solving Process

Given the importance of viewing assessment as a broad problem-solving process, as well as the lack of an adequate theoretical model for viewing social-emotional assessment in this regard, a four-phase model of assessment as a problem-solving process is proposed. This model, illustrated in Table 1.1, was developed to be specifically relevant to the problems inherent in assessing social and emotional behavior of children and adolescents. However, it is broad enough in its scope that it can easily accommodate other applications of assessment. This model is based on the premise that within the four basic phases of assessment, a series of basic questions can help guide assessment practice into appropriate actions so that assessment truly becomes a process of problem solving.

model = Questions that lead to problem solving

TABLE 1.1
A Proposed Model for Assessment as a Problem-Solving Process

Phase I: Identification and Clarification
  Who is the client (or who are the clients)?
  From the client's perspective, what is the problem?
  What is the intended purpose of the assessment?

Phase II: Data Collection
  What information is needed?
  What assessment methods, procedures, and tests will best provide this information?
  Which of the potential means of gathering information are most appropriate for this specific client, problem, and situation?

Phase III: Analysis
  Does the assessment information confirm the problem?
  What other information do the assessment data provide regarding the problem?
  How can the assessment information be used to answer specific referral questions?
  What are the factors that appear to contribute to the problem?
  Is there any missing assessment information that is needed to help analyze this problem? If so, how can it be obtained?

Phase IV: Solution and Evaluation
  Based on all the available information, what should be the target for intervention?
  What appear to be the most appropriate types of intervention?
  What resources are available to implement the intervention?
  Which means of assessment can be used to collect data continuously during intervention?
  Which means of assessment can be used to evaluate the effectiveness of the solution?

Phase I: Identification and Clarification.   The first phase is titled *Identification and Clarification.* Within this phase it is critical to answer some basic questions that will lead to clearly articulating the purpose of assessment. First, it is essential to identify the client. In reality, this identification is often complex. Everyone would agree that the referred child or adolescent is the client, but it is also likely that the referral agent, such as parents or teachers, is the client as well, given that they have a specific interest in the outcome of the assessment. Second, it is critical to clearly delineate the nature of the problem from the client's perspective. Sometimes the perceived problem is anything but straightforward, and there may actually be multiple problems from the client's perspective. Third, the clinician must identify what is the intended purpose or purposes of the assessment. Again, it is possible that there will be more than one purpose, such as diagnosing the problem, determining eligibility for specific services, and helping to develop a plan of intervention.

What assess. measures to use?

Phase II: Data Collection.   The second phase of the model is where the assessment data are actually gathered. Rather than mindlessly gathering information through administration of a standard battery of procedures that is the same for everyone, the problem-solving clinician will let the purposes of the assessment and the characteristics of the client and problem guide the selection of assessment procedures. First, it is essential to clearly identify what information is needed. Second, the clinician should determine which assessment methods, procedures, and tests will best provide the needed information. Third, after some basic decisions have been made regarding what information is needed, the clinician should analyze carefully the specific nature of the client, problem, and situation to determine whether some means of information gathering may be more appropriate than others. For example, if the main referral issue is inattentive and hyperactive behavior problems, it would make sense to select a behavior rating scale for completion by parents or teachers that is specifically designed to evaluate the characteristics of attention deficit hyperactivity disorder (ADHD). However, in some cases, there may also be evidence of co-occurring conduct problems such as aggressive and antisocial behavior. Thus, in the latter situation, a broad-band externalizing behavior problem rating scale would be a better choice than a scale designed solely to evaluate ADHD characteristics.

Phase III: Analysis.   In the third phase of the process, the obtained assessment data are analyzed in detail. Some of the questions that may be most useful in guiding this process involve whether or not the data confirm the problem, what other information the data provide regarding the problem, how the data can be used to answer specific referral questions, what other factors appear to be contributing to the problem, and what, if any, assessment data are missing. If any assessment information is missing, the clinician must also ask if this information can be obtained, and if so, how.

Phase IV: Solution and Evaluation.   The final phase of assessment as a problem-solving process is perhaps the most difficult, using the obtained assessment information to develop a solution to the problem, and ultimately, to evaluate the effectiveness of the solution. First, the main target or targets for intervention should be selected, based on all the available information. Second, the most appropriate types of intervention for these targets should be identified, as should the potential resources for implementing such intervention. These second and third questions in the phase should guide the development of a specific intervention plan. The fourth and fifth questions in the phase are often overlooked, but should be considered essential if assessment will truly result in problem solving. Once an intervention plan has been developed, it is also essential to consider how data can be continuously collected during the intervention to help determine whether the desired effect is occurring. This type of continuous data collection is closely linked to the process of *formative evaluation*, or making decisions that will guide instruction or treatment practices on an ongoing basis. Finally, it is often appropriate to use assessment procedures to assist in *summative evaluation* of the intervention, or whether it has produced the desired changes after it has been implemented.

This proposed model represents a practical commonsense approach to assessment as a broad process for solving problems. Other models, including models developed individually by clinicians to serve their own purposes, may have the same effect. Regardless of which specific questions are asked, or what specific theoretical approach is used to guide the assessment, assessment should be approached from a broad perspective that is a means to an end, rather than a simple testing perspective where the means becomes an end, or where the end purpose is never clearly defined.

LEGAL AND ETHICAL ISSUES IN ASSESSMENT

Although a truly comprehensive overview of the legal and ethical issues in assessment is beyond the scope of this book (see Bersoff, 1982a; DeMers, 1986; Jacob & Hartshorne, 1994, for more complete treatments of the topic), it is still useful to take a brief look at some issues that are particularly relevant for assessment of behavioral, social, and emotional problems. By definition, legal issues involve aspects of assessment that are affected by either constitutional or statutory constraints. Ethical issues, on the other hand, do not always involve legal constraints, but what is considered to be "right" professional practice, as dictated by the codes for ethical conduct developed by professional organizations such as the American Psychological Association, National Association of School Psychologists, and American Counseling Association. Although it is sometimes possible to separate law from ethics, in reality, the two areas are intertwined. Legal constraints affecting assessment practices have often been developed from the basis of professional practice codes, and these codes of ethics for professionals typically take into account important legal constraints that affect the profession.

Basis for Legal Constraints on Assessment

According to DeMers (1986), there are two basic ways that testing and assessment practices can be affected by the law. The first means of jurisdiction involves constitutional protections to citizens. In this regard, the *equal protection* and *due process* clauses from the 14th Amendment to the U.S. Constitution are the areas most likely to constrain assessment practices, particularly if the individual conducting the assessment is employed by the "state" (e.g., public school districts, corrections agencies, hospitals, clinics, etc.). The equal protection clause forbids the state to treat persons who are similarly situated in a different manner, unless there is a justifiable reason. Examples of assessment practices that would violate the equal protection clause would be those that result in members of a specific gender or racial/ethnic group receiving inferior assessment, classification, or treatment services (i.e., the use of an assessment procedure that was *systematically biased* against a particular group). The due process clause was designed to prevent "the government from denying life, liberty, or property without

law prevents differential assessment of equal people.

(a) a legitimate reason, and (b) providing some meaningful and impartial forum to prevent arbitrary deprivations of those protected interests" (DeMers, 1986, p. 37). Property and liberty interests have been defined quite broadly through a number of supreme court decisions—the concept of liberty is now thought to encompass rights to privacy, personal security, and reputation. In the assessment process, a number of activities could potentially infringe on liberty rights, including the actual conducting of the assessment and the writing and maintaining of confidential assessment reports.

The second way that assessment practices can be affected by law involves various statutory provisions that may be invoked at the state and federal level. These types of legal constraints typically do not directly involve constitutional provisions, but consist of the passage of specific laws by legislative bodies that are considered to be useful in governing professional practices. At the state level, laws for licensing or certifying psychologists and other service providers usually contain specific regulations pertaining to who can provide services, how privileged information and confidentiality must be handled, and to what extent clients must be informed of the procedures in which they might become involved. Another example of state-level law that affects assessment practices would be school law, where specific procedures and safeguards governing consent for assessment and release of assessment records are often included. At the federal level, assessment practices in school settings are affected by the Individuals with Disabilities Education Act (IDEA), and the 1974 Family Educational Rights and Privacy Act (FERPA). Both of these laws contain provisions relating to parental access to student records and release of records to third parties. Additionally, the IDEA contains provisions for selection of appropriate assessment instruments and procedures.

Specific Assessment Practices Affected by Ethics and Law

To be more specific about how social-emotional assessment practices can be affected by legal and ethical constraints, consider three distinctive areas that have been addressed in this realm: informed consent, validity of assessment procedures, and right to privacy. These areas are discussed in this section, with specific comments regarding assessment practices with children and adolescents.

Informed Consent. The area of informed consent is broadly construed to mean that prior to any assessment services being conducted, the client (and/or their parent or guardian, in the case of a minor) must receive a sufficient explanation of the purpose and nature of the procedures that will be done as well as the risks involved, if any, and must give their express consent for participation. Informed consent regulations are a major feature of the due process stipulations in the Individuals with Disabilities Education Act (IDEA). Within the regulations of IDEA, there are three components: *knowledge* (parents are to be given complete explanation about the purposes and procedures of the assessment), *voluntariness* (consent is willfully granted and not obtained through coercion or misrepresentation), and *competence* (parents must be legally competent to give consent, which is usually assumed by school officials). Even when psychologists or other professionals are engaging in assessment activities outside the scope of the IDEA, there are similar ethical expectations for utilizing informed consent procedures, as indicated by Principle 2 and Principle 4 of the American Psychological Association's 1992 code of ethical principles (APA, 1992), and Section 3.5.4 of the National Association of School Psychologists Standards for the Provision of Psychological Services (NASP, 1984).

For many years, the concept of informed consent applied to children and adolescents was relatively straightforward and uncomplicated; it has traditionally been assumed that parents or guardians are the ultimate holders of the informed consent right, and the children or adolescents play a secondary role in this process—if any at all. However, in recent years, evolving ethics and values in society, as well as some new legal and philosophical concepts, have begun to put a new spin on how informed consent issues should be handled with minors. Legally speaking, the right of informed consent still belongs to parents or guardians of minors, especially when considering service delivery under specific systems and laws, such as IDEA. However, in legal circles, the static nature of informed consent for children and adolescents has been increasingly challenged by a gradually evolving concept that is sometimes referred to as the "mature minor" doctrine. The basis of this doctrine is that decisions regarding competence and consent should be made on the basis of cognitive capacity (and perhaps emotional maturity) and not age (Hesson, Bakal, & Dobson, 1993; Shields & Johnson, 1992). Therefore, adolescents who are intellectually advanced and possess reasonable emotional maturity might, in some circumstances, be allowed to provide their own informed consent, even without prior parent notification. The most likely situations in which such informed consent might be considered legitimate are not in the realm of IDEA and other federal or state laws that provide specific statements regarding parent rights to informed consent, but in the voluntary seeking of mental health treatment by the adolescent client (T. H. Murray, 1995; Shields & Johnson, 1992), particularly in Canada and a few U.S. states where the mature minor doctrine has been given some legitimacy. However, this concept is still evolving, and it is certainly at odds with several sectors of society that are seeking to increase parental empowerment in decisions regarding their children. Until the mature minor concept becomes widely recognized and better defined, practitioners should be aware of this option but should be very cautious in thinking about utilizing it; they should attempt to stay abreast of informed consent laws in their own state and with federal laws that span the various states. *ASSENT= not just guardian consent, but child also !*

Another evolving legal-ethical concept involving children and adolescents in mental health research and services is the *assent* doctrine. Simply stated, this concept embodies the idea that researchers and practitioners should, in addition to obtaining appropriate parental consent, allow children or adolescent participants to have a voice in whether or not they will be involved in research or the receipt of services (Levine, 1995; Powell & Vacha-Haase, 1994; Range & Cotton, 1995). For example, if this concept were being implemented fully, the child or adolescent for whom research or services are targeted would have the opportunity to agree to or decline such participation. Certainly this concept is a complicated and potentially thorny. Although most persons would probably agree that a mature minor should be able to voluntarily decline or agree to participate in a research study, the point at which an individual is considered mature enough for self-determination is unclear. Additionally, there are serious potential problems involved when moving assent from the realm of research to service delivery. If children or adolescents provide their assent for treatment, then they will likely feel more empowered and positive about the process. But what about refusal of assent? Should a seriously emotionally disturbed 14-year-old who has been referred by parents for assessment and possible diagnosis and treatment be allowed to refuse the assessment? These are tough but important questions. As the concept of assent continues to evolve, practitioners and researchers should strive to stay current with laws in their own state or province, as well as stay aware of the current Zeitgeist involving this issue.

Validity of Assessment Procedures. Regarding legal and ethical aspects of validity of assessment procedures, there is substantial agreement and overlap between the provisions of the IDEA, APA's Principle 2, and NASP's standards 3.5 and 4.3. Some of the conditions stated in the public law and in the professional codes include that tests must be validated for the specific purposes for which they are being used, tests must have adequate technical (psychometric) properties, obsolete assessment results should not be used, and assessment procedures must be administered only by persons with specific and adequate training. Although there have been many criticisms of the technical aspects of many social-emotional assessment instruments (particularly those in the personality and projective-expressive technique realm) (Bersoff, 1982b; Gregory, 1996; Salvia & Ysseldyke, 1995), it is interesting to note that, unlike their counterpart instruments in the domain of cognitive assessment, there have been few legal complaints stemming from the use of inadequate measures in the social-emotional domain (DeMers, 1986). The education and mental health professions, as well as society at large, generally have been much less vocally critical of social-emotional assessment procedures as compared to intellectual and academic achievement tests, despite the fact that the latter category of tests tends to be better researched and possess higher levels of reliability and validity. Whatever the reason for this relative lack of controversy, the potential for future litigation regarding social-emotional assessment procedures appears to be great, and practitioners and researchers are advised to stay current on changing laws and ethics codes regarding validity of assessment procedures.

Right to Privacy/Confidentiality. The third area involves the broad domain of what is most commonly referred to as the *right to privacy*, but also includes the concept of *confidentiality*. In this area, procedures and principles have not only been outlined by the IDEA and APA and NASP standards, but by the Family Educational Rights and Privacy Act of 1974 (FERPA), numerous state statutes, and court decisions related to the right to privacy inferred from or carved out of the 14th Amendment to the U.S. Constitution. Within the general area of right to privacy, the following are some key components relating to assessment practices: (a) Clients (and the parents of minor clients) are provided access to their records and assessment results. (b) Assessment results are not released to third parties without the express consent of the client (or parents of a minor client). (c) Communications between the professional and client are regarded as confidential unless the client has voluntarily waived their right to confidentiality, or the information obtained in the professional relationship reveals a clear and imminent danger to the client or to other persons (the "duty to warn" principle). Moreover, each U.S. state and Canadian province has laws mandating that reasonable evidence or suspicions of child abuse be reported to the proper legal authority. Therefore, within the context of information obtained during a social-emotional assessment, such information would constitute an instance where confidentiality must be breached.

Given the various provisions and exceptions to the laws and ethical codes, clinicians must be very careful about the way that promises of confidentiality are stated to their child and adolescent clients. It has been argued that mental health professionals have a primary obligation to respect the wishes expressed by a mature minor in relation to the provision of counseling services, including confidentiality. However, given the uncertainties and evolving nature of the mature minor doctrine, and given the legal status of children and adolescents, confidentiality of communication does not exist in a strict sense, given that parents have a right to be informed of what information is obtained in most situations (DeMers, 1986), and there are certain legal exceptions to the rule. This statement is particularly true when service provision is under the blanket of specific federal and state laws that mandate parents' ultimate right to information. Therefore, clinicians should avoid making unrealistic promises that what they say will be kept in strict confidence to their child or adolescent clients, and instead should help them to understand the limits of confidentiality by giving them the power to participate in the process in the most informed way possible.

An additional area to consider regarding privacy and confidentiality involves a long-standing concern among psychologists that using personality assessment instruments, and presumably other social-emotional measures, may result in unjustifiable encroachment of privacy rights (Jacob & Hartshorne, 1994; Messick, 1965). Within this line of reasoning, the argument is that because they are designed to obtain highly private, personal information, some personality or social-emotional assessment methods may routinely violate privacy rights. This concern, although certainly important, is difficult to clearly define and operationalize, and would obviously lead to very difficult distinctions among various assessment instruments (i.e., which are justifiable and which are not). In practice, adhering to the three component areas outlined in this section, and always acting to "do no harm" will reduce the likelihood of invading privacy rights within the context of assessing social and emotional behavior.

Some Concluding Comments on Legal and Ethical Issues

As stated earlier, it is interesting to note that the type of assessment instruments that have most often been the targets of legal action are intellectual ability and academic achievement tests rather than social-emotional behavior measures (Bersoff, 1982b). There is a peculiar irony to this imbalance of legal action. Tests of intellectual ability, as a whole, tend to have better psychometric properties and a more extensive research base than do most behavioral-emotional assessment instruments. When projective personality measures are included, the difference in psychometric quality becomes even more pronounced (Salvia & Ysseldyke, 1995). A possible reason for behavioral-emotional or personality measures not being legally targeted as extensively as intellectual tests has been articulated by DeMers (1986), who suggested that there is a limited legal basis for complaint against these types of measures. They have seldom been found to systematically discriminate against particular groups, and are most often administered in the context of voluntary work by private citizens, rather than as an action of the state. Therefore, although the potential legal entanglements of social-emotional assessment remain high, they are probably not as likely to be targeted for action until their use is found to *systematically* bias opportunities for specific groups of people.

A final interesting point to think about in regard to legal and ethical issues is that they can and do change over time. The codes of ethical practice adopted by professional organizations tend to be influenced by changes in social thought, and statutory regulation at the state level tends to be influenced by changes in the ethical codes of professional organizations. An example of such changing social thought is the mature minor and assent concepts discussed previously in this section, which for all practical purposes did not exist only a few years ago. These concepts have begun to evolve as society has begun to seriously consider the notion of self-determination for children and adolescents. Another example of changing legal and ethical standards is that until the mid-1970s, both the American Psychiatric Association and the American Psychological Association officially viewed homosexuality as a form of mental illness. Today, as attested to by many recent journal articles, letters to the editor in professional newsletters such as the *APA Monitor*, and news stories regarding policy-making at professional conventions, there is considerable controversy regarding whether it is ethical for therapists to work with clients who desire to change their sexual orientation (i.e., *reparative therapy*). This shift in direction over a 20- to 30-year period has mirrored changing social trends that have become more accepting of homosexuality as an alternative lifestyle (G. Corey, M. S. Corey, & Callanan, 1993). In terms of social-emotional assessment practices, it is difficult to predict how legal and ethical constraints will change over time, but it is likely, if not given, that such changes will indeed occur.

THE DIRECT AND OBJECTIVE APPROACH TO ASSESSMENT

As the title of this book indicates, a conscious choice has been made to emphasize assessment approaches within the text that are *direct* and *objective*. Although this book does include a comprehensive chapter on projective-expressive assessment techniques (chap. 8), it is clearly oriented more toward direct and objective methods. Given this emphasis, what are the key characteristics of direct and objective assessment, how do they differ from nondirect and nonobjective methods, and what advantages does such an approach offer?

Bases of Direct and Objective Assessment

Direct approaches to assessment tend to deemphasize mediating steps between obtaining and interpreting assessment data. For an example of how a direct approach differs from a less direct approach, compare two techniques for assessing social status or peer relationships. Sociometric assessment methods (use of peer nominations or peer ratings) could be considered to be direct in this example. The obtained assessment data provide direct information about how children or adolescents are perceived by their peers. On the other and, the use of a human figure drawing test to provide information on social status or peer relations would be a less direct means. With this technique, the drawings are the obtained assessment data, but to convert the information into hypotheses about social functioning and peer relationships, several intermediary steps are involved (e.g., measuring the size of the drawings, looking at the qualitative aspects of the drawings, looking at the placement of the different figures in relation to each other) before the issue is addressed.

Assessment methods that are objective in nature deemphasize the need for making qualitative inferences in order to interpret the obtained data, whereas less objective methods require a greater degree of inference on the part of the examiner to make an interpretation. Using the example of sociometric assessment versus human figure drawings, notice the difference in the inference level required by the two methods. Whereas some inference is needed in order to interpret the sociometric data and to link it with actual social status and peer relationships, a much higher level of inference is needed to accomplish the same means with drawing tests, which assume that certain qualitative features of the drawings, their size, or their placement on the paper have some intrinsic meaning that will shed light on child or adolescent social functioning. In sum, direct and objective methods of assessment tend to allow for data gathering and interpretation with a minimal amount of intermediary steps, and with a minimal amount of subjective inference.

Nomothetic Versus Idiographic Assessment and the Empirical Approach

(Individual)   *(group)*   *(direct, objective)*

To understand what this discussion is getting at when direct and objective assessment are emphasized, it is also necessary to examine some related assessment concepts, namely, the difference between *nomothetic* and *idiographic* assessment, and the *empirical approach* to assessment. The division of assessment methods into a dichotomous nomothetic-idiographic breakdown dates to the early part of the 20th century, and has been the subject of considerable debate over the years. The issue was popularized and became the point of much discussion in psychology with the publication of Meehl's (1954) *Clinical vs. Statistical Prediction.* Meehl argued that clinical judgment was often a poor substitute for quantitative or actuarial prediction based on objective data. According to Barnett and Zucker (1990), nomothetic assessment focuses on actuarial and quantitative data, objective tests, and statistical prediction. Idiographic assessment in the social-emotional behavior domain, on the other hand, focuses more on individual and qualitative data, projective tests, and clinical judgment.

The empirical approach to assessment is more in line with nomothetic than idiographic assessment. The term *empirical* originates from the Greek word *empeiria*, which refers to *experience* (Achenbach, McConaughy, & Howell, 1987). Empirical data is based on experience or observations, and it can be proven or disproven through direct experimentation or observation. In Achenbach et al.'s conceptualization of empirical assessment, this approach "follows psychometric principles, including the use of standardized procedures, multiple aggregated items, normative-developmental reference groups, and the establishment of reliability and validity" (1987, p. 16). In essence, empirical assessment epitomizes many of the characteristics that are referred to under the title "direct and objective."

Why Emphasize Direct and Objective Assessment?

↳ *reduce amt. of ERROR, more legal + ethical*

Given the discussion thus far, it is fair to say that the direct and objective approach to social-emotional assessment favors nomothetic methods, and is compatible with empirically based assessment. But what advantages are found in the direct and objective approach to justify it being emphasized in this book? Perhaps the greatest value in using direct and objective approaches is that they help to reduce the amount of error that a clinician brings into the assessment. Particularly when used in an aggregated, multimethod manner, direct and objective methods help to diminish the problem of bias that may be introduced by overreliance on subjective clinical judgment, or overreliance on a limited number of assessment techniques. Thus, the use of direct and objective assessment methods allows the clinician to be more confident in the integrity of the assessment results and any intervention recommendations that stem from them.

Another advantage of the direct and objective approach to social-emotional assessment is that it puts the clinician on more solid ground when it comes to adherence to legal and ethical principles of assessment. The organizational ethical standards of both the American Psychological Association and National Association of School Psychologists stress the need to use assessment methods that are technically adequate, and to use them only for the purposes for which they have been validated. These

Direct + objective = more measurement integrity.

sentiments are echoed by the guidelines stated in the Individuals with Disabilities Education Act (IDEA) and in the *Standards for Educational and Psychological Testing* (1985). It is necesary to be careful not to overgeneralize on this point—not all direct and objective approaches to assessment are technically sound and validated, and not all assessment methods that are less direct and objective do not meet acceptable levels of measurement integrity. However, as a general rule, the more direct and objective an assessment method is, the more measurement integrity it is likely to have (Salvia & Ysseldyke, 1995; Worthen, Borg, & White, 1993).

To conclude this section, it is important to emphasize that although the focus here is on direct and objective methods of assessment, there is a place for clinical judgment, and the abandonment of all assessment methods that are less direct and objective in nature is not advocated here. There are some projective assessment techniques that meet acceptable technical standards, and the use of subjective clinical techniques can sometimes provide useful and interesting assessment information within the context of a comprehensive assessment. It is also true that not every method of assessment for behavioral, social, and emotional problems can be broken into categories of empirical-direct and objective-nomothetic versus nondirect and objective-idiographic. Whereas there are varying amounts of objectivity and directness in each possible assessment method, the focus is on methods that lean toward directness and objectivity.

DESIGNING A MULTIMETHOD, MULTISOURCE, MULTISETTING ASSESSMENT

Since about 1980, there have been significant advances in the research and technology base for conducting assessments with children and adolescents. One of the major developments has been the articulation of a model for a broad-based assessment design. The essential feature of this broad-based model is that by using various assessment methods with different informants or sources and in several settings, the amount of error variance in the assessment is reduced, and the result is a comprehensive representation of the referred client's behavioral, social, and emotional functioning. This type of broad-based assessment design has been referred to by various names, including *multifactored assessment* (Barnett, 1983), *multisetting, multisource, multi-instrument assessment* (R. P. Martin, 1988; R. P. Martin, Hooper, & Snow, 1986), and *multiaxial empirically based assessment* (Achenbach, McConoughy, & Howell, 1987). Although there are some differences between the ways these different models have been articulated, the critical feature of obtaining assessment data on a client through a number of different instruments, methods, sources, informants, and settings remains the same.

The term *multimethod, multisource, multisetting assessment*, first introduced in a previous edition of this text (Merrell, 1994a), has been chosen to represent the features of conducting broad-based assessment that are most relevant to the topic of social-emotional assessment. In Fig. 1.2, a graphic representation of the model is displayed. For an example of how a multimethod, multisource, multisetting assessment would be conducted in actual practice, look at the hypothetical case of a child client who is referred to a clinic setting because of a variety of behavioral and emotional problems. In terms of method, it would probably be desirable to include behavioral observation, interviews, rating scales, and self-report instruments as part of the assessment from the onset, and within each method, a variety of instruments or specific techniques should be used when possible. In the event that the client was experiencing social

use methods to reduce error

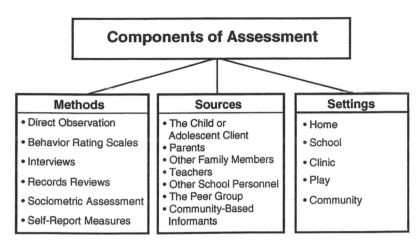

FIG. 1.2. Potential components of a multimethod, multisource, multisetting assessment.

adjustment problems and there was easy access to a social group (i.e., school or playground) for assessment, it might also be desirable under some circumstances to gather sociometric assessment data. In terms of source, it would be necessary to gather assessment data from both clients and their parent(s) at a minimum, and if possible, it would be desirable to include other relevant sources who know the children as well as informants. These other sources might include school personnel, other family members, and community-based individuals such as clergy, youth group leaders, and so on. And, in terms of setting, clinic, home, and school would be included in an optimum assessment, and when feasible, community-based and play settings as well.

In reality, it is often difficult or impossible to include all of the possible relevant sources and settings, and it is sometimes a problem to even include more than a couple of methods. The main point to remember in this regard is that as the assessment becomes more diverse and broad based, an aggregated picture of the child's behavioral, social, and emotional functioning is obtained. Such an assessment design is considered to be a best practice that has the possibility of reducing error variance and providing a more comprehensive picture of the child (Achenbach & McConaughy, 1987; R. P. Martin, 1988; R. P. Martin et al., 1986; Merrell, Merz, Johnson, & Ring, 1992).

Some caution is warranted in considering the possibilities and advantages of an aggregated multimethod, multisource, multisetting assessment. Although most current thinking purports that such a design is indeed a best practice and the most sophisticated way of implementing the assessment, there is some divergence of professional opinion here. Some experts in the field of child and adolescent psychopathology (e.g., Arkes, 1981; Loeber, Dishion, & Patterson, 1984; Reid, Baldwin, Patterson, & Dishion, 1988; Wiggins, 1981) have presented persuasive arguments that, in some cases, aggregated multiple assessment data may actually *increase* error variance due to covariation among different assessment sources and the inability of clinicians to effectively aggregate assessment data that is contradictory. This is indeed a compelling and interesting argument, and is at least partially the impetus behind efforts that advocate sequential or multiple gating approaches to assessment, which are reviewed in chapters 2 and 13. Even some experts who advocate the aggregated multiple assessment model (e.g., Achenbach & Edelbrock, 1984) have acknowledged this possibility. So, in light of these somewhat contradictory arguments, what is the best clinical practice? The position advocated throughout this book is that the informed and judicious use of an aggregated

Aggregated assessments is still best — but beware!

multiple assessment model is still the best practice for general referral and assessment cases. However, clinicians and researchers need to be informed of the potential liabilities of their assessment design. In the meantime, additional empirical evidence on this assessment issue would be very useful in helping those in the child and adolescent assessment field articulate a state-of-the-art assessment model for the next century. Because most of these contradictory arguments on assessment design are theory based but not yet empirically validated, being aware of both positions and their possibilities seems to be a prudent step at the present time.

CRITERIA FOR INCLUSION OF ASSESSMENT METHODS AND INSTRUMENTS

Throughout this book, five general assessment methods are emphasized: direct behavioral observation, interviewing techniques, behavior rating scales, sociometric approaches, and self-report procedures. To varying degrees, each of these methods can be considered direct and objective, as the terms have been defined in this book. Additionally, chapter 8 provides a comprehensive overview of projective-assessment techniques and their use with children and adolescents. Given that there are many more specific procedures and instruments within each method than can be included in any book, the guidelines for including them within this text follow three general sets of criteria. These are as follows:

tech.
adequacy
   1. Any procedure or instrument that is included must have met at least minimum standards for technical adequacy (i.e., must have sufficient research behind it demonstrating psychometric properties and clinical utility).

usability
   2. Any procedure or instrument included must have a high degree of "usability" for the clinician. In other words, any particular techniques or tests requiring a particularly extensive amount of specialized equipment or training to the point that it is overly burdensome for clinicians to use day to day were not included, regardless of the technical properties.

good
norm
sample
   3. In the case of standardized, norm-referenced instruments (such as behavior rating scales and self-report tests), to be included in this text, these instruments must include reasonably large and representative normative populations, and be easily available (i.e., commercially published or easily accessible within the public domain). Of course, this third criterion is in addition to the first two being met.

In some cases, the number of possible instruments or techniques that meet the inclusion criteria are well in excess of the capacity to all be included within one book. Thus, in some cases, instruments or specific approaches that are generally representative of their general domain were included as examples of what is available.

CONCLUSIONS

Assessment (or at least testing) may be conducted with minimal thought regarding a theoretical foundation for social and emotional behavior, but such practice is discouraged, as it relegates the assessment professional to the role of a technician. Numerous theories regarding human behavior and personality have influenced psychology, education, and related fields, ranging from behaviorism to psychodynamic theory to humanistic theory. Social cognitive theory, stemming from the work of Bandura, is proposed as a foundation for much of this book, and is briefly overviewed. Assessment professionals are urged to integrate theory into their assessment practices, regardless of whether they adopt the orientation of this book or select a competing theory to guide their work.

Referrals for assessment of child and adolescent social-emotional behavior often occur because of a discrepancy between the child's or adolescent's current level of functioning and an optimum level of functioning desired by the referral source. Such discrepancies may be from standards desired by society in general, by community subgroups, or by specific families or teachers. It is critical to recognize these perspectives of the referral source when proceeding with assessment referrals.

Although there have been some previous attempts made to integrate assessment into an overall process of problem solving, surprisingly little attention has been paid to this area. All too often, assessment practitioners tend to view assessment as both a means and an end, rather than as one part of an overall process, and administrative practices in many school districts and mental health agencies tend to reinforce this limited view. A four-phase model of assessment as a problem-solving process is proposed. This model includes various practical questions within the phases of Identification and Clarification, Data Collection, Analysis, and Solution and Evaluation.

There are numerous legal and ethical constraints on assessing children, based on specific statutes or administrative laws of individual states, federal laws affecting educational practice, certain provisions of the U.S. constitution, and the ethics codes of various professional organizations. Specifically, the areas of informed consent, validity of assessment procedures, and right to privacy/confidentiality are involved with legal and ethical constraints when assessing social and emotional behavior of children and adolescents. Legal and ethical constraints regarding assessment and related professional practices are constantly in a state of change, based on the changing values of society. Therefore, professionals are advised to keep current on changes that may affect their assessment practices.

A direct and objective approach to social-emotional assessment of children and adolescents is proposed and emphasized throughout this book. Direct and objective approaches to assessment emphasize objective data, actuarial prediction, and statistical relations among assessment data. As compared to assessment methods that are more indirect and subjective in nature, direct and objective approaches minimize the amount of inference required to interpret assessment results.

Additionally, a multimethod, multisource, multisetting model of assessment design is proposed and emphasized throughout this book. This type of assessment design is aimed to overcome error variance associated with specific types of assessment practices by building an aggregated assessment design to the greatest extent that is feasible. By including multiple methods of assessment, various sources of data, and by basing the assessment on more than one setting, the limitations of any one type of assessment may be overcome, and a broad-based picture of the social-emotional behavior of the referred child or adolescent is likely to be obtained.

REVIEW AND APPLICATION QUESTIONS

1. Compare and contrast social learning theory with any other prevailing theory of social-emotional behavior (e.g., behavioral, psychodynamic, humanistic, etc.). When it comes to using either theory as a foundation for conducting and reporting an assessment, what are the limitations and advantages of each?

2. What are the three components of triadic reciprocity within social learning theory, and how do they affect each other?

3. What are some ways that social and emotional behavior of children and adolescents can be assessed as part of a comprehensive process of problem solving?

4. What are the three components of informed consent, and how might they need to be addressed prior to conducting a child or adolescent assessment?

5. With respect to the legal and ethical mandates for using assessment procedures that have adequate validity, what types of instruments or procedures commonly used for social-emotional assessment might be problematic?

6. Regarding confidentiality between the clinician and child or adolescent clients, what are some reasonable statements that could be made to help the client understand the limits and ramifications of confidentiality when an assessment is being conducted?

7. Of the assessment procedures commonly used for evaluating child and adolescent social-emotional behavior, which could be characterized as more direct and objective, and which could be characterized as more indirect and subjective?

8. For social-emotional assessment of children and adolescents, what are some potential components within a broad-based multimethod, multisource, multisetting assessment design?

9. A 14-year-old student who has been receiving special education services as "emotionally disturbed" since grade 2 enters the records office of the school, and in a highly emotional and agitated state, demands to see her permanent behavioral file. This file includes several psychological, social work, and psychiatric reports, all of which contain some very sensitive information about the student and her family. What is an appropriate way to deal with this situation, maintaining a balance between what is legal and what is in the best interests of the student?

10. A 16-year-old boy is participating in a diagnostic interview with a psychologist in a community mental health center. He was referred to the center by his parents because of their concerns regarding serious depression. During the interview, the boy talks about being very jealous and angry with a former girlfriend who broke up with him, and he seems almost obsessed with his anger toward her. At one point in the interview, he angrily states that "if she makes me look like a fool one more time I'll kill her!" What is an appropriate way to handle this situation?

2

ASSESSMENT AND CLASSIFICATION

One of the traditional primary purposes of assessing social and emotional behavior is to determine an appropriate diagnosis or classification. The term *diagnosis* is historically linked with the medical model of psychological disorders, whereas the term *classification* is utilized more in education and by behaviorally oriented researchers. Both terms imply a common element of categorizing and codifying an observable phenomena based on an existing taxonomy or scheme. Without splitting hairs over conceptual or definitional differences between the two terms, both are subsumed under the more generic term, *classification*, in this chapter. Debate over the practice of classification

There has been extensive debate within the field regarding the usefulness of the process of classification. The traditional view of classification is that the behavioral sciences, like the natural sciences, should develop and utilize classification taxonomies to create order, to provide a common ground for different practitioners to use in describing problems, to help predict the future course of behavior, and ideally, to prescribe a treatment scheme. Unfortunately, the state of the behavioral sciences is still far from being at the point where these goals for classification are being met (Gresham & Gansle, 1992). The problems with traditional classification systems have led to great dissatisfaction by behaviorally oriented practitioners and researchers, as exemplified by Kauffman's (1989) statement that "the usual psychiatric systems of classification have been quite unreliable . . . [and have] had little or no implications for treatment, particularly educational treatment" (p. 122).

This chapter deals with several important issues regarding the role of classification in assessment. First, a rationale for conducting classification activities is proposed, which is followed by a discussion of differential diagnosis and classification error. The majority of the chapter is devoted to descriptions of current classification systems. Three major classification systems are overviewed, including the *DSM* system, special education classification, and the emerging behavioral dimensions approach. Following the presentation of current classification systems, this chapter includes an overview of a promising development in systematic assessment and selection for classification and treatment—a series of procedures and decision points referred to as *multiple gating*.

It concludes with a brief discussion of some additional issues relating to the assessment-classification process.

WHY CLASSIFY?

There is no doubt that current classification systems in psychology, psychiatry, and education are imperfect. And yet, despite their present flawed state, there may be some wisdom in the thought that disregarding current systems due to their imperfections may be throwing out the proverbial baby with the bathwater. There are some solid pragmatic reasons why classification is often necessary and useful as part of the assessment process. The following four examples are reasons why doing a formal classification as part of an evaluation is often important:

Reasons FOR classifying

1. Classification can provide some common ground of understanding for different professionals working with the same client.
2. Classification can provide access to services for clients.
3. Educational and health service institutions often require classification to remunerate the client or service providers for services.
4. In the absence of a totally reliable and valid classification taxonomy for behavioral and emotional problems, continuing to work with and refine present systems is a step in the right direction toward developing improved systems.

Although it is true that there are many problems with current classification systems, and they are often used and implemented cynically, abandoning the use of classification simply because the state of the art is currently marginal is shortsighted at best, and may lead to professional anarchy at worst. Therefore, the purpose of this chapter is to orient the reader to the more commonly used classification systems that are often used as part of the assessment process, and to provide a rational argument for how current classification systems can be best utilized in assessment.

DIFFERENTIAL DIAGNOSIS AND CLASSIFICATION ERROR

problem = norm or abnorm + what to classify it as?

Although the term *differential diagnosis* is often used in the psychiatric and psychological literature, it is often misunderstood. The process of differentially diagnosing or classifying a behavioral, social, or emotional problem essentially involves two steps: making a binary decision as to whether or not the problem is considered normal or abnormal in nature, and reaching a decision regarding how to specifically classify the problem (e.g., conduct disorder vs. oppositional-defiant disorder; learning disabilities vs. serious emotional disturbance). This differential process is often difficult, and is considered to be one of the most technically demanding aspects of the assessment process (R. P. Martin, 1988).

Given the imperfect nature of the current classification systems, it is inevitable that some error will be found in many differential diagnostic and classification decisions. Two types of error are of particular interest for clinicians making classification decisions. A *false-positive* error occurs when an individual is classified as having a particular disorder, but in fact does not. A *false-negative* classification error occurs when individu-

Flawed classification system → false-neg + false-pos. Errors!

In large screenings – a false positive is the better error b/c it can be corrected. In indiv. a false-positive can be very bad!

als are classified as being "normal" or not having a specific disability or disorder, when they in fact do.

Which type of error is worse? The answer to this question depends on what type of classification decision is being made, and the potential consequences of such errors. For example, when conducting initial screening (e.g., to identify children who are in the early stages of developing behavioral, social, or emotional problems), the primary goal is to narrow down who is a *good suspect*, and then look at the narrowed population in more detail. For a screening process, it would be preferable to make a false-positive error rather than a false-negative error, because overselection can be corrected at a later point, but underselection may mean that a child who is in need of help may go some time without receiving it. On the other hand, if the clinician is making a decision as to whether or not an individual has a psychotic disorder, making a false-positive error sets up a potentially insidious situation where the client is improperly labeled, has a good chance of being stigmatized for a long period of time, and may even end up being the recipient of a treatment that is not needed and may have negative side effects (e.g., the prescription psychotropic medications).

In general, it is recommended that the higher the risks and consequences are in a differential diagnosis and classification decision, the more conservative the approach to making the decision. In cases where a great deal of adverse consequences are potential, a clinician should even go so far as to take a disconfirmatory approach, which involves approaching the classification decision with the hypothesis that the disorder or disability under question is not present, and only rejecting that premise when the evidence to the contrary clearly overwhelms the initial working hypothesis.

not present until proven otherwise

Higher risk → be more conservative in classification

CURRENT CLASSIFICATION SYSTEMS

Three different classification systems for arranging behavioral, social, and emotional problems of childhood and adolescence are overviewed in this section. First, the psychiatric-based *DSM* system, which is widely used by psychiatrists, clinical psychologists, and in hospital-based day or residential treatment programs is overviewed. Then, the classification categories and definitions based on special education law are discussed. Finally, a relatively recent and promising approach to classification of behavioral, social, and emotional problems is introduced—namely, the *behavioral dimensions* method.

The *DSM* System

Assumptions and Structure of **DSM.** Without question, the most widely used system for classification of behavioral, social, and emotional problems in North America is the psychiatric-based *Diagnostic and Statistical Manual for Mental Disorders* (*DSM*), currently in its fourth edition (American Psychiatric Association, 1994). The first edition of the *DSM* was published in 1952, and like subsequent editions, was based on a *medical model* of behavioral and emotional problems, which views such disturbances as *mental disease*. The traditional underlying assumption of this model is that behavioral and emotional problems reside within the individual, although this assumption has been tempered to a great extent in recent years by the influence of behavioral psychology, which provides an alternative framework in which problems are viewed as a product of eliciting and reinforcing stimuli within a person's environment.

The *DSM–III–R* uses a *multiaxial* approach to classification. That is, individuals are classified according to five different dimensions or axes, rather than as simply experiencing a given problem. The first two axes refer to types of psychological/psychiatric disorders. The other three axes refer to general medical conditions, psychosocial and environmental problems, and level of adaptive functioning. Within Axes I (clinical disorders) and II (personality disorders and mental retardation), several of the disorders within the classification system are relevant to children and adolescents, and other disorders are either specific to the developmental years, or are at least considered to be first evident during childhood or adolescence. Table 2.1 provides a brief overview of the five axes of the *DSM–III–R* system, whereas Table 2.2 specifies the diagnostic categories usually considered to be first evident during infancy, childhood, or adolescence. In addition, it is important to recognize that many other *DSM* categories may have an onset during childhood or adolescence, and most *DSM* disorders apply a single criterion to children, adolescents, and adults. "The provision of a separate section for disorders that are usually first diagnosed in infancy, childhood, or adolescence is for convenience only and is not meant to suggest that there is any clear distinction between 'childhood' and 'adult' disorders" (APA, 1994, p. 37). However, it is also important to realize that the manifestation of symptoms of specific *DSM* disorders that are generically diagnosed without respect to age may differ according to developmental level. For example, the criteria for Major Depressive Disorder do not vary by age, but *DSM–IV* notes that "certain symptoms such as somatic complaints, irritability, and social withdrawal are particularly common in children" (APA, 1994, p. 324).

Using the* DSM *System in Assessment. Virtually any type of moderate to severe behavioral or emotional problem that might be experienced by a child or adolescent is potentially *DSM–IV* diagnosable under one of the many categories available. The all-inclusive nature of this system is both an advantage and a problem. The advantage lies in a clinician being able to use the system to classify a broad range of problems, to provide a common framework of understanding with other professionals, and to have possible implications for treatment (although many would argue this third point). The problem with such an all-inclusive system is that clinicians using it may end up making classification decisions (and potentially, intervention recommendations) that

TABLE 2.1
An Overview of the Multiaxial Structure of the *DSM–IV*

Axis I	Clinical Disorders, Other Conditions That May Be a Focus of Clinical Attention Includes 16 general categories of disorders, with some categories having several subcategories.
Axis II	Personality Disorders, Mental Retardation Includes 11 different categories of personality disorders, and mental retardation.
Axis III	General Medical Conditions The clinician reports current general medical conditions that are potentially relevant to the understanding or management of the individual's mental disorder. ICD–9–CM codes are included.
Axis IV	Psychosocial and Environmental Problems Psychosocial and environmental problems that may affect the diagnosis, treatment, and prognosis of mental disorders (e.g., education, occupational, housing problems) are reported.
Axis V	Global Assessment of Functioning The clinician rates the individual's overall level of functioning on a 1 (most severe) to 100 (most adaptive) scale. DSM–IV provides descriptive anchor points at 10-point intervals.

TABLE 2.2
DSM–IV Categories of Disorders Considered to Usually
Be First Evident in Infancy, Childhood, and Adolescence

Mental Retardation: Mild, Moderate, Severe, and Profound Mental Retardation

Learning Disorders: Reading Disorder, Mathematics Disorder, Disorder of Written Expression, Learning Disorder Not Otherwise Specified

Motor Skills Disorder: including Developmental Coordination Disorder

Communication Disorders: Expressive Language Disorder, Mixed Receptive-Expressive Language Disorder, Phonological Disorder, Stuttering, Communication Disorder Not Otherwise Specified

Pervasive Developmental Disorders: Autistic Disorder, Rett's Disorder, Childhood Disintegrative Disorder, Asperger's Disorder, Pervasive Developmental Disorder Not Otherwise Specified

Attention Deficit and Disruptive Behavior Disorders: Attention Deficit Hyperactivity Disorder (3 types), Conduct Disorder, Oppositional Defiant Disorder, Attention Deficit Hyperactivity Disorder Not Otherwise Specified, Disruptive Behavior Disorder Not Otherwise Specified

Feeding and Eating Disorders of Infancy or Early Childhood: Pica, Rumination Disorder, Feeding Disorder of Infancy or Early Childhood

Tic Disorders: Tourette's Disorder, Chronic Motor or Vocal Tic Disorder, Transient Tic Disorder, Tic Disorder Not Otherwise Specified

Elimination Disorders: Encopresis, Enuresis

Other Disorders of Infancy, Childhood, or Adolescence: Separation Anxiety Disorder, Selective Mutism, Reactive Attachment Disorder of Infancy or Early Childhood, Stereotypic Movement Disorder, Disorder of Infancy, Childhood, or Adolescence Not Otherwise Specified

---

are outside of their areas of professional expertise. For example, how many psychiatrists have sufficient training and experience with reading, writing, and arithmetic problems? And, how many psychologists or clinical social workers have any special training or expertise in diagnosing and treating speech and language problems? Thus, the broad, all-inclusive nature of the *DSM* system, along with potential problems of unreliability between different raters (Achenbach & Edelbrock, 1983) does present some potential difficulties when using the system in assessment. DSM doesn't link to interventions!

Another quandary that the *DSM* system poses is that the specific criteria for each category of disorder are not tied to specific assessment techniques, nor are the classification categories clearly linked to common intervention techniques. Therefore, the responsibility for selecting and using specific assessment techniques or instruments, and eventually developing an appropriate intervention plan, is fully on the shoulders of the clinician or team conducting the assessment. However, the *DSM* does provide relatively objective criteria for clinicians to follow in making a classification decision.

Consider the diagnostic criteria for *DSM–IV* code 313.81, Oppositional Defiant Disorder, which is a type of problem classification often seen in older children and adolescents who have been referred for psychological or other mental health services. The diagnostic criteria specify a clear time element (the condition must have lasted at least 6 months) and a list of behavioral conditions (in which at least four of eight specified conditions must be present). The criteria also list conditions that would rule out a classification of Oppositional Defiant Disorder (presence of certain other *DSM*

TABLE 2.3
An Example of Criteria for a *DSM–IV* Diagnostic Category:
Oppositional Defiant Disorder (313.81)

A. A disturbance of at least 6 months during which at least four (or more) of the following are present:
   1. Often loses temper.
   2. Often argues with adults.
   3. Often actively defies or refuses adult requests or rules.
   4. Often deliberately annoys other people.
   5. Often blames others for his or her mistakes or misbehavior.
   6. Is often touchy or easily annoyed by others.
   7. Is often angry or resentful.
   8. Is often spiteful or vindictive.

   Note: Consider a criterion met only if the behavior occurs more frequently than is typically observed in individuals of comparable age and developmental level.

B. The disturbance in behavior causes clinically significant impairment in social, academic, or occupational functioning.

C. The behaviors do not occur exclusively during the course of a Psychotic or Mood Disorder.

D. Criteria are not met for Conduct Disorder, and, if the individual is age 18 years or older, criteria are not met for Antisocial Personality Disorder.

Note. From *Diagnostic and Statistical Manual of Mental Disorders* (4th ed.). Copyright ©1994, American Psychiatric Association. Reprinted by permission of the American Psychiatric Association.

classifications). So, the classification criteria do have at least the appearance of objectivity. Nevertheless, by viewing the complete criteria for Oppositional Defiant Disorder shown in Table 2.3, it becomes clear that classification decision making also involves a fair amount of subjectivity. For example, what does "often loses temper" mean—once a week, once a day, or several times a day? And, how easy is it in certain cases to determine if the "deliberately" in "often deliberately annoys people" is indeed deliberate? Obviously, the *DSM* system of classification, though it is most widely used, has inherent in it many potential pitfalls that clinicians need to be aware of, but, if used judiciously, can help the clinician achieve many of the goals and necessities of assessment.

***Improvements and Changes in* DSM.** Each subsequent edition of the *DSM* has contained various changes in content and format, sometimes substantial changes. Assumably, these changes involve improvements to the system. For example, one of the primary purposes of the change to a fourth edition of the *DSM* was to develop more consistency with the World Health Organization's *ICD–10* health classification system, which was published in 1992. Presumably, this type of change would make the *DSM* system more useful outside of North America. During the development of the *DSM–IV* it was reported that the threshold for adding new categories under this revision was higher than in previous revisions of the *DSM* (Spitzer, 1991), an attempt to produce a relatively conservative document that would integrate changes from the *DSM–III–R* only when it was necessary to ensure consistency with the *ICD–10* or to integrate new findings.

Earlier in this section some of the problems of the *DSM* system relating to assessment and classification were discussed, and to be sure, there has been no shortage of criticisms of the use of the *DSM* system, particularly when used with children and in school settings (e.g., Gresham & Gansle, 1992). However, there has been considerable optimism that the changes in the *DSM* system over the years have resulted in a more reliable and valid classification system, and have been a significant step toward reducing or eliminating some of the problems associated with earlier versions of the manual. One of the aims of the revision resulting in the *DSM–IV* was to provide substantial reliability and validity data for proposed revisions (Sartorius, 1988). The National Institute of Mental Health (NIMH) supported at least 11 reliability and validity studies for the *DSM–IV*, and additional similar studies were conducted through other means. Widiger, Frances, Pincus, Davis, and First (1991) noted that the major emphasis in this latest revision of the *DSM* was to maximize the impact of the accumulating research evidence and to document the rationale and empirical support for any changes. Any substantial revision, addition, or deletion to the manual was preceded by a comprehensive literature review in which the reviewers were encouraged to follow standard meta-analytic procedures (Widiger, Frances, Pincus, & Davis, 1991). Thus, the continuing refinements in the *DSM* system appear to be positive steps in improving the empirical integrity of this influential system. If the procedures utilized to develop *DSM–IV* are indicative of a trend, the possibilities for the long-term refinement of a scientifically sound taxonomy of human behavioral and emotional disorders appear to be improving and the ultimate goal of a scientifically precise and reliable classification system appears to be within closer reach than ever before.

Classification Under Special Education Law   *Federal Law affects school practices ex-PL 94-142 + IDEA*

Whereas the *DSM* system is the most commonly used classification structure for behavioral, social, and emotional problems within the mental health professions, professional practice in these areas is governed by an additional definition and classification structure within the public educational systems of the United States. In 1975, the U.S. Congress passed the Education for All Handicapped Children Act (also referred to as P.L. 94-142) as a result of "constitutionally based challenges to the exclusion of handicapped children" (Rothstein, 1990, p. xxiii). Now after more than two decades of existence, the federal law has had a profound impact on assessment and classification practices within school settings. This law, which is now referred to as the Individuals with Disabilities Education Act (IDEA), is designed to ensure a free and appropriate public education and related educational services to all children and youth with disabilities. As part of IDEA, specific classification criteria for disability conditions have been adopted, and specific guidelines for assessment have been enacted. It is beyond the scope of this book to provide a comprehensive understanding of IDEA, but it is important for both school-based and community-based practitioners to have a basic understanding of how IDEA impacts assessment and classification. Therefore, this section provides a basic outline of the assessment and classification procedures of IDEA that are pertinent to assessing behavioral, social, and emotional problems. A specific emphasis is placed on the classification category *emotionally disturbed*, as it is obviously the area most pertinent to this topic.

General Assessment Guidelines in IDEA. Before a student with a disability can receive special education services under the auspices of IDEA, they must first be identified as having a disability, and this process typically involves formal assessment practices. Within IDEA itself, and through a number of court decisions that have been reached over the years, certain assessment requirements and safeguards have been put into place. Eight of these requirements and procedures that are most pertinent to the general topic are listed as follows:

Safeguards for assessments ↷⤵ *(handwritten annotation)*

1. Parent consent must be obtained before the assessment is conducted.

2. When the school district requests that an evaluation be done, it is paid for at public expense.

3. Tests must be valid for the purpose for which they are being used.

4. No single evaluation procedure may be used as the sole criterion for classification or program eligibility.

5. The assessment procedures must be culturally and racially appropriate; children must be tested in their native language or mode of communication unless it is infeasible.

6. The evaluation is conducted by a *multidisciplinary team* (MDT) or group of individuals, including at least one team member who is knowledgeable about the child's specific area of disability.

7. The student is assessed in all areas pertinent to the suspected disability.

8. The identified student's program must be reviewed annually, and the child must be reevaluated at least once every 3 years (although this does not necessarily mean a formal assessment, unless it is suspected that the child's disability condition has changed).

Examples from IDEA (handwritten annotation)

These eight examples from IDEA are deceptively simple and straightforward. It is easy to understand the law's intent, but often it is difficult to implement. As an example, look at guideline 5. It is not uncommon for Anglo clinicians to conduct an assessment with Hispanic, Native American, or Asian American children who have been raised in cultural conditions much different from those of the majority Anglo culture, and for whom English is not their primary language. Given that few, if any Anglo assessors have a proficient command of all the potential languages that might be needed to meet this requirement, their first inclination when approached with cases like these may be not to take them on. And yet, there is a competing pressure that makes it difficult to refer a difficult case. Particularly in isolated rural areas, the assessment professional in question may be the only person available at the time with technical training in educational and psychological assessment, and there may be no prospect of a qualified person who is also bilingual. In such a situation, the examiner is faced with a variety of ethical, technical, and legal dilemmas, of which the solution is often complex (for a good discussion of best practices in considering cultural factors, see Nuttall, DeLeon, & Valle, 1990).

problems w/ safeguards is that they are easy to understand but complex to implement (handwritten annotation)

Another good example of how these eight guidelines are easy to understand but complex to implement can be demonstrated by considering guideline 3, that test procedures must be valid for the purpose for which they are being used. How many of the assessment instruments utilized by an examiner in attempting to determine whether or not a child is emotionally disturbed have been validated for that purpose? Many, if not most procedures typically used for this purpose are not adequately validated. For example, given the level of reliability and validity evidence that most projective techniques have, it is doubtful that most, if any, would hold up under the scrutiny of a due process hearing or court decision, particularly if they are used in isolation.

Item 6 should be of special interest to clinicians working in private practice or some other nonschool mental health setting. The law is clear in stating that the school MDT has the ultimate responsibility for conducting the evaluation and determining program eligibility; it is not appropriate for one person to make a unilateral decision, even though one person may have conducted a majority of the evaluation. Many professionals working in community mental health centers or private practices may be unaware of this requirement, much to the consternation of school personnel when they receive a psychological report that states a child is eligible for special education services as emotionally disturbed, before the child has even been made a focus of concern by the MDT!

   IDEA Definition of "Emotionally Disturbed." In looking at all of IDEA's potential special education service categories, it is the category "emotionally disturbed" (ED, as it is commonly described) that is most relevant to the practice of clinical assessment of social and emotional behavior. It is true that such problems often occur concomitantly with other disability conditions (most notably, mental retardation, which does include guidelines for adaptive behavior assessment within the criteria), but it is the ED category that most specifically addresses disturbances of behavior, social adjustment, and emotion. *this area applies most to Soc/Emo/Behav Assessment + is co-morbid w/ MR*

   Students classified as ED receive the same federal protections as students with other disability conditions (right to a free and appropriate public education and related services), and are potentially provided with a "cascade" of placement and service, ranging from regular classroom placement with the assistance of a behavioral consultant, to full-time placement in a residential treatment center. The specific type of placement and service an ED student would receive would vary depending on the nature and severity of their disability, and what they would require in order to benefit educationally.

   In developing the rules and regulations for implementing the original Education of the Handicapped Act (P.L. 94-142), Congress adopted the following definition (which has since been revised to remove the term *autism*, which is now a subcategory of "Other Health Impaired"). This definition was an adaptation of an earlier proposed definition developed by Bower (1981), based on his widely influential research with delinquent and disturbed youth in California. The adaptation of Bower's definition that was originally embraced in the federal law is as follows:

Def of Emo Disturbed:

"(Seriously) emotionally disturbed" is defined as follows:
   (i) the term means a condition exhibiting one or more of the following characteristics over a long period of time and to a marked degree, which adversely affects educational performance:
   (A) An inability to learn which cannot be explained by intellectual, sensory, or health factors;
   (B) An inability to build or maintain satisfactory interpersonal relationships with peers and teachers;
   (C) Inappropriate types of behavior or feelings under normal circumstances;
   (D) A general, pervasive mood of unhappiness or depression, or,
   (E) A tendency to develop physical symptoms or fears associated with personal or school problems.
   (ii) The term includes children who are schizophrenic or autistic. The term does not include children who are socially maladjusted, unless it is determined that they are also seriously emotionally disturbed.

Note that "seriously" appears before "emotionally disturbed" in parentheses. The law originally passed by Congress and the resulting regulations that integrated Bower's definition referred to this category as "seriously emotionally disturbed." However, the 1997 reauthorization of IDEA resulted in the word "serious" being dropped from the title (Dwyer & Stanhope, 1997), but otherwise retained the same essential definition of the term that has been in use for over 20 years.

problems of the definition

A careful reading of the federal ED definition shows that using these criteria to make a classification decision is a process, like using the *DSM* criteria, that is at least superficially objective, but also involves a great deal of subjectivity. For example, what is a "long period of time" over which the problems must have occurred? Is 6 weeks too little time to be considered "a long period"? Is 1 year too much time? How about the statement "to a marked degree"? What kind of objective criteria can a clinician use to determine how marked the degree of a problem is? Obviously, the definition of ED from the federal law, like many of the *DSM* diagnostic criteria, does carry with it some problems of interpretation and implementation, and requires the clinician and members of the MDT to use a fair amount of professional judgment.

The ED Versus SM Issue. One of the continuing controversies surrounding the federal definition of ED stems from a brief statement in Part ii of the definition: The term does not include children who are socially maladjusted unless it is determined that they are also seriously emotionally disturbed. What exactly does this statement mean, and what are the ramifications? Interestingly, whereas IDEA does include the term *socially maladjusted* within the definition of ED, no operational definition is provided in the law. Traditionally, social maladjustment has been used as a term to indicate a pattern of behavioral problems that are thought to be willful, goal oriented, and to possibly be reinforced as part of an individual's immediate social reference group—a gang member being encouraged by peers to attack a member of a rival gang. The volitional nature of the antisocial behavior engaged in is often linked with social maladjustment, as characterized by Kelly's (1989) statement: "The term socially maladjusted encompasses . . . most individuals described as 'conduct disordered' who demonstrate knowledge of appropriate family, social, and/or school rules and *choose* (emphasis added) not to conform to them" (p. 3). Another traditional feature of the way social maladjustment has been conceptualized is that it is antisocial in nature, as typified by the type of behaviors exhibited in the *DSM–IV* diagnostic categories Conduct Disorder and Antisocial Personality Disorder.

socially maladjusted LOOPHOLE for denying service!

Because students identified as ED cannot easily be expelled from school, and because considering a student with severe behavioral problems as socially maladjusted provides a "loophole" for not providing special education services to them, there has been a great deal of professional interest in this topic. Although earlier studies of state special education regulations indicated that more than half of all states had ignored or chosen not to deal with the social maladjustment issue in their state definitions of ED (Mack, 1985), more recent surveys have shown that the majority of state definitions now include the social maladjustment exclusionary clause or some other form of exclusion (Skiba, Grizzle, & Minke, 1994). Although the federal ED definition provides no guidelines on how to identify social maladjustment, a number of professionals in education, psychology, and law have developed suggested classification procedures. A common approach, stemming from a legalistic interpretation of the *DSM* system, is characterized by the opinions of Slenkovitch (1983, 1992a, 1992b), who contended that a *DSM* diagnosis of Conduct Disorder should be equated with social maladjustment, and could legitimately serve to disqualify students from being identified as ED. There have also been attempts to develop psychometric instruments that are purported to be able to distinguish ED from social maladjustment (Kelly, 1986).

In view of the tremendous interest in this particular aspect of the ED definition (the third edition of the 1990 volume of *Behavioral Disorders*, and the first edition of the 1992 volume of *School Psychology Review* are both specifically devoted to the issue), it is interesting to note that the term *socially maladjusted* was not a part of Bower's original definition, and in fact, he was on record as being opposed to its inclusion in the federal definition because he considered it unworkable (Bower, 1982). There have been other compelling arguments made for eliminating the social maladjustment clause from the federal ED definition (Council for Children with Behavioral Disorders, 1987; C. M. Nelson, Rutherford, Center, & Walker, 1991; Skiba, 1992). However, there is no evidence that such a change is imminent, given that the most recent (1997) reauthorization of IDEA retained the social maladjustment exclusion. For now, professionals conducting school-related assessments of children and youth with behavioral, social, and emotional problems should be aware that there are no psychometrically valid and defensible assessment procedures that can be used to make this distinction. Clinicians and program administrators who are forced to deal with this issue must walk a perpetual fine line between empirically validated professional practices and the necessity of making pragmatic decisions based on policies and resource constraints. Of course, it should be recognized that the final addendum in the current federal definition does allow students who are considered to be socially maladjusted to receive special education services if it is determined that they are also emotionally disturbed, but the interpretation of this particular statement has been problematic, and the statement itself may be construed as using circular logic. In commenting on this and related statements in federal definition discussion of social maladjustment, Kauffman (1989) remarked that "the final addendum regarding social maladjustment is incomprehensible" (p. 25).

All states go by IDEA but switch up labels + don't use all the same categories

State Adaptations of the Federal Definition.   In practice, IDEA is carried out by each of the states, which are given a fair amount of leeway in adapting and implementing specific aspects of the rules and regulations. It is interesting to note that not all states have adopted this classification category by the "emotionally disturbed" title, or its predecessor, "seriously emotionally disturbed." Given that these terms tend to elicit images of psychiatric hospitals and highly disturbing behaviors, many individuals believe the term is pejorative at best, and some states have adopted this part of IDEA by the use of other terms. The state of Washington, for example, utilizes the term "Seriously Behaviorally Disabled," and the state of Utah refers to the category as "Behavior Disordered." Examples of some other terms used by states and by local education agencies include "Emotionally Impaired" and "Behaviorally-Emotionally Handicapped." There is also some variation among states in terms of specific assessment procedures that are to be utilized in making a classification of ED. For example, several states require documentation of appropriate intervention plans being implemented with a student prior to ED classification. Other states require specific assessment procedures such as direct behavioral observation or rating scales, and some states require an evaluation from a psychiatrist or other medical doctor prior to classification being allowed.

Regarding the differences among labels used to describe and implement ED from state to state, there is some evidence that "behaviorally disordered" is less stigmatizing and more accurate as a definitional term than "seriously emotionally disturbed" (Feldman, Kinnison, Jay, & Harth, 1983; Walker, 1982). Also, there seems to be a professional preference among special educators for the term *behavior disordered*. Nevertheless, widely varying terms and practices continue to be the norm. The confused state of the field as to definitions and assessment criteria reflects the confused state of the field in general; there is no question that professions that provide psychological and educational services to children and youth with behavioral, social, and emotional problems are continually evolving, and for good reason.

A Proposed New Definition. Given that there is widespread dissatisfaction with both the title (emotionally disturbed) and functional definition (the federal adaptation of Bower's definition) used to classify students with behavioral, social, and emotional problems under IDEA, it is not surprising that proposals for new terms and definitions have been developed. The most influential alternative definition proposed to date has been developed by the National Mental Health and Special Education Coalition, which comprises some 30 professional mental health and education associations. This coalition made modifications on the final definition from an earlier draft proposed by the Council for Children with Behavioral Disorders (CCBD) (1991). This new proposed definition, which uses the term *emotional, or behavior, disorder*, was detailed by Forness and Knitzer (1992) and is as follows:

Proposal for new def. of EMO. DISTURB.

(i) The term *emotional or behavioral disorder* (EBD) means a disability characterized by behavioral or emotional responses in school so different from appropriate, age, cultural, or ethnic norms that they adversely affect educational performance. Educational performance includes academic, social, vocational, and personal skills. Such a disability

(A) is more than a temporary, expected response to stressful events in the environment.

(B) is consistently exhibited in two different settings, at least one of which is school-related; and

(C) is unresponsive to direct intervention in general education or the child's condition is such that general interventions would be insufficient.

(ii) Emotional and behavioral disorders can co-exist with other disabilities.

(iii) This category may include children or youth with schizophrenic disorders, affective disorders, anxiety disorders, or other sustained disturbances of conduct or adjustment when they adversely affect educational performance in accordance with section (i).

Groups within the National Mental Health and Special Education Coalition have actively lobbied to have this definition adopted into IDEA, to replace the current term and definition of emotionally disturbed. For example, the National Association of School Psychologists has adopted the Mental Health/Education Coalition's proposed new definition as an official position (Dwyer & Stanhope, 1997). Because this alternative definition was not adopted by Congress during the past two reauthorizations of IDEA, despite some fairly extensive support and lobbying, it is unclear if and when such a change might occur, but there does seem to be widespread support for it among professional organizations. In many respects, the proposed definition appears to be a definite improvement over the definition currently used in IDEA. While still retaining the open features of a general definition, the proposed new definition better operationalizes certain aspects of the definition (e.g., EBD can co-exist with other disability conditions; the problems must be exhibited in a school-related setting and at least one other setting). The term *EBD* itself has face validity of being more descriptive and less stigmatizing than ED. Moreover, the proposed new definition does not allow the troublesome loophole for refusing service to "socially maladjusted" children and youth, which has been discussed.

Behavioral Dimensions: An Alternative Classification Paradigm

In addition to the *DSM* and special education classification systems, a third type of classification system has been making inroads in recent years, which appears to show considerable promise as an empirically sound way of taxonimizing behavioral, social, and emotional problems exhibited by children and youth. This method has been referred to by various terms, but is specifically referred to as the *behavioral dimensions* approach in this book. The paradigm utilized in the behavioral dimensions approach is rooted in empirical methods of measuring behavior, and complex statistical procedures that allow for the identification of *behavioral clusters*, which refer to clusters of highly intercorrelated behaviors. The statistical techniques most important in identifying intercorrelated behavioral syndromes are factor analysis, cluster analysis, and more recently, structural equation modeling. The use of these techniques in the behavioral dimensions approach to classification became prominent between the late 1960s and early 1980s, mainly through the pioneering work of Achenbach and his colleagues (Achenbach, 1982a; Achenbach & Edelbrock, 1981, 1983, 1984) and Quay and his colleagues (Quay, 1975, 1977; Quay & Peterson, 1967, 1987). These researchers developed and refined behavioral dimensions approaches to classifying behavioral problems through the utilization of sophisticated rating scales with empirically derived factor structures.

Behavioral Dimensions and the Child Behavior Checklist System. Through the development of both parent and teacher rating forms of the *Child Behavior Checklist* (CBCL) (Achenbach, 1991a; Achenbach & Edelbrock, 1984), Achenbach and his colleagues originally utilized factor analytic studies to identify two general classification areas within the behavior dimensions approach. The first general classification scheme is referred to as *broad-band syndromes*, which indicates the existence of large general behavioral clusters accounting for many types of related behavioral problems. The two broad-band syndromes utilized in the CBCL system include *internalizing* behavioral problems, which relate to *overcontrolled* behavior, and *externalizing* behavioral problems, which relate to *undercontrolled* behavior. Examples of internalizing behavior problems include anxiety, depression, and social withdrawal. Examples of externalizing behavior problems include delinquent behavior, aggressive behavior, and hyperactivity. The second general classification scheme is referred to as *narrow-band syndromes*, which are smaller behavioral clusters indicating more specific types of behavior, social, or emotional problems. The narrow-band problem syndromes utilized in the current CBCL system include Withdrawn, Somatic Complaints, Anxious/Depressed, Social Problems, Thought Problems, Attention Problems, Delinquent Behavior, and Aggressive Behavior.

The most recent CBCL system includes a variety of different rating and report forms, and these are discussed more specifically in subsequent chapters. Earlier versions of the instruments in the CBCL system utilized different narrow-band syndromes for different age and gender breakdowns, which were based on separate factor analytic studies, but the most current version utilizes the same "cross-informant" syndromes for each instrument, regardless of gender and age range. The CBCL system is arguably the most sophisticated series of behavior rating scales available, but it is certainly the most extensively researched. These instruments have become widely used by practitioners in both school and clinical settings, as well as by researchers. Table 2.4 shows the division of broad-band and narrow-band problem cross-informant syndromes utilized in the CBCL system.

TABLE 2.4
Cross-Informant Syndrome Categories Utilized in
Achenbach's Child Behavior Checklist System

Broad-band Syndromes
    Internalizing (overcontrolled)
    Externalizing (undercontrolled)

Narrow-band Syndromes
    Aggressive Behavior
    Anxious/Depressed
    Attention Problems
    Delinquent Behavior
    Social Problems
    Somatic Complaints
    Thought Problems
    Withdrawn

Quay's **Behavioral Dimensions Approach to Classification.** Another well-known dimensional approach to behavioral, social, and emotional problems of children and youth is based on the work of Quay and his colleagues. Originally, this line of research began through empirical analyses of the data sets obtained in developing the Behavior Problem Checklist (Quay, 1975, 1977; Quay & Peterson, 1967, 1987), a well-researched and historically important measure that appears to be diminishing in use at the present time. The first widely circulated version of the Behavior Problem Checklist (BPC) was developed during the 1960s (Quay & Peterson, 1967), and research associated with this instrument constituted one of the first large-scale efforts at developing a behavioral dimensions taxonomy. A 1987 revision of this instrument, known as the Revised Behavior Problem Checklist (RBPC; Quay & Peterson, 1987) included a modified rating format, new factor analytic and construct validity studies, and additional and reworded items. The overall dimensional structure of the RBPC was relatively similar to that of the BPC, with some exceptions. In addition to four major dimensions, two minor dimensions (which consist of fewer behavioral items) were included that described psychotic-like behaviors and unusually high rates of motor behavior. The several years of research with the BPC and RBPC resulted in the identification of the following four general dimensions of child problem behavior:

1. *Conduct Disorder*: Physical and verbal aggressiveness, defiant behavior, disruptiveness in classroom settings, and a pervasive attitude of irresponsibility and negativity.
2. *Anxiety-Withdrawal*: Social withdrawal, shyness, oversensitivity, a general pattern of retreat from the environment.
3. *Immaturity*: Passiveness, attentional problems, daydreaming, preoccupation, and delays in emotional development.
4. *Socialized Aggression*: Gang activities, stealing in groups, truancy from school, and identification with antisocial/delinquent subculture.

These four general areas were consistently identified as separate dimensions through several years of research. An interesting difference between the BPC system and the CBCL system is that the former has tended to focus more on overt conduct problems and less on the general class of internalizing problems than the latter. For example, the BPC contains fewer items measuring physical symptoms, sensory distortions, and the general area of social withdrawal than does the CBCL system.

Quay's pioneering work in the area of behavioral dimensions classification was not limited to findings from his own data sets with the BPC and RBPC. Perhaps the most influential of his work in this regard was his landmark review of 61 multivariate studies of child psychopathology characteristics (Quay, 1986). Quay matched the results of these various studies by examining both the factor labels and the actual behaviors subsumed by the factors to develop an integrative classification system of children's problem behavior. Like the work of Achenbach and his colleagues, Quay's work in this review identified the two broad-band dimensions of internalizing (over-controlled) and externalizing (undercontrolled) problems. Additionally, various types of narrow-band syndromes or disorders were identified. Some of the particular syndromes that Quay found are discussed in more detail in chapter 9 (externalizing disorders) and chapter 10 (internalizing disorders).

An Example of Behavioral Dimensions Approaches to Specific Classes of Behavior. The behavioral dimensions systems advocated by Achenbach and Quay conceptualize dimensions of behavior problems in a global sense by attempting to define and validate overall classes of behavioral, social, and emotional problems. However, some additional work by these researchers has demonstrated that a behavioral dimensions approach to smaller and more discrete classes of behavior is also possible. Using the specific class of delinquent behavior as an example, both researchers (Achenbach, 1982a, 1982b; Quay, 1975, 1986) identified subtypes of delinquent behavior using the same general behavioral dimensions methodology that has been overviewed.

Achenbach (1982) identified three dimensions of subtypes of delinquent activity: *socialized-subcultural* (low IQ and SES, bad companions, gang activities, maintain social status through illegal behavior), *unsocialized-psychopathic* (aggressive, assaultive, irritable, defiant, insensitive, feel persecuted), and *neurotic-disturbed* (overly sensitive, shy, worried, unhappy). Likewise, Quay's (1975) dimensional findings on delinquent behavior are extremely similar to those of Achenbach's, often using the same labels and terminology. One minor difference between the two dimensional approaches is that Quay suggested the existence of a fourth category, namely, what is referred to as *inadequate-immature* (passivity, dependence, tendency toward daydreaming). Because both of these dimensional classification systems for delinquency subtypes are so similar, they are presented in an integrated manner by four major categories in Table 2.5.

The purpose of presenting this overview of dimensional approaches to subtypes of delinquent behavior is to illustrate how the behavioral dimensions approach to classification extends to not just the overall conceptualization of behavior into several broad classes, but how it can be used within each dimensional class of behavior. One can assume that other general classes of behavioral, emotional, or social problems can also be further developed into dimensional subtypes. These empirically derived findings are intriguing, and suggest that the behavioral dimensions approach to classification may hold great promise in the future development of classification.

Additional Comments on the Behavioral Dimensions Approach. One thing to consider when looking at the examples of behavioral dimensions clusters overviewed in this chapter is that the names or titles of the specific dimensions are developed somewhat subjectively by the researchers involved, and can be misleading if taken too literally. When a researcher, through factor analytic studies, identifies the existence of specific behavioral clusters, the researcher develops a name for the factor based on

TABLE 2.5
An Overview of Dimensional Subtypes of Delinquent Behavior
Merging the Findings of Achenbach (1982a) and Quay (1975)

Dimensional Subtype	Behavioral Description
Socialized-Subcultural	Peer-oriented, group or gang activities, delinquent value orientation, lower in IQ and socioeconomic status, and experience less parental rejection than other subtypes
Unsocialized-Psychopathic	Unbridled aggression, assaultive, hostile, defiant, explosive, insensitive to feelings of others, impulsivity, thrill-seeking, respond poorly to praise or punishment, feel persecuted
Neurotic-Disturbed	Anxiety, guilt, overly sensitive, social withdrawal, worrying, unhappy
Inadequate-Immature	Highly dependent, passive, tendency toward daydreaming

the types of specific behaviors in the cluster. Sometimes, the cluster can be labeled in a way that directly indicates the specific behaviors involved. For example, a cluster of behaviors that includes "threatens others," "physically fights," "argues," and related behaviors may be labeled as "Aggressiveness," which seems to make good clinical sense. On the other hand, some clusters of behaviors may fit together well in a statistical sense, but coming up with an equally descriptive label for the cluster can be problematic. For example, one of the narrow-band clusters identified through the work of Achenbach and his colleagues was labeled "Thought Problems." Intuitively, one might think at first glance that high scores on this cluster may indicate the presence of schizophrenia or other types of psychoses, but this is seldom the case. Some of the actual behaviors found in this cluster include "can't get his/her mind off certain thoughts," "strange ideas," and "stares blankly." Although these characteristics might be commonly seen in severely thought-disordered or psychotic individuals, they may also occur with frequency in individuals with lesser problems. Clinicians using assessment and classification systems based on behavioral dimensions need to always look at the specific endorsed behaviors in a cluster to make decisions, rather than strictly going by the label or name a behavioral cluster has been given.

THE USE OF MULTIPLE GATING IN ASSESSMENT AND CLASSIFICATION

In chapter 1, a model for using multiple sources of assessment data, obtained from multiple sources and in multiple settings, was introduced as a "best practice" in assessing behavioral, social, and emotional problems. The advantages of this multiaxial model were presented, and there is little doubt that its use is preferable to single source assessments from both a clinical and research standpoint. And yet, despite the obvious advantages it presents, there are some potential obstacles. One of the problems in conducting assessments using many sources and instruments is the problem of *behavioral covariation*. If many different sources of information are utilized in an assessment, a diverse, if not contradictory, portrait of a given child's behavioral, social, and emotional status may result. This may present a serious problem for data interpretation, because it is generally agreed that most clinicians are not very efficient or skilled at effectively aggregating the multiple data sources and detecting covariation across the

assess that is too diverse may be contradictory!

instruments (Achenbach & Edelbrock, 1984; Reid, Patterson, Baldwin, & Dishion, 1988). Another problem that may become amplified with a multisource, multisetting, and multi-instrument assessment design is that detection of a class of target behavior or a specific syndrome that has a very low base rate is difficult. If multiple data sources are not used in a sequential and methodical fashion, the amount of error in classification may possibly be increased due to the behavioral covariation problem.

However, new developments in assessment technology are showing great promise in reducing the types of assessment problems that have just been described. One of the most exciting and innovative developments in assessment and classification during the past several years has been the development and refinement of a model for sequentially obtaining multiple sources of behavioral, social, and emotional assessment data, and then systematically using this information to make screening and classification decisions. This assessment model has come to be known as *multiple gating*. It is based on the sequential assessment strategy first introduced by Cronbach and Gleser (1965) for applications in personnel selection. Multiple gating in the assessment and classification of child and adolescent psychopathology was first formally articulated and presented by research scientists at the Oregon Social Learning Center (Loeber et al., 1984; Reid et al., 1988).

The basis of multiple gating is that through a series of assessment and decision steps (gates), a large population is sequentially narrowed down to a small population of individuals who are highly likely to exhibit the behavioral syndromes in question across settings and over time. The first step or gate generally consists of screening a large population of interest using time- and cost-effective measures, such as rating scales or teacher ranking procedures, for the behavioral syndrome of interest (e.g., antisocial behavior, aggression, hyperactivity, internalizing problems). This screening data is used to narrow down the larger population to a more reasonable number by only allowing those whose scores are at a specified level (e.g., over the 50th percentile) to pass through the first gate and on to the second. The initial criteria are established in a fairly liberal fashion, as to result in a number of false-positive errors (identification of individuals who do not exhibit the behavioral syndrome in question in a serious manner), but few or no false-negative errors (failure to identify individuals who should be identified). The next gate in the sequence might be additional low-cost data that are obtained across different situations, for example, using more lengthy rating scales completed by persons who know the subject in different settings. Again, a cutoff criterion is established to determine which individuals will pass through the second gate. Those who pass through the second gate (and their numbers should be fairly small at this point) are then assessed using more time intensive procedures, such as structured interviews with parents and behavioral observations at home and/or school. The final gate(s) also contain established decision rules for passing through, and those who do pass through the final points are considered to almost certainly exhibit the behavioral syndrome of interest to a serious degree. These individuals are then referred for additional assessment, final classification, and potentially, a program of intervention. The final classification does not necessarily have to be a *DSM* or special education category, but could consist of any formal operational definition of specific problem areas of interest.

Two examples of published multiple gating procedures are presented to illustrate the potential uses and steps involved. The first example is a community or clinic-based multiple gating procedure developed at the Oregon Social Learning Center to identify youths at risk for delinquency. The second example is a school-based multiple gating procedure to identify students with severe behavioral disorders.

A Community- and Clinic-Based Multiple Gating Procedure

A number of risk factors and behavioral variables have been found to correlate with juvenile delinquency. Loeber and Dishion (1983) ranked these etiological variables in terms of their predictive power, and noted that the composite measures of parental family management techniques, early childhood conduct problems, poor academic performance, and parental criminality or antisocial behavior were the most powerful predictors. They then attempted to apply this predictive information to a sequential multiple gating procedure using data from 102 twelve- to sixteen-year-old boys (Loeber et al., 1984). The result was a three-stage screening procedure that showed evidence of a high correct classification rate that was significantly less expensive than traditional methods of screening and assessment. This multiple gating procedure is illustrated in Fig. 2.1.

Gate 1 in the procedure consisted of teacher ratings obtained for each boy in the study. These ratings were conducted using a brief 11-item scale that required the teachers to rate the boys on both academic competency and social-behavioral characteristics at school. Boys whose ratings were at the 47th percentile or higher ($N = 55$) were selected to be assessed at Gate 2. The second gate consisted of telephone interviews with the parents of the remaining 55 boys. There were at least five interviews with each family, wherein questions regarding family organization, the whereabouts of the target child, and the occurrence of problem behaviors within a 24-hour period were asked. A risk score for this procedure was established, and boys scoring above the 47th percentile ($N = 30$) were moved on to the final gate. Gate 3 involved structured interviews with both the parents and target children. The content of the interviews was focused on family management procedures, such as parental monitoring of child activities, parental discipline practices, and perceived disobedience of the target boys. Again, a risk score for the procedure was developed, and boys whose scores were at the 47th percentile or higher ($N = 16$) were passed through this final gate. Subjects who were passed through this final gate were found to have an extremely low false-positive error rate when follow-up data on involvement by all subjects in delinquent activities was pursued. The authors concluded that this study provided strong initial evidence for the use of multiple gating in classification, both from empirical and cost-effectiveness standpoints. Since the publication of the Loeber et al. (1984) study, researchers at the Oregon Social Learning Center have continued

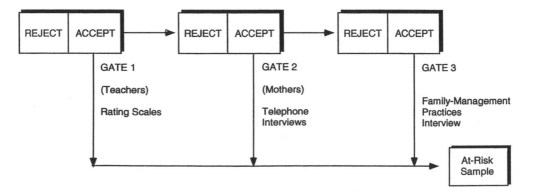

FIG. 2.1. Diagram of a clinic-based multiple gating procedure used to identify youths at risk for delinquency. Adapted from Loeber, Dishion, and Patterson (1984).

to refine the use of multiple gating assessment in additional investigations. A revised multiple gating model was articulated by Reid et al. (1988).

The SSBD: A School-Based Multiple Gating Procedure

Beginning in the mid-1980s, attempts were made to utilize multiple gating in the development of reliable and cost-effective screening procedures to identify students with serious behavioral disorders in the school setting. The initial development of these procedures was based on methodology modeled after the findings of researchers at the Oregon Social Learning Center (Loeber et al. 1984; Reid et al., 1988). The rationale for the development of a school-based model was the desirability of identifying severe behavioral problems at early grade levels, and thus being able to provide appropriate interventions in the incipient stages of developmental psychopathology rather than waiting until problems become extremely serious. The researchers involved in the early stages of this effort had noted that formal assessment and identification of students with severe behavioral disorders usually did not occur until about the middle school years, but a review of these students' behavioral records often found strong evidence for the existence of severe problems as early as kindergarten or first grade (H. Severson, personal communication, August 18, 1992).

The result of these efforts was the development of a multiple gating procedure that showed strong evidence of several forms of reliability and validity, and was found to have high classification accuracy in screening students with severe behavioral problems (Todis, Severson, & Walker, 1990; Walker, Severson, Stiller, et al., 1988; Walker, Severson, Todis, et al., 1990). This multiple gating system has since been revised and commercially published as the *Systematic Screening for Behavior Disorders* (SSBD; Walker & Severson, 1992). The SSBD is a three-gate system that includes[1] teacher screening (using a rank ordering procedure) of students with internalizing and externalizing behavioral problems (Gate 1),[2] teacher ratings of critical behavioral problems (Gate 2), and[3] direct behavioral observation of students who have passed the first two processes (Gate 3). The observational procedure used in Gate 3 includes both academic behavior in the classroom and social behavior on the playground. The end result of the SSBD system is that students who are passed through all three gates become the focus of prereferral interventions, and are potentially referred to child study teams for formal assessment and special education classification. Figure 2.2 displays a diagram of the gates and procedures in the SSBD.

The complete SSBD package includes procedural, training, and technical manuals, normative data, recommendations for behavioral interventions, complete forms and protocols, and a videotape for training in the observational system. It is a unique and exemplary system that shows some of the best possibilities of how school-based assessment and subsequent special education classification of students with severe behavioral and emotional problems can be accomplished.

SOME CONCLUDING COMMENTS ON DIAGNOSIS AND CLASSIFICATION

Attempts have been made in this chapter to delineate suitable reasons for making diagnostic and classification decisions as part of the assessment process, and to provide an overview of three major systems of classification: the *DSM*, special education service

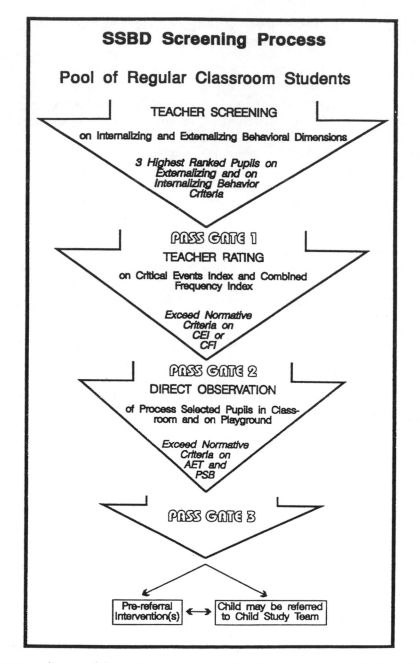

FIG 2.2. A diagram of the multiple gating stages of the Systematic Screening for Behavior Disorders. From *Systematic Screening for Behavior Disorders*, by H. M. Walker, H. H. Severson, 1992, Longmont, CO: Sopris West. Copyright © 1995 by Sopris West. Reprinted with permission.

categories, and the emerging behavioral dimensions approach. This chapter concludes by questioning how classification activities help link assessment of behavioral, social, and emotional problems to the process of intervention. Although attempts have been made to impress the reader with the necessity and advantages of conducting classification activities during the assessment process, the answer to this question is not as hopeful as it could be. At the present time, the evidence supporting the *treatment validity* (usefulness in developing intervention or treatment plans) of current classification schemes is neither abundant nor compelling. Whereas classification systems and activities may serve several appropriate purposes, being able to take a given classification category and automatically translate that into a set intervention is seldom possible. Classifying human behavior is inherently more simple than changing it. Because of the wide degree of individuality and variation in the biology, behavior, and temperament that human beings exhibit, developing effective interventions for behavioral, social, and emotional problems requires a tremendous understanding of the conditions under which those problems are occurring, as well as a great deal of clinical sensitivity on the part of the therapist. It will be an extraordinary challenge to the emerging generation of researchers and practitioners to develop classification systems that not only reliably codify a wide array of problems, but will provide information that might directly translate into valid treatment planning. On the other hand, the use of multiple gating procedures in assessment and classification is one development that shows tremendous promise in conducting systematic screening and assessment procedures that can be connected to various classification systems and subsequent programs of intervention.

CONCLUSIONS

Classification of behavioral, social, and emotional problems continues to be an important aspect of the overall assessment process. Although current psychological/psychiatric classification systems are imperfect, classification continues to be an important function because it can provide some common ground of understanding for professionals, and help provide access to services and remuneration for clients. Continuing to work with and refine present systems is a step in the right direction toward developing improved systems.

Differential diagnosis is a two-step process that involves making a decision regarding whether a problem is considered normal or abnormal, and then reaching a decision regarding how to classify the problem. In making classification decisions, there are two major types of errors. False-positive error involves making a determination that individuals have a particular disorder when in reality they do not, whereas false-negative error involves failure to diagnose individuals with a particular condition or disorder that they in fact have. The stakes involved in making particular decisions will determine which type of error is less onerous. The higher the risks and consequences are in a differential diagnosis and classification decision, the more conservative the approach to making the decision.

The *DSM* system, currently in its fourth edition, is the most widely used psychological/psychiatric classification system in North America. Historically, it has been based on the medical model, wherein emotional and behavioral disorders are viewed as manifestations of an underlying disease process residing within the individual. In more recent editions, the medical model outlook of the *DSM* has been tempered by the influence of behavioral psychology, and more attention is now given to situational and environmental factors in diagnosing many types of disorders. Although the *DSM* system has been rightly criticized in the past for problems of unreliability and lack of treatment validity, there have been substantial improvements with the most recent editions.

Within the public education system in the United States, the Individuals with Disabilities Education Act (IDEA) has substantial implications for assessment and classification of children and adolescents. Of particular interest to assessing social and emotional behavior in school settings is the IDEA special education eligibility category "emotionally disturbed" (ED). The definitional criteria for this category are broad enough to allow for classification of children with a variety of challenging social-emotional behaviors. One of the continuing controversies regarding the IDEA definition of ED is the so-called social maladjustment exclusion clause, which not unlike the definition of ED, has come under intense criticism but was never changed by Congress.

A more recent approach to classification of child and adolescent social-emotional problems is what has been referred to as the behavioral dimensions approach. This approach, typified by the pioneering work of Achenbach and Quay, relies on sophisticated statistical models to empirically derive clusters or syndromes of child behavior.

A promising and innovative approach to assessment and classification of social-emotional problems of children and adolescents is multiple gating methodology. By using a sequential series of systematic and increasingly time-consuming screening procedures, multiple gating methods allow for narrowing a large population down to a small group of candidates who are likely to exhibit behavioral and emotional problems to the point of needing further assessment and intervention. Multiple gating approaches have been developed and validated for use in both community and school settings. Although this methodology is time consuming, multiple gating and sequential assessment may theoretically reduce error variance associated with using aggregated multiple assessment sources.

Despite the substantial improvements in classification systems for emotional and behavioral disorders of children and adolescents, many challenges remain. Perhaps the foremost challenge in this area is the development of classification systems and categories that are not only reliability and scientifically taxonomic, but have strong treatment validity as well.

REVIEW AND APPLICATION QUESTIONS

1. What are the primary purposes of classifying emotional and behavioral disorders of children and adolescents?

2. Define the term *differential diagnosis*. Illustrate how it is utilized in the assessment and classification process.

3. Give examples of how *false-positive* and *false-negative* classification errors might occur in assessing behavioral, social, and emotional problems. Is one type of error less damaging than the other?

4. The *DSM* classification system has been widely criticized over the years, but continues to be refined and is without question the preeminent classification system in the North America. List the major positive and useful aspects of the *DSM* that have helped expand its influence.

5. What are some of the continuing problems with the *DSM* approach to classification?

6. What are some ways that the social maladjustment "exclusion" clause in the definition of emotionally disturbed in IDEA can be implemented?

7. Compare and contrast the definition of *Emotionally Disturbed* from the Individuals with Disabilities Education Act, with the proposed definition of *Emotional or Behavioral Disorder* from the National Mental Health and Special Education Coalition. What differing implications do each of these definitions have for assessing behavioral, social, and emotional problems?

8. What are the assumptions and procedures behind the *behavioral dimensions* approach to classification, and how do they differ from those of other classification methods?

9. Two different *multiple gating* procedures for assessment and classification were described in this chapter. Identify the potential problems involved with instituting and utilizing a multiple gating procedure, and determine what steps could be taken to reduce these problems.

3

DIRECT BEHAVIORAL OBSERVATION

Direct Behav. Observations = one of the most empirically sound assess. techniques [handwritten annotation]

This chapter provides a detailed introduction to the principles, specific uses, and problems of direct behavioral observation. This is one of the primary tools of many clinicians and researchers who are involved in assessing the behavioral, social, and emotional problems of children and adolescents, and it holds a prominent position as one of the most empirically sound assessment techniques.

This chapter first provides an overview of the basic principles and concepts of behavioral observation, and then takes a detailed look at both the general methods and typical coding procedures of behavioral observation. After the general foundations and methods of direct behavioral observation have been described, a review of six different formal observational coding systems is provided. These systems were selected based on their general purpose design and their utility in conducting assessments in school, home, and clinic settings. The chapter then includes an analysis of some of the major problems and issues in behavioral observation. Issues ranging from observer reactivity to situational specificity of behavior are covered, and specific suggestions for overcoming these problems and limitations of behavioral observation are provided. The exploration concludes with a discussion of how direct behavioral observation can be useful in making various decisions related to the assessment process.

BEHAVIORAL OBSERVATION: BASIC PRINCIPLES AND CONCEPTS

Dir. Behav. obser. = direct & objective method [handwritten annotation]

Direct observation of behavior is one of the cornerstone tools for the assessment of behavioral, social, and emotional problems exhibited by children and adolescents. Whether the observation involves formal behavioral recording in naturalistic settings, or whether it is done informally as part of other measurement strategies, behavioral observation provides the clinician with one of the most direct and objective assessment tools available. Direct behavioral observation is a procedure in which observers develop operational definitions of the targeted behaviors of interest, observe the subjects, and systematically record their behaviors. Behavioral observation is one of the strongest

judge against self — not to large group   *linked to interventions*

nomothetic methods of assessment, and has the advantage of being easily linked to the development of interventions.

The roots of behavioral observation are firmly grounded in behavioral psychology, as advocated by Watson, Skinner, and others. Researchers and clinicians who embrace behavioral psychology in its most radical forms go so far as to contend that direct observation is the only empirically sound method of behavioral assessment. However, since the 1970s, there have been increased efforts at integrating behaviorism and direct observation into more broad models of conceptualizing human behavior. To that end, direct observation has been found to be compatible with social learning theory (Patterson, 1969; Bandura, 1977, 1978), applied behavior analysis (Baer, 1982), and cognitive behavior therapy (Meichenbaum & Cameron, 1982). Even an approach to treatment as different from behaviorism as Rogers' (1951) client-centered therapy relies on clinical observation by the therapist as an important part of understanding and treating the problems of the client, even though it is not as systematic as many behaviorists prefer. *Behav. observation is linked to several theories of ψ*

Keller (1986) noted that the unifying factor of different behavioral approaches appears to be "their derivation from experimentally established procedures and principles" (p. 355). As such, most methods of behavioral observation, and specifically those methods and techniques covered in this chapter, have a strong emphasis on sound empirical methodology and a high degree of treatment validity. Alessi (1988) noted that one of the critical characteristics of observation methods for emotional and behavioral problems is that they permit a *functional analysis of behavior*, and as such, are intrinsically linked to valid interpretation of assessment data and development of systematic intervention plans. Additionally, it is important to recognize that direct behavioral observation methods are particularly suited to assessing the behavior of individuals as opposed to groups, even though groups of individuals may be involved, because these methods are particularly adept at taking into account the unique context and the repertoire of responses exhibited by individuals (Sulzer-Azaroff & Mayer, 1991).

permit a FUNCTIONAL ANALYSIS of BEHAVIOR → allows interventions!

DIRECT BEHAVIORAL OBSERVATION AS "ECOBEHAVIORAL ASSESSMENT"

what natural support systems elicit + maintain the behavior?

Perhaps the foremost advantage of direct behavioral observation is that it allows the observer to gather functional information regarding not just individual behavior, but also about how this behavior exists as part of an interactive environment. During the past two decades, substantial efforts by behavioral scientists have demonstrated that behavior is best understood and predicted when taking into account the natural support systems within the environment that elicit and maintain the behavior, because "those (behaviors) that run counter to natural support systems are less likely to prevail for very long" (Sulzer-Azaroff & Mayer, 1991, p. 46). For example, take the case of an elementary-age student who exhibits aggressive and antisocial behavior in the various settings at school. A superficial observation of this student's behavior will merely define when, where, and how the problem behavior is occurring. In contrast, a sophisticated observation that takes into account the surrounding environment or ecology in which these behaviors exist is more likely to provide information on conditions that elicit and maintain the problem behaviors, such as interactions from teachers and peers, the physical aspects of the classroom, or particular activities or

sophisticated observations take the surrounding environment into account...

individuals. A skilled clinician can use this type of information not only to describe and classify the behavior in detail, but to develop intervention plans that may have a good chance of succeeding.

Rogers-Warren (1984) labeled the type of behavioral assessment that takes into account environmental variables as *ecobehavioral assessment*. She proposed an assessment matrix that included the following four levels:

[handwritten left margin: Eco-Behavioral Assess.]

1. *Discrete level.* Individual initiations and responses. *[handwritten: = 1 person]*
2. *Exchange level.* Initiation–response–reciprocation between two people. *[handwritten: = 2 people]*
3. *Episodes.* Events immediately preceding and following the target behaviors.
4. *Standing patterns.* Similar series of events or episodes. *[handwritten: = events before behav.]*

[handwritten: → similar episodes elicit same behav.]

Following the collection of observational data within this matrix, the four behavioral levels are analyzed to ascertain relations between behavior and the environment, to determine which environmental events co-occur with the behavior, and whether or not these events facilitate or inhibit behavior. Such identified relations are then examined in more detail to determine whether or not they might be helpful in planning and evaluating an intervention.

Although the model articulated by Rogers-Warren (1984) is innovative and appears to have a great deal of merit, it is also important to recognize that in reality, comprehensive behavioral assessment is (or should be) ecobehavioral assessment, irrespective of its title. The notion of examining environmental antecedents and consequences of behavior has existed for many years, even though it occasionally becomes infused with new energy through concepts like the ecobehavioral assessment model, or more recently, what has been referred to as *functional assessment* of behavior (e.g., Reep, 1994; Vollmer & Northrup, 1996). Thus, researchers and practitioners who utilize direct behavioral observation should always consider that behavior does not occur in a vacuum; examining environmental relations within the entire behavioral ecology should be a standard practice if the observation is meant to result in anything more useful than simple description of behavior.

[handwritten left margin: always observe what's going on around the indiv.]

GENERAL METHODS OF BEHAVIORAL OBSERVATION

Although there are a number of specific techniques and systems for use in observing behaviors, most can be included in the categories of naturalistic observation, analogue observation, and self-monitoring. This section illustrates the main characteristics and uses of each of these three general methods.

Naturalistic Observation   *[handwritten: = no/little inferring required.]*

The most direct and desirable way to assess child and adolescent behavior in most cases is through naturalistic observation. The essential elements of naturalistic observation have been outlined by Jones, Reid, and Patterson (1979), and include observation and recording of behaviors at the time of occurrence in their natural setting, the use of trained, objective observers, and a behavioral description system that requires only a minimal amount of inference by the observers-coders. Naturalistic observation differs from the other two general methods of observation in that there is a premium on obtaining observational data in typical, day-to-day situations, with strong efforts to minimize any obtrusiveness or reactivity caused by the presence of an observer.

Analogue or self-monitoring methods require more inference than naturalistic observation in determining whether or not observed behaviors are representative of what actually occurs in the subject's day-to-day environment.

What type of observational settings can be considered to be naturalistic? Perhaps more than any other setting, school-based assessments offer many opportunities for naturalistic observation. Whether the observation takes place in the classroom, on the playground, during recess, in the cafeteria, or in the halls between classes, the school environment has great potential for unobtrusive data collection in situations that are encountered by children and adolescents on a regular basis. For younger children who are not yet in school, there are other possibilities for naturalistic observation settings, including day care and play groups.

The home setting also offers opportunities for naturalistic observation, but on a more limited basis. Observing subjects as they interact with their family in the home environment has the potential for being an excellent means of gathering data, but there are significant obstacles that must be overcome: the increased probability of obtrusiveness and reactivity, and the physical circumstances of the home. Because most families are not used to having strangers enter their home and watch their ongoing activities, it is a given that they will behave differently under these conditions; most likely, they will make an effort to minimize the occurrence of any maladaptive or coercive behaviors by putting their "best foot forward." The design of most American houses and apartments, with the resulting lifestyles that are shaped, also create considerable challenges for conducting observation. A typical middle-class home is sufficiently large and compartmentalized so that family members can distance themselves from each other (and from an observer) with relative ease by going into different parts of the home. Investigators at the Oregon Social Learning Center (OSLC; Reid, Baldwin, et al., 1988) have worked extensively on the problems of conducting effective naturalistic observations in home settings and have developed methods of minimizing reactivity and physical barriers with their coding systems. A typical in-home observation by the OSLC team is structured so that family members agree to stay in a common area of the home and do some activity together (other than watching television) during the observation period. In a sense, conducting a home observation in this manner is somewhat contrived, and is akin to analogue observation, but it still allows for highly effective observation and coding of family interactions in the home setting (Patterson, Ray, Shaw, & Cobb, 1969).

Analogue Observation = simulation of real, natural conditions

Unlike naturalistic observation, which is designed to capture behavior as and where it normally occurs, analogue observation methods are designed to simulate the conditions of the natural environment, and to provide a highly structured and controlled setting where behaviors of concern are likely to be observed (Keller, 1986). The analogue observation might occur in a clinic or laboratory, but the specific environment developed for the observation is structured to simulate everyday situations in the natural environment. In many cases, the participants in analogue observation might be requested to role play or engage in the observation activity in a specific way. Examples of situations that have been developed for analogue observation include parent–child interactions, family problem-solving approaches, and children's task orientation.

There is no question that analogue observation carries with it problems and obstacles. Compared to naturalistic observation, a greater deal of inference is required in

Con of analog = more inferences required
Pro "   " = can structure so that ↑ eliciting behav.

52

CHAPTER 3

drawing conclusions about behavior; many questions are likely to arise concerning the validity of the observational data. However, analogue observation offers enough advantages that clinicians who conduct child and adolescent assessments are advised to become competent in its use. One of the chief advantages of the analogue method is that the observer can exert much greater control over the environment than with naturalistic observation, thus increasing the opportunities for eliciting important but low frequency behaviors. For example, if one of the stated referral problems is noncompliance to teacher or parent directions, the observer can create a large number of analogue situations where the subject must react to directions. A related advantage that the control aspect of analogue observation offers is that extraneous stimuli—those things that are inconsequential to or detract from the behavior in question—can be reduced or eliminated. Overall, the analogue method offers many advantages and possibilities, if the observer considers its limitations.

One of the most important aspects of conducting an analogue observation is to structure the observational conditions so that they closely resemble those of the setting(s) in which the problems are most likely to occur. By doing this, similarity in stimuli and responses between the two settings is maintained, and the observation is more likely to be conducive to the behavior in question. For example, if the assessment goal is to obtain observational data of interactions between a mother and her child, it would be important to have them engage in activities that they are likely to be doing at home, by having them role play, or work with materials they are likely to utilize at home. By carefully structuring the conditions of the analogue observation, the similarity between the natural environment is increased, and the resulting validity and usefulness of the observation data is enhanced.

Self-Monitoring

A third general method of observing behavior is self-monitoring. The essential feature of self-monitoring is that subjects are trained in observing and recording their own behavior. The advantages apparent with self-monitoring include its relatively low cost and efficiency, its utility in the measurement of covert of private events such as thoughts and subtle physiological changes, and its lack of intrusiveness (Shapiro & Cole, 1994). It would be extremely difficult to conduct valid observations of mild seizures a subject experienced unless they were constantly connected to physiological measurement instruments, but the subject might be easily trained to record the occurrence of these events.

Of course, there are a number of drawbacks to self-monitoring, including the reliability and validity of the self-monitored observations (Keller, 1986). It is difficult enough to train impartial observers-coders in the reliable use of observation technology, and when the observation is extended to include self-scrutiny by the subject (particularly with children), the implementation problems are likely to increase. These potential reliability and validity problems can be decreased through specific procedures, including providing a sufficient amount of training to the subject, using systematic and formal observation forms, using self-monitoring procedures that require a minimum of time and energy by the subject, conducting occasional reliability checks with the subject, and reinforcing the subject for conducting accurate observations.

Self-monitoring tends to be used to a much greater extent in behavioral treatment programs than as part of a multimethod, multisource, multisetting assessment, and as such, is not addressed in more detail here. For a more complete treatment of the use of self-monitoring procedures, readers are referred to Alberto and Troutman (1990), Shapiro and Cole (1994), Sulzer-Azaroff and Mayer (1991), or the *Journal of Applied Behavior Analysis*. The first three sources are textbooks that include a number of school-based applications of self-monitoring in assessment and treatment, and the latter is a scholarly journal that has included articles detailing many uses of self-monitoring.

OBSERVATIONAL CODING PROCEDURES

Now that the general methods of behavioral observation have been analyzed, it is useful to look at the specific ways that behavioral observation data may be recorded or coded. As many as seven different observational coding procedures and useful combinations of procedures have been identified (Sulzer-Azaroff & Mayer, 1991), but in this chapter the number of recording categories has been collapsed into four general types of procedures. A brief summary of these four coding procedures is found in Table 3.1.

TABLE 3.1
A Guide to Selecting Observational Coding Procedures

Coding Procedure	Definition	Example	Advantages and Disadvantages
Event Recording	Recording the number of times a specific behavior occurs during the length of an observational period	Number of times students leave their seat	A: Can be used to determine antecedents and consequences of behavior D: Not useful with behaviors that occur frequently
Interval Recording	Dividing the observational period into intervals, and recording specified behaviors that occur at any time during the interval (partial interval) or during the entire interval (whole interval)	Number of intervals in which students are out of seat at any point (partial interval) or during entire time (whole interval)	A: Good choice for behaviors that occur at a moderate but steady rate D: Requires complete attention of observer
Time-Sampling Recording	Dividing observational period into intervals, and recording if specified behavior occurs momentarily at interval	Number of intervals in which students are out of seat at exact point of interval	A: Requires only one observation per interval D: May miss some important low frequency behaviors
Duration/Latency Recording	Recording how long a particular behavior lasts (duration), or how long from the end of one behavior to the beginning of another (latency)	How long students are out of seat (duration); how long the students are out of seat after the teacher tells them to return to seat	A: Simple to do with a stopwatch or wall clock D: Difficult for behaviors without a clear beginning or end

Event Recording   = FREQUENCY RECORDING

Event recording is simply a measure or count of how many times specified target behavior(s) occur during the length of the observational period. Event recording is also known as *frequency recording*. Barton and Ascione (1984) suggested that this type of recording procedure is best suited for use with behaviors that meet three criteria. First, the behaviors should have a clear beginning and end. Within the behavioral domains of physical aggression or asking for help, it is normally quite simple to determine starting and stopping points, but with behaviors such as making noise, this task becomes more difficult. Second, it should take approximately the same amount of time to complete each response every time the behaviors occur. If the observer is recording a class of behaviors that vary considerably in time from occurrence to occurrence, another recording technique (such as duration recording) should be used. Because event recording yields a simple tally of how many times the behavior(s) occurred, it is not useful for gauging such aspects of behavior as intensity or length. Third, the behaviors should not occur so frequently that it becomes difficult to separate each occurrence. For example, if an observer was using event recording to measure self-stimulatory behavior (e.g., hair twirling, rocking, or lip rubbing) of a child with severe disabilities, and these behaviors were occurring every few seconds, the event recording procedure would become too cumbersome. On this third criteria, the observer will have to make a decision if the frequency of the behavior is so high that event recording will be difficult to implement.

Certain techniques can be used with event recording to maximize its usefulness as an observational recording procedure. One way that the utility of event recording can be increased is to record events sequentially, or in the exact order in which they occur. By developing a sequential analysis of observed events, behaviors can be categorized according to antecedents and consequences, which may be helpful in fully understanding the behaviors and in developing intervention plans. A useful way of transcribing event recording into an analysis of behavioral antecedents and consequences is through the use of an A–B–C (antecedent–behavior–consequence) evaluation, which follows these steps: (a) Divide a sheet of paper into three columns, one each for antecedents, behaviors, and consequences; (b) list the specific behaviors that were recorded in the middle column (behaviors); and (c) note what events or behaviors preceded the recorded behaviors (antecedents), and what events or behaviors followed the recorded behaviors (consequences). Using this A–B–C procedure requires some flexibility in the observation system—in some cases, a targeted behavior that was recorded in the "B" column will also appear in the "A" column as an antecedent to another important behavior or event. However, the payoff of using this technique will come in the form of an ecologically sensitive observational recording system that has strong implications for treatment. An example of using the A–B–C breakdown sheet with event recording is provided in Fig. 3.1.

Another way that the use of event recording can be fine-tuned to yield more useful data is to report the events in different ways, depending on the length of the observation period. Barton and Ascione (1984) suggested three length-based ways of reporting data: (a) If each observation period is of the same length, report the actual frequency that each event occurred; (b) if the observation periods differ to some extent in length, the data should be reported by rates of occurrence, or the number of responses divided by the time period that the observations took place in; and (c)

A-B-C Event Recording Sheet

ANTECEDENT	BEHAVIOR	CONSEQUENCE
Teacher asks students to take out their workbooks	S does not take out workbook, talks to neighbor	teacher reprimands S
Teacher reprimands S	S removes workbook from desk	Teacher focuses attention away from S
	S raises hand to ask question	Teacher works with another student
	S continues to raise hand	Teacher responds to S's question
Teacher responds to S's question	S puts head down on desktop	
S puts head down on desktop	S begins to tap leg against desk	Neighbor tells S to be quiet
Neighbor tells S to be quiet	S tells neighbor "shut up"	Teacher tells S "get back to work"
Teacher tells S "get back to work"	S puts book in desk, places arms and head on desktop	Teacher again tells S to get back to work
Teacher again tells S to get back to work	S pounds hand on desk and swears at teacher	Teacher tells S to go to time-out chair in back of room
Teacher tells S to go to time-out chair in back of room	S kicks chair and goes to time-out chair	

FIG. 3.1. An example of behavioral observation data that were collecting using an event recording procedure and the A–B–C (antecedent–behavior–consequence) technique.

behavioral events that are supposed to follow specific cues (such as compliance with directions from the teacher) should be reported as a percentage of opportunities that the behavior occurred, as in three compliances for five commands. Event recording in its most basic form is very easy to use, but by using some of these modifications, the observer will be able to make the observation more insightful and useful.

Interval Recording — Best for moderate rates of behav.

The essential characteristics of interval recording involve selecting a time period for the length of the observation, dividing the observational period into a number of equal intervals, and recording whether or not the specified target behavior(s) occur during each interval. Interval recording is considered to be a good choice for use with behaviors that occur at a moderate but steady rate, but is not as useful for behaviors that occur with relatively low frequency. It does not provide an exact count of behaviors, but is a good choice for use with behaviors that occur on a very frequent basis. An example of a typical interval-based observation would be a 30-minute observation period divided into 90 equal intervals of 20 seconds each.

Interval recording requires the complete attention of the observer, and can be difficult to implement if the intervals are too short, or the number of behaviors targeted for observation are too great. Normally, the observational period will be less than 1 hour long, and the intervals will be no more than 30 seconds long (Cooper, 1981). The most simple form of interval recording involves using the procedure with one targeted behavior, and recording a plus (+) or minus (–) in boxes that have been drawn for each interval to indicate whether or not the target behavior occurred. If the intervals are short, or if the number of behaviors that are targeted for observation are so many that it creates difficulty in making an accurate recording, brief recording intervals can be placed between each observation interval (Alberto & Troutman, 1990). For example, observers might use 10-second intervals for the observation, but place a 5-second scoring interval between each observation interval, thus giving themselves the time to accurately record the behaviors and prepare for the next interval.

Whole and Partial Interval Recording.   Interval recording can be divided into two general types: *whole interval recording* and *partial interval recording*. With whole interval recording, the behavior being coded must be observed during the entire interval in order to be recorded. The whole interval method is considered to be a good choice if the behaviors being coded are continuous (such as on-task behavior) and the intervals are short to medium in length (Shapiro & Skinner, 1990). With partial interval recording, the observer codes the target behavior in question if it occurs at any time during the interval; once a specific behavior has been coded, it is no longer necessary to monitor that behavior until the next interval begins. The partial interval method is considered to be a good choice for recording low frequency behaviors that are observed over fairly long intervals of time (Shapiro & Skinner, 1990). An example of behavioral observation data obtained with a partial interval coding system is found in Fig. 3.2. Both types of interval recording, whole and partial, may result in error. Whole interval recording tends to overestimate the frequency and underestimate the prevalence of behavior, whereas partial interval recording tends to underestimate the frequency and overestimate the prevalence of behavior (Salvia & Hughes, 1990; Salvia & Ysseldyke, 1995). Which is the best of these two methods of interval recording? It depends on the behaviors being observed, and the purposes for which the observation is being conducted.

A final consideration of interval recording is that its effective use may depend on special timing devices. If the observation intervals are long enough, and if the number of targeted behaviors is limited, then it is possible to get by with the use of a digital or hand watch with second timers. However, as the time intervals decrease, or as the number of behaviors targeted for observation increases, using a typical watch with a second timer becomes increasingly frustrating (if not maddening), and the reliability and validity of the observation inevitably suffers. Although they are difficult to find, special timing devices have been developed for interval recording that use small battery-powered electronic timers that provide a cue (i.e., a beep or a tone) to the observer when the interval has elapsed. Some of these instruments are sophisticated enough to allow the observer to adjust the time intervals to varying lengths, and to deliver the time cues through a small earplug, which reduces the obtrusiveness of the observation. Obviously, these types of instruments, like certain musical recordings advertised on late-night television, are "not sold in any store." To obtain them, a practitioner must either look in specialized psychological testing equipment catalogues, or have a local electronics technician specially design them.

PLAYGROUND SOCIAL BEHAVIOR RECORDING FORM

Name and Grade: *Justin T., Grade 4t*   **Date:** *October 17*
Location: *Central School Playground*   **Activity:** *Morning Recess*
Observer: *Chris Thompson*   **Start/Stop Time:** *10:05 - 10:18 AM*
Interval Length/Type: *20 seconds, partial interval*

INTERVAL	PA	VA	INT	ISO		INTERVAL	PA	VA	INT	ISO
1				X		21				X
2				X		22				X
3				X		23				X
4			X			24				X
5		X				25				X
6		X				26			X	
7				X		27			X	
8				X		28			X	
9				X		29			X	
10				X		30			X	
11				X		31				X
12			X			32				X
13			X			33				X
14			X			34				X
15		X				35			X	
16	X					36				X
17			X			37				X
18	X					38		X		
19				X		39		X		
20				X		40		X		

CODING KEY:
PA=physically aggressive   **VA**=verbally aggressive
INT=appropriate social interaction   **ISO**=socially isolated

FIG. 3.2. An example of behavioral observation data that were collecting using a partial interval coding procedure for social behavior in a school playground setting.

only observe momentarily +
Intervals can be randomly spaced

Time-sampling Recording

Time-sampling recording is similar to interval recording in that the observation period is divided into intervals of time. The essential difference between the two procedures is that with time-sampling, behavior is observed only momentarily at the prespecified intervals. An additional difference between the two procedures is that with interval recording, the observation intervals are generally divided into equal units, whereas it is not unusual to divide time intervals randomly or in unequal units with time-sampling. As with interval recording, time-sampling is most useful for observing behavior(s) that occur at a moderate but steady rate.

Time-sampling recording can be illustrated using assessment of on-task academic behavior as an example. The observation might occur during a 20-minute time period of academic instruction that has been divided into 20 intervals of 1 minute each. As each minute ends, the observer records whether or not the subject was on-task. In this example, the time units were divided into equal intervals, but these intervals do not need to be equal, and could even be generated randomly. If the time intervals used in time-sampling are short or complex, then the type of electronic timing devices mentioned in the discussion of interval recording would be useful. Some innovative researchers and clinicians have even developed electronic timing devices that randomly generate audible tones at varying time intervals within a given range.

A major advantage of the time-sampling recording procedure is that it requires only one observation per interval, and is thus less subject to the problems of getting off-track that are easily encountered with interval recording. If the intervals are large enough, the time-sampling method may even free up the observer to engage in other activities. For example, a teacher could still go about directing an instructional activity while conducting an observation using time-sampling, provided the intervals are large enough and the recording is simple. Interestingly, the major advantage of time-sampling is closely related to its most glaring drawback. Because time-sampling only allows for recording of behavior that occurs occasionally, an observer may end up not recording many important behaviors, and invalid conclusions may be reached. The longer the interval used with time-sampling, the less accurate the data; as the interval increases, the sample of behavior decreases. Reaching an appropriate balance between the length of the interval needed and the necessity of freeing up the observer for other activities is the most reasonable way to use time-sampling.

don't observe too much behavior. — shorter time = better results,

Duration and Latency Recording

Event recording, interval recording, and time-sampling recording all have the similarity of focusing on obtaining exact or approximate counts of targeted behaviors that occur during a given time frame. Two additional techniques, duration and latency recording, differ from the first three because their focus is primarily on the *temporal* aspects of the targeted behaviors rather than on how often the behaviors occur. Duration and latency recording are best used with behaviors that have a discrete beginning and end, and last for at least a few seconds each time they occur (Barton & Ascione, 1984).

How long behav is.

Duration Recording. In duration recording, the observer attempts to gauge the amount of time a subject engages in a specific behavior. In other words, the most critical aspect of the observation is how long the behavior lasts. For school-based assessment, a good example of how duration recording might be used is provided by the observation of out-of-seat behavior. If a student leaves their workspace during an instructional activity to wander around the classroom, it may be useful to understand how long the out-of-seat behavior is lasting. There is a big difference between students who get out of their seat three times during a 30-minute observation but who are still academically engaged for most of the period, and those who get out of their seat only once during the observation but who stay out of their seat for most of the period. For clinic-based assessment, a good example of the use of duration recording is provided by observation of child temper tantrums. The parent of a 6-year-old who engages in temper tantrums two to three times per week lasting for 20 minutes or longer can provide the clinician with valuable information by measuring the length of the tantrums. A treatment that reduces the average number of tantrums from three to two per week might be less valuable than a treatment that reduces their duration to 5 minutes each.

Latency Recording. In latency recording, the observer attempts to gauge the amount of time from the end of one behavior to the beginning of another. In other words, the most critical aspect of the observation is how long it takes for the behavior to begin. A typical example of how latency recording could be used comes from observation of a child referred for noncompliant behavior. In this case, it might be important to observe how long it takes from the parent or teacher request for action to the enactment of the behavior. Treatment progress could be gauged through seeing a consistent trend of a decreased amount of time between the request and the compliance.

A REVIEW OF SELECTED OBSERVATIONAL CODING SYSTEMS

This section provides introductions and reviews of six relatively general different observational coding systems. Observational coding systems that are useful for highly specific purposes, such as the measurement of hyperactivity or social withdrawal, are reviewed in chapters 9 through 13. The six observational coding systems described here, which are summarized in Table 3.2, are divided into three types—school-based,

TABLE 3.2
Characteristics of Six Selected General Purpose Observational Coding Systems

Code Name	Setting	Measures	Uses
Child Behavior Checklist, Direct Observation Form	School	96-item rating scale, event recording, interval recording	Internalizing and externalizing behavior problems and on-task behavior
Behavior Coding System	School	8 categories, interval recording	Coercive and aggressive behavior
Social Interaction Scoring System	Home	12 categories, continuous event recording	General social-behavioral problems
Family Interaction Code	Home	29 categories, interval recording	Aversive family behavior
Child's Game and Parent's Game	Clinic	7 parent behavior and 3 child behavior categories, coded in 30-second intervals	Child noncompliance, behavior problems during interactions with parent
Teacher Behavior Code	Clinic/ Home	9 categories, interval-based "teaching trials"	Change in parent teaching behavior following training

home-based, and clinic-based—with two representative coding systems selected for each category. With the exception of the Child Behavior Checklist–Direct Observation Form (Achenbach, 1986), these observation coding systems are not commercially published products. Most of these coding systems were reported in professional journals as one part of the research methodology employed in a study. Thus, to obtain complete information on most of these observational systems, readers will need to locate the reference cited with them.

School-Based Observation Systems

Child Behavior Checklist–Direct Observation Form. The Direct Observation Form (DOF) was developed by Achenbach (1986) and his colleagues as the observational component of the multiaxial Child Behavior Checklist system for assessing child psychopathology. It was developed specifically for use in classrooms and in other group activities. The DOF, unlike many observational coding systems, is at least partially based on rating scale technology, because it includes 96 items rated on a 4-point scale following a 10-minute observation period. The rating scale items are completed based only on what was observed during the observation period, and not on a rater's general knowledge of a subject. In addition to the rating format, the DOF merges the use of event recording and time-sampling recording. The event recording aspect of the DOF is included by having the observer write a narrative description of the child's behavior as it occurs during the observation period. The time-sampling aspect of the DOF is included by having the observer record whether or not the subject was on-task at the end of each 1-minute interval.

The DOF is a norm-referenced instrument, which sets it apart from most other observational coding systems. A norm group of 287 children from age 5 to 14 is used as the basis for comparing individual observation scores. The norm group data was also used to develop a factor structure for the 96 rating items on the DOF, which, in addition to a total problems score, includes *Internalizing* and *Externalizing* scores, consistent with the other measures in the CBCL system. Six additional narrow-band factor scores are also available through the use of an optional computer-scored profile.

The DOF, like the other components of the CBCL system, is a thoroughly researched instrument that represents an empirically sound approach to assessment of behavior problems. It is easy to use, and requires only a modest amount of training. The recommended observation and scoring procedure for the DOF allow for the obtaining of social comparison data with two observed control children on the checklist and on-task ratings. The psychometric properties of the DOF are good to excellent, with very acceptable levels of interrater reliability and discriminant validity (McConoughy, Achenbach, & Gent, 1988). The DOF is a good choice for group-based observations where rather serious behavioral or emotional problems are likely to be observed in short time periods. However, it is not particularly useful for observing children or adolescents in individual or solitary situations, and is not a good choice for assessing low frequency behaviors that are unlikely to occur within a 10-minute period.

Behavior Coding System. Developed by Harris and Reid (1981), the Behavior Coding System (BCS) was designed to measure patterns of coercive behavior and aggression in classroom and playground settings. The BCS uses an interval recording system with eight behavioral categories. The coding system of the BCS is easy enough to use so that paraprofessionals or trained undergraduate students could be effective observers.

The reported psychometric properties of the BCS are quite good, with interobserver agreement at 93% in classroom settings, and at 86% on playground settings. Harris and Reid (1981) also reported satisfactory consistency in behavioral categories across different settings. An interesting aspect of the BCS is that it was designed to not only provide a general observational measure of aggressive and coercive behaviors, but provides data on the stability of these behaviors across different settings. As such, the BCS might be effective in helping to determine whether aggressive behavior problems are setting specific, or whether they appear to generalize across settings.

The BCS also gives info about stability of behavior

Home-Based Observation Systems

Social Interaction Coding System. Designed to assess family interaction behaviors along different dimensions and on general classifications, the Social Interaction Coding System (SICS; Weinrott & Jones, 1984) provides an interesting and useful format for conducting home-based observations. The SICS uses a continuous event recording procedure wherein 12 different behavioral categories are targeted. The methodology employed in field testing the SICS was somewhat unique; the reliability of the coding system was studied using both *covert* and *overt* observation techniques. In both cases, the reliability of the SICS proved to be adequate to good, though it was somewhat higher for overt observations (.91) than for covert observations (.73).

continuous event recording

Family Interaction Code. Another observational recording system developed by Weinrott and Jones (1984) for home-based observation, and discussed in the same research report as the SICS, is the Family Interaction Code (FIC). Although the FIC was field tested along the same dimensions as the SICS (overt vs. covert observations), its focus is somewhat different, and its design and use varies considerably. The FIC uses a 6-second interval recording system wherein 29 different behavioral categories are targeted. As such, the complexity and difficulty of use of the FIC is great, and it should be used by experienced trained observers. The general area measured through the FIC is family interactions, with its specific focus being aversive family behaviors. Like the SICS, the reliability level was somewhat higher on the FIC for overt (.87), rather than covert (.69), observations.

6 sec intervals recording 29 diff behav categories

Clinic-Based Observation Systems

Child's Game/Parent's Game. An innovative coding procedure useful for observing parent–child interactions in clinic settings was developed by Forehand and his colleagues (Forehand & McMahon, 1981; Forehand, Peed, Roberts, McMahon, Griest, & Humphreys, 1978). This coding system has not been formally named, but is referred to herein as the Child's Game/Parent's Game, due to the focus of tasks. The recommended setting for use of this observational coding system is a sound-wired clinic playroom that has a supply of toys and is equipped with a one-way window, where an observer codes parent–child interactions from an adjoining room. Alternatively, observations could be videotaped and coded at a later time. Parent–child pairs are observed in two different situations that may last 5 or 10 minutes each. The first situation is referred to as the *Child's Game*, which is an unstructured or free-play setting where the child chooses the activity and rules. The second situation is the *Parent's Game*, in which the parent is instructed to choose an activity and rules. Therefore, the Parent's Game is a situation in which the parent delivers commands to the child.

observing parent-child play in 2 diff ways ① child leads ② parent leads

Freq. count= 30sec interval
(6 parental behav. domains / 3 child behav domains)

For both games, parent and child behaviors are coded using frequency counts in 30-second intervals. The only exception to this is inappropriate behavior, which is coded as occurring or not occurring during each interval. Six parent behavioral domains are coded, including rewards, attends, questions, commands, warnings, and time out. Three child behavioral domains are coded, including compliance, noncompliance, and inappropriate behavior. These codes are later summarized into rate per minute of various parent behaviors, and percentages of child behaviors to various parent commands. An additional summary statistic includes the percentage of parental attention that was contingent on child compliance.

Several studies have demonstrated the Child's Game/Parent's Game coding system to have adequate technical properties, including an average interobserver agreement rate of 75% (Forehand & Peed, 1979), strong stability over time (Peed, Roberts, & Forehand, 1977), sensitivity to treatment effects (McMahon & Forehand, 1984), and discriminant validity for differentiation of clinic-referred and nonreferred children (Griest, Forehand, Wells, & McMahon, 1980). In sum, this clinic-based observational coding system is relatively easy to implement, requires a small amount of parent and child time, is unobtrusive, and appears to be a reliable and valid method of conducting behavioral assessment.

Teacher Behavior Code. Unlike other observation systems reviewed here, the focus of the Teacher Behavior Code (TBC; Weitz, 1981) is on the parent or caregiver rather than the child. Specifically, the TBC was designed to be used in assessing the amount of change in "teaching behavior" by parents who have participated in a parent training program. Though developed specifically for use with parents of developmentally disabled children, there is no reason why the TBC could not be used as a measure for parents of children with different types of problems. The TBC was selected for review in this chapter for a very pragmatic reason; in clinical treatment of children with behavioral, social, or emotional problems, the parent is often the mediator or initial target of treatment. As such, it is important to have a measurement technique that will assess their responsiveness to consultation or parent training, rather than focusing only on the resulting child behavior. *measure parent responsiveness...*

The TBC can be used in home as well as clinic settings, and includes nine targeted behavioral categories that are recorded using an interval measurement system during "teaching trials." The TBC can be used by trained graduate students, and perhaps even trained paraprofessionals, as well as by experienced observers. The reported technical properties of the TBC are adequate to good, with an average interobserver agreement of 87%, and a range across categories from 69% to 98%. The TBC is a unique observation system that is very worthwhile for consideration by clinicians or researchers who provide consultation or training to parents, and who desire a formal system for assessing the level of change in parents' behaviors.

interval measurement system during "teaching trials"

VALIDITY ISSUES IN DIRECT BEHAVIORAL OBSERVATION

Despite the strong empirical support and practical utility of using behavioral observation as a primary means of assessment, there are a number of potential limitations, problems, and cautions that should be kept in mind. Two decades ago, J. D. Cone (1981) noted that the state of behavioral assessment methodology was still relatively primitive, and things have not changed that much in the years since then. Even the strongest advocates of observational assessment concede that the accuracy, validity, and reliability of behavioral observation data are often not adequately established, and there are several potential threats to the integrity of observational data (Merrell, 1989a; Sulzer-Azaroff & Mayer, 1991). This section addresses some of the potentially problematic issues surrounding the use of behavioral observation.

Potential threats to the integrity of observational data

Defining the Observation Domain

↳ problematic if too narrow OR too broad.

One of the first tasks in developing an observational coding system, or in using an existing system, is defining what types of behaviors are important in the observation, and then developing appropriate operational definitions for those behaviors. In defining behaviors to observe, the domain of behavior can be viewed as a continuum, with broadly defined behaviors on one end and narrowly defined behaviors on the other end. Although defining each behavioral domain in a highly narrow manner may seem to make empirical sense, it may be impractical when it comes time to actually conduct the observation. For example, if aggressive behavior is of particular importance in an observational assessment, and the general category of "aggressiveness" is broken down into 15 different subcategories of behavior, then the observational coding system will probably be cumbersome and of little use for all but the most esoteric scientific purposes.

On the other hand, defining a behavioral domain too broadly might increase the ease of coding by the observer, but will tend to reduce the validity and reliability of the observational system (Epps, 1985). Using the example of the general category of aggressive behavior, it is easy to see how two behaviors that are qualitatively different might be coded in the same way if the domain of "aggressiveness" is defined too broadly. Both arguing with and physically attacking another person are generally considered to be forms of aggression, but for most purposes coding them as the same will not be particularly helpful either for the assessment or for intervention planning.

To reduce the potential problems associated with defining the behavioral domain to be observed, care should be taken to ensure that the observational coding categories are neither defined too broadly nor too narrowly; the scope of the behavioral definition should be linked to the specific purposes of the observation, and treatment implications should be considered in creating definitions if the purpose of the assessment is to evaluate a problem and develop an appropriate intervention. If the observational domain must be defined broadly, then the validity of the assessment can be increased by employing multiple measures. The use of multiple measures allows for the measurement of a broad range of behaviors while avoiding the practice of equating behaviors that are related but still qualitatively different (Kent & Foster, 1977).

Keep in mind, the specific purpose of the observation

Observer Training and Reliability

One of the universes of generalization in behavioral assessment in J. D. Cone's (1978) widely influential conceptualization of a Behavioral Assessment Grid is referred to as *scorer generalization*. This term indicates that behavioral assessment data may vary due to differences between persons who score or code the data. Therefore, once the observational system has been developed or selected, it is imperative that those individuals who will be actually conducting the observations are properly trained so that the resulting observational data are both reliable and valid. Failure to properly train observers in the use of specific coding systems and procedures may result in behavioral assessment data that are of questionable use.

make sure the behav data do not vary as a function of the observer.

"observer drift" = changing def of observation over time...

After the observers are properly trained in the reliable use of an observational coding system, there is still potential for scorer generalization problems. It has been shown that over time there is a tendency for observers to gradually depart from their original definitions of how to score or code particular behaviors (Kent, O'Leary, Diament, & Deitz, 1974), a phenomenon referred to as *observer drift*. As is the case for observations carried out by observers who are poorly trained in the first place, a great deal of observer drift will produce observational data that are of questionable utility. In order to reduce the tendency of different observers to "drift" from original definitions of behavior, it is suggested that retraining or reliability checks of observers be conducted from time to time (Kazdin, 1981; Reid, 1982). Common procedures that might be used in observer retraining might include periodic group meetings, conducting observations on actual sets of events ("live" or using videotaped situations), calculating the rate of interobserver agreement (agreements divided by agreements plus disagreements), discussing points of disagreement and coming to common decision rules, and practicing until an acceptable criterion of reliability is reached. The following is a simple procedure for calculating interobserver agreement:

Interobserver agreement

$$\frac{\text{number of agreements}}{\text{number of agreements} + \text{number of disagreements}}$$

Although the problem of observer drift can be dealt with through the five steps that have been noted, these steps are seldom possible for practitioners who work independently. Clinicians who employ direct observation procedures in assessment who work under more solitary conditions can overcome this disadvantage in several ways. Enlisting the assistance of a colleague to act as a reliability check is one possibility. Other possibilities include doing an occasional self-check on observational reliability by videotaping observational situations, and striving to keep aware of new information pertinent to the observational techniques being used.

Use of Social Comparison Data — *to ensure proper perspective on observations*

During the observational process, the target of the assessment is generally a specific child or adolescent who has been referred for a variety of problems. So naturally, the observation should focus on that particular individual. However, if the observation does not also include the use of *social comparison data*, the results may lead to inappropriate conclusions about the nature and severity of problems, and the validity of the observation might therefore be jeopardized. The use of social comparison data is important to determine whether the problem behaviors exhibited by particular subjects deviate significantly from those of their peers who are in similar situations (Epps, 1985). In practice, obtaining social comparison data can be a relatively simple part of the observation. The observer might randomly pick two or three nonreferred subjects in the same setting, and alternate the observation between the referred subject and the social comparison subjects on a rotating basis. The social comparison data obtained from rotating the alternate observation intervals may be considered to represent the behavior of a "typical" peer in a situation similar to the target subject's.

It has been suggested by Alessi and Kaye (1983) that obtaining observational social comparison data from the referred person's peer group may serve as a basis for identifying individuals whose behavioral problems are severe enough to warrant intervention. An important factor to keep in mind in obtaining social comparison data is the type of setting in which the behavior was observed. For example, if the assessment was conducted in a school setting wherein the referred student was placed in both regular education and special education classroom settings, then it would be important to obtain social comparison data in both settings, as the behavioral norms in the two settings might vary considerably (Walker, 1983). Reaching an inappropriate conclusion on the basis of observational data without social comparison information could threaten the overall validity of the observational system.

The Problem of Reactivity

- subject behaves differently b/c he/she is aware he/she is being observed.

Anyone with experience in observing child and adolescent behavior in naturalistic settings can attest to the fact that their presence as an observer can easily influence the behavior of the subjects, a problem referred to as *observer reactivity*. With uncanny perceptiveness, children seem to understand and react to the presence of a "stranger" in the observational setting, sometimes with amusing results. For example, when conducting behavioral observations in classroom settings, the target subject, on several occasions, may walk directly over to the clinician and say something to the effect of "you're here to watch me, aren't you?" Other examples of children being aware of the presence of an observer are more subtle, but equally illustrative of the reactivity problem—it is not uncommon for a particular child who is not the target of the observation to spend a good deal of time during the observational period staring at the observer, asking questions like "what are you doing here?", and even showing off or trying to impress the observer. These examples serve to illustrate the fact that obtrusiveness by the observer can cause a change in subject performance, due simply to the presence of a new person in the environment (Kazdin, 1981).

In situations where there is a high degree of obtrusiveness in the observation, it is unwise to interpret the observational data without taking into account the possible reactivity effects. In cases where the presence of the observer has created significant reactivity, the data should be used with extreme caution, and attempts should be made to gather observational data that is more valid, if possible. As with other threats to observational validity, the use of data obtained under conditions of significant observer reactivity might result in reaching unwarranted conclusions.

Several steps can be taken to reduce the potential effects of observer reactivity. One possibility is to select observational settings where the presence of the observer does *non-overt observation* not create an unusual circumstance. For example, observations in playground settings can be done in a way so that the targeted subject(s) might not even be aware of the presence of the observer, whereas observations in the home setting are very likely to result in significant reactivity—the more private the observation setting, the more likely that observer reactivity will become a factor. In classroom observation situations, where the observation is usually considered to be naturalistic in character, the fact that subjects are being observed doing routine tasks is by itself a factor in reducing reactivity. Other commonsense measures can be employed to reduce the potential reactivity in classroom observations, such as entering the classroom at the end of a recess period or other activity rather than during the middle of instructional time, conducting the observation in an inconspicuous location such as the back of the room, avoiding any unnecessary use of observational equipment that might attract the attention of the students, and observing informally for a short period of time in order for the students to adjust to the observer's presence before the formal observation is conducted (Merrell, 1989a).

Situational Specificity of Behavior — *Behavior may change drastically depending on the setting.*

The concept of *situational specificity of behavior* is central to assessment from the behavioral perspective, and has certain implications for conducting behavioral observations. Kazdin (1979, 1981, 1982) has written extensively on this topic, and regards the essence of situational specificity as behavior exhibited by individuals in one particular setting that may or may not parallel their behavior in other settings. In other words, the ecological differences and varied stimulus control between settings may create very specific conditions for behavior. For example, students might behave somewhat differently in two different classrooms. Classroom rules, teacher expectations and management style, composition of students, and physical circumstances of the two classrooms might vary considerably, thus creating differences in the overall ecology of the classrooms that elicit, shape, and maintain behaviors in a different manner.

The idea of situational specificity of behavior has been supported by findings from several research projects. Wahler (1975) found that child behavior tends to "cluster" between school and home settings. Even when deviant or antisocial behaviors are present in both the school and home setting, the specific types of deviant behavior tend to differ. Stokes, Baer, and Jackson (1974) found that subject responses tended to be specific to the presence of individual experimenters and observers. The important point from both of these studies is that changes in setting were found to lead to different behavior patterns, indicating that generalization of behavior needs to be programmed into assessment and intervention strategies (Baer, Wolf, & Risley, 1968).

problem w/ generalizing behav. inferences

The problems relating to situational specificity occur during behavioral observation assessment under two conditions: when generalized inferences are drawn based on behaviors observed in specific settings, and when the observer selects a setting for the observation that is inappropriate and does not adequately represent the behavioral responses exhibited in other settings. Both of these problems can be minimized when observations occur in multiple settings, and when caution is used in making behavioral inferences based on what was observed in only one setting.

Use of Inappropriate Recording Techniques

Earlier in this chapter, four general observation coding procedures were discussed: event, interval, time-sampling, and duration or latency recording. Some authors (e.g., Barton & Ascione, 1984) have suggested that there are as many as six different categories of recording techniques. Whether or not one collapses or expands the categories of recording procedures, observation data can be recorded using at least four, and possibly more procedures.

In addition to looking at specific recording procedures, behaviors can be categorized according to the dimensions under which they occur, which tend to correlate with specific recording techniques of choice. Alberto and Troutman (1990) identified six specific dimensions under which behaviors may occur, including rate, duration, latency, topography, force, and locus. The various dimensions under which behavior occurs might be expressed differently than these six categories, but the overall concept is still the same: Behaviors occur under several dimensions. There is also a general similarity between systems for recording behavior and systems for explaining behavior, which leads to the conclusion that a specific category of behavior is probably best chronicled through the use of a related recording system.

A potential threat to the validity of an observation may occur when the observer chooses a system for recording the behavior that is not parallel with or appropriate to it. For example, low frequency but important behavioral occurrences are normally best recorded using event recording techniques. Use of interval or time-sampling techniques would probably result in these behaviors not even being recorded. The dimension under which the behavior occurs and the recording system must mesh to a reasonable degree, or inappropriate conclusions may be reached.

Biased Expectations and Outside Influence *Subtle biases may affect observation*

An additional potential threat to the validity of data obtained through direct behavioral observation may occur as a result of the observer or someone who might influence the observer expecting behavior to occur or change in a specific manner. Very little has been written on this potential problem, but it should nevertheless be considered as a real threat. There is a humorous old adage regarding biased expectations in behavioral science research that goes something like "I wouldn't have seen it if I hadn't believed it." Essentially, an observer who expects to see subjects engaging in aggressive behavior is more likely to record their behavior as being aggressive, even if the observational coding system used is quite objective. In this scenario, subtle biases in perceptions may occur wherein behavior that is a borderline or questionable fit with a particular coding category may indeed by coded in that direction because the observer believes it should fit.

Another situation that may lead to biased results in observational data is when researchers, supervisors, or someone else with a vested interest in the outcome of the observational assessment communicates to observers their satisfaction, disappointment, or annoyance with the content of behavioral observation data, or their expectations regarding the child's behavior. For example, in making plans for an observer to come into the classroom to assess a particular child, a teacher might make a comment something like "Karen is *always* off-task at least two or three times as much as other students in my class," with an empathic emphasis on the word "always." Or, a supervisor might mention to the observer that the referral source for a specific case "almost always exaggerates how bad a problem is," setting up a situation in which the observer may feel pressure to not observe and code substantial problem behavior. This type of communication may set up a situation in which the observer feels some pressure to satisfy the stated expectations, which in turn might subtly bias the way that observed behavior is coded.

There are no simple solutions to this particular threat to validity. About the only things that can be done to reduce this threat is for observers to make overt efforts to maintain their objectivity, be scrupulously precise in the way they objectively code behavioral data, and to actively resist pressures toward a specified given outcome.

In sum, although there are several potential threats to the reliability and validity of systems for observing behavior directly, there are also a number of potential solutions. The major threats to validity, along with their potential consequences and some possible solutions, are presented in Table 3.3. Becoming aware of what problems might be encountered as part of direct behavioral observation, and then taking the appropriate preventative steps, will greatly enhance the usefulness of the obtained behavioral assessment data.

TABLE 3.3
Some Potential Threats to the Validity of Behavioral Observations

Problem	Potential Consequences	Possible Solutions
Poorly Defined Observational Domains	Observational recording system is either too cumbersome or too vague	Carefully define and select behaviors to be observed based on assessment problem and intervention goals
Unreliability of Observers	Observers drift from original definitions; interrater reliability decreases	Provide high quality initial training; conduct periodic reliability checks and retraining
Lack of Social Comparison Data	Interpretations of behavior are not based on a normative perspective; deviancy may be under- or overestimated	Include typical or randomly selected subjects in the same setting for behavioral comparison
Observer Reactivity	Subject behavior is influenced by the presence of the observer	Select and participate in observational settings in a discrete, unobtrusive manner
Situational Specificity of Behavior	Interpretations of observational data may not represent the larger picture	Conduct observations in multiple settings; do not overgeneralize from limited data
Inappropriate Recording Techniques	Behaviors are not adequately depicted; inappropriate conclusions are reached	Select recording systems to carefully match the behavioral domain
Biased Expectations of the Observer	Borderline behaviors may be systematically coded in a biased manner	Resist pressure to confirm expectations of persons with vested interests; remain scrupulously objective in coding behavior

DIRECT BEHAVIORAL OBSERVATION AND DECISION MAKING

As previously stated, the most important and powerful contribution that direct behavioral observation assessment methods can make to psychoeducational decision-making processes is in the arena of intervention and treatment planning. Because behavioral observation has the capability, if done with great care, of being the most ecologically valid assessment method, fewer inferences and intervening steps are potentially needed in translating the observational data to intervention planning because of the functional type of data that result from such an observation. Given that observation data may be capable of not only pinpointing specific problem behaviors, but in gauging the antecedent stimuli and controlling consequences of these behaviors, this assessment method can provide a great deal of information relevant to modifying the environment for the purpose of behavioral change.

In terms of screening and assessment decisions, direct behavioral observation is potentially useful, but may be too costly (in terms of professional time) to effectively implement on a large scale. For example, observational data obtained during the course of a formal assessment may provide clues that further types of assessment are warranted, but using direct observation during the initial stages of a large-scale screening would typically be unmanageable and too costly. During the initial screening stages of assessment, a quicker method such as behavior rating scales is desirable.

In making diagnosis or classification decisions, behavioral observations may provide useful information, but will probably be insufficient alone. Two problems are likely to emerge if observational data are used exclusively in making diagnostic decisions: Child behavior tends to be variable across situations and time, and thus an observational picture of child behavior may be incomplete. Therefore, to be used most effectively in making reliable diagnostic decisions, direct behavioral observation would need to occur in several settings and over several time periods, which could be an expensive and difficult proposition (Doll & Elliott, 1994). Situational specificity of behavior appears to be a particularly important issue with young children.

For making placement decisions with children and adolescents, observational data are often necessary. In implementing the Individuals with Disabilities Education Act (IDEA), several states have required that direct behavioral observations must be conducted prior to placing a student in a more restrictive educational setting. For making placement decisions that involve psychiatric hospitalization or residential treatment facilities, few (if any) credible institutions would consent to such placements without having a staff member or associate first obtain a direct assessment of the referred child's behavior through observation.

CONCLUSIONS

Direct behavioral observation is one of the key assessment tools of scientifically minded clinicians and researchers. Grounded in the tradition of behavioral psychology, particularly the work of B. F. Skinner and the field of applied behavior analysis, direct behavioral observation is potentially useful in many situations, without respect to the theoretical orientation of the observer.

Perhaps the greatest advantage of direct behavioral observation is the fact that it can be highly functional and ecologically valid, or in other words, be used to identify important antecedent stimuli and controlling consequences of behavior. In the hands of a skilled and theoretically grounded observer, direct observation data can be thus used to help in planning and implementing interventions. Essentially, high quality direct behavioral observation assessment can be "ecobehavioral assessment."

There are three major types of direct behavioral observation: naturalistic observation, analogue observation, and self-monitoring observation. Naturalistic observation, or observing subjects in their natural environment and using an objective and impartial coding procedure, is the preferred method for most purposes. Analogue observation, or simulating the circumstances of the natural environment within a lab or clinic, has some advantages for research, and may be used when naturalistic observation is not possible. Self-monitoring observation is a process whereby the subject is trained to monitor and record their own behavior. Self-monitoring has the advantage of being strongly linked to intervention, and may serve to change behavior in and of itself. However, it is difficult to maintain reliability and objectivity over time with self-monitoring.

Several types of coding systems have been developed for use in direct behavioral observation. In this chapter, these types of coding systems are circumscribed into four general areas: event recording, interval recording, time-sampling recording, and duration/latency recording. Each of these types of coding systems is useful for different purposes, and the choice of a specific system should be guided by the characteristics of the behavior under observation.

Six formal observation coding systems were reviewed in some detail. These six systems are representative of the variety found in direct behavioral observation, and show how specific observational systems may be developed for specific purposes. Unlike some other types of assessment methods, most direct behavioral observation systems are not commercially produced or norm referenced. Rather, they tend to be developed for specific purposes and settings. A skilled clinician may therefore develop their own observational systems to address the specific problems and situations they encounter.

Although, at its best, direct behavioral observation is highly ecologically valid and functional, there are several potential threats to the validity of observational data that must be considered. These threats include poorly defined observational systems, unreliability of observers, lack of social comparison data, observer reactivity within observation settings, situational specificity of behavior, use of inappropriate recording techniques, and biased observer expectations. There are specific practices that may be employed to reduce these various threats to observational validity. Perhaps the most important practice in reducing threats to observational validity is to simply consider these various threats when planning and implementing the observation, and taking specific steps to counter problems as they arise.

Direct behavioral observation data may be used in various ways in making decisions regarding the delivery of psychological or educational services. Perhaps the greatest advantage of direct observation in this regard is use of ecologically valid and functional information for intervention planning and implementation. Direct observation procedures are typically so time consuming and costly that they are best used in the later stages of the classification process. In doing so, it is critical to consider the potential problems of situational specificity of behavior and unreliability of some behavior over time.

REVIEW AND APPLICATION QUESTIONS

1. Define the term *ecobehavioral assessment*. What practices should be considered and implemented in behavioral observation to truly make the resulting data functional and ecologically valid?

2. Three types of general observational procedures were outlined, namely, naturalistic observation, analogue observation, and self-monitoring. For each of these three types, describe an appropriate and inappropriate situation for using them.

3. What are some of the most potentially useful ways that direct behavioral observation data may be used in decision making? Conversely, in what situations will direct behavioral observation data be less useful in decision making?

4. Perhaps the best way to integrate an understanding of the best uses of various types of observational and coding procedures is to work on cases requiring the development of various methods and procedures. Therefore, for each of the five scenarios listed at the bottom of this item, do the following:

   • Select and specify one setting that would be appropriate for conducting a 20-minute observation.

- Select what you consider to be the most appropriate observation method (naturalistic, analogue, or self-monitoring observation).
- Select what you consider to be the most appropriate coding procedure (event, interval, time-sampling, duration, or latency recording).
- Provide a rationale or justification for the methods and procedures you select.
- List what behavior(s) you would specifically target for observation.

Scenarios

a. Observation of a primary-grade student who was referred because of frequent off-task behavior, difficulty "staying put," and problems completing academic work.

b. Observation of a 4-year-old child who was referred because of severe social withdrawal, significant interpersonal communication problems, and stereo-typic self-stimulating behavior (rocking, twirling, and hand-flapping). The child attends a developmental preschool 3 hours per day.

c. Observation of an adolescent client who was referred because of self-reported depression. This client has made two suicide gestures or attempts in the past 6 months (cutting wrists, eating a bottle of aspirin).

d. Observation of a ninth-grade student who was referred due to severe acting-out and aggressive behavior at school, including attacking other students and throwing chairs or other objects. These types of behaviors are reported to occur an average of three to five times per week.

e. Observation of a fifth-grade student who was referred due to peer relationship problems, including teasing classmates, difficulty making friends, and being rejected by other students.

4

BEHAVIOR RATING SCALES

In recent years there has been a substantially increased amount of interest in using parent and teacher rating scales as a method of assessing behavioral, social, and emotional problems of children and youth. School and clinical psychologists frequently employ behavior rating scales either as a primary component of an assessment battery, or as a key means of obtaining information on the child or adolescent client prior to the onset of treatment. At the same time that behavior rating scales have become more widely used, there have been numerous advances in research on rating scale technology that have strengthened the desirability of using this form of assessment (Elliott, Busse, & Gresham, 1993).

The purpose of this chapter is to acquaint readers with the theoretical-technical aspects and applied clinical use of behavior ratings scales as a method for assessing behavioral, social, and emotional problems of children and adolescents. First, a brief discussion on the nature and characteristics of rating scales is presented. Next, sections on advantages and problems of rating scales, and some of the measurement and technical issues involved in rating scale technology, are provided to assist readers in developing a broader understanding of some important measurement issues. After the initial foundation-laying part of the chapter, reviews and discussions of several of the most widely used general purpose problem behavior rating scales for children and youth are provided. Some "best practices" in using rating scales are then discussed, and the chapter ends with a discussion of the use of behavior ratings in making various decisions related to the assessment process.

CHARACTERISTICS AND NATURE OF BEHAVIOR RATING SCALES

Definitions and Foundations

Behavior rating scales provide a standardized format for the development of summary judgments regarding a child or adolescent's behavioral characteristics, by an informant who knows them well. The informant is usually a parent or teacher, but other individuals

Behav. Rating scales measure perceptions

who are familiar with the child or youth might also legitimately be a source for behavior rating scale data. Behavior rating scales also could be used with work supervisors, classroom aides, temporary surrogate parents, and other direct-care persons.

As an assessment methodology, behavior rating scales are less direct than either direct observation or structured behavioral interviewing (McMahon, 1984) in that they measure *perceptions* of specified behaviors rather than providing a firsthand measure of the existence of the behavior. However, rating scales are an objective method and yield more reliable data than either unstructured clinical interviewing or projective techniques (R. P. Martin, Hooper, & Snow, 1986; Merrell, 1994a). As behavior rating scales became more widely used during the 1970s, they were typically viewed with suspicion and used as a "last resort" by behaviorally oriented clinicians (Cone & Hawkins, 1977). But, as the research base and technological refinements in rating scales have become more advanced, there appears to be a more broad acceptance of their use (Elliott et al., 1993).

At this point, it is useful to differentiate rating scales from a related term, *checklist*. A checklist format for identifying behavioral problems lists a number of behavioral descriptors, and if the rater perceives the symptom to be present, they simply "check" the item. After completing the checklist, the number of checked items can be summed. Hence, checklists are considered to be *additive* in nature. Rating scales, on the other hand, not only allow the rater to indicate whether a specific symptom is present or absent, but also provide a means of estimating to what degree the symptom is present. A common 3-point rating system (and there are many variations) allows the rater to score a specific behavior descriptor from 0 to 2, with 0 indicating the symptom is "never" present, 1 indicating the symptom is "sometimes" present, and 2 indicating the symptom is "frequently" present. Because rating scales allow the rater to differentially weight the specified symptoms, and each weighting corresponds with a specific numerical value and frequency or intensity description, rating scales are said to be *algebraic* in nature. Conners and Werry (1979) defined rating scales as an "algebraic summation, over variable periods of time and numbers of social situations, of many discrete observations" (p. 341). In general, the algebraic format provided by rating scales is preferred to the additive format provided by checklists, because it allows for more precise measurement of behavioral frequency or intensity (Merrell, 1994a). The difference between the additive nature of a checklist format and the algebraic character of a rating scale format are illustrated by the sample items in Table 4.1. Clearly, a wider range of possible scores and variance is possible using the algebraic rating scale

rating scales = algebraic

TABLE 4.1
An Example of Differences Between Checklist and Rating Scale Format and Scoring

Behavioral Descriptor	Checklist Format		Rating Scale Format		
1. Is noticeably sad or depressed	Y	N	0	1	2
2. Feels hopeless about his or her problems	Y	N	0	1	2
3. Wants to be left alone	Y	N	0	1	2
4. Has had a change in eating or sleeping habits	Y	N	0	1	2
5. Is irritable or disagreeable	Y	N	0	1	2
Total Values					

Note. Key to Checklist Format: Y = symptom is present; N = symptom is not present. Key to Rating Scale Format: 0 = never occurs; 1 = sometimes or to some degree occurs; 2 = frequently or to a great degree occurs.

format as opposed to the less sophisticated checklist format, which seems to have continually lost favor during the past two decades.

Advantages of Behavior Rating Scales

The widespread popularity of behavior rating scales is not incidental—they offer many advantages for clinicians and researchers conducting child and adolescent assessments. The main advantages of behavior rating scales are summarized in the following six points:

1. In comparison with direct behavioral observation, behavior rating scales are less expensive in terms of professional time involved, and amount of training required to utilize the assessment system (Merrell, 1992, 1994a).

2. Behavior rating scales are capable of providing data on low frequency but important behaviors that might not be seen in a limited number of direct observation sessions (Sattler, 1988). An example that serves to illustrate this point is violent and assaultive behavior. In most cases, these types of behavior do not occur on a constant or consistent schedule, so they might be missed within the constraints of conducting two brief observations. Nonetheless, it is extremely important to know about them.

3. As mentioned earlier, behavior rating scales are an objective assessment method that provide more reliable data than unstructured interviews or projective techniques do (R. P. Martin et al., 1986).

4. Behavior rating scales can be used to assess subjects who cannot readily provide information about themselves (Merrell, 1992, 1994a). For example, consider the difficulty in obtaining valid assessment data on an adolescent who is in a lock-up unit in a psychiatric hospital or juvenile detention center, and who is unavailable or unwilling to be assessed through interviews and self-reports.

5. Rating scales capitalize on observations over a period of time in a child's or adolescent's natural environment (i.e., school or home settings) (McMahon, 1984).

6. Rating scales capitalize on the judgments and observations of persons who are highly familiar with the child's or adolescent's behavior, such as parents or teachers, and are thus considered to be "expert" informants (R. P. Martin et al., 1986).

Rating Scales get at the BIG PICTURE

With these six advantages of using rating scales illustrated, it is easy to see why they are widely used—they get at the "big picture" of the assessment problem in a short amount of time, at moderate cost, and with a good deal of technical precision and practical utility.

Problems Associated With Using Behavior Rating Scales

Despite the several advantages of behavior rating scales, there are some problems or disadvantages as well. The most sophisticated rating scales can help provide objective, reliable, and socially valid information on both broad and narrow dimensions of behavioral, social, and emotional problems, but the nature of rating scale technology contains several potential flaws, which are important to understand. At the onset of discussing problems associated with behavior rating scales, it is useful to remember that by their nature (i.e., assessing *perceptions* of problems), rating scales provide *idiographic* as well as *nomothetic* information. They are capable of providing a portrait of a general idea or conception of behavior, but do not provide actual observational

Problems of rating scales =
Bias of response + Error Variance

data, even though their technical characteristics allow for actuarial prediction of behavior.

R. P. Martin et al. (1986) categorized the measurement problems of behavior rating scales into two classes: *bias of response* and *error variance*. Bias of response refers to the way that informants completing the rating scales may potentially create additional error by the way they use the scales. There are three specific types of response bias, including *halo effects* (rating a student in a positive or negative manner simply because they possess some other positive or negative characteristic not pertinent to the rated item), *leniency or severity* (the tendency of some raters to have an overly generous or overly critical response set when rating all subjects), and *central tendency effects* (the proclivity of raters to select midpoint ratings and to avoid end points of the scale such as "never" or "always").

Bias

Error variance is closely related to and often overlaps with response bias as a form of rating scale measurement problems, but provides a more general representation of some of the problems encountered with this form of assessment. According to R. P. Martin et al. (1986), there are four types of variance that may create error in the obtained results of a rating scale assessment. These variance types are outlined in Table 4.2, and are overviewed as follows. *Source variance* refers to the subjectivity of the rater and any of the idiosyncratic ways that they complete the rating scales. *Setting variance* occurs as a result of the situational specificity of behavior (Kazdin, 1979) in that humans tend to behave differently in different environments due to the differing eliciting and reinforcing properties present. *Temporal variance* refers to the tendency of behavior ratings to be only moderately consistent over time—partly due to changes in the observed behavior over time and partly due to changes in the rater's approach to the rating task over time. Finally, *instrument variance* refers to the fact that different rating scales measure often related but slightly differing hypothetical constructs (e.g., aggressive behavior vs. delinquent behavior), and a severe problem behavior score on one scale may be compared with only a moderate problem behavior score on a different rating scale for the same person. Another problem that creates instrument variance is the fact that each rating scale utilizes different normative populations to make score comparisons with, and if the norm populations are not randomly selected and representative of the population as a whole, then similar score levels on two different rating scales may not mean the same thing.

Error Variance

Although there are several types of problems inherent in using behavior rating scales, there are also effective ways of minimizing those problems. Notwithstanding the argument (considered in chap. 1) that in some cases it might actually increase

TABLE 4.2
Types of Error Variance Found With Behavior Rating Scales

Type of Error Variance	Examples
Source Variance	Various types of *response bias*; different raters may have different ways of responding to the rating format.
Setting Variance	Related to *situational specificity* of behavior; eliciting and reinforcing variables present in one environment (e.g., classroom 1) may not be present in a closely related environment (e.g., classroom 2).
Temporal Variance	Behavior is likely to change over time, and an informant's approach to the rating scale task may also change over time.
Instrument Variance	Different rating scales may be measuring different hypothetical constructs; there is a continuum of continuity (ranging from close to disparate) between constructs measured by different scales.

error variance, the *aggregation principle* is particularly important to understand and implement in utilizing behavior rating scales, and this principle is considered in some detail in the "best practices" later in this chapter.

Measurement and Technical Issues

Thus far, some of the uses, advantages, and disadvantages of using behavior rating scales have been reviewed. This section provides a brief overview of some of the measurement and technical issues that can affect the psychometric properties of rating scales. One of the measurement characteristics of rating scales that can produce variation in the reliability and validity of a measure is the time element involved in making the rating. This is related to, but not the same as, the issue of temporal variance already discussed. According to Worthen et al. (1993), there is a tendency for recent events and behavior to be given disproportionate weight when a rater completes a rating scale. It is easier to remember behavioral, social, and emotional characteristics during the previous 2-week period than during the previous 2-month period. Rating scales differ as to the time period on which the ratings are supposed to be based. For example, the Child Behavior Checklist specifies that the rater should complete the rating items based on the observation of the child over the previous 6-month period. The Walker–McConnell Scales of Social Competence and School Adjustment (Walker & McConnell, 1995a, 1995b), on the other hand, are examples of rating scales that do not specify a precise time period for the observations, although the test manual does specify that at least 2 months of the new school year should have elapsed before a teacher completes the scale on a student. A related measurement issue raised by Worthen et al. (1993) is that it is easier for raters to remember unusual behavior than ordinary behavior. Thus, typical uneventful behaviors may be assigned less proportional weight during the rating than novel, unusual, or highly distinctive behaviors.

Another measurement and technical variable that can affect the psychometric properties of rating scales is the construction of the actual rating format. The two rating formats that appear to be the most common for behavior rating scales are 3-point and 5-point scales. Typically, each numerical value in the rating format is keyed or anchored to a descriptor (for example, 0 = never, 1 = sometimes, 2 = frequently). As a rule, more accurate ratings are obtained when there is a tangible and understandable definition for each quality level. In terms of deciding how many rating points or levels of rating are appropriate in constructing a rating scale, Worthen et al. (1993) suggested that a common error in scale construction is to use too many levels; the higher the level of inference needed in making the rating, the more difficult it becomes to reliably discriminate among the rating levels. Therefore, another good rule of thumb is for scale developers to use the fewest rating levels needed to make the rating discrimination, and for scale consumers to avoid rating scales that include an extremely high number of inference points. It is also important to carefully review the descriptors or anchor points in a rating format to ensure that they are clear and meaningful before adopting a new behavior rating scale.

A final technical characteristic of behavior rating scales to consider includes the directions for use. Some scales provide highly detailed instructions for completing the ratings, such as what persons should use the rating scale, the time period involved, how to approach and interpret the items, and so on. Other scales may provide a minimum of directions of clarifications. It is recommended that users of behavior rating scales select instruments that provide clear and tangible directions for conducting the rating, as well as decision rules for interpreting blurred distinctions (Gronlund & Linn, 1990). In sum, the characteristics of rating scale technology that make behavior rating scales appealing may also negatively impact the consistency and utility of the measure. As with any type of measurement and evaluation system, consumers of behavior rating scales are advised to evaluate a potential instrument based on the important technical characteristics.

REVIEW OF SEVERAL GENERAL PURPOSE PROBLEM BEHAVIOR RATING SCALES

Now that the technical foundation for understanding the technology, uses, and problems of rating scales has been covered, this section takes an in-depth look at several selected behavior rating scales or rating scale systems that are widely available and frequently employed as child assessment tools in school and clinical settings. The instruments or systems selected for review and discussion in this chapter include the Behavior Assessment System for Children, the Child Behavior Checklist and related Teacher's Report Form, the Conners Rating Scales, and the Revised Behavior Problem Checklist. Besides the fact that these scales or systems are frequently used and widely available, they have been selected for inclusion in this chapter because they are general purpose problem behavior assessment instruments. That is, they provide measures of a variety of behavioral, social, and emotional problems, including a range of internalizing and externalizing symptoms. Another reason these instruments have been singled out for inclusion as examples in this chapter is that they represent some of the best constructed and widely researched instruments currently available. Finally, these instruments can be completed by either parents or teachers, and thus are useful in a variety of assessment and treatment settings. Several other general problem behavior scales are available but are not reviewed here because of space limitations and a judgment call regarding which scales or systems are most technically sound, widely influential, and clinically useful. Some of the more widely used general purpose problem behavior rating scales that are available but not reviewed here include the Behavior Dimensions Scales (McCarney, 1995a, 1995b), Behavior Rating Profile (R. T. Brown & Hammill, 1983), Burks' Behavior Rating Scales (Burks, 1977), and the Devereux Rating Scales (Naglieri, LeBuff, & Pfeiffer, 1993). Several other behavior rating scales have been developed for more specific purposes such as assessing social skills, hyperactivity, depression, anxiety, antisocial behavior, and school-based behaviors that could be referred to as specific purpose instruments. Many of these instruments are reviewed and discussed in subsequent chapters during discussions of assessment of specific problems or constructs.

Behavior Assessment System for Children *BASC*

The Behavior Assessment System for Children (BASC; C. R. Reynolds & Kamphaus, 1992) is, as the title implies, a comprehensive system for assessing child and adolescent behavior. Included in the BASC system are parent and teacher rating scales for preschool-age children (4–5), children (6–11), and adolescents (12–18). These behavior rating scales are separately normed and somewhat unique across age range and informant versions, but still share a common conceptual and practical framework, and have many items in common across versions. Also included in the overall BASC system are comprehensive self-report forms for children (age 6–11) and adolescents (age

12–18), a structured developmental history form, and a student observation system. The preschool versions of the BASC are discussed in chapter 13, and the self-report forms are discussed in chapter 7. This chapter provides an overview of the parent and teacher versions of the child and adolescent rating forms.

Description. The BASC behavior rating scales are comprehensive instruments designed to assess a variety of problem behaviors, school problems, and adaptive skills. The parent and teacher rating forms for children and adolescents include the PRS–C (parent rating scale for ages 6–11), PRS–A (parent rating scale for ages 12–18), TRS–C (teacher rating scale for ages 6–11), and TRS–A (teacher rating scale for ages 12–18). These instruments are relatively long in terms of number of items, ranging from 126 to 148 items. The items are rated by circling adjacent letters indicating how frequently each behavior is perceived to occur, based on N = "Never," S = "Sometimes," O = "Often," and A = "Almost Always." The test form is self-scoring and very easy to use. After the rating is completed, the examiner tears off the top perforated edge and separates the forms, which reveals an item scoring page and a summary page with clinical and adaptive profiles. Norm tables in the test manual are consulted for appropriate raw score conversions by rating form and age and gender of the child.

Scoring System and Scale Structure. Raw scores on BASC rating scales are converted to *T*-scores (based on a mean score of 50 and standard deviation of 10). *T*-scores for clinical scales are converted to five possible classification levels, ranging from "Very Low" (*T*-scores of 30 and lower) to "Clinically Significant" (*T*-scores of 70 or higher). Classification levels for the BASC adaptive scales are in the opposite direction of those for the clinical scales, but retain the same names. For example, an adaptive skill *T*-score of 70 or higher is considered "Very High," whereas a *T*-score of 30 or lower would be considered "Clinically Significant." In other words, higher scores on the clinical scales always indicate more problems, whereas higher scores on the adaptive scales always indicate greater competencies. Other classification levels include "Low," "Average," and "At-Risk." In addition to the clinical and adaptive scales, the BASC rating scales contain an *F* index, which is a validity scale designed to detect excessively negative responses made by a teacher or parent.

The empirically derived scale structure of the BASC rating scales is relatively complex, consisting of composite and scale scores. The *Externalizing Problems* composite includes the *Aggression, Hyperactivity,* and *Conduct Problems* scales. The *Internalizing Problems* composite includes the *Anxiety, Depression,* and *Somatization* scales. The *School Problems* composite includes the *Attention Problems* and *Learning Problems* scales. There are two other problem scales, namely *Atypicality* and *Withdrawal,* that do not fall into either the Externalizing or Internalizing composites. The *Adaptive Skills* composite includes the scales of *Adaptability* (for the child version only), *Leadership, Social Skills,* and *Study Skills* (for the teacher rating scales only). The *Behavioral Symptoms Index,* sort of a composite problem behavior total score, includes the *Aggression, Hyperactivity, Anxiety, Depression, Attention Problems,* and *Atypicality* scale scores. For comparison purposes, the scale structure of the TRS–C of the BASC is presented in Table 4.3, with a brief description of item content.

Development and Standardization. Extensive development procedures for the BASC rating scales are detailed in the test manual. An initial item pool was constructed using literature reviews, existing rating scale items, and the clinical expertise of the

TABLE 4.3

Scale Structure of the Teacher Rating Scale–Child (TRS–C) of the Behavior
Assessment System for Children, with Brief Description of Item Content

Name of Scale*	Brief Description of Item Content

Externalizing Problems
  Aggression
  Hyperactivity
  Conduct Problems
	Arguing, cheating, bullying other students, stealing things at school, school suspensions, various overt symptoms of ADHD.

Internalizing Problems
  Anxiety
  Depression
  Somatization
	Fearfulness, nervousness, excessive worries, complaints of physical symptoms, aches, and pains, depressed or sad affect.

School Problems
  Attention Problems
  Learning Problems
	Attention seeking behavior, does schoolwork too quickly and carelessly, poor attention span, poor study habits and organization skills.

(Other Problems)
  Atypicality
  Withdrawal
	Stares with blank expression, makes odd noises, is shy and withdrawn, avoids others, appears to be "out of touch" with reality, has strange ideas.

Adaptive Skills
  Adaptability
  Leadership
  Social Skills
  Study Skills
	Active in school organizations, is viewed as a leader, is considered a "good loser," asks for assistance in appropriate manner, has a good sense of humor, is liked by peers, volunteers to help.

Behavioral Symptoms Index	Includes scores from Aggression, Hyperactivity, Anxiety, Depression, Attention Problems, and Atypicality scales.

*Composite scores are listed in italics, with subordinate scale scores listed directly below in regular type.

authors as a basis for selection. Two separate item tryout studies were conducted that resulted in extensive deletion and revision of items. Final item selection was determined empirically through basic factorial analysis and covariance structure analysis to determine appropriate item fit within their intended domain. Readability analyses and bias analyses were also conducted during the item development phase of the BASC, which also resulted in the deletion of some items.

The child and adolescent versions of the BASC rating scales are based on extensive and well-stratified norm samples. A total of 116 testing sites in the United States and Canada were used for standardization, representing a geographically diverse standardization process. Extensive data in the test manual is presented regarding race/ethnicity, gender, and special education classification characteristics of the BASC norm samples, including comparisons along these dimensions with the 1990 U.S. census. In general, the BASC norms are quite representative of the general U.S. population in these domains. The BASC parent rating scale norms include 2,084 respondents for the child form and 1,090 respondents for the adolescent form. The BASC teacher rating scale norms include 1,259 respondents for the child form and 809 respondents for the adolescent form. The standardization process and level of attention to detail in developing the BASC should be considered exemplary. The norm samples for the BASC parent and teacher rating scales, child and adolescent forms, should be considered adequate to good.

Psychometric Properties. Because the BASC is a relatively new instrument and was commercially published before any external research was disseminated in peer-reviewed journals, there are only a small handful of external studies providing reliability and validity evidence. However, the BASC test manual provides highly detailed and comprehensive evidence of the psychometric properties of the various parts of the system. The parent and teacher versions of the child and adolescent forms are probably the most widely researched components of the BASC. Internal consistency reliability estimates for the PRS–C, PRS–A, TRS–C, and TRS–A are impressive. Most scale score coefficients are in the .80 and .90 range, with a few in the .70 range. Internal consistency estimates for the Behavioral Symptoms Index are very solid, ranging from .88 to .97, depending on the specific demographic breakdown analyzed. Short-term test–retest coefficients were calculated for both versions, with time intervals ranging from 2 to 8 weeks. These temporal stability indices are adequate to good, with median values for the four forms typically ranging from .70 to .80. Long-term stability (7 months) of the TRS–C was investigated, with coefficients ranging from .27 (Atypicality) to .90 (Study Skills). Interrater reliability studies across different teachers conducted with the TRS–C yielded coefficients ranging from .44 (Depression) to .93 (Learning Problems), and similar studies across mothers and fathers conducted with the PRS–C and PRS–A yielded coefficients ranging from .46 (Somatization, PRS–C) to .76 (Externalizing Problems, PRS–C). As would be expected, the lowest test–retest and interrater reliability coefficients tend to be in relation to behavioral clusters that are not as easily observable through objective means (internalizing problems) or are not highly stable (Atypicality). A review of the BASC by Merenda (1996), although generally positive, was critical of the test–retest and interrater reliability of the measures within the system. However, it is my opinion that Merenda's review did not adequately take into account the overall evidence regarding source and setting variance and expected reliability performance with behavior rating scales. In reality, both of these areas of reliability for the BASC child and adolescent forms are in the expected range or higher in comparison to other widely researched behavior rating scales, and taking into account the yield of evidence regarding cross-informant and cross-setting reliability of third-party ratings.

Numerous types of validity evidence are presented in the BASC technical manual. As stated earlier, the factorial structure for the scales was based on strong empirical evidence derived from extensive covariance structure analyses, and the empirically derived scale structure truly appears to be robust. Studies reported in the BASC test manual showing correlations between the TRS and PRS with several other behavior rating scales provide strong evidence of convergent and discriminant construct validity, as do studies regarding intercorrelation of scales and composites of the various TRS and PRS forms. BASC profiles of various clinical groups (conduct disorder, behavior disorder, depression, emotional disturbance, ADHD, learning disability, mental retardation, autism), when compared with the normative mean scores, provide strong evidence of the construct validity of the TRS and PRS through demonstrating sensitivity and discriminating power to theory-based group differences. This type of construct validity for the BASC has also been demonstrated through an externally published study by Lett and Kamphaus (1997) in evaluating the sensitivity of the TRS in classifying children with and without ADHD.

Additional Comments. Although some other components of the BASC system are not as strong as the TRS–C, TRS–A, PRS–C, and PRS–A rating scales, overall, the system is extremely impressive and there is very little room for criticism of these four general purpose problem behavior rating scales. These instruments were developed with the latest and most state-of-the-art standards and technology, have an impressive empirical research base, and appear to be very easy to use and practical. They truly represent the best of the newer generation of behavior rating scales, and they have been positively reviewed in the professional literature (e.g., R. Flanagan, 1995; Sandoval & Echandia, 1994). One of the very few drawbacks of the BASC rating scales may be that their extensive length (as many as 148 items) may make these instruments difficult to use for routine screening work, and certainly a poor choice for weekly progress monitoring, which requires a much briefer measure. Therefore, routine screening and progress monitoring may call for the use of shorter measures, such as the shorter versions of the Conners and revised Conners rating scales. However, for a thorough and comprehensive system of behavior rating scales, the BASC is representative of the best of what is currently available.

Child Behavior Checklist and Teacher's Report Form *CBCL + TRF*

Among the most sophisticated and technically sound general purpose problem behavior rating scales are those incorporated into the Achenbach's empirically based child assessment system. This collection of instruments is referred to as a system because it incorporates several rating scales, self-report forms, interview schedules, and observation forms for children and adolescents. Several of these instruments use a common cross-informant system of similar subscales and items. Two of the instruments in this system, namely the Child Behavior Checklist for ages 4–18 (CBCL; Achenbach, 1991a), and the Teacher's Report Form (TRF; Achenbach, 1991b) are conceptually very similar and are reviewed herein. Although the CBCL and TRF have different names and not entirely common normative groups, the items and format are very similar. In combination, these two instruments are clearly the most widely researched parent and teacher behavior rating scales in existence. To date, more than 800 studies have been published wherein the CBCL was used as a primary measure, and more than 60 studies using the TRF have been published. More than any other measures, these two instruments have been the moving force behind the increased interest and acceptance of behavior rating scales and the advances in technical adequacy that have occurred since the late 1970s.

Description.   The CBCL and TRF both include 120 problem behavior items that are rated on a 0 = "Not True," 1 = "Somewhat or Sometimes True," or 2 = "Very True or Often True" format. The 120 items on the two checklists have a high degree of continuity, though some on the TRF were modified or changed to make them more directly applicable to use in school settings. The original CBCL provided norms on children from ages 4 to 16, but the scoring profile, norms, and manual were revised in 1991 to include an upward extension up through age 18. Likewise, whereas the original TRF provided a behavioral profile based on norms from ages 6 to 16, the scoring profile, norms, and manual were revised in 1991 to include an age extension so that it can now be used with students from age 5 to 18. Downward extensions of both of these measures have been developed for use with younger children, and these instruments are discussed in chapter 13.

In addition to the problem behavior rating scales on the CBCL and TRF, both instruments contain sections wherein the informant provides information on the adaptive behavioral competencies of the subject. On the CBCL, this section is referred to as *Social Competence*, and allows for ratings pertinent to the child's preferred activities, social interaction patterns, and school competence. On the TRF, this section is referred to as *Adaptive Functioning*, and is a measure of adaptive school-related skills.

Scoring System and Scale Structure. Raw scores for both the CBCL and TRF are converted to broad-band and narrow-band scores that are based on a *T*-score system (a normalized distribution with a mean of approximately 50 and standard deviation of 10). Both rating scales can be hand scored using the test manuals and appropriate versions of the Child Behavior Profile, which includes scoring keys for the internalizing/externalizing total scores, plus the various subscales scores, as well as a graph to plot the scores. The hand scoring process with both the CBCL and TRF is somewhat tedious, taking at least 15 minutes for an experienced scorer, and longer for a scorer who is not familiar with the system. However, available hand scoring templates make this job quicker and easier, and computerized scoring programs and machine-readable forms for mail-in scanning are also available at an additional cost. These latter two scoring methods provide convenient and easy-to-read printouts of score profiles.

For both instruments, three different broad-band problem behavior scores are obtained. The first two are referred to as *Internalizing* and *Externalizing*, and are based on the behavioral dimensions breakdown of overcontrolled and undercontrolled behavior discussed in chapter 2. The third broad-band score is a total problems score, which is based on a raw score to *T*-score conversion of the total ratings of the 120 problem behavior items. The total problems score is not obtained by merely combining the Internalizing and Externalizing scores because there are several rating items on each instrument that do not fit into either of two broad-band categories, but are included in the total score. The CBCL and TRF scoring systems also provide *T*-score conversions of the data from the Social Competence and Adaptive Functioning portions of the instruments, which were previously discussed.

In terms of narrow-band or subscale scores, the CBCL and TRF score profiles both provide a score breakdown into eight common subscale or syndrome scores, which are empirically derived configurations of items. These eight cross-informant syndromes include *Aggressive Behavior, Anxious/Depressed, Attention Problems, Delinquent Behavior, Social Problems, Somatic Complaints, Thought Problems,* and *Withdrawn*. These eight syndromes are listed in Table 4.4, with examples of specific areas measured within the

TABLE 4.4

Cross-Informant Syndrome (Subscale) Structure of the Child Behavior Checklist and Teacher's Report Form with Brief Description of Item Content

Name of Syndrome	Brief Description of Item Content
Aggressive Behavior	Arguing, cruel behavior toward persons and animals, bullying or meanness to others, physically fighting.
Anxious/Depressed	Unhappy, sad, or depressed affect, frequent crying, verbal report of suicidal ideation, nervous tension.
Attention Problems	Impulsive behavior (acts without thinking), difficulty concentrating, fidgety or restless behavior, inattention.
Delinquent Behavior	Keeps company with children who get into trouble, runs away from home, school truancy, lying and cheating.
Social Problems	Does not get along well with other children, is not well liked by other children.
Somatic Complaints	Reports feeling dizzy, feels overtired, reports physical problems without known medical cause (list of 8 problems).
Thought Problems	Hears sounds or voices that aren't there, acts confused or seems to be in a fog, sees things that aren't there.
Withdrawn	Likes to be alone, withdrawn and isolated, doesn't get involved with other people.

syndrome. Raw scores for the eight cross-informant syndromes are also converted to *T*-scores and percentile ranks.

The 1991 versions of the CBCL and TRF behavior profiles allow for the plotting of subscale scores in a manner that is a departure from previous versions. The eight cross-informant syndromes are scored from all instruments, for all age levels, and both sexes. At least in the clinical and practical sense, this system of constant subscale configuration is a definite improvement over the previous versions of the score profiles. Until 1991, the names of and items in the CBCL and TRF subscales varied depending on age levels and gender, and they were not constant between the instruments. This inconsistency made for some confusion in comparing scores obtained over several years and between teachers and parents, and also made it difficult to compare score profiles obtained on children of different genders or age levels. The most recent versions of the CBCL and TRF behavior profiles are still based on different norms for males and females and by age group. However, the names of the narrow-band syndromes are constant, and the general item content within these syndrome scores is similar. For both the narrow-band and broad-band scale scores of these measures, clinical cutoff points have been established based on empirically validated criteria.

Development and Standardization.   The CBCL was developed based on an extension and revision of Achenbach's (1966) Behavior Problem Checklist that was generated from a survey of the literature and case histories of over 1,000 psychiatric patients. In the original construction of the CBCL, Achenbach (1978) and Achenbach and Edelbrock (1979) used data from clinic-referred samples from a large number of eastern U.S. community mental health centers, and analyzed the data using principal components analyses based on various gender and age configurations. This initial wave of analysis led to the development of the original narrow-band syndrome configurations that were used in the CBCL. The 1991 edition of the CBCL included large new nationwide normative samples consisting of 2,368 cases, with additional clinical cases used for construction of the narrow-band subscales and establishment of clinical cutoff criterion. The 1991 CBCL norm sample appears to be a substantial improvement over previous versions of the CBCL, which tended to be heavily urban and geographically concentrated in a few areas.

The origins of the TRF are rooted in the CBCL. The construction of items for the TRF were modeled after, revised from, and in many cases directly adapted from the CBCL. Correlations between the two instruments that were reported in the original TRF manual were statistically significant at the $p. < .001$ level, yet modest, ranging from .26 to .45 on the three broad-band scores. These modest correlations show that even with similar rating items, the differences in behavioral ecology between school and home settings, as well as the differing normative perspectives of parents and teachers, can be significant. The 1991 TRF national norm sample of 1,391 cases is considered to be more nationally representative than the pre-1991 TRF norms. In addition to the national norm sample, the TRF manual describes the use of supplementary norm groups (special education, clinical cases) that were used to construct the subscales and develop clinical cutoff criterion.

Psychometric Properties.   The psychometric properties of both the CBCL and TRF, as reported in the scale manuals and in externally published research reports, range from adequate to excellent. In terms of test–retest reliability, the majority of the obtained reliabilities for the CBCL, taken at 1-week intervals, are in the .80 to mid

.90 range, and are still quite good at 3-, 6-, and 18-month intervals (.47 to .76 mean reliabilities at 18 months). On the TRF, the median test–retest reliability at 7-day intervals was .90, and at 15-day intervals was .84. The median TRF test–retest correlation at 2 months was .74, and at 4 months it was .68. These data suggest that ratings from the CBCL system can be quite stable over short to moderately long periods of time.

Interrater reliabilities (between fathers and mothers) on the CBCL were calculated, with the median correlation across scales being .66. On the TRF, interrater reliabilities (between teachers and teacher aides) on combined age samples ranged from .42 to .72. Although lower than the test–retest reliabilities, the interrater agreement is still adequate. On a related note, a highly influential study by Achenbach, McConaughy, and Howell (1987) looked at cross-informant correlations in ratings of child/adolescent behavioral and emotional problems, and discussed the problem of situational specificity in interpreting rating scale data. Based on the data from this study, average cross-informant correlations across all forms was found to be closer to the .30 range.

Various forms of test validity on the CBCL and TRF have been inferred through a number of studies. Through demonstration of sensitivity to theoretically based group differences, strong construct validity has been inferred for each instrument. Both the CBCL and TRF have been shown to distinguish accurately among clinical and normal samples, and among various clinical subgroups. The convergent construct validity for both scales has been demonstrated through significant correlations between the scales and other rating scales, such as the Revised Behavior Problem Checklist (.92 correlation on total scores), the Conners Parent Rating Scale (.91 correlations on total scores), and the Conners Teacher Rating Scale (.85 correlation on total scores). In addition to the extensive research shown in the CBCL and TRF manuals, numerous externally published validity studies have been reported in the professional literature. For example, the factor analytic evidence regarding the validity of the eight subscale cross-informant syndrome structure has been replicated externally with independent samples for both the CBCL (Dedrick, 1997) and TRF (deGroot, Koot, & Verhulst, 1996).

Additional Comments. The CBCL and TRF appear to have a great deal of clinical utility in that they provide both general and specific information on the nature and extent of a subject's rated behavioral, social, and emotional problems. Used in combination with parents and teachers, these rating scales have been shown to be powerful predictors of present and future emotional and behavioral disorders of children and adolescents (Verhulst, Koot, & Van-der-Ende, 1994). It has been the opinion of several reviewers (e.g., Christenson, 1990; Elliott & Busse, 1990) that the CBCL system is a highly useful clinical tool for assessing child psychopathology.

However, it should be recognized that the CBCL and TRF are probably more useful for some types of assessment purposes and problems than others. Many of the behavioral symptoms on the checklists are rather psychiatric or clinical in nature (e.g., hearing voices, bowel and bladder problems, handling one's own sex parts in public) and certainly have a great deal of relevance in assessing childhood psychopathology. However, many of these more severe low rate behavioral descriptions on the scales are not seen on a day-to-day basis with most children who have behavioral or emotional concerns, and some teachers and parents tend to find certain CBCL/TRF items irrelevant, if not offensive, for the children they are rating. In addition to limited sensitivity of these instruments to identify less serious problems, other weaknesses of the CBCL/TRF cross-informant system have also been pointed out, including limited (and perhaps misleading) assessment of social competence, possible bias in interpreting data regarding physical symptoms, subjectivity in the scoring system, and difficulties raised by combining data across informants (Drotar, Stein, & Perrin, 1995). Therefore, although Achenbach's empirically based assessment and classification system is the most widely researched and perhaps most sophisticated child rating scale currently available for assessing substantial childhood psychopathology (and has much to commend it), it may not be the best choice as a rating scale for social skills and routine behavioral problems in home and school settings.

Conners Rating Scales and Conners Rating Scales–Revised

The Conners Rating Scales (Conners, 1990) are referred to as a system because they form a set of four different behavior rating scales (two parent rating scales and two teacher rating scales) that share many common items, and are conceptually similar. These original scales vary in length from 28 to 93 items. Several versions of these scales have been in use since the 1960s (Conners, 1969) and were originally developed by Conners as a means of providing standardized objective behavioral assessment data for children with hyperactivity, attention problems, and related behavioral concerns. Research on the Conners scales has been widely reported in the research literature. The scales have also found wide acceptance by clinicians. Although a broad range of behavioral, social, and emotional problem descriptions are included in the scales, they have been touted primarily as a measure for assessing attentional problems and hyperactivity, and they have historically been considered to be the most widely used scales for that purpose. It was not until 1990 that the scales became widely commercially available and that a manual was published that integrated the description, use, and scoring of the four scales into one source.

In 1997, a revised, expanded, and completely restandardized version of the Conners Ratings Scales was published. This most recent revision is truly considered to be a comprehensive behavior assessment system because it contains numerous parent and teacher rating scales as well as an adolescent self-report scale. The revised Conners scales may have been designed to ultimately replace the original Conners scales, but certainly not in the short term. The publisher is still promoting both versions, and the original Conners Rating Scales are probably still in much wider use than the revised version. Therefore, this review focuses primarily on the original Conners Rating Scales, for which there is much more empirical evidence available, and concludes with a description and brief review of the Conners Rating Scales–Revised.

Description. The Conners system includes 39-item (CTRS–39) and 28-item (CTRS–28) rating scales for use by teachers, and 48-item (CPRS–48) and 93-item (CPRS–93) rating scales for use by parents. Because the CTRS–39 and CTRS–48 have been the most widely used versions of the scales, and because much more is known about their psychometric properties, these are discussed here, and the CTRS–28 and CPRS–93 are not discussed any further, though much of the information presented on the first two scales is also relevant to these others. The Conners scales all use a common 4-point rating scale, where 0 = "Not at All," 1 = "Just a Little," 2 = "Pretty Much," and 3 = "Very Much." Although both scales have been used with a number of different age groups, the age ranges in the manual norms for the CTRS–39 is 3 through 14, and the CPRS–48 age norm range is 3 through 17.

The CTRS–39 includes six subscales, whereas the CPRS–48 includes five subscales. Additionally, both scales (as well as the other two rating scales within the Conners system) include a scale that has been referred to for years as the *Hyperactivity Index*, a group of 10 items consistent between the four rating scales that is not technically part of the factor structure of the scales, but includes items taken from various subscales that have been grouped in this manner to conduct research on the effects of stimulant medication on child behaviors. The Hyperactivity Index was empirically constructed because these 10 items were found to be most sensitive to behavioral and emotional changes brought on by pharmacological treatment. This 10-item scale was also originally conceptualized as a brief and efficient general psychopathology measure that could be used by both parents and teachers. It should be noted that the revised Conners scales also include these same 10 items as a separate index, but the name has been changed to the *Conners Global Index*.

Scoring System and Scale Structure. Raw scores are converted to subscale scores using the *T*-score method (i.e., mean scores of 10 and standard deviations of 5) for all scales in the Conners system. Total scores are typically not obtained and used with the Conners scales, and are not part of the published scoring systems, though some investigators and clinicians have utilized a total score in interpreting scores. The six basic subscales of the CTRS–39 include *Hyperactivity, Conduct Problem, Emotional-Indulgent, Anxious-Passive, Asocial*, and *Daydream-Attention Problem*. The five basic subscales on the CPRS–48 include *Conduct Problem, Learning Problem, Psychosomatic, Impulsive-Hyperactive*, and *Anxiety*. For comparison purposes, the subscale structure of the CTRS–39, with a brief description of item content, is presented in Table 4.5.

The rating scales in the Conners system are easily scored and converted to standardized subscale scores based on gender and age level breakdowns, using an innovative "Quickscore" format on the ratings forms that require a minimum of time and reduces the chance of committing scoring errors. Microcomputer online administration and scoring programs for the Conners scales are also available from the publisher. The computer programs provide not only administration and scoring possibilities, but the generation of brief interpretive summary paragraphs related to individual score configurations and levels.

Computer scoring

It should be noted that although the subscale structures of the two rating scales illustrated in this chapter are the configurations presented in the 1990 system manual,

TABLE 4.5
Subscale Structure of the 39-Item Version of the Conners
Teacher Rating Scales with Brief Description of Item Content

Name of Scale	Brief Description of Item Content
A. Hyperactivity	Fidgets constantly, makes odd noises such as humming, quarrels with others.
B. Conduct Problems	Acts sassy or impudent, has destructive behavior, stealing, temper outbursts and other explosive behavior.
C. Emotional-Indulgent	Temper outbursts, acts overly sensitive, gets easily frustrated, is demanding.
D. Anxious-Passive	Appears to be easily led by others, appears to lack leadership qualities, submissive behavior.
E. Asocial	Socially isolates self from other children, peer relationship problems, rejected by social group.
F. Daydream-Attention Problem	Does not finish things that s/he initiates, has a short attention span, daydreams and related off-task behavior.
I. Hyperactivity Index	Cries often and cries easily, disturbs activities of other children, has quick and drastic mood changes.

the items in each factor and the number of factors in each instrument have varied somewhat in the research reported throughout the years. In fact, R. P. Martin (1988) stated that it was a common practice for investigators using the Conners scales to independently develop their own factor structure, and report it in their research reports. For example, M. Cohen and Hynd (1986) identified a factor structure for the CTRS–39 as used with special education students that varied somewhat from the subscale structure most commonly used. In general, the factor structures for the Conners scales presented in the 1990 manual are the structures most commonly reported and widely used in the research literature (e.g., M. Cohen, 1988). With the 1990 publication of an integrated manual with set scoring systems for the scales, the use of various factor configurations for these scales by individual researchers and clinicians appeared to diminish. These and other standardized changes that were incorporated into the 1990 manual were a major improvement over what was previously available for the Conners scales.

Development and Standardization. The development of the first version of the Conners Rating Scales commenced during the 1960s by clinicians at Johns Hopkins Hospital in Baltimore, Maryland. These clinicians, who were implementing and re-searching psychopharmacological and psychotherapeutic interventions with children, developed a set of rating scale items that were used informally and qualitatively to obtain further information from teachers. In discussing how the scales progressed from this earlier informal prototype to the standardized versions now in use, Conners (1990) noted that "when I compared data from normal children and clinical cases, it was clear that they differed on several different dimensions, not just in the number of total symptoms. Factor analysis confirmed that existence of stable clusters of items, . . . having much more clinical interest than a simple catalogue of problems" (p. vi). Research on this first standard version of the scales was published by Conners in 1969, and this version was essentially the same as the present version of the CTRS–39. The 28-item version of the teachers rating scale was later developed as a shorter form with slightly different content and properties. The first version of the parents rating scale was the 93-item version, with the 48-item version being later developed "after a careful consideration of accumulated psychometric evidence of the original version" and was thought to "represent a more abstract, and consequently abbreviated, formu-lation of child problem behaviors" (Conners, 1990, p. 1).

One of the drawbacks of the normative standardization data for the scales in the Conners system is that these instruments were not originally developed with the idea of creating widely available norm-referenced instruments from random, stratified populations. As such, comparative normative data and factor structures were devised later in the development process, sometimes after several iterations of the original instrument. Therefore, reviews of the Conners scales and the integrated 1990 manual include a number of different studies using diverse research methodologies that sometimes report slightly different results.

The factor structure and normative data reported in the 1990 manual for the CTRS–39 were based on an extremely large stratified random sample (9,583 Canadian schoolchildren) obtained by Trites, Blouin, and Laprade (1982). Factor analytic data and gender- and age-based score norms for the CPRS–48 were developed by Goyette, Conners, and Ulrich (1978), and included 570 children from age 3 to 17. This normative population was obtained from the Pittsburgh, Pennsylvania area, using a stratified sampling procedure.

Psychometric Properties. Test–test reliability for the scales of the CTRS–39 has been reported to range from .72 to .91 at 1-month intervals (Conners, 1969), and from .33 to .55 at 1-year intervals (R. A. Glow, P. A. Glow, & Rump, 1982). No test–retest data on the CPRS–48 had been reported at the time of publication of the 1990 manual, or located in subsequent computer-assisted literature searches. Several studies of in-terrater agreement on the CTRS–39 have yielded reliabilities ranging from a low of .39 (on the *Inattentive-Passive* scale) to as high as .94 (on the *Hyperactivity Index*). Agreement between parents on the CPRS–48 was reported in the Goyette et al. (1978) study, with the obtained reliability coefficients ranging from .46 to .57, with a mean correlation of .51.

Evidence for several forms of validity for the various Conners scales has accumulated in a large number of published research reports. For example, several studies have documented the efficacy of the Conners scales in differentiating between distinct diagnostic groups—hyperactive and normal children (King & Young, 1982), learning disabled and regular education students (Merrell, 1990), boys referred to juvenile court and a normal control group (L. Berg, Butler, Hullin, R. Smith, & Tyrer, 1978), and behavior disordered and non-special education students (Margalit, 1983). The CTRS–39 scores have been found to be highly predictive of hyperactivity at age 10, based on behavior ratings obtained at age 7 (C. Gillberg, 1983). Finally, the convergent construct validity of various versions of the Conners scales has been demonstrated through several studies that found significant correlations between them and other instruments, such as the Child Behavior Checklist (Edelbrock, Greenbaum, & Conover, 1985), the Behavior and Temperament Survey (Sandoval, 1981), the Behavior Problem Checklist (Campbell & Steinert, 1978), the School Behavior Survey, and the School Social Behavior Scales (Merrell, 1993a). It should be noted that the majority of the validity studies cited have involved the use of the CTRS–39, and less is known about the properties of the CPRS–48. An annotated bibliography of over 450 studies using the Conners rating scales has been assembled by the publisher (Wainwright & MHS Staff, 1996), which provides extensive documentation evidence for the many reliability and validity studies that have been conducted.

Additional Comments. In sum, the CTRS–39, CPRS–48, and the other two rating scales in the Conners system have been and continue to be widely utilized in clinical practice, and have been tested in various ways in a significant amount of published studies. There is no question that the CTRS–39 is the particular version of the Conners scales for which there is the most externally published empirical evidence. Less has been demonstrated about the CPRS–48 and the other two Conners scales. However, there is a good deal of overlap between the different scales that comprise the Conners system, which should lend at least a substantial degree of "face validity" to the versions of the scales that have not been as extensively researched. One caution to consider is that the size of the CPRS–48 norm population is relatively small, and the geographic and racial composition of the CPRS–48's norm sample is limited to the extent that the generalizability of norm-based scores should be questioned. Clinicians using the CPRS–48 for assessment of children and youth should be aware of these limitations, and should also become familiar with the properties of the other Conners scales so that proper interpretations can be made.

The 1990 publication of an integrated manual and standard scoring systems for the Conners scales filled a very large void in the understanding and use of these instruments, and clearly resulted in their increased clinical use, and also paved the way for the 1997 revisions. Because the CTRS–39 and CPRS–48 are relatively brief instruments (half as many or fewer items than the other scales reviewed in this chapter), they are an excellent choice for conducting initial screenings, but it is important that they be supplemented with other evaluation methods in conducting comprehensive clinical assessments.

→ designed as a comprehensive assessment system

1997 Conners Rating Scales–Revised. The Conners Rating Scales–Revised (CRS–R; Conners, 1997) is a comprehensive revision and expansion of the original Conners scales. The CRS–R, like the BASC and Achenbach's empirically based assessment system, is designed as a comprehensive assessment system, because it contains six main scales and five brief auxiliary scales, including adolescent self-report scales. In terms of general problem behavior rating scales, this discussion focuses on long and short forms of the Conners Parent Rating Scale–Revised (CPRS–R:L, 80 items, and CPRS–R:S, 27 items, respectively), as well as long and short forms of the Conners Teacher Rating Scale–Revised (CTRS–R:L, 59 items, and CTRS–R:S, 28 items, respectively). These instruments are all designed for assessment of children and adolescents from age 3 to 17.

Conners revisions are compatible w/ DSM-IV ADHD ratings

The revised Conners scales are similar in many respects to their predecessors, the CTRS–39, CTRS–28, CPRS–48, and CPRS–93. Even though there is much similarity in item overlap between the original and revised rating scales, some items were added or deleted to make the revised scales specifically compatible with the *DSM–IV* diagnostic criteria for Attention Deficit Hyperactivity Disorder (ADHD). The rationally derived subscale structure of the revised Conners scales also differs somewhat from that of the predecessor instruments. Specifically, in addition to the general subscales, the long-form scales contain the 10-item Conners Global Index (CGI; formerly referred to as the Hyperactivity Index), a 12-item ADHD index, and an 18-item *DSM–IV* Symptom Scale for ADHD. The CGI is now specifically touted as a brief measure of psychopathology that is useful for screening or progress monitoring. These 10 items are embedded into the long-form rating scales, and are also available on a separate short scale for screening use. The ADHD index includes critical items that are considered to be important in determining the existence of ADHD. The *DSM–IV* Symptoms Subscales, however, are used specifically in determining whether ADHD characteristics fall into the Inattentive or Hyperactive-Impulsive subtypes from *DSM–IV*. The ADHD and *DSM–IV* scales on the longer versions of the Conners scales are also packaged separately as a specific ADHD assessment instrument, which is reviewed in chapter 9. The long- and short-forms scales of revised Conners system include the same 4-point rating format and the same *T*-score/percentile rank score conversion format that is used with the original versions. Scoring of these instruments is accomplished in the same variety of ways as the original Conners scales.

The standardization sample for the CRS–R system is extremely large, with over 8,000 normative cases in aggregate, and between about 2,000 and 4,000 for the specific rating scales reviewed in this section. The normative sample is well stratified, including extensive samples from the United States and Canada. Extensive data are provided in the technical manual regarding gender and racial/ethnic breakdowns of the various samples, as well as the effects of gender and ethnicity on CRS–R scores. Internal consistency reliability for all CRS–R scales is adequate to excellent. For example, the internal consistency coefficients for the CPRS–R:L subscales range from .73 to .94. Obviously, the scales with lower reliability coefficients tend to be the scales with fewer items. Test–retest reliability at 6- to 8-week intervals for the CPRS–R:L and CTRS–R:L has been shown to range from .47 to .88 for the various subscales. Extensive factorial validity evidence (including confirmatory factor analyses) for the CRS–R scales is presented in the technical manual. Additional validity evidence for the CRS–R scales is presented in the form of extensive convergent and divergent validity coefficients among various scales within the system, and correlations with scores from the Children's Depression Inventory. Given that the CRS–R is based heavily on the already extensively researched original Conners Rating Scales, it as assumed that the developers did not consider it essential to gather as extensive validity evidence as would be needed with a totally new system of instrumentation. It can probably be assumed that much of the existing validity evidence for the original Conners scales will translate reasonably well to the revised scales.

Utility of rating scales

In sum, the rating scales within the revised Conners system show considerable promise and utility. The extensive new norms are a definite plus, as is the integration of *DSM–IV* criteria for ADHD into subscales on the longer version scales. These instruments should prove to be particularly useful in assessing children who have attention problems and hyperactivity, but have broader applications as well. According to Connors (1997), "The main use of the Conners' Rating Scales–Revised will be for the assessment of ADHD. However, the CRS–R can have a much broader scope, as they also contain subscales for the assessment of family problems, emotional problems, anger control problems, and anxiety problems" (p. 5). Although the original Conners scales should continue to be viewed as valid and important measures, the revised system is poised to eventually replace them, and to set a new research and clinical standard for the next decade or two.

Revised Behavior Problem Checklist *RBPC*

The Revised Behavior Problem Checklist (RBPC; Quay & Peterson, 1987, 1996) is a well-researched, widely used, and highly respected problem behavior rating scale. Like Achenbach's Child Behavior Checklist, development and refinement of the RBPC was one of the pioneering efforts in modern child behavior assessment that opened the door to increased development, acceptance, and use of behavior rating scales. The RBPC is a revision of the original Behavior Problem Checklist (Quay & Peterson, 1967), which was one of the first child behavior rating scales to gain wide acceptance by clinicians and researchers in the United States. The original version was a 55-item scale, including five subscales, developed and based on empirical behavioral data. The revision process included increased number of items in the scale, increased length and quality of item descriptions, change from a checklist format to a rating scale format, a new standardization group, and a new factor or subscale structure.

Description. The RBPC includes 89 problem behavior items that are rated according to a 3-point scale (0 = "Not A Problem," 1 = "Mild Problem," and 2 = "Severe Problem"). The scale may be completed by anyone who is familiar with the child's behavior, and is appropriate for use by either parents or teachers. It is designed to be used with children and adolescents from age 5 to 16. Completion of the RBPC typically takes about 10 minutes. The scale includes six empirically derived factor or subscale scores.

Scoring System and Scale Structure. For the most recent version of the RBPC raw scores are converted to the six factor scores (Conduct Disorder, Socialized Aggression, Attention Problems-Immaturity, Anxiety-Withdrawal, Psychotic Behavior, and Motor

6 Factor Scores

Excess) through the use of a removable self-scoring template that is self-scored as the items are completed. To obtain subscale raw scores, the examiner needs only to total the values on the self-scoring template. For pre-1996 versions of the published test protocol, subscale scores are obtained through the use of a set of acetate scoring keys, which are relatively easy to use and straightforward. After the 6-factor raw scores are obtained, they are converted to *T*-scores using the conversion tables in the professional manual for differing types of normative groups. There is no configuration for converting the total raw score to a *T*-score; only the six subscale scores are typically used. The RBPC subscale structure with a brief description of item content is presented in Table 4.6. The factor structure was developed by comparing factor analyses of the instrument that were obtained on four separate sets of data of children and adolescents with behavioral, emotional, and learning problems. The number of subjects in the four factor analytic samples ranged from 114 to 276. The factor loading data presented in the RBPC manual indicates that the six subscale factor structure is sound, despite the modest number of subjects in each analysis sample, even across differing populations of children and adolescents.

Development and Standardization. The technique used by Quay and Peterson in the development of normative data for the RBPC was to provide descriptive statistics (*n*'s, means, standard deviations, and score ranges) for several different specific populations, as well as to provide raw to *T*-score conversion charts based on grade level ranges and gender. The specific populations available for comparison purposes include gifted fourth-grade students, middle-elementary-age students from a university laboratory school, rural middle school students, children in public school classrooms for seriously emotionally disturbed students, students in a special school for children with behavior disorders, learning disabled students, general population ratings by mothers, outpatient clinical cases rated by parents, inpatient psychiatric cases rated by staff, and institutionalized juvenile delinquents. The raw score to *T*-score conversion tables are based on teacher ratings of a sample of 869 cases of nonreferred public school children in South Carolina, New Jersey, and Iowa.

Psychometric Properties. Technical data presented in the RBPC manual and in subsequent published studies indicate that the instrument has adequate to excellent psychometric properties. To date, there have been more than 80 externally published

TABLE 4.6
Subscale Structure of the Revised Behavior Problem
Checklist with Brief Description of Item Content

Name of Scale	Brief Description of Item Content
Conduct Disorder	Fighting, bragging/boasting, domination of others, teasing others, uncooperative.
Socialized Aggression	Staying out late at night, cheating, stealing, gang membership, school truancy with other persons.
Attention Problems-Immaturity	Difficulty following directions, lack of responsible behavior, not dependable, inattentive, impulsive.
Anxiety-Withdrawal	Feels inferior to others, shyness, lacking in self-confidence, feels that he or she is not loved, afraid of failure.
Psychotic Behavior	Has strange or bizarre beliefs and ideas, engages in repetitive or incoherent speech.
Motor Excess	Squirms or has fidgety behavior, is restless or not able to sit still, tense disposition, difficulty relaxing.

studies using the RBPC. Several types of reliability data on the RBPC have been demonstrated. Internal consistency coefficients from six different samples range from .70 to .95 for the six scales. Interrater reliability coefficients from a small number of teachers range from .52 to .85 for the six scales, while agreement between mothers and fathers of 70 children ranges from .55 to .93. Test–retest stability of the RBPC was determined by obtaining teacher ratings of 149 elementary-age children at 2-month intervals, with the resulting coefficients ranging from .49 to .83.

Validity of the RBPC has been ascertained through research presented in the test manual, and numerous external published research reports. The major evidence regarding the construct validity of the RBPC involves its sensitivity to theoretically based group differences. Numerous studies with the RBPC and its predecessor have demonstrated its ability to differentiate between clinical or special education groups and typical youth. Several studies have demonstrated strong convergent validity between the RBPC and other assessment instruments. An interesting recent study that provided predictive validity evidence for the RBPC was conducted by Steele, Forehand, Armistead, and Brody (1995). These researchers demonstrated that various combinations of RBPC scores in adolescence significantly predicted substance various abuse patterns in young adulthood. Comparisons between RBPC scores and direct observational data presented in the scale manual indicate that the Conduct Disorder scale correlates highly with playground observations of aggressive behavior (.60). Various scales of the RBPC have been found to correlate highly with peer nomination data for aggression, withdrawal, and likability. Hagborg (1990) found four of the six RBPC scales to be significantly correlated with sociometric ratings of peer acceptance.

Additional Comments. The RBPC is a well-respected instrument that has strong psychometric properties and a notable history of research that has validated it for many purposes. At its face value, the instrument appears to be highly relevant for the assessment of conduct disorders and general antisocial behavior. In fact, numerous studies with incarcerated, delinquent, antisocial, and conduct disordered youth have provided strong validity evidence for this use of the RBPC. However, there is some question regarding the effectiveness of the RBPC in assessing internalizing symptoms and disorders. It is true that many of the problems included in the internalizing dimension are represented in the RBPC items, but they are not as numerous or as prevalent in the factor structure as problem items included in the externalizing dimension. Therefore, if the major focus of concern in conducting an assessment are problems relating to social withdrawal, depression, and somatic complaints, then it is recommended that specific rating scales for these problems be included in the assessment battery, and that interviews and objective self-report tests also be used. This concern has been validated through research demonstrating that the RBPC was not sensitive to differences in depressive symptoms among students with and without learning disabilities (Maag & Reid, 1994). However, out of fairness to the RBPC, it must be recognized that as a general rule, internalizing disorders are quite difficult to assess adequately through the use of third-party rating scales.

The RBPC descriptive statistics for specific populations are informative and quite useful for comparison purposes. However, the raw to T-score conversion tables are based on a modest number of cases, with unknown ethnic, cultural, and socioeconomic backgrounds, and are not representative or the geographic breakdown of the U.S. population. Therefore, some caution should be used in making inferences based on the T-score conversions from the normative group.

① use rating scales routinely for early screening
② obtain from a variety of sources
③ use to assess progress...

BEST PRACTICES IN USING BEHAVIOR RATING SCALES

This chapter has included an overview of the uses, advantages, and cautions of behavior rating scales, as well as reviews of several of the most widely used commercially published general purpose problem behavior rating scales. To effectively use behavior rating scales requires more than just a cursory understanding of their characteristics. Thus, three "best practices" are suggested for using rating scales in a useful manner.

The first suggestion is to use rating scales routinely for early screening. Effective screening practices involve being able to systematically pick out children who are in the early stages of developing behavioral, social, or emotional problems with a high degree of accuracy. The identified subjects are then evaluated more carefully to determine whether their problems warrant special program eligibility and intervention services. The purpose of screening for social-emotional problems is usually for *secondary prevention*, which is prevention of the existing problem from becoming worse (Kauffman, 1989). Screening for early intervention is one of the best uses of behavior rating scales, given that they cover a wide variety of important behaviors and take very little time to administer and score. For general screening purposes, it is recommended that children or youth whose rating scale scores are one or more standard deviations above instrument normative means in terms of problem behavior excesses be identified for further evaluation. This practice will narrow the screening pool down to approximately 16% of the overall population, and this selected group can then be evaluated more comprehensively.

The second suggestion offered is to use the "aggregation principle." This principle involves obtaining ratings from a variety of sources, each of which might present a slightly differing picture. When using rating scales for purposes other than routine screening, obtaining aggregated rating scale data is recommended to reduce bias of response and variance problems in the assessment. In practice, using aggregated measures means to obtain rating evaluations from different raters in different settings, and to use more than one type of rating scale to accomplish this (R. P. Martin et al., 1986; Merrell, 1994a).

A final suggestion is to use behavior rating scales to assess progress during and after interventions. It has been demonstrated that continuous assessment and monitoring of student progress following the initial assessment and intervention is very important in successful implementation of behavioral interventions (Kerr & C. M. Nelson, 1989). Progress toward behavioral intervention goals can be easily assessed on a weekly or biweekly schedule using appropriate rating scales. Although behavior rating scales may not be the best measurement choice for daily assessment data (unless they are shortened considerably), there are a number of other simple ways of assessing progress daily, such as using performance records or brief observational data. Additional assessment following the intervention can also be a useful process. The main reason for follow-up assessment is to determine how well the intervention effects have been maintained over time (e.g., after 3 months), and how well the behavioral changes have generalized to other settings (e.g., the home setting and other classrooms). In actual practice, a follow-up assessment might involve having teacher(s) and parent(s) complete behavior rating scales on a child after a specified time period has elapsed following the student's participation in a social skills training program. The data obtained from this follow-up assessment can be used to determine whether or not follow-up interventions seem appropriate, and may be useful in developing future intervention programs if it is determined that social-behavioral gains are not being maintained over time or generalized across specific settings.

BEHAVIOR RATING SCALES AND DECISION MAKING

One of the major advances in the development and use of behavior rating scales over the past two to three decades is considered to be effective use of such scales in decision making regarding children and youth (Elliott et al., 1993). There are several potential ways that behavior rating scales may be used in decision making. Perhaps their most natural use for decision making involves decisions regarding screening and additional assessment. Behavior rating scales are an excellent choice for use in either individual or large group screening, because they tend to be quick and easy to administer, and if the screening criteria are set low enough, they will result in very few false-negative errors (failure to identify children and youth who do indeed meet behavioral criteria). For making decisions regarding additional assessment that may need to occur, behavior rating scales are capable of identifying specific dimensions or behavioral clusters that may need to be investigated in more detail. The multiple gating systems described in chapter 2 utilize rating scales as one of the important first steps in narrowing down a large population to a smaller population of potentially at-risk individuals before additional assessment methods are utilized. In actual screening practice, behavior rating scales completed by parents or teachers would be either the first or second gate in the assessment process, and would be followed by more time-intensive measures such as direct behavioral observation and interviewing.

Although behavior rating scales should never be used alone for making classification or placement decisions, they are capable of providing some potentially useful information in this regard. Given the development of the behavioral dimensions approach to classification, and the application of sophisticated multivariate statistical techniques to rating scales, they are capable of isolating specific dimensions of problem behaviors that would be useful in making classification decisions, particularly if used across raters and settings. Several state education agencies have recommended or required that local education agency personnel utilize behavior rating scales in systematic or prescribed ways in the identification of students for special education services under certain classification categories.

Behavior rating scales are increasingly being considered useful for making intervention planning decisions (Elliott et al., 1993). Primarily because they are quite effective at identifying specific areas of behavioral deficits or excesses a child or youth may exhibit, behavior rating scales may be used effectively in a general way for intervention planning. In terms of methods for effectively linking assessment results to intervention planning, data obtained through the use of behavior rating scales seem to line up most effectively with two specific intervention linkage strategies described by Shapiro (1996). The first of these strategies is referred to as the *Keystone Behavior Strategy,* and was originally described by R. O. Nelson and Hayes (1986). This strategy involves identification of a group or cluster of responses that appear to be clearly linked to a particular disorder, and then selecting interventions that are known to be functionally linked to impacting that particular problem or disorder. For example, if Child Behavior Checklist scores on a referred youth consistently showed them to have behavioral excesses in a cluster of items related to aggressive behavior and antisocial conduct problems, then it would be logical to select one of the several contingency management interventions that have been found to be effective in altering this group of behaviors with antisocial-aggressive youth. Another potentially useful strategy in this regard that was discussed by Shapiro (1996) is referred to as the *Template-Matching Strategy,* which was originally described by Hoier and J. D. Cone (1987) and J. D.

Keystone Behav. strategy - clusters

Template Matching Strategy
- Comparing

Cone and Hoier (1986). This strategy involves comparing objective behavioral data (i.e., rating scale data) on referred children with similar data obtained on children who have high functioning levels of the desired social-behavioral competencies. The areas of largest discrepancy between the two sets of data would then become the prime targets for intervention. For example, suppose that RBPC ratings on a referred child were compared to those obtained from behaviorally high functioning children, and the largest discrepancy area was items related to attention problems and motor excesses. Appropriate behavioral strategies for increasing on-task and attentive behavior would then be the obvious intervention choices.

In addition to these particular decision-making uses for behavior rating scales, it is also important to consider their use in monitoring and modifying interventions that have been put in place. Behavior rating scales are an excellent choice for summative evaluation of intervention efficacy, and if modified appropriately (i.e., using shortened versions), may also be useful for monitoring intervention progress on a weekly (and perhaps daily) basis.

CONCLUSIONS

Behavior rating scales have become an increasingly prominent assessment method for measuring child and adolescent behavior. Particularly since the late 1970s and early 1980s, technical advances with behavior rating scales have considerably advanced their popularity and prominence. Rating scales provide a structured format for making summary evaluative judgments regarding perceptions of child or adolescent behavior. Because rating scales do not measure behavior per se, but measure perceptions of behavior, they are probably more of an idiographic than a nomothetic measurement tool. The earlier generation of rating scales tended to use simple additive checklist formats. However, during the past two decades, use of an algebraic-style rating scale has become the standard, allowing for more precision in measurement of degree and intensity of behavior.

Behavior rating scales offer many advantages for researchers and practitioners. These advantages include low cost and efficiency; increased reliability and validity in comparison with some other methods of assessment; opportunity for assessment input from parents, teachers, and other important social informants; and the possibility of obtaining assessment data on individuals who are not in a position to be directly observed or to provide high quality self-report information. However, rating scales are not without their disadvantages. Foremost among the limitations and disadvantages of rating scales are various types of error variance (source, setting, and instrument variance), as well as response bias from raters, such as halo effects, leniency or severity effects, or central tendency effects. Many of these limitations and problems associated with behavior rating scales can be effectively combated by using rating scales as one part of a comprehensive assessment design, and by obtaining aggregated measures, or ratings across sources, instruments, and settings. Careful attention to the technical aspects of measurement in designing rating scales can also reduce potential problems.

Several widely used commercially published general purpose problem behavior rating scales were reviewed and discussed. These instruments, including the Child Behavior Checklist and Teacher's Report Form, Behavior Assessment System for Children, Conners Rating Scales, and Revised Behavior Problem Checklist, represent some of the best of what is currently available. However, many other technically sound and clinically useful behavior rating scales that are not as widely known as these measures have been developed for various purposes. The Child Behavior Checklist and Teacher's Report Form are both components of Achenbach's empirically based classification system, and comprise the most extensively researched of any combination of rating scales. The validity of these measures has been well documented and they are useful for many purposes. However, they have also been criticized for not being as useful for routine behavioral concerns as they are for severe psychopathology. The Revised Behavior Problem Checklist is also an extensively researched instrument that has found many important clinical uses, particularly regarding assessment of externalizing behavior problems. There is some question concerning how effective this instrument, and rating scales in general, are for assessing internalizing problems. The various forms and versions of the Conners rating scales have also been extensively researched and used clinically for nearly three decades. Although the reputation of these instruments was built largely through research and clinical applications with children who have ADHD characteristics, they are also considered to have broader applications for assessing emotional and behavioral problems. The recent revisions to the Conners scales have included several positive changes while building on the solid empirical tradition of the previous versions. The more recently developed Behavior Assessment System for Children (BASC) is representative of a new generation of behavior rating scales linked to a comprehensive assessment system. The BASC rating scales offer numerous advantages. Although they are not yet as extensively researched as the more established rating scales, they appear to be technically sound and potentially useful for varied research and clinical purposes.

Three best practices in using behavior rating scales were recommended. First, behavior rating scales should be used extensively for screening and early identification purposes. Second, the aggregation principle of gathering rating scale data from multiple informants across multiple settings is encouraged to provide a comprehensive portrait of perceptions of child behavior. And third, the use of rating scales to monitor progress during and following interventions is encouraged to provide empirical evidence of the efficacy (or lack thereof) of planned interventions, as well as to help guide formative changes in such interventions.

Behavior rating scales are potentially useful in clinical and education decision making, in several respects. Examples of the types of decisions that may be aided through the use of behavior rating scales include screening and assessment, classification and placement, and intervention decisions. Regarding intervention decisions, there appears to be an increasing acceptance of the usefulness of behavior rating scales for this purpose. Use of specific intervention linkage strategies, such as the Keystone Behavior Strategy and the Template Matching Strategy, may be helpful in making effective links between behavior rating scale data and subsequent intervention decisions.

REVIEW AND APPLICATION QUESTIONS

1. Describe the major differences between behavior rating scales and behavior checklists. Related to this first point, what is considered to be the major advantage of using rating scales instead of checklists?

2. For each of the four types of *error variance* described in this chapter, describe at least one practical way to implement the assessment to minimize or overcome potential error.

3. Assume that the same behavior rating scale has been completed on the same child by three different teachers, but the obtained scores from the three sources are considerably different. What are some potentially effective ways of interpreting this pattern of data?

4. The Child Behavior Checklist and Teacher's Report Form comprise the most widely and well-researched combination of child behavior rating scales. However, they are probably not a good choice for some purposes. In what situations or with what problems would it be more advantageous to use a different rating scale?

5. The Revised Behavior Problem Checklist, like many other behavior rating scales, may not be as effective for assessing internalizing problems (e.g., anxiety, depression, somatic problems) as for externalizing problems such as aggressive behavior, hyperactivity, and conduct problems. What are some reasons for this difference in efficacy across symptom domains?

6. Why is test–retest and interrater reliability of internalizing problem subscales of behavior rating scales typically lower than for externalizing problem subscales?

7. What are some ways that item-level data on behavior rating scales could be used to establish and monitor I.E.P. goals? Provide some specific examples.

8. For screening purposes, a cutoff point on behavior rating scales of one standard deviation or higher is recommended. If two separate rating scales are used for screening, and they produce differing results (one meets screening criteria, one does not), then how can a screening decision be made, and what are the risks and advantages of making yes/no decisions?

9. What is the *Template Matching Strategy*, and how might it be best implemented using data obtained through the use of behavior rating scales?

CLINICAL INTERVIEWING

Whether meeting informally with the teacher of a referred student, conducting a problem identification interview with a parent, or undertaking a diagnostic interview with a child or adolescent, interviewing is one of the most widely used and valuable assessment methods. The popularity of interviewing is no fluke because it offers many advantages to clinicians. This chapter provides a broad overview of clinical interviewing of children and adolescents, including problem identification and developmental history interviewing with the parents of children and adolescents. Additionally, it provides specific recommendations for procedures and techniques that may be useful in conducting high quality interviews.

The term *clinical interviewing* is the title of this chapter, and thus encompasses the broad range of interview techniques discussed. What does this term mean, and how does clinical interviewing differ from other types of interviewing? To help answer these questions, it is important to recognize that the term *clinical* in this case refers to a purpose rather than a place. Clinical interviewing is conducted in a variety of settings: schools, hospitals, homes, detention centers, and clinics. The purpose reflected in the title "Clinical Interviewing" is to gather specific information regarding behavioral, social, and emotional functioning, particularly regarding problems in functioning that may be occurring in any of these areas. But, in contrast to other methods of assessment that may be used for these same purposes, clinical interviewing is unique in its emphasis on direct face-to-face contact and interpersonal communication between the clinician and the client. As such, it places some very unique demands on the clinician. As Sattler (1998) explained, "Clinical assessment interviewing is a critical part of the assessment process. And even more than other assessment techniques, it places a premium on your personal skills, such as your ability to communicate effectively and your ability to establish a meaningful relationship" (p. 3).

This chapter begins with a discussion of the role of the interview as an assessment method, including sections on developmental issues in interviewing, factors or contexts that affect overall interview quality, and how to select specific interview methods for specific purposes. Much of this chapter is devoted to discussions of three types of interviews: the traditional or unstructured interview, behavioral interviewing, and structured or semistructured diagnostic interviews. Because the clinical interview is clearly the most useful assessment technique for working with children and adolescents who are suicidal, a specific section is devoted to this topic. The chapter concludes with a brief discussion of how interviews can be used in decision-making processes.

THE ROLE OF THE INTERVIEW IN ASSESSING CHILDREN AND ADOLESCENTS

There is no question that as an assessment method, clinical interviewing holds a place of prominence in the fields of psychology, psychiatry, social work, and counseling. This venerated attitude toward the interview process has been perpetuated in popular media, and thus has strongly shaped the beliefs of the public. It is even fair to say that public beliefs and attitudes regarding clinical interviewing are often shaped to the point of nearly mystifying what is actually done and accomplished in the interview process. Many psychologists and psychiatrists have experienced this public mystification of the interview process and the supposed diagnostic powers possessed by clinicians, sometimes to the point of hilarity. Even when conducting such mundane business as standing in line at the supermarket, getting a haircut, or having a major appliance serviced, when clinicians are queried by strangers as to what their occupation is, the answer frequently draws responses such as "are you analyzing me now?" or "oh no, you'll figure out what all my problems are by talking to me!" Of course, an honest reply to such questions is usually disappointing to both the professional and those inquiring about their skills—both would like to believe that the clinicians' prowess in interpersonal communications allows them more "clinical insight" than is usually the case. *Interview= a purposeful conversation.*

If the process of clinical interviewing is not always a mystical conduit to the secrets of the human soul, then what is it? Essentially, interviewing is structured communication, mainly verbal, but nonverbal as well. R. P. Martin (1988) noted that an interview resembles a conversation, but differs from day-to-day conversation in that it is purposeful; is usually "controlled" by the interviewer through the initiating of interchanges and the posing of questions; and has unity, progression, and thematic continuity. In other words, clinical interviews should have direction and structure, and are driven by very specific goals related to obtaining relevant information and using it to make decisions.

Interviews come in several forms, ranging from less structured stream-of-consciousness interchanges to formalized and highly structured interview schedules used for exploring very specific problem areas. Although the purposes, underlying theories, and level of structure among different types of interviews may vary considerably, all forms of clinical interviewing share some commonalities, and have specific advantages when compared with other assessment methods. Perhaps the most salient advantage of interviewing as an assessment method is the flexibility it provides. Throughout the course of an interview, the clinician has the opportunity to shorten or lengthen it, to change directions when needed, and to focus on specific aspects of the clients' thought, behavior, or emotion that emerge as being most important at the time. With other methods of assessment, this type of flexibility is rarely, if ever, possible. Another advantage of clinical interviewing is that it provides the clinician with the opportunity to directly observe the client under structured conditions. Client characteristics such

Flexibility + observation

as social skills, verbal ability, insight, defensiveness, and willingness to cooperate can all be assessed to a degree throughout the course of an interview. When interviewing children, the observational advantage of the interview process is particularly important, because their limited experiences and typically unsophisticated verbal mediation skills make it difficult for children to directly express their concerns, needs, and problems. In cases where the client is not available or otherwise incapable of providing high quality information in an interview context (a typical concern with young children), interviews can be conducted with individuals who know them well, such as parents or teachers. Finally, the process of interviewing can be an important bridge in the therapeutic process. Unlike any other method of assessment, clinical interviewing provides the opportunity to establish rapport, trust, and security with clients, which may be critical to the eventual implementation of an intervention plan.

Of course, like other methods of assessment, clinical interviewing does have its flaws or weaknesses. Perhaps the most easily criticized feature of interviewing is that the flexible, nonstandardized nature of many interviews, which is also considered to be an advantage, may easily lead to unreliability or inconsistency over time and between interviewers. Another potential problem with interviewing is that to be effective, it requires a great deal of training and experience, particularly when less structured interview formats are used. Finally, there are some important limitations in clinical interviewing related to distortion and bias. Clinicians and clients may have personal biases that may result in selective or faulty recall of information, lack of attention to important details, and even subtle cues from the clinician that may lead clients to distort the information they provide (Sattler, 1998).

DEVELOPMENTAL ISSUES AND CLINICAL INTERVIEWING

Stated simply, interviewing children or adolescents is a much different task than interviewing adults. Although there may be some superficial similarity, a qualitatively different approach is required to obtain a useful and informative verbal report. As children develop and mature in their physical, cognitive, social-emotional functioning, their ability to respond to the tasks required of them in an interview format likewise changes. To effectively interview children and adolescents, interviewers must have a knowledge of some of the basic aspects of these developmental issues. This section provides a general discussion of some basic developmental issues that may affect the interview process, some of which is summarized in Table 5.1. For a more complete discussion of developmentally sensitive interviewing, readers are referred to Bierman (1983) and J. N. Hughes and Baker (1990).

Preschool- and Primary-Age Children

Young children tend to be particularly difficult to interview and pose perhaps the greatest challenge to the interviewer. As Bierman (1983) noted:

> Young children are able to describe their thoughts and feelings, but they require specialized interview techniques to do so. Moreover, characteristics of conceptual organization and information processing associated with cognitive and linguistic development result in a phenomenological world for the young child that is qualitatively different from the adult's world. Clinicians who are unfamiliar with the thought processes associated with various developmental levels are likely to find children's reasoning extremely difficult to follow

TABLE 5.1

Developmentally Sensitive Interviewing: Considerations and Suggestions

Developmental Period	Developmental Considerations		Suggested Practices
	Cognitive Functioning	Social-Emotional Functioning	
Early Childhood	Easily confused by distinctions between appearance and reality, *egocentric*, tendency toward *centration*, memory is not fully developed.	Actions considered right or wrong based on consequences, limited verbal ability to describe range of emotions, learns to initiate tasks, some difficulty in self-control.	1. Use combination of open and closed questions. 2. Don't attempt to maintain total control of interview. 3. Reduce complexity of questions. 4. Use toys, props, manipulatives. 5. Establish familiarity and rapport.
Middle Childhood	Increased capability for verbal communication, simple logic attained, mastery of *reversibility*, *decentration*, *conservation*.	May view right or wrong based on rules and social conventions, *industry vs. inferiority* struggle based on how well new challenges are mastered, peer group becomes increasingly important.	1. Avoid abstract questions. 2. Rely on familiar settings and activities. 3. Avoid constant eye contact. 4. Provide contextual cues (pictures, examples) and request language interaction. 5. Physical props in context may be useful.
Adolescence	Ability for abstract reasoning and formal logic usually emerges, systematic problem solving.	May develop *postconventional* moral reasoning, identifies confusion and experimentation, high emotional intensity and lability is not unusual, peer group usually becomes extremely important.	1. Consider the possibility of emotional lability and stress. 2. Avoid making judgments based solely on adult norms. 3. Show respect.

101

or comprehend. To conduct effective child interviews, clinicians must acquire an understanding of the characteristics of developing social-cognitive processes, and they must make some major adjustments in their interviewing techniques and strategies. (pp. 218–219)

2–7

In Piagetian terms, children between age 2 and 7 are in the *Preoperational* stage of cognitive development. A child in this stage is able to represent things with words and images but is lacking in logical reasoning abilities (Piaget, 1983). These children can be easily confused by distinctions between reality and appearance, find it easier to follow positive instructions ("hold the blocks carefully") than negative ones ("don't drop the blocks"), and tend to be *egocentric*, in that they have difficulty in taking or understanding the viewpoint or experience of another person. They tend to have difficulty recalling specific information accurately, because they have usually not developed memory retrieval strategies (McNamee, 1989). Preoperational children tend to focus on just one feature of a problem, neglecting other important aspects, a tendency referred to as *centration*. They often exhibit difficulty understanding that actions can be reversed. These cognitive aspects of early childhood may often lead young children to provide incomplete accounts of past events, and also make them particularly susceptible to acquiescing to "leading" questions from an interviewer, such as "Does your mom get really mad at you?" (Saywitz & Snyder, 1996).

To most young children, behavioral actions are considered to be right or wrong depending on what consequences they bring on ("stealing is wrong because you get put into jail"). Kohlberg (1969) referred to this type of moral reasoning as being at a *preconventional level*. In terms of emotional development, younger children may experience a wide range of emotions and affect, but typically can only describe these experiences along a limited number of dimensions (i.e., happy or sad, good or bad, mean or nice).

Interestingly, recent evidence has put into question some of the absolutist aspects of developmental stage theories with young children. J. N. Hughes and Baker (1990) reviewed several studies from the 1970s and 1980s demonstrating that the apparent cognitive limitations of young children are often artifacts of the way they are questioned, or the way that tasks are presented to them. It is now thought that young children are capable of producing higher quality self-report information than was previously thought. The chances of obtaining high quality interview information from young children are increased if they are comfortable in the interview situation, and are questioned by an interviewer who understands cognitive development and appropriately modifies interview tasks for them (Gelman & Baillargeon, 1983). Because social-emotional assessment in early childhood poses many singular challenges and requires a high level of specific skills, this topic is treated separately in this book. Thus, specific techniques and recommendations for increasing the quality of interviews with young children are presented in chapter 13.

Elementary-Age Children

↑ verbal = higher quality interview info.

7–11

As children move from the preschool and primary years into the elementary years, their capabilities for verbal communication tend to increase *dramatically*. Thus, although conducting an effective interview with elementary-age children is a challenging endeavor that requires special understanding and methodology, the probability of obtaining high quality interview information is increased in comparison with the same probability for younger children.

In developmental terms, elementary-age children tend to be in what Piaget (1983) referred to as the *concrete operations* stage of cognitive development, which extends roughly from 7 to 11 years. Children at this developmental stage are able to use simple logic, but can generally perform mental operations only on images of tangible objects and actual events. During the concrete operations stage, many principles are mastered that were formerly elusive to children while they were in the preoperational stage, including *reversibility*, *decentration*, and *conservation* (understanding that a change in appearance does not always change a quantity). Concrete operational children learn to develop simple hierarchical classification abilities, but still do not have the ability to use formal logic or abstract reasoning. For example, a child at this stage of development may understand that anger is an emotion and that acting-out is a behavior, but they may often demonstrate little insight into the connection among the two realms.

Elementary-age children are challenged by the task of learning to function socially beyond the family into a broader social realm, a developmental stage that Eriksen (1963) referred to as *industry vs. inferiority*. If they are able to master these new social challenges, elementary-age children will develop a strong sense of self-competence. However, lack of such mastery may lead to feelings of low self-esteem and poor self-efficacy.

Most elementary-age children learn to make moral decisions in a more complex way than they did during their preschool and early primary grade years. Kohlberg (1969) suggested that most children in this age range reach what he referred to as *conventional morality*, wherein rules and social conventions are viewed as absolute guidelines for judging actions. For example, whereas a preschool-age child may respond to the question "why is it wrong to steal?" by stating something like "because you will get in trouble if you do that," a typical elementary-age child might respond by saying "because it is against the school rules." *Effective interview methods*

Effective interviewing of elementary-age children can be greatly facilitated by using specific methods and techniques that are developmentally appropriate for this age level. Establishment of adequate rapport and familiarity with the child prior to the actual assessment has been found to be a critical variable in influencing the amount and quality of responses presented in standardized assessment situations (D. Fuchs & L. S. Fuchs, 1986). Although elementary-age children have generally developed a reasonable mastery of language, the interviewer should avoid the use of abstract or symbolic questions, which will probably serve to confuse the child. J. N. Hughes and Baker (1990) suggested that interviews with elementary-age children may be enhanced by relying on familiar settings and activities during the interview, allowing them to use manipulatives and drawings during the interview, avoiding constant eye contact (which elementary-age children are not typically used to), and providing contextual cues (such as pictures, colors, and examples) along with requests for language interaction. Use of physical materials and familiar contexts in interviewing children has also been empirically studied. For example, Priestley and Pipe (1997) found that the use of toys and other physical props in interviews with children may facilitate their accurate accounts of events they have experienced, particularly when many props are provided and the physical similarity of these objects is similar to what was experienced in the actual event. Use of toys, props, and other physical materials is likely to enhance the quality of interviews with preschool and primary age children as well as those in the elementary age range.

Adolescents

12 - 14   By the time adolescence has been reached, which is typically around age 12 to 14, children are usually capable of participating in an interactive interview situation to a much greater extent than are younger children. In many ways, the interview task becomes similar to that of interviewing an adult. However, clinicians who assume that interviewing adolescents is the same as interviewing adults seriously risks the chance of reaching invalid conclusions or obtaining low quality information based on their lack of sensitivity to the unique development aspects of adolescence.

In Piagetian terms, most individuals move toward the *formal operations* stage of cognitive development at about age 12 (Piaget, 1983). This stage is characterized by the ability to use formal logic and to apply mental operations to abstract as well as concrete objects. Adolescents tend to become more systematic in their problem-solving efforts, rather than using quick trial-and-error methods for attacking problems. It is important to consider that some individuals (i.e., those with impaired cognitive functioning or developmental disabilities) do not reach this advanced stage of cognitive functioning; there is no guarantee that because subjects are 17 years old they will be able to think abstractly and logically, and clinicians should screen subjects' academic/intellectual history prior to the clinical interview.

Depends on the academic, intellectual history

During adolescence, many persons reach what Kohlberg (1969) referred to as *postconventional moral reasoning*, which is a stage where actions are judged based on individual principles of conscience rather than potential consequences or social conventions. Thus, some adolescents (particularly older adolescents) may make decisions regarding what is considered right or wrong behavior based on abstract internalized ideals, rather than conventional guidelines such as school or family rules, or fear of consequences. Although there is not a great deal of empirical evidence regarding how many adolescents make decisions in postconventional terms, it can be generalized that this stage is more likely to be reached toward the end of adolescence, and many individuals do not reach this stage of moral reasoning development at all. In practical terms, an example of a postconventional response to the question "why is stealing wrong?" might be "because stealing violates the personal property rights of other people." Related to the area of moral reasoning, adolescence is a time when many individuals experience personal shifts in their religious and political thinking, a developmental issue that may sometimes create stress in relationships with parents (Dusek, 1996).

Since the time of the industrial revolution in Western industrialized societies, prominent thinkers as disparate as the European philosopher Jean Jacques Rousseau and the pioneering American psychologist G. Stanley Hall have characterized emotional development during adolescence as a period of "storm and stress" because of the challenging adaptions that must be made. In his theory of psychosocial development, Eriksen (1963) characterized adolescence as a time of *identity vs. confusion* crisis, wherein young persons struggle to find themselves and may experience a wide variation in emotional intensity. Teachers and clinicians who work frequently with adolescents usually tend to agree with these assessments of age-related emotional stress. However, the empirical evidence regarding adolescence as a period of emotional storm and stress has been characterized as being less than convincing (Dusek, 1996). One of the tragic aspects of adolescence in the United States is that compared to childhood, it is accompanied by substantial increases in suicidal ideation and suicide attempts (Dusek, 1996). This evidence is often cited to characterize adolescence as a time of emotional difficulty. However, it is important to consider that even with this age-related increase, adolescent suicide rates are still low compared to older age groups (Weiten, 1997). Therefore, it is unclear whether adolescence constitutes a developmental period of unique emotional turbulence. Notwithstanding, clinicians who interview adolescent-age individuals should consider that adolescence is a time of many challenges and changes, and they need to be sensitive to and aware of these issues.

Conducting interviews with adolescent clients can be a very rewarding experience. It is usually less constrained or frustrating than interviewing younger children. Nevertheless, clinicians must consider the unique developmental aspects of adolescence to elicit and receive useful interview information and to make sound inferences. Whereas many adolescents may be very adultlike in their approach to the clinical interview, and may actually enjoy the unique one-to-one attention that comes from this process, others may find the process to be intimidating or upsetting. It is extremely important to at least consider the possibility of intensely variable emotionality during adolescence. Although most *DSM–IV* diagnostic categories may apply to both adolescents and adults, clinicians should still exert extra care and caution in making significant inferences. Any diagnoses of severe affective or behavioral problems should be tempered by the understanding of normal adolescent development, and adult standards of behavior and emotionality should not be exclusively applied. There is actually evidence that making decisions on an adolescent's social and emotional behavior in the same manner that is done with adults may lead to faulty conclusions. For example, Archer (1987) demonstrated that about 25% of adolescent subjects responded to the Minnesota Multiphasic Personality Inventory (MMPI) in a manner that would be suggestive of psychotic behavior when interpreted strictly according to adult norms. Regardless of whether or not clinicians subscribe to the notion that adolescence is by its nature an emotionally difficult and variable period, this type of evidence compels them to consider adolescence as a time of unique challenges and adaption.

FACTORS THAT MAY AFFECT THE QUALITY OF THE INTERVIEW

Knowledge of child development and methods of making interviews developmentally appropriate do not by themselves result in effective and useful interviews with children or adolescents. In addition to developmental issues and interview format, there are a number of other factors that may contribute to the overall quality of the interview. Several of these factors are discussed in this section.

The Interpersonal Context

Whether the interview is with a child, parent, or teacher, the interpersonal relationship established prior to and during the course of the interview may significantly affect the extent and quality of client self-report data. One of the key tenets of Rogerian *person-centered therapy* is that the development of a positive relationship between the interviewer and the client is critical to both the quality of client self-disclosure and the effectiveness of therapy. Three core relationship conditions are considered essential: *empathy*, or accurate understanding of the client's concerns; *respect*, or positive regard for the client; and *genuineness*, which can be described as congruence between the interviewer's verbal and nonverbal messages toward the client (Rogers, Gendlin, Kiesler, & Truax, 1967). Although these interpersonal considerations were first described and used within the context of person-centered therapy, they obviously have value for other forms of interviewing and therapy as well.

W. H. Cormier and L. S. Cormier (1985) elaborated further on the relationship-building aspect of the interview, and suggested that *expertness, attractiveness,* and *trustworthiness* are additional characteristics that enhance the interpersonal context of communication. Expertness is related to the client's perception of how competent the interviewer is, with an emphasis on characteristics of interviewer competence that are immediately evident to a client. Attractiveness goes far beyond the client's perception of the interviewer's physical characteristics and includes such attributes as friendliness, likability, and similarity to the client. Trustworthiness includes such variables as the interviewer's reputation for honesty, the congruence of their nonverbal behaviors, and the amount of accuracy, openness, and confidentiality that is evident during the interview process. Clinicians who successfully incorporate these interpersonal characteristics and behaviors into their interviewing methods will likely increase the value of their interviews with clients.

It is worth considering the idea that children may have a different perspective than adults on what interpersonal qualities make a good and trusted interviewer. For example, take the concept of expertness. Whereas many adults might be swayed toward positive appraisal of a clinician who comes across as a highly knowledgeable expert, it is no stretch of the imagination to consider that these same characteristics will not necessarily impress children as much, and in some cases may even hinder communication. C. L. Thompson and Rudolph (1992) stated that "adults are often too aggressive in trying to initiate conversations with children" (p. 33). Although some adults might respond well to a clinician who seems confident and eager to engage in conversation, this same behavior may be intimidating to many children. Likewise, consider how perceptions of what constitutes expertness relate to professional dress standards. A clinician who is dressed in relatively formal business-type attire might impress many adults as being groomed like a professional, but it is highly doubtful that the same effect will result with children. In attempting to develop an appropriate and effective interpersonal context for clinical interviews with children, always consider these and other potential differences between children and adults, and place a premium on helping the child client feel comfortable and safe.

The Ethnocultural Context

The United States is a uniquely diverse nation in terms of the racial, ethnic, and cultural diversity of its inhabitants, and all demographic indicators point to this diversity increasing rapidly over the next several decades. In fact, the U.S. Bureau of the Census has projected that the proportion of Americans who are White or caucasian (sometimes referred to as European American), which currently includes from 70% to 75% of the general U.S. population, will shrink to slightly over 50% by the year 2050, and growth in the population of Hispanic Americans and Asian Americans will account for most of this shift (Rosenblatt, 1996). Clearly, it is critical for clinicians to consider cultural factors that may affect clinical interviewing.

In discussing information about differences between different racial, ethnic, or cultural groups, it is important to consider that much of the information on group differences is based on generalizations from studies. There are always individuals who do not fit the "typical" group characteristics. Therefore caution is essential to avoid stereotypical overgeneralizations of group differences.

Two of the dimensions of the clinical interview that may have immediate cultural relevance include the degree of eye contact and the amount of physical distance between the interviewer and the client. D. W. Sue and D. Sue (1990) noted that White, U.S. Americans make eye contact with the speaker about 80% of the time, but tend to avoid eye contact about 50% of the time when speaking to others. This is in contrast to the eye contact patterns of many African Americans, who tend to make greater eye contact when speaking, and less frequent eye contact when listening. On the other hand, American Indians are more likely to have indirect eye contact when speaking or listening, whereas Asian Americans and Hispanics are more likely to avoid eye contact altogether when speaking to persons who they perceive to have high status.

In terms of comfortable physical proximity or distance between persons, D. W. Sue and D. Sue (1990) also noted that there may be important cultural differences. For Latino Americans, Africans, African Americans, Indonesians, South Americans, Arabs, and French, a much closer physical stance between communicators than most White/Anglo clinicians are comfortable with is normal. Clearly, degree of eye contact and physical proximity between interviewee and interviewer may be variables that can greatly affect the overall quality of the interview. Some of the culturally based aspects of interpersonal communication styles among U.S. cultural groups are reflected in the information presented in Table 5.2. Additionally, because cultural diversity is such a critical issue in conducting effective social-emotional assessments, the topic is dealt with separately in chapter 14.

The Behavioral Context

It is also known that some specific interviewer behaviors are likely to enhance or detract from the amount and quality of interview information that is obtained from a client during a clinical interview. Whether the interview will be of a structured or unstructured format, there is some evidence that by preparing the client and instructing them in desirable ways of responding, the interviewer will increase the amount, quality, and accuracy of self-disclosure by the client (Gross, 1984; Saywitz & Snyder, 1996). For example, at the beginning of an interview with the parent of a referred child, the clinician might say something like "when you tell me about problems you are having with Sari, I would like you to be very specific—tell me exactly what she does that you see as a problem, how it affects you, and what you generally do about it."

The use of reinforcement also may increase the quality of the interview. With both children and adults, the selective use of praise or appreciative statements have the effect of increasing both the amount and quality of subsequent self-disclosure (Gross, 1984). For instance, a clinician who is interviewing a child about how the divorce of his parents has affected him might say something like:

> Scott, you really did a good job of telling me what it was like for you when your mom and dad got divorced. I know that was a very hard thing for you to talk about, but you were able to tell how you feel about it in a very clear way. The more you can tell me about how you feel and what has happened to you, the better I can understand you and help you.

Other forms of reinforcement may also be effective with younger children, edible primary reinforcers such as raisins, nuts, or small pieces of candy are one possibility, though they should be used with caution to avoid satiation effects, and to avoid having the reinforcers take center stage during the interview. An alternative is stickers, which are often popular with children, or tokens that can be exchanged for small rewards following the interview.

TABLE 5.2

Generalized Communication Style Differences Between Major Cultural Groups in the United States: Overt Activity Dimension, Nonverbal and Verbal Communication

American Indians	Asian Americans and Hispanics	Whites	African Americans
1. Speak softly/slower	1. Speak softly	1. Speak loud/fast to control	1. Speak with affect
2. Indirect gaze when listening or speaking	2. Avoidance of eye contact when listening or speaking to high-status persons	2. Greater eye contact when listening	2. Direct eye contact (prolonged) when speaking, but less when listening
3. Interject less, seldom offer encouraging communication	3. Similar rules	3. Head nods, nonverbal markers	3. Interrupt (turn-taking) when can
4. Delayed auditory (silence)	4. Mild delay	4. Quick responding	4. Quicker responding
5. Manner of expression low key, indirect	5. Low keyed, indirect	5. Objective, task-oriented	5. Affective, emotional, interpersonal

Note. From *Counseling the Culturally Different* (2nd ed.), by D. W. Sue and D. Sue. Copyright © 1990 by John Wiley & Sons, Inc. Reprinted by permission of John Wiley & Sons, Inc.

Finally, consider the type of questioning used. The use of closed questions (those that can be answered with a one-word response) should be avoided except when very specific information is needed. A barrage of closed questions from an interviewer may leave clients feeling as though they are being interrogated. With adults, adolescents, and older children, the use of open-ended questions (e.g., "tell me about what you like to do with your friends") is generally preferred. With very young children, it is generally most useful to use a combination of open and closed questions (J. N. Hughes & Baker, 1990).

The Physical Context

A final aspect of the interview that should also be considered is the physical context of the interview setting, and likewise, the physical or topographical aspects of communication. The issue of degree of eye contact has already been discussed, which involves both the physical context and the ethnocultural context. Related to degree of eye contact is physical proximity between clinician and client. This issue may become particularly important with children. It is widely held that children prefer to talk to adults at the same eye level as they are, and it has been recommended that to increase their comfort during an interview, children should, in most cases, be allowed to control the distance between them and the interviewer (C. L. Thompson & Rudolph, 1992). Therefore, clinicians are encouraged to allow the child to determine how close they want to sit to the interviewer in most situations, and to be willing to sit lower to the ground to avoid intimidating the child. With younger children and those children who are not comfortable in formal assessment situations, this advice may become especially crucial.

An additional aspect of the physical context is the seating arrangement, or how to arrange tables, chairs, and desks for optimum comfort and effectiveness. Although no empirical evidence has been reported regarding this issue, clinicians who are experienced in counseling children tend to agree that having a barrier such as a desk between the clinician and a child client tends to make the child see the clinician as an authority figure, which in some cases may inhibit communication. Also, having the clinician and child client seated directly across from each other with no physical barrier between them is seen as being problematic, because it can be too intimidating for the child. Regarding appropriate seating arrangements for counseling and interviewing with children, C. L. Thompson and Rudolph (1992) recommended that the preferred arrangement is to "use the corner of a desk or table as an optional barrier for the child, allowing them to retreat behind the desk or table corner or to move out around the corner when he or she feels comfortable doing so" (p. 33). These general guidelines may be useful as a starting point, but the optimal interview situation may vary from child to child and situation to situation. Thus, clinicians are encouraged to pay complete attention to the comfort and level of disclosure of their client, and to make modifications to the physical setup or interview technique as needed. Essentially, what works is what is best in any given situation, and that will certainly vary.

[handwritten margin note: no evidence]

SELECTING AN APPROPRIATE INTERVIEW METHOD   *[handwritten: 3 types of Interviews...]*

Within this chapter, clinical interviewing methods are divided into three general categories: traditional interview techniques, behavioral interviews, and structured or semistructured interviews. It is certainly possible to divide or categorize interview methods into more classifications than this, but this three-part division provides a useful grouping into general methods that might typically be used in most clinical interviews.

The particular choice of the interview method will depend on several factors, including the theoretical orientation of the clinician, the level of training and experience the clinician has in conducting interviews, and the overall goals and specific objectives for conducting the interview. The clinicians' theoretical orientation will ~~theoretical~~ influence the choice of interview methods in that their personal beliefs and biases ~~orientation~~ may limit the level of comfort they have in using different methods. For instance, clinicians who have a very strong behavioral orientation may not be comfortable using a traditional, open-ended interview format with a client, perceiving that the type of information obtained will be of little use in identifying key elements and sequences of problem behaviors and in developing an intervention. Conversely, a psychodynamic or humanistic-oriented clinician may perceive that some of the highly structured diagnostic interview schedules are restrictive and confining.

The clinicians' level of training and experience may affect their choice of methods as well. Being able to effectively conduct a traditional, open-ended interview without a great deal of pre-imposed structure requires a significant amount of clinical judgment, ~~training~~ which is only gained through experience and specific training. Conducting an effective ~~level~~ behavioral interview requires a solid grounding in behavioral psychology, if the results are to be useful in identifying factors that elicit and maintain problem behaviors, and the subsequent development of an intervention plan. Some of the available structured and semistructured interview schedules require a high degree of specific training, but some can be easily and effectively used by paraprofessionals and laypersons with minimal training.

In addition to the clinician's theoretical orientation and level of training, the choice ~~purpose~~ of interview techniques will also be shaped by the specific purposes for conducting ~~of~~ the interview. Traditional interview formats are considered to be useful when there ~~interview~~ is a premium on obtaining historical information, and in establishing rapport with the client within the arrangement of a less formal, client-focused interview. Behavioral methods of interviewing are considered to be particularly useful when the preeminent goal is to develop an immediate intervention wherein the critical behavioral variables can be identified and modified. If diagnostic or classification purposes are of paramount importance for the interview, many of the semistructured or structured interview schedules are considered to be a good choice, particularly if the purpose is psychiatric diagnoses via the *DSM* system.

TRADITIONAL INTERVIEWING TECHNIQUES

What is referred to here as *traditional interviewing* is not really a specific format or type of interview. Rather, this term represents the broad range of clinical interviews that are relatively open-ended, less structured, and highly adaptable depending on the situation. Traditional interviewing techniques may include a wide range of specific types of approaches to interviewing, such as psychodynamic, case history, psychosocial status, and so forth. Within the discussion of traditional clinical interviewing techniques, two areas are covered that are germane to virtually any specific type of interview: obtaining background information from parents and teachers and methods of developing the interview with child or adolescent clients.

Obtaining Relevant Background Information From Parents and Teachers

In addition to identifying specific problems and developing intervention plans, both of which are covered in the section on behavioral interviewing, one of the main purposes for interviewing the parent(s) or teacher(s) of a referred child is to obtain a report of relevant background information. Why should background information be obtained? Although an argument could be made for using only information that is current and directly linked to the presenting problem, such an approach is shortsighted. By carefully reviewing important historical information, clues are sometimes provided to both the causes of and potential solutions to child behavior or emotional problems. An additional advantage of obtaining comprehensive background information is that it can help to provide links to seemingly unrelated problems. For example, some behavioral or physical side effects of medications a child is taking may be mistakenly misunderstood unless the clinician is aware that the medication is being taken in the first place. Another benefit of interviewing parents or teachers is that it creates an opportunity to build trust and rapport with them, which is a crucial ingredient when it is time to implement interventions.   *info + rapport w/ parent interview*

What type of background information should be obtained? The answer to this question will depend to some extent on the nature of the presenting problems, but there are some standard areas that are typically explored in the process. Table 5.3 includes five general areas of inquiry, each with some specific recommended areas of questioning. The general areas include medical history, developmental history, social-emotional functioning, educational background, and community involvement. Of course, this format is not all-inclusive; other general areas and specific questions can *5 areas of INQUIRY* be identified as the need arises. It is also important to consider that the five general areas of inquiry presented here are not equally applicable to all adults being interviewed. Specific medical and developmental history may not be known to a foster caregiver or a teacher. Likewise, when interviewing a teacher, the focus on educational background and performance will of necessity be the major area of discussion.

A wide array of forms have been developed and are in use for obtaining developmental history information. These forms range from being self-produced to commercially produced, and short and informal to long and formal. An example of a comprehensive formal developmental history interview form that has been commercially published is the Structured Developmental History form from the Behavioral Assessment System for Children (C. R. Reynolds & Kamphaus, 1992). This is a 12-page form covering everything from prenatal history to family health history to adaptive skills of the child.

Developing the Interview With Children and Adolescents

Interviewing a child or adolescent client provides the opportunity for two important elements of the assessment: directly observing their behavior under controlled conditions and obtaining their self-report regarding their concerns, problems, goals, and hopes. The interview also provides an opportunity to develop rapport with the child or adolescent client, which may prove to be especially important if the interviewer will also be functioning as a counselor-therapist following the completion of the assessment.

Areas for Observation. Although the specific aspects of client behavior that are most important for the interviewer to observe will depend to a great extent on the purpose of the interview and the nature of the presenting problems, there are four

TABLE 5.3
Recommended Questioning Areas for Obtaining Background Information

Medical History
  Problems during pregnancy and delivery?
  Postnatal complications?
  Serious illnesses/high fevers or convulsions?
  Serious injuries or accidents?
  Serious illnesses in family history?
  Allergies or dietary problems?
  Current health problems or medications?
  Vision and hearing OK?

Developmental History
  Ages for reaching developmental milestones—crawling, talking, walking, toilet-training, etc.
  Developmental delays (communication, motor, cognitive, social)?
  Development in comparison with siblings or peers

Social-emotional Functioning
  Temperament as an infant/toddler
  Quality of attachment to caregiver(s) as infant/toddler
  Quality of relationships with parents
  Quality of relationships with siblings and peers
  Discipline methods: what works best, who does s/he mind the best?
  Behavioral problems at home or in community?
  Number and quality of friendships with peers
  Any traumatic/disturbing experiences?
  Any responsibilities or chores?
  Who provides afterschool care?

Educational Progress
  Initial adjustment to school
  Academic Progress: delayed, average, high achieving?
  School grades
  Any school attendance problems?
  Behavioral problems at school?
  Quality of peer relationships at school
  Favorite subjects, classes, or teachers
  Extracurricular activities

Community Involvement
  Belong to any organizations or clubs (scouts, YMCA, etc.)?
  Organized team sports?
  Parttime job? (for adolescents)
  Church attendance/religious background
  Relationships with extended family

4 areas to observe

general areas that are almost always useful to target. These include *physical characteristics, overt behavioral characteristics, social-emotional functioning*, and *cognitive functioning*. Table 5.4 includes a more complete breakdown of child characteristics to observe within each of these four general areas. Of course, in some cases, the clinician will need to add to or subtract from this list, depending on the specifics of the interview. Many clinicians who routinely conduct interviews as part of a broader assessment find it useful to make notes of the important characteristics that were observed during the interview, so that they can be detailed in the report at a later time.

TABLE 5.4
Important Child Characteristics to Observe During Interviews

Physical Characteristics
    Unusual or inappropriate attire
    Gang-related attire
    Height and weight in comparison to same-age peers
    Obvious physical problems
    Direct signs of possible illness
    Motor coordination
    Tics (vocal, facial, motor)

Overt Behavioral Characteristics
    Activity level
    Attention span
    Interaction with environment
    Distractibility
    Impulsivity

Social-emotional Functioning
    Range and appropriateness of affect
    Mood state during interview
    Reaction to praise
    Reaction to frustration
    Apparent social skills
    Obvious anxiety or nervousness
    Ease of separation from caregiver (for young children)

Cognitive Functioning
    Communication skills
    Overall intellectual competence, estimated
    Intrapersonal insight
    Logic of reasoning
    Temporal and spatial orientation
    Level of organization in activities
    Inferred planning ability

Areas for Questioning. As already discussed, the traditional child interview is amenable to some very specific types of interviews, ranging from psychodynamic to basic rapport building. The use of questioning strategies (e.g., open vs. closed questions), as well as developmental considerations to consider when conducting clinical interviews with children and adolescents, have also been discussed.

Although traditional interview techniques for specific purposes and problems, and with specific ages of clients, will vary to some extent, there are still some commonalities and some general areas of questioning that can remain constant. Table 5.5 lists five general areas that are usually important to target when interviewing children or adolescents. These five areas include *intrapersonal functioning, family relationships, peer relationships, school adjustment,* and *community involvement.* Within each of these areas some specific areas for recommended questioning are provided, which can be increased or decreased as needed. When conducting traditional open-ended interviews, many clinicians find it useful to develop the interview and make notes according to a breakdown such as that shown in Table 5.5. It allows for a degree of structure and a logical progression in the interview, while still leaving it flexible and open-ended.

TABLE 5.5
General Areas of Questioning for Child/Adolescent Interviews

Intrapersonal Functioning
  Eating and sleeping habits
  Feelings/attributions about self
  Peculiar or bizarre experiences (e.g., hearing or seeing things)
  Emotional status (depressed, anxious, guilty, angry, etc.)
  Clarity of thought/orientation to time and space
  Insight into own thoughts and concerns
  Defensiveness/blaming
  Understanding of reason for interview

Family Relationships
  Quality of relationships with parents
  Quality of relationships with siblings
  Family routines, responsibilities, chores
  Involvement with extended family members
  Level of perceived support from family
  Perceived conflicts within family

Peer Relationships
  Number of close friends
  Preferred activities with friends
  Perceived conflicts with peers
  Social skills for initiating friendships
  Reports of peer rejection and loneliness

School Adjustment
  Current grade, teacher, school subjects
  General feelings about school
  Previous and current academic performance
  Favorite or preferred subjects or teachers
  Difficult or unliked subjects or teachers
  Involvement in extracurricular activities
  School attendance patterns
  Perceived conflicts or unfairness at school

Community Involvement
  Involvement in clubs or organizations
  Participation in community activities
  Church attendance/activities
  Level of mobility within community
  Parttime jobs (for adolescents)
  Relationships with other individuals in the community

THE BEHAVIORAL INTERVIEW

Behavioral interviewing differs from traditional interview methods in both the level of structure imposed by the interviewer, and the purposes for conducting the interview. The roots of behavioral interviewing are found in behavioral psychology. As noted by Gross (1984), "The primary objective of behavioral assessment is to obtain descriptive information about problem behavior and the conditions maintaining it" (p. 62). The behavioral interview, then, is viewed as a specific type of behavioral assessment with the same objectives as other behaviorally oriented assessment methods. The clinician who conducts a behavioral interview is interested in pinpointing the problem behaviors,

Requires a relatively high degree of **115** *structure*

and identifying variables that may have controlling or maintaining effects on those behaviors. As such, the behavioral interview requires a relatively high degree of structure by the interviewer in order for the primary goals to be met.

Several models of behavioral interviewing have been proposed, and each model has a different level of emphasis of such variables as cognitive competency of the client, other within-client variables, analysis of the environment, and historical information. What the different models of behavioral interviewing seem to have in common is their emphasis on description and clarification of the problem behaviors, and the identification of antecedent stimuli and consequences of those behaviors. Haynes and Wilson (1979) identified the essential elements of the behavioral interview as an organized interaction between the subject or a mediator and the behavioral interviewer for eight specific purposes ranging from gathering information about client concerns to communicating specifically about the procedures and goals of the assessment and any subsequent intervention. With some additional modifications, the eight specific purposes of behavioral interviewing originally outlined by Haynes and Wilson are illustrated in Table 5.6.

8 specific purposes of an interview

As a clinical interviewing technique, the behavioral method offers several advantages over other forms of assessment, including other interview techniques. Behavioral interviewing has been touted as the most economical method of obtaining behavioral information (Wahler & Cormier, 1970), especially in comparison to direct observation. Given that interviews can be conducted with an informant who is familiar with the client, behavioral interviewing offers flexibility in the event that the child or adolescent client is not directly available to observe or interview, or is not capable of providing detailed interview information. Another advantage of behavioral interviewing is that when conducted directly with the client, it allows the clinician to directly observe various social behaviors and communication skills of the client, which may be useful in developing intervention strategies. Additionally, conducting a comprehensive behavioral interview with a *mediator* (i.e., parent or teacher) allows the clinician to assess how receptive they might be to the idea of implementing an intervention, and the specific types of intervention to which they may be amenable (Gresham & Davis, 1988). Finally, in comparison with such behavioral assessment techniques as direct observation and rating scales, interviewing is flexible enough to allow the clinician the opportunity to expand or narrow the scope of the assessment, depending on what areas emerge as specific problems.

Interview= Economical

low freq. behav.

Implementing the Behavioral Interview With Parents and Teachers

When the client is a child or adolescent, it is almost always necessary and desirable to interview the parent(s) as part of the initial assessment, and it is often useful to interview a teacher as well. Interviewing the parent(s) or teacher of the referred child or adolescent can be an extremely important part of the assessment, for several reasons: They are a potential rich source of behavioral data due to their daily observations of the child's behavior in naturalistic settings; they may be able to provide information on the child's behavior that is not available to the interviewer through other methods of assessment; and because they will often function as mediators in the intervention process, it is critical to obtain their report and assess their ability to implement an intervention. Although conducting behavioral interviews of parents and teachers have been treated as separate topics, the processes involved have much in common, and will be dealt with together in this chapter.

TABLE 5.6
Specific Purposes of Behavioral Interviewing

1. Gather information about client concerns and goals.
2. Identify factors that elicit and/or maintain problem behaviors.
3. Obtain relevant historical information.
4. Identify potential reinforcers within the environment.
5. Assess the *mediation potential* of the client.
6. Educate the client regarding behavioral principles and the particular problem situation.
7. Obtain informed consent from the parent/guardian of child or adolescent client (and obtain assent from the child or adolescent client).
8. Communicate about the goals and procedures of assessment and intervention.

Conceptualizing the behavioral interview process as part of an overall behavioral consultation model for working with parents and teachers, Gresham and Davis (1988) identified three different types of behavioral interviews that might occur: the problem identification interview, the problem analysis interview, and the problem evaluation interview. Because the problem evaluation interview is designed to be implemented following the implementation of an intervention, it is beyond the scope of this text. Therefore, this chapter will deal only with the first two types of behavioral interviews. And, although it is possible to treat problem identification and problem analysis together, they are overviewed individually for purposes of conceptual clarity.

The Problem Identification Interview. Identification of the problem is considered to be the most important phase in the consultation process because it defines the focus and how the problem will be envisioned (Gresham & Davis, 1988). In beginning the problem identification interview, a clinician will typically start by obtaining demographic information and asking general questions about the child ("what concerns do you have about your child?"), but will soon begin to probe for more specifics and in more depth ("how often does this student engage in aggressive behavior?"). The main idea is for the interviewer to assess the variety of problems reported, identify the problems that are of most concern, and then obtain very specific behavioral information relating to those problems.

Gresham and Davis (1988) identified six major objectives for the problem identification interview, which are listed as follows:

1. Specification of the problem to be solved in consultation.
2. Elicitation of an objective description of the target behavior.
3. Identification of environmental conditions surrounding the target behavior.
4. Estimation of the frequency, intensity, and duration of the problem behavior.
5. Agreement on the type of data collection procedures that will be used, and who will collect the data.
6. Setting a date for the next interview, which will be the problem analysis interview.

In addition to identifying and gathering specific information on the problem behavior exhibited by the child or adolescent, Gross (1984) suggested that it is also important to obtain information on their behavioral assets. By specifically asking the parent(s) or teacher what behavior is desired in place of the problem behavior, the interviewer can then work on assessing whether or not the child or adolescent has that behavior within their repertoire. Another example of gathering information on behavioral assets involves the interview focusing on what things the child or adolescent finds particularly enjoyable or rewarding. This information could then be used later in developing a menu of potential reinforcers.

The Problem Analysis Interview.   Ideally, problem analysis will occur after a problem identification interview, which sets the stage for an appropriate plan for obtaining baseline data. Gresham and Davis (1988) identified four objectives for the problem analysis interview, which are as follows:

1. Validation or confirmation of the problem through an examination of the baseline data. If the problem is confirmed, then this step would also include determining any discrepancies between the child's existing performance and what is desired.
2. Analysis of conditions surrounding the behavior. In other words, what are the antecedents, sequences, and consequences that affect the behavior?
3. Design of an intervention plan to alter the identified problem behavior. This objective includes developing both general approaches and precise plans for how the interventions will be implemented.
4. Setting a date for the problem evaluation interview, assuming that an appropriate intervention plan has been developed and agreed on.

Admittedly, it is often difficult to divide the problem identification and problem analysis aspects of the behavioral interview into two separate interview sessions, with the parent or teacher agreeing to gather appropriate baseline data between sessions. In practice, there are often strong time pressures and needs to develop interventions immediately that make it necessary to combine both aspects of the behavioral interview into one extended session. However, by doing this, there is no opportunity for the gathering of baseline data, and the clinician will need to rely on the verbal report of the client and rating scale data, and then work on gathering progress data as the intervention is implemented and modified. The following interchange of dialogue between a therapist and the parent of a 6-year-old boy serves to illustrate how the elements of a problem identification interview and a problem analysis interview can be merged into one session:

Therapist: You've told me about several problems that are happening with Marcus. Which behavior do you see as being the biggest problem?
Parent: The temper tantrums.
Therapist: Tell me, very specifically, what Marcus does when he is having a tantrum.
Parent: It usually starts out with screaming and yelling, kind of mixed with crying. He'll call me names, make threats, and if it is a really bad one, he'll sometimes kick the walls, push over furniture and lamps, and even try to kick me or hit me.
Therapist: What kinds of things are usually going on just before Marcus behaves like this?
Parent: It's usually when he wants something that I won't let him have or do, or when he has been in an argument with his older brother.
Therapist: And where does it usually happen?
Parent: Always at home. Usually inside the house.

Therapist: Is it more likely to happen at particular times?

Parent: Well, most of the time it happens at night.

Therapist: How long do these tantrums last?

Parent: Oh, maybe 10 or 20 minutes. A really bad one might go on for almost an hour.

Therapist: Tell me what kinds of things you do, both just before the tantrums happen, and then during or after them, as a way to get them stopped.

Parent: It seems like the when the arguments start that happen before the tantrums, I am usually tired or in a bad mood, and I might be kind of snappy with him. But not always. Once it gets started, it all depends on the situation and how I am feeling—it seems like if I'm worn-out and irritated, I yell back at him, and sometimes even try to hold him or give him a spank. If I'm not so out-of-sorts, I might try and send him to the other room, or just sit down and try to listen to him.

Therapist: And what seems to work best?

Parent: Well, it does seem like the thing that works best is to not let the argument get so bad, like try and distract by getting him to do something else, or to sit down calmly and listen to him. But I usually only do that when I'm not tired or irritated. Once it gets going, I know that the worst thing I can do is to get into it with him, but sometimes I don't care. It seems like moving him into his room for a few minutes until he settles down works better than that.

This example is an excerpt from a 50-minute intake interview with a parent. Obviously, much more ground was covered during the interview, but the dialogue shows how a therapist can ask specific questions to pinpoint the greatest problem, and determine its intensity, duration, locus, and environmental variables that might be eliciting or maintaining it.

Implementing Behavioral Interviews With Children and Adolescents

Because behavioral interviewing techniques are strongly associated with the behavioral consultation model of problem identification and treatment, there is a definite emphasis on conducting the interview with parents and teachers, who will ultimately serve as mediators in the intervention process. However, in many cases, the referred child or adolescent can also become an important participant in the behavioral interview process. As a general rule, the younger the client is, the more difficult it is to obtain useful behavioral data from them in an interview, and the more important other behavioral assessment sources will be (e.g., parent interviews, direct observations, rating scales). Although interviews with young children may lead to the establishment of rapport and to the clinician being able to directly observe their social behavior, Gross (1984) suggested that interviews with children under age 6 typically provide little in the way of content information.

As children become older and more sophisticated in their verbal mediation skills, the likelihood increases that they will be able to provide valuable descriptive information in the behavioral interview process. When conducting a behavioral interview with a child client, it is important to carefully move from a general to a more specific level of questioning. The interview might start out with some general questions about why clients think they are being interviewed, and an opportunity for them to talk about their interests, but ultimately lead to specific probes of suspected problem behavior (e.g., "Tell me what usually happens before you get into fights"). As is true in the case of interviewing parents or teachers, it is important to ask questions pertaining to the child or adolescent client's behavioral assets. Obtaining their perspective on what positive and appropriate behaviors they can do, as well as what their strongest likes and dislikes are, may be important when it is time to construct an intervention plan. The following example illustrates some of the elements of conducting a behavioral interview directly with the child-client. In this case, the client is an 11-year-old girl who has been referred for peer relationship problems, and the clinician is a school psychologist, who is conducting a formal assessment:

Psychologist: Tiffany, tell me what happens when you get into fights with the other girls you told me about?

Stacy: Well, on Friday I got into a bad fight with Monica and Janeece. It was during recess, and I knew they were talking about me behind my back. I walked up to them and told them to just shut up.

Psychologist: You said you knew they were talking about you. Why did you think that?

Stacy: I could see them talking, while they were walking away from me, and they were looking at me.

Psychologist: So you figured they were talking about you, even though you couldn't hear what they were saying. What happened next?

Stacy: Well, Janeece told me to shut-up, so I said "why don't you make me?" She called me a bitch, so I pushed her away, then Monica hit me and we started to really fight. The recess supervisor sent me to the principal's office, and I told her that I wasn't the one who started it, but she never believed me.

Psychologist: Do these kind of fights usually happen during recess?

Stacy: Mostly. But sometimes during lunch and one or two times while I was waiting for the bus.

Psychologist: But not during class?

Stacy: Not usually, cause the teachers won't let me sit by kids who bother me all the time, and my homeroom teacher has my desk away from them. The teacher is usually there to stop it right away.

Like the previous example, this excerpt illustrates how the clinician can ask specific questions regarding the circumstances and location of specific problem areas.

It also may be useful to conduct a brief joint interview with the adult and child. Particularly in the case of clinic-based assessments of child behavior problems, observing the parent and child together can provide the clinician with a rich source of direct observation data. Being able to observe the extent and quality of parent–child interactions and how they react to each other in both positive and negative situations affords the opportunity for a valuable merging of behavioral interviewing and direct behavioral observation.   *joint interviews to see relationships*

STRUCTURED AND SEMISTRUCTURED INTERVIEWS

Although child interviewing techniques have historically been rather informal or unstructured, since about the 1970s there have been a number of efforts aimed at developing highly structured and standardized interview schedules for use with children and adolescents. Many of these structured or semistructured clinical interview instruments (or *schedules*, as they are sometimes called) have been designed for use in psychiatric settings or for epidemiology research, but they may have a degree of usefulness in other settings and for other purposes. Three interview schedules that are representative of what is currently available are reviewed in some detail, and some comments follow on additional interview schedules.

Schedule for Affective Disorders and Schizophrenia, School-Age Children

Also referred to as the Kiddie–SADS, or K–SADS, the Schedule for Affective Disorders and Schizophrenia for School-age Children (Puig-Antich & Chambers, 1978) is a semistructured diagnostic interview for children and adolescents in the 6- to 17-year-old age range. It was developed as a downward extension of the Schedule for Affective Disorders and Schizophrenia (SADS; Endicott & Spitzer, 1978). Although the title of this instrument implies that it for the purpose of assessing affective and psychotic disorders, the K–SADS is a broadly based interview that has been used for eliciting information on a wide range of emotional and behavior problems, and then classifying these problems according to *DSM* diagnostic criteria.

Three versions of the K–SADS have been in use. The Present Episode version (K–SADS–PL) was designed for use in assessing current or present (within the past year) episodes of psychopathology. The Epidemiologic version (K–SADS–E) was designed for use in assessing psychopathology that has occurred over the course of the subject's entire life. J. N. Hughes and Baker (1990) noted that both versions of the schedule should be utilized when the K–SADS is used to diagnose disorders that require detailed historical information, and the interviewer should be particularly careful to ensure that the child or adolescent subject is appropriately oriented to time when administering the K–SADS–E. A revised version of the K–SADS is referred to as the Present and Lifetime version (K–SADS–PL). This latest version integrates some components of the other two versions, and also includes a number of improvements, such as improved probes and anchor points, diagnosis-specific impairment ratings, *DSM–IV* diagnostic classification linkage, and a wider variety of disorder screening capabilities. This review focuses on elements of the K–SADS that are common to all versions, or are specific to the K–SADS–PL, given that it is the most recent version.

The K-SADS should be used only by experienced interviewers who have received specific training. The format is fairly complex and requires a degree of sophisticated judgment. All versions of the K–SADS first include a parent interview, and then follow with an interview of the child or adolescent. Each interview takes approximately 1 hour (or longer), so one must plan on 2 to 3 hours for the entire interview process. The interviews include a combination of unstructured or open-ended questions and questions regarding highly specific symptoms, which are scored on a rating scale. The K–SADS allows for skipping certain areas of questioning that are not relevant for the particular client. In addition to providing specific open-ended and structured interview questions, the K–SADS provides a format for rating the overall behavioral characteristics and performance of the subject.

Data reported by Chambers et al. (1985) indicate that the K–SADS–P has moderate test–retest reliability with both parents and children over a 72-hour period (average = .54 across symptom categories), and adequate interrater reliability (.86 for parent interviews and .89 for child interviews) across symptom categories. A study of the validity of the K–SADS–E by Orvaschel, Puig-Antich, Chambers, Tabrizi, and Johnson

(1982) compared K–SADS–E diagnoses of 17 subjects who were previously diagnosed using an earlier version of the K–SADS, and found that 16 of the 17 subjects received the same diagnosis. More recent evidence on the K–SADS–PL indicates good concurrent validity with diagnostic classification and standard self-report measures, and has excellent test–retest reliability (Kaufman, Birmaher, Brent, & Rao, 1997). In general, the evidence regarding the K–SADS indicates that it has adequate to good reliability and validity, and it has been recommended as one of the better structured interview schedules for use with children and adolescents (Hodges, 1993). The K–SADS may be a good choice for use in some situations where *DSM* diagnostic criteria are important.

Diagnostic Interview for Children and Adolescents–Revised   DICA – R

The Diagnostic Interview for Children and Adolescents–Revised (DICA–R) (Reich & Welner, 1989) is a highly structured interview schedule for children from age 6 to 17. The DICA–R is a revision of the original DICA, which was developed by Herjanic and her colleagues (B. Herjanic & Reich, 1982). The original DICA was patterned after the adult Diagnostic Interview Schedule (DIS; Robins, Helzer, Croughan, & Radcliff, 1981).

The DICA–R includes three closely related interview schedules designed to be used with children from 6 to 12 years of age, adolescents from 13 to 17 years of age, and parents of children from age 6 to 17, respectively. The three versions are essentially similar, with the only notable differences being changes in item wording to make them more appropriate to the specific age group of child and adolescent clients, or for use by parents in evaluating their children on specific symptoms. In terms of differences between the DICA–R and the original DICA, J. N. Hughes and Baker (1990) noted that the items on the DICA–R were modified in order to "produce a more conversational style between the examiner and respondent" (p. 70).

Administration of the DICA–R takes approximately 1 hour. The instrument contains 267 items that are coded in a structured manner (i.e., "yes," "no," "sometimes," and "rarely"). The DICA–R is structured so that the interview begins with a brief demographic session that includes both the parent(s) and child, after which it is recommended that separate interviewers concurrently meet with the parent(s) and child for the completion of the separate interview forms. The interviews conclude with an assessment of psychosocial stressors, and an observational checklist and clinical impressions section completed by the examiner. The interview data are scored according to specific criteria included in the interview booklet, and the obtained scores are used to diagnose *DSM* Axis I disorders. Although the DICA–R can be administered by interviewers who are only minimally trained, it is recommended that training of interviewers be conducted in order to increase the reliability and validity (Reich & Welner, 1989).

Studies published on the original DICA have indicated relatively high percentages of interrater agreement (85% to 89%) on child symptoms (B. Herjanic & Reich, 1982) and within-interviewer agreement (80% to 95%) on child symptoms at 2- to 3-month intervals (B. Herjanic, M. Herjanic, F. Brown, & Wheatt, 1975). The rate of agreement on symptoms between children and parents has also been explored (B. Herjanic & Reich, 1982), with the results showing rates of agreement ranging from very modest to quite strong, depending on the particular diagnostic category and number of subjects. B. Herjanic and Campbell (1977) reported data on the DICA showing that it can differentiate to a moderate to strong degree between children referred to psychiatric and pediatric clinics.

↳ good @ differentiating

Two published reports to date have been identified regarding the psychometric properties of the revised version of the DICA. Ezpeleta, de-le-Osa, Domenech, and Navarro (1997) found low to moderate diagnostic agreement between clinicians' judgment and DICA–R scores, with the exception of Conduct Disorder, which was higher. Boyle, Offord, Racine, and Sanford (1993) demonstrated that test–retest reliability of DICA–R scores over 10- to 20-day time intervals was moderate, and also found that agreement between parents and children tended to be low, whereas agreement between trained lay observers and child psychiatrists was generally high. Interestingly, DICA–R interview data in this study from children tended to be too unreliable for classification of internalizing disorders. Edelbrock and Costello (1988) noted that although the DICA has several strong features, further validation is needed before it can be strongly recommended for use as a clinical research tool. This sentiment has been echoed by Hodges (1993), who stated that the validity data for the DICA and DICA–R are questionable, and evidence on psychometric properties is sparse. Therefore, some caution is warranted in selecting and using the DICA–R.

Child Assessment Schedule — CAS

The Child Assessment Schedule (CAS) (Hodges, Kline, Stern, Cytryn, & McKnew, 1982; Hodges, 1987) is a semistructured interview designed for use with children from age 7 to 16. Although most of the research on the CAS has been on its direct use with children, a modified version for use with parents is also available. Like most of the other interview schedules reviewed here, the CAS is useful for making *DSM* diagnostic classification decisions, as many of the items are similar to the diagnostic criteria found in *DSM* childhood disorders.

The CAS is utilized in evaluating the child or adolescent client's functioning in several areas, and scores are yielded in 11 different content areas (school, friends, activities and hobbies, family, fears, worries and anxieties, self-image, mood and behavior, physical complaints, acting out, and reality testing). It includes 75 questions that are coded "yes," "no," "ambiguous," "no response," or "not applicable." The CAS takes approximately 45 to 60 minutes to administer, including a 53-item observational rating that is completed by the examiner following the interview. The developers of the CAS recommend that interviewers with clinical training be used in administering the interview schedule, but satisfactory results have also been obtained with the use of interviewers without formal clinical training (Hodges, McKnew, Burbach, & Roebuck, 1987).

Published studies relating to the stability of the CAS have demonstrated moderate to high interrater reliability (90% and above) on CAS total scores (Hodges, 1990a, 1990b; Hodges et al., 1982), and adequate test–retest reliability through showing statistically significant correlations on diagnostic classifications and instrument scores (Hodges, Cools, & McKnew, 1989). Internal consistency reliability of CAS scores has also been demonstrated (Hodges & Saunders, 1989). Concurrent validity of the CAS has been demonstrated through finding significant relations with self-report measures of anxiety and depression (Hodges et al., 1982). Construct validity of the CAS has been demonstrated by showing that the instrument differentiated between groups of normal, behaviorally disturbed, and psychosomatic children (Hodges, Kline, Barbero, & Flanery, 1985; Hodges, Kline, Barbero, & Woodruff, 1985). There is probably a greater amount and variety of published reliability and validity research on the CAS than other structured or semistructured interview schedules currently available. It is interesting to note that diagnostic utility and interrater agreement on the CAS, like that of other structured interview schedules, tends to be higher for problems in the externalizing domain than for problems in the internalizing domain (R. J. Thompson, Merritt, Keith, & Murphy, 1993). Therefore, when internalizing problems are a major concern, the CAS (and other structured interview schedules) should be supplemented with an appropriate self-report measure.

Concluding Comments on Formal Interview Schedules

NIMH - DISC

In Table 5.7, some of the major characteristics of the three reviewed interview schedules are included for comparison purposes. As was stated earlier, these three interview schedules do not represent the entire domain of semistructured and highly structured interview schedules that are available for use with children and adolescents. The National Institute of Mental Health Diagnostic Interview Schedule for Children (DISC; Fisher, Wicks, Shaffer, Piacentini, & Lapkin, 1992) is another widely known structured interview schedule for use in assessing child and adolescent behavioral emotional problems. However, the validity data for the DISC has been described as notably weak (Hodges, 1993), and it is not reviewed in detail in this text. Other structured interview schedules that have been reported in the child psychiatry and psychology literature include the Interview Schedule for Children (ISC; Kovacs, 1982), and the Mental Health Assessment Form (MHAF; Kestenbaum & Bird, 1978). The three interview schedules reviewed in this chapter were featured due to factors such as availability, amount and quality and psychometric data, ease of use, and general purpose design. A more recent instrument, the Semistructured Clinical Interview for Children (SCIC; McConaughy & Achenbach, 1990) appears to have a great deal of promise as a clinical tool. This schedule is designed for use with 6- to 11-year-old children, and takes 60 to 90 minutes to administer. However, the SCIC is still considered to be a provisional instrument, as there are not yet extensive training materials or published research studies available.

The development of formal structured and semistructured interview schedules are an important development in the area of child and adolescent assessment. For the most part, they represent high quality attempts to integrate a stronger empirical base into the process of clinical interviewing. At the present time, most of the formal interview schedules have a decidedly psychiatric bent, in that they are utilized specifically for generating *DSM* diagnoses, and have been developed and validated primarily in psychiatric settings. It remains to be seen how useful these efforts will be in general school and clinic-based assessment, but there is some cause for optimism that appropriate applications in these areas will be found.

CLINICAL INTERVIEWING AND SUICIDAL IDEATION/BEHAVIOR

Suicide, or the act of deliberately killing oneself, is one of the most disturbing phenomena faced by mental health professionals. It is particularly troubling when a person who makes a suicide attempt is a child or adolescent. Many persons simply cannot understand why young people—individuals with "their whole lives ahead of them"—would even consider taking their own life. Indeed, to most individuals, suicide is an intensely irrational act. However, the evidence regarding suicide convincingly demonstrates that it cannot be dismissed, and children, and especially adolescents, are not

TABLE 5.7

An Overview of Three Selected Semistructured and Structured Interview Schedules for Use with Children and Adolescents

Name	Format	Purpose	Level of Structure	Time Required	Comments
Schedule for Affective and Schizophrenic Disorders for School-age Children (K–SADS)	Combination of open-ended and structured questions; interviews for both parent and child subject	Diagnosis of major child disorders according to DSM criteria	Semistructured	2–3 hours for complete interviews with parent and child	Three versions available; requires extensive training
Diagnostic Interview for Children and Adolescents–Revised (DICA–R)	267 highly structured items that are systematically coded; interviews begin with a joint demographic interview with both subject and parent	Diagnosis of major child disorders according to DSM Axis I categories	Highly structured	About 1 hour	Parent, adolescent, and child versions available; requires some training; still lacking in reported validity data; some concerns regarding validity
Child Assessment Schedule (CAS)	75 items coded according to 5 different criteria; child and parent versions are available	Evaluation of various aspects of child functioning; DSM diagnoses	Semistructured	45 minutes to 1 hour	Can be administered by interviewers with limited experience and training; relatively large amount of reliability and validity data

immune to it. Because suicide attempts and completions by children and adolescents appear to be increasing in the United States, and because clinical interviewing is clearly the most widely used and direct method of assessing for suicidal ideation (thinking about suicide) and potential suicidal behavior (specific behaviors aimed at suicide), this section is included in this chapter on clinical interviewing. First, some facts regarding suicidal ideation and suicidal behavior among young people are provided. Second, recommendations for conducting clinical interviews with children and youth who may be suicidal are offered. This treatment of clinical interviewing and suicide is necessarily brief. Readers who desire a more in-depth treatment of the topic are referred to chapters by Brock and Sandoval (1997) and Sattler (1998); books by Berman and Jobes (1991), Davis and Sandoval (1991), and Poland (1989); and articles by Peach and Reddick (1991) and Shaffer, Garland, Gould, Fischer, and Trautman (1988).

Facts Regarding Suicidal Behavior Among Children and Youth

When discussing statistics concerning suicide among young persons, it is important to recognize that there are many problems with the data. Many (if not most) suicide attempts go unreported, and many suicides are mistakenly interpreted through other causes, such as accidents. However, the available evidence does indicate that suicide among children and adolescents is an increasing problem in U.S. society. Sattler (1998) and Brock and Sandoval (1997) have cited extensive statistics from the U.S. federal government (Bureau of the Census and Centers for Disease Control and Prevention) indicating that suicide rates among young people have increased substantially during the past three to four decades. In some cases and in some age ranges, the prevalence rates have quadrupled during this period. Statistics for younger children are virtually nonexistent. However, for midelementary and middle school age children (age 10–14), the Bureau of the Census reported a 1990 suicide rate of 1.5 per 100,000, which was up from 0.6 per 100,000 in 1970. For high school age youth (age 15–19), the reported 1990 suicide rate of 11.1 per 100,000 was up from 5.9 per 100,000 in 1970, and 2.7 per 100,000 in 1950. Although these rates are not as high as the suicide rates for any adult age group in the United States, they are extremely troubling, not only because of their mere existence, but because of their continually increasing trend.

Although suicidal ideation and suicidal behavior may potentially affect young persons from virtually any demographic, it is important to recognize that there are clear demographic trends regarding who is more likely to make and complete suicide attempts. Regarding gender, a simple summary statement is that females are more likely than males to make suicide attempts, but males are more likely than females to actually complete suicide attempts. In fact, among adolescents of all racial/ethnic groups, females were about twice as likely as males to make a suicide attempt, but males were about five times as likely as females to actually commit suicide (U.S. Bureau of the Census data, cited in Sattler, 1998). Two explanations are typically given for this gender difference. First, males are more likely to use highly lethal means of attempting suicide than females. Second, females are thought to be more likely to use suicide attempts as a "cry for help." Regarding race and ethnicity, there are also some substantial group differences. According to Sattler's (1998) analysis of the 1990 U.S. Bureau of the Census data, the highest rates for completed suicides for both males and females were among Native American youth, with varying ascendancy of rates among other racial/ethnic groups according to gender. However, other researchers have reached differing conclusions regarding the effects of race and ethnicity. For example, Brock and Sandoval (1997) cited data from several sources indicating that the highest rates of suicidal attempts and completions are among non-Hispanic caucasians.

There are numerous risk factors that may increase vulnerability among young people to suicidal ideation and behavior. Although these risk factors are complex and in many cases interactive, some of the major ones are thought to include: psychological disorders, particularly depression and conduct disorder; substance abuse; family history of suicide; family history of significant medical and psychiatric illness; chronic and debilitating illness; feelings of hopelessness; and severe life stress, especially involving perceived losses. It should be stressed that these risk factors, when they exist in isolation, may be relatively weak predictors of suicide. However, they may have an interactive effect on each other. In other words, the presence of additional risk factors may increase vulnerability to suicide in more of a multiplicative than additive manner.

Experts in the area of child and adolescent suicide have noted that although suicide attempts may occur suddenly after a single traumatic stressor, they are usually preceded by a number of signals or warning signs that may predict the suicide attempt (Ramsay, Tanney, Tierney, & Lang, 1990). Although it is critical to recognize that such warning signs may be numerous, complex, and weakly predictive in individual situations, they nevertheless should be carefully scrutinized. Some of the most commonly identified suicide warning signs include:

- Suicide notes
- Suicide threats, suicidal statements, both direct and indirect
- Preoccupation with death and related themes
- Romanticizing and glorifying death
- Making final arrangements (saying goodbye, giving possessions away, putting affairs in order)
- Feelings of helplessness and hopelessness
- Withdrawal from family and friends
- Loss of interest in activities that were previously important
- Heavy use/abuse of drugs, including alcohol
- Marked changes in temperament and/or behavior

It is interesting to note that there is some overlap between the list of risk factors and the list of warning signs. Some characteristics or behaviors seem to serve both purposes. Most children and adolescents who become suicidal are not likely to be observed by persons who are highly familiar with the warning signs of suicide. It is more realistic to think that the persons most likely to observe suicide warning signs will be parents, friends, and teachers. Therefore, professional education and outreach activities regarding warning signs are imperative.

Recommendations for Clinical Interviewing

Some semistructured interview checklists for assessing potentially suicidal children or youth have been previously developed. However, the reality of the situation is that most clinicians will end up using a more unstructured interview format for such an assessment. If this is the case, it is critical that particular questions be asked, and that

Suicide interview should not be @ 127
the universal level

particular areas of content be included in the interview. It certainly is not appropriate to routinely ask questions regarding suicidal behavior to all child and adolescent clients. There should be some strands of evidence within the overall assessment or the content of the interview that first tip off the interviewer that the client may be suicidal. Questions regarding the client's affect, level of engagement in activities, substance abuse, changes in routines and behavior, and especially feelings of helplessness and hopelessness, may serve to drive hypotheses regarding potential suicidal characteristics. These areas of questioning may be part of a standard clinical interview, but may certainly be formed by analysis of other assessment data, such as self-report tests and behavior rating scales. Prior conversations with parents and teachers may also serve to provide information that may help focus the content of the interview toward suicide assessment.

Once the clinician has enough evidence to justify some concern or suspicion regarding the client's potential suicidal ideation or behavior, it is critical to simply "jump right in" and conduct a suicide assessment interview. A common mistake that is made by inexperienced clinicians is that clients will be too hesitant to respond to questions regarding suicide, or they may become extremely upset if such questions are asked. In reality, the inexperienced clinician is the one who is more likely to feel uncomfortable or upset by such questioning. The experience of most clinicians who work with emotionally and behaviorally troubled children and youth is that they are relatively candid regarding suicidal thought and action, and in fact, may be very willing to discuss it because of their ambivalent feelings or desire to receive help. Therefore, if there are reasonable concerns, simply initiate a suicide assessment interview, and take all statements regarding suicidal ideation and thought seriously. If there are no valid reasons for such concern, this will become manifest quickly enough during such an interview, and you will be able to move on to a more relevant topic.

There are a number of ways that suicide assessment questions may be asked, and these will need to be modified depending on the developmental characteristics of the client. However, certain areas of questioning are deemed critical in conducting a suicide assessment interview.

Thinking About Suicide. The first area of questioning is to simply ask child or adolescent clients if they have been thinking about killing themselves. For younger and less cognitively sophisticated clients, this area of questioning may need to be modified, because the concept of death may be difficult for them to fully comprehend. In such cases, questions such as "have you been thinking about wanting to be dead?" or "do you sometimes wish you could make yourself be dead?" might be appropriate.

Suicide Plan. If there is sufficient evidence that the client has been having suicidal thoughts, it is critical to ascertain whether or not a particular plan for suicide is in place. Questions such as "do you have a plan?", "have you thought about how you might kill yourself?", or "do you have specific ideas about how you might kill yourself?" may be useful in this regard. Clinicians should be particularly aware of how concrete or detailed such plans may be. It is generally agreed that the more specific or detailed the plan, the more the individual has thought about suicide.

Means and Preparations for Suicide. If clients indicate they have a plan, the next area of questioning should be aimed at determining if they actually have the means at hand (or specific preparations) to carry out such a plan. Questions such as "do you have the means to carry out your plan with you now, at school, or at home?" might be used. If the plan is very specific, and for example, involves a gun, simply ask "do you have a gun?" or "is there somewhere you can get a gun?" At this point, it is necessary and critical to become very specific. Clinicians should find out the exact location of the lethal means (i.e., "in my dad's gun rack in his den").

Intended Place or Setting. Assuming a suicide plan is in place, the clinician should ask where the client intends to commit the act. Such specificity in questioning has resulted in a prevented suicide on many occasions. It may also be helpful to ask whether the client has written a suicide note, and if so, what it says and where it is: "You told me that you were seriously thinking about killing yourself, and that you would probably do it with the sleeping pills in your mother's medicine cabinet. Have you thought about *where* you might take the pills?"

Immediate Protective Action. If clinicians have proceeded through a suicide assessment interview and become convinced that clients have been seriously considering the possibility of killing themselves, then ethics, law, and professional practice dictate that there is responsibility to take further action to support and protect the client. In the most serious cases, where it is apparent that clients are clearly intent on killing themselves and have a plan and lethal means in place, immediate and direct action must be taken. First, never leave a suicidal client alone in an unsecured setting, even for a short time. Second, clinicians should follow whatever protocol or policy is in place for such emergencies at their place of practice. According to Sattler (1998), "If you decide there is a risk of imminent danger, notify the parents immediately, ask them to come to your office to get their child, and advise them to hospitalize their child" (p. 441). All U.S. states have provisions within licensing and certification laws regarding protecting clients from harming themselves. Be aware of the laws and policies in your area, and be prepared to follow them in such emergency situations. In most areas, law enforcement officers may be called for assistance in situations where there is clearly imminent danger and there is no reasonable means to get the in-danger person to the proper evaluation and treatment facility (i.e., their parents are not available or are not willing to provide assistance).

Suicide Contract and Follow-up Planning. Assuming that clinicians ascertain that child or adolescent clients have been thinking seriously about suicide, but there is no evidence of imminent danger, another set of supportive and protective actions is called for. First, it is recommended that clinicians elicit a promise or contract from the clients that they will not engage in a suicide attempt or any related harmful behavior, and that they will call their clinician (or their counselor/therapist) if they begin to think seriously about it. Such contracts may be in formal written form, or in the form of a verbal agreement, at the discretion of the clinician, based on the present circumstances. Some clinicians have found it useful to seal a verbal nonsuicide contract with clients through a handshake, which may serve to impress on them the importance of the agreement into which they have just entered. In addition to a nonsuicide contract with the client, certain other steps are appropriate and necessary in this type of situation. It is important to provide the client with a card containing appropriate names and phone numbers to call for help (including any local crisis lines). It has also been suggested that the clinician should make plans to see the child/adolescent (or have them seen by another professional) as early as the next day (Peach & Reddick, 1991).

Even if child/adolescent clients do not appear to be imminently dangerous to themselves, it is still recommended that their parent(s) be called and asked to visit with the clinician.

Although clinicians may have made an agreement with clients that their conversations would be held in confidence, danger of suicide is always considered an exception to confidentiality rules, and prudent clinicians will make sure their clients understand this fact (and related exceptions to confidentiality) up front. The discussion with the parent(s) should be frank, and clinicians should assist in determining what support and resources the family is capable of providing, as well as educating them regarding appropriate actions to take. Most parents in such a situation will be very fearful and upset, and may need substantial confidence and support.

In situations where there is clear risk but no apparent immediate danger, it is important to discuss what resources the client may have to help them through this difficult time. Is there someone or something that would stop them from making a suicide attempt? Is there someone who they are comfortable talking to regarding their feelings? Have they talked to family or friends about their feelings? These types of questions help to set the stage for getting clients to think in terms of available support and appropriate courses of action to take when they are distressed. Finally, it is critical for clinicians to consult with other professionals (especially their supervisor) regarding suicidal clients, and to jointly determine an appropriate course of action, such as follow-up plans or making a referral. The burden of clinical interviewing with a suicidal child or adolescent is simply too great to carry alone, and in this case, the old adage "when in doubt, consult" is particularly important.

In sum, clinical interviewing of children and adolescents who may be suicidal is a special circumstance, and requires specific interviewing behavior and follow-up actions. Regardless of the setting in which they work, it is essential that clinicians who work with emotionally and behaviorally troubled youth become familiar with best practices for interviewing suicidal clients, and that they establish and follow a practice or agency protocol for dealing with such situations.

INTERVIEWS AND DECISION MAKING   *Interviews alone are not sufficient*

How useful are interviews when it comes to decision making? They can range from moderately useful to extremely useful, depending on the specific decision-making process. For making additional assessment decisions, interviewing can provide excellent information regarding specific additional areas that need to be assessed. During the process of interviewing, additional information may surface that will persuade the interviewer of the necessity for observation or other objective assessment in specific areas. Interview information can be important for diagnosis and classification decision making, though it should seldom be used alone. For special education classification, it is essential that decisions not be made based on a single assessment method. For making *DSM* diagnostic decisions, the interview will normally serve as an important aspect, perhaps as a keystone of a comprehensive assessment, although in some cases, *DSM* diagnoses can be made based on interview data alone. In making placement decisions, interview data can provide necessary clues and be used to support inferences drawn from additional information sources, but is seldom sufficient to do so by itself. One of the best uses of information obtained through interviews is for intervention or treatment decisions. If the interviews were carefully structured to identify specific problems and the environmental conditions eliciting and maintaining those problems (e.g., behavioral interviewing), there may be obvious implications for developing an intervention plan. In the case of developing prevention or intervention responses for suicidal youth, interviewing will likely be the single best source of information.

CONCLUSIONS

Interviewing holds a special place of prominence as an assessment method among mental health professionals. Even among the lay public, interview assessments by specially trained professionals are accorded high status, and may even be the object of unrealistically high expectations. Although interviews appear to simply be special cases of a conversation, they are in fact much more complex in that they are goal oriented, and the interviewer will attempt to shape or lead the direction of the conversation to fulfill specific information-gathering purposes. There are several methods of interviewing, ranging from being very loose to very tight in structure. Interviews have a number of advantages. However, they have disadvantages as well, and foremost among these disadvantages is the well-known problem of unreliability across interviewers.

Effective clinical interviewing of children and adolescents absolutely requires the clinician to have knowledge of developmental issues, and to use this knowledge to inform their interviewing technique. Each of the three major developmental stages of early childhood, middle childhood, and adolescence includes major cognitive development milestones, as well as changes and challenges in social-emotional functioning. Regardless of the chronological age of the child or adolescent client, it is essential to quickly ascertain their functioning in the various developmental areas, and to build the interview format and activities based on developmentally appropriate expectations and tasks.

Several key factors may affect the overall quality of the interview. Perhaps most critical among these factors is the interpersonal context, or the relationship established between the interviewer and the interviewee. Clients' culture may decidedly shape their interpersonal communication style and characteristics, and clinicians must therefore show appropriate understanding of and sensitivity to race, ethnicity, and other cultural variables that may be important in establishing effective communication. Behavior of the client during an interview may be shaped by the clinician to optimize the validity of the interview through making specific requests and through modeling appropriate ways of responding. The physical context of the interview is also an important factor in affecting interview quality. Clinicians should arrange and modify the physical circumstances of the interview setting to make the child or adolescent client feel comfortable, safe, and secure.

Traditional interviewing techniques tend to be relatively unstructured, highly flexible, and are probably the most commonly used of any of the interviewing techniques. In conducting traditional unstructured interviewing techniques, clinicians should strive to obtain appropriate relevant historical and developmental information from parents, develop the interview in a manner that meets their goals for interviewing, and carefully observe certain key behaviors of the interviewee. Traditionally, there are several specific areas of questioning that are useful to focus on in conducting clinical interviews.

Behavioral interviewing tends to be more structured than traditional interviewing, and is clearly aimed at identifying critical events and behaviors that elicit, shape, or maintain the presenting social-emotional problems. Behavioral interviews tend to involve parents and teachers in a consultation model of service delivery. Various models have been presented for conducting behavioral consultation interviews, but most are oriented toward identifying and analyzing the problem in behavioral terms, and most importantly, identifying possible intervention agents and factors to change problem behaviors.

In recent decades, several structured interview schedules have been developed for use with children and adolescents. These structured interview schedules (such as the K–SADS, DICA–R, and CAS) tend to be scripted, somewhat time consuming, and require extensive interviewer training. However, in their better manifestations, such structured interview schedules can yield high reliability across interviewers, something that is notoriously difficult with less structured interview methods. Also, some of these structured interview methods, particularly the K–SADS and CAS, have been shown to have good diagnostic validity from a *DSM* diagnostic perspective.

For assessing children and youth who may be suicidal, clinical interviewing is clearly the preeminent method, and offers many advantages over other methods such as rating scales, self-report tests, and direct behavioral observation. Suicide among children and youth appears to be a rapidly increasing phenomenon in U.S. society. It is essential that clinicians who work with troubled children and adolescents become knowledgeable in conducting a suicide assessment interview. Such an interview requires specific areas of direct questioning to ascertain if the individual may be suicidal, if they have a specific plan and lethal means in place, and what supports may be available to them to help them cope with their suicidal feelings and thoughts. Ethically, there are specific obligations that professionals take on when interviewing a suicidal child or adolescent—specifically, the duty to protect. In the most serious cases, immediate protective action must be taken, which in some cases will involve immediate hospitalization or asking for the assistance of law enforcement officers. In cases where the threat of danger to oneself seems less clear and imminent, but is still probable, other precautionary and follow-up measures should be taken. When dealing with suicidal children and adolescents, it is often necessary to break the confidentiality of the communication, and to notify other persons, particularly the child's parent(s). Working with suicidal clients is too great of a burden for one professional to deal with in isolation. Discussing suicidal cases with a supervisor is a given, and practices and agencies should have clear guidelines in place for such situations. Even for clinicians in solo private practices, it is critical to consult with trusted colleagues regarding the appropriate course of action. "When in doubt, consult."

REVIEW AND APPLICATION QUESTIONS

1. Regarding physical circumstances of clinical interviews with children, what is the recommended optimal furniture and space setup to facilitate comfort and communication?

2. Several typical interpersonal communication styles and behaviors related to the racial or ethnic background of individuals were described in this chapter. How well do such generalities predict individual behavior, and what are some problems from overgeneralizing such inferences regarding group differences?

3. Regarding cognitive development of children and adolescents, how should knowledge of developmental stages shape specific interviewing practices with

preschool- and kindergarten-age children, with elementary-age children, and with adolescents?

4. Regarding social-emotional development of children and adolescents, how should knowledge of developmental stages shape specific interviewing practices with preschool- and kindergarten-age children, with elementary-age children, and with adolescents?

5. What are some practical ways that behavioral interviewing might be useful in developing future intervention plans?

6. For what purposes are structured clinical interview schedules such as the K–SADS, DICA–R, and CAS most appropriate?

7. When should a child's or adolescent's statement regarding suicide be taken seriously?

8. If there is concern that an interviewee may be suicidal, then what are the most essential areas of questioning to pursue?

9. What prior preparations are recommended for breaking confidentiality between clinicians and minor clients in the case of suicidal ideation or behavior?

SOCIOMETRIC TECHNIQUES

[handwritten annotation: procedures used w/in social groups to measure related constructs]

Assessment using sociometric techniques includes a variety of procedures used within social groups to measure such related constructs as social status, popularity, peer acceptance or rejection, and reputation. Sociometric techniques are not new, having been utilized in educational-clinical practice and research on a fairly wide basis since the 1930s. However, a number of important research efforts in this area have occurred since the 1960s. These studies (e.g., Cowen, Pederson, Babigan, Izzo, & Trost, 1973; Dodge, Coie, & Brakke, 1982; Roff, 1961) have emphasized the importance of social functioning in childhood, and thus have underscored the importance of clinicians who work with children having a knowledge of sociometric assessment methods.

This chapter begins with a discussion of the conceptual and historical foundations of sociometric assessment, along with some information on what is known about the validity of sociometry for various clinical and research purposes. The largest section is devoted to four general types of sociometric methods, including peer nominations, peer ratings, sociometric rankings, and alternative sociometric procedures. Both general and specific aspects of assessment using these four approaches are discussed, and numerous examples are presented. Following the overview of specific sociometric assessment techniques, some of the ethical and pragmatic issues that have surfaced in recent years regarding sociometric assessment are explored. The chapter ends with a discussion on how sociometric assessment can best be used in making various types of clinical and educational decisions.

SOCIOMETRIC ASSESSMENT: ITS IMPORTANCE, HISTORY, AND EMPIRICAL BASE

[handwritten annotation: directly gathering info concerning social dynamics]

Sociometric assessment procedures involve directly gathering information from within a peer group (usually in a classroom setting) concerning the social dynamics of that group. The key ingredient of sociometric assessment is that data on various aspects of social status of persons within the peer group is obtained directly from its members

tap directly into group members —

rather than through observations or ratings by impartial outside evaluators. These procedures allow the assessor to tap directly into the ongoing social dynamics of a group, which is an obvious advantage, because there are many aspects of social relationships within a group that are not easily discernable to the casual observer (Worthen, Borg, & White, 1993).

not norm-referenced or standardized

Sociometric assessment provides an avenue for measuring constructs such as level of popularity, acceptance or rejection status, and attribution of specific positive and negative characteristics like leadership ability, athletic or academic prowess, aggressiveness, and social awkwardness. Unlike many other assessment methods, sociometric procedures are not usually norm referenced, standardized, or commercially published. Instead, they tend to consist of different variations of a few relatively simple methods originally developed for use by researchers, but fully capable of being translated into school or clinical practice.

Why Study Social Status?

In 1917, C. R. Beery, a prominent educator, published a series of books titled _Practical Child Training_. This offered some practical advice to mothers who had children with few friends and difficulty approaching peers. Beery suggested that mothers could help these children by facilitating opportunities for peer interaction, such as picnics that would include their children's classmates. He noted that these types of activities would help children to "have a royal good time," and further suggested that if a child shows fear in approaching other children, the mother should "not scold or make any scene, but simply appear to pay no attention to him" (Asher & Parker, 1989, p. 5). This anecdote demonstrates that concern regarding the quality of children's social interactions with their peers has been of academic and practical importance for many years.

10% of children experience significant peer relation. difficult.

The study of social status is indeed important, inasmuch as peer relationship problems during childhood may have a potentially large and lasting positive or negative impact on later adjustment in life. But, how extensive are peer relationship problems during childhood? Based on research by Hymel and Asher (1977), wherein typical elementary schoolchildren were asked to nominate their three best friends, Asher (1990) provided a conservative estimate that about 10% of all children experience significant peer relationship difficulties, based on his findings indicating that about 10% of children are not named as anybody's best friend in sociometric research. Asher (1990) noted that if the criterion of reciprocal friendship nominations is used, the estimated percentage of children with peer relationship problems is substantially higher. Thus, a conservative estimate would mean that at least 10% of all school-age children experience problems in developing friendships and in gaining social acceptance. Given the poor long-term prognosis that may follow these children, this figure is alarming.

The study and assessment of children's social status is also important because of the positive developmental purposes that children's friendships serve. Fine (1981) noted that children's friendships serve an important purpose by making a significant contribution to the development of their overall interactional competence. In other words, through the processes that friendship building requires and refines, children learn to not only interact effectively with their friends, but develop social-interactional skills that may also generalize to many other situations and persons. Fine (1981) specifically identified three functions of preadolescent friendships that contribute to general interactional competence:

First, friendships provide a staging area for behavior. Friendships are situated in social environments that have implications for the acquisition of interactional competencies. Second, friendships are cultural institutions, and as such they provide didactic training. Third, friendships provide a context for the growth of the child's social self, a context within which he or she can learn the appropriate self-image to project in social situations. (p. 49)

Understanding some of these dynamics regarding the positive developmental aspects of children's friendships allows for a better understanding of why peer relationship problems in childhood can be so detrimental. Essentially, the development of positive peer relationships via friendship making is a critical aspect of a youngster's overall cognitive and social development.

Historical Development of Sociometric Assessment

The use of sociometric assessment procedures dates back to the 1930s with the first clinical and research uses of these techniques being conducted by educators and sociologists. One of the first published works on sociometry was Moreno's (1934) highly influential book with the ominous title of *Who Shall Survive?* The earliest attempts to use sociometric assessments were experimental and novel, but by the late 1930s and early 1940s, reports of the systematic use of sociometry began appearing in scholarly journals. The journal *Sociometry* began publication in the 1930s, and included a mix of articles showing applications of sociometric techniques in both educational practice and sociological research. Several research reports using sociometric assessment were published in the *Journal of Educational Psychology* in the early 1940s, as exemplified through articles by Bonney (1943) and Young and Cooper (1944).

By the 1950s, the state of sociometric assessment had advanced considerably, and a number of books were published dealing with the topic (e.g., Cunningham, 1951; Laughlin, 1954; Taba, Brady, Robinson, & Vickery, 1951). During this time period, and probably through the early to mid-1960s, sociometric procedures were commonly used as a means of measuring social adjustment in public school settings. Starting in about the mid-1960s, the use of sociometrics as a typical school-based assessment procedure appears to have declined. Possible reasons for the declining clinical or practical use of sociometrics may include the advancement of other forms of assessment (specifically behavior rating scales and objective self-report measures), public and professional concerns that sociometric assessment may have some negative effects on some children, and the increasingly stringent nature of ethical guidelines for research and human subjects institutional review boards. Interestingly, though concerns do exist about the potential negative effects of sociometric assessment, these concerns have not been substantiated through research. The ethical-professional concerns associated with sociometric assessment are discussed later.

Presently, although sociometric techniques are still widely used by researchers in the fields of child development, education, sociology, and psychology, their use as a standard method for assessing social adjustment problems in schools appears to occur less than it did two to three decades ago. In fact, surveys of school psychologists during the 1980s (Goh & Fuller, 1983) and 1990s (Hutton, Dubes, & Muir, 1992) indicated that sociometric procedures were so seldom used by practitioners that they did not appear on tables of survey results. Whether or not there will be increased use of sociometric assessment in the future remains to be seen. But, it is doubtful that sociometry will regain the level of popularity it enjoyed during the 1940s and 1950s, if for no other reason than the advent and refinement of so many other competing assessment procedures, coupled with the sometimes complicated nature of using sociometrics.

Validity of Sociometric Assessment

Dimensions of Social Status. According to Landau and Milich (1990), early researchers in the use of sociometrics tended to view social status in a fairly unidimensional manner. However, more recent efforts in this area have led investigators to conclude that the construct of social status is both complex and multidimensional. Coie, Dodge, and Coppotelli (1982) used peer preference questions in a sociometric technique with a large number ($N = 537$) of elementary and middle school children, and analyzed the obtained data to develop five different social status groups: *popular, rejected, average, neglected,* and *controversial.* An analysis of characteristics of the students indicated that although there was some overlap between categories, each category had some distinct features. Popular children were those who were rated by peers as being cooperative, having leadership ability, and engaging in very little disruptive behavior. Rejected children were rated as frequently fighting and being disruptive, and not being cooperative or having leadership traits. Neglected children were those who were largely ignored by other children and were seen as being socially unresponsive. The fourth nonaverage group, controversial children, tended to exhibit features of both the popular and rejected group, being considered disruptive and starting fights, but were also being perceived as being assertive leaders. This widely cited and influential conceptualization of social status ratings shows how complex social dynamics within peer groups can be, and indicates that sociometric procedures can indeed provide complex and compelling social assessment data.

Table 6.1 presents the four nonaverage groups from the Coie et al. study, with a listing of the social-behavioral characteristics found to be pertinent for each group. In viewing this interesting conceptualization of children's social status groupings, it is important to recognize that this system is not without criticism. Because Coie et al.'s system has been so widely influential, it has been adopted by researchers for various purposes in several investigations. Not all of these studies have produced results supportive of the classification system. For example, Gresham and Stuart (1992) found that the categories in the Coie et al. system (particularly the Controversial category) were relatively unstable over a 1-year interval, and produced unacceptably high reclassification errors. Additionally, Foster, Bell-Dolan, and Berler (1986) maintained

TABLE 6.1
Descriptions of Four Nonaverage Child and Adolescent Social Status Groups

Group	Sociometric Findings and Social-Behavior Characteristics
Popular	Receive the most positive and fewest negative nominations; described by peers in prosocial terms and perceived as leaders
Rejected	Receive the most negative nominations; described by peers as being disruptive and likely to fight; perceived as having poor leadership skills and being uncooperative
Neglected	Receive few positive or negative peer nominations; described by peers as being shy and unassertive; perceived as having poor social skills
Controversial	Have characteristics similar to both popular and rejected groups; described by peers as being active and assertive leaders, but also perceived as being disruptive, demanding, and frequently not liked

Note. Based on research by Coie, Dodge, and Coppotelli (1982).

that the Coie et al. classification system produced subject selection bias, and overlapped poorly with teacher nomination and assessment methods. These two studies do not necessarily negate the usefulness of the classification system, but should serve to promote careful consideration and caution in its use.

Technical Adequacy of Sociometric Procedures. The technical and psychometric aspects of various sociometric procedures have been investigated in numerous studies. In general, the yield of this research has shown favorable evidence of the technical adequacy of sociometrics, leading the authors of one comprehensive review of sociometrics to state that "we find clear evidence of the importance and utility of sociometrics" (McConnell & Odom, 1986, p. 275). Temporal stability of sociometric assessments has been shown to be relatively high, at both short- and long-term stability periods (Hartup, 1983; Roff, Sells, & Golden, 1972). Landau and Milich (1990) reviewed several studies of interrater correspondence in sociometric procedures, and noted that moderate to high levels of correspondence between raters has generally been found. However, there is one interesting and peculiar finding in this regard—a gender difference on social convergence in ratings wherein both boys and girls tend to attribute more positive attributes to members of their own sex, and more negative attributes to members of the opposite sex. *gender differences on favorable attributes?!*

A methodologically sophisticated study on this topic by Hayden-Thomson, Rubin, and Hymel (1987) went a step beyond simply identifying the fact that boys and girls tend to provide more positive nominations and ratings to each other than to members of the opposite sex. In this study, sex biases in children's sociometric preferences were examined developmentally. The authors used a two-study cross-sectional design to obtain rating scale data from 195 girls and 191 boys in kindergarten through third grade, and 91 girls and 88 boys in third through sixth grade. As expected, the results indicated that children at each grade level rated their classmates of the opposite sex significantly lower than same-sex peers. However, a significant linear trend for these sex biases were found, wherein the negative sex biases of both boys and girls increased with age. This trend was particularly evident at the early grade levels. Therefore, the generally strong interrater correspondence in sociometric assessment may not generalize well when cross-gender data are considered, particularly as children move from early childhood to the intermediate elementary grades. *↑ sex biases w/ age!*

Predictive Validity of Sociometric Assessment. Predictive validity, or ability to predict future social outcomes, of sociometric assessment procedures has been established through several widely cited studies. Cowen et al. (1973) used the Class Play peer assessment procedure in their longitudinal study of 537 children who were tested in three different cohorts in either the first or third grade. The children who were nominated more frequently for negative roles in the Class Play assessment were more likely to receive psychiatric services as adults, based on their names appearing on registers of psychiatric services.

Roff (1961) conducted a prospective study of 164 boys who were referred to child guidance clinics, and who later served in one of the branches of the U. S. military. Based on a review of the participants' case histories as children and their adult service records, those who were reported to have poor peer adjustment were significantly more likely to receive bad conduct discharges from the military than the children who were reported to have good peer relationships. Interestingly, approximately half of the subjects in this study ultimately received bad conduct discharges. Another widely cited study by Roff and his colleagues (Roff & Sells, 1968; Roff et al., 1972) used a longitudinal design in studying various social-behavioral characteristics of approximately 40,000 children who were enrolled in grades 3 through 6 in public schools in Minnesota and Texas. The sociometric assessment data for this study included peer nominations and teacher ratings. When records of delinquency were evaluated 4 years following the completion of the sociometric assessments, it was found that low rated children were significantly more likely to appear on juvenile delinquency rosters. These classic studies from the watershed era of sociometric assessment clearly indicate that important future social outcomes are strongly associated with sociometric assessment information obtained during childhood and adolescence.

Sociometric status has also been shown to be a significant factor in predicting school dropout patterns. Ullman (1957) studied peer and teacher sociometric ratings of students in 11 ninth-grade classes, and found that positive sociometric ratings were predictive of being named on honor rolls at graduation, and negative sociometric ratings were predictive of the students dropping out of school prior to graduation.

In sum, whereas sociometric assessment procedures tend to not be standardized or commercially published like many other forms of assessment, they have nevertheless been demonstrated to have favorable technical properties, and should be viewed as a potentially useful method of assessing peer relations and social status.

AN OVERVIEW OF SPECIFIC SOCIOMETRIC ASSESSMENT PROCEDURES

Because most sociometric assessment procedures are nonstandardized and have a considerable amount of overlap with each other, it is difficult to divide them into distinct categories. However, there are some distinctive similarities and differences among various methods that make a general categorization possible. This section provides an overview of some commonly used sociometric procedures based on a division into four categories: peer nomination procedures, peer rating procedures, sociometric ranking procedures, and alternative sociometric procedures. In some cases, these categories involve general descriptions common to many methods within the category. In others, the categorical description is unique to a specific procedure that has been developed.

Peer Nomination Procedures

The oldest and most widely used sociometric approach, and the basis for most other types of sociometric measures, is the nomination method, originally introduced by Moreno (1934). The essential characteristic of the peer nomination technique is that students are asked to nominate or name classmates they prefer according to specific positive criteria. This approach typically involves the student naming one or more classmates they would most like to study with, play with during free time, work with on a class project, or participate with in some other positive way. For children with sufficient reading and writing ability, peer nomination procedures can be administered by either an item-by-peer matrix, or a questionnaire wherein they fill in names of classmates on blank lines following questions.

The item-by-peer matrix consists of having the names of all children in the class across the top of the page, and the social interaction items listed vertically on the left side of the page. The students are instructed to put an "x" under the name(s) of the other students to whom they think the item applies (e.g., "which student would you most like to have as your best friend?"). Use of a questionnaire format accomplishes essentially the same thing (e.g. "Write the names of three students in your class that you would most like to have as your friends" followed by three numbered blank lines). Scoring of peer nominations is typically done by totaling the number of nominations that each child receives.

Worthen et al. (1993) suggested that the results of positive peer nomination procedures can be classified and interpreted according to a frequently used set of criteria. *Stars* are individuals who are frequently chosen. *Isolates* are individuals who are never chosen in the process. *Neglectees* are those who receive only a few nominations. The results can also be graphically plotted using a *sociogram*, which shows the patterns of choice for each student, and helps to identify not only frequently and never nominated students, but cliques or small groups as well. A *mutual choice* occurs when an individual is chosen by the same student that they selected. A *cross-sex choice* occurs when a boy chooses a girl or a girl chooses a boy. A *clique* is identified by finding a small group of students who choose each other and make few or no choices outside of that group. *Cleavage* is said to occur when two or more groups within the class or social unit are identified who never choose someone from the other group(s).

Using these scoring and classification criteria, it is easy to see how a procedure as deceptively simple as the peer nomination method can yield information that is both striking and complex. Figure 6.1 presents an example of an anonymous item-by-peer matrix that could be used in a peer nomination assessment in a classroom setting, and includes both positive and negative items. Figure 6.2 presents an example of a sociogram that was plotted based on a positive nomination procedure used with 15 elementary-age boys who were asked to select two boys with whom they would most like to be friends.

Although the peer nomination technique has historically most often involved the use of positive items indicative of high social status, many practitioners and researchers have used variations of this method by employing negative nominations, using items that are created to identify students who are socially rejected by peers (e.g., "who would you least like to play with," or "who would you never want to be friends with"). Negative nominations are scored and interpreted in a variety of ways, including finding specific patterns of social rejection within a group, and identifying rejected students who receive a large number of negative nominations. When used in conjunction with positive nominations, negative nominations can provide more detailed information about the subtle dynamics of social status within a group, as exemplified by Coie et al.'s (1982) division of social status into five different groups.

Peer Rating Procedures

The use of peer ratings, also referred to as the roster rating method, constitutes a form of sociometric assessment that is conceptually and psychometrically quite different from peer nominations. In the peer rating procedure, the children within a group are asked to respond to a sociometric question for each child in the group. A typical procedure for implementing the peer rating method involves providing each member of a group with a roster that has the names of all other group members and a list of sociometric questions, and then rating each member of the group on each question using a 5-point scale (Connolly, 1983). For younger children, a variation of the 5-point scale is often used, which consists of a series of 3 or 5 faces ranging from frowning

PLEASE LIST THE NAME OF YOUR TEACHER _____

WHAT GRADE ARE YOU IN? _____

I AM A (circle one): BOY / GIRL

DIRECTIONS: We are interested in finding out how well children are able to notice the behavior of other children. Please help us by answering some questions about the other children in your class. Follow along as the questions are read out loud, and try to answer each question the best you can. For each question, you will be asked to pick one student that you think the question is most like, and then put an **X** in the box under their name for that question. Remember, there are no right or wrong answers, and the way you answer these questions will not affect your grade. Your classmates and your teacher will not know how you answered the questions. If you don't understand what to do, or need help, please raise your hand.

	Tina	Jan	Cal	Ole	Ken	Tim	Kim	Sari	Jon	Tia	Kyle	Sue	Erin	Pat	Eli
Who would you most like to be best friends with?															
Who is angry or mad a lot?															
Who would you like to invite over to your home?															
Who gets in fights?															
Who gets along well with the teacher?															
Who is in trouble a lot?															

FIG. 6.1. An example of an item-by-peer matrix for a peer nomination procedure that includes both positive and negative items.

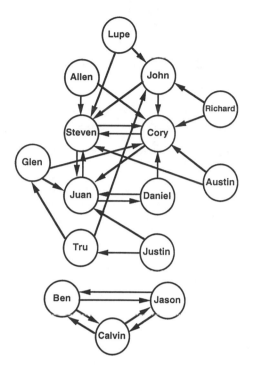

FIG. 6.2. An example of a sociogram plotted for a group of 15 elementary-age boys who were asked to select the two boys in the classroom that they would most like to be friends with.

to smiling, that are anchored to different scale values. Using this method, the children are asked to circle one of the faces in lieu of a numerical rating (Asher, Singleton, Tinsley, & Hymel, 1979). A sample peer rating assessment form is displayed in Fig. 6.3. This particular example shows a rating scale format peer rating that might be used with children in grades 3 through 6.

Psychometrically and statistically, peer rating methods are considerably different than peer nomination methods. Each child's score is based on an average of all the ratings they receive. Because children are rated by all their classmates, a broader picture of their social status is obtained. Compared with peer nomination methods, ratings are more stable within a group, and are less affected by the size of the group (Connolly, 1983). In general, peer ratings tend to yield higher reliability/stability coefficients than do nomination methods (McConnell & Odom, 1986), and with younger children, the increase in score stability with rating methods is particularly noticeable (Asher et al., 1979). Another interesting measurement characteristic of peer ratings is that they tend to provide distributions that are less skewed than are distributions provided by some other forms of sociometric assessment (Hops & Lewin, 1984).

In addition to having measurement qualities that are different from peer nomination procedures, peer rating methods are conceptually different as well, and may measure a somewhat different construct. Peer ratings are thought to produce a measure of *average likability*, whereas peer nominations are thought to produce a measure of *popularity*. Although likability and popularity have some obvious similarities, there are some subtle yet important differences between these constructs. For example, using

likability   v. popularity
(ratings)   (niminations)

RATING FORM

Please List the Name of Your Teacher:_____

What Grade Are You In?_____

I AM A (circle one): BOY / GIRL

DIRECTIONS: We are interested in finding out how much the students in your class would like to work with each other or play with each other. For each student on this list, circle one of the numbers to show **how much you would like to play with them** and circle one of the numbers to show **how much you would like to work with them**. This is what the numbers mean:

1 = NOT AT ALL (I definitely would not to work or play with this person)
2 = NOT VERY MUCH (I don't think I would want to work or play with this person)
3 = DON'T CARE (it really wouldn't matter to me if I played with this person or not)
4 = SORT OF (I think I would like to work or play with this person)
5 = VERY MUCH (I definitely would like to work or play with this person)

Your teacher and the other students in the class will not know how you answered. There are no right or wrong answers, and the way you fill this form out will not affect your grade. If you have any questions, or if you need help, raise your hand.

NAME	WORK WITH?					PLAY WITH?				
1._____	1	2	3	4	5	1	2	3	4	5
2._____	1	2	3	4	5	1	2	3	4	5
3._____	1	2	3	4	5	1	2	3	4	5
4._____	1	2	3	4	5	1	2	3	4	5
5._____	1	2	3	4	5	1	2	3	4	5
6._____	1	2	3	4	5	1	2	3	4	5
7._____	1	2	3	4	5	1	2	3	4	5
8._____	1	2	3	4	5	1	2	3	4	5
9._____	1	2	3	4	5	1	2	3	4	5
10._____	1	2	3	4	5	1	2	3	4	5

FIG. 6.3. A sample peer rating assessment form.

the peer rating method, a child might receive scores that indicate an average amount of likability, yet it is possible that they might not receive any positive nominations. In this case, if the sociometric interpretation were based on the peer nomination data alone, the child might be considered to be socially isolated or neglected, which might not be the case. There is a relatively large degree of measurement overlap between these procedures—Oden and Asher (1977) reported a correlation of .63 between the two measures. Yet, in another study (Asher & Hymel, 1981), 11 of 23 children who received no positive nominations did receive high positive ratings from their peers.

By combining the nomination and rating procedures in conducting a sociometric assessment, the obtained sociometric data may be more powerful in differentiating popular/likable and unpopular/unliked children than would be single-source data (Asher & Renshaw, 1981). Another advantage of using peer rating procedures is that they can provide information regarding both positive and negative social status without the use of negative questions. This can be done by wording questions positively or neutrally, and simply looking at the distribution of scores. This advantage may be particularly important when attempting to obtain consent from parents or program administrators who are uncomfortable with the use of negative nomination methods.

Sociometric Ranking Procedures

↑ adults rather than peers

Unlike the peer nomination and peer rating procedures that have just been overviewed, sociometric ranking procedures are designed to provide information on child social status and peer relations through data contributed by adults rather than peers. In most instances of sociometric ranking procedures that have been reported in the literature, the informant is a teacher and the peer group consists of same-grade classmates. However, it would also be possible to implement sociometric ranking assessment procedures in nonschool settings as well, such as group homes, residential or day treatment programs, and perhaps in clinic-based therapy groups.

Because the object of sociometric assessment is to obtain information on status and relations within a peer group, what advantage is there in going outside of the peer group to an adult informant to collect this data? Connolly (1983) noted that when using the peer group as a source of information, it must be assumed that children are capable of making accurate social distinctions. With typical children who are elementary age or older, this assumption appears to be valid. However, with younger children, and perhaps with older children who have moderate to severe intellectual disabilities, the completion of sociometric tasks may be difficult, and may result in lower reliability. Hence using teachers as sociometric informants may actually increase reliability in some instances (Foster et al., 1986; Hagborg, 1994). Another reason for employing teachers as sociometric informants is that they tend to be expert objective observers of child behavior, and thus understand the social dynamics within their classroom. Additionally, educators are understandably often hesitant to commit blocks of academic time for nonacademic student tasks, and might be more willing to provide sociometric ranking data themselves rather than have their students spend instructional time on it. *adults ↑ reliability + don't take away from academic time*

There are two general ways that sociometric rankings can be completed by classroom teachers. The first method involves the teacher rank ordering every student in their classroom according to some sociometric criteria, such as popularity with classmates or positive interactions with peers. Previous studies that have employed this type of ranking procedure have shown that the obtained data tends to be highly reliable, and may correlate better with independent ratings and observations of child social behavior than do peer nominations or ratings (Connolly & Doyle, 1981; Greenwood, Walker, Todis, & Hops, 1979). It is interesting to note that when the object of interest is negative social interactions or peer rejection, teacher rankings have been found to correlate with independent ratings and observations of child behavior to a lower degree than negative peer nominations (Connolly, 1983).

A related method for obtaining teacher sociometric rankings involves first determining which students in a classroom fit a given social-behavioral description, and

multiple
gating

then rank ordering those students according to the severity or strength of how they fit those criteria. Using this method of ranking, not all students in a classroom are ranked, but only those who are found to meet given criteria. An example of this method of selective rank ordering is found in Stage 1 of Walker and Severson's (1992) Systematic Screening for Behavior Disorders (SSBD), a multiple gating screening and assessment procedure discussed in chapter 2. This rank ordering procedure involves teachers selecting 10 students in their classroom whose behaviors most closely match an objective description of internalizing behavior problems, and then rank ordering those students according to the severity of their symptoms. Examples from the description of internalizing problems include not talking with other children; being shy, timid, or unassertive; not participating in games and activities; and being unresponsive to social initiations by others. Following the rank ordering along the internalizing dimension, a separate rank ordering procedure is conducted in a similar manner for students who exhibit externalizing social-behavioral problems. Examples from the description of externalizing problems include arguing, forcing the submission of others, disturbing others, and stealing. The instructions for rank ordering students with internalizing behavior problems are presented in Fig. 6.4.

Research reported in the SSBD technical manual indicates that the Stage 1 rank ordering procedures have adequate to strong interrater agreement between teachers and classroom aides (.89 to .94 for the externalizing dimension and .82 to .90 for the internalizing dimension) and good test–retest reliability at 10- to 30-day intervals (.81 to .88 for the externalizing dimension, and .74 to .79 for the internalizing dimension). Additionally, the Stage 1 ranking procedure of the SSBD has been found to have a strong degree of sensitivity in discriminating students with behavioral disorders from peers with normal levels of problem behaviors.

Alternative Sociometric Procedures

In addition to peer nominations, peer ratings, and sociometric rankings, other sociometric procedures have been developed that may have some similarities with one or more of these categories, but are in many ways unique. Three of these alternative sociometric assessment procedures are reviewed in this section—picture sociometrics, the Class Play, and "guess who" techniques.

Picture Sociometrics. Picture sociometric procedures involve individually presenting each child in a classroom with an arbitrary assortment of photographs of each child in the class, and then asking the child to answer a series of questions by pointing to or selecting a photograph of a peer. This method is an adaptation of other peer nomination methods that is useful for work with preliterate clients. Landau and Milich (1990) stated that it is the preferred method for preschool through second-grade level subjects. Examples of questions that have been used with this technique include "who do you like to play with the most?", "who is your best friend?", and "who is the best student in your class?" As with most other sociometric techniques, specific questions can be developed based on the clinical or research questions, and these questions can be produced to indicate either social acceptance or social rejection.

The original picture sociometric technique and minor variations of it are scored based on totaling the number of times each child was nominated by classmates based on questions indicating positive social status. Using this scoring scheme, rejected or neglected children would have significantly lower scores than accepted children with

Rank Ordering on Internalizing Dimension

Internalizing refers to all behavior problems that are directed inwardly (i.e., away from the external social environment) and that represent problems with self. Internalizing behavior problems are often self-imposed and frequently involve behavioral deficits and patterns of social avoidance. *Non-examples* of internalizing behavior problems would be all forms of social behavior that demonstrate social involvement with peers and that facilitate normal or expected social development.

Examples include:

- having low or restricted activity levels,
- not talking with other children,
- being shy, timid, and/or unassertive,
- avoiding or withdrawing from social situations,
- preferring to play or spend time alone,
- acting in a fearful manner,
- not participating in games and activities,
- being unresponsive to social initiations by others, and
- not standing up for one's self.

Non-Examples include:

- initiating social interactions with peers,
- having conversations,
- playing with others, having normal rates or levels of social contact with peers,
- displaying positive social behavior toward others,
- participating in games and activities,
- resolving peer conflicts in an appropriate manner, and
- joining in with others.

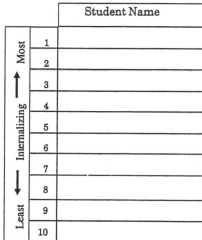

Column One
List Internalizers

Student Name

(Most Exemplifying Internalizing Behavior)

Column Two
Rank Order
Internalizers

	Student Name
1	
2	
3	
4	
5	
6	
7	
8	
9	
10	

(Most ↑ Internalizing ↓ Least)

Instructions:

1. First, review the definition of internalizing behavior and then list of all students in your class.

2. Next, in Column One above, enter the names of the ten students whose characteristic behavior patterns most closely match the internalizing behavioral definition.

3. Finally, in Column Two, rank order the students listed in Column One according to the degree or extent to which each exhibits internalizing behavior. The student who exhibits internalizing behavior to the greatest degree is ranked first and so on until all ten students are rank ordered.

FIG. 6.4. Instructions for rank ordering students with internalizing social-emotional problems, from Stage 1 of the SSBD multiple gating system. A rank ordering procedure for externalizing problems is also included in Stage 1. From *Systematic Screening for Behavior Disorders*, by H. M. Walker and H. H. Severson, 1992, Longmont, CO: Sopris West. Copyright © 1992 by Sopris West. Reprinted with permission.

higher social status. Of course, variations in scoring procedure would be needed if there were any significant deviations in administration method from the original study by McAndless and Marshall (1957). For example, questions that reflect both positive (e.g., "who do you most like to do schoolwork with") and negative (e.g., "who are you afraid to be around on the playground") social status could be mixed, and the scoring system could be divided into positive and negative status categories.

The use of picture sociometrics was first reported by McAndless and Marshall (1957), and has been used in a number of other published studies. The psychometric properties of picture sociometric techniques have been shown to be quite good, with relatively high interrater reliability, very high short-term test–retest reliability, and adequate long-term test–retest reliability (see Landau & Milich, 1990). Validity of the picture sociometric method has been demonstrated by producing significant discriminations between groups of aggressive, aggressive-withdrawn, and normal boys (Milich & Landau, 1984). Interestingly, with young children, picture sociometrics have been shown to produce more effective discriminations of social status than information provided by teachers, particularly when negative ratings or nominations are involved. Because picture sociometrics are of particular use with young children, their use is discussed further in chapter 13.

The Class Play. The Class Play procedure was first utilized and described by Bower (1969) and was then revised further by Masten, Morrison, and Pelligrini (1985). It is a frequently used sociometric technique that has been employed in several large-scale investigations, including the classic 11- to 13-year follow-up study of elementary-age children by Cowen and his colleagues (Cowen et al., 1973). The basis of this procedure is that children are asked to assign their peers to various roles (usually both positive and negative roles) in an imaginary play. The original Class Play described by Bower (1969) included both positive (e.g., "someone who will wait their turn") and negative (e.g., "someone who is too bossy") roles, but consisted of a scoring procedure wherein only a single score (negative peer reputation) was derived, which was done by calculating the number of negative roles given to a child and dividing that by the total number of roles given to the child. Large percentages are supposed to indicate a high degree of peer rejection, whereas low percentages are meant to indicate that the child has higher social status. As is the case with most sociometric approaches, the specification of roles in the Class Play procedure (as well as the method of scoring) can be manipulated by clinicians or researchers to suit their specific assessment goals. It should be noted that the scoring system advocated by Bower has been criticized as being flawed (Landau & Milich, 1990).

The use of Class Play sociometric procedures is attractive for two reasons other than its measurement capabilities. One advantage is that children seem to truly enjoy participating in make-believe plays and casting their peers into the various roles. The second advantage is that teachers and administrators seem to view this type of procedure more positively than some other sociometric methods, and as such, it is more likely to be supported and approved than some other approaches. Masten et al. (1985) suggested that because of the diversity of roles needed in a play, this procedure will reduce any probability of disapproving labels on children with high negative scores by other children in the rating/casting process.

"Guess Who" Measures. The "guess who" technique is a sociometric approach wherein brief descriptive statements are provided to students, and they are then asked to write down names of a few other students (usually three or fewer) who they think

best fit the descriptions. For example, the students might be asked to respond to descriptions such as "guess who is often in trouble," "guess who does the best job on schoolwork," "guess who no one knows very well," or "guess who is often angry at other children." The descriptions can be provided to the students either verbally or in written format. The content of the "guess who" items can be made up by the teacher, clinician, or researcher based on specific characteristics they are interested in identifying. Scoring of these types of measures is done by making simple frequency counts of each question/description. More elaborate scoring methods are also possible, such as grouping descriptions into categories of similar content (e.g., antisocial behaviors, helping characteristics, peer popularity, etc.) and obtaining frequency counts within each broader category.

An example of a "guess who" measure that has been used with a large number of students and has been carefully investigated is the Revised PRIME Guess Who Measure, which was developed for use in Project PRIME, a large-scale investigation of students with disabilities who had been integrated in regular education classrooms for part of their instructional day (Kauffman, Semmell, & Agard, 1974). The original instrument consisted of 29 questions/descriptions, and was administered to over 13,000 students in grades 3 through 5. Factor analytic procedures conducted on the instrument divided the items into four major factors, which were labeled "disruptive," "bright," "dull," and "well behaved." A revised scale including 20 items (the 5 items contributing the most to each factor) was developed by Veldman and Sheffield (1979), who reported reliability coefficients ranging from .56 to .77 for each factor score, and developed a satisfactory concurrent validity procedure for the instrument by correlating the instrument items with teacher ratings along similar dimensions.

In sum, the "guess who" technique is flexible, easy to administer and score, has been used in a large number of studies and projects, and has been found to have satisfactory technical properties. Clinicians and investigators desiring an adaptable, easy to administer sociometric measure may find "guess who" techniques to be a useful choice in assessment instrumentation.

ETHICAL CONCERNS IN USING SOCIOMETRIC PROCEDURES

[handwritten margin note: negative criteria are a concern — fear that indiv. will be further isolated!]

The sociometric assessment approaches detailed in this chapter, as well as other types of sociometric measures, have a great deal of appeal to clinicians and researchers, and have a long history of use in psychology, sociology, and education. However, these approaches are not without controversy. Many sociometric methods involve negative ranking or nomination procedures, or having children single out peers based on negative characteristics. Largely because of the use of these negative nomination procedures, parents, teachers, and administrators may be hesitant or alarmed at the possibility of their children participating in sociometric assessments for fear of their child or other children being singled out by peers and further ostracized because of it. The use of negative criteria clearly is the most controversial aspect of sociometric assessment (McConnell & Odom, 1986). The gist of this controversy is that there seems to be a common concern that children will compare their responses after the assessment to find out which children were singled out for negative nominations, and this process will end up in increased isolation or social exile for the children who were commonly perceived in negative terms. For example, some research projects had to undergo major methodological modifications or be stopped altogether because of threats by parents and some educators to "shut the study down" because of outrage over the use of negative peer ranking or nomination procedures.

Although concerns regarding negative effects from sociometric assessment are understandable, it is important to recognize that such concerns have never been substantiated through empirical evidence. Landau and Milich (1990) noted that several large-scale longitudinal investigations with at-risk children have been conducted wherein sociometric procedures have been employed (e.g., Pekarik, Prinz, Liebert, Weintraub, & Neale, 1976; Serbin, Lyons, Marchessault, Schwartzman, & Ledingham, 1987) with no reports of negative consequences to the participants. An ambitious and intriguing investigation by Hayvren and Hymel (1984) found that there were no observable negative consequences within peer groups immediately following the use of sociometric assessment procedures. However, this study was conducted with a population of preschool-age children, and it is unclear whether the same results would generalize to elementary- or secondary-age children.

More recently, an ambitious study was conducted by A. M. Iverson and G. L. Iverson (1996) to gauge children's long-term reactions to participating in sociometric assessment. In this study, 82 children in the fifth grade completed a positive and negative peer nomination procedure during the last week of the school year. Following the summer vacation period, 45 of the participants (who were by then in the sixth grade) were individually interviewed to assess their reactions to the sociometric procedures. As many as one third of the participants indicated they had indeed discussed the measures with their peers, despite specific instructions that they were not to do so. However, the participants stated that they enjoyed participating in the sociometric procedure, particularly the positive nomination procedure. Because the original nomination procedure was used to assign participants to social status groups based on the Coie et al.'s (1982) five category breakdown of Average, Controversial, Neglected, Popular, and Rejected, their responses were analyzed by group. No evidence of reactions indicating any harm to any of the participants was found.

Given the combined evidence in this area to date, two things can be surmised. First, it does appear likely that a substantial number of children who participate in sociometric assessments, perhaps one third or more of participants, will discuss their choices with peers, even if they are instructed not to do so. Second, despite the reasonable possibility of children comparing their responses, there is no empirical evidence that negative nomination or rating procedures are harmful to individuals who participate in the assessment. However, even with the fairly recent addition to the literature of the interesting study by Iverson and Iverson, there is still a lack of evidence on the effects of sociometric assessment in general. Clinicians or researchers who are considering the use of sociometrics would do well to interpret the available evidence as indicating that "it seems very unlikely that it is harmful, but we don't know" rather than "we know for sure that it is not harmful." Of course, concerns regarding the use of sociometrics may be reduced through not using negative criteria, but such a course of action may greatly reduce the utility of sociometric assessment. Before deciding to do entirely away with the use of any negative criteria in sociometric assessment, consider McConnell and Odom's (1986) point: "Because the efficiency of peer nomination assessments will decrease markedly when negative nominations are not used, it is imperative that they be included in the assessment process" (p. 233).

Whether or not concerns about the effects of sociometric assessment are founded, clinicians and researchers desiring to utilize sociometric approaches are advised to carefully pick the most appropriate method for their purposes, communicate closely and carefully with their constituent groups, and educate those involved on the purposes and procedures involved. Landau and Milich (1990) suggested that the use of positive nomination procedures or peer ratings instead of negative nomination procedures may be necessary (but certainly not optimal) when working with systems or individuals who are suspicious of the use of sociometrics. In the meantime, additional research on any potential peer effects of sociometric measurement involving negative ranking or nomination would be extremely useful.

SOCIOMETRIC APPROACHES AND DECISION MAKING

sociometrics can be used for screening + confirming hypotheses.

Perhaps the best use of sociometric assessment is in making decisions about screening and assessment. As a screening tool, various sociometric approaches can quickly help identify individuals who might be at heightened risk for developing social-behavioral problems. As part of a comprehensive assessment system, sociometric methods can help to confirm or disconfirm hypotheses about peer relationship problems or other social risk factors that have been developed through the use of other assessment methods.

Sociometric assessment may have some use as a means to identify individuals who might benefit from special social skills interventions, but if used for this purpose, it would be important to augment the sociometric approaches with other objective assessment methods. It would also be important to word the sociometric assessment questions or instructions very carefully in order to match the intended type of intervention. For example, if a school counselor or psychologist was attempting to identify potential participants for an anger control group, a peer nomination question such as "list five students who easily lose their temper" might be useful in conjunction with other selection data. For making specific intervention decisions, it is difficult to see how sociometric data would be very useful. In fact, it has been suggested by some researchers that a clear link between sociometric assessment and social-behavioral intervention is simply not clearly founded (e.g., Foster et al., 1986; Gresham & Stuart, 1992; Hagborg, 1994). *linkage of sociometrics to interventions is questionable*

An intriguing potential use of sociometric assessment data is for grouping students together in classroom settings for maximizing cooperation and providing appropriate modeling. For example, a student who lacks social skills and comes out as socially neglected in a sociometric assessment might be strategically paired with another student with strong social competence and who is identified in the sociometric assessment as being well liked and accepting. Such a pairing might potentially result in the socially neglected student being exposed to a positive social model and a potential source of social support. Likewise, a teacher who is assigned to teach an intact group of students but who does not yet know these students might use a sociometric assessment to ensure that seat assignments and workgroup pairings include an appropriate mix of students, and that students at heightened risk for engaging in negative social behavior (e.g., rejected and controversial students) are not clustered together.

For making diagnosis/classification or placement decisions, sociometric assessment procedures appear to be even less useful. These types of decisions tend to require objective information on whether or not an individual meets specific criteria. The only possible use of sociometrics in this regard would be as a means of confirming or disconfirming other data used in determining whether or not the criteria have been met. *not good for diagnosis*

In sum, sociometric assessment, like other forms of assessment used to gauge emotional and behavioral problems, is more relevant for certain types of decision-making processes. The decision-making process that appears to be most relevant to sociometric assessment is screening and assessment decision making. Sociometric assessment may also have some relevance when used in conjunction with other forms of assessment and for making general decisions about interventions for peer relationship problems, but the current link in this regard is questionable.

CONCLUSIONS

Sociometric assessment is comprised by a collection of related measurement techniques that allow for the gathering of social information from within an intact peer group, such as students within a classroom. Social status, popularity, social acceptance or rejection, and average likability are the most common constructs that are assessed with sociometrics. Sociometrics comprise a potentially important assessment method because the constructs being measured are critically important and highly predictive of future social and emotional outcomes. Sociometric assessment has a rich history within developmental psychology, education, and sociology, and became widely used in the 1950s and 1960s. However, the use of sociometrics appears to have declined since that era, perhaps partly because of the increasing availability of other social assessment methods, and partly because of increasing difficulty in obtaining acceptance and approval for using sociometrics.

The empirical base for sociometrics is generally quite solid. There have been numerous studies conducted over the years that have documented the reliability and validity of various sociometric procedures. Perhaps the most compelling of these studies supporting the use of sociometrics were the classic studies conducted by Cowen, Roff, Ullman, and their respective colleagues. These studies demonstrated in a very compelling way that sociometric assessment not only is capable of having sound technical adequacy, but more importantly, is strongly predictive of important future social-emotional outcomes. There have been some studies conducted that have highlighted the shortcomings of sociometric assessment, but it has held up surprisingly well to some fairly intense scrutiny.

The peer nomination procedure is the oldest sociometric technique, and provides the basis for most other sociometric techniques as well. Peer nominations involve presenting a child with a series of positive and negative statements or questions such as "who would you most like to play or work with?" or "who are you afraid to be around?" and asking them to nominate someone from their peer group who they think best fits the specific question. In addition to the peer nomination procedure, other common sociometric techniques include peer rating scales and sociometric ranking procedures. These methods vary somewhat in terms of how they best tap underlying constructs, as well as their technical or psychometric properties. Additional alternative sociometric techniques, such as picture sociometrics, "guess who" techniques, and the Class Play, have been developed for use with specific populations and problems.

During the past two decades, there has been increasing concern regarding the ethics of using sociometric techniques for assessment of children. Prompted primarily by concerns regarding the use of negative criteria and the fear of children comparing their responses and ostracizing other children, many institutional review boards and school administrators have been reluctant to approve projects involving sociometric assessment. As a result, many practitioners or researchers do not view sociometry as a viable method, or compromise by removing all negative criteria, which has the effect of reducing the power and efficiency of sociometric assessment. These concerns are understandable, but are simply not founded on empirical evidence. None of the very few studies that have attempted to investigate negative effects resulting from participation in sociometric assessment have identified any short- or long-term negative consequences for participants.

Perhaps the best use of sociometric assessment to assist in psychoeducational decision making is for making decisions regarding additional screening and assessment. Sociometrics have been clearly demonstrated to have substantial accuracy in identifying at-risk children and youth who may be in need of additional assessment or intervention services.

REVIEW AND APPLICATION QUESTIONS

1. What are some advantages of obtaining peer-referenced sociometric assessment data rather than relying solely on teacher ratings or observations of social interaction patterns?

2. Briefly describe some of the evidence attesting to the predictive validity of sociometric assessment.

3. Compare and contrast peer ranking and peer rating procedures. Under what circumstances might each procedure be best utilized?

4. Describe two ways of using positive nomination procedures. Under what circumstances might each procedure be best utilized?

5. What are some ways of implementing sociometric assessment procedures with children who cannot yet read or write?

6. Develop a list of five different "guess who" questions that you might utilize to help select the three students in a third-grade classroom who are most likely to benefit from participation in a social skills training group wherein friendship making and peer interaction skills are stressed.

7. The use of negative peer nomination procedures and other negative criteria in sociometrics has generated a great deal of controversy. Regarding this issue, respond to the following questions: (a) What are some of the possible negative outcomes of using negative nomination procedures?, (b) What evidence exists attesting to the negative effects of these procedures?, and (c) What are some potential alternatives to negative nominations?

7

SELF-REPORT INSTRUMENTS

This chapter addresses the development and use of a broad category of assessment instruments referred to herein as objective self-report tests, or simply self-report tests. This assessment category is inextricably linked to the field of personality assessment. Some assessment texts define self-report assessment separately from personality assessment, whereas other texts include additional categories of assessment methods in this vein. This book refers to this general category of assessment instruments as self-report tests because the term is descriptive of the type of activity the assessment involves, and because many (if not most) of the self-report tests reviewed here and in later chapters are not designed to measure the broad construct of "personality," but to assess very specific aspects of social and emotional behavior based on the child or youth's own perceptions.

Even with this relatively broad and functional way of defining self-report assessment, the fact that it is so strongly linked to personality assessment may be troublesome, if not distasteful, to some behaviorally oriented practitioners or researchers. This skeptical view is mirrored by Salvia and Ysseldyke (1995), who began their chapter on personality assessment as follows: "Personality development is a nebulous concept, ill-defined and subjectively measured. In fact, you could probably debate long and hard about the meaning of adequate personality development. Personality is never assessed. Rather, we observe and/or measure behaviors and infer a thing called personality" (p. 324). This chapter lays the groundwork for understanding self-report assessment, an important field within psychology and within subsequent chapters of this book. In the introductory chapter, the notion of *direct* and *objective* assessment was highlighted as an important focus of this text. In this chapter, there is a clear emphasis on objective (and relatively direct) methods of self-report assessment, consistent with the overall emphasis of this volume. However, indirect and subjective methods of assessment are not totally neglected. Chapter 8 provides a comprehensive discussion of the use of various projective-expressive techniques for assessing personality and affect of children and youth, including recommendations for best practices in using these techniques within the context of a broader and relatively direct assessment design.

This chapter begins with a broad examination of the important foundations of self-report assessment, including historical and psychometric considerations. The largest share of the chapter is dedicated to evaluative reviews and discussion of several self-report instruments designed for assessing children and youth. These instruments differ from the types of self-report measures reviewed in chapters 9 through 12, because they are omnibus or general purpose assessment instruments designed for measuring overall personal adjustment and psychopathology. Conversely, the self-report instruments discussed in later chapters include instruments developed for assessing very specific constructs, such as ADHD, depression, anxiety, social competence, and self-concept. This chapter ends with a discussion on how data from self-report tests can be used in making decisions regarding screening and assessment, classification, and intervention.

FOUNDATIONS AND METHODS OF SELF-REPORT ASSESSMENT

To best appreciate the uses of self-report tests in the assessment of behavioral, social, and emotional problems, it is first necessary to develop a general understanding of them. This section presents a historic and psychometric overview of the basis of objective self-report assessment. First, a brief historical account of the personality testing movement is presented, followed by some basic definitions and a discussion of objective measurement. Then, information specific to methods of objective test construction and some associated measurement problems is presented.

Historical Foundations of Personality Testing

As previously mentioned, self-report assessment is closely linked to, if not an integral part of, the field of personality assessment. As noted by McReynolds (1986), interest in the assessment of personality may actually be older than the field of psychology. Primitive attempts to measure personality have been identified in antiquity, as exemplified by the work of some of the ancient Greek philosophers. The first formal efforts connected to assessing personality structure were found in free association techniques, such as those developed by Freud and Jung in their psychoanalytic work, and Kraepelin's (1892) use of the technique in studying physiological effects of hunger, fatigue, and drugs (cited in Anastasi & Urbina, 1997). As advances in the study of personality continued in the early 1900s, there became more of a distinction between projective methods (such as the Rorschach test, apperception tests, and drawing tests) and objective methods of personality assessment, the latter of which are the focus of the remainder of this historical overview.

Anastasi (1988) and Anastasi and Urbina (1997) noted that the prototype of the modern personality/self-report inventory was the Personal Data Sheet, which was developed by Woodworth during World War I as a test to screen men with serious emotional problems from military service. By the late 1920s and early 1930s, a number of objective personality questionnaires, surveys, and inventories had been developed for research and clinical purposes. Many of these early efforts did not meet the current criteria for being considered objective self-report measures, but they were objective in the sense that they incorporated methods that were distinctly different from associative and projective techniques. By the late 1930s and early 1940s, advances in personality theory, psychometric theory, and statistical analysis set the stage for major advances in objective personality assessment. In the first edition, Cronbach (1949) noted that the publication of Berneuter's Personality Inventory in the 1930s resulted in an instrument based on four personality traits and was widely used in clinical and other applied settings. This assessment instrument became the prototype for a number of later objective self-report measures. The most notable of these later measures was the Minnesota Multiphasic Personality Inventory (MMPI), which was first published in 1943 and was subsequently revised and updated. The MMPI was the first widely used instrument to use the sophisticated *empirical criterion keying* method of construction, a technique on which many later tests were constructed.

During the 1950s, 1960s, and 1970s, there were many challenges to the validity of traditional personality assessment. Some of these challenges arose from the increasing influence of behaviorism in graduate psychology training, a school of thought that was often seen as highly dogmatic and parochial in those days. The growth of humanistic psychology in the 1950s and 1960s also posed some challenges to traditional personality assessment, because many humanistic practitioners considered personality assessment to be impersonal and invasive. Some of the challenges to personality assessment during these three decades arose from the fact that many assessment instruments that were commonly used had very poor psychometric/technical qualities, and limited evidence of validity. During the past three decades, the field of personality assessment has undergone many changes but has not seen its demise (as some predicted). In fact, there has clearly been a resurgence of interest in personality assessment since the 1970s (Anastasi & Urbana, 1997; Knoff, 1986). Currently, there are numerous professional organizations and scholarly journals devoted specifically to the assessment of personality or social-emotional behavior. Some of the reasons for this apparent revitalization of personality assessment include increasing eclecticism among practitioners and researchers, a decline in dogmatism and parochialism in specific schools or fields of psychology, and the development and refinement of sophisticated mathematical models and statistical techniques for studying personality and developing self-report instruments. Regarding the relatively recent improvements in technical sophistication and research regarding personality assessment, Anastasi and Urbina (1997) stated:

> The 1990s have witnessed a resurgence of research that faced up to the complexities of personality assessment and sought innovative solutions to these long-standing problems. The period is characterized by significant theoretical and methodological advances. The earlier critiques of personality measurement undoubtedly had a salutary effect and in part stimulated the subsequent development in this area of psychometrics. We must, however, guard against the danger that, in the zeal to eradicate fallacious thinking, sound and useful concepts may also be lost. The occasional proposal that diagnostic personality testing and trait concepts be completely discarded, for example indicates an unnecessarily narrow definition of both terms. (p. 385)

Psychometric Foundations of Objective Test Construction

Chapter 1 discussed the notion of direct and objective assessment in general. However, these concepts have not been addressed in detail at this point. Because the focus of this chapter is on objective self-report tests rather than projective-expressive techniques (see chap. 8), it appropriate and necessary to discuss objective assessment more fully in this section.

R. P. Martin (1988) proposed that the following four essential characteristics or criteria must be present for an assessment instrument to be considered an objective test:

Characteristics of an OBJECTIVE assessment...

1. There must be individual differences in the responses of persons to the test stimuli, and these differences must be sufficiently consistent over time, across test items, and in different assessment situations.

2. The measurement must involve the comparison of one person's responses to those of other individuals, and the items must be presented to different persons in a consistent manner.

3. The assessment device must include normative data so that individual scores can be assigned a place on a scale for purposes of comparison against a larger group of persons.

4. The test responses must be shown to be related to other meaningful behavior. In other words, the measurement must be shown to be useful in predicting behavior. This criterion is referred to as the *validity requirement.*

Therefore, an objective self-report test is one in which subjects respond to various items or questions about their own social-emotional behavior in a standardized manner, wherein their responses are compared to those of a normative group, and evidence is provided as to the psychometric properties (reliability and validity) of the measure. R. P. Martin's (1988) four criteria and the subsequent summation of these key points show that the assessment methods discussed in previous chapters (behavioral observation, rating scales, interviewing, and sociometric measures) are not usually considered to be objective self-report measures in the strictest sense of the term, though they sometimes meet several of the essential characteristics. To these four characteristics, it is useful to add a brief definition of how self-report responses are scored using objective procedures: Each possible response on an item is associated with a predetermined score, and there is no room for inference or individual judgment in the scoring process. *Predetermined scores.*

It is interesting to note that with regard to the first essential criterion of objective measurement (consistent measurement of individual differences) self-report personality/affective measures tend to have special difficulties when compared to tests that measure various forms of cognitive functioning, such as intelligence and achievement tests (Anastasi & Urbina, 1997). Part of the problem with the greater difficulty in obtaining high reliability coefficients on personality or behavioral measures is that social and emotional behavior in humans tends to be less stable or predictable than human cognitive functioning (F. G. Brown, 1983). A second potential reason for psychometric problems on self-report tests noted by Brown is that these tests have all too often been accepted uncritically or used for purposes for which they were not intended. Given the differences in predictability between social-emotional and cognitive functioning in humans, the psychometric gap between the two areas may be reduced in time, but perhaps never closed. According to Anastasi and Urbina (1997):

problems

> The behavior measured by personality tests is also more changeable over time than that measured by tests of ability. The latter fact complicates the determination of test reliability, since random temporal fluctuations in test performance are less likely to become confused with broad, systematic behavioral changes. Even over relatively short intervals, it cannot be assumed that variations in test responses are restricted to the test itself and do not

characterize the area of nontest behavior under consideration. A related problem is the greater situational specificity of responses in the noncognitive than in the cognitive domain. (p. 385).

Three Approaches to Developing Objective Tests

Experts in the field of personality assessment are in agreement that the number of approaches for constructing objective self-report tests is quite small, with most experts listing only three categories of test construction methods. In this regard, the only variable that differs to any significant extent is the name assigned to each category or type of approach. For a further analysis of the basic types of test construction categories and names, readers are referred to works by Anastasi (1988), Anastasi and Urbina (1997), Gregory (1996), Lanyon and Goodstein (1984, 1997), and Goldberg (1974). In the present text, the names assigned to the three basic categories of objective test construction include the *rational-theoretical* approach, the *factor analytic* approach, and the *empirical criterion keying* approach.

Rational-Theoretical Approach. The rational-theoretical approach to developing self-report tests involves the assumption by the test developer that a given set of personality traits and behavioral correlates can be measured by developing a set of items or scales that logically appear to fit within the definitions for those traits and behaviors. If the test developer simply uses their own ideas about what constitutes appropriate items or scales, the test is said to be *intuitively* developed. If the test developer uses the judgments of experts in developing and selecting items, the process is referred to as a *content validation* method. The development process is said to be *theory based* if the construction of items or scales is done according to a recognized theory of personality or personal social-emotional functioning.

The rational-theoretical approach can be illustrated using the example of developing a self-report test for measuring depression. Test developers might generate a list of items that they believe represent the construct of depression (intuitive), ask a group of mental health professionals to evaluate or generate potential items thought to measure depression (content validation), or develop potential items based on how closely they concur with an accepted theory of depression (theory based). In reality, these rational-theoretical test construction methods are often used in conjunction with each other. And, in many cases, an objective measure is initially developed using rational-theoretical methods and then subjected to other forms of developmental validation.

The main advantage of the rational-theoretical approach is that if the item and scale development proceeds thoughtfully, the end result is a group of items or scales that have strong face validity and appear to be psychologically meaningful and theoretically unified. The main disadvantage of this approach is that, regardless of how much face validity they may appear to have, the resulting items or scales may not necessarily have acceptable psychometric properties or be able to differentiate between normal and abnormal behavior.

Factor Analytic Approach. This approach to test construction is characterized by reliance on a sophisticated group of statistical procedures referred to as factor analysis or principle components analysis to sort and arrange individual test items into groups that are mathematically related. These clusters are referred to as factors. Presumably, the arrangement of test items into statistically related groups allows for more precise measurement and interpretation of various personality or behavioral constructs. Normally, the test developer also utilizes a rational-theoretical approach in developing the test items prior to subjecting them to factor analysis and subsequent interpretation.

Chapter 4 provided several examples of how factor analytic procedures were used in the development of some of the most commonly used behavior rating scales, and how the obtained factor solutions are commonly interpreted. The same general procedures and practices are also true of factor analytic approaches to the development of self-report measures. An example of a well-known objective personality test for adults that employs factor analytic procedures is Cattell's 16PF Questionnaire (Cattell, Eber, & Tatsuoka, 1970). Additionally, virtually all individually administered tests of cognitive ability (such as the Wechsler and Stanford–Binet scales, the Woodcock–Johnson Psychoeducational Battery, and the Kauffman Assessment Batteries) rely on factor analytic procedures to group subtests into interpretable factors or area scores. Increasingly, test developers are not only using factor analytic techniques, but employing the added sophistication of more recently developed techniques of confirming or testing the models created through exploratory factor analysis by using structural equation modeling, covariance structure analysis, and similar methods of confirming or testing existing structures.

The major advantage of the factor analytic approach is that it is capable of producing mathematically precise groups of items, and thus may bring a high degree of scientific precision to self-report measurement of behavioral, social, and emotional characteristics. This mathematical sophistication can also be a disadvantage. Even among psychologists who have received graduate training in measurement and psychometrics, very few have the skills to understand the nuances of factor analysis and make consistently good decisions on factor analytic test data produced by computer programs. Factor analysis is difficult to understand and even more difficult to adequately implement in the development of a clinical test. The use of more recent statistical methods for testing or confirming factor structures presents additional challenges for clinicians and researchers who are not conversant in the latest statistical thinking (Crowley & Fan, 1997). And, if the test items themselves are poorly constructed, then the mathematical sophistication offered by factor analysis will be of little use in making the test useful, and may only confuse matters. It is not unusual to find test items in the same factor that do not appear to have a great deal of clinical similarity based on their face validity. Thus, factor analysis cannot enhance a test that was poorly constructed in the first place. As the old adage goes, "garbage in, garbage out."

③ *comparing traits of 2 known groups.*

Empirical Criterion Keying Approach. Anastasi and Urbina (1997) referred to the third major objective test construction method as empirical criterion keying. This term alludes to the development of scoring keys in terms of some external criterion. The manner in which this procedure is actually implemented typically involves administering a large number of test items to two groups of persons who are known to differ in some psychologically meaningful way (e.g., those who are clinically depressed and those who are not clinically depressed, or those who have conduct disorders and those who do not have conduct disorders). After the pool of items is administered, they are analyzed to determine which items reliably discriminate or differentiate between the two groups. The discriminating items are then considered to be a scale that is used in predicting or classifying membership in the particular groups. Of course, the pool of items that are initially administered to the two groups are not just random descriptions of behavior; typically, they are carefully developed and selected using rational-theoretical construction methods.

The actual steps in the empirical criterion keying approach are more complex than this brief description might indicate. Readers interested in learning more about the specific steps in empirical criterion keying are referred to more thorough descriptions found in general texts on psychological test construction. Some of the most widely used and influential self-report measures (such as the various versions of the MMPI and the Millon inventories) are based on the empirical criterion keying approach.

The major strength of the empirical criterion keying approach is that it relies on the empirical properties of particular test items or scales rather than the presumed clinical expertise of the test developer or the observed behavior of the person who takes the test. With this approach, the clinical implications of the actual contents of items is less important than the fact that the items are known to meaningfully "sort" among different groups of persons. For example, if the item "I do not sleep well at night" is found to differentiate between persons who are highly anxious and those who are not, it is not actually known whether the anxious individuals have trouble sleeping. The important consideration is that they report not sleeping well, and this discriminates them from nonanxious persons. Of course, the empirical criterion keying approach also has a number of drawbacks. R. P. Martin (1988) reported that the scales of many tests constructed in this fashion do not have high internal consistency. Another problem to consider is the precision with which different diagnostic groups used to develop scales were selected in the first place. For example, if the tests or other selection procedures used to identify depressed and nondepressed persons are unreliable or are only reliable within specific geographical and cultural constraints, then the utility of an empirical criterion keying scale that will differentiate these groups is suspect.

Response Bias and Error Variance

Although each of the three major forms of objective test construction have some advantages and disadvantages, trying to determine the "best" method is typically not a fruitful endeavor. In fact, there have been some empirical attempts to answer this question (Burisch, 1984; Hase & Goldberg, 1967), which have concluded that the psychometric properties and validity evidence of individual tests are more important markers of their usefulness than the method employed in their construction. And, regardless of the approach or method to test construction, objective self-report measures are invariably subject to some degree of *response bias* on the part of the examinee, a phenomenon that leads to *error variance*.

Error variance has been defined by R. P. Martin (1988) as "variation of responses that is uncorrelated with the trait being assessed and with any nontest behavior of interest" (p. 60). This problem is created by the response bias of the examinee, which can be defined as either conscious or unconscious attempts to respond to items in particular directions or to create a specific type of impression. So, response bias may be either deliberate or unconscious on the part of the examinee, but it can have the effect of increasing the error present in the assessment.

Response bias can take several forms. One of the most well researched is *acquiescence*, which is a tendency of some test takers to answer true/false or yes/no items consistently in one direction. Acquiescence is particularly a problem when test items are ambiguous or unclear. A common method of attempting to control for acquiescence involves developing items and scales so that there are equal numbers of true/false or yes/no responses keyed into specific scales. Another well-known type of response bias is referred to as the *social desirability response set*. This term refers to the conscious or unconscious tendency of most test takers to endorse items in a socially desirable direction. For example, virtually all test takers faced with the statement "boys and girls should both be treated equally and fairly by teachers" would answer "true," regardless of their personal awareness or convictions regarding sexism, gender roles, and public policy. It is interesting that both well-adjusted and poorly adjusted persons tend to respond to items in the socially desirable direction, and their responses are usually indicative of their true behavior or feelings (R. P. Martin, 1988). Therefore, it is difficult to gauge how much, if any, error variance is created through this response set.

Another form of response bias is *faking*, which involves deliberate attempts by test takers to manipulate or distort their responses to test items in order to create a particular impression. Faking usually takes the direction of manipulation to create a favorable or positive impression (e.g., a test taker applying for a job, or a person accused of a crime undergoing pretrial assessment), but it can also involve deliberate distortion by the examinee to create a negative impression or exaggerate their psychopathology (e.g., a "cry for help" or malingering). Several adolescent and adult self-report instruments incorporate sophisticated methods for detecting faking. The most notable example is the MMPI and its predecessors, with the various validity scales that are designed to detect falsification, random answering, defensiveness, and related styles of deliberate distortion. Some of the more recently developed self-report tests for children (e.g., the BASC self-report scales) include lie or fake detection scales, but these efforts are generally not as well researched or understood as are scales used with adults. *some reports can test for faking, distortion, etc.)·*

Another type of response bias is *deviation*, or the tendency to answer test items in unusual or unconventional ways. The deviation hypothesis was proposed by I. A. Berg (1967), who argued that deviation in test responses is content free, and can be found on either verbal or nonverbal tasks. Little is known about deviation as a form of response bias, and it is unclear how it contributes to error variance in self-report testing.

It has thus far been demonstrated that several forms of response bias exist in testing, and they may contribute to the error variance found in a given assessment situation. Test construction methods can potentially include efforts to reduce or control response bias. But what is the probable overall effect of response bias? Whereas response bias in self-report assessment continues to be a problem, Anastasi (1988) contended that some aspects of it may be "a tempest in a teapot" (p. 554). Perhaps the best solution to reducing error variance through response bias is to make systematic efforts to detect response styles and response sets, and then evaluate the examinee's responses to individual test items in terms of their motivations, cognitive ability, and social-emotional status. *— maybe look @ response styles systematically?*

REVIEWS OF SELECTED GENERAL PURPOSE SELF-REPORT TESTS

Chapters 9 through 12 include reviews and comments regarding several self-report tests for children and adolescents that are designed for assessing specific types of behavioral and emotional problems. Several psychometrically sound and clinically useful self-report instruments for children and adolescents have been developed for assessing specific theoretical constructs and types of problems, such as depression, anxiety, social competence, and self-concept. Until very recently, there have been very

general purpose self-reports

few general purpose self-report tests for children and youth that meet the criteria of acceptable psychometric and technical properties (see Merrell, 1994a). With regard to the preadolescent age group (i.e., age 8–11), the dearth of good general purpose self-report measures has been particularly noticeable. However, recent research and development efforts in this arena have been encouraging. The number of technically sound and useful general purpose self-report instruments developed for use by children and adolescents has increased during the 1990s from barely a handful to several.

This section includes descriptions, technical information, and evaluative comments regarding eight general purpose self-report instruments, including the child and adolescent self-report forms of the Behavior Assessment for Children, Millon Adolescent Personality Inventory, Millon Adolescent Clinical Inventory, Minnesota Multiphasic Personality Inventory (original and adolescent versions), Personality Inventory for Youth, and Youth Self-Report. These measures were each included for review here because they represent the best of what is available in the area of self-report instruments. Each test is recommended, but they are useful for various purposes. Thus, this section provides a framework for selecting among several potentially useful measures by comparing their strengths and weaknesses.

① BASC

Behavior Assessment System for Children: Child and Adolescent Self-Reports

Description. The Behavior Assessment System for Children (BASC; C. R. Reynolds & Kamphaus, 1992), a comprehensive system of child and adolescent assessment instruments, was discussed in chapter 4, and is addressed to some extent in other chapters as well. Of interest here are two self-report instruments that are part of the system: the self-report for children from age 8 to 11 (SRP–C), and the self-report for adolescents from age 12 to 18 (SRP–A). These two self-report measures, like the behavior rating scales of the BASC, are comprehensive instruments that include a variety of items and scales reflecting clinical problems, interpersonal adjustment, and adaptive competencies. The SRP–C includes 152 items, whereas the SRP–A includes 186 items. Many of the items on these two instruments are similar, but they were obviously developed specifically for differing age and developmental groups rather than being just slightly reworded. Thus, they can be considered separate instruments, although they share many common features.

The SRP–C and SRP–A take approximately 30 minutes to complete in most situations. Audiotapes are available to help youths complete the tests who have limited English reading ability but who can understand the spoken language. All SPR items are rated T (True) or F (False) by the examinee. The forms are scored using scoring forms that tear off from the rating forms after they are completed. Raw scores are converted to various Clinical Maladjustment, School Maladjustment (Other Problems), and Personal Adjustment scales, as well as a composite Emotional Symptoms Index (a global index of emotional distress), which are based on a *T*-score system. The Composites and Scales of the two SRP forms are shown in Table 7.1. In addition to the SRP scale scores, these instruments both include various validity scales. Both forms include an *F index*, a "fake bad" index that is designed to detect abnormally high levels of symptom endorsement, as well as a *V index*, consisting of nonsensical items like "I drink 60 glasses of milk a day" to help detect random responding or failure to understand the directions. The SRP–A also includes an *L index* designed to detect "faking good" or a social desirability response set.

TABLE 7.1
Composites and Scales of the Child and Adolescent Versions of the
Self-Report Form of the Behavior Assessment System for Children

Composite/Scale	Child (SRP–C)	Adolescent (SRP–A)
Clinical Maladjustment	X	X
Anxiety	X	X
Atypicality	X	X
Locus of control	X	X
Social stress	X	X
Somatization		X
School Maladjustment	X	X
Attitude to school	X	X
Attitude to teachers	X	X
Sensation seeking		X
(Other Problems)		
Depression	X	X
Sense of inadequacy	X	X
Personal Adjustment	X	X
Relations with parents	X	X
Interpersonal relations	X	X
Self-esteem	X	X
Self-reliance	X	X
Emotional Symptoms Index	X	X

Technical Characteristics. The highly detailed and well-written BASC manual provides extensive information regarding the development, standardization, and supporting empirical base for the BASC. The standardization samples for both the SRP–C (5,413) and SRP–A (4,448) are extremely large, geographically diverse, and reasonably similar to the general U.S. population in terms of racial/ethnic group, socioeconomic status, and special education participation. Additional clinical norm samples for both forms were obtained to assist in validity research.

Internal consistency reliability coefficients of the SRP forms are very high, with data from the standardization sample showing median alpha coefficients for the scale scores in the low .80 range, and median coefficients for the composite scores in the mid .80 to mid .90 range. Test–retest reliability of both scales was evaluated with medium size subsamples at 0- to 1-month intervals. The resulting stability coefficients ranged from .57 to .81 and .67 to .83 for the child and adolescent version scale scores, respectively, and from .78 to .84 and .81 to .86 for the composite scores, respectively. Predictably, longer term stability of the self-report forms is lower. One study is reported in the BASC manual wherein the SRP–C was administered to a group of children at 7-month retest intervals. In this case, the range of scale score retest coefficients was .36 to .66, and the range of composite score coefficients was .38 to .69.

Various types of validity evidence for the SRPs are presented in the BASC manual, including extensive factorial validity and covariance structure analysis studies, convergent and discriminant validity correlations with scores from the MMPI, Youth Self-Report, Behavior Rating Profile, and Children's Personality Questionnaire. Additionally, mean scores of seven clinical group samples (conduct disorder, behavior disorder, depression, emotional disturbance, attention deficit hyperactivity disorder, learning disability, and mild mental retardation) who completed the SRP–C or SRP–A are presented, with the results providing construct validity evidence regarding sensitivity to theory-based group differences.

The only externally published empirical study regarding the self-report forms of the BASC was conducted by Dalton (1996), who used the SRP–C with a small group of male sex offenders, and failed to find any atypical score patterns on any of the scales. This study by itself should not raise substantial questions regarding validity of the SRP–C, given the very small sample size and other methodological limitations.

Evaluation. The SRP–C and SRP–A are both exemplary self-report instruments in every respect, and constitute much needed additions to the arsenal of available assessment tools. The SRP–C, in particular, filled a tremendous void because before its publication there was virtually no psychometrically adequate general purpose self-report instruments for children from age 8 to 11. Even though the SPR–A did not fill as large a void for adolescent self-report instruments because several other good quality measures are in existence, it is definitely a positive addition, and it should be seriously considered against such instruments as the MAPI, MACI, MMPI–A, PIY, and YSR. The self-report forms of the BASC are practical, easy to use, psychometrically strong, and have many other positive qualities to support them. Even though the externally published research base for these measures is very small to nonexistent at the present time, the very extensive supporting technical evidence in the BASC manual should give practitioners and researchers confidence in using the SRP–C and SRP–A for a variety of purposes.

Millon Adolescent Personality Inventory

Description. The Millon Adolescent Personality Inventory (MAPI; Millon, Green, & Meagher, 1982) is a 150-item true–false format test for use with adolescents from age 13 to 19. The test was designed to assess and predict a wide range of psychological characteristics of adolescents. The MAPI includes 20 subscales that are located along three basic dimensions, including *Personality Style, Expressed Concerns,* and *Behavioral Correlates.* The eight subscales that comprise the Personality Style dimension are based on Millon's (1969, 1981) theory of personality, which is built on the notion that personality styles consist of combinations of reactive and proactive behavior patterns (e.g., passive detached, active detached). The Expressed Concern dimension also includes eight subscales, and appears to measure various developmental concerns of adolescents. The Behavioral Correlates dimension consists of empirically derived scales that were developed to discriminate between the probability of membership in various troubled or clinical groups of youth. The three dimensions of the MAPI with the corresponding subscales are shown in Table 7.2. The MAPI also includes three validity measures: a reliability index based on responses to three items that directly inquire about how honestly or attentively the subject is completing the test, a validity index based on three nonsensical items that is designed to detect random responding, and an adjustment score that alters the scores on either the Expressed Concern or Personality Style dimensions. Raw scores are converted to Base Rate (cutoff) scores, rather than standard scores, based on the test authors' theory that the dimensional scores are not normally distributed. Separate norms are used for males and females, and for younger (age 13–15) and older (age 16–18) subjects.

The test protocol is completed on a NCS response form, and all scoring and interpretation are done through NCS computerized scoring procedures. Hand-scoring

TABLE 7.2
Dimensions and Scales of the Millon Adolescent Personality Inventory

Personality Styles
Introversive
Inhibited
Cooperative
Sociable
Confident
Forceful
Respectful
Sensitive
Expressed Concerns
Self-concept
Personal esteem
Body comfort
Sexual acceptance
Peer security
Social tolerance
Family rapport
Academic confidence
Behavioral Correlates
Impulse control
Societal conformity
Scholastic achievement
Attendance consistency

keys are not available at the present time. Prepaid mail-in scoring sheets are available from NCS in both clinical and guidance forms. The guidance form is designed for use in counseling with an adolescent, and the clinical form provides more detailed interpretative information for clinicians. In addition to mail-in scoring, the MAPI can be scored and interpretive reports generated on-site using special NCS software, or through the use of uploading and downloading software and a modem. Regardless of the method of scoring and report generation utilized, the MAPI is relatively expensive. When purchased in small quantities, test scoring and clinical interpretive reports cost $22.50 to $23.50 each, whereas scoring and guidance interpretive reports cost $12.50 each (these prices are based on information from the 1998 NCS catalogue).

Technical Characteristics. The test manual for the MAPI is well written and comprehensive. Normative data for the MAPI were obtained from a sample of over 2,000 subjects. The manual includes both test–retest and internal consistency reliability data, with subtest reliabilities ranging from .45 to .84, and most in the low .60s to upper .70s. Concurrent validity data between the MAPI and other personality tests (i.e., the California Psychological Inventory, 16PF test, and Edwards Personal Preference Schedule) indicate adequate to strong relations between particular MAPI subscales and various subscales for the other tests. The test manual also includes factor analytic data via an intercorrelation matrix of the test's subscales. More recent external validity research for the MAPI includes studies showing specific score patterns and levels among adolescents with disruptive behavior disorders and among inpatient adolescents with substance abuse problems (L. R. Hart, 1993, 1995), significant relations and differing diagnostic patterns in comparison to MMPI scores (Johnson, Archer, Sheaffer, & Miller, 1992), and effectiveness as a treatment outcome measure (Piersma, Pantle, A. Smith, & Boes, 1993).

Evaluation. The MAPI has many strong points, and can be recommended for use as a personality assessment instrument for research and guidance work with adolescents, specifically normal (nonclinical) youths, the population for which this test was developed. The test takes approximately 20 minutes to complete, is written at about a sixth-grade reading level, and consists of language that most adolescents should be able to relate to and understand. The development and publication of the MAPI was an important development in the area of adolescent personality assessment, given that it was one of the first comprehensive personality assessment instruments utilizing modern measurement technology and psychometric standards that was developed specifically for use with adolescents.

Although the MAPI can be recommended for use and has many strengths, it also has some potential drawbacks. One of the chief (and perhaps most annoying) complaints about the MAPI is that it can be scored only by National Computer Systems mail-in service or special scoring software. The lack of hand scoring keys has probably inhibited external research efforts as well as more widespread use of the test. The sole reliance on the MAPI report is a problem given that interpretations are primarily based on deductive inference, and not so much on actuarial prediction and empirical evidence. Although there has been concern that the empirical evidence for many of the MAPI subscales is weak (Lanyon, 1984), and its commercial production preceded adequate empirical evaluation (Widiger, 1985), it is also true that the external research base on the MAPI has grown substantially since these criticisms were first registered. Therefore, the MAPI appears to have withstood the test of time, and the quantity and quality of evidence supporting it is strong.

Millon Adolescent Clinical Inventory

Description. The Millon Adolescent Clinical Inventory (MACI; Millon, 1993) is a more recently developed companion instrument to the MAPI. Whereas the MAPI was developed for assessment of personality in normal adolescents, the MACI was designed with a more clinical focus. Although it shares many features in common with the MAPI (from which it evolved), the MACI was normed specifically with clinical samples, and includes clinical scales aligned to *DSM–IV* diagnostic categories and areas that the MAPI does not include. It was designed to be used for adolescent assessment, treatment planning, and progress monitoring in outpatient, inpatient, or residential treatment settings.

The MACI includes 160 items written at about a sixth-grade reading level. For most adolescents with the requisite reading ability, this test takes approximately 30 minutes to complete. The MACI scales, which appear to have been developed through various construction methods, are based on a combination of clinical diagnostic categories and personality patterns from Millon's comprehensive theory of personality. The MACI scales, illustrated in Table 7.3, are built within the areas of *Personality Patterns*, *Expressed Concerns*, *Clinical Syndromes*, and *Modifying Indices*. Additionally, a reliability scale is provided to detect consistency in responding.

Unlike the MAPI, the MACI can be hand scored using scoring keys available from the publisher. And like the MAPI, mail-in or on-site software scoring of the MACI is also available, at a cost (from the 1998 NCS catalogue) of $12.50 for a basic Profile Report, and $21.95 for a more comprehensive Clinical Interpretive Report. MACI scores are based on gender and age group (13–15 and 16–19) breakdowns.

TABLE 7.3
Dimensions and Scales of the Millon Adolescent Clinical Inventory

Personality Patterns
  Introversive
  Inhibited
  Doleful
  Submissive
  Dramatizing
  Egotistic
  Unruly
  Forceful
  Conforming
  Oppositional
  Self-demeaning
  Borderline tendency
Expressed Concerns
  Identity diffusion
  Self-devaluation
  Body disapproval
  Sexual discomfort
  Peer insecurity
  Social insensitivity
  Family discord
  Childhood abuse
Clinical Syndromes
  Eating dysfunctions
  Substance abuse proneness
  Delinquent predisposition
  Impulsive propensity
  Anxious feelings
  Depressive affect
  Suicidal tendency
Modifying Indices
  Disclosure
  Desirability
  Debasement

Technical Characteristics. The MACI was standardized with 1,107 subjects from age 13 to 19 in 28 U.S. states and Canada. As mentioned earlier, the standardization sample was based entirely on clinical samples from various treatment settings. Cross-validation samples were also constructed from the normative data for developing the final reliability/validity statistics and for cross-validating base rate conversions for MACI scores. Research presented in the MACI manual, though relatively limited in scope, provides evidence of acceptable reliability and validity, as well as basic support for the scale structure. Unfortunately, there has been very little external validity evidence published to date. A computer-assisted search of the literature resulted in the location of only one published study using the MACI, an investigation of MACI score profiles of inpatient adolescents with and without substance abuse problems (Grilo, Fehon, Walker, & Martino, 1996). This study found that the substance abusing sample had differing MACI score patterns from the other inpatient sample with regard to greater delinquent characteristics, lower levels of anxiety, and some related features.

comprehensive assessment

Evaluation. The MACI appears to have great potential as a comprehensive self-report clinical assessment instrument for use with adolescents. The particular strength of this test is that is was developed specifically for use with clinical issues and with troubled or disturbed youths. Therefore, clinicians and researchers working with clinical populations may find the MACI to be particularly useful. Some of the same criticisms that were made of the MAPI shortly after its publication in the early 1980s appear to be true of the MACI at the present time, particularly the lack of extensive externally published empirical evidence. However, the evidence in the test manual, the reputation of the MACI author, and the mounting evidence supporting the MAPI certainly bolster confidence in the MACI. It is likely that within the next several years the MACI will become a widely used and solidly supported self-report instrument.

MMPI and MMPI–A

The Minnesota Multiphasic Personality Inventory (MMPI) in its various versions and editions has for many years been the most widely used objective self-report measure of adult personality and psychopathology in the world. Its clinical applications, research uses, and psychometric properties have been the subject of thousands of published research studies and dozens (if not hundreds) of widely read professional books. It is arguably the most widely used and researched psychological assessment instrument of any type in existence. A computer-assisted search of the MMPI literature conducted in early 1998 resulted in an astounding number of entries—nearly 8,000! Given that entire volumes have been devoted to the description, development, uses, and properties of the MMPI, this section only briefly focuses on uses of the original MMPI and the 1992 adolescent version of the instrument (MMPI–A) as they apply to the assessment of adolescents. Readers who desire more complete information on the various versions of the MMPI (i.e., the original MMPI and the MMPI–2) are referred to the many volumes devoted specifically to the instrument, especially the excellent books by Archer (1987, 1992, 1996), Ben-Porath (1996), Butcher (1990, 1992), J. R. Graham (1987, 1990), and Greene (1980, 1991). Because the MMPI is such a vast and complex topic, this description and evaluative review follows a different format than what is used for the other instruments covered in this chapter.

Development of Various Versions of the MMPI. The original MMPI was first published in 1943 as a paper-and-pencil test for use in diagnostic personality assessment with adults. The authors of the MMPI utilized the empirical criterion keying method, a new technique at that time, in developing the various validity and clinical scales. As time went on, the MMPI with its 566 true/false statements became very widely used, and as previously mentioned, has been the subject of scores of research reports and books. In addition to these basic validity and clinical scales of this instrument, numerous additional scales have been developed for the MMPI, ranging from those being highly experimental in nature to those being widely used and researched. Perhaps the most commonly used of these additional scales have been the 21 supplementary scales and the 28 Harris–Lingoes subscales.

By the late 1970s, it became apparent that in spite of the tremendous body of validation literature that had evolved on the MMPI, it was in need of a revision and restandardization. There were two main concerns that drove this need. First, the original 1943 MMPI normative group, though exemplary for its time, did not meet modern standards for test development. The original normative group consisted of 724 persons who were visiting friends or relatives at the University of Minnesota Hospitals in Minneapolis, and this group was very racially, socioeconomically, culturally, and geographically homogenous. The second major concern involved problems with the MMPI item content. Some of the language and many of the references in the 566 statements had become obsolete and archaic, many of the original items used sexist language, and a number of items were considered to be objectionable for reasons such as focusing on bowel and bladder functions, Christian religious beliefs, and sexual behavior. There was also a lack of items in areas considered important in modern personality assessment, such as suicide gestures/ideation, alcohol and other drug use, and treatment-related behaviors. The MMPI revision process was conducted during the 1980s, and the revised and restandardized instrument (the MMPI–2) was published in 1989. Although retaining the same basic validity and clinical scale configurations as the MMPI, the MMPI–2 included a large representative normative sample, as well as numerous changes in item wording and content.

The original MMPI had become widely used with adolescents, but the MMPI–2 was never intended to be used with this group. During the same general time period that the MMPI–2 project was conducted, separate adolescent norms were gathered using an experimental restandardization booklet, and additional research and development efforts continued on the uses of the MMPI with adolescents for some time. In late 1992, 3 years after the publication of the MMPI–2, the Minnesota Multiphasic Personality Inventory–Adolescent (MMPI–A) was published. It was the first version of the MMPI designed specifically for use with adolescents. ↳standardized for adolescents too!

Use of the Original MMPI With Adolescents. Although the original MMPI was designed to bc used with adults, it has a long history of clinical and research applications with adolescents. The MMPI was administered to large groups of adolescents in Minnesota as early as 1947 (Hathaway & Monachesi, 1963), and a large number of research studies were published in the 1960s, 1970s, and 1980s detailing specific empirical findings and clinical applications of the instrument with adolescent populations (e.g., Archer & Gordon, 1988; Ball, 1962; Baughman & Dahlstrom, 1968; Ehrenworth & Archer, 1985; Marks, Seeman, & Haller, 1974; Rutter, P. Graham, Chadwick, & Yule, 1976). Most comprehensive books on the MMPI include sections on its applications with adolescent populations (e.g., J. R. Graham, 1987, 1990; Greene, 1991), and several chapters in edited works on the MMPI have detailed the uses of the instrument with adolescents (e.g., Reilley, 1988; C. L. Williams, 1985). Perhaps the most comprehensive treatment of the use of the original MMPI with adolescents was Archer's (1987) *Using the MMPI with Adolescents.* In addition to the numerous research reports and books that have dealt with the MMPI and adolescents, a number of test publishing and scoring companies have offered products such as special adolescent MMPI profile forms and interpretative score reports. In sum, although the MMPI was intended primarily for use with adults, there can be no doubt that it has been used and investigated with adolescent populations more than any self-report instruments developed to date specifically for use with adolescents, including the more recent MMPI–A.

Although the uses of the MMPI with adolescents have a strong historical and empirical basis, there are numerous potential problems that may be encountered along the way. As Archer (1987) noted, the MMPI is at the same time the most widely used and widely abused personality inventory for adolescents.

Perhaps the key to understanding and preventing the misuse of the MMPI (and to some extent, other self-report tests) with adolescent clients is to develop a strong understanding of normal adolescent development. Archer (1987) stated that there are

Factors to consider when admin. MMPI to

three essential developmental factors that must be considered when the MMPI is administered to adolescents:

adolescents ?

1. *Cognitive changes.* Piaget observed that most children move from the concrete operations stage of cognitive development to the formal operations stage between the ages of about 11 and 13. The emergence of formal operational thinking allows for abstract reasoning, formal logic, and advanced symbolism. Many of the items on the MMPI may be answered differently by individuals simply based on their level of cognitive development. Two examples of such MMPI items are "My father was a good man" and "I loved my father." If adolescent clients completing the MMPI are still in the concrete operations stage, then they are likely to interpret the past-tense meanings of the words "was" and "loved" on a very concrete level, perhaps not knowing how to answer the items if their father is still alive.

2. *Physical and sexual maturation.* Adolescence is a time of great physical change, and it is not unusual for the adolescent years to include gains in height and body weight of 25% and 100%, respectively. Some of the questions on the MMPI must be considered within this context of rapid physical change. For example, the item "I am neither losing nor gaining weight" when endorsed negatively (false), appears on the MMPI Depression scale. And yet, it would be expected that an adolescent would answer "false" to this item because of the weight gains that typically occur. A related area is sexual maturation. As children reach puberty and enter into adolescence, they are likely to be preoccupied with their sexual maturation and they may not be entirely comfortable with it. Thus, typical adolescent responses to MMPI items dealing with sexuality may be different in character from those of typical adults.

3. *Emotional and social changes.* In Western culture, adolescence is often accompanied by a period of increasing independence from the family, increased attention to the peer group, and perhaps greater emotional lability. Eriksen (1963) referred to this social-emotional transition as an identity versus role confusion crisis; the adolescent typically begins to deal with internal questions such as "who am I?" and "what do I want out of life?" This period has been viewed by many as a time of great emotional turmoil. Thus, MMPI items that refer to conflict with family (e.g., "No one seems to understand me," and "My relatives are all in sympathy") or emotional intensity (e.g., "At times I feel like smashing things," and "Often I can't understand why I have been so cross and/or grouchy") may be answered differently by typical adolescents than typical adults, simply as a function of normal developmental changes.

The three developmental areas of adolescence noted by Archer (1987) provide some clear examples of why clinicians should exercise caution in administering the MMPI to young clients. Additionally, Reilley (1988) suggested that because adolescence often involves extreme sensitivity to what others think, conflicts with authority, and unresolved self-concept issues, young subjects may approach the test-taking task in a defensive or uncooperative manner. Using these potential issues as examples, it is easy to see the possibility of a young client faking good or faking bad on the MMPI to either present themselves in a particular manner or to obstruct the validity of the testing altogether. Therefore, clinicians who use the MMPI with adolescent clients must be constantly aware of the potential effects of normal adolescent development on MMPI responses, and should remain vigilant for threats to test validity.

Given the numerous challenges faced in administering the MMPI to adolescent subjects and then appropriately interpreting their MMPI profiles, how should one go about this process? The first step is deciding whether it is appropriate to administer the MMPI to an adolescent client. Given Archer's (1987) comments on developmental cognitive changes that occur during adolescence, an attempt should be made to discern whether the adolescent client is still cognitively functioning on a concrete level. This decision can usually be made by reviewing current school records, or by directly interviewing the client. Archer (1988) suggested that the MMPI should never be administered to a subject who has an IQ score below 70, and for adolescents this criterion appears to be almost too liberal. The reading level of the subject should also be taken into account. J. R. Graham (1990) estimated that effective completion of the MMPI–2 requires about an eighth-grade reading level. It can be assumed that the original MMPI items require a similar level of reading competence, if not slightly higher, due to some of the dated language they contain. Therefore, if an adolescent subject cannot read at about an eighth-grade level, then the MMPI should not normally be administered to them. The reading level of the client can be estimated by reviewing recent academic testing records or administering brief formal or informal reading screens to the client prior to the MMPI administration. Archer (1988) suggested that having clients read a few of the MMPI items and the directions out loud is an easy way to determine if their reading level is high enough to take the test.

Once the decision has been made to administer the MMPI to an adolescent client, examiners should make themselves available to answer questions that may arise during the testing, and should provide clear directions to the subject. Archer (1988) suggested that the adolescent client simply be told that the MMPI is a widely used test with many questions, and that they simply be instructed "I'd like you to take a test which will tell us a little bit about yourself and how we can help you."

In terms of interpreting the adolescent profile, a number of procedures have been researched and suggested, but perhaps the most advisable procedures are those proposed by Archer (1987), who recommended the following four steps:

1. Examine the completed protocol for unanswered items and unusual response sets in order to determine if it is a valid profile.

2. Sum the raw score values for each scale using standard scoring procedures.

3. Convert the raw score totals to *T*-scores by using supplementary adolescent norm tables that are found in books by Archer (1987), J. R. Graham (1990), and others. Make sure the conversion table is age and gender appropriate. The supplementary adolescent norms do not include *K*-corrections.

4. If scores are plotted on adult profile sheets, do not use *K*-correction procedures or *T*-score conversion based on adult norms. Special adolescent MMPI plotting sheets have been developed and are available through various assessment materials catalogues.

Given that the use of adolescent norms without *K*-corrections will result in lower *T*-scores, and thus increase the possibility of *false-negative* error, Archer (1987) suggested that 65 be considered a critical *T*-score value (the lower limit of the abnormal range on a given scale) rather than the traditional value of 70, if the recommended adolescent scoring procedure is followed. To conduct a comprehensive interpretation of the obtained MMPI scale scores, the use of MMPI code type comparisons rather than simple evaluations of individual MMPI scale score levels is recommended. MMPI interpretation based on code types is beyond the scope of this chapter, and the reader is thus referred to Archer (1987), Butcher (1990), J. R. Graham (1987, 1990), and Green (1980, 1991).

The MMPI–A. In 1992, National Computer Systems released the long-awaited adolescent version of the MMPI, the MMPI–A. Although the original MMPI had been used for many years with adolescents, the MMPI–A was the first version of the test designed specifically for this age group.

The MMPI–A contains 478 true/false items, a reduction of nearly 100 from the MMPI and MMPI–2. The items in the MMPI–A are based on the original MMPI, but with items, scales, and norms specific to the adolescent population included. These new items cover areas considered critical in adolescent assessment, such as alcohol and other drug use, school adjustment problems, family conflict, and maladaptive eating behavior. As in the case of the MMPI–2 revision, several of the items of the MMPI–A that were retained from the original MMPI were reworded to make them more applicable and contemporary. The MMPI–A was designed specifically for use with adolescents from age 14 to 18, and the new norms reflect this age group composition. These norms are based on a representative nationwide sample of 805 boys and 815 girls in the 14- to 18-year age range. Additionally, a clinical sample of 420 boys and 293 girls from age 14 to 18 was obtained, recruited from clinical treatment facilities in Minnesota. As is the case with the MMPI and MMPI–2, the adolescent version of the instrument includes separate norms for males and females, and utilizes a T-score system.

Many of the features of the original MMPI were retained in the MMPI–A, such as the L and K validity indicators, and slightly revised versions of the F validity scale and the basic clinical scales. However, a number of significant changes in scale structure are found on the MMPI–A, including some new validity scales and 15 new "content" scales that were developed to reflect content that is highly specific to adolescent concerns and problems. In addition to the basic validity-clinical scales and the content scales, the MMPI–A includes several supplementary scales and 27 Harris–Lingoes subscales that are quite similar to those developed for the MMPI and MMPI–2. The basic and content scale breakdown of the MMPI–A is presented in Table 7.4. Like the MMPI and MMPI–2, the MMPI–A can be hand scored using answer keys or may be scored on-site or through prepaid mailers with computer software from NCS that also generates interpretive reports. An interesting and useful change in the MMPI–A from the MMPI is that uniform T-scores across eight of the clinical scales (the exceptions being Mf and Si) and the content scales are provided for percentile ranking equivalency.

The MMPI–A manual is comprehensive in detail, and provides substantial evidence regarding the psychometric properties of the test, which are adequate. The test–retest reliability studies presented in the manual show strong evidence of short-term temporal stability of MMPI–A scores, although the internal consistency coefficients of some of the scales are disappointingly low (in the .40 to .60 range in some cases). The evidence presented in the manual regarding clinical sensitivity of MMPI–A scores is quite supportive. Because the manual was written to coincide with the 1992 publication of the test, it does not include the fairly extensive research the has accrued since that time. Also, it may not be as helpful in clinical interpretation as some of the externally published books.

Although the MMPI–A was introduced relatively recently, a substantial amount of published research on it in addition to what appears in the test manual has begun to accrue. As of early 1998, over 30 published research studies on the MMPI–A could

TABLE 7.4
Basic and Content Scales of the MMPI–A

Scale Abbreviation	Scale Name
Basic Validity Scales	
VRIN	Variable Response Inconsistency
TRIN	True Response Inconsistency
F1	Infrequency 1
F2	Infrequency 2
F	Infrequency
L	Lie
K	Defensiveness
Basic Clinical Scales	
Hs	Hypochondriasis
D	Depression
Hy	Conversion Hysteria
Pd	Psychopathic Deviate
Mf	Masculinity-Femininity
Pa	Paranoia
Pt	Psychasthenia
Sc	Schizophrenia
Ma	Hypomania
Si	Social Introversion
Content Scales	
A-anx	Anxiety
A-obs	Obsessiveness
A-dep	Depression
A-hea	Health Concerns
A-aln	Alienation
A-biz	Bizarre Mentation
A-ang	Anger
A-cyn	Cynicism
A-con	Conduct Problems
A-lse	Low Self-esteem
A-las	Low Aspirations
A-sod	Social Discomfort
A-fam	Family Problems
A-sch	School Problems
A-trt	Negative Treatment Indicators

[handwritten annotation: MMPI-A will replace MMPI as most widely used person. invent for adolescents]

be referenced in the professional literature. Two of these journal articles are particularly noteworthy for potential users of the MMPI–A. Archer (1997) summarized the important research to date on the MMPI–A and provided suggestions for specific areas of productive research. Janus, Tolbert, Calestro, and Toepfer (1996) examined issues regarding score plotting and interpreting with both the MMPI and MMPI–A. Additionally, several books have been published regarding clinical use of the MMPI–A, including Archer (1992, 1996), Ben-Porath (1996), and Butcher (1992). These are probably the best sources for guidance in clinical use and interpretation of the test.

Publication of the MMPI–A was a much needed major development in the assessment of adolescent personality and psychopathology, and promises to eventually replace the MMPI as the most widely used instrument of this type for use with adolescents. The technical and psychometric properties of the instrument are adequate to good, the heritage from the original MMPI is strong, and there is a growing body of literature attesting to the MMPI–A's concurrent and predictive criterion validity.

⑤ **Personality Inventory for Youth**

Description. The Personality Inventory for Youth (PIY; Lachar & Gruber, 1995) is a comprehensive objective self-report measure designed to be used with children and adolescents from 9 to 18 years of age, or from 4th through 12th grades. It consists of 270 true–false statements that are written at about a mid-third-grade reading level. Most of these statements describe personal and family difficulties, whereas a small percentage of the statements describe positive or prosocial characteristics. The test authors state that administration of the PIY generally takes between 30 and 60 minutes, depending on various characteristics of the subject. The PIY is easily administered with a reusable booklet that clusters items into groups of about 15 on several narrow cardstock pages. Scoring of the PIY is accomplished through the use of either mail-in service from the publisher, or hand scoring forms. The scoring process for the PIY involves converting clusters of item responses to an array of clinical and validity scales that are based on the T-scores (with a normative mean of 50 and standard deviation of 10). The clinical scales and subscales of the PIY are presented in Table 7.5. The initial development of the PIY evolved from the Personality Inventory for Children (Lachar, 1990; Wirt, Lachar, Klinedinst, & Seat, 1990), a behavior rating scale for parents that includes a large number

TABLE 7.5
Clinical Scales and Subscales of the Personality Inventory for Youth

Cognitive Impairment
  Poor achievement and memory
  Inadequate abilities
  Learning problems
Impulsivity and Distractibility
  Brashness
  Distractibility and overactivity
  Impulsivity
Delinquency
  Antisocial behavior
  Dyscontrol
  Noncompliance
Family Dysfunction
  Parent–child conflict
  Parent maladjustment
  Marital discord
Reality Distortion
  Feelings of alienation
  Hallucinations and delusions
Somatic Concern
  Psychosomatic syndrome
  Muscular tension and anxiety
  Preoccupation with disease
Psychological Discomfort
  Fear and worry
  Depression
  Sleep disturbance
Social Withdrawal
  Social introversion
  Isolation
Social Skill Deficits
  Limited peer status
  Conflict with peers

of true–false statements and aims to assess child personality characteristics through parent endorsement of child-focused statements. Thus, the PIY was designed to be a true self-report personality measure rather than a hybrid behavior rating scale and personality questionnaire.

Technical Characteristics.   The PIY was standardized using a norm group of 2,327 children and youth from age 9 to 18. The participants in the standardization were regular education students from 13 public school districts in five U.S. states. The standardization information presented in the extensive technical guide for the PIY indicates that the sample adequately represents the general U.S. population in terms of race/ethnicity and parent education levels across various age groups. In addition to the regular education normative sample, a large clinical research base for the PIY was established with 1,178 clinically referred subjects from more than 50 treatment facilities.

Extensive evidence regarding the technical characteristics of the PIY is presented in the comprehensive test manuals. The median internal consistency coefficient for the clinical scales is reported at .82 for regular education samples and .85 for clinical samples, whereas the median coefficients for the clinical subscales are reported at .70 for the regular education samples and .73 for the clinical samples. Median test–retest reliability at 7- to 10-day intervals is reported at .85 for the clinical scales (with both the regular education and clinical samples), and .80 and .73 for the clinical subscales, for the regular education and clinical samples, respectively. Validity evidence for the PIY includes demonstration of significant relations with other self-report tests (such as the MMPI), significant score differences between regular education and clinical samples, and extensive evidence for the clinical scale and subscale structure of the instrument, including exploratory factor analyses and various structural modeling studies. The one externally published validity study located since the 1995 publication of the PIY (Wrobel & Lachar, 1998) explored relations between self-report and parent report data (on the PIC), and found that PIY self-report data were sensitive to mood disturbances and social withdrawal.

Evaluation.   Although the PIY is a relatively new instrument and the externally published empirical evidence has not yet accrued at a substantial level, this test appears to have much to offer, and is recommended as a general purpose self-report test for use with children and adolescents. The excellent user's guide and technical manual that accompany the PIY are extensively detailed and documented, and provide a great deal of information regarding its potential uses and its supporting evidence. One of the unique aspects of the PIY is that it is one of the only (and perhaps the only) general purpose self-report tests that spans the age ranges of middle childhood through adolescence with a common set of items. It is anticipated that the supporting empirical evidence for the PIY will continue to mount, and clinicians and researchers may find it useful for a variety of purposes as part of a comprehensive assessment battery.

Youth Self-Report   *(of CBCL)*

Description.   The Youth Self-Report (YSR; Achenbach, 1991c) is the self-report component of Achenbach's empirically based Child Behavior Checklist system. Although the YSR can be used alone, it is intended for use as a cross-informant assessment instrument in conjunction with the CBCL and TRF, and was designed and normed for use by subjects between 11 and 18 years of age. The YSR requires about a fifth-grade reading level to complete. The first section includes seven adaptive competency items where subjects provide information about their interests, hobbies, peer and family relationships, and school performance. These first seven items yield several competence scale scores. The remaining 119 items are descriptive statements that are rated by the subject using a 3-point scale ("Not True" to "Very True"). Of these 119 items, 103 are statements about various problem behaviors, whereas 16 reflect socially desirable items that are endorsed by most subjects. The socially desirable items are not scored, but were placed in the checklist to provide a balance to the problem items and to help detect indiscriminate responding. The 103 problem items are scored along two broad-band scales (Internalizing and Externalizing), eight narrow-band syndromes, and a total problem score. The narrow-band cross-informant syndrome scores are the same as those used with the CBCL and TRF (see chap. 4). All raw scores are converted to T-scores in the scoring process, and the YSR can be scored using scoring templates, a computer-based scoring program, or machine-readable scoring forms that require separate software and scanning devices. The scoring system provides separate score norms for boys and girls, although the same cross-informant subscale configuration is used with each gender.

Technical Characteristics. The most recent version of the YSR is based on a large standardization sample ($N = 1,315$) that is nationally representative with respect to socioeconomic status (SES), race, and urbanicity. This norm sample was obtained from nonreferred youth, although clinical cases were used in development of the subscales.

Data reported in the YSR manual are indicative of acceptable levels of test–retest reliability at 1-week intervals (median $r = .81$; range of broad-band and total score reliabilities = .83 to .87), although the range for narrow-band and competence scores is somewhat large (.39 to .83). Evidence of validity of the YSR presented in the manual includes sufficient factorial validity data, and correlational data between the YSR, CBCL, and TRF (which are in the .40 range). Several independent studies using the YSR have been published since the late 1980s. These studies have increasingly demonstrated the technical adequacy and psychometric properties of the YSR. For example, Gresham and Elliott (1990) found moderate correlations between the YSR with social competence instruments. Hepperlin, Stewart, and Rey (1990) found strong correlations between the YSR internalizing scale and a self-report measure of depression. Merrell, Anderson, and Michael (1997) used the YSR as a criterion measure in the validation of the Internalizing Symptoms Scale for Children, and found very strong convergent validity coefficients between the ISSC scores and the internalizing broad-band score of the YSR. Other studies have shown significant relationships between *DSM–III* diagnoses of conduct disorders and the YSR delinquency scale (Weinstein, Noam, Grimes, & Stone, 1990), good cross-cultural generalizability of the cross-informant syndromes with a large population of Dutch youth (deGroot et al., 1996), and convergent validity evidence between YSR scores and several of the MMPI–A clinical scales (Belter, Foster, & Imm, 1996). However, some studies have produced findings that raise questions regarding the validity of the YSR for specific purposes. For example, the YSR was found to have only limited usefulness in screening for childhood psychopathology in a community screening procedure (Bird, Gould, Rubio-Stipec, & Staghezza, 1991), and was found to have poor discriminant validity and elevated rater variance in a study of 108 adolescent girls who were hospitalized because of various emotional and behavioral problems (Thurber & Snow, 1990). And, although the subscale structure of the YSR was generally supported in a study by Song, Singh, and

Singer (1994), these researchers also demonstrated that there were important differences in the scale structure between boys' and girls' score structures that were not addressed in the test manual.

Evaluation. Despite some potential cautions raised by a few researchers, the YSR has become widely used and well supported. It appears to be valid for numerous clinical and research purposes, especially when used in conjunction with other forms of assessment. Clinical experience shows that it is quite easy for youths with externalizing behavior problems (i.e., conduct disorders) to manipulate their responses on the YSR so that their scores tend to minimize any problems (i.e., they may look normal). This potential problem is exacerbated because the YSR does not contain any validity scales to detect deviant responding styles. However, the YSR has a number of strengths and features that warrant its use, including an easy to use response format, a well-written manual with a great deal of technical information, a large and increasing body of research documentation, and the empirical connection between the YSR and the other components of Achenbach's multiaxial assessment system.

SELF-REPORT TESTS AND DECISION MAKING

[handwritten: ✓ screening process + red flags]

Like each of the other forms of assessment covered in this book, self-report tests can be very useful for screening purposes and for making decisions about additional forms of assessment that may be warranted. Not only can the administration of self-report tests provide "red flags" that may be indicative of general social or emotional distress, but in some cases, they can isolate specific areas of concern where additional assessment is needed. For example, each of the general purpose self-report tests reviewed in this chapter can provide specific information that can be used to generate hypotheses about additional assessment of depression, low self-esteem, anxiety, conduct problems, and even psychotic behavior. Anastasi and Urbina (1997) emphasized that self-report personality inventories are best used as "an aid for describing and understanding the individual, identifying her or his problems, and reaching appropriate action decisions" (p. 385). In assessing children and youth, obtaining their own perspective through self-report assessment should often be a critical part of the assessment design, and may yield information pertinent to decision making that is not possible through other sources.

Like most other forms of assessment, self-report tests should never be used by themselves to make diagnoses or classification and placement decisions. These types of decisions require a broad, multifactored assessment design wherein specific aspects of the decision process are weighed against specific pieces of evidence obtained through a carefully planned and implemented assessment process. *[handwritten: not sufficient- evidence alone]*

In terms of intervention or treatment planning decisions, self-report tests are normally used to generate broad hypotheses about what to do in conjunction with other forms of assessment data, but seldom provide sufficient evidence by themselves to warrant the design and implementation of intervention plans. The possible exception to this rule may be the use of the MMPI and MMPI–A. Because of the vast history of research and clinical use of the MMPI, a great deal is understood about using actuarial assessment data from this instrument in developing treatment plans, and the MMPI–A promises to eventually yield the same type of extensive database. Butcher (1979, 1990) and others wrote extensively on the actuarial application of MMPI data to treatment planning, and there is currently a great deal of interest in expanding and refining work in this area. A related decision-making use of self-report tests is their administration as treatment outcome measures. Several studies with the MMPI, MMPI–A, and MAPI (and other specific purpose self-report tests) have shown that adolescent self-report measures may serve as sensitive indicators of subjective changes that may occur as a result of treatment. Therefore, readministration of a self-report test following treatment may provide some useful information regarding the efficacy of the intervention, at least from the clients' own reports of their symptoms.

[handwritten margin note: sensitive indicators of subjective changes from Tx]

[handwritten note: clients own reports.]

CONCLUSIONS

Although there has been interest in personality assessment since antiquity, empirical efforts at objective self-report assessment have only been in place since the early to mid 1900s. The Personal Data Sheet and Berneuter Personality Inventory of the 1920s and 1930s served as prototypes for modern objective self-report measures. The development and popularization of the MMPI in the 1930s and 1940s served as a model stimulus for developments in this emerging field. Although the area of objective personality assessment has faced many challenges, there has been increased interest in it in recent decades, and important new technological developments in recent years.

Although there are many approaches to assessing behavioral, social, or emotional status through self-report means, there are specific technical criteria that must be in place for a test to be considered an objective self-report measure. In comparison with other forms of objective assessment, such as aptitude or ability testing, self-report assessment of social-emotional characteristics presents many unique challenges. Perhaps the greatest difference is that social-emotional characteristics of humans are much less stable and much more subject to variations through situations than are cognitive characteristics.

Three major approaches to developing objective self-report tests have been identified. These include the rational-theoretical approach, factor analytic approach, and empirical criterion keying approach. There are substantial differences in how each approach is used to develop test items and scales. However, in reality, many test developers use combinations of these approaches, and it is difficult to identify any one approach as being superior. Rather, the characteristics and predictive power of particular tests is a better indicator of quality than the method used to construct the test.

Several types of response bias and error variance have been identified relative to self-report tests. Clinicians and researchers who use self-report tests should always consider the possibility of how these phenomena may affect obtained test scores, either overtly or subtly, and take these potential problems into consideration when interpreting results.

Descriptions and evaluative reviews of eight self-report tests for use with children and youth were provided in this chapter. These instruments include the child and adolescent self-report forms of the Behavior Assessment for Children, Millon Adolescent Personality Inventory, Millon Adolescent Clinical Inventory, Minnesota Multiphasic Personality Inventory (original and adolescent versions), Personality Inventory for Youth, and Youth Self-Report. Of these instruments, only two (the SRP–C of the BASC and the PIY) are aimed at the preadolescent population. These instruments represent the best of what is currently available, and they also represent major advances in self-report assessment of youth. Prior to 1990, virtually nothing was available for children under the age of 11 or 12 in the way of psychometrically adequate general purpose self-report forms. And, although more instruments have been available for use with adolescents, the recent developments in this area have been very encouraging as well. It is safe to say that the field of self-report assessment of children adolescents is substantially more advanced today than it was even a decade ago. Clinicians and researchers now are able to choose among several high quality measures for specific assessment issues.

Self-report measures may provide information useful in making various decisions, such as screening, diagnosis, and treatment planning. An emerging decision-making use of self-report measures stems from their increasing use as treatment outcome measures. One caution that should be considered in making decisions with self-report data is the fact that these data are sometimes at odds with assessment data supplied from other sources, such as parent and teacher reports. Clinicians and researchers should include self-report assessment as one aspect of the assessment design, and consider the overall picture provided by all sources of data when making decisions.

REVIEW AND APPLICATION QUESTIONS

1. What characteristics are considered to be essential for an assessment instrument to be considered an objective self-report test?

2. Compare and contrast the three major methods of objective test construction: rational-theoretical, empirical criterion keying, and factor analysis. Which, if any, is the preferred method for constructing self-report tests?

3. What are the major forms of response bias discussed in this chapter, and how may they be manifest in self-report assessment of children and youth?

4. Of the several general purpose self-report tests reviewed in this chapter, only two (the SRP–C of the Behavior Assessment System for Children, and the Personality Inventory for Youth) were developed for extensive use with children younger than age 12. If clinicians were determining which of these two instruments to administer to a 9- or 10-year-old child, how would the relative merits and drawbacks of each test play into the decision?

5. What is the major difference between the intended uses of the Millon companion instruments, the MAPI and MACI?

6. Although the MMPI–A, a newer version of the MMPI developed specifically for use with adolescents, has been available for several years, the original MMPI continues to be used with this age group and is still considered a valid measure for this purpose when used appropriately. What are the possible advantages and disadvantages of each that might play into a decision regarding which instrument to use with a young client?

7. How might child and adolescent self-report tests be best used in making decisions regarding the effectiveness of treatment?

8. It is not uncommon for youth self-report instruments to yield data that differs markedly from assessment data provided through other sources (i.e., parent and teacher reports). What are some realistic ways of treating these differences in assessment results?

PROJECTIVE-EXPRESSIVE TECHNIQUES

Given that the major emphasis of this volume is on direct and objective methods of assessing social and emotional behavior of children and adolescents, the inclusion of a chapter on projective techniques, at first glance, may seem out of place. After all, there appears to be very little (if any) philosophical continuity between direct/objective and projective assessment methods. Indeed, the immediate predecessor to this volume, *Assessment of Behavioral, Social, and Emotional Problems: Direct and Objective Methods for Use With Children and Adolescents* (Merrell, 1994a) did not include a chapter on projective techniques. As the subtitle of the previous volume indicated, it was devoted exclusively to a model of direct and objective assessment that did not include projective techniques. However, by the time the current volume was being planned, it became apparent that a comprehensive chapter covering the most widely used projective techniques for children and adolescents was necessary.

Some of the impetus for this chapter came from former graduate students, who had been trained in social-emotional assessment with primary emphasis in direct and objective methods. Some of these students, who obtained positions as school, clinical child, and pediatric psychologists, found they were now working in systems where they were expected to be at least minimally conversant in projective assessment, and they lacked background in this area. Additional impetus came from academic colleagues in school and clinical child psychology at various universities across the country. Some of these colleagues liked the emphasis on direct and objective assessment in the first edition, but thought that a brief overview of projective assessment for comparison purposes would be useful. Other colleagues believed that a comprehensive chapter on projective assessment should be critically important in a text for training graduate students, and that a child-focused assessment of their "inner life" through projectives should always be an important part of a comprehensive assessment. Finally, an examination of research assessment practices of school and clinical psychologists (e.g., Lubin, Larsen, & Matarazzo, 1984; Watkins, Campbell, & McGregor, 1988; Wilson & Reschly, 1996) makes it apparent that despite the controversies surrounding them, projective-expressive and related social-emotional assessment techniques remain wildly popular among clinicians. Therefore, it was clear that this chapter was needed, and it should provide a well-reasoned analysis of the evidence supporting projective techniques, as well as a proposal for defensible recommended best practices in using such techniques. This chapter should be considered an adjunct to chapters 3 through 7, and projectives are not specifically included in the main methods these chapters detail, which are again specified in terms of specific assessment problems in chapters 9 through 13.

This chapter begins with a brief introduction to the theory and practice of projective-expressive techniques, and then includes sections on using thematic approaches, drawing techniques, and sentence completion tasks as methods of assessing social-emotional behavior of children and adolescents. The chapter concludes with a set of recommendations for best practices in using projective-expressive techniques, emphasizing appropriate and defensible practices. In making a determination of which projective techniques were most important to include in this chapter, some prominent techniques were left out because of space considerations. One technique that is prominently missing from this chapter is the Rorschach inkblot test. There are two reasons for this omission. First, the use of the Rorschach has evolved to the point where it is not as loosely projective as it once was, and the best methods for scoring and interpretation treat it as a highly structured perceptual task (e.g., Exner & Weiner, 1994). Second, given the complexity of modern methods of using the Rorschach (i.e., the Exner system), readers should be advised that a cursory overview of the Rorschach in a general chapter will in no way prepare them to even begin administering this test. Rather, effective use of the Rorschach with subjects of any age requires intensive training and study. Clinicians who desire to become more familiar with it should refer to the appropriate comprehensive books.

PROJECTIVE ASSESSMENT: AN INTRODUCTION

some projectives were being used in the 1920s (handwritten annotation)

According to Gregory (1996), the *projective hypothesis* was first formally detailed by Frank (1939) to describe a category of psychological tests designed to study personality through responses to unstructured stimuli. As demonstrated throughout this chapter, actual use of assessment techniques that might be considered to be projective substantially predates the term itself, and some projective techniques were clearly in use with both children and adults by at least the 1920s, if not earlier. The projective hypothesis is based on the assumption that "personal interpretations of ambiguous stimuli must necessarily reflect the unconscious needs, motives, and conflicts of the examinee" (Gregory, 1996, p. 511). Therefore, the task involved in projective assessment is to evaluate information and products (i.e., statements, drawings, key words) that are provided by the examinee in response to an ambiguous task, for the purpose of deciphering their underlying personality processes and social-emotional functioning. Without question, this task is formidable, and by the very nature of the procedures designed to enable it, will often become a highly speculative pursuit. There is wide variation in how structured or unstructured the processes of elicitation and interpretation are within the various projective methods.

The term *"projective-expressive techniques"* is used throughout this chapter. The addition of "expressive" to the constellation of projective techniques signifies that some methods that are often lumped together with projectives are not truly projectives in the strict sense, in that they are not based singularly on the projective hypothesis. Rather, *"projective-expressive" - examinees express themselves in response to ambiguous or loosely structured stimuli*

expressive social-emotional assessment techniques are procedures in which the examinees are allowed to express themselves in response to ambiguous or loosely structured stimuli, but their responses may not necessarily be used in a true projective manner. Examples of techniques that may be considered more expressive than projective include certain drawing tasks and specific sentence completion tests. Throughout this chapter, the term *projective-expressive* is used to denote a category of assessment techniques that do not strictly meet the criteria for being considered direct and objective, and allow for individualized administration and interpretation by the clinician.

projections of unconscious mental processes

Most advocates of projective-expressive assessment have been strongly influenced by psychodynamic theory. Perhaps the most central psychodynamic tenet that is incorporated into projective-expressive assessment is the assumption that responses to ambiguous stimuli represent projections of the examinees' unconscious mental processes. Within this psychodynamic-projective paradigm, the responses that examinees make to ambiguous stimuli may be quite revealing (to the trained clinician) regarding their "inner processes," but the examinees may not be aware that the information they have provided is so revealing. Although psychodynamic theory has clearly been in the forefront of projective testing, more recently, humanistic theory has also been incorporated. However, in a strict sense, the purpose of the test is no longer truly projective when the psychodynamic theory is deemphasized. The major difference between psychodynamic and humanistic approaches to assessment is that humanistic-based techniques do not rely as much on the latent or hidden content of an examinees responses (i.e., their unconscious projection). Rather, assessment techniques that are underpinned by humanistic theory are more likely to view the responses of examinees as a direct statement about who they are as a person. An example of a humanistic approach to this type of assessment would be human figure drawings for the purpose of identifying an examinee's overt body image.

Psycho-dynamic v. Humanistic approach

Indirect measure = less discomfort

Projective-expressive assessment appears to be as widely used with children and adolescents as it is with adults. Some projective techniques have been developed or adapted specifically to one age group or another, but many are adaptable across various age ranges. Some of the presumed advantages of using projective-expressive techniques with children and adolescents are that the examinee does not need to understand the specific purposes of the task, and they may be less suspicious and defensive when asked to engage in tasks like drawing, finishing sentences, and telling stories about pictures than they might be when asked specific questions about their social-emotional behavior (Chandler & Johnson, 1991).

unconscious personality & poor psycho-metrics

Like no other method of social-emotional or personality assessment, the use of projective techniques has been controversial. It is interesting to note that most of the controversy regarding projective assessment has been from within the professional community rather than from the lay public (unlike the controversies surrounding IQ and academic achievement tests). There have been many points of contention regarding projectives, but the essential controversies involve two main issues. First, many psychologists and other professionals simply do not believe the argument that is evident in the projective hypothesis, namely, that responses to ambiguous stimuli may reveal important information about the personality that is unconsciously projected. Second, and perhaps more importantly, projective-expressive assessment does not fare particularly well in comparison with direct and objective assessment from the standpoint of scientific psychometric criteria (Gregory, 1996).

Despite years of controversy that has surrounded projective assessment, these techniques continue to be incredibly popular, and in many cases are more popular than direct and objective methods that fare much better in terms of empirical evidence. The studies by Lubin et al. (1984), Watkins et al. (1988), and Wilson and Reschly (1996) all indicate that projective-expressive techniques are among the most widely used of all psychological assessment methods, and they show no sign of declining. In commenting on this paradox between evidence and use, Gregory (1996) stated that "the essential puzzle of projective tests is how to explain the enduring popularity of these instruments in spite of their generally marginal (often dismal) psychometric quality. After all, psychologists are not uniformly dense, nor are they dumb to issues of test quality. So why do projective techniques persist?" (p. 512). In answering his own question, Gregory proposed two explanations for the continued popularity of projective-expressive techniques. First, human beings are likely to cling to preexisting notions and stereotypes, even after they are exposed to contradictory findings. And, second, there is a tendency toward illusory validation (L. J. Chapman & J. P. Chapman, 1967), a phenomenon that is best put into context by the deceptively ironic statement "if I didn't believe it, I wouldn't have seen it." In essence, clinicians who believe strongly in using assessment methods that have questionable validity are more likely to clearly notice instances of findings that confirm their hypotheses, and at the same time are likely to ignore findings that contradict their expectations. With this cautionary interpretation to the continued popularity of projectives as a preamble, this chapter provides a comprehensive overview to three of the most popular areas of projective assessment with children: thematic approaches, drawing techniques, and sentence completion tasks.

THEMATIC APPROACHES

Thematic approaches to assessing personality and psychopathology are clearly based on the projective hypothesis, and their use became specifically associated with the study of ego psychology as advocated by Henry Murray and Leopold Bellak and their associates at the Harvard University Psychological Clinic in the 1940s. In a thematic-based assessment, the examinee is presented with a series of drawings or pictures showing unstructured ambiguous characters and situations, and is then asked to tell a story about each picture. The basis of interpreting responses to thematic storytelling tasks is that examinees are assumed to project their own needs, drives, conflicts, and emotions that form the foundation of the personality into the picture stimulus and the resulting story.

It is interesting to note that many of the early clinical and research uses of thematic storytelling approaches were heavily oriented toward assessing creativity and imagination, and instructions to examinees typically encouraged them in this regard (Gregory, 1996). However, as thematic approaches became increasingly popular in the 1950s and 1960s, the emphasis on creativity and imagination was soon replaced with a stronger emphasis on personality assessment, particularly from a psychodynamic orientation.

Because there are so many thematic techniques available, and because there are no dominant standardized methods of administration, scoring, and interpretation, it is best to refer to this category of assessment as thematic *approaches* rather than thematic *tests*. Therefore, unlike the other projective-expressive techniques covered, it is difficult to include a separate section on administration, scoring, and interpretation, because there is so much variation from one clinician to another, and among various thematic approaches (Gregory, 1996; Obrzut & Boliek, 1986; Worchel, 1990). Thus, this section provides information on administration, scoring, and interpretation within the description of each of the three specific approaches overviewed herein (the Thematic Apperception Test, Children's Apperception Test, and Roberts Apperception Test for Children). Following the description of these three approaches, additional sections on reliability-validity and concluding comments on using thematic approaches are provided.

Before proceeding with this discussion, it is important to recognize that it is a relatively cursory and limited overview, and cannot possibly do justice to the vast body of literature on research and clinical applications of thematic approaches. Readers who desire to become highly familiar and skilled in the use of thematic approaches should therefore refer to some of the recent volumes that have been written to provide in-depth explorations of thematic approaches (e.g., L. Bellak, 1975; Rabin, 1986; Teglasi, 1993).

Thematic Apperception Test

The Thematic Apperception Test (TAT) should be considered "the mother of all thematic approaches," and is clearly the most influential and researched. Most other widely used thematic approaches are modifications or extensions of the TAT. Developed by Murray and his colleagues at the Harvard Psychological Clinic (Morgan & H. A. Murray, 1935; H. A. Murray, 1938), the TAT was originally designed to assess personality constructs such as *needs* and *press*, and *thema*, which were essential elements to Murray's personality theory. In this theory, needs include processes that organize thought, action, and behavior to be energized to satisfy underlying needs. Press refers to to the power of environmental events that may influence a person. Themas are described as themes of combined needs and presses into a pattern that is played out in a story.

The TAT includes 31 black-and-white picture cards that contain a variety of unstructured and ambiguous characters, situations, and objects. The entire collection of cards is never administered to an examinee; an individualized administration battery ranging from 10 or fewer cards to as many as 20 cards is selected. The cards are numbered, and many cards include letters with the number to identify cards that are recommended for specific use with boys (B), girls (G), adult males (M), and adult females (F), or some combination thereof (i.e., GF). Obrzut and Boliek (1986) recommended that when administering the TAT to children from age 8 to 11, the following cards were particularly important: 1, 3BM, 7GF, 8BM, 12M, 13B, 14, and 17BM. For adolescents, Obrzuit and Boliek recommended cards 1, 2, 5, 7GF, 12F, 12M, 15, 17BM, 18BM, and 18GF. Teglasi (1993) noted that cards 1, 2, 3BM, 4, 5, 6BM, 7GF, and 8BM were appropriate for use with children and adolescents of either gender. Other writers have expressed similar and differing preferences for constructing TAT batteries for child and adolescent use, but ultimately, clinicians will need to select an appropriate set of cards from the TAT that make sense for use with their specific examinee. An important consideration in selecting an appropriate battery of TAT cards is the presenting issues and problems of the examinee. For example, if the examinee "appears depressed, those TAT pictures related to depression and suicide should be used" (Obrzut & Boliek, 1986, p. 178).

Administration instructions for the TAT tends to be nonstandardized, and many uses of the TAT tend to deviate from H. A. Murray's (1938) original directions emphasizing creativity and imagination. Some writers have expressed the opinion that

TAT directions should provide as few cues as possible, thus permitting examinees great leeway in expressing themselves (Peterson, 1990). However, Teglasi (1993) argued that TAT administrations with children and adolescents should include more structure because it will allow for better follow-up questions by the examiner. Teglasi recommended the following general instructions from H. A. Murray (1943) for administering the TAT to children and adolescents:

Younger Children:
I am going to show you some pictures, and I would like you to tell me a story for each one. In your story, please tell: What is happening in the picture? What happened before? What are people thinking and feeling? How does it all turn out in the end? So I'd like you to tell a whole story with a beginning, a middle, and an ending. You can make up any story you want. Do you understand? I'll write down your story. Here's the first card.

Older Children and Adolescents:
I am going to show you some pictures, one at a time, and your task will be to make up a story for each card. In your story, be sure to tell what has led up to the event shown in the picture, describe what is happening at the moment, what the characters are feeling and thinking, and then give the outcome. Tell a complete story with a beginning, middle, and end. Do you understand? I will write your stories as you tell them. Here's the first card.

After each TAT card story, a series of clarifying questions is recommended so the examiner will better understand the examinee's story. This process is referred to as the *inquiry phase* of administration. Questions may involve such areas as further clarification of the characters' thoughts and feelings, and how the story was generated (e.g., whether examinees created the story or adapted it from something they read or watched on television). True to the unstandardized nature of the TAT, some writers have expressed a preference for conducting the inquiry phase only after all cards have been administered, so as to not interfere with the examinees storytelling while it is happening (e.g., L. Bellak, 1975). If the clinician considers the TAT to be a true projective test, then it should be considered that the more structure that is imposed on the administration process, the less projective or spontaneous will be the examinee's responses (Obrzut & Boliek, 1986).

Interpretation of the TAT tends to be even more unstandardized than administration. Numerous interpretation approaches have been proposed, and it is beyond the scope of this chapter to overview them. In their review of using the TAT with children and adolescents, Obrzut and Boliek (1986) recommended the *inspection technique* as being "the simplest and, perhaps, most useful for TAT interpretation" (p. 179). This method is fairly straightforward, and involves the clinician simply treating the stories as being meaningful psychological communications from the child/adolescent examinee. Data that appear to be significant, specific, or unique are noted. This technique also incorporates the widely used suggestion of the original TAT authors to identify a *hero* or main character within each story, which is presumably the character that examinees will identify with and on which they will project their unconscious motives and needs. "The motives, trends, and feelings of the hero; the forces within the hero's environment; the outcome of the stories; simple and complex themes; and interests and sentiments attributed to the hero" (p. 180) are all considered to be important aspects of interpretation. Common themes among the stories should be identified, and the expressive manner in which the examinee relates the story should be carefully noted. This method of interpretation is simple, allows the clinician extensive leeway,

Common themes

and if used conservatively, should provide an effective bridge of understanding into the examinee's stories.

Children's Apperception Test

The Children's Apperception Test (CAT; L. Bellak & S. Bellak, 1949) was developed as a downward extension of the TAT, specifically targeted for use with children from age 3 to 10. The CAT includes 10 cards that depict animal characters (lions, bears, chimps, dogs, etc.) rather than human characters. The theory behind the use of animal characters by the authors of the CAT is that young children would be better able to relate to animal characters rather than human characters, and might find them to be less threatening. A parallel form of the CAT (the CAT–H) was also developed that includes human rather than animal figures (with the same picture scenarios as the CAT), and is thought to be more appropriate for older children and preadolescents.

Because the CAT is conceptually and theoretically similar to the TAT, the same general administration and general interpretation methods that were outlined for the TAT are recommended. L. Bellak (1975), the author of the CAT, recommended that interpretation of CAT stories should focus on identification of 10 variables: the main theme, the main hero, main needs and drives of the hero, the conception of the environment, how figures are seen, significant conflicts, nature of anxieties, main defenses against conflicts and fears, adequacy of superego as manifested by "punishment for crime," and integration of the ego. Obviously, Bellak's recommendations for interpretation are heavily influenced by psychoanalytic-psychodynamic theory. Clinicians who are not so psychodynamically inclined who desire to use the CAT are advised to focus on the inspection technique of interpretation, focusing on the issues and variables in the story content with which they are most comfortable.

Roberts Apperception Test for Children

The Roberts Apperception Test for Children (RATC; McArthur & Roberts, 1982) is the most recently developed thematic technique for children that is in wide use. The authors of the RATC intend for it to be used with children from age 6 to 15. Its stated purpose is to assess child and adolescent perceptions of interpersonal situations, such as the thoughts, concerns, conflicts, and coping styles of examinees. The RATC includes 27 stimulus cards. Some cards are specifically labeled for use with boys or girls, and only 16 cards are actually administered at one time. The content of the RATC cards is more modern and less ambiguous than that of the TAT and CAT, depicting very specific scenes involving such themes as parental discord and harmony, the observation of nudity, aggression, peer rejection, and so forth.

Administration of the RATC is quite similar to what has been discussed for the TAT and CAT. However, scoring and interpretation is much more of a structured process for the RATC. The test includes a standardized *T*-score scoring system, and results in four areas of scores:

1. *Adaptive Scales*: reliance on others, support others, support child, limit setting, problem identification, and three types of problem resolution.
2. *Clinical Scales*: anxiety, aggression, depression, rejection, unresolved.
3. *Critical Indicators*: atypical response, maladaptive outcome, refusal.
4. *Supplementary Measures*: ego functioning, aggression, levels of projection.

[handwritten: RATC = innovative b/c standardized scoring + interpretation]

The RATC appears to be a well-designed assessment technique that may be useful as a clinical tool when used with caution. The innovation and contribution of the RATC is its emphasis on a standardized scoring and interpretation system that is more empirically based than most thematic approaches (although it must be recognized that the normative sample is comprised of only 200 cases). Worchel (1990) concluded that the RATC "appears to have significant benefits over its predecessors" (p. 424), while acknowledging that the standardized scoring system is admittedly "lacking in validity evidence compared to more objective personality tests" (p. 424). Clinicians who are interested in using thematic approaches with children and young adolescents and who desire to use an objective scoring and interpretation approach may find the RATC to be a potentially useful addition to their assessment design.

Reliability and Validity

The technical adequacy of thematic approaches has been difficult to evaluate not only because there are numerous competing thematic techniques, but because of the plethora of nonstandardized scoring and interpretation methods. In their review on psychometric properties of thematic approaches, Obzrut and Boliek (1986) stated that much less in this area has been investigated with children and adolescents than with adults. They stated that the available evidence indicates that thematic approaches have demonstrated substantial reliability and evidence of clinical validity. Obzrut and Boliek's review is notable because of the assertion they made in several instances that traditional standards of reliability and validity are not highly relevant with thematic approaches. Other writers have been less charitable in their assessment of the psychometric properties of thematic approaches: "In large measure, then, the interpretation of (thematic techniques) is based on strategies with unknown and untested reliability and validity" (Gregory, 1996, p. 523). *[handwritten: non-standardized interpretations]*

Concluding Comments on Thematic Approaches

Thematic approaches to personality assessment have a fascinating history, and are quite interesting to administer and interpret. It is significant to consider that child and adolescent examinees often seem to enjoy the process of making up stories to thematic stimulus cards, and tend to find this assessment technique nonthreatening. One drawback to using thematic approaches with younger and less intellectually sophisticated children is that they often respond to the stimulus cards in a very short, concrete, and unenlightening manner, making for difficult interpretation if a true projective approach is followed.

As the review of psychometric properties of thematic approaches indicated, the evidence regarding reliability and validity is certainly mixed, and even advocates of such techniques tend to be cautious in their appraisals. Therefore, caution is advised when using thematic approaches with children and adolescents, particularly regarding making strong interpretive statements in the absence of any additional supporting evidence. However, it is clear that a thematic approach to assessment may help facilitate communication and rapport with children and adolescents, who often find such activities to be fun and nonthreatening. Therefore, clinicians may find thematic approaches to be a useful part of a comprehensive social-emotional assessment design that may serve to provide insight into young examinees from their own perspective and in their own words.

DRAWING TECHNIQUES

Drawing techniques for children are perhaps the oldest category of assessment procedures that can be placed in the general domain of projective-expressive assessment. Psychologically based drawing techniques have been in use nearly as long as the field of psychology has existed, as early as the 1890s by some accounts (Barnes, 1892). Historically, the first uses of psychologically based drawing techniques were not necessarily for assessment of social-emotional status or personality. Rather, the earliest uses of drawing techniques were primarily focused on intellectual and developmental assessment (Cummings, 1986). According to Hammer (1981), use of drawing techniques for projective-expressive assessment of children began to occur gradually, as clinicians noted interesting qualitative differences in specific features of drawings (e.g., facial expression, size, position on page) produced by children. These qualitative differences in drawings did not necessarily result in differential scoring when intellectual or developmental screening procedures were being used, but rather led to interpretations by clinicians that such differences should be considered important emotional or affective expressions within the drawing. It was this type of reasoning that led to the widespread clinical use of children's drawings for projective social-emotional and personality assessment.

Cummings (1986) stated that the literature indicates the use of four major functions for projective drawing tests:

1. To allow graphic, symbolic communication between a nonverbal child and a clinician.
2. To allow the clinician to develop an understanding of the inner conflicts, fears, family interactions, and perceptions of others from the child's perspective.
3. To provide a medium for understanding the child from a psychodynamic perspective (e.g., sexual identification, ego strength).
4. To assist in planning for further evaluation through the generation of hypotheses regarding the child.

As is true regarding virtually all projective-expressive techniques, despite widespread use, a great deal of controversy exists regarding projective drawing techniques. Many of the historical and current uses of projective drawing techniques with children are indefensible, and in general, the technical properties (i.e., reliability and validity evidence) of such techniques tend to be inferior to those of many of the more recently developed social-emotional assessment technologies that have refined since the 1980s. However, it is also naive to think that clinicians will simply abandon projective drawing techniques. It becomes evident that these techniques remain enormously popular despite criticism and supporting evidence that is mixed at best. Given this set of conditions, it is important to include a review of the major projective drawing techniques for children in this chapter, with a specific focus on evaluating the supporting evidence and identifying the most appropriate uses for these techniques. The discussion in this chapter includes separate overviews of three of the most widely used drawing techniques: the Draw-A-Person technique, the Kinetic Family Drawing technique, and use of the Bender–Gestalt Test as a social-emotional screening device. Additionally, some related drawing techniques are also mentioned.

The Draw-A-Person Technique

The most widely used drawing procedure in social-emotional assessment of children is the Draw-A-Person technique (DAP). The preeminent position of this drawing technique was verified through Wilson and Reschly's (1996) national survey of assessment practices of school psychologists. The results of this survey indicated that in both the 1980s and 1990s the DAP was not only the most widely used drawing technique for social-emotional assessment of children, but it was also the fourth most widely used psychological assessment technique overall.

The exact origins of human figure drawings (the predecessor to the current DAP technique) are somewhat unclear, but they have been in use by psychologists since the early part of the 20th century. Although human figure drawings were formally used by Goodenough in the 1920s as a measure of cognitive development (Goodenough, 1926), they also appear to have been used clinically for social-emotional assessment during this time period (Chandler & Johnson, 1991). The first widely disseminated technique for using human figure drawings in social-emotional assessment was Machover's highly influential book, *Personality Projection in the Drawing of a Human Figure* (Machover, 1949). This book has clearly been a major force behind the DAP as a social-emotional assessment technique, and it continues to be an influential foundation for current methods of using the DAP. Another book that has also been widely influential as a force behind the DAP for social-emotional assessment is Koppitz's *Psychological Evaluation of Children's Human Figure Drawings* (1968), which was published two decades after Machover's seminal text.

The basis of the using the DAP as a social-emotional assessment technique is similar to that of other drawing tests. Proponents of human figure drawings such as the DAP purport that the quality of drawings made by children through these tasks may provide important information regarding their psychosocial adjustment, including nonverbal symbolic communication of their conflicts, fears, family interactions, and so forth. The theoretical foundations and assumptions underlying DAP social-emotional assessment techniques are varied, but psychodynamic and humanistic theories have clearly been in the forefront in this regard.

Administration, Scoring, and Interpretation. Most advocates of DAP techniques suggest a similar administration method. The child is given a blank sheet of 8½" × 11" paper and a #2 lead pencil with eraser. The child is then instructed to "draw a picture of a whole person" (Cummings, 1986, p. 202). Some variations on DAP instructions have been suggested by various DAP advocates. Koppitz (1968) suggested that the examiner add the statement "It can be any kind of person you want to draw. Just make sure that it is a whole person and not a stick figure or a cartoon figure" (p. 6). This clarification was suggested to discourage older children from drawing a stick figure just to avoid the task. Chandler and Johnson (1991) recommended that younger children (i.e., kindergarten-age and younger) be allowed to use a thick pencil, crayon, or felt-tip pen for ease of drawing. An example of a DAP produced by a child through this instructional procedure is presented in Fig. 8.1.

Most DAP advocates suggest that the examiner use the words "draw a person" rather than the less ambiguous instructions to draw a man, a woman, a girl, and so forth. The ambiguity of the more general instructions has been considered to result in increased psychological projection regarding the subject's identification of gender,

FIG. 8.1. A human figure drawing produced by a 5-year-old girl, using standard DAP directions.

which has been the object of several empirical studies in and of itself (e.g., Dickson, Saylor, & Finch, 1992; Zabach & Waehler, 1994). Most advocates of the DAP favor having the child make two (or more drawings), in a process whcre the second drawing is requested to be a person of the opposite sex of the person depicted in the first drawing (Cummings, 1986). The entire DAP process typically takes 5 to 10 minutes to complete.

Scoring of the DAP tends to be nonstandardized, and is usually done in conjunction with interpretation. The exception to this statement is Naglieri, McNeish, and Bardos' (1991) structured scoring system for using the DAP as a screening procedure for emotional disturbance, referred to as the DAP:SPED. The structured DAP:SPED system includes scoring templates and specific scoring rules for various features of drawings. However, most DAP advocates and users tend to favor a nonstandardized holistic manner of scoring that is connected directly to interpretation. Machover (1949) and Koppitz (1968) provided general guidelines for scoring DAP figures, and are still widely influential.

Interpretation of the DAP is a process that also tends to be nonstandardized, and is often done in conjunction with a particular text or technique (i.e., Machover or Koppitz). Despite the influence of one interpretation technique or another, many practitioners who use the DAP for clinical assessment use holistic, self-styled interpretation methods, occasionally borrowing from various interpretation guidelines that have been integrated during their career.

Machover's (1949) technique for interpretation of human figure drawings proposed that interpretation should be based on a combination of indicators rather than individual signs or characteristics. From this perspective, the social features of the drawing are symbolically represented in the head. For example, "closed eyes may suggest an attempt to shut out the world," and "large, accentuated eyes may be associated with hostility" (Cummings, 1986, p. 203). From this perspective, the *contact features* of a drawing (i.e., the fingers, hands, arms, toes, feet, and legs) are said to represent a child's interactions with their environment. For example, "a relative lack of attention to feet and legs or their omission may reveal a child's insecurity about his or her problems dealing with sexual impulses," whereas irrelevant emphasis of pockets in drawings is seen in "infantile and dependent individuals" (Cummings, 1986, p. 203). The Machover method also emphasizes such factors as figure size, placement of figures on the paper, and drawing themes.

The Koppitz (1968) method of interpretation is clearly psychodynamically oriented and built on Machover's (1949) technique. One important difference in the Koppitz method is the increased emphasis on empirical identification of low frequency *emotional indicators* through systematic investigation of clinical cases and normal cases. In the Koppitz system, a particular characteristic on human figure drawings is considered an emotional indicator if three criteria are met:

1. It must possess clinical utility through differentiating between drawings of children with and without emotional problems.
2. It must be unusual, or in other words, be something that is infrequently found in the drawings of normal children.
3. It must not be related to developmental maturation.

Using these three criteria as a guide, Koppitz' (1968) guide lists 38 different emotional indicators, divided into the areas of *quality signs, special features,* and *omissions.* A summary of these emotional indicators is provided in Table 8.1. It is important to recognize that the Koppitz method of scoring and interpretation is complex and comprehensive, and requires a more in-depth study than simply referring to a table of emotional indicators.

A more recent system for scoring and interpreting the DAP is Naglieri et al.'s (1991) DAP:SPED method, which differs substantially from traditional methods of interpreting human figure drawings because of its emphasis on objective scoring and reliance on empirical criteria within a normative standardization group. Within this system, specific scoring indicators—such as legs together, placement of figure, various omissions, objects in mouth, fists, nude figures, and so forth—were developed through identification of low frequency indicators that were significantly more likely to be found in clinical samples. Specific criteria are provided for the presence of these figures (including objective scoring keys), and each indicator is given a score of 1. The total raw score is then converted to *T*-scores and percentile ranks, based on gender and age breakdowns. Using this system, interpretation is based on "the higher the score, the more likely it is that emotional disturbance exists" (Naglieri et al., 1991, p. 64). Therefore, indicators are interpreted in a combined manner from a normative perspective, and individual indicators are not generally considered to have a great deal of clinical meaning in and of themselves.

Reliability and Validity. With the DAP and other specific types of human figure drawing techniques, there is no question that particular scoring systems can be used reliably across raters. In his review of the DAP, Cummings (1986) integrated the results of 13 interrater reliability studies, which revealed a range of agreement among judges from 75% to 95% (.75 to .95), with a median reliability in the 80% range. Naglieri et al.'s (1991) test manual for the DAP:SPED also presents internal consistency reliability evidence, which was relatively modest, with alpha coefficients ranging from .67 to .78 at various age and gender levels. Test–retest reliability of human figure

TABLE 8.1

Summary of 38 Emotional Indicators for Human Figure Drawings
from the Koppitz (1968) Scoring and Interpretation System

Quality Signs
  Broken or sketchy lines
  Poor integration of parts of figure
  Shading of the face or part of it
  Shading of the body and/or limbs
  Shading of the hands and/or neck
  Gross asymmetry of limbs
  Figure slanting by 15 degrees or more
  Tiny figure, 2″ or less in height
  Big figure, 9″ or more in height
  Transparencies
Special Features
  Tiny head, $\frac{1}{10}$ or less of total height of figure
  Large head, as large or larger than body
  Vacant eyes, circles without pupils
  Side glances of both eyes, both eyes turned toward one side
  Crossed eyes, both eyes turned inward
  Teeth
  Short arms, not long enough to reach waistline
  Long arms that could reach below kneeline
  Arms clinging to side of body
  Big hands, as big as face
  Hands cut off, arms without hands and fingers
  Hands hidden behind back or in pockets
  Legs pressed together
  Genitals
  Monster or grotesque figures
  Three or more figures spontaneously drawn
  Figure cut off by edge of paper
  Baseline, grass, figure on edge of paper
  Sun or moon
  Clouds, rain, snow
Omissions
  Omission of eyes, nose, mouth, body, arms, legs, feet, neck

drawings has been a more problematic area, with stability coefficients typically much lower than those obtained for behavior ratings scales and objective self-report tests. Naglieri et al. (1991) reported a test–retest reliability coefficient of .67 at a 1-week interval with a sample of 67 children, using the DAP:SPED objective scoring system. Cummings (1986) integrated the findings of eight test–retest reliability studies from 1926 to 1978 with intervals ranging from 1 day to 3 months, with the resulting reliability coefficients ranging from .68 to .96. However, these studies were all based on Goodenough and Harris' scoring approaches for using human figure drawings to evaluate cognitive development and intellectual maturity. Few studies have been conducted wherein the more common use of the DAP as a social-emotional assessment technique was evaluated over time. In discussing the little evidence available in this area, Cummings (1986) commented that "drawings are subject to mood changes or a trait variable may be manifested by varying indicators" (p. 214).

Validity evidence of using human figure drawings like the DAP for social-emotional assessment of children is mixed. Koppitz' (1968) comprehensive book on children's

(handwritten in left margin, rotated) Validity for DAP is uncertain

human figure drawings was one of the first efforts to systematically provide empirical evidence for the validity of emotional indicators of DAP productions, and reported several studies wherein specific types of emotional indicators were found to differ significantly among emotionally disturbed and normal children through chi-square analyses. Cummings' (1986) review of validity evidence of the DAP concluded that the evidence was mixed and sometimes contradictory regarding the ability of DAP drawings to differentiate among clinical and normal groups. In the manual for Naglieri et al.'s (1991) adaptation of the DAP, the results of four separate validity studies are presented, wherein DAP:SPED standard scores of various clinical groups were compared with those of normal children. Each of these studies showed statistically significant differences among groups, with the clinical groups always receiving higher scores. Taken in combination, these studies provide some support for the construct validity of the DAP:SPED scoring system. However, several authors of recent reviews and empirical investigations have provided evidence that various adaptations of the DAP fail to discriminate accurately among clinical and nonclinical subjects (e.g., Bricceti, 1994; Feyh & Holmes, 1994; Klein, 1986), causing one expert in assessment to assert that DAP techniques are "tests in search of a construct" (Kamphaus, 1991, p. 395).

Additional Comments on the DAP. The DAP technique and related human figure drawing tests are clearly popular among clinicians, and may be the most widely used social-emotional assessment procedure for children at the present time. However, it is fair to state that both the reliability and validity evidence for these procedures is mixed at best, and there will continue to be controversy surrounding their use, even as they continue in popularity and widespread use. It is interesting to note that very little is actually known regarding how clinicians actually use the DAP in practice. Some clinicians clearly make the DAP and related techniques a centerpiece of their assessments, and make sweeping interpretations of the child's social-emotional status based on little else. However, it is the experience of the author that many practitioners simply "throw in" the DAP and related projective drawing tests into the assessment battery to build rapport with the child and form some tentative hypotheses, but are quite conservative when it comes to clinical interpretation of these drawings. An important but missing piece of evidence regarding social-emotional assessment with DAPs is how they are actually used (and perhaps abused) in clinical practice.

The Kinetic Family Drawing Technique

Another adaptation of human figure drawings is the use of family drawings. As a social-emotional assessment technique for children and adolescents, family drawings have been popular with clinicians during the past half century, and have been advocated since at least the 1930s (e.g., Appel, 1931). By the 1950s, the use of family drawings in psychological assessment of children had become widespread, as typified by widely cited articles by Hulse (1951, 1952). The basic idea behind family drawings has always been that through the process of drawing a pictorial representation of their family, children may provide important information regarding their perspective on such issues as family dynamics, emotional relationships, and their place within the family.

In the 1970s, a major new approach to children's family drawings was introduced by R. Burns and Kaufman (1970, 1972), which was described as the Kinetic Family Drawing technique (KFD). Unlike earlier approaches to family drawings, which tended to provide a relatively open format for making the drawings, the KFD included a

Basic ideas behind kinetic family drawing

carefully circumscribed set of directions with a clear goal: to draw everyone in the family doing something. Thus, with the introduction of the KFD, which eventually became the most widely used family drawing techniques, the emphasis was on actions. According to a critical review by Handler and Habenicht (1994), "This seemingly minor modification of the instructions results in some surprisingly revealing data concerning family dynamics, allowing a clearer picture to emerge of interpersonal interactions and emotional relationships among family members" (pp. 440–441). Compared to the Draw-A-Person and House-Tree-Person techniques, the KFD has been said to "often reveal conflicts and difficulties when the other two procedures indicate the absence of problems" (Handler & Habenicht, 1994, p. 441). The hypothesized reason for the more revealing nature of the KFD is that it allows the clinician to view the children as they feel they are reflected and expressed in the family, enabling the children to depict the family as an active unit, and enabling the clinician to see the children's impressions of family interactions (R. Burns, 1982; R. Burns & Kaufman, 1970, 1972).

Administration, Scoring, and Interpretation. The actual procedures for administering the KFD are quite simple. The examiner provides the examinee a plain white sheet of 8½" × 11" paper and a #2 lead pencil with an eraser. The paper is set ambiguously on the table so the child can determine whether to draw on it lengthwise or widthwise. The examiner then gives the following directions: "Draw a picture of everyone in your family, including you, DOING something. Try to draw whole people, not cartoons or stick people. Remember, make everyone DOING something—some kind of actions" (R. Burns & Kaufman, 1972, p. 5). An example of a KFD drawing produced by an elementary-age child is shown in Fig. 8.2.

While the drawing is being completed, the examiner is expected to carefully observe the examinee, record verbal statements, and make other behavioral observations. There is no specified time limit for the KFD, and if the examinee asks questions regarding the procedure, the examiner is supposed to respond in a noncommittal manner.

After the drawing is completed, it is recommended that the examiner ask a series of postdrawing questions (the inquiry phase) for the purpose of finding out the child's perspective on additional information related to the drawings. As recommended by Knoff and Prout (1985), the areas of questioning should attempt to find out about who the figures in the drawing represent, and what the child's relationship is to them; what the persons in the drawing are doing, feeling, and thinking; what is good and bad about each person; what the child was thinking about while drawing; what the drawing makes the child think of; what the weather is in the picture; and what the child would like to change about

the picture.

Various scoring systems have been used for the KFD, including many derivations on what was originally proposed by R. Burns and Kaufman (1970, 1972). The most recent KFD scoring system proposed by one of the original authors (R. Burns, 1982) is distinctly psychodynamic in nature and includes four major scoring categories: *Actions; Distances, Barriers, and Positions; Physical Characteristics of the Figures;* and *Styles.* The Actions category refers to the type of activity depicted for each figure, and Burns grouped possible actions into activities that are said to symbolize cooperation, communication, masochism, narcissism, nurturance, sadism, or tension. The Physical Characteristics category represents such formal aspects of the drawings as inclusion of essential body parts, the size of figures, the size of figures relative to other figures, the

FIG. 8.2. A Kinetic Family Drawing produced by an 8-year-old boy.

size of various body parts, and facial expressions. The Distances, Barriers, and Positions category involves such things as numbers of barriers between key figures in the drawing, the direction each figure faces, and the distance between the figures. The Styles category involves the organization of figures on the page. Some of the Style variables proposed by Burns to reflect psychopathology or emotional disturbance include intentional separation of family figures, encapsulation of figures by lines of objects, folding the paper into segments and placing each figure on individual segments, including more than one line across the entire bottom or top of the drawing, underlining individual figures, and presenting figures from an aerial or bird's-eye view. In listing these scoring categories and major indicators, it is important to also note that the KFD scoring system is complex and requires careful study from the original sources for effective and meaningful interpretation.

Reliability and Validity. When the original KFD technique was proposed in the early 1970s, it was criticized for having insufficient psychometric data available. Because the KFD has now been in widespread use for nearly three decades, reliability and validity studies have accrued, and much more is known about its psychometric properties. In terms of reliability, the yield of research on the KFD indicates that it has acceptable to excellent interrater reliability with specific scoring systems, but its test–retest reliability is often poor or marginal. In Handler and Habenicht's (1994) review it was noted that median percentages of interrater agreement on the KFD typically ranged from .87 to .95 across studies, indicating that "the various KFD scoring systems can be scored with a high degree of interrater reliability" (p. 443). However, test–retest reliability studies of the KFD have raised many questions and concerns. A number of test–retest studies at short-term intervals (i.e., 2 weeks) have been conducted with specific scoring systems, and the reliabilities have ranged from the .40 range to the .90 range, which is a considerable spread. It is certain that test–retest reliabilities in the .40 and .50 range at short-term intervals with other types of social-emotional assessment procedures (e.g., objective self-report tests, behavior rating scales) would be construed as evidence of extreme inconsistency. However, with the KFD, poor to marginal test–retest findings have been interpreted in various other ways. For example, Mangold (1982) suggested that the KFD is very sensitive to antecedent testing conditions, and performances may vary substantially depending on when and where it is administered. Cummings (1980) stated that the KFD's is probably a very state-dependent measure in that it may tap a child's feelings, perceptions, and general affect for only a very specific point in time. Other interpretations of the marginal test–retest reliability of the KFD are certainly possible, but it is sufficient to observe that it is likely that children will produce qualitatively different KFDs from one occasion to another.

In terms of test validity of the KFD, the evidence is equally mixed. In Handler and Habenicht's (1994) comprehensive review, it was noted that most of the validity studies on the KFD involved comparisons of drawings of children who had been identified as having some form of psychopathology or poor adjustment status and normal comparison children, and that various scoring systems have been used in these comparisons. In evaluating the yield of research of this type, it appears that many studies have shown significant differences among clinical status groups, whereas many others have not. There have also been a few studies wherein KFD scores were correlated with other types of social-emotional measures, such as self-concept tests, family relationship tests, and behavior rating scales. Some of these studies have shown significant but modest correlations between the KFD and criterion measures, providing some evidence of construct and criterion-related validity.

Most of the validity studies of the KFD have used very specific aspects of formal scoring systems, a practice that has come under closer scrutiny in recent years. According to Handler and Habenicht (1994), the best trend in KFD scoring is toward the use of a "holistic, integrative approach rather than one that emphasizes the mere addition of signs or symbols" (p. 458). Examples of these more holistic scoring systems are those used in studies by Cook (1991) and Tharinger and Stark (1990), both of which were able to differentiate clinical from nonclinical children. Obviously, the use of such systems necessitates a great deal of creativity and flexibility, given the statement of the latter authors that "the clearest sense of these characteristics can be gained through placing oneself in the drawing, preferably in place of the child" (Tharinger & Stark, 1990, pp. 370–371).

The Kinetic School Drawing. One of the variations on the KFD is a technique known as the Kinetic School Drawing (KSD). This technique was first proposed by Prout and Phillips (1974), was refined by Sarbaugh (1983), and was integrated with the KFD by Knoff and Prout (1985). The basic premise of the KSD is similar to that of the KFD in that children who draw themselves within their school environment in an action-oriented manner may provide important information on relationships and other dynamics within the school environment.

The directions for the KSD are very similar to those for the KFD. The examiner provides the child with a standard size piece of white paper, a #2 lead pencil with an eraser, and then states "I'd like you to draw a school picture. Put yourself, your teacher, and a friend or two in the picture. Make everyone doing something. Try to draw whole people and make the best drawing you can. Remember, draw yourself, your teacher, and a friend or two, and make everyone doing something" (Cummings, 1986, p. 229).

As with the KFD, various procedures have been proposed for interpreting the KSD, and both formal scoring systems and qualitative-holistic methods of interpretation are possible. However, much less is known about the psychometric properties of the KSD in relation to those of the KFD, as much less research has been reported. In general, the KSD does not appear to have caught on to the extent of the KFD. Because the tasks are so similar and because there is similar variation in scoring and interpretation methods, it can probably be assumed that the KSD has relatively similar psychometric characteristics and problems to the KFD. Although the use of the KFD has become incredibly popular among clinical child psychologists and school psychologists, it remains to be seen whether the KSD will attain this level of use.

Additional Comments on the KFD. Although the reliability and validity evidence regarding the KFD is certainly mixed to say the least, perhaps the most salient issue is "for what purposes are the KFD valid" rather than whether or not it is valid per se. As with any of the drawing and other techniques reviewed in this chapter, some uses are clearly indefensible, whereas other uses may be prudent and helpful in a diagnostic sense. In addition to basic reliability and validity evidence, Handler and Habenicht's (1994) review evaluated examinee variables that may strongly influence KFD production. Specifically, it was noted that age, gender, and culture/ethnicity have all been shown to be significant factors in the quality of children's KFDs. Therefore, clinicians who desire to use the KFD should become familiar with the literature in this area, and always take into account these factors in scoring and interpretation. Based on the current state of the art in using the KFD, it appears that there is definitely a trend toward the use of more naturalistic clinical methods of scoring and interpretation, as well as methods that integrate various scoring techniques rather than relying on single summative scoring systems. Therefore, although caution regarding the clinical use of the KFD is certainly advised, there also appears to be some promise of improved clinical validity evidence in the future.

The Bender–Gestalt Test as a Measure of Social-Emotional Status

Another drawing test that has been used for social-emotional assessment of children is the Bender–Gestalt Test (BGT), which has also been referred to as the Bender Visual-Motor Gestalt Test. The origins of this test stem from the foundation of Gestalt psychology. The BGT was developed by Bender (1938, 1946), who adapted nine figures that were being used in perceptual experiments and added specific administration, scoring, and interpretation guidelines so that this drawing technique could be used as a standardized psychological test. This test quickly became one of the most popular and widely used of all psychological assessment techniques, and it remains very popular today (Wilson & Reschly, 1996). *9 figures*

Because of its widespread use and continued popularity, numerous scoring and interpretation systems have been developed for the BGT. The vast majority of com-

Bender-Gestalt → visual motor perception → test for brain injury

prehensive scoring and interpretation systems are clearly not designed to aid in social-emotional assessment of children, and thus are not discussed in this chapter. The BGT has primarily been used as a measure of visual perception, visual-motor perception, and motor coordination for such diverse purposes as screening for brain injury, assessing developmental motor coordination levels, and providing rough estimates of intellectual functioning. The major force behind the use of the BGT as a social-emotional assessment technique for children was the work of Elizabeth Koppitz. In her two-volume series of books, *The Bender–Gestalt Test for Young Children* (Koppitz, 1963), and *The Bender–Gestalt Test for Young Children: Vol. 2. Research and Application, 1963–1973* (Koppitz, 1975), Koppitz outlined the theory and practice of using the Bender–Gestalt Test to screen for *emotional indicators* (EIs). These EIs are defined as drawing characteristics that tend to occur primarily with emotionally disturbed and behaviorally disordered children, and are associated with specific types of emotional-behavioral problems, such as impulsivity, mental confusion, low frustration tolerance, and so forth. Other social-emotional or psychopathology methods have been developed for the Bender–Gestalt Test, but none have been nearly as influential for social-emotional assessment of children as the Koppitz method. Therefore, this section is exclusively devoted to a brief description and overview of the Koppitz method for EIs.

Administration, Scoring, and Interpretation. Koppitz (1963, 1975) suggested that the original administration method advocated by Bender (1938, 1946) be used. This method of administration is straightforward and easy to follow. The examiner provides a sheet of 8½″ × 11″ white paper (more than one sheet may be used if needed) and a #2 lead pencil to the child, and sits with them at a table suitable for drawing. The examiner states to the child that the task of this test is for them to carefully make copies of the figures that will be shown to them, on the paper. The examiner then presents the child with the nine BGT figures, one at a time in succession as they complete them. There is no time limit for this test, although most children complete the task in about 6 minutes (Koppitz, 1975). The examiner should provide minimal direction for the child, allowing them to copy the drawings any way they want, while carefully observing their behavior during the testing task. An example of a child's reproduction of the BGT figures is presented in Fig. 8.3.

With the Koppitz system, it is recommended that both the developmental scoring system and identification of possible emotional indicators be used by the examiner. Because the developmental scoring system is not a primary concern of this text, it is not discussed here, and readers are referred to Koppitz (1963, 1975) for more detailed instruction. Koppitz' system for identifying emotional indicators is the major emphasis of this section, and therefore is briefly presented herein. However, users of this book who desire to become proficient in the Koppitz EI identification method should carefully study the original texts and supporting evidence, and not rely on this chapter alone as a training guide.

Koppitz (1963) presented 10 emotional indicators for the BGT. In Koppitz (1975), the original 10 emotional indicators were presented, with new supportive evidence, and two more indicators were also presented, bringing the total number of EIs to 12. These EIs are described briefly as follows:

Emotional indicators of BGT

1. *Confused Order.* This EI is considered to be present if the designs are scattered arbitrarily on the paper, and if there is no logical sequence or order to the drawings. Koppitz noted that Confused Order is associated with a lack of planning ability and

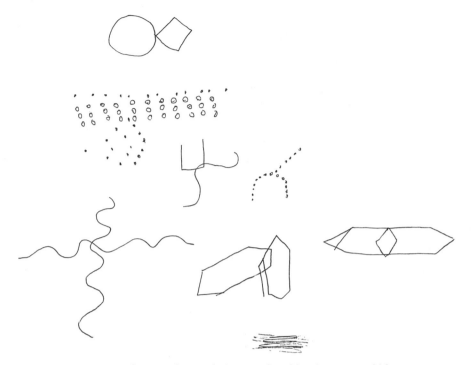

FIG. 8.3. Bender–Gestalt Test designs produced by an 11-year-old boy.

poor organizational skills, but emphasized that it is not uncommon among younger children (age 5–7).

2. *Wavy Line in Figs. 1 and 2.* If there are two or more abrupt changes in the direction of the lines of dots or circles in BGT Figs. 1 or 2, then this EI is considered to be present. Koppitz noted that Wavy Line appeared to be associated with both poor motor coordination and emotional instability.

3. *Dashes Substituted for Circles in Fig. 2.* If at least half of all the circles in Fig. 2 are replaced with dashes 1/16" long or more, then this EI is considered to be present. Koppitz noted that Substitution of Dashes for Circles in Fig. 2 has been associated with impulsivity and lack of interest, particularly with younger children.

4. *Increasing Size of Figs. 1, 2, or 3.* If the dots or circles of drawings of Figs. 1 through 3 progressively increase in size until the last ones are three times as large or more than the first ones, then this EI is considered to be present. Koppitz stated that increasing size on these BGT designs is associated with low frustration tolerance and explosiveness, particularly as children become older (e.g., age 10 vs. age 7).

5. *Large Size.* According to Koppitz, if the area covered by any one BGT figure drawing is at least twice as large as the design area on the stimulus card, then this EI, which is said to be associated with acting-out behavior in children, is considered to be present.

6. *Small Size.* If the area covered by any BGT figure drawing is half as large or less than the original stimulus area on any of the figures, then the Small Size EI, which is thought to be related to anxiety, withdrawal, timidity, and constriction in children, is considered to be present.

7. *Fine Line.* If the pencil line for any BGT figure drawing is so fine that it requires considerable effort to view the design, then the Fine Line indicator is considered to

be present. Koppitz noted that this EI is associated with timidity, shyness, and with-drawal, specifically in young children.

8. *Careless Overwork or Heavily Reinforced Lines.* This EI is considered to be present if a design or part of a design is redrawn with heavy lines. This category is not scored if the drawing is erased and then redrawn, or if it is corrected with careful lines that improve the drawing. Koppitz noted that Careless Overwork and Heavily Reinforced Lines have been associated with impulsivity, aggressiveness, and acting-out behavior.

9. *Second Attempt.* The Second Attempt EI is considered to be present if a BGT design or part of it is abandoned before or after its completion, and a new drawing is made. This EI should only be scored if there are two distinct drawings from one design on two locations on the paper. Koppitz stated that the Second Attempt EI is associated with impulsivity and anxiety.

10. *Expansion.* The Expansion EI, which is said to be associated with impulsivity and acting-out behavior, is scored when two or more sheets of paper are used to complete the nine BGT drawings.

11. *Box Around Design.* Koppitz noted that this EI is quite rare, but suggested that children who exhibit it have "weak inner control; they need to be able to function in school and at home" (Koppitz, 1975, p. 86). This EI is considered to be present when a box is drawn around one or more BGT designs after they have already been copied.

12. *Spontaneous Elaboration or Additions to Designs.* This EI is scored when a child makes spontaneous changes on BGT test figures that "turn them into objects or combine them into bizarre designs" (Koppitz, 1975, p. 88). Koppitz noted that this EI, which is also quite rare, "occur[s] almost exclusively on Bender Test records of children who are overwhelmed by fears and anxieties or who are totally preoccupied with their own thoughts. These youngsters often have a tenuous hold on reality and may confuse fact with fantasy" (Koppitz, 1975, p. 88).

When scoring and interpreting EIs on the BGT using the Koppitz system, it is important to consider some of her suggestions and warnings (Koppitz, 1975). First, emotional indicators "are clinical signs that should be evaluated individually like any other clinical symptom" (p. 89). Second, "EIs lack internal consistency and cannot, therefore, be added together into a meaningful total EI score" (p. 89). And, finally, there is a concern that single EIs on BGT drawings are not always indicative of emotional problems. In fact, Koppitz noted that "three or more EIs are necessary before one can say with some degree of confidence that a child has serious emotional problems and will need further evaluation" (p. 89). Obviously, with a process so tenuous as inferring emotional adjustment from a drawing task, these three recom-mendations should be considered absolute minimum considerations.

Reliability and Validity. Ample evidence exists indicating that the BGT can be scored reliably across different scorers, and is also relatively stable over short periods of time. Koppitz (1975) summarized numerous studies showing that the interrater reliability validity of the BGT is often in the .80 to .90 range, and that test–retest reliability of the BGT at short time intervals is often in the .70 to .80 range (although younger children often demonstrate less reliable performances). These strong findings regarding reliability of the BGT are typically based on overall developmental scoring system results, and not just on the presence of EIs. Therefore, the stability of EIs on BGT drawings is less clear.

Koppitz (1975) also provided some empirical support for each of the 12 EIs. Given the 1975 publication date, these supporting references were all based on research published in the 1960s and 1970s. A computer-based review of the PSYCHLIT database revealed only a few additional studies regarding the validity of the Koppitz EI system. Most of the studies' support of the validity of EIs on BGT is based on methodology where frequency counts of specific EIs are compared between clinical and nonclinical groups, and the clinical groups evidenced a higher EI prevalence. In some of these studies, chi-square analyses were used to provide evidence of statistical significance of these differences, whereas other studies analyzed the frequency counts qualitatively. A substantial number of these studies are in the form of unpublished master's thesis and doctoral dissertation projects from the 1960s and 1970s, and are virtually impossible to obtain for evaluation. Therefore, it is difficult to make strong conclusions regarding the validity of the BGT as a social-emotional assessment procedure.

Additional Comments on the BGT. It is fair to say that the Koppitz system for using the BGT for social-emotional assessment has some supporting evidence, but it is also fair to state that most of this evidence is substantially dated, and does not meet current research standards for providing evidence of clinical validity (i.e., large effect sizes among clinical and nonclinical groups, use of multiple regression and discriminant function analyses for prediction purposes). Therefore, caution is certainly advised in using the BGT for social-emotional assessment of children. Although the BGT is still widely popular, even as a social-emotional assessment technique, research on this particular use of the test appears to have diminished substantially within the years following the publication of Koppitz' two books (1963, 1975). These books are very well written, documented to a substantially greater degree than most related books, and quite interesting. Given that the BGT is easy to administer and is typically a nonthreatening if not enjoyable experience for children, it is no surprise that it continues to be widely used, even for social-emotional assessment. However, potential users of the BGT for social-emotional assessment purposes are cautioned that the state of the art in social-emotional assessment has advanced considerably during the past two decades, and the evidence supporting the BGT for this purpose has simply not kept pace with the burgeoning evidence supporting other methods, such as behavior rating scales, direct observation, and objective self-report tests.

↳ BGT is a bit outdated ...

Concluding Comments on Drawing Techniques

This section outlines the history, rationale, and theory of using drawing tests for social-emotional assessment of children and adolescents, and provides an overview of three of the most popular techniques within this area. These three techniques included human figure drawing techniques (specifically the Draw-A-Person technique), the Kinetic Family Drawing technique and a related school-based procedure, and the use of the Bender–Gestalt Test as a social-emotional assessment procedure.

In addition to these three techniques there are various other drawing techniques that are popular for social emotional assessment that were not discussed in this chapter. For example the House-Tree-Person drawing technique continues to be a widely used procedure that has many conceptual and practical similarities to the Draw-A-Person technique. Likewise, Burns (1982), the most influential early proponent of the Kinetic

Family Drawing technique, expanded his work in this domain to what he refers to as Family-Centered-Circle Drawings. These and other variations of projective-expressive drawing techniques are not included here because of space constraints, their overlapping content with the procedures that were reviewed, and because the quantity of both use and research on these procedures appears to be substantially less than the DAP, KFD, and BGT. It is sufficient to note that many variations and adaptations of social-emotional drawing tests are possible, and they vary substantially in terms of their popularity and availability of supporting evidence.

For the foreseeable future, it appears that projective-expressive and other types of drawing tests will continue to be widely used by clinicians in the United States and throughout the world. During the early 1980s, R. P. Martin (1983), an authority in the field of social-emotional assessment of children, asserted that the use of projective-expressive drawing techniques is unethical, and such practices reduce the overall reliability of an assessment and may simply serve to reinforce biases held by the clinician. Such arguments are not new. Two decades earlier, Roback (1968) made a similar assertion against some uses of projective-expressive drawing tests, stating that "many clinicians apparently entertain grandiose delusions that they can intuitively gain a great deal of information from figure drawings about the personality structure and dynamics of the drawer" (p. 16). Such criticisms, and the questionable validity and mixed research base of many of these procedures, have failed to quash the desire of clinicians to use such techniques, as evidenced by their continued widespread popularity among psychologists who work primarily with children (Wilson & Reschly, 1996). Therefore, it seems futile to berate clinicians for continuing to use drawing tests for social-emotional assessment of children and adolescents. Perhaps a better approach is to focus on appropriate or best uses of these tests.

SENTENCE COMPLETION TASKS

Like thematic approaches and drawing techniques, sentence completion tasks also appear to be widely used for social-emotional and personality assessment (Lubin et al., 1984). In a sentence completion task, the examinee is presented a list of *sentence stems* (the beginning of a potential sentence) with a blank space after each stem. The task of the examinee is to complete the sentence. The typical way to complete sentence completion tasks is for the examinee to read the stems and then provide a written response, but oral administration and response is also an option. Sentence completion tasks may consist of only a few items (10–15), and may range in length to as many as 50 or more items. The basis of all sentence completion tasks is that either qualitative or systematic inspection of an examinee's responses may provide insight into their self-image, developmental characteristics, interpersonal relationships, needs, and perceived threats (Chandler & Johnson, 1991). A sample sentence completion task with 20 stems is presented in Table 8.2. These stems are representative of the range of stems found in various sentence completion tasks that have been advocated for use with children and adolescents. Notice that there are several recurring types of stem content in these sample items. Most advocates of sentence completion tasks advocate making inferences on *clusters* of items rather than on individual items or responses in isolation.

There has been some debate regarding how to best conceptualize and use sentence completion tasks. Some advocates of this assessment technique advocate a holistic, qualitative method of analyzing and interpreting responses (Chandler & Johnson, 1991),

TABLE 8.2
20 Sample Stems Typical of the Content of Sentence Completion
Tasks Advocated for Use with Older Children and Adolescents

1. I wish . . .
2. Most people are afraid of . . .
3. I usually get mad when . . .
4. If I could only . . .
5. At school . . .
6. Other kids think I . . .
7. I feel best when . . .
8. I am the . . .
9. The best thing about school . . .
10. When mom and dad are together . . .
11. I often feel . . .
12. Girls seem to . . .
13. I am most proud about . . .
14. My mom . . .
15. I feel worse when . . .
16. Kids should . . .
17. Teachers usually want you to . . .
18. The worst thing that could happen . . .
19. My dad . . .
20. When I go to sleep . . .

whereas other advocates contend that scoring and interpretation is best done using standardized systems (D. H. Hart, 1986). Furthermore, there has been substantial disagreement regarding how sentence completion tasks should be conceptualized (Koppitz, 1982), and they have been alternately described as projective, semiprojective, and nonprojective techniques (D. H. Hart, 1986). Regardless of how these tasks are conceptualized and actually used, it is evident that they have been and continue to be widely used with older children and adolescents, and thus deserve attention in this chapter.

Sentence completion tasks appear to have been in use since the early 1900s. Like drawing techniques, the first uses of sentence completion tasks were for mental ability testing, but interest in this use gradually waned and gave way to personality assessment (D. H. Hart, 1986). Most of the early sentence completion tasks were developed for use with adults and older adolescents. The Rotter Incomplete Sentence Blank (e.g., Rotter & Rafferty, 1950) is perhaps the most influential of all sentence completion tasks in terms of the amount of research published on it and the influence it maintained in shaping subsequently developed sentence completion tasks. This test—which includes high school, college, and adult forms—has 40 items, an objective scoring system, yields a single adjustment score, and has been shown to have exceptionally high reliability (Gregory, 1996).

Although older adolescents have been specifically targeted for development and use of sentence completion tasks since the early days of this procedure, specific extensions of such tasks to the child population occurred much later. One of the challenges in administering sentence completion tasks to children is that a certain reading level is required. In this regard, McCammon (1981) found that by the sixth grade, most children are capable of reading sentence completion tests, and oral administration is probably not necessary. Another challenge is that preoperational children (i.e., most children below 12 or 13 years old) tend to think in a concrete manner, and will thus tend to provide very factual, concrete responses to sentence completion stems, possibly defeating the projective-expressive purpose of the technique. Despite this history and the stated limitations, numerous clinicians use sentence completion tasks with children and adolescents. It is significant to note that most of the sentence completion tasks in use by practitioners are nonstandardized and not commercially published or widely available (Gregory, 1996). They also tend to be used in a qualitative, nonobjective manner.

In addition to the general orientation on sentence completion tasks that was just provided, this discussion includes sections on administration, scoring, and interpretation procedures; a brief overview of reliability and validity evidence; short descriptions of two sentence completion tasks that have been widely used with children (the Hart Sentence Completion Test) and adolescents (the Washington University Sentence Completion Test); and some concluding comments on the clinical uses of sentence completion tasks with children and adolescents.

Administration, Scoring, and Interpretation

Administration, scoring, and interpretation of sentence completion tasks tends to be highly dependent on the specific test used. Some tests have highly structured procedures, whereas others provide only minimal guidelines and structure for clinicians. From a projective psychodiagnostic perspective, a frequently used administration technique includes the clinician reading the sentence stem to the examinee, who is then encouraged to verbally complete the stem with whatever words come to mind (D. H. Hart, 1986). If such an approach is used, the clinician is encouraged to carefully record the responses of the examinee, as well as observations of behavior during the task. An *inquiry phase* often follows the initial administration technique, in which the clinician inquires regarding the content of the response. Such inquiry is for the purpose of clarifying meaning, identifying reasons why an examinee responded in a particular way, and "tracking feelings or perceptions to deeper levels and causes" (D. H. Hart, 1986, p. 252). Various approaches to interpreting sentence completion tasks have been proposed. The most structured tests include standardized scoring systems that are linked directly with specific interpretative criterion. A common approach to interpretation has been rating each response according to the degree of conflict apparent (e.g., negative to neutral to positive) using a weighted scoring system such as that proposed for use in the Rotter Incomplete Sentence Blank. Many (if not most) clinicians tend to score and interpret sentence completion task responses in a subjective and qualitative manner by reviewing each item to develop clinical impressions regarding the underlying dynamics of the response, and to cluster sentence stems with similar content, and then focus on the specific impressions obtained from examining those item clusters.

Reliability and Validity

In terms of reliability or stability, sentence completion tasks share a common characteristic with other projective-expressive techniques discussed in this chapter: They tend to have good to excellent interrater reliability with specific scoring systems, but poor stability of children's responses over even short-term time intervals. Reliability of sentence completion tasks has been reviewed by Gregory (1996) and by D. H. Hart (1986), who noted that interscorer or interrater reliability in the .70 to .90 range with specific tests and structured scoring systems is not uncommon. However, test–retest reliability of sentence completion tasks is typically not reported, and the few studies that have investigated this phenomenon have found that children's responses are quite unstable over time. Thus, it is best to view sentence completion tasks as a means of eliciting information from a child that may be meaningful at that moment, but will probably not generalize over time.

Validity of sentence completion tasks is also an area of inquiry that has yielded mixed results. Sentence completion tasks tend to have very low convergence with other types of social-emotional assessment data. However, numerous investigations with adult-focused sentence completion tasks have found them to differentiate among clinical and nonclinical groups to at least a modest degree (Gregory, 1996). Thus, it is fair to say that there is some support for the construct validity of sentence completion tasks. However, it is difficult to generalize this validity evidence across the many tests that have been developed, because they tend to vary greatly in terms of purpose, procedures, and scoring and interpretation methods.

Hart Sentence Completion Test for Children

The Hart Sentence Completion Test for Children (HSCT; D. H. Hart, 1972, 1980; D. H. Hart, Kehle, & Davies, 1983) is a 40-item sentence completion task for children and adolescents from age 6 to 18. According to the author of this test, it was developed for two reasons: to provide a sentence completion task developed specifically for children and adolescents rather than modifying adult sentence completion tasks for child use, and because "other child-oriented sentence completion tests had poorly developing scoring systems or no standardized scoring systems at all and little documentation of any reliability and validity data" (D. H. Hart, 1986, p. 257). The HSCT was developed based on a four-dimensional theory of areas that are important to child social-emotional adjustment: family environments, social environments, school environments, and intrapersonal or internal conditions. The HSCT appears to have been developed with a great deal of care, and is clearly the most objective, comprehensive, and clinically useful sentence completion task for children currently available. Two scoring approaches are used with the HSCT: a scale rating system and an item-by-item rating system. Information provided in the test manual and research reports in the public domain both indicate that the HSCT has demonstrated an excellent interrater reliability, moderate test–retest reliability, and evidence of construct validity, including significant differentiation of responses of emotionally disturbed, learning disabled, and regular education students. For clinicians who desire a relatively objective, well-documented sentence completion task for use specifically with children, the HSCT appears to be peerless. However, this test is currently not available. Hart does not consider the HSCT to be complete at the present time, and is not distributing it publicly until such a time when additional research efforts are conducted for validation purposes (D. H. Hart, personal communication, April 25, 1997). Therefore, researchers and clinicians interested in the HSCT will have an obviously difficult time obtaining it, but may desire to study the references provided in this section for more information on its development, structure, and use.

Washington University Sentence Completion Test

The Washington University Sentence Completion Test (Loevinger, 1976, 1979) has been widely used with adults and adolescents. It is considered to be the most theory driven of all the sentence completion tasks (Gregory, 1996) because of its stated purpose of assessing ego development. Using a relatively objective scoring system, responses are classified according to seven stages of ego development, including presocial and symbiotic, impulsive, self-protective, conformist, conscientious, autonomous, and integrated. A review of the literature using the computer-assisted PSYCHLIT program indicated that more scholarly journal articles had been published using Loevinger's sentence completion test than any other sentence completion task with the adolescent population. Consistent with the stated purposes of this test, most of the published studies using it involved the assessment of adolescent and adult ego development from a psychodynamic perspective. Although this sentence completion test is one of the best constructed and most widely researched, little is known regarding its ability to differentiate between emotionally disturbed or behaviorally disordered and normal adolescents.

Concluding Comments on Sentence Completion Tasks

Although sentence completion tasks have been among the most widely used projective-expressive assessment techniques of this century, theoretical and research interest in them seems to have waned in recent decades. It is interesting and telling to note that most of the seminal research and development efforts and important literature on sentence completion tasks occurred in the 1940s, 1950s, and 1960s. The last two decades of the 20th century have seen very little in the way of new innovations with sentence completion tasks. One of the few potentially valuable innovations during this period has been the development and dissemination of the Hart Sentence Completion Test for Children, one of the few sentence completion tasks designed to consider the unique characteristics of childhood. This test also has the advantage of good standardization and an objective scoring and interpretation scheme. However, research and development efforts on the HSCT have waned, and it is no longer available in the public domain. Clinicians who desire to develop or modify sentence completion tasks to meet their own needs and use them in a qualitative-holistic manner may find them to be an interesting addition to their assessment design, particularly when results are interpreted in a conservative manner.

BEST PRACTICES

This chapter has provided an overview of theory, practice, and research regarding some of the most popular projective-expressive assessment techniques for use with children and adolescents, including thematic approaches, drawing techniques, and sentence completion tasks. After reading this chapter, two facts should be obvious: Projective-expressive techniques have been and continue to be an extremely popular and widely used form of social-emotional assessment among clinicians. And, there continues to be considerable controversy regarding the use of these techniques, primarily because of a combination of extremely mixed psychometric evidence and the vagueness or difficulty operationalizing some of the constructs purported to be measured by these techniques. It also appears as though there have been very few new innovations in this area during the past two decades. Most of the cutting edge developments in assessing psychopathology and personality of children during the past two decades have been in the realm of empirically based multiaxial assessment techniques, as illustrated by research and innovation in such areas as behavior rating scales, objective self-report measures, and multiple gating systems. Thus, projective-expressive techniques are in a unique and paradoxical position, being among the most popular assessment techniques used by clinicians, but also becoming outdated, and perhaps even archaic.

Because of these issues and related concerns, prominent writers in the area of social-emotional assessment of children have issued strong statements against the continued use of projective-expressive techniques, and in some cases, calling for a moratorium on their use (R. P. Martin, 1983). In this vein, Wilson and Reschly (1996) commented on the results of their survey of assessment practices of school psychologists:

> The persistence of using measures with poor technical adequacy and dubious relationships to psychological constructs and to current child disability classification systems criteria is difficult to explain, other than to note that some psychologists seem to be tied to poor assessment instruments. The Bender-Gestalt and Draw-A-Something projective measures have poor technical adequacy, and, if used as a primary basis for any decision, render the psychologist vulnerable to challenge in legal proceedings such as due process hearings. Use of these measures, especially in personality assessment, is difficult to justify from ethical as well as psychometric grounds. (pp. 18–19)

Despite such strong and clearly defensible statements, it is naive to think that projective-expressive assessment techniques will just go away, or that clinicians will simply abandon them. There is obviously something about these techniques that appeals to so many clinicians, and that they must find to be useful. After looking at all the evidence, it seems as though the problem with projective-expressive assessment techniques may not be in the techniques themselves, but rather in how they may be used. Much of the heated dialogue regarding the pros and cons of projective-expressive assessment has stemmed from either proponents who will blindly argue for the merits of these techniques without regard to the evidence, or opponents who are diametrically opposed to their use on virtually all grounds. Very little has actually been written regarding how to make the best use of these assessment techniques that are both popular and under close scrutiny. Therefore, this chapter concludes with some basic suggestions for best practices in using projective-expressive techniques in an appropriate and defensible manner.

One appropriate use of projective-expressive techniques in social-emotional assessment of children and adolescents is to establish rapport with the examinee. As a general rule, children find these assessment procedures to be safe and nonthreatening, and in many cases actually find them to be fun or enjoyable. Therefore, projective-expressive techniques such as thematic approaches, drawing techniques, and sentence completion tasks may serve the purpose of helping the examinee feel comfortable during the initial stages of the assessment, and helping to establish a positive relationship between the clinician and the child.

Another appropriate and potentially effective use of projective-expressive techniques is to use them as a means of communication with extremely shy or verbally reluctant children, or very young children who are not yet verbally sophisticated enough to engage in such processes as meaningful interviews. Even the most experienced and skilled clinicians will have difficulty from time to time in getting some children to communicate with them through traditional means such as a clinical interview. Drawing techniques may be especially useful in this regard, given that they make few or no demands on the child to engage verbally with the clinician, yet provide the opportunity for observation under structured conditions. This latter area may prove to be highly advantageous in some cases; observing a child's behavior under the semistandardized and structured conditions of completing a drawing technique allows for making observations regarding comparison with the behavior of numerous other children who may have been observed under the same conditions.

If projective-expressive techniques have been used to fulfill either of the first two general purposes just stated, then a natural and defensible use would be to help form hypotheses about the child's social-emotional functioning for additional assessment with more direct and objective approaches. For example, children are sometimes referred for assessment without a clear assessment problem or stated objective, and such children or the referral source are sometimes not particularly helpful in pinpointing specific areas to target in the assessment. In such situations, recurring themes found in nonthreatening projective-expressive assessment results may provide a basis for shaping future assessment directions (i.e., whether to target the internalizing or externalizing domain, or whether to include specific objective self-report measures within the battery).

Some clinicians find projective-expressive assessment techniques to be helpful in developing an understanding of their child or adolescent client, particularly from the examinee's own worldview and personal perspective. Perhaps this sort of experiential understanding of the child may be helpful in forming counseling goals, or in developing the rapport that will be useful in future counseling sessions.

Finally, it is important to clearly articulate the inappropriate uses of projective-expressive assessment techniques. Perhaps the most egregious use of these techniques (and the use that continues to raise the most controversy) is to make factual inferences based on inconclusive "signs." For example, let's say that a 6-year-old girl produces a kinetic family drawing in which she is separated from her father by a thick barrier of some kind. Let's also suppose that her picture of herself in this drawing includes supposed signs of powerlessness (i.e., thin, weak arms), and that her picture of her father includes some supposed signs of hostility or anger (i.e., large arms). Furthermore, suppose that in the final report, the clinician states "this child feels weak, alienated, and separated from her father, who she views as domineering and aggressive." In the absence of any corroborating defensible evidence, this type of use of projective-expressive techniques is unsupportable at best, and inflammatory and unethical at worst. This is the worst and most indefensible use of projective-expressive techniques, yet it seems to happen routinely. A related misuse of projective-expressive techniques is to use them as the sole basis for making a diagnosis or classification decision. Although various ethical and legal guidelines for assessment state that no single test or technique should be the basis for such a decision, using assessment techniques for this purpose that have questionable reliability and validity puts the clinician even further at-risk. Such inappropriate uses of projective-expressive techniques should be avoided at all costs.

CONCLUSIONS

Although projective-expressive techniques differ substantially from the direct and objective methods of assessment that are emphasized in this volume, they are among the most widely used of all social-emotional assessment methods, and have an important place in the history of social-emotional assessment. The basis of projective-expressive techniques is that examinees may "project" their unconscious motives, conflicts, and needs either verbally or in drawings when they are presented with ambiguous stimuli and tasks. Most of these techniques are heavily influenced by psychodynamic theory. Although projective-expressive techniques are very popular among clinicians, they have been surrounded in controversy because of the difficulty in defining specific constructs they may purport to assess, and because of psychometric properties that are often tenuous.

Thematic approaches to personality assessment are among the most widely used projective-expressive technique, and have a long and storied history. The Thematic Apperception Test (TAT) is among the oldest and most widely used techniques, and is the basis for most other thematic approaches. The Children's Apperception Test (CAT) was the first downward extension of the TAT for use with younger children, and includes pictures of animal characters for use with very young children. The Roberts Apperception Test for Children (RATC) is a more recently developed thematic approach that includes less ambiguous stimulus cards and a relatively objective scoring system. The evidence regarding thematic approaches is mixed, but they continue to be quite popular among clinicians, and have the potential advantage of facilitating communication with shy or reluctant examinees.

Drawing techniques for projective-expressive assessment have also been in existence nearly as long as the field of psychology. The Draw-A-Person (DAP) technique for personality assessment is a later variation on human figure drawing tests, which were originally developed for cognitive and developmental assessment. Numerous methods have been articulated for interpreting DAP drawings, including some more recently developed objective methods of scoring and interpretation. The Kinetic Family Drawing System (KFD) is a relatively recent technique for drawing members of a family in action situations. The KFD has been purported to provide revealing information on the child's perception of the inner dynamics and conflicts of a family constellation. The Bender–Gestalt Test (BGT) has primarily been used for perceptual motor and intellectual screening, but also has been advocated as a projective-expression test of social-emotional functioning. The most influential BGT technique in this regard is that proposed by Koppitz (1963, 1975). Overall projective-expressive drawing techniques remain very popular with clinicians. They evidence good interrater reliability using specific scoring systems, but evidence of test–retest reliability and construct validity has been less convincing.

Sentence completion tasks as a projective-expressive technique peaked in popularity in the 1940s and 1950s, and very little has occurred in the way on new innovations during the past two or three decades. The most acclaimed sentence completion task specifically for children is the Hart Sentence Completion Test for Children (HSCT), but it was never considered fully complete by its author, and is not currently available in the public domain. The Washington University Loevinger Sentence Completion Test is currently the most widely used sentence completion task with adolescents. It is privately published by its author and may be difficult to obtain. Most clinicians who utilize sentence completion tasks clinically develop their own lists of stems, and interpret them in a qualitative manner.

In sum, projective-expressive assessment techniques are among the most popular forms of social-emotional assessment currently used, but they still exist in a swirl of controversy because of their occasional misuse and because of their technical properties, which are often weak according to traditional psychometric conceptions. However, projective-expressive techniques will likely be in use for the foreseeable future, and do seem to have certain advantages and benefits. Thus, clinicians who use them should focus on the recommended best practices provided in this chapter, and avoid their misuse.

REVIEW AND APPLICATION QUESTIONS

1. What is the *projective hypothesis*? How can this hypothesis be operationally defined in assessment practice?

2. How can the continuing popularity of projective assessment be explained in the face of questionable empirical evidence?

3. If using the Thematic Apperception Test with an adolescent girl, what would be recommended stimulus cards?

4. How is the *inspection technique* best used in interpreting the Thematic Apperception Test and other thematic approaches?

5. How can the accumulated reliability and validity evidence regarding thematic approaches to assessment be best characterized?

6. For interpretation of the Draw-A-Person test and other human figure drawing tests, what should be considered when attempting to determine if a specific characteristic is a significant emotional indicator?

7. In comparison with the Draw-A-Person test, what is the *active* nature of the Kinetic Family Drawing test purported to predict?

8. How can the accumulated reliability and validity evidence regarding human figure drawing tests as social-emotional measures be best characterized?

9. What evidence exists to support the validity of Koppitz's *emotional indicators* on the Bender–Gestalt test?

10. How reliable over time are sentence completion tasks?

11. What are the most defensible and empirically supportable uses of projective-expressive assessment techniques?

ASSESSMENT OF SPECIFIC
PROBLEMS, COMPETENCIES,
AND POPULATIONS

CHAPTER

9

ASSESSMENT OF
EXTERNALIZING PROBLEMS

The domain of externalizing disorders and its related symptoms is a particularly troubling area for parents and teachers. By their nature, externalizing behavior problems are difficult to overlook, and are usually annoying and disruptive, if not dangerous at times. These behaviors often create problems for other individuals who are in the same environments as the children or adolescents who exhibit them. Fortunately, externalizing behavior problems can be effectively assessed, and some of these best assessment methods for these problems may be quite useful in developing intervention plans.

This chapter begins with an overview of externalizing problems, including discussions of specific disorders from both the behavioral dimensions and *DSM* approaches to classification. Following this introduction to the externalizing domain, some of the prevalence, etiology, developmental course, and prognosis indicators associated with externalizing disorders are reviewed. The bulk of the chapter is devoted to discussions of five methods of assessment and how they may be best utilized in evaluating the externalizing domain of problems. Additionally, there is a brief discussion on how well the five methods of assessment are linked to developing interventions to externalizing disorders and problems. A case study is presented to help readers to integrate the theory and technique discussed in this chapter into practical assessment applications based on an actual case.

EXTERNALIZING DISORDERS: AN OVERVIEW

aka undercontrolled + outer-directed

Experts in the field of child psychopathology generally agree that the behavioral dimension of *externalizing* disorders includes a broad array of aggressive behavior, antisocial characteristics, and hyperactivity (Cicchetti & Toth, 1991). Other terms that have been used to identify this behavioral dimension include *undercontrolled* and *outer-directed* behavior. Without respect to the terms used by researchers to classify this broad behavioral dimension, the essential characteristics are the same: aggressive, acting-out, disruptive, defiant, oppositional, and hyperactive behaviors. A youth who exhibits externalizing problems will not necessarily demonstrate all of these types of

211

behaviors, but the congruence or relatedness among such symptoms has been well-established.

The area of externalizing behavior problems has received significantly more attention than internalizing problems in the research literature, perhaps due to the debate over the reliability and long-term implications of internalizing disorders (Cicchetti & Toth, 1991), as well as the practical consideration that externalizing problems are seldom difficult to overlook. A number of historically important empirical studies have provided solid support for the construct of an externalizing dimension of behavior problems (e.g., Achenbach, 1985; Ackerson, 1942; Coie, Belding, & Underwood, 1988; Robins, 1966; Sroufe & Rutter, 1984). In addition to the types of externalizing symptoms noted at the beginning of this section, most of these sources identified another commonality of externalizing disorders, namely, peer rejection that stems from aggressive behavior.

Behavioral Dimensions Approach to Classifying Externalizing Disorders

Several prominent researchers, most notably Achenbach and Quay, have developed empirical behavioral dimensions classification taxonomies of externalizing behavior disorders (see chap. 2 for more details). Quay's model for externalizing disorders has been particularly influential. Quay (1986a) reviewed over 60 studies that applied multivariate statistical approaches to the classification of child psychopathology. These studies commonly identified several narrow-band dimensions of symptoms, with each area of symptomatology consisting of core behaviors and characteristics that were replicated at least several times. Under the broad-band domain referred to as externalizing, Quay isolated three major narrow-band dimensions of disorders, including Undersocialized Aggressive Conduct Disorder, Socialized Aggressive Conduct Disorder, and Attention Deficit Hyperactivity Disorder. These three disorders are briefly overviewed here. In addition, Table 9.1 provides examples of specific behaviors that fit within these domains.

Undersocialized Aggressive Conduct Disorder. The narrow-band externalizing dimension that Quay (1986a) referred to as Undersocialized Aggressive Conduct Disorder includes a cluster of behaviors that involve aggression, violation of rules, temper tantrums and irritability, attention seeking and impertinence, and a variety of other negative and oppositional behavioral characteristics. Quay (1986a) noted that this particular domain has emerged in multivariate classification studies "almost without exception" (p. 11), indicating that it is a relatively stable confluence of associated behaviors. In addition to a pattern of aggressive, disruptive, and noncompliant behaviors, the undersocialized aggressive conduct syndrome includes two other noteworthy features. The first feature is that hyperactive and restless behaviors (but usually not full-blown Attention Deficit Hyperactivity Disorder) often occur concomitantly with this syndrome, indicating an element of motor overactivity within the domain, but not necessarily attentional problems. The second noteworthy feature is that "stealing has not been found at all central to this dimension" (Quay, 1986a, p. 11). Instead, stealing behaviors are more central to socialized aggressive conduct disorder.

Socialized Aggressive Conduct Disorder. The second type of conduct disorder identified in Quay's (1986a) review and analysis is referred to as Socialized Aggressive Conduct Disorder. This cluster of behavior is seen less frequently than undersocialized aggressive conduct disorder, but has still received strong empirical support (Loeber &

TABLE 9.1
Major Characteristics of Three Domains of Externalizing
Behavior Disorders Derived from Quay's (1986) Literature Review

Undersocialized Aggressive Conduct Disorder
  Assaultive behavior (fights, hits)
  Disobedient and defiant behavior
  Temper tantrums
  Destructive behavior
  Impertinent or "sassy"; uncooperative
  Attention seeking
  Domineering/threatening behavior
  Demanding/disruptive behavior; loud and boisterous
  Irritable and explosive
  Negativity and refusal
  Restlessness, hyperactivity
  Dishonest and undependable
Socialized Aggressive Conduct Disorder
  "Bad" companions
  Truancy from home and school
  Gang membership
  Steals with others; steals at home
  Lies and cheats
  Stays out late at night
  Loyalty to delinquent friends
Attention Deficit Hyperactivity Disorder
  Poor concentration, short attention span, distractibility
  Daydreaming
  Poor coordination and clumsiness
  Stares into space; preoccupied
  Passivity and lack of initiative
  Fidgeting and restless behavior
  Fails to complete tasks
  Lazy or sluggish behavior, drowsiness
  Impulsivity
  Lack of interest, general boredom
  Hyperactive motor behaviors

hanging w/ a bad crowd

Schmaling, 1985). The principal features of this narrow-band dimension include involvement with peers in illegal or norm-violating behaviors. Some of the specific characteristic
behaviors of Socialized Aggressive Conduct Disorder include having "bad" companions,
truancy from school and home, stealing (both at and away from home), lying, and gang
activity. The essential feature of the behavior problems in this disorder is that they
occur as a way of maintaining social acceptance within a deviant or antisocial peer group. *maintain social acceptance*
Given that these conduct problems are often aimed at violating the rights of other persons
and social institutions, delinquent behavior and involvement with juvenile justice systems
often results. The onset of socialized aggressive conduct problems typically occurs at
a later developmental stage than the undersocialized variety, usually in late childhood
or early adolescence (Quay, 1986a). Another interesting feature of this dimension is
that it is much more likely to occur with males, and it is often accompanied by deficits
or lack of development in moral reasoning (Smetana, 1990). *later; ♂ = lack of morals.*

Attention Deficit Hyperactivity Disorder. The third narrow-band dimension of
externalizing behavior disorders identified by Quay (1986a) is Attention Deficit Hyperactivity Disorder, characterized by notable problems in maintaining concentration

and attention, and often including associated behavior features such as impulsivity,
clumsiness, and passivity. It is interesting to note that overt motor overactivity (what
is commonly thought of as hyperactivity) is not always a feature of this disorder. In
fact, behaviors that are characteristic of *underactivity* are often a prominent feature.
Essentially, Attention Deficit Hyperactivity Disorder is a diverse group of behaviors
and characteristics, and there are extremes in how the level of motor activity is manifest
in individual cases. Some children who exhibit this disorder are constantly "on the
move," fidgety, restless, and may be at heightened risk for developing other conduct
problems. On the other hand, the disorder may be exhibited in children who are more
withdrawn and passive, and who seldom engage in aggressive or antisocial behaviors.
As such, this particular disorder does not fit into the broad band of externalizing
problems as neatly as unsocialized and socialized aggressive conduct disorders. However, Attention Deficit Hyperactivity Disorder has more often been lumped in with
the externalizing than the internalizing broad-band dimension, based on both statistical
and clinical evidence. In fact, one of the principal problems in classification of the
behavioral symptoms of Attention Deficit Hyperactivity Disorder has been in distinguishing them from conduct disorders, due to the existence of so many overlapping
behaviors (Campbell & Werry, 1986). There is strong evidence that active and aggressive behavior usually coexist at a very early developmental stage (Campbell, 1991).

DSM Approach to Classifying Externalizing Disorders

Although Quay's behavioral dimensions approach to classification of externalizing
disorders is empirically supportable and has enjoyed wide influence among researchers,
the *DSM* system of classification is clearly the most widely used among practitioners in
the United States and Canada. *DSM–IV* includes three major categories of externalizing
behavior disorders relevant to children and youth that are found under the general
heading Attention Deficit and Disruptive Behavior Disorders. These three categories
include Attention Deficit Hyperactivity Disorder, Conduct Disorder, and Oppositional
Defiant Disorder. These three categories of externalizing behavior problems are reviewed
briefly in this section. Two additional *DSM–IV* classification categories, namely Adjustment Disorder with Disturbance of Conduct, and Other Conditions That May Be a Focus
of Clinical Attention, are also used to classify or diagnose externalizing behavior
problems. However, these categories are not an integral part of the domain of externalizing behavior disorders, and will not be discussed further here.

Attention Deficit Hyperactivity Disorder.   The *DSM–IV* diagnostic criteria for Attention Deficit Hyperactivity Disorder (ADHD) are shown in Table 9.2. The major behavioral characteristics of this disorder are quite similar to the major characteristics identified through Quay's (1986a) behavioral dimensions approach, although more
detailed, comprehensive, and specific. "The essential feature of Attention-Deficit/Hy-
peractivity Disorder is a persistent pattern of inattention and/or hyperactivity-impulsivity that is more frequent and severe than is typically observed in individuals at a
comparable level of development" (APA, 1994, p. 78). Perhaps the most notable
difference between the current *DSM* criteria and earlier editions of the *DSM* is the
separation of symptom areas into two major groups (inattention and hyperactivity),
with the resulting implication that the two symptom areas may be independent to
some extent. The previous edition (*DSM–III–R*; APA, 1987) did not separate symptoms
into clusters by type, but simply required that a diagnosis be based on the presence

TABLE 9.2
Diagnostic Criteria for Attention Deficit Hyperactivity Disorder from the *DSM–IV*

A. Either (1) or (2)
  1. Six (or more) of the following symptoms of *inattention* have persisted for at least 6 months to a degree that is maladaptive and inconsistent with developmental level:
  Inattention
     a. often fails to give close attention to details or makes careless mistakes in schoolwork, work, or other activities
     b. often has difficulty sustaining attention in tasks or play activities
     c. often does not seem to listen when spoken to directly
     d. often does not follow through on instructions and fails to finish schoolwork, chores, or duties in the workplace (not due to oppositional behavior or failure to understand instructions)
     e. often has difficulty organizing tasks and activities
     f. often avoids, dislikes, or is reluctant to engage in tasks that require sustained mental effort (such as schoolwork or homework)
     g. often loses things necessary for tasks or activities (e.g., toys, school assignments, pencils, books, or tools)
     h. is often easily distracted by extraneous stimuli
     i. is often forgetful in daily activities
  2. Six (or more) of the following symptoms of *hyperactivity-impulsivity* have persisted for at least 6 months to a degree that is maladaptive and inconsistent with developmental level:
  Hyperactivity
     a. often fidgets with hands or feet or squirms in seat
     b. often leaves seat in classroom or in other situations in which remaining seated is expected
     c. often runs about or climbs excessively in situations in which it is inappropriate (in adolescents or adults, may be limited to subjective feelings of restlessness)
     d. often has difficulty playing or engaging in leisure activities quietly
     e. is often "on the go" or often acts as if "driven by a motor"
     f. often talks excessively
  Impulsivity
     g. often blurts out answers before questions have been completed
     h. often has difficulty awaiting turn
     i. often interrupts or intrudes on others (e.g., butts into conversations or games)
B. Some hyperactive-impulsive or inattentive symptoms that caused impairment were present before age 7 years.
C. Some impairment from the symptoms is present in two or more settings (e.g., at school or work and at home). +
D. There must be clear evidence of clinically significant impairment in social, academic, or occupational functioning.
E. The symptoms do not occur exclusively during the course of a Pervasive Developmental Disorder, Schizophrenia, or other Psychotic Disorder and are not better accounted for by another mental disorder (e.g., Mood Disorder, Anxiety Disorder, Dissociative Disorder, or a Personality Disorder).

Code Types:

Attention-Deficit/Hyperactivity Disorder, Combined Type: If both Criteria A1 and A2 are met for the past 6 months.
Attention-Deficit/Hyperactivity Disorder, Predominantly Inattentive Type: If Criterion A1 is met but Criterion A2 is not met for the past 6 months.
Attention-Deficit/Hyperactivity Disorder, Predominantly Hyperactive-Impulsive Type: If Criterion A2 is met but Criterion A1 is not met for the past six months.

Note. From *Diagnostic and Statistical Manual of Mental Disorders* (4th ed.). Copyright © 1994, American Psychiatric Association. Reprinted by permission of the American Psychiatric Association.

of a minimum number of symptoms out of a larger broad symptom list. Current thinking on ADHD is that this disorder is often manifest as a distinct pattern of either inattentiveness or hyperactivity-impulsivity, although many individuals will exhibit characteristics of both types. Another significant change from previous editions in the *DSM–IV* criteria for ADHD is the requirement that symptoms must be pervasive (Hinshaw, 1994). This change was apparently intended to ensure that ADHD would not be diagnosed unless the associated problems were substantial. *DSM–IV* includes an age of onset criterion by age 7 for diagnosis of ADHD. However, it has been argued that no support exists for this age of onset criterion, and the primary symptoms of ADHD do not necessarily have to be manifest by age 7 (Barkley & Biederman, 1997).

[age 7]

Conduct Disorder. The *DSM–IV* diagnostic criteria for Conduct Disorder are presented in Table 9.3. In *DSM* terms, the essential feature of this disorder is "a repetitive and persistent pattern of behavior in which the basic rights of others or major age-appropriate societal norms or rules are violated" (APA, 1994, p. 85). In other words, Conduct Disorder is characterized by high levels of antisocial behavior. Unlike Quay's (1986a) behavioral dimensions approach to classification of conduct disorders, the current *DSM* criteria do not differentiate among various possible subtypes (other than age of onset and severity). However, previous versions of the *DSM* have included various typologies for conduct disorders. For example, the *DSM–III–R* (APA, 1987) included code types for *group type* and *solitary aggressive type,* two categories that roughly correspond to Quay's typology of Socialized Aggressive Conduct Disorder and Undersocialized Aggressive Conduct Disorder, respectively. To make a diagnosis of Conduct Disorder, a minimum of three characteristics from the diverse list of 15 symptoms must be present. Such generality in classification precision presents some obvious challenges. One such classification issue is the required existence of three (as opposed to, say, four or five) symptoms in the absence of any compelling empirical evidence to justify the criterion of three (Kazdin, 1995). Another issue exists regarding the diversity of symptoms on the list of 15 and the lack of any developmental anchors for these symptoms. As Kazdin (1995) noted,

persistently violating rights of others

> the symptoms are delineated in a fixed way so that they are applied equally across the full period of childhood to adolescence. Yet perhaps symptoms required to meet the diagnosis should vary with age. It is unlikely that a 4-year-old would steal or confront a victim or force sex on someone. Does this mean that Conduct Disorder does not emerge before the age of 4 years or that the criteria for a 4-year-old ought to be different? (p. 26)

Despite these and other concerns regarding the current *DSM* approach to classifying Conduct Disorder, it still results in identification of youth who, as a group, tend to show remarkable distinguishing behavioral characteristics when compared to "normal" youth (Walker, Colvin, & Ramsey, 1995), and who often have an amazingly poor prognosis.

Oppositional Defiant Disorder. The *DSM–IV* diagnostic criteria for Oppositional Defiant Disorder (ODD) are found in Table 9.4. There is no parallel behavioral dimensions category corresponding to ODD, but its symptoms appear to be subsumed under the Undersocialized Aggressive Conduct Disorder category. According to the *DSM–IV*, "The essential feature . . . is a recurrent pattern of negativistic, defiant, disobedient, and

neg. behavior against authority figures

TABLE 9.3
DSM–IV Diagnostic Criteria for Conduct Disorder

A. A repetitive and persistent pattern of behavior in which the basic rights of others or age-appropriate societal norms or rules are violated, as manifested by the presence or three (or more) of the following criteria in the past 12 months, with at least one criterion present in the past 6 months:
Aggression to people and animals
   1. Often bullies, threatens or intimidates others.
   2. Often initiates physical fights.
   3. Has used a weapon that can cause serious physical harm to others (e.g., a bat, brick, broken bottle, knife, gun).
   4. Has been physically cruel to people.
   5. Has been physically cruel to animals.
   6. Has stolen while confronting a victim (e.g., mugging, purse snatching, extortion, armed robbery).
   7. Has forced someone into sexual activity.
Destruction of property
   8. Has deliberately engaged in fire setting with the intention of causing serious damage.
   9. Has deliberately destroyed others' property (other than by fire setting).
Deceitfulness of theft
   10. Has broken into someone else's house, building, or car.
   11. Often lies to obtain goods or favors or to avoid obligations (i.e., "cons" others).
   12. Has stolen items of nontrivial value without confronting a victim (e.g., shoplifting, but without breaking and entering; forgery).
Serious Violations of Rules
   13. Often stays out at night despite parental prohibitions, beginning before age 13 years.
   14. Has run away from home overnight at least twice while living in parental or parental surrogate home (or once without returning for a lengthy period).
   15. Is often truant from school, beginning before age 13 years.
B. The disturbance in behavior causes clinically significant impairment in social, academic, or occupational functioning.
C. If the individual is 18 years or older, criteria are not met for Antisocial Personality Disorder.

Code Types
Childhood-Onset Type: Onset of at least one criterion characteristic of Conduct Disorder prior to age 10 years.
Adolescent-Onset Type: Absence of any criteria characteristic of Conduct Disorder prior to age 10 years.
Severity
Mild: Few if any conduct problems in excess of those required to make the diagnosis *and* conduct problems cause only minor harm to others.
Moderate: Number of conduct problems and effect on others intermediate between "mild" and "severe."
Severe: Many conduct problems in excess of those required to make the diagnosis or conduct problems cause considerable harm to others.

Note. From *Diagnostic and Statistical Manual of Mental Disorders* (4th ed.). Copyright © 1994, American Psychiatric Association. Reprinted by permission of the American Psychiatric Association.

hostile behavior toward authority figures" (APA, 1994, p. 91). Although some researchers and clinicians may doubt the existence of ODD as an empirical category that is unique from Conduct Disorder (some have derisively referred to ODD as a "weeny conduct disorder"), *DSM–IV* considers it to be a developmental precursor to Conduct Disorder. However, it is interesting to note that *DSM–IV* considers ODD and Conduct Disorder to be mutually exclusive classifications. If symptom criteria for both disorders are met, then Conduct Disorder should be the appropriate classification. Making a differential diagnosis between the two disorders would surely be a problem, because of their apparently hierarchical relation. Perhaps the most salient feature that might separate ODD from Conduct Disorder is the absence of overtly aggressive behavior, which is also a major predictor of future problems.

ODD → CD
less severe   more severe

TABLE 9.4
DSM–IV Diagnostic Criteria for Oppositional Defiant Disorder

A. A pattern of negativistic, hostile, and defiant behavior lasting at least 6 months, during which four (or more) of the following are present:

   1. often loses temper
   2. often argues with adults
   3. often actively defies or refuses to comply with adults' requests or rules
   4. often deliberately annoys people
   5. often blames others for his or her mistakes or misbehavior
   6. is often touchy or easily annoyed by others
   7. is often angry and resentful
   8. is often spiteful or vindictive

   Note: Consider a criterion met only if the behavior occurs more frequently than is typically observed in individuals of comparable age and developmental level.

B. The disturbance in behavior causes clinically significant impairment in social, academic, or occupational functioning.
C. The behaviors do not occur exclusively during the course of a Psychotic or Mood Disorder.
D. Criteria are not met for Conduct Disorder, and, if the individual is age 18 years or older, criteria are not met for Antisocial Personality Disorder.

Note. From *Diagnostic and Statistical Manual of Mental Disorders* (4th ed.). Copyright © 1994, American Psychiatric Association. Reprinted by permission of the American Psychiatric Association.

PREVALENCE, ETIOLOGY, AND PROGNOSIS OF EXTERNALIZING DISORDERS

Prevalence

Prevalence estimates for externalizing disorders vary depending on definitional criteria, specific populations studied, and assessment methodology. However, there is a general consensus that externalizing problems tend to be quite common, and a surprisingly high percentage of children and adolescents are thought to exhibit externalizing symptoms. The *DSM–IV* states that for school-age children, ADHD occurs in an estimated 3% to 5% of the general population, a range consistent with the empirical evidence (e.g., Barkley, 1990). ADHD is known to occur much more frequently in males than in females, with prevalence ratios for the genders ranging from 4:1 to 9:1, respectively, depending on the type of setting. Regarding Conduct Disorder, *DSM–IV* states that in the child and adolescent population, the prevalence rate ranges from 6% to 16% for males, and 2% to 9% for females. B. Martin and Hoffman (1990) cited conservative prevalence studies placing the range of estimation for conduct disorders from about 4% to 8% in the entire school-age population, with males outnumbering females at about a 3:1 ratio on average. Less information is available regarding the prevalence of ODD. *DSM–IV* provided a very wide range (2% to 16%) for the estimate of prevalence, and noted that it "is more prevalent in males than in females before puberty, but the rates are probably equal after puberty" (APA, 1994, p. 92). In contrast with what is known regarding the prevalence and gender features of ADHD and Conduct Disorder, relatively little evidence exists in the professional literature regarding Oppositional Defiant Disorder. When viewed as a whole, the prevalence estimates for externalizing disorders indicate that this band of disorders is relatively common in school-age children, that boys are more likely to exhibit them than are girls, and that Conduct Disorder is more common than ADHD.

Comorbidity   *— of externalizing disorders in children*

A well-known fact that has emerged from the literature on externalizing disorders in children is that they tend to occur in a comorbid pattern, meaning that two or more of these disorders will coexist in a substantial percentage of cases. This finding has been verified with respect to the relation between ADHD and Conduct Disorder (Hinshaw, 1987, 1994; Kazdin, 1995; Loney & Milich, 1982; Paternite & Loney, 1980), Conduct Disorder and Oppositional Defiant Disorder (Biederman, Faraone, Milberger, & Jetton, 1996; Kazdin, 1995), and Oppositional Defiant Disorder and ADHD (Biederman et al., 1996). Although the existence of one of these disorders does not necessarily mandate the presence of another (remember that a diagnosis of Conduct Disorder precludes a diagnosis of Oppositional Defiant Disorder), they have been linked through theory and research for many years. Loeber (1985a) posited an interesting speculation on the link between ADHD and Conduct Disorder, suggesting that ADHD symptoms (and particularly hyperactive behavior) may be a necessary precursor for the development of severe forms of Conduct Disorder in many children. In addition, *DSM–IV* regards Oppositional Defiant Disorder as "a developmental antecedent to Conduct Disorder" (p. 92). Whatever the relation among the various externalizing disorders, it is clear that they share extensive common ground. Of course, the substantial comorbidity of specific forms of externalizing disorders "raises questions about the categories themselves and about what is the most meaningful and useful way to delineate disruptive behaviors" (Kazdin, 1995, p. 25).   *ADHD may be a precursor to other disorders*

Etiology   *cause of externalizing disorders*

The etiology or origin of externalizing disorders has been the focus of much speculation and a good deal of research. The major models for explaining causation have been social learning, biochemical/neurological, and familial/genetic approaches, or variants thereof. Hinshaw, in his excellent overview of the various competing etiological models for ADHD, noted that researchers are "actively searching for unifying themes that could account for the symptomatology, associated features, and course of the disorder" (1994, p. 51). With respect to ADHD, Campbell and Werry (1986) noted that although there has been a tremendous amount of speculation that a biological basis for the disorder exists, "specific conclusions remain elusive" (p. 116). If there is a biological basis for ADHD as Deutsch and Kinsbourne (1990) contended, it may be obscured due to its heterogeneous nature, and by the fact that there may be differing causal factors and risk factors for diverging subgroups of children with ADHD (Hinshaw, 1994). An interesting recent theory regarding the etiology of ADHD, one that promises to be highly influential, has been postulated by Barkley (1997a, 1997b), who argued that the root of this disorder is not attentional, but rather a developmental problem of self-control, or a deficit in behavioral inhibition. It is anticipated that the tremendous surge of interest in recent years regarding ADHD will result in continued theoretical developments and empirical advances regarding etiology.

With respect to conduct disorders (including Conduct Disorder and Oppositional Defiant Disorder), there has been increasing speculation of a biologically based etiology (Kazdin, 1995; Werry, 1986), but again, specific conclusions are difficult at this point.

Like ADHD, conduct disorders may have a familial/genetic connection (Deutsch & Kinsbourne, 1990; Plomin, Nitz, & Rowe, 1990). However, even with the inclusion of some well-designed twin studies and adoption studies, ferreting out the specific contributions of social learning and genetics has been problematic (Deutsch & Kinsbourne, 1990; Hetherington & B. Martin, 1986; Werry, 1986). Despite the increasing amount of attention and interesting evidence regarding the possible biochemical or neurological basis for conduct disorders, the social learning model may offer a more clear-cut model of etiology at the present time. For example, Patterson's research group at the Oregon Social Learning Center conducted a number of studies demonstrating that such factors as harsh and inconsistent discipline practices, lax parental monitoring, and exposure to adult models of antisocial behavior are all powerful predictors of the development of aggressive and antisocial behavior in children (e.g., Patterson, 1976, 1982, 1984; Patterson & Bank, 1986; Patterson & Dishion, 1985; Patterson et al., 1992). Another influential social learning-based model of the development of childhood conduct problems has been proposed by Wahler and colleagues (e.g., Wahler, 1994; Wahler & Dumas, 1986). This model includes many of the features identified by Patterson and colleagues, but takes a somewhat differing approach, focusing on social continuity and predictability of coercive interactions between parents and children as key variables in developing and maintaining antisocial-aggressive child behavior. Despite efforts to identify single essential variables that lead to development of conduct disorders, researchers who investigate this area appear to be focusing less on specific sole etiologic factors, and are viewing these possible causes as being *risk factors,* or factors that increase vulnerability to the development of the disorders. Thus, perhaps the most useful method of approaching the etiology of Conduct Disorders and Oppositional Defiant Disorder for assessment purposes is to integrate the various findings and speculations into a reciprocal determinism model consistent with Bandura's (1986) social cognitive theory. It is likely that behavioral, environmental, and personal factors all contribute to development of externalizing disorders, and that they work together in an interactive fashion.

Developmental Course and Prognosis

There is more evidence regarding developmental patterns and long-term implications of externalizing disorders than for internalizing disorders (Cicchetti & Toth, 1991). The general developmental course of ADHD appears to include several components, including onset in infancy or early childhood, continuation during childhood and adolescence with concomitant academic, behavioral and social problems, and marginal adjustment to the disorder during adulthood (Campbell & Werry, 1986; Hinshaw, 1994). "Overall, ADHD is far from a benign disorder: It carries significant risk for antisocial outcomes and for continuing patterns of disinhibited behavior, cognitive dysfunction, and interpersonal difficulties" (Hinshaw, 1994, p. 87). Longitudinal studies of ADHD (e.g., Weiss, 1983; Weiss, Hechtman, Perlman, Hopkins, & Wener, 1979) have shown that although individuals with ADHD may exhibit less impulsivity, restlessness, and antisocial behavior as adults than they did as adolescents, they are more likely to be "underemployed" than individuals without ADHD. These same studies have indicated that ADHD by itself is not necessarily predictive of severe psychopathology later in life. A related review of studies by Whalen and Henker (1998) concluded that although adults who were diagnosed with ADHD as children may have continuing problems with ADHD symptoms and related externalizing problems, there

prognosis depends on what else ADHD is occurring with

is no compelling evidence that children with ADHD are at increased risk for later development of internalizing disorders, such as mood or anxiety disorders. However, if ADHD during childhood is accompanied by other externalizing disorders, substance abuse, familial discord, and low levels of intelligence and academic achievement, the long-term prognosis is poorer, and there is a greater likelihood of criminal behavior and psychiatric problems (Barkley, 1990; Whalen & Henker, 1998).

With respect to conduct disorders (including Conduct Disorder and Oppositional Defiant Disorder from the *DSM* system), their developmental course and long-term prognosis appear to be related strongly to the amount and intensity of aggressive behavior that is present. Quay (1986b) suggested that aggression is more likely to be a major characteristic of unsocialized rather than socialized types of conduct disorders, and the best prognosis for long-term adjustment is likely with individuals who have socialized aggressive conduct disorder in conjunction with high intelligence and good social skills. Previous research on aggressive behavior has resulted in findings that indicate reasonably strong stability over time. The likelihood that children's aggressive behavior will persist into adulthood increases with age. In other words, there is a modest probability that very young children (e.g., preschoolers) who exhibit persistent patterns of aggressive behavior will also exhibit aggressive behaviors as adults. But, if these children are still exhibiting the same pattern of behavior by age 10 or 12, then the probability of them continuing aggressive behavior as adults increases significantly. This pattern of continuity was demonstrated in a classic review of the literature from 1935 to 1978 by Olweus (1979), who found that stability of aggressive behavior was almost as strong over 10-year periods (.60) as that of intelligence (.70). Quay (1986b) suggested that the pattern of persistence of aggressive behavior is stronger for males than for females. Interestingly, whether or not aggressive and antisocial conduct results in involvement with the justice system (i.e., reported delinquent and criminal behavior) seems to be strongly related to whether or not the child or adolescent has a parent who was convicted of a crime before the child reached age 10 (Farrington, 1978).

Thus, the long-term developmental course of Conduct Disorder leads to the conclusion of a poor prognosis: "Longitudinal studies have consistently shown that conduct disorder identified in childhood or adolescence predicts a continued course of social dysfunction, problematic behavior, and poor school and occupational adjustment" (Kazdin, 1995, p. 69). Although considered to be a less severe disorder than Conduct Disorder, Oppositional Defiant Disorder also appears to have a poor long-term prognosis, primarily because it is considered to be a developmental antecedent to Conduct Disorder. Again, the amount and intensity of aggressive behavior that develops over time may be a key to understanding the long-term prognosis. It is important to recognize that the change in development from childhood to adolescence to adulthood of children who develop and maintain patterns of antisocial behavior is *additive*. That is, these children usually "do not *change* the types of behaviors they display but instead *add* the more severe conduct problem behaviors" (italics added; Frick, 1998, p. 215).

To sum up this discussion on the long-term implications of conduct disorders, it is important to consider two major findings: Present aggressive behavior is the most important variable in the prediction of future aggressive and antisocial behavior (Quay, 1986b; Robins, 1966); and although almost all adults with antisocial aggressive behavior exhibited these same patterns as children, many antisocial children do not become antisocial adults (Frick, 1998; B. Martin & Hoffman, 1990; Robins, 1974). Therefore, a diagnosis of Conduct Disorder, though often associated with a poor prognosis for future adjustment, does not necessarily mandate such a prognosis.

CD ≠ poor prognosis for future in all cases.

METHODS OF ASSESSING EXTERNALIZING PROBLEMS

Each of the five major assessment methods emphasized in this book can be used with success in measuring externalizing disorders and problems. In terms of the state of the art and the utility of each method for day-to-day assessment of externalizing problems, direct observation and rating scales have received more attention in the literature. In terms of interview techniques, the behavioral interview with parents or teachers offers a great deal in the assessment of externalizing problems, and the structured interview schedules that have been developed over the past two decades also have shown some promise. Sociometric techniques have been shown to be extremely strong predictors of externalizing behavior disorders, but may not be as easily implemented in routine assessment designs. Objective self-report assessment may also be used in evaluating externalizing problems, but it does appear to be more limited in scope and utility than observation, rating scales, and interviews. Each of these five methods is discussed in this section.

Behavioral Observation

There is widespread professional agreement that direct behavioral observation is one of the most useful procedures for assessing externalizing behavior disorders (Alessi, 1988; Reid et al., 1988). McMahon and Forehand (1988) suggested that behavioral observation is "the most reliable and valid assessment procedure for obtaining a functional analysis of conduct disorders in children" (p. 138). There are two major reasons that direct behavioral observation is a preferred method for assessing externalizing problems. The first reason has to do with the nature of externalizing disorders. Unlike internalizing disorders, which often involve highly subjective perceptions and internal states, externalizing disorders are characterized by overt behavior patterns that are easy to observe, such as excessive motor activity, physical aggression, and verbal intimidation and opposition. Therefore, behavioral observation is an assessment method that easily measures externalizing target behaviors and is highly objective. The second reason for preference of direct observation in assessing externalizing disorders has to do with behavior–environment interactions and the need to identify aspects of the environment that may be usefully modified in a treatment plan. Like internalizing problems, externalizing behavior problems do not occur in a vacuum; they are elicited and maintained in a very complex interaction between the person, the behavior, and the environment, as illustrated in Bandura's (1977, 1978, 1986) notion of reciprocal determinism. However, unlike internalizing problems, these interactive relations in externalizing behavior problems are easier to directly observe. Therefore, specific interactions and environmental variables that may play a role in the development of interventions are relatively easy for a skilled observer to identify.

Chapter 3 includes a detailed discussion of general observation methods and coding procedures, including examples of systems useful in clinic, home, and school settings. This information is not repeated in this chapter. This section does provide an example of a direct observation system that has been successfully employed in the assessment of externalizing disorders in clinic settings. Although home- and school-based observation systems for externalizing problems have been successfully demonstrated (see chap. 3 for examples), the focus is on a clinic-based example in this section of the chapter, because this is a setting that can be easily utilized in by the majority of clinicians on a day-to-day basis.

Although mental health, medical, or school psychology clinics are usually not considered to be naturalistic settings for conducting observations, these clinic environments can serve as very effective atmospheres for observing externalizing behavior problems (H. M. Hughes & Haynes, 1978). Clinic observations are usually analogue in nature, in that they can create conditions where behavior can simulate the home setting. A major advantage of clinic-based observation is that it is more efficient and cost-effective and less obtrusive than home-based observations (McMahon & Forehand, 1988).

DPICS

Dyadic Parent–Child Interaction Coding System. An example of an excellent clinic-based observation system is Eyberg and Robinson's (1983) Dyadic Parent–Child Interaction Coding System (DPICS), which is a coding procedure that has proven to be a highly reliable and valid method for assessment of externalizing problem behaviors of children. What makes the DPICS particularly interesting is that it goes beyond simply focusing on child behavior problems and assesses these behaviors in the context of parental interactions in the parent–child dyad. The DPICS requires observation of the parent–child dyad in three different situations in the clinic: a free-play situation (Child-Directed Interaction); a situation in which the parent guides the child's activity (Parent-Directed Interaction); and a situation referred to as Clean-Up, where the parent attempts to get the child to clean up the toys in a playroom. The observations occur for 5 minutes in each of the three settings using a continuous frequency recording system, for a total of 15 minutes of direct behavioral observation. Parent behaviors are coded along 12 domains, including direct and indirect statements, descriptive and reflective statements, descriptive and reflective questions, acknowledgment, irrelevant verbalization, unlabeled and labeled praise, positive and negative physical interactions, and critical statements. Child behaviors are coded along seven different domains, including cry, yell, whine, smart talk, destructive, physical negative, and change activity. Robinson and Eyberg (1981) also developed composite behavioral coding variables (total praise, total deviant, total commands, command ratio, no opportunity ratio, compliance ratio, and noncompliance ratio), which consist of specific combinations of individual coding domains.

Results of several studies have shown the DPICS to have solid psychometric properties. The interrater reliability of the DPICS has been found to range from .65 to 1.00 (Aragona & Eyberg, 1981; Eyberg & Matarazzo, 1980), with mean reliability coefficients of .91 and .92 for parent and child behaviors in the standardization study (Robinson & Eyberg, 1981). Although the DPICS has been primarily utilized in clinic-based observations, one investigation (Zangwill & Kniskern, 1982) found overall cross-setting interobserver agreement of .68 and .69 between home and clinic observations.

In terms of validity evidence, Robinson and Eyberg (1981) demonstrated that the DPICS can accurately discriminate groups of children with conduct disorders from their siblings and from normal children, and it has a high correct classification rate for each of these child groups and their families. This finding has been replicated through other studies (e.g., Forster, Eyberg, & G. L. Burns, 1990). Other studies have shown the DPICS to be sensitive to treatment effects (Eyberg & Matarazzo, 1980; Webster-Stratton, 1984). It appears to be relatively easy to implement with trained observers, and to provide assessment data that are not only descriptive of problems, but can be used to build treatment plans as well.

The DPICS is just one example of a clinic-based coding procedure that has proven useful in assessing externalizing problems. A number of other clinic-based systems

flexibile observational coding systems

that have been empirically validated for assessing externalizing disorders have been reported in the literature. Of course, one of the main advantages of behavioral observation is that the methodology is flexible and easily tailored to the specific assessment problem in question. Observational coding systems that have been well researched offer certain advantages, but clinicians and researchers who understand the dynamics of observational assessment are able to develop systems that are uniquely suitable for the settings in which they are working. If the referred child/adolescent client is reported to exhibit serious behavioral problems at school as well as at home, it may also be necessary to observe directly in the classroom, using an observation system similar to the school-based examples in chapter 3. As McMahon and Forehand (1988) suggested, the therapist usually does not have the option of observing teacher–child interactions in the clinic, and as a result, naturalistic observation in the classroom may be warranted. Of course, if the problem behavior is related to a school-based referral, direct observation in the classroom should be a high priority, if not an essential part, of the assessment.

Behavior Rating Scales

Behavior rating scales are potentially one of the most useful methods of assessment for externalizing behavior problems. Because externalizing behavior is usually directly observable, an informant who knows the child or adolescent well may be in a position to provide a comprehensive rating of a wide variety of problem behaviors. Like direct observation, rating scales can provide relatively objective measurement, yet they are much less time intensive to utilize. As a method of initial screening of problem behaviors and subsequent hypothesis generation, behavior rating scales may be one of the best choices. Theoretically though, there are some important differences between even the best rating scales and direct observation, and these differences usually indicate the need for using both types of measures. Rating scales usually provide a *retrospective* method of assessment, given that a parent or teacher rates child or adolescent problem behaviors according to their observations and perceptions over a past time period, say, the preceding 6 months. On the other hand, direct observation provides a format for measuring behaviors as they occur over a limited time period. Thus, rating scales will seldom provide information on environmental variables relating to problem behaviors, whereas direct observation over short time periods is likely to miss low frequency but important behaviors. The multimethod, multisource, multisetting assessment model described in chapter 1 provides a format for overcoming the limitations of individual assessment sources and still utilizing their strengths.

For most purposes, the general problem behavior rating scales or systems illustrated in chapter 4 (Behavior Assessment System for Children, Child Behavior Checklist and Teacher's Report Form, Conners Rating Scales and Revised Conners Rating Scales, and Revised Behavior Problem Checklist) are excellent choices for screening externalizing behavior problems. These rating scales all have a number of items and scales specific to the externalizing domain. Additionally, the School Social Behavior Scales, discussed in chapter 12, may also prove useful in certain cases when assessing externalizing problems. Scale B of this instrument (the Antisocial Behavior scale) provides a specific format for measuring aggressive, disruptive, and antisocial behavior in conjunction with a rating of social skills from Scale A. And, the Preschool and Kindergarten Behavior Scales, discussed in chapter 13, provide an excellent means for screening externalizing behavior problems with preschool and kindergarten-age children.

good info w/o too much trouble

There may be times when it is useful to assess externalizing problems using rating scales designed to measure specific components of the externalizing domain. Thus, this section includes brief overviews of some "narrow purpose" rating scales. These include the Attention Deficit Disorders Evaluation Scales and the Conners ADHD/*DSM–IV* Scales, both of which are parent and teacher rating scales designed for assessing the behavioral symptoms of ADHD specifically based on the *DSM–IV* diagnostic criteria; the Eyberg Child Behavior Inventory, a measure for assessing conduct problems and general externalizing characteristics; and the Home and School Situations Questionnaires, which are related measures for assessing the situational aspects of externalizing behavior problems.

specific disorder

Attention Deficit Disorders Evaluation Scales. The Attention Deficit Disorders Evaluation Scales (ADDES; McCarney, 1989a, 1989b, 1995a, 1995b) are a set of instruments designed specifically for measuring the behavioral characteristics of ADHD in children, adolescents, and young adults, and for making program planning and intervention decisions. The 1989 references to the ADDES are for the original versions of this instrument (reviewed in Merrell, 1994a), and the 1995 references are for the second edition, which was developed based on the changes in ADHD diagnostic criteria that were implemented in *DSM–IV*. Although many of the features of the two editions are similar, this discussion of the ADDES focuses solely on the second editions of these measures.

Two versions of the ADDES are available: a 50-item home version designed to be completed by parents, and a 56-item school version designed to be completed by teachers and other school-based professionals. The items on the ADDES are descriptions of a variety of behaviors reflecting inattentiveness and hyperactivity-impulsivity. The items are divided into two sections and scales consistent with this *DSM–IV* symptom area breakdown. The items are rated using a rather unique 5-point scale where each rating point is anchored to a specific time element under which the behaviors may occur (0 = "does not engage in the behavior," 1 = "one to several times per month," 2 = "one to several times per week," 3 = "one to several times per day," and 4 = "one to several times per hour"). Raw scores are converted to standard scores (with a range of 0–20, and representing a mean of 10 and standard deviation of 3) and percentile ranks based on the two subscale breakdown and a total score. These scores are keyed to three different diagnostic levels (normal score, some problems, serious problems), based on standard deviation units from the normative population.

rating scales

The brief technical manuals for the home and school versions of the ADDES provide a variety of information on the technical properties of each instrument. Both versions of the ADDES were normed on very large nationwide population samples. The Home Version standardization sample includes ratings of 2,415 youth provided by 3,932 parents. The School Version standardization sample includes ratings of 5,795 students provided by 2,414 teachers. The stability of the ADDES across time, settings, and raters appears to be very good. Test–retest reliability at 30-day intervals is in the low .90 range for the total scores, and ranges from .88 to .97 for the subscales. Mean interrater reliabilities of the ADDES are also very high, with an average *r* of .85 between pairs of teachers on the school version, and .82 between parents on the home version. Internal consistency coefficients are in the .90 range for the scales on each version of the ADDES. Although the subscale structure of the ADDES was developed using rational-theoretical methods, the data were subjected to factor analysis procedures, which provide strong support for the *DSM–IV* symptom area breakdown of the measures. Diagnostic validity data gathered during the standardization of the ADDES show

[handwritten: ADDES correlates w/ other measures of ADHD]

that each version of the instrument can discriminate between groups of children who have been diagnosed as having ADHD and randomly selected comparison subjects. The technical manuals present strong convergent construct validity evidence for both versions, including moderate to very strong correlations between them and various instruments from the Conners Rating Scale System (CTRS–28 and CPRS–48, CPRS–93), strong correlations between the Home Version and the externalizing subscales from the Child Behavior Checklist, and strong correlations between both versions and the Children's Attention and Adjustment Survey (Lambert, Hartsough, & Sandoval, 1990), a measure not discussed in this book.

Although there are no externally published validity studies to date on either version of the ADDES, the reliability and validity evidence presented in the technical manuals is adequate to very good, and the normative standardization samples are very impressive. Thus, the ADDES is recommended as a narrow-band behavior rating scale for screening and assessment of children and adolescents where ADHD symptoms are the sole or primary concern. Parents and teachers will likely find the scales easy to use, and clinicians will likely find both versions of the ADDES to be quite practical. However, the addition of some externally published research studies supporting the ADDES would bolster the confidence with which researchers and clinicians might use these instruments, and would bolster their reputation within the professional community.

Conners ADHD/DSM–IV Scales. The Conners ADHD/*DSM–IV* Scales (CADS) are part of the revised Conners Rating System (CRS–R; Conners, 1997) overviewed in chapter 4. These instruments, including a 26-item parent version and a 27-item teacher version, are similar measures designed specifically to evaluate symptoms of ADHD in children and adolescents. The CADS include the ADHD index and the 18 ADHD Symptom Scales from the full-length versions of the CRS–R. The parent and teacher versions of the CADS are quite similar and contain several overlapping items. The main difference between them are a few items specific to each that are focused exclusively on either the home or school setting. These instruments use the same rating format, scoring system, and scoring options that were described for the CRS–R in chapter 4. They typically require 5 to 10 minutes for administration, and are organized so that the respondent may either complete all 26 or 27 items, or just the items pertinent to the ADHD issue in question (ADHD index, *DSM–IV* inattentive items, or *DSM–IV* Hyperactive-Impulsive items).

Because these instruments are simply domain-specific briefer versions of the full-length CRS–R instruments, they were standardized using the same large normative sample. Based on information provided in the CRS–R technical manual, the psychometric properties of the CADS are adequate to very good, as was stated in chapter 4. There are currently no externally published studies documenting the validity of the CADS, but based on the extensive information provided in the technical manual, there is no reason to doubt that they are potentially useful in assessing behavioral symptoms associated with ADHD. For assessment situations in which the referral questions are very specific to attentional problems and/or hyperactivity, and in which there is no indication of coexisting conduct or affective problems, the CADS may be a good choice for a narrow-band behavior rating scale.

Eyberg Child Behavior Inventory. The Eyberg Child Behavior Inventory (ECBI; Eyberg, 1980) is a 36-item scale designed to obtain parent ratings of externalizing conduct problems in children from age 2 to 16. The 36 items are rated using a 7-point scale that

[handwritten margin note: parents rate externalizing conduct problems]

assesses frequency of occurrence, as well as a yes–no problem identification checklist. The original ECBI normative data were divided into 2–12 and 13–16 age groups. Since the original publication of ECBI norms, new standardization data have been published for large samples of children and adolescents (G. L. Burns, Patterson, & Nussbaum, 1991). The ECBI was originally considered to be a unidimensional scale primarily measuring overt conduct problems. However, a more recent analysis (G. L. Burns & Patterson, 1991) has indicated that the ECBI may in fact be a multidimensional scale, with three factors isolated that approximate the *DSM* diagnostic categories of Conduct Disorder, Oppositional Defiant Disorder, and Attention Deficit Hyperactivity Disorder.

Several early research reports demonstrated the ECBI to have strong internal consistency and adequate test–retest reliability (e.g., Eyberg & Robinson, 1983; Robinson, Eyberg, & Ross, 1980). A more recent study (Eisenstadt, McElreath, Eyberg, & McNeil, 1994) demonstrated that the ECBI had adequate interrater reliability between mothers and fathers. Evidence for validity of the ECBS has come from numerous published studies. For example, the ECBS has been shown to differentiate among groups of conduct problem, clinic control, and normal children (Eyberg & Robinson, 1983), to be sensitive as an outcome measure to various treatment effects (e.g., Eyberg & Robinson, 1982a; McGain & McKinzey, 1995; Mullin, Quigley, & Glanville, 1994), and to correlate significantly with the broad-band scales of the Child Behavior Checklist, especially the externalizing dimension (Boggs, Eyberg, & L. A. Reynolds, 1990).

The ECBI is easy to administer and score, and appears to be a useful instrument for inclusion in assessment batteries where measuring externalizing disorders is the primary or only concern. The ECBI has not been commercially published, and clinicians or researchers will need to obtain copies of the various published research articles in order to effectively utilize this instrument. *measures behaviors and environments!*

Home and School Situations Questionnaires. The Home Situations Questionnaire (HSQ) and School Situations Questionnaire (SSQ) are a set of related behavior rating scales introduced by Barkley (1981) in his book on diagnosis and treatment of hyperactivity in children. These scales are different in nature from most problem behavior rating instruments because they help to assess the settings in which children exhibit problem behaviors. Thus, the HSQ and SSQ are designed to measure both *behaviors* and *environments*. These instruments were developed from a parent interview format for obtaining information on problem behaviors often exhibited by hyperactive children (Barkley, 1981). The HSQ asks parents about 16 situations around the home and in public where problem behaviors of their children are exhibited (e.g., mealtimes, getting dressed in the mornings, when child is asked to do a chore, etc.). Parents first respond in a yes/no fashion as to whether each item constitutes a specific problem, and then rate the severity of each situation using a 1 (mild) to 9 (severe) rating scale. The SSQ is similar in format to the HSQ, but specifies 12 situations specific to school settings (e.g., in the hallways, during small group work, etc.). Both instruments yield two scores: the total number of problem settings (from the yes/no checklist) and a mean severity rating (the average score of the 1–9 ratings).

Published studies have provided normative data for elementary-age children for the HSQ and SSQ, and have demonstrated that these instruments have adequate psychometric properties, treatment sensitivity, and discriminant validity in differentiating children with ADHD from other children (Barkley & Edelbrock, 1987; Barkley, Karlsson, Pollard, & Murphy, 1985; Befera & Barkley, 1985; Danforth & DuPaul, 1996;

DuPaul & Barkley, 1992; Pollard, Ward, & Barkley, 1983). Additional research efforts have included examinations of the factor structures of both scales (Breen & Altepeter, 1991), provision of additional normative data and verification of psychometric properties (Altepeter & Breen, 1989), and development and initial standardization of a version of the instruments specific to the adolescent age range (C. D. Adams, McCarthy, & Kelly, 1995). Although the HSQ and SSQ are much briefer and more specific in scope than the broad purpose rating scales in chapter 4, they are innovative, unique, and potentially very useful for assessing externalizing behavior problems. They appear to have a great degree of clinical and research utility in assessing situational factors for treatment planning and evaluation, particularly surrounding behaviors often seen in children with attention deficit hyperactivity disorder.

Interviewing Techniques   *— an important 1st step, but limited …*

Of the interviewing techniques discussed in chapter 5, the behavioral interview appears to be the most effective approach for assessing the various externalizing disorders. Although traditional (i.e., unstructured) interviewing techniques may be useful in getting a general appraisal of the cognitive and affective status of the client or informant, they are not as likely to result in a clear picture of the specific problems that are occurring. Given that child and adolescent conduct problems tend to be conceptualized in terms of interaction with others (McMahon & Forehand, 1988), the behavioral interview should include input from parents, and input from teachers if the conduct problems are present in the school setting. The characteristics externalizing disorders may make conducting an effective interview directly with the child or adolescent client very difficult. For conduct disorders, characteristic problems such as lying, defiance of authority, and oppositional behavior may result in the child/adolescent client providing information that is suspect. On the other hand, children or adolescents with ADHD may not necessarily show such overt defiance to the interview, but may still provide poor quality data because of typical difficulties in concentration, self-awareness, and behavioral self-control. Thus, behavioral interviews with parents and/or teachers will be an important first step in the assessment of externalizing disorders.

Whether the externalizing problems in question involve conduct disorders, attention deficit hyperactivity disorder, or some combination thereof, the effectiveness of the behavioral interview will be greatly enhanced by the specificity of questions. For assessing ADHD, DuPaul (1992) and DuPaul and Stoner (1994) have suggested using a semistructured behavioral interview format where teachers and/or parents are asked questions pertaining to the presence or absence and intensity of symptoms from the *DSM* criteria. Such an interview format is simple, yet potentially very effective in ruling in or out various diagnostic criteria. Forehand and McMahon (1981) described the use of *The Problem Guidesheet*, a semistructured format for conducting behavioral interviews to assess child conduct problems. This interview format, which is shown in modified format in Fig. 9.1, assists the clinician in structuring questions so that specific information on the frequency, duration, and parent or child responses to the problem behaviors can be obtained. The Problem Guidesheet also provides a format for asking questions about problem behaviors in specific settings and at specific times (e.g., mealtime, public places, etc.). The Problem Guidesheet is not intended to be a standardized interview instrument, but simply a format to help clinicians structure behavioral interviews so that effective information about conduct problems can be obtained.

In terms of using standardized structured and semistructured interview schedules to assess externalizing problems, the instruments overviewed in chapter 5 may be of

| Name of Child: | | | Interviewer: | | |
| Name of Interviewee(s): | | | Date of Interview: | | |
Setting/ Time	Description	Frequency	Duration	Parent Response	Child Response
At bedtime					
At mealtime					
At bath time					
With parent on the phone					
With visitors at home					
When visiting others					
Traveling in the car					
In public places					
At school					
With siblings					
With peers					
With other parent/ relative					
Disciplinary procedures					
Other:					

FIG. 9.1. An adaptation of Forehand and McMahon's (1981) *Problem Guidesheet,* a format for conducting behavioral interviews to assess child conduct problems.

some use. These instruments were all designed to assess a broad range of child disorders along the lines of *DSM* criteria, and thus are not specifically designed for assessing externalizing problems. However, Conduct Disorder, Oppositional Defiant Disorder, and Attention Deficit Hyperactivity Disorder are all mainstay childhood disorders in the *DSM–III–R* and *DSM–IV*, and thus, various characteristics of these disorders are covered within the K–SADS, DICA–R, and CAS.

The National Institute of Mental Health Diagnostic Interview Schedule for Children (DISC; Fisher et al., 1992) is an additional structured interview schedule that appears to be highly relevant for assessing externalizing problems. The DISC is an interview schedule for use with children from age 9 to 17 and their parents. This interview schedule was originally designed as a screening instrument for research purposes, but its clinical uses are currently being refined and investigated. The DISC provides scores in 27 symptom areas that are outlined according to *DSM* classification criteria. The child version of the DISC has 264 items and requires from 40 to 60 minutes to administer, whereas the parent version includes 302 items and takes 60 to 70 minutes to administer. Both versions are highly structured and include specific codes for each item. The DISC requires very little training to administer and score, though interpretation is a somewhat more difficult task. Edelbrock and Costello (1988) reviewed several studies indicating that the DISC has very strong interrater reliability, fair to adequate test–retest reliability, and modest agreement between parent and child forms. The DISC has also been shown to have strong concurrent validity with the DICA–R, and weaker but still significant concurrent validity with the parent version of the Child Behavior Checklist (Costello, Edelbrock, Dulcan, & Kalas, 1984). For version 2.3 (Fisher et al., 1992), a comprehensive user's manual and IBM PC-compatible *DSM–III–R* computer diagnostic program are available. Additionally, researchers who have been developing the DISC for the National Institute of Mental Health periodically offer training seminars in the use of the DISC at various locations. If an easy to use and highly structured interview schedule is needed for assessing externalizing problems, the DISC appears to be a potentially good choice.

Sociometric Techniques

In chapter 6, four types of sociometric assessment techniques are examined in detail, including peer nomination, peer rating, sociometric ranking, and alternative procedures such as picture sociometrics, the Class Play, and "guess who" measures. If properly applied, any one of these sociometric procedures is a potentially good choice for screening and assessment of externalizing disorders.

The utility of sociometrics for assessing externalizing problems depends on two things: the specific design of the sociometric question or task, and the purposes for which the sociometric assessment will be used. To be most effective in assessing conduct disorders or attention deficit hyperactivity disorder, the sociometric tasks will need to be carefully structured so that the peer or teacher informants will make selections based on the most salient behavioral characteristics. For instance, negative ranking or rating procedures where participants are asked to list or rate peers who "fight a lot" will likely be more effective in externalizing assessment than procedures where participants are asked to list or rate peers who "don't get along with other students." The latter example could obviously have a great deal of correlation with internalizing problems. Sociometric assessment of externalizing problems is generally a more useful procedure for screening purposes or research than it is for individual assessment. It is true that conducting a sociometric procedure as part of an individual assessment in the classroom of a referred student might provide some useful data on that student, but the amount of time and intrusiveness involved in doing this would rarely be warranted.

Because chapter 6 provides an overview of the specifics of conducting sociometric assessments, this information will not be repeated in this chapter. However, some examples of studies employing sociometric procedures to assess externalizing characteristics and outcomes are provided. In their review of studies documenting the predictive validity of sociometrics, McConnell and Odom (1986) cited several investi-

least liked students- nominated
most juvenile delirg.

gations where sociometric procedures were employed in the assessment of externalizing problems. One of the most frequently cited of these studies is Roff, Sells, and
Golden's (1972) longitudinal investigation of peer and teacher ratings of 40,000
children. One of the interesting findings of this classic study was that children rated
least liked by their peers were significantly more likely to appear on registers of
juvenile delinquency than children who were rated most liked by peers. Other
longitudinal studies have found that peer ratings or nominations of classmates as
mean, noisy, or quiet (Victor & Halvorson, 1976) and troublesome or dishonest (West
& Farrington, 1973) were significantly related to conduct problems and juvenile
delinquency at a later age. Roff (1961) conducted a prospective study of 164 male
children who were referred to child guidance clinics and later served in the military,
and found that children whose records indicated poor peer adjustment were significantly more likely to receive bad conduct discharges from military service than children
with good peer relationships. Other studies documenting the utility of sociometric
procedures in assessing externalizing problems could be cited, but these four classic
studies provide sufficiently strong evidence. In sum, sociometric assessment procedures
have been demonstrated to be highly effective in the assessment of a variety of
externalizing conduct problems, and are particularly useful for screening and research
purposes.

Self-Report Instruments

problems of self reports + external disorders

As is demonstrated in chapter 10, the use of objective self-report instruments is often
the primary method of choice for assessing internalizing problems. However, a much
different picture of the usefulness of self-report assessment emerges when it is applied
to the measurement of externalizing behavior disorders. There are three measurement
problems that emerge in using self-report tests for assessing conduct disorders and
attention deficit hyperactivity disorder. First, externalizing problems are usually best
assessed through direct measurement and unbiased reporting by objective observers
(McMahon & Forehand, 1988). Second, children and adolescents with externalizing
disorders may not always be reliable or insightful reporters of their own behavior
because of social perception deficits or because of oppositional defiance to the assessment process (Barkley, 1981). And third, the very nature of most objective self-report
tests requires that a fair amount of inference be used in applying the results to actual
behaviors exhibited, particularly with conduct problems. Thus, whereas objective
self-report tests may be very useful in the assessment of internalizing problems, they
do present substantial challenges in assessing externalizing behavioral problems.

Despite the apparent limitations of using self-report instruments in assessing externalizing problems, there are times when it is highly desirable to include a suitable
self-report instrument in an assessment battery. For instance, a clinician may want to
gather systematic data on a child or adolescent client's perceptions of their behavior,
or compare their personality profile to that of a normative or clinical group. Another
possible advantage of self-report assessment of youth with externalizing disorders exists
with regard to obtaining their own report of covert conduct problems (such as
vandalism, theft, drug use, etc.) that may not be easily observed by third-party
informants (Kazdin, 1995).

↳ somethings that may not be observable
covert in self reports

Fortunately, there are a few standardized self-report instruments that are a potentially valuable addition to the multimethod, multisource, multisetting assessment
design for measuring externalizing disorders. The general purpose self-report instru-

ments examined in chapter 7—namely, the Self-Report Forms of the Behavior Assessment System for Children (BASC), Millon Adolescent Personality Inventory (MAPI), Millon Adolescent Clinical Inventory (MACI), Minnesota Multiphasic Personality–Adolescent (MMPI–A), Personality Inventory for Youth (PIY), and Youth Self-Report (YSR)—may all be useful to some extent in assessing externalizing problems and their correlates. Each of these instruments includes subscales associated with externalizing and antisocial behavior problems, such as the Psychopathic Deviate and Conduct Problems scales of the MMPI–A, the Impulse Control and Societal Conformity scales of the MAPI, and the Aggressive Behavior, Attention Problems, and Delinquent Behavior scales of the YSR. The MAPI, MMPI–A, and PIY are best described as measures of personality that may be useful in predicting psychopathology. The YSR and BASC, on the other hand, require that youth actually rate their own levels of specified problem behaviors. The MACI is unique among these instruments, given that it is a personality inventory based on a specific personality theory, but designed for use in assessing clinical populations.

It is extremely important, however, to stress that these and other self-report instruments do not directly assess externalizing behaviors. Rather, they measure self-perceptions of externalizing problems, as well as patterns of responding associated with these problems. For example, a number of investigations have shown that the MMPI 2-point code type of 4-8 or 8-4 (Psychopathic Deviate-Schizophrenia) is a common pattern of individuals who have been incarcerated for severe antisocial acting-out behavior. In fact, this MMPI 2-point code type is the most common code type among male rapists (J. R. Graham, 1990). Yet, the MMPI does not actually assess antisocial and violent behavior; the vast amount of research on the instrument has merely identified response patterns that are correlated with these behaviors based on group research.

In addition to the general purpose self-report instruments just described, this section provides brief evaluative reviews of three instruments designed expressly or primarily for self-report assessment of youth with externalizing behavior problems. These instruments, including two forms of the Conners–Wells' Self-Report Scale and the Jesness Inventory, are described next.

Conners–Wells' Adolescent Self-Report Scales. The Conners–Wells' Adolescent Self-Report Scales (CASS) are a recent addition to the comprehensive Conners assessment system. They were commercially published for the first time with the 1997 Conners Rating System–Revised (CRS–R; Conners, 1997). The CASS was designed to provide a self-report evaluation of various symptoms central to and associated with ADHD. There are two forms of the CASS. The Long Form (CASS:L) contains 87 items and is designed for use with youths from age 12 to 17. The Short Form (CASS:S) contains 27 items, and is also designed for use with youths from age 12 to 17. Both measures utilize the same rating format, *T*-score conversion system, and scoring options and features as the other instruments in the Conners Rating System.

The CASS:L contains the following 10 subscales: Family Problems, Emotional Problems, Conduct Problems, Cognitive Problems, Anger Control Problems, Hyperactivity, ADHD Index, and Inattentive and Hyperactive-Impulsive *DSM–IV* Symptom Scales. The CASS:S, on the other hand, contains the following four subscales: Conduct Problems, Cognitive Problems, Hyperactive-Impulsive, and ADHD Index. Although both versions of the CASS are designed to measure self-perceptions of the core symptoms and associated features of ADHD, the longer version includes many more items that are more loosely associated with ADHD, reflecting various aspects of internalizing problems, social problems, and emotional distress. The shorter version, however, is limited to the core symptoms and most closely associated behavioral features.

Information regarding the standardization and psychometric properties of the CASS are presented in the technical manual. The normative samples for both the long and short versions of the CASS are very large (over 3,000 cases each) and representative. Internal consistency reliability coefficients for the CASS:L scales range between .75 and .92, whereas these coefficients range from .75 to .85 for the CASS:S scales. Test–retest reliability for both measures was investigated at 6- to 8-week intervals, with scale stability coefficients ranging from .73 to .89 for the CASS:L and from .72 to .87 for the CASS:S. These reliability data indicate that both versions of the CASS have adequate stability. The empirically derived scales of the CASS appear to have sound factorial validity. Convergent and discriminant construct validity evidence is presented in the technical manual for the CASS, including correlations with parent and teacher ratings (which predictably tend to be low to moderate), correlations with the Children's Depression Inventory self-report scores (which tend to be moderate), and comparisons between nonclinical and various clinical samples (which tend to be significant). No externally published research on the CASS has appeared in the literature at this point in time.

In sum, both versions of the CASS appear to be technically adequate, although there is still a lack of information regarding some of the finer points of construct validity, such as how strongly the scales correlate with general purpose and externalizing self-report measures. These instruments may be useful for assessment of adolescents with ADHD symptoms who also are reported to exhibit related behavioral and emotional problems. However, additional research regarding specific applications and validity issues appears to be needed.

oldest, best respected

Jesness Inventory. The Jesness Inventory (JI), also referred to as the Jesness Adolescent Personality Inventory (Jesness, 1962, 1996) is one of the oldest, best respected, most empirically documented, and widely used self-report instruments specifically developed for youth with conduct disorders and antisocial behavior. This instrument is a 155-item true/false questionnaire designed to measure attitudes and personality characteristics associated with antisocial and delinquent behavior. This test was originally developed during the early 1960s, based on outcome research with delinquent youths in California (Jesness, 1962, 1963, 1965). Although the 155 items and original normative samples for the original instrument remain the same, the manual has recently been updated to include a variety of more recent validity and reliability evidence. The 155 items yield *T*-scores on 11 scales. Three of the scales (Social Maladjustment, Values Orientation, Immaturity) were developed using methods similar to the empirical criterion keying approach used on the MMPI clinical scales. Seven of the scales (Autism, Alienation, Manifest Aggression, Withdrawal, Social Anxiety, Repression, Denial) were developed using cluster analysis, a statistical procedure for identifying clusters of similar items that Jesness chose to employ rather than factor analysis. The remaining scale (the Asocial Index) includes items from all the scales that were combined using a discriminant function analysis procedure in order to develop a single measure to discriminate between delinquent and nondelinquent populations. As with all arbitrarily named test scales, the scales on the JI may not necessarily measure what literal interpretations of the scale names might suggest, and because of the age of this test, the names of some scales may not reflect the most current associations of the titles. For example, the Autism scale is not designed to measure the developmental disorder Autism, but includes items where the central theme is a distortion of reality, or superficial self-enhancement. Also, the Asocial Index is described by Jesness (1996) as a measure that identifies general tendencies to behave in ways that transgress social rules. The term *asocial* is a somewhat dated description for what most of today's clinicians consider to be *antisocial* characteristics.

Normative data for the JI are based on samples of 970 delinquent and 1,075 nondelinquent males from age 8 to 18, and 450 delinquent and 811 nondelinquent females from age 12 to 19. The normative data were gathered during the initial development of the JI in California during the early 1960s. Additional large samples of JI normative data have been collected with both delinquent and nondelinquent youth (Jesness & Wedge, 1984). Reliability of the JI has been criticized as being insufficient (Shark & Handel, 1977), but is close to the same general range as the MMPI clinical scales, with split-half coefficients ranging from .62 to .88, and test–retest coefficients ranging from .40 to .79. The JI scales that show the most stability include Values Orientation, Manifest Anger, Social Maladjustment, Alienation, and Depression. A number of studies have demonstrated various forms of validity of the JI. Concurrent validity has been demonstrated through strong correlations between specific JI scales and various scales of the MMPI and California Psychological Inventory (CPI). The JI has been shown in several outcome studies to be sensitive to treatment changes with delinquent youths (e.g., Kahn & McFarland, 1973; Roberts, Schmitz, Pinto, & Cain, 1990; Shivrattan, 1988). Other validity evidence found in the JI test manual indicate that the test has been effective in differentiating delinquent from nondelinquent youths, but the JI has been criticized in this regard as having a high false-positive error rate because of the relatively low base rate of serious delinquent behavior (Mooney, 1984).

The JI can be recommended as an objective self-report test for assessing conduct problems and delinquent attitudes, but with some reservations and cautions. Some of the techniques employed to develop the JI scales are not in line with current thinking and technology applications for test development, and this problem is particularly true for the JI scales developed through cluster analysis. As a result, some of the JI scales have relatively poor or modest psychometric properties. The normative data were gathered over 30 years ago, and are geographically limited. Because the JI was developed over three decades ago, some of the items may be dated, and may not reflect the complexity of organized antisocial and delinquent behavior that has emerged in the United States since the 1980s (i.e., large-scale and highly organized gang activity).

Despite some of the reservations concerning the JI, this test has withstood many criticisms, primarily because of years of sophisticated research on it. As Mooney (1984) stated, "the research on the Jesness Inventory shows it is remarkably resilient to these potential 'insults' to its functioning. A number of its scales, most notably Social Maladjustment, Value Orientation, and the Asocial Index, appear to tap into delin- quent attitudes and degree of delinquent involvement. . . . As a personality inventory relevant to delinquent attitudes and behavior, it appears to have no rivals" (p. 391). Mooney's comment was made several years ago, but continues to be relevant. In sum, the JI has the potential of being a very good addition to assessment designs aimed at evaluating externalizing conduct disorders, particularly socialized aggressive types of conduct disorder.

LINKING ASSESSMENT TO INTERVENTION

Each of the five general methods for assessing externalizing disorders discussed in this chapter have their own advantages and limitations, and are useful for various purposes and situations. However, when it comes to linking assessment data to interventions for externalizing problems, it is fairly clear that the five methods are not equal. Direct behavioral observation, particularly observational coding systems that take into account environmental variables and interactions between the subject and significant others, is the method that is potentially most useful in developing intervention plans. Because a carefully designed and implemented observation system allows for direct measurement of environmental situations and interpersonal interactions that help to elicit and maintain problem behaviors, it will also help to generate hypotheses about methods for reducing problem behaviors and increasing desired behaviors. Behavioral interviewing with parents and teachers of the referred child/adolescent client is another assessment method that allows for collection of the same type of intervention-linked and functional assessment data, albeit in a somewhat less direct fashion.

Behavior rating scales are typically less useful than direct observation or behavioral interviews in designing interventions for externalizing problems, but they are also potentially useful. If rating scales completed by different raters in different settings consistently portray certain behaviors or situations as significant problems, then the clinician will have some salient clues as to what specific behaviors or situations to focus on in the intervention plan. The Keystone Behavior Strategy (R. O. Nelson & Hayes, 1986) is an intervention selection strategy for which behavior rating scales may be potentially useful. This strategy is based on the idea that identification of a group of critical behaviors or responses linked to a particular disorder, something that is quite possible with rating scales, leads to the immediate targeting of those responses as "keystone" behaviors for intervention. The developers of two of the rating scale systems reviewed in this chapter (Home/School Situations Questionnaires and Attention Deficit Disorders Evaluation Scales) have produced intervention manuals that are to a great degree keyed to the behavioral descriptions on these instruments, and these materials appear to be potentially useful in designing intervention plans.

Sociometric assessment of externalizing problems is perhaps best used as a descriptive method for screening or research, and offers a much weaker link to intervention planning. Objective self-report tests also provide a most tenuous link to treatment planning for externalizing disorders, due to the fact that they assess responding and personality patterns rather than actual behaviors. There have been some attempts to link MMPI profile types to treatment planning (e.g., Butcher, 1990), but these efforts cover only one specific self-report instrument, and are in need of further empirical validation. In sum, by their very nature, externalizing disorders are distinctly suited to the most direct methods of assessment, which in turn are capable of providing the most useful links to intervention planning.

It is important to view the idea of linking assessment to intervention for externalizing behavior disorders within a realistic perspective. Certainly, the more direct approaches to assessment (direct observation, behavioral interviews, behavior rating scales) offer the promise of linkage to intervention planning. However, a large body of evidence clearly indicates that externalizing behavior disorders present many challenges for effective intervention. Recent reviews of the treatment literature on conduct disorders (Frick, 1998; Kazdin, 1995) and ADHD (Hinshaw, 1994; Whalen & Henker, 1998) have reached a consensus that although there are several promising treatments for externalizing disorders, they typically do not produce extremely large and long-lasting effects, because these disorders tend to be relatively intransigent. Therefore, treatment of externalizing disorders should be viewed in many cases as more of a long-term management strategy than as a cure.

CONCLUSIONS

The area of externalizing disorders is perhaps the most clearly defined broad-band domain of child psychopathology. Externalizing disorders, which are typically thought of as being behavior problems rather than emotional problems (although the two categories are not exclusive), involve a variety of acting-out, aggressive, antisocial, disruptive, and overactive behaviors. This domain of behavioral problems has been referred to as undercontrolled and outer-directed in nature.

The two major approaches to classification of child psychopathology have resulted in similar, though slightly differing, diagnostic and classification categories, all of which tend to co-occur with each other in a large percentage of cases. Quay's behavioral dimensions classification scheme for the externalizing disorders includes three categories: Undersocialized Aggressive Conduct Disorder, Socialized Aggressive Conduct Disorder, and Attention Deficit Hyperactivity Disorder. The *DSM–IV*, on the other hand, includes the major diagnostic categories of Attention Deficit Hyperactivity Disorder (ADHD), Conduct Disorder, and Oppositional Defiant Disorder. Refinements in the *DSM* classification system for externalizing disorders of children have occurred from the two previous editions, and will likely continue as better empirical evidence mounts.

Externalizing disorders typically begin early in life, with the developmental antecedents sometimes present as early as infancy (difficult temperament) and early childhood (attention-seeking and acting-out behavior). There are many competing theories regarding etiology of these disorders, ranging from biological to behavioral, but most recent notions of causality tend to view specific etiological components as risk factors rather than sole causes. With respect to conduct disorders, earlier development and the presence of aggressive behavior tend to be associated with a poorer long-term prognosis, whereas later onset, less aggressive behavior, the presence of good social skills, and higher levels of intelligence tend to be associated with a better prognosis. With ADHD, the presence of other externalizing disorders, substance abuse, and antisocial-aggressive behavior tend to be associated with a poorer long-term prognosis. All forms of externalizing behavior disorders tend to present substantial challenges for long-term adjustment.

Behavioral observation is one of the best and most direct methods for assessing externalizing problems, because they tend to be readily observable, and because observation may be more functionally linked to intervention than other methods. Behavior rating scales are another potentially useful method for assessing externalizing problems, for many of the same reasons as behavioral observation. Each of the general purpose behavior rating scales discussed in chapter 4 are potentially useful in assessing externalizing problems, as are the externalizing-specific rating scales discussed here. Interviewing, particularly behavioral interviewing and structured interview schedules, is another excellent assessment for externalizing problems. The advantage of behavioral interviewing for this purpose is that it allows for identification of possible behavior–environment relations that may be useful in treatment planning. Sociometric assessment techniques have a long history of successful use with externalizing problems, but are often impractical to use as part of individual assessment; their best uses in this regard tend to be for research and for general screening. Self-report instruments are probably the most tenuous of the five assessment methods for externalizing problems, but even this method has some advantages, such as obtaining self-report of covert conduct problems that may not be readily observed by parents, teachers, or observers. The general purpose self-report instruments discussed in chapter 7 all appear to have some degree of relevance for assessing externalizing problems, as do the externalizing-specific self-report instruments discussed in this chapter.

Although treatment for externalizing disorders tends to be quite difficult, and is usually more of a long-term management proposition than a short-term "cure," there are some promising treatment modalities. Linkage between assessment and effective treatment of externalizing problems is most direct when using behavioral observation, behavioral interviewing, and behavior rating scales.

REVIEW AND APPLICATION QUESTIONS

1. What are some possible reasons why the externalizing domain of child psychopathology is more easily defined and well documented than the internalizing domain?

2. Contrast Quay's behavioral dimensions approach to classifying externalizing disorders with the *DSM* approach. Does either approach present any salient advantages for assessment or treatment planning?

3. For children with conduct disorders, what characteristics tend to be associated with the poorest long-term prognosis? What characteristics tend to be associated with a more favorable long-term prognosis?

4. Substantial research efforts have been directed at identifying specific etiologic factors in the development of externalizing disorders. Why do you suppose that the current trend is to view specific possible causes as risk factors rather than a sole causal explanation?

5. If one were to design an optimal observation coding system for detecting the broad-band of externalizing disorders, what critical observable behaviors would need to be separately coded?

6. Contrast the narrow-band externalizing behavior rating scales discussed in this chapter with the general purpose rating scales presented in detail in chapter 4. Under what circumstances would an assessment design be enhanced by one of these more externalizing-focused instruments?

7. Regarding covert conduct problems such as vandalism, stealing, drug use, and so forth, what advantages do interviews and self-report instruments offer over direct observation, parent–teacher interviews, and behavior rating scales? How much confidence should a clinician have regarding the truth or accuracy of self-report statements obtained from a youth with serious conduct problems?

8. What are the critical components needed to most effectively link assessment of externalizing problems to intervention planning?

CASE STUDY: MICHAEL C.

Background Information

Michael C., an 8-year-old boy in the second grade, was referred for assessment by the multidisciplinary child study team at his elementary school. The primary referral concerns focused on acting-out and aggressive behavior in the school setting. Michael's second-grade teacher, who originally initiated the referral, noted that although Michael is performing "average" on his academic work, he has difficulty completing assignments. However, the primary problems in the classroom are reported to involve intimidation of and physical aggression toward his classmates, as well as constant violations of classroom and school rules. Michael's teacher reports having documented a behavior management plan using rewards for nonaggressive and compliant behavior and time-out from the classroom for aggressive-noncompliant behaviors, but noted that the "behavior management doesn't work with Michael."

Michael lives with his parents (Mr. and Mrs. C.) and his 3-year-old sister in the suburbs of a large metropolitan area. Michael's father is a long-haul truck driver, and is often away from home for up to 10 days at a time. He has had minimal contact with the school staff, but was at Michael's last parent–teacher conference when the issue of the behavior problems was discussed at length, and permission to conduct the assessment was processed. Mr. C. was willing to grant permission for the assessment, but wrote on the form "I don't want my boy labeled or put on any drugs." Mr. C.'s opinion is that Michael's aggressive behaviors are "just like most boys." Mrs. C. appears to be somewhat more concerned about Michael's behavior at home than is Mr. C.; she agreed that he is sometimes difficult to manage at home and that he occasionally "plays too rough with his sister and other kids in the neighborhood."

Assessment Data

The following assessment data were gathered as part of this initial assessment.

Behavior Rating Scales. Michael was rated by his each of his parents using the Child Behavior Checklist, and by his classroom teacher using the Teacher Report form of the Child Behavior Checklist. Additionally, Michael's mother and teacher rated him using the Revised Behavior Problem Checklist. The obtained T-scores (based on a mean of 50 and standard deviation of 10) for these tests are shown in Tables 9.5 and 9.6.

Behavioral Observation. Michael was observed during two different 15-minute time periods by a special education resource teacher; once during a reading and spelling activity in the classroom, and once during the recess playground period. The classroom observation was conducted utilizing a series of behavioral codes at 20-second intervals using the partial-interval method (45 intervals total). Michael was out-of-seat during 12 different intervals, which was more than three times as much as the social comparison students who were observed. He was coded as being off-task during 17 intervals, which was more than two times as much as the social comparison students. He was also coded as engaging in physically negative behavior during six intervals (pushing or kicking classmates near him), whereas the social comparison students did not receive

TABLE 9.5
Child Behavior Checklist Scores

Cross-Informant Syndromes and Broad-Band Areas	Michael's Teacher	Michael's Father	Michael's Mother
Aggressive Behavior	78	62	70
Anxious/Depressed	55	55	57
Attention Problems	72	70	72
Delinquent Behavior	72	63	68
Social Problems	70	60	62
Somatic Complaints	57	55	55
Thought Problems	55	55	58
Withdrawn	55	55	55
INTERNALIZING PROBLEMS	57	56	57
EXTERNALIZING PROBLEMS	74	64	69
TOTAL PROBLEMS	68	60	65

TABLE 9.6
Revised Behavior Problem Checklist Scores

RBPCL Subscale	Michael's Teacher	Michael's Mother
Conduct Disorder	72	65
Socialized Aggression	70	62
Attention Problems-Immaturity	68	71
Anxiety-Withdrawal	46	52
Psychotic Behavior	68	62
Motor Excess	70	70

this coding at all. The playground observation consisted of an event recording procedure with a checklist of observed problem behaviors completed at the end of the 15 minutes. Michael was observed engaging in various forms of physically aggressive behavior eight times during the observation, and was also observed as being rejected by peers (who ran away from him) three times. The critical problem behaviors that were checked at the end of the observation included "physically aggressive," "threatens peers," "violates playground rules," and "peer problems." No social comparison data were collected during this observation.

Interviews. Behavioral interviews were conducted by the school psychologist with Michael's teacher and with Michael's parents, using a problem identification model of interviewing to pinpoint the most significant or bothersome problems. Stated briefly, the "most bothersome" problem behaviors identified during the interviews included:

Teacher Behavioral Interview	Parent Behavioral Interview
Physically aggressive to classmates	Plays rough with other children
Intimidates and bullies other children	Difficulty following directions
Frequently out-of-seat	"Doesn't think before he acts"
Frequently off-task	
Difficulty completing assignments	

Questions to Consider

1. The assessment data that have been presented here are preliminary screening data. What other information regarding Michael's social-emotional behavior would be useful, and what assessment tools would best provide this information?

2. Based on the behavioral dimensions and *DSM–IV* approaches to classification and the various types of externalizing disorders identified in Table 9.1 through 9.4, do Michael's behavioral characteristics fit in with any of these types? If so, which are the most likely, and why?

3. Are the assessment data congruent with the reasons for referral? Do these data suggest the presence of problems that were not noted in the reasons for referral and background information?

4. Compare the scores from the three CBCL profiles. What do the differences and similarities between these scores suggest about source and setting variance?

5. Compare the scores from the two RBPCL profiles. What do the differences and similarities between these scores suggest about source and setting variance?

6. Compare the scores from the CBCL and RBPCL profiles. What do the differences and similarities between the scores of these two rating scales suggest about instrument variance in this case?

7. Based only on the data presented in this case study, how severe do Michael's externalizing behavior problems appear to be?

10

ASSESSMENT OF
INTERNALIZING PROBLEMS

Internalizing problems, which include a broad domain of symptoms related to depression, anxiety, social withdrawal, and somatic complaints, are an intriguing and sometimes problematic area for assessment. It becomes evident that internalizing problems can be difficult to detect, and the symptoms of various specific internalizing disorders are often mingled together. One expert in this area has even referred to internalizing problems in children as *secret illnesses* (Reynolds, 1992a). After carefully reading this chapter, readers will gain a greater understanding of the complexity and various dimensions of internalizing problems, and how various assessment strategies are utilized in the investigation, identification, and classification process.

This chapter begins with a theoretical discussion of the nature of internalizing problems, including overviews of each major area of internalizing symptomatology. This introductory overview is followed by discussions of the implications of developing internalizing problems, and how this broad band of symptoms is related to the self-concept. The chapter then provides detailed information on direct and objective methods of assessing internalizing problems, using behavioral observation, rating scales, interview techniques, sociometric approaches, and self-report tests. A special assessment section is also provided for methods of measuring the self-concept. The chapter ends with a brief discussion of the challenges of linking assessment of internalizing problems to intervention.

INTERNALIZING PROBLEMS: AN OVERVIEW

As is indicated in chapters 2 and 9, recent efforts at creating sophisticated and empirically sound taxonomies of child psychopathology (i.e., the behavioral dimensions approach) have tended to sort general types of behavioral and emotional problems along two broad dimensions, usually referred to as *internalizing* (overcontrolled) and *externalizing* (undercontrolled) disorders (Cicchetti & Toth, 1991).

The domain of internalizing problems or disorders includes a seemingly wide variety of symptomatology, such as dysphoric or depressive mood states, social withdrawal, anxious and inhibited reactions, and the development of somatic problems (physical symptoms with no known organic basis). And yet, although these various internalizing conditions may at least superficially appear to be distinct symptoms, there has long been strong historical evidence that they often tend to exist together in a *comorbid* or *co-occurring relationship* (Ackerson, 1942; Fish & Shapiro, 1964). Currently, there is a large and growing body of evidence that strongly indicates a great deal of behavioral covariation between the characteristics of mood disorders, anxiety disorders, and somatic complaints (e.g., Achenbach & McConoughy, 1992; Maser & Cloninger, 1990). Thus, the chances may be quite high that a youth who presents the obvious symptoms of depression may also experience anxiety, social inhibition and withdrawal, and physical concerns. Therefore, it is useful, if not necessary, to study the assessment of these types of problems together within a common framework.

Behavioral Dimensions Classification

Consistent with previous discussions of the behavioral dimensions classification approach (see chaps. 2, 4, and 9), specific areas of internalizing problems have been identified using multivariate statistical techniques. Quay (1986a) identified the two major dimensions that coincide with internalizing problems as *Anxiety-Withdrawal-Dysphoria* and *Schizoid-Unresponsive*. The major characteristics of these two internalizing behavioral dimensions are illustrated in Table 10.1. As can be seen from an inspection of this table, there is a fair amount of overlap in characteristics between the two major internalizing domains from this perspective. Other researchers have described the domains within internalizing problems in a somewhat differing manner (e.g., Achenbach, 1982b; Achenbach & McConaughy, 1992), but Quay's description serves to illustrate the point of overlapping characteristics within types of internalizing problems.

DSM Classification

The *DSM* system includes several general diagnostic categories that fit very specifically within the internalizing domain, such as Mood Disorders, Anxiety Disorders, and Somatoform Disorders. An overview of the major *DSM–IV* diagnostic categories for

TABLE 10.1
Major Characteristics of Two Dimensions of Internalizing Problems
Identified Through Quay's (1986a) Review of Multivariate Classification Studies

Anxiety-Withdrawal-Dysphoria	*Schizoid-Unresponsive*
Anxious, fearful, tense	Won't talk
Shy, timid, bashful	Withdrawn
Depressed, sad, disturbed	Shy, timid, bashful
Hypersensitive, easily hurt	Cold and unresponsive
Feels inferior, worthless	Lack of interest
Self-conscious, easily embarrassed	Sad
Lacks self-confidence	Stares blankly
Easily flustered and confused	Confused
Cries frequently	Secretive
Aloof	Likes to be alone
Worries	

TABLE 10.2

Major Diagnostic Categories of Internalizing Disorders from *DSM–IV*

DSM

Mood Disorders
  Major Depressive Disorder
  Dysthymic Disorder
  Depressive Disorder, Not Otherwise Specified
  Bipolar I and Bipolar II Disorders
  Cyclothymic Disorder
  Mood Disorder Due to Medical Condition or Substance Use
Anxiety Disorders
  Panic Disorder without Agoraphobia
  Panic Disorder with Agoraphobia
  Agoraphobia without History of Panic Disorder
  Specific Phobia (list type)
  Social Phobia
  Obsessive-Compulsive Disorder
  Posttraumatic Stress Disorder
  Acute Stress Disorder
  Generalized Anxiety Disorder
  Anxiety Disorder Due to Medical Condition or Substance Inducement (specify)
Other Disorders of Infancy, Childhood, or Adolescence
  Separation Anxiety Disorder
  Selective Mutism
Somatoform Disorders
  Somatization Disorder
  Undifferentiated Somatoform Disorder
  Pain Disorder
  Hypochondriasis

internalizing disorders is presented in Table 10.2. More details on the some of the major *DSM–IV* diagnostic categories for internalizing disorders are presented later. The classification categories presented in Table 10.2 do not include the more general "not otherwise specified" categories, nor do they include several classification categories that are not primarily internalizing in nature, but may have very specific internalizing manifestations, such as Psychotic Disorders, Eating Disorders, Pervasive Developmental Disorders, and Tic Disorders. Many of these other disorders are discussed in chapter 11. It is interesting to note that, unlike the externalizing disorders discussed in chapter 9, these *DSM–IV*-based classification categories for internalizing disorders bear very little resemblance to the corresponding behavioral dimensions classification categories discussed previously and presented in Table 10.1. This lack of similarity among the major classification approaches to internalizing disorders indicates that this domain is still somewhat amorphous or difficult to define precisely to clinicians and researchers.

DSM + the 2 internalizing dimensions are very dissimilar

Prevalence

(more difficult to determine than extern. disorders)

Prevalence rates for internalizing disorders of children and youth have been much more difficult to ascertain accurately than prevalence estimates for externalizing disorders. In fact, these rates tend to vary considerably from one investigation to another depending on the particular disorder under investigation and the diagnostic criteria used (Michael & Merrell, in press). Examples of prevalence rates from epidemiologic studies of specific internalizing disorders of children have ranged from 1% to 5.9% for depression, to 8.9% for anxiety disorders in normal samples (Costello,

1989). The *DSM–IV* does provide some general prevalence estimates for specific internalizing disorders, but these data reveal nothing about the prevalence of such problems in child and adolescent populations. It is important to recognize that there are many children and youth who are significantly affected by internalizing symptoms, but whose problem characteristics do not neatly fit into a specific diagnostic category. And, perhaps unfortunately, the *DSM* system does not have a category for Childhood Internalizing Disorder, Not Otherwise Specified. Despite the lack of precision of current prevalence rates for internalizing disorders in children and youth, even the more conservative estimates are cause for alarm. For example, assume that there is a median prevalence rate of about 5% of the general school-age population that either has a specific internalizing disorder, or has significant enough internalizing symptoms to interfere with their academic and personal adjustment. This figure would represent an average of 1 or 2 children who are afflicted in each class of 30 students. Perhaps most distressing is the fact that, unlike children with externalizing disorders, many of these internalizing children will be overlooked or not identified as needing help, and their suffering will go unmitigated.

Gender Issues in Prevalence

Most prevalence estimates for internalizing disorders indicate that they occur with greater frequency in females than in males, particularly in the case of depression. For example, in summarizing prevalence studies, *DSM–IV* states that the point prevalence for a major depressive disorder is from 5% to 9% for women and from 2% to 3% for men, and from 55% to 60% of persons who are identified as having generalized anxiety disorder are female. These adult gender prevalence patterns appear to be true for adolescents as well as for adults, and it appears that "girls show an enhanced susceptibility for a number of internalizing disorders" (W. M. Reynolds, 1992c, p. 314). However, gender characteristics of internalizing disorders among younger children are much more speculative, with some studies showing no gender difference, some studies showing a higher prevalence among boys, and some studies showing a higher prevalence among girls (Merrell & Dobmeyer, 1996). In general though, there is a belief among professionals that internalizing disorders are more common among girls than among boys, but the evidence is still lacking in some respects.

MAJOR INTERNALIZING DISORDERS

To more clearly identify and define the major subcomponents of internalizing problems, this section includes brief discussions of symptomatology based on a breakdown into three areas: depression, anxiety, and related problems. When using this three-part breakdown of internalizing problems, it is important to consider that there is more confusion among researchers over terminology and classification subtypes for internalizing problems than for externalizing problems (e.g., Merrell, Crowley, & Walters, 1997). Therefore, any categorical breakdown in the internalizing domain will certainly have some level of imprecision. This section thus follows a hybrid of behavioral dimensions and *DSM* approaches to categorization. This discussion of general characteristics of internalizing disorders only addresses etiology and developmental course of specific problems at a superficial level; a thorough treatment is beyond the scope of this book. Some excellent sources for a comprehensive treatment of various internalizing problems include books or chapters by Craig and Dobson (1995), Lewis and Miller (1990), W. M. Reynolds (1992a), Schwartz, Gladstone, and Kaslow (1998), and Silverman and Ginsburg (1998).

Depression

To better understand what the target is when assessing depression, some definitions and distinctions are needed. The term *depression* may be construed to indicate a broad range of behaviors, characteristics, and symptoms. This broad and imprecise use of the term has been a problem in the research literature, resulting in many studies that have used the same basic terminology to describe differing facets of behavioral and emotional functioning. Three common uses of the term *depression* have been noted by Cantwell (1990): depression as a symptom, depression as a syndrome, and depression within the context of a depressive disorder.

Depression as a Symptom. As a symptom, depression involves a dysphoric mood state—feeling unhappy or sad, being "down in the dumps," feeling miserable, or feeling melancholic or "blue." These subjective states are only a smaller part of the syndrome or disorder of depression. It is important to recognize that depressive symptoms are very typical across the life span of most persons, are typically transient, and are usually not part of a depressive disorder or serious problem. It is also possible that depressive symptoms may exist as part of other disorders. Thus, symptoms of depression alone usually will not provide the impetus for conducting an assessment of depression.

Depression as a Syndrome. The term *syndrome* is used to describe something that is more than a dysphoric mood state. This term is usually understood to describe the coexistence of behavioral and emotional symptoms that often occur together, and are thus not simply associated by chance. Cantwell (1990) noted that a depressive syndrome commonly involves not only mood changes, but additional changes in psychomotor functioning, cognitive performance, and motivation. These additional changes usually occur in a negative direction, reducing the functional capacity of the person who experiences them. Depression as a syndrome is less common than depression as a symptom. It may be brought on by certain types of life stress, exist concurrently with various medical problems, or occur in conjunction with psychological and psychiatric disorders such as disruptive behavior disorders, schizophrenia, and anxiety disorders. Depression as a syndrome may also occur as the primary problem, with no preexisting or comorbid syndromes. And, of course, depressive syndromes may also be a part of depressive disorders.

↱ longterm experience of depressive syndrome + incapacitating

Depression as a Disorder. The distinction between depressive syndromes and depressive disorders is not quite as clear as the distinction between depressive symptoms and depressive syndrome. Whereas depressive syndromes are typically part of depressive disorders, more is usually implied by the latter term. By saying that a depressive disorder exists, there is an implication that a depressive syndrome exists, but that the syndrome has occurred for a specified amount of time, has caused a given degree of functional incapacity, and has a characteristic outcome such as duration and responsiveness to treatment (Cantwell, 1990). The most common way of referring to depression as a disorder is within the context of the *DSM* classification system. As seen in Table 10.2, the *DSM–IV* has several general categories for diagnosis of mood disorders, including three categories for the diagnosis of depressive disorders. To make a diagnosis of a Major Depressive Episode, which is most commonly considered a way of looking at depression, at least five out of nine possible specified symptoms (ranging from a depressed mood to recurrent thoughts about death) must have occurred within a 2-week period, in addition to certain exclusionary criteria being met (as is shown in Table 10.3).

One of the major challenges of using standard criteria like the *DSM* system for diagnosing depressive disorders with children and youth is that these systems may not be equally effective or useful across various age ranges (Carlson & Garber, 1986). Thus, assessment of depression as a disorder in children and adolescents requires particular care, skill, and caution. It is interesting to note that *DSM–IV* states that "certain symptoms such as somatic complaints, irritability, and social withdrawal are particularly common in children, whereas psychomotor retardation, hypersomnia, and delusions are less common prepuberty than in adolescence and adulthood" (APA, 1994, pp. 324–325). Although this information supports the notion that depression may present differently in children than in adults, there is still no alternative method

DSM criteria may not be best for children [handwritten marginal note]

TABLE 10.3
Diagnostic Criteria for Major Depressive Episode from the *DSM–IV*

A. Five (or more) of the following symptoms have been present during the same 2-week period and represent a change from previous functioning; at least one of the symptoms is either (1) depressed mood or (2) loss of interest or pleasure.
Note: Do not include symptoms that are clearly due to a general medical condition, or mood-incongruent delusions or hallucinations.
   1. depressed mood most of the day, nearly every day, as indicated by either subjective reports (e.g., feels sad or empty) or observation made by others (e.g., appears tearful). *Note:* in children and adolescents, can be irritable mood.
   2. markedly diminished interest or pleasure in all, or almost all, activities most of the day, nearly every day (as indicated by either subjective account or observations made by others)
   3. significant weight loss when not dieting or weight gain (e.g., a change of more than 5% of body weight in a month), or decrease or increase in appetite nearly every day. *Note:* in children, consider failure to make expected weight gains.
   4. insomnia or hypersomnia nearly every day
   5. psychomotor agitation or retardation nearly every day (observable by others, not merely subjective feelings of restlessness or being slowed down)
   6. fatigue or loss of energy nearly every day
   7. feelings of worthlessness or excessive or inappropriate guilt (which may be delusional) nearly every day (not merely self-reproach or guilt about being sick)
   8. diminished ability to think or concentrate, or indecisiveness, nearly every other day (either by subjective account or as observed by others)
   9. recurrent thoughts of death (not just fear of dying), recurrent suicidal ideation without a specific plan, or a suicide attempt or a specific plan for committing suicide
B. The symptoms do not meet criteria for a Mixed Episode.
C. The symptoms cause clinically significant distress or impairment in social, occupational, or other important areas of functioning.
D. The symptoms are not due to the direct physiological effects of a substance (e.g., a drug of abuse, a medication) or a general medical condition (e.g., hyperthyroidism).
E. The symptoms are not better accounted for by Bereavement, i.e., after the loss of a loved one, the symptoms persist for longer than 2 months or are characterized by marked functional impairment, morbid preoccupation with worthlessness, suicidal ideation, psychotic symptoms, or psychomotor retardation.

Note. From *Diagnostic and Statistical Manual of Mental Disorders* (4th ed.). Copyright © 1994, American Psychiatric Association. Reprinted by permission of the American Psychiatric Association.

of classification for youth, and the *DSM* system does not include any of the internalizing disorders in separate categories usually first diagnosed in infancy and childhood.

✓ causes of depression.

Causal Factors. Given that entire volumes have been devoted to the etiology of depression, treating these topics in such a short space is highly presumptuous, to say the least. The purpose of this discussion is to simply provide a brief description of some of the recent key findings on causal factors. Reviews of the literature on etiology of childhood depression by Miller, Birnbaum, and Durbin (1990) and Schwartz et al. (1998) articulated some of the critical psychosocial variables, or issues, such as parental influences, life events, and family interaction patterns associated with depression in children. A relation has been found to exist between what is commonly referred to as "loss" and childhood depression, with this relation most readily verified by studies of mother or father loss due to death or family separation. Children of parents who are themselves depressed have been shown to be at heightened risk for developing depression, as well as other psychological disorders. High rates of parental stress and family conflict have been found to be associated with childhood depression as well. There is some evidence that negative events that occur outside the family context in the lives of children, such as school and friendship problems, may also influence the development of depression.

"loss"

parents depress.

neg events

Additionally, children who become depressed may develop maladaptive or unhealthy cognitive styles, and concurrent impaired coping skills. The *learned helplessness* model, first proposed by Seligman (1974), posits that some forms of depression may occur under learning conditions where the child does not recognize a relation between their actions and the consequences of these actions. Lewinsohn (1974) proposed a highly influential model suggesting that the disruption of pleasurable and otherwise reinforcing events may predispose a person to depression, an idea definitely worth considering when conducting a comprehensive child assessment wherein environments as well as behavioral characteristics are evaluated. Additionally, strong evidence is emerging in the psychobiology literature indicating that some forms of childhood depression are related to biologic variables, namely, the interrelated areas of family genetics and brain chemistry (Schwartz et al., 1998).

learned helpless.

disrupt ☺

Bio

Anxiety

feelings, behaviors + physiological symptoms.

Anxiety is a class of internalizing responses that may involve subjective feelings (e.g., discomfort, fear, dread), overt behaviors (e.g., avoidance, withdrawal), and physiological responding (e.g., sweating, nausea, general arousal). Anxiety is closely related to two other areas: *fears* and *phobias.* Although anxiety, fears, and phobias have a great deal of overlap, there have been some historical distinctions drawn between these three categories. Fears have been described as "reactions to perceived threats that involve avoidance of the threatening stimuli, subjective feelings of discomfort, and physiological changes" (Barrios & Hartmann, 1988, p. 197). Fears are usually distinguished from anxiety because the former involves distinctive reactions to very specific stimuli (such as darkness or noise), whereas the latter tends to involve a more diffuse type of reaction (apprehension) to stimuli that are not as specific in nature. Phobias are similar to fears in that they involve intense reactions to specific stimuli, but are differentiated from fears in the sense that they are more persistent, maladaptive, and debilitating (Barrios & Hartmann, 1988; Morris & Kratochwill, 1983). Because the

Fears are specific / Anxiety is diffuse

focus of this section of the chapter is a general treatment of the subject, anxiety is the topic of this overview, rather than the more specific categories of fears and phobias.

It is interesting that the topic of anxiety in children has often been overlooked. Particularly in view of evidence that a significant portion of child clients at mental health clinics are treated for anxiety disorders (Miller, Boyer, & Rodoletz, 1990), and that childhood anxiety may be predictive of adult psychopathology (Bowlby, 1973), the topic deserves attention. One of the reasons that anxiety in children may be overlooked is the belief that it is both common and transient (Wolfson, Fields, & Rose, 1987). In reality, many anxiety problems experienced by children are quite stable, with the combined literature indicating that from 20% to 30% of anxiety disorders diagnosed during childhood show strong stability over intervals of 2 to 5 years (Silverman & Ginsburg, 1998).

With the publication of the *DSM–IV* in 1994, significant changes were made in the *DSM* classification criteria for anxiety disorders in youth. Perhaps the most significant of these changes was the elimination of the *DSM–III* and *DSM–III–R* broad diagnostic category of Anxiety Disorders of Childhood and Adolescence. From this former diagnostic category, Overanxious Disorder was incorporated into the adult General Anxiety Disorder, and Avoidant Disorder was removed. The only childhood-specific anxiety disorder that remained from *DSM–III–R* was Separation Anxiety Disorder, but this category was also reclassified under another broad category, Other Disorders of Childhood and Adolescence. The *DSM–IV* general and specific categories of anxiety disorders, all of which may potentially pertain to youth, are outlined in Table 10.2. It is still somewhat unclear what prompted the changes between *DSM–III–R* and *DSM–IV* with regard to child and adolescent anxiety disorders, but these changes may potentially have some unintended effects. Silverman and Ginsburg (1998) noted that although research regarding anxiety in youth has historically lagged behind comparable research with adults, "research interest in anxiety in youth burgeoned with the establishment of the broad diagnostic category, Anxiety Disorder of Childhood and Adolescence (in *DSM–III* and *III–R*)" (p. 239). Although it is still too early to tell, it would be most unfortunate if the elimination of youth-specific diagnostic categories for anxiety disorders in the *DSM* resulted in a lessened amount of research in the area.

The current *DSM* classification categories for anxiety disorders, as shown in Table 10.2, are extensive and broad—yet, in some cases, they are also very specific and narrow. Clinicians who work extensively with young children will probably end up using the diagnostic category of Separation Anxiety Disorder at least occasionally, and clinicians working with children and adolescents of various ages will undoubtedly occasionally encounter a specific type of anxiety disorder. Realistically, however, most clinicians who work with anxious youth will probably classify most cases of anxiety under the more general category of Generalized Anxiety Disorder (see Table 10.4).

Causal Factors. Although a fair amount of effort has been devoted to exploring the etiology of depression, comparatively little has been done in this area related to the development of anxiety, particularly in relation to children. One of the problems in making a few general statements about the causes of anxiety in children is that they have been viewed very differently by professionals from different theoretical orientations, such as psychoanalytic, behavioral, and cognitive perspectives (Miller, Boyer, & Rodoletz, 1990). A review of etiologic perspectives by Silverman and Ginsburg (1998) divided the major areas of etiologic research into genetic and neurobiology, psychosocial, psychoanalytic, behavioral, cognitive, family, and peer influence, and

DSM-IV eliminated almost all child-specific anxiety disorders

little info on causal factors for anxiety

TABLE 10.4
Diagnostic Criteria for Generalized Anxiety Disorder from the *DSM–IV*

A. Excessive anxiety and worry (apprehensive expectation), occurring more days than not for at least 6 months, about a number of events or activities (such as work or school performance).
B. The person finds it difficult to control the worry.
C. The anxiety and worry are associated with three (or more) of the following six symptoms (with at least some symptoms present for more days than not for the past 6 months). *Note: Only one item is required in children.*
   1. restlessness or feeling keyed up or on edge
   2. being easily fatigued
   3. difficulty concentrating or mind going blank
   4. irritability
   5. muscle tension
   6. sleep disturbance (difficulty falling or staying asleep, or restless unsatisfying sleep)
D. The focus of the anxiety and worry is not confined to features of an Axis I disorder, e.g., the anxiety or worry is not about having a Panic Attack (as in Panic Disorder), being embarrassed (as in Social Phobia), being contaminated (as in Obsessive-Compulsive Disorder), being away from home or close relatives (as in Separation Anxiety Disorder), gaining weight (as in Anorexia Nervosa), having multiple physical complaints (as in Somatization Disorder), or having a serious illness (as in Hypochondriasis), and the anxiety and worry do not occur exclusively during Posttraumatic Stress Disorder.
E. The anxiety, worry, or physical symptoms cause clinically significant distress or impairment in social, occupational, or other important areas of functioning.
F. The disturbance is not due to the direct physiological effects of a substance (e.g., a drug of abuse, a medication) or a general medical condition (e.g., hyperthyroidism) and does not occur exclusively during a Mood Disorder, a Psychotic Disorder, or a Pervasive Developmental Disorder.

Note. From *Diagnostic and Statistical Manual of Mental Disorders* (4th ed.). Copyright © 1994, American Psychiatric Association. Reprinted by permission of the American Psychiatric Association.

indicated that with the exception of psychoanalytic, there is at least a small body of empirical evidence to support each perspective. However, given that relatively little empirical work has been devoted to the causes of anxiety in children, perhaps the most appropriate statement about causation, and one that is compatible with the social learning perspective of this book, is that "the child's temperamental characteristics, in combination with early socialization experiences and the nature of the current . . . environment, probably account for the development (of anxiety-related problems)" (Kauffman, 1989, p. 334).

Related Internalizing Disorders

In addition to the characteristics of depression and anxiety, the broader category of internalizing disorders includes a number of other associated behavioral, social, and emotional problems. This section provides some additional discussion on some of the more prominent of these associated problems.

Social Withdrawal. One of the major correlates of depression and anxiety is social withdrawal or isolation. As Kauffman (1989) noted, social isolation can result from either behavioral excesses (e.g., aggression or hyperactivity) or behavioral deficits. It is the category of behavioral deficits that is most closely linked with internalizing disorders. Children who are socially isolated or withdrawn due to behavioral deficits tend to lack responsiveness to the social initiations of others—in other words, they lack the specific social skills to make and keep friends. Often, a severe lack of social skills is accompanied by immature or socially inadequate behavior that further compounds the problem by making the child an easy target of ridicule (Kauffman, 1989). Internalizing social withdrawal and isolation seems to be related not only to exposure to incompetent adult social models, but to a temperamental characteristic referred to by Kagan, Reznik, and Snidman (1990) as *behavioral inhibition to the unfamiliar*. When present, this characteristic appears to emerge in infants at about 8 months, and leads to a tendency to become inhibited or withdrawn when presented with unfamiliar stimuli. There may be biological contributions to this temperamental characteristic, but it probably interacts with behavior and environment in a complex manner to result in characteristic social withdrawal.

broad range of physical symptoms

Somatic Problems. Another common correlate of internalizing disorders is a broad range of physical symptoms and problems that are collectively referred to as *somatic* complaints. There is a strong probability that persons who experience significant depression or anxiety will have concurrent physical symptoms. These somatic symptoms associated with internalizing characteristics are presumably based on a psychological origin, although physical infections or injuries may cause similar symptoms. One of the subscales of the Child Behavior Checklist that turns up primarily along the internalizing dimension is labeled *Somatic Complaints*, and includes rating items such as "feels dizzy," "overtired," and "physical problems without known medical cause." This last item has seven possible specifications, including aches and pains, headaches, nausea, problems with eyes, rashes or other skin problems, stomachaches or cramps, and vomiting. Any or all of these physical symptoms may be reported by children are who experiencing depressive, anxious, or withdrawn symptoms. Interestingly, the congruence of somatic complaints and anxious-depressed-withdrawn characteristics in psychological assessment even predates the use of factor analytic assessment techniques. The first three of the MMPI–2 and MMPI–A clinical scales (Hypochondriasis, Depression, and Hysteria), sometimes referred to as the "Neurotic Triad," all contain items relating to physical complaints as well as statements about depressive, anxious, and withdrawn symptomatology. First developed in the 1940s using empirical criterion keying procedures, these three scales have been shown to reliably differentiate among different psychiatric groups in numerous studies.

Fears and Phobias. Fears and phobias, a more specific group of characteristics that relate to anxiety, were touched on briefly earlier in this chapter. However, what is commonly referred to as *school phobia* deserves some additional discussion because it is a set of problems commonly encountered by mental health professionals who work with children and adolescents. The *DSM–IV* does not have a separate diagnostic classification for school phobia, but considers it one of the nine key features of Separation Anxiety Disorder. Thus, traditional thinking considers that fear of and subsequent refusal to attend school are internalizing problems that relate to a child's inner state of anxiety. More recently, this traditional anxiety-based view of school phobia has come under criticism, and the problem has been reconceptualized as *school refusal*, a broader term that indicates the possible heterogeneity of symptoms.

Pilkington and Piersel (1991) conducted a comprehensive review of the literature on school phobia, and criticized the separation anxiety based theory on three grounds: methodological problems of the research, lack of generalizability concerning pathological mother–child relationships, and lack of emphasis on possible external or ecological variables. With respect to this third criticism, an alternative conceptualization of school phobia has been presented in which many cases of refusal to attend school

School Phobia + School Refusal

can be explained as "a normal avoidance reaction to a hostile environment" (Pilkington & Piersel, 1991, p. 290). Realistically, avoidance of or refusal to attend school probably includes a more heterogeneous group of conditions than was once thought, and anxiety problems as well as avoidant behavioral reactions are likely both culpable explanations. The implication of this new conceptualization of school phobia is that clinicians should consider assessing the school environment as well as child characteristics when refusal to attend school is a presenting problem. This implication is compatible with the transactional-interactional model within social learning theory and suggests that refusal to attend school may be explained by an interaction of parent and child characteristics, coupled with the environmental and behavioral conditions that occur at school. *Social learning theory → interaction of parent + child characteristics + environment + behav. conditions of school*

Other Problems. Finally, there are a few additional conditions that are often part of the larger internalizing syndrome. Obsessive thought processes and compulsive behavioral rituals are closely related to the anxiety disorders, and in *DSM–IV*, Obsessive-Compulsive Disorder is included as a diagnostic category under the broad category of Anxiety Disorders. Various forms of eating disorders, including anorexia nervosa, bulimia, pica, and rumination disorders, have all been shown to be related to the broad internalizing syndrome (Kauffman, 1989). Some stereotypical movement disorders, such as motor tics, may also be a part of the internalizing picture. Finally, elimination disorders (enuresis and encopresis) may occur with other internalizing problems, although there are also a number of physiologic causes for these problems. Some of these problems are discussed in more detail in chapter 11.

OCD, eating disorders, stereotypical movement disorders + elimination disorders

Implications of Internalizing Disorders

There has been some disagreement in the developmental psychopathology literature as to the potential long-term consequences of internalizing disorders, and more research in this area is needed. At the present time, there seems to be general agreement in the field that serious internalizing symptoms of childhood may persist for long periods of time, perhaps as long as 2 to 5 years (Silverman & Ginsburg, 1998; Quay & Werry, 1986). In terms of the persistence of these characteristics into adulthood, there is much less agreement. Quay and Werry stated that symptoms of anxiety-withdrawal "do not have the rather foreboding prognosis that is associated with undersocialized conduct disorders" (1986, p. 101), and cited Robins' (1966) long-term follow-up research of neurotic children as an example that internalizing symptoms during childhood may not accurately predict the presence of internalizing problems during adulthood. However, other researchers have found evidence for a less optimistic prognosis for children with internalizing disorders. Social withdrawal and inadequate levels of social competence have been found to be associated with a number of later negative outcomes, although the evidence to date suggests that the prognosis is worse for aggressive than nonaggressive socially withdrawn children (Kauffman, 1989; Pullatz & Dunn, 1990). When childhood depression is the internalizing disorder of interest, there seems to be stronger evidence for persistence across the life span, particularly in the case of adolescent depression (Cantwell, 1990). Thus, there may be some hope that the existence of internalizing disorders during childhood does not hold as poor a prognosis as does that of externalizing disorders, but there is nevertheless evidence to suggest the potential for negative outcomes later in life (W. M. Reynolds, 1992b).

long term is questionable

persistence of disorder across the lifespan

POSITIVE AND NEGATIVE AFFECTIVITY:
A NEW SPIN ON INTERNALIZING PROBLEMS

An interesting development during the past several years regarding the understanding of internalizing disorders is the research that has been conducted on cognitive and mood states of these disorders. The constructs of *positive and negative affectivity* (also referred to as affect) involve the positive or negative presentations of various mood symptoms. This conceptualization of affectivity is not considered to be a specific dimension of internalizing disorders, but it is considered to be an important characteristic that may help differentiate among various types of internalizing disorders. Watson and Tellegen (1985) originally proposed this two-dimensional model of affect in an attempt to discriminate empirically between depression and anxiety. Positive affect (PA) has been defined as "the extent to which a person avows a zest for life" (Watson & Tellegen, 1985, p. 221), and is reflected by such descriptors as *active, alert, energetic, enthusiastic, interested, joyful,* and *determined.* Conversely, descriptors such as *drowsy, dull, fatigued, lethargic,* and *sluggish* reflect low levels of PA. In contrast, Negative Affect (NA) has been defined as "the extent to which a person reports feeling upset or unpleasantly aroused" (Watson & Tellegen, 1985, p. 221). The terms *distressed, fearful, hostile,* and *nervous* reflect high levels of NA, whereas adjectives such as *calm, placid,* and *relaxed* reflect low levels of NA.

In various studies on expressions of affectivity with internalizing disorders (e.g., Blumberg & Izard, 1986; T. C. Carey, Finch, & M. P. Carey, 1991; Jolly, Dyck, Kramer, & Wherry, 1994; Stark, Kaslow, & Laurent, 1993; Tellegen, 1986; Watson, 1988; Watson & Clark, 1984), a general consensus has emerged, notwithstanding the fact that there have been some minor differences among findings. In general, it is understood that measures of depression and anxiety both tap negative affectivity. In other words, persons who report high symptoms of either depression or anxiety are also likely to report high levels of negative affect. However, there also seems to be a general consensus that individuals with high levels of depressive symptoms are likely to be low in positive affect, whereas individuals with high levels of anxiety but no depression will not necessarily be low in positive affect. In other words, in cases where anxiety and depression can actually be differentiated, it may be that the presence or absence of positive affect is a key distinguishing feature.

Although there is still much that is not understood regarding the role of affectivity in child emotional and behavioral disorders, it appears to be an important element, particularly with respect to the internalizing domain. One of the self-report instruments discussed in this chapter (the Internalizing Symptoms Scale for Children) was developed specifically to assess the global construct of internalizing symptomatology in children, and includes specific items and subscales aimed at differentiating positive and negative affect. Although including dimensions of affectivity within clinical assessment and diagnostic practices is an endeavor that is still quite unrefined, future developments in this area may prove to be essential to furthering the assessment and intervention practices with children and adolescents who exhibit internalizing problems.

INTERNALIZING PROBLEMS AND SELF-CONCEPT

Because internalizing problems have sometimes been thought of as being self-related or inner-directed, a psychological construct that is particularly relevant to this discussion is *self-concept.* The constructs of depression and self-concept have been clearly

Self esteem, self worth and depression

linked in the professional literature, because diminished self-esteem is often a prominent feature of depression (Kazdin, 1988), because particular styles of self-esteem
beliefs are likely to substantially increase the risk of depression (Hammen, 1995), and
because irrational beliefs regarding self-worth often constitute a clear target for cognitive treatment of depression (Swallow & Segal, 1995). Although less is known
regarding specific links between other variations of internalizing problems (e.g., anxiety, social withdrawal, and somatic problems) and self-concept, it is logical to assume
that self-concept and internalizing symptoms in general may be negatively associated,
given the strong overlap among various internalizing symptoms and disorders.

Harter (1990) noted that self-concept can have a number of different definitions
depending on the theoretical framework that is adopted. The definition of self-concept
that is utilized in this book is that of *multidimensional* self-concept. When defined from
a multidimensional viewpoint, self-concept includes not only overall self-evaluation
and level of self-esteem, but a person's self-evaluation of particular aspects of functioning, such as physical appearance and skills, academic competence, and social-emotional functioning. In a multidimensional framework, people's overall self-concept is
not merely a summation of how they feel about or evaluate any of these different
aspects of life. Rather, individuals' evaluation of a particular aspect of self-functioning
may contribute somewhat to their overall view of themselves, but each dimension of
self may operate somewhat independently. For example, people might have a very
negative evaluation of some particular dimensions of the self (e.g., their physical
appearance and athletic competence), but still have a relatively high global self-concept, or overall view of themselves. *Self-concept = multidimensional*

Earlier work in the area of self-concept, as typified by research and theoretical
writing prior to the 1970s, tended to regard self-concept in a *unidimensional* fashion.
The unidimensional view indicates that self-concept is best assessed by presenting the
subject with a number of different items that tap various aspects of self-functioning,
giving each different aspect of the self-concept equal weight, and then providing a
global estimate of self-concept by simply summing the item responses. The assessment
of self-concept from this unidimensional viewpoint is typified by two instruments
originally developed during the 1960s—the Coopersmith Self-Esteem Inventory (Coopersmith, 1981) and the Piers–Harris Children's Self-Concept Scale (Piers & Harris,
1969)—neither of which are reviewed in this text because they are based on somewhat
archaic notions of self-concept and its assessment. *2 self-concept scales → Archaic*

During the 1970s and 1980s, a number of researchers began to explore self-concept
in a manner that identified specific domains of self-evaluation, which were thought to
operate somewhat independently while at the same time correlate moderately with each
other. This multidimensional approach to self-concept was typified during this time
period by the work of Harter (1985a, 1986) and Marsh (1987). Proponents of this view
contend that overall self-concept is affected by individual areas of self-evaluation, but
the contribution from each individual area is not necessarily the same. From a practical
standpoint, viewing self-concept from a multidimensional perspective has important
implications for a clinician who is conducting an assessment. For example, children or
adolescent clients may have a very negative view of their academic competence, but may
not consider it to be very important and thus feel okay about themselves in a general
sense. On the other hand, youths may see themselves as being very competent and
successful in most areas of functioning, but assign great or undue weight to their
unfavorable self-concept in the area of physical appearance, and thus have a poor global
self-concept, despite the many other areas in which they feel competent and successful.

*diff areas worth diff weight to
people + self-concept.*

functional role of self concept

The best evidence to date indicates that self-concept does indeed have a strong functional role that may impact such diverse aspects of human development as affect, motivation, and energy level, all of which have strong implications when it comes to internalizing problems. Commenting on this functional role of the self-concept, Harter (1990) stated:

> We have also been concerned with the mediational role that self-worth may play in impacting both affective state, along a dimension of depressed to cheerful, and motivation, along a dimension of low to high energy. Our studies provide strong support for the impact that self-worth has on affect, which in turn influences the child's energy level. The implications of these findings for childhood depression as well as adolescent suicide have also been explored within this context. (p. 319)

self-concept and academic achievement

The construct of self-concept not only has significant implications in relation to internalizing problems, but in relation to a number of other aspects of life. Since about the 1970s, there have been strong efforts nationwide to provide affective education in public schools, with the goal of enhancing student's self-concept. Bloom (1976) suggested that academic self-concept is the single most powerful affective predictor of academic success, accounting for about 25% of the variance in academic achievement after the elementary school period. More recently, many school-based intervention programs designed to prevent substance abuse and gang membership have focused on enhancing children's self-esteem as one preventative measure. Although there has been some disagreement regarding how to best enhance the self-concept, there is no question that the construct holds a place of prominence in the goals of most educators. Thus, clinicians working with children and adolescents should have a basic understanding of the issues involved in assessing self-concept. Some multidimensional self-concept assessment instruments for children and adolescents are discussed later in this chapter.

METHODS OF ASSESSING INTERNALIZING PROBLEMS

difficult to assess internal, subjective states.

The assessment of internalizing problems presents a peculiar problem for clinicians and researchers. By definition and practice, internalizing problems tend to involve internal states and subjective perceptions. Not surprisingly then, assessing characteristics such as depression and anxiety using external methods (e.g., direct observation, sociometrics, and to some extent, rating scales) can be quite problematic (Links, Boyle, & Offord, 1983). Partially as a result of this problem, the research base on internalizing problems has historically lagged behind that of externalizing problems (Cicchetti & Toth, 1991). In terms of clinical practice with internalizing problems, this state of affairs has created similar problems. Because they are for the most part assessing internal and subjective states when evaluating internalizing problems, clinicians have tended to rely on various forms of self-reporting. But with child and adolescent clients (particularly very young children), there is often a reluctance to relinquish the use of external methods of assessment, due to the supposed questionable accuracy of information obtained with self-report methods.

Thus, although this chapter covers assessment of internalizing problems using each of the five methods of direct and objective assessment, the larger focus is on the use of objective self-report tests and interview methods.

Behavioral Observation

[handwritten: There are some behaviors that can be observed to represent depress. + anxiety]

Although assessment of internalizing problems through methods other than self-report (interviewing and objective tests) presents a number of problems, some internalizing characteristics can be directly observed, and there has been some experimentation with the use of behavioral observation codes for assessment. Unlike self-report methods, which assess client perceptions of internalizing symptoms, or rating scales, which assess third-party perceptions of internalizing symptoms retrospectively, the aim of direct behavioral observation is to assess these symptoms as they actually occur. Kazdin (1988) listed several symptoms of depression that are measurable through direct behavioral observation. Some of these include *diminished motor and social activity, reduced eye contact with others*, and *slowed speech*. Additional anxiety-related internalizing symptoms that might be assessed through direct observation include *avoidance of feared or anxiety-provoking stimuli, facial expressions*, and *stance* (Miller, Boyer, & Rodoletz, 1990). Using these characteristics as examples, it becomes very clear how important some of the basic rules of conducting effective observations might be, such as defining the observation domain and selecting an appropriate recording system, which were discussed in chapter 3.

An interesting observational technique that has been used in the assessment of anxiety and related symptoms since the 1930s (Jersild & Holmes, 1935) is the Behavioral Avoidance Test (BAT). The BAT can be implemented in a variety of ways, and is quite simple to use. The original BAT technique involved having the subject enter a room where the anxiety or fear provoking stimulus is present (e.g., an animal, insect, separation from parent, darkness) and then having them approach the feared stimuli. The observational measures that can be taken include latency of approach, duration of time in the presence of the stimulus, and number of approaches completed (Miller, Boyer, & Rodoletz, 1990). A variation of the BAT involves having the subject imagine the feared stimuli or situation, and then recording their overt responses to the task. This variation of the BAT may be particularly useful for assessing overt responses to anxiety provoking situations that cannot be contrived in a clinical setting, such as fear of imagined "monsters," injury or death of a caregiver, or clouds. *[handwritten: BAT way to assess fears/anxiety w/ observat. + clinical settings]*

There are three general classes of behavioral codes that may be used for direct observational assessment of childhood depression. These general codes are listed as follows, with types of specific target codes that might be included under each class: *[handwritten: 3 classes of Behavior to observe in Depressed children]*

1. *Social Activity*: Talking, playing a game, participating in a group activity.

2. *Solitary Behavior*: Playing a game alone, working on an academic task, listening and watching, straightening one's room, grooming.

3. *Affect-Related Expression*: Smiling, frowning, arguing, complaining.

These types of observational target codes have been successfully used in the measurement of depression and related internalizing problems in several studies. For example, J. G. Williams, Barlow, and Agras (1972) found significant negative correlations with self-reports of depression and observations of verbal activity, smiling, and motor activity in depressed patients. Kazdin, Esveldt-Dawson, Unis, and Rancurello (1983) used behavioral codes from these three general categories to observe inpatient children (age 8–13) over a 1-week period, and found that those children who were high in depression engaged in significantly less social behavior and exhibited significantly less affect-related

observable behaviors are only a small part of internalizing disorders. [handwritten annotation]

expression than other children. These two studies show that internalizing problems can be effectively assessed through direct observation. However, it is important to always consider that overt or easily observable characteristics of internalizing problems are only a part of the picture (and often a very small part). The subjective emotional state and cognitive processes of the subject are also extremely important, and these must be assessed primarily through client self-report. Because so many aspects of internalizing problems are subtle or covert, it is very important to carefully design the observation, using procedures like those outlined in chapter 3.

self monitoring [handwritten annotation]

Self-monitoring, a specific facet of direct behavioral observation, has not been widely researched as an assessment method for internalizing problems, but it appears to hold some promise in this regard. Because there is considerable evidence that children and adolescents can be trained to accurately monitor and record their own behavior (Gettinger & Kratochwill, 1987; Shapiro & Cole, 1994), there is no a priori reason why they could not also be trained to accurately monitor and record internal or private events. For example, a clinician working with a depressed adolescent might train them to periodically record the number of positive and negative internal self-statements they make, and use this data to chart both baseline rates and treatment progress. Likewise, children or adolescents could be trained to record their own perceptions of various somatic complaints, their pulse rate, engagement in pleasurable activities, or positive self-affirming thought processes. Of course, there may be some important limitations of self-monitoring observation with internalizing problems. Self-monitoring may be *reactive* in the sense that it may produce change in the subject (Kratochwill, 1982). Thus, self-monitoring may be more useful in assessment during a follow-up or intervention period than during baseline data gathering. An obvious concern with self-monitoring of internalizing problems may surface when working with children or adolescents who exhibit obsessive-compulsive behaviors. Logically and intuitively, obsessive thought or compulsive behavior could potentially be strengthened because of the increased focus placed on it. Despite these potential problems, self-monitoring of internalizing problems appears to be a plausible alternative to direct observation by an independent observer, though it has not been widely reported for these uses in the professional literature.

Behavior Rating Scales

Each of the general purpose behavior rating scales or rating scale systems discussed in chapter 4 includes rating items and subscales specifically directed at measuring internalizing problems, and all of these instruments have been validated to some extent for this purpose. Thus, there are several widely used general purpose rating instruments that are very pertinent to the assessment of such varied internalizing symptom areas as anxiety, depression, and social withdrawal. Although a few research instruments have been reported in the literature that are aimed at specific types of internalizing symptomatology, for the most part these behavior rating scales have not been validated or are not in wide enough use to justify their inclusion in this chapter. Therefore, the general purpose instruments evaluated in chapter 4 are recommended as the instruments of choice when objective third-party behavior ratings of internalizing problems are desired.

Another potentially useful behavior rating scale for assessing internalizing problems is the Preschool and Kindergarten Behavior Scales, which are discussed in chapter 13. These scales include a broad-band internalizing problems subscale with two internal-

types of internalizing disorders [handwritten annotation]

rating scale. [handwritten annotation]

izing problems subscales, and may be useful for objective evaluation of internalizing problems of young children. Also, it may be useful to consider the use of any of the social competence rating scales or systems that are discussed in chapter 10 (the Social Skills Rating System, School Social Behavior Scales, and Walker–McConnell Scales of Social Competence and School Adjustment) when there are concerns about assessing internalizing problems. Given that social withdrawal often accompanies depression and anxiety, and that deficits in social competence may be correlated with internalizing problems, such an assessment strategy may be very useful.

Although the use of behavior rating scales is recommended as part of a comprehensive assessment design for evaluating internalizing problems of children and youth, this recommendation is not without caution. As has been mentioned numerous times in this chapter, many aspects of internalizing problems are *not readily detectable* to an external observer, even one who knows the child or youth well. Because many of the core symptoms of internalizing disorders are not externally observable in any reliable way, behavior rating scales should be used for this purpose with a great deal of caution. Because the evidence indicates that parent reports (and by inference, teacher reports) may be more accurate for assessing externalizing problems, but child self-reports may be more accurate for assessing internalizing problems (Kolko & Kazdin, 1993), there should always be a strong assessment emphasis on the latter method when internalizing symptoms are concerned. *Emphasis on self reports when problems are not readily detectable by others...*

Clinical Interviewing

Whether structured, traditional, or behavioral in nature, the clinical interview is perhaps the most widely used method for the assessment of internalizing problems (Miller, Boyer, & Rodoletz, 1990). Virtually any of the interview techniques discussed in chapter 5 can be useful in the assessment of depression, anxiety, social withdrawal, and related internalizing symptoms. In terms of structured or semistructured interview schedules, each of those discussed in chapter 5 (e.g., K–SADS, DICA–R, CAS, and DISC) are directly relevant for assessing internalizing symptomatology, and include a number of areas of questioning that are very specific to this area. As such, any of these interview schedules are worthy of consideration for assessing internalizing problems. An example of the utility of these structured interview schedules in assessing internalizing problems is a recent study by King (1997), who examined the diagnostic efficacy of the DISC (version 2.3) for diagnosing depressive disorders in a large sample of inpatient adolescents, and found it to have strong concurrent validity for this purpose. It is interesting to note that this study found that the highest rates of diagnostic accuracy were obtained when results from both parent and adolescent versions of the interview were combined. Another interesting facet of this investigation is that parents reported a higher prevalence of depressive symptoms in their children than the adolescents themselves reported. *parents reported child as more depressed than the child reported about self.*

An interview schedule that has been developed specifically for use in assessing depression is the Children's Depression Rating Scale (CDRS), which was originally developed by Poznanski, Cook, and Carroll, 1979, but has since been revised and also developed into a short form (e.g., Overholser, Brinkman, Lehnert, & Ricciardi, 1995). This instrument was developed as a downward extension and adaption of the Hamilton Rating Scale for Depression, an instrument for use in assessing depression in adults. Although the CDRS may not be as widely used as the interview schedules reviewed in chapter 5, it is of interest because of its specificity of design. The CDRS includes

CDRS

17 interview items that cover a range of depressive symptoms, such as inability to have fun and the appearance of sad affect. The clinician who conducts the interview questions the child regarding each item, but may also consult other informants such as parents or teachers. Each interview item is ultimately rated for symptom severity by the clinician, using an 8-point scale (0 = *unable to rate*, to 7 = *severe symptoms*). The research base on the CDRS is growing, and there have been some encouraging findings. For example, the CDRS has been found to have relatively high interrater agreement (.75 and higher), high correlations with global clinical ratings of depression (.85 and higher), high test–retest reliability at up to 6-week intervals (.81), and good convergent validity with other diagnostic interview schedules. This instrument appears to be useful for research purposes or as part of a comprehensive assessment battery when measurement of depressive symptoms is specified.

Sociometric Techniques

problem- Internalizing is difficult to be observed + recognized.

Like direct behavioral observation, sociometric approaches may be used to assess internalizing problems, but also poses some difficult challenges in the process. As is true in the case of behavioral observation, a major difficulty with the use of sociometric assessment for measuring internalizing problems is that subjective internal states, thought patterns, and other covert characteristics may not be easily observed and perceived by peers. An additional difficulty in this regard surfaces when young children are being assessed. Given their experiential limitations due to their age, very young informants may lack the maturity to make differentiations among subtle emotional characteristics. Whereas it may be relatively easy for a child to name three classmates who are likely to fight on the playground, the identification of peers who are sad, lonely, or nervous may become confounded with a number of other personality characteristics. With adults, sociometric assessment of internalizing characteristics is perhaps more effective. Kane and Lawler (1978) reviewed 19 peer assessment studies where the subjects were adults, and concluded that several of the investigations were reasonably valid in measuring various internalizing type characteristics.

Although sociometric approaches will seldom be the first method of choice for assessing internalizing problems, they nevertheless can and have been useful for this purpose. As an assessment component for internalizing problems, sociometric approaches are probably best used as a screening device for identifying potentially at-risk children who might be administered further assessments. Virtually all of the general sociometric assessment methods presented in chapter 6 are flexible enough to be appropriately implemented in this manner. The teacher ranking procedure for internalizing problems from the Systematic Screening for Behavior Disorders (Walker & Severson, 1992) discussed in chapter 6 is an example of a sociometric type method targeted specifically at internalizing characteristics. Typical peer nomination, rating, or ranking methods could all be used to target specific internalizing characteristics. As is true in using behavioral observation, it will be necessary to carefully define the target characteristic for a valid assessment. For example, a nomination procedure used to screen for social withdrawal by wording the statement something like "write down the names of three students who always seem to be alone," might also screen in children who are socially isolated because of their antisocial-aggressive behavior.

Despite the challenges inherent in doing so, several studies have shown that sociometric assessment approaches can effectively screen for internalizing problems in children. McConnell and Odom (1986) reviewed 46 investigations that utilized so-

sociometrics useful for screening.

ciometric methods with children for various research purposes, and several of these studies directly assessed at least some internalizing characteristic, such as withdrawal or depression. It is interesting to note that several of the studies reviewed by McConnell and Odom found that targeted subjects were likely to exhibit both internalizing and externalizing symptoms. Thus, the distinction between these two domains of problems that has been found through behavioral dimensions research does not always exist in individual cases. *Sociometrics have difficulty separating depress + anxiety*

An additional sociometric assessment procedure that has been used in the measurement of depression on a fairly wide basis for research is the Peer Nomination Inventory for Depression (PNID; Lefkowitz & Tesiny, 1980). The PNID consists of 20 statements that comprise three subscales (Depression, 14 items; Happiness, 4 items; *Peer* and Popularity, 2 items). Individuals within a group (usually a classroom) are asked *Nomin.* to identify peer(s) that the statements apply to. Examples of some of the statements *Invent.* on the Depression subscale include "Often plays alone," "Often sleeps in class," *for* "Worries a lot," and "Often looks sad." Kazdin (1988) noted that the PNID has solid internal consistency (.85 or higher), acceptable test–retest reliability at 2- to 6-month *Depression* intervals, and adequate interrater agreement, and that normative data on the PNID have been gathered for over 3,000 children in grades 3 through 5. Several validation studies of the PNID (e.g., Crowley & Worchel, 1993; Lefkowitz, Tesiny, & Gordon, 1980; Lefkowitz & Tesiny, 1985; Tesiny & Lefkowitz, 1982) have shown that it has relatively weak correlations with self-report and teacher ratings of depression, but strong correlations with measures of school performance, self-concept, teacher ratings of social behavior, and other peer ratings of happiness and popularity. An interesting finding from the PNID validation research is that children who evidence greater depressive symptoms as measured by self-report instruments are more likely to rate other children as more depressed on the PNID (Crowley & Worchel, 1993). This instrument is an innovative assessment technique that is one of the few sociometric measures designed specifically or solely for assessing internalizing problems. However, at the present time, it is probably best used as a research or broad screening tool.

Self-Report Instruments

Best uses of sociometrics

In addition to the general purpose self-report instruments discussed in chapter 7, numerous self-report instruments have been developed for assessing specific internalizing disorders and symptoms in children and adolescents. However, there are many more objective self-report instruments for assessing this area than can be adequately addressed in this chapter. Six of these self-report instruments have been selected for further discussion and evaluation in this chapter. Three of these instruments are designed specifically to assess symptoms of depression, two of them are designed to assess symptoms of anxiety, and one is designed to assess the broad range of internalizing symptomatology. These six instruments were selected over other potential measures for inclusion due to their commercial availability, psychometric properties, ease of use, and amount and/or sophistication of available research evidence. Table 10.5 presents summary information regarding the major characteristics of each of these instruments.

Children's Depression Inventory. The Children's Depression Inventory (CDI; Kovacs, 1980–1981, 1991) is a 27-item self-report measure of depressive symptomatology for use with school-age children and adolescents (age 6–17). Without question, this

TABLE 10.5

Self-Report Instruments for Assessing Internalizing Problems and Self-Concept:
Summary of Instruments Reviewed in Chapter 10, Listed in Order of Review

Instrument	Focus	Age Range	Items and Format	Norm Sample	Technical Properties
Children's Depression Inventory	Depressive Symptomatology	6–17	27 items, forced choice between three statements	1,463 (Florida)	good
Internalizing Symptoms Scale for Children	General Internalizing Symptoms	8–13	48 statements responded to on a 4-point scale	2,149 (national)	good
Revised Children's Manifest Anxiety Scale	General Anxiety	6–17	37 yes/no statements	5,000 (national)	fair to good
Reynolds Child Depression Scale	Depressive Symptomatology	8–12	30 statements responded to on a 4-point scale	1,600 (midwest and west)	good
Reynolds Adolescent Depression Scale	Depressive Symptomatology	13–18	30 statements responded to on a 4-point scale	2,400 (national)	good
State-Trait Anxiety Inventory for Children	State Anxiety and Trait Anxiety	9–12	2 scales with 20 items each; forced choice between 3 statements	1,554 (Florida)	good
Multidimensional Self-Concept Scale	Dimensions of Self-Concept	9–19	150 items rated using a Likert-type scale	2,501 (national)	good
Self-Perception Profile for Children	Dimensions of Self-Concept	9–14	36 statement pairs with two score options each	1,543 (Colorado)	fair to good
Self-Perception Profile for Adolescents	Dimensions of Self-Concept	13–18	45 statement pairs with two score options each	651 (Colorado)	fair to good

instrument is the most widely used and researched child self-report depression scale, with nearly 400 studies using the CDI appearing in the professional literature by 1998. The CDI was developed as a downward extension of the Beck Depression Inventory, and was first reported in the research literature in the early 1980s. For several years, the instrument and an accompanying unpublished manuscript were available in various versions from the author, but it was only in 1991 that the CDI became commercially published and thus more easily available.

Each of the 27 items of the CDI has three statements about a particular depressive symptom, and respondents choose the statement that best describes their feelings during the past 2 weeks. Each item is scored 0, 1, or 2, with the statements reflecting the greater severity of symptoms receiving the higher value. The following is an item similar to those found in the CDI, to illustrate the structure of the items and how they are scored:

_____ I feel very unhappy (scored 2)

_____ I feel somewhat unhappy (scored 1)

_____ I feel happy (scored 0)

The CDI is easy to administer and score, usually taking no more than 10 to 20 minutes for the entire process. The CDI manual suggests that a cutoff score of 11 be used if the purpose of the administration is to screen for depression while making few false-negative errors. If the purpose of the administration to assess the presence of depression in children with behavioral and emotional problems, 13 is suggested as the appropriate cutoff score.

Normative data for CDI score conversions are based on a study by Finch, Saylor, and Edwards (1985), wherein CDI score norms for 1,463 Florida public schoolchildren in grades 2 through 8 were reported. These normative data are broken down by gender and grade level. Previous versions of the unpublished CDI manual manuscript provided score norms based on a sample of 860 Canadian schoolchildren from age 8 to 13. Additional samples have also been reported in the literature. Although the CDI total score is the measure of interest, various factor analyses of the CDI have been reported in the literature, wherein five to seven factors have typically been extracted. The current version of the CDI manual advocates a five-factor solution.

The psychometric properties of the CDI have been documented in a large number of published research reports. Most studies have found the internal consistency of the CDI to be in the mid to upper .80s. With some exceptions where lower correlations were obtained, test–retest reliability of the CDI has typically been found to be in the .70 to .85 range at short (1-week to 2-month) intervals, and in the same general range at several-month intervals. The relative stability of the CDI over time is an interesting trend, considering that the author of the instrument has recommended it as a measure of _state_ depression rather than _trait_ depression. Perhaps the CDI measures trait depression as well.

The most common method of determining the validity of the CDI has been through obtaining correlations of concurrent scores from other internalizing measures, and a plethora of studies have found the CDI to have significant relations to other depression instruments and techniques purported to measure depression and related constructs. Other types of validity studies have included finding negative correlations between the CDI and measures of self-esteem (e.g., Kovacs, 1983) and social competence (e.g., Helsel & Matson, 1984), using CDI scores as a predictive measure of psychiatric diagnoses (e.g., Hodges, 1990a; Cantwell & Carlson, 1981), and using CDI scores to predict future emotional and behavioral adjustment problems (e.g., Mattison, Handford, Allen, Kales, & Goodman, 1990). Also, the CDI has been used as a treatment outcome measure in several studies.

There have been numerous criticisms of the CDI—particularly on the basis that the cutoff score criteria may be problematic and the instrument lacks a nationally standardized normative group (e.g., Kavan, 1990; Knoff, 1990). However, the CDI has the distinct advantage of being perhaps the most widely researched child self-report instrument in existence, and its psychometric properties and discriminant abilities are generally quite good. The commercial publication of the CDI with the concurrent development of a standard test manual that incorporates much of the vast research on the instrument is a positive and major development. The CDI should continue to have wide use in research. For clinical applications, a conservative approach to the use of cutoff scores is recommended, given the lack of nationwide norms and some previous criticisms of the predictive value of the cutoff scores.

Internalizing Symptoms Scale for Children. The Internalizing Symptoms Scale for Children (ISSC; Merrell & Walters, 1998) is a recently developed self-report measure designed to assess the broad range of internalizing symptomatology and affect of children in grades 3 through 6. It has 48 items that reflect symptoms of various internalizing disorders and include statements regarding positive and negative affect. The items are responded to on a 4-point scale: "Never True," "Hardly Ever True," "Sometimes True," and "Often True." The scale can be administered individually and in groups and can be completed in approximately 10 to 15 minutes. Items may be read by students, or read aloud by an administrator (Walters & Merrell, 1995). Raw scores are converted to subscale and total score percentile ranks, standard deviation equivalent scores, and interpretive score levels though the use of any easy-to-use scoring key and reference to two tables in the appendix of the ISSC manual.

The ISSC has two subscales or factors that were derived from several multivariate analyses (Merrell, Crowley, & Walters, 1997): Factor 1, *Negative Affect/General Distress*, and Factor 2, *Positive Affect*. Items in Factor 1 represent symptoms of negative affect (i.e., depression, anxiety, negative self-evaluation) and general emotional and physical distress. Items in Factor 2 represent positive affect or self-evaluative statements that are incompatible with internalizing disorders. Positively worded items on Factor 2 are reverse scored; thus the scoring throughout the ISSC is such that higher scores reflect greater levels of internalizing distress or the absence of positive affect. The ISSC national norm sample includes 2,149 students in grades 3 through 6 (1,109 boys and 1,040 girls) from several U.S. states. This norm sample is generally representative of the U.S. population in terms of socioeconomic status, special education participation, and racial/ethnic group membership.

Extensive information regarding the technical and psychometric properties of the ISSC is presented in the manual and in other published studies. Internal consistency reliability of the total score is .91, with reliabilities for Factor 1 and Factor 2 being .90 and 86, respectively. A study regarding the ISSC's test–retest reliability found strong stability at six differing time intervals over a 12-week period (Michael & Merrell, 1998). Mean stability coefficients from this study include .83 for the ISSC total score, .81 for Factor 1, and .80 for Factor 2. Convergent validity studies by Merrell, Anderson, and Michael (1997), and by M. S. Williams (1997) demonstrated strong correlations between the ISSC and the Internalizing broad-band score of the Youth Self-Report, the Revised Children's Manifest Anxiety Scale, Children's Depression Inventory, and Reynolds Child Depression Scale. Other validity studies that have involved the ISSC include an evaluation of sensitivity to theory-based gender differences in internalizing symptoms (Merrell & Dobmeyer, 1996), comparisons of internalizing symptoms and affectivity of gifted and nongifted students (Merrell, Gill, H. McFarland, & T. McFarland, 1996), and strong discriminating power between seriously emotionally disturbed and regular education students (Sanders, 1996).

The ISSC is unique among child self-report instruments because it is the only one designed specifically and solely to assess the broad band of internalizing symptomatology as well as to include dimensions of positive and negative affect, which are increasingly being viewed as critical variables in distinguishing depression from anxiety. It is best used as a screening measure, and appears to be potentially useful for research purposes and for clinical evaluation of emotional problems of children.

ISSC= only broad band, internalizing scale that includes por + neg affect dimension

Revised Children's Manifest Anxiety Scale. The Revised Children's Manifest Anxiety Scale (RCMAS; C. R. Reynolds & Richmond, 1985) is a self-report instrument for use with children from age 6 to 17. It includes 37 statements that are responded to in a yes/no fashion, and is designed to be a measure of trait anxiety (the tendency to be anxious over settings and time). Scoring the RCMAS simply involves summing the number of "yes" responses for each of three subscales (Physiological Anxiety, Worry and Oversensitivity, Concentration Anxiety) and a Lie scale, and calculating a total score. The three RCMAS subscales were developed through factor analytic research (C. R. Reynolds & Paget, 1981), whereas the Lie scale consists of nine items that are socially desirable but almost never true (e.g., "I never say things I shouldn't").

Normative data for the RCMAS are from nearly 5,000 cases obtained in the United States, with each geographical region being represented. These data were first reported in a study by C. R. Reynolds and Paget (1983), and include separate norm samples based on age, gender, and Black/White racial breakdowns.

Psychometric properties of the RCMAS as reported in the test manual and in numerous published studies are indicative of generally adequate levels of reliability and validity. Internal consistency reliability of the total RCMAS score has been reported at .79 for males and .85 for females in a study with kindergarten children (C. R. Reynolds, Bradley, & Steele, 1980). Internal consistency coefficients for the RCMAS subscales are at a somewhat troubling lower level than for the total score, ranging from .50 to .70 across groups for Physiological Anxiety and from .70 to .90 for the Lie scale. One test–retest reliability study of the RCMAS found short-term reliability coefficients of .88 (1 week) and .77 (5 weeks) (Wisniewski, Mulick, Genshaft, & Coury, 1987), whereas another study found a coefficient of .68 at a 9-month interval (C. R. Reynolds, 1981). Evidence for the convergent validity of the RCMAS comes from a large number of studies comparing the RCMAS with other self-report measures of anxiety and related internalizing symptoms. Evidence for theory-based sensitivity to group differences of the RCMAS (an indicator of construct validity) comes from studies such as one that found the scores of gifted children to be lower than the scores of average children (C. R. Reynolds & Bradley, 1983), and one that found scores of learning disabled children to be higher than those of average children (Paget & C. R. Reynolds, 1982). A number of other studies have found RCMAS score elevations in children with various internalizing disorders.

Although the reported psychometric data for the RCMAS are relatively sparse for the amount of research that has gone into it, and the internal stability of the RCMAS subscales is somewhat lower than desirable (although it is still acceptable), this instrument can be recommended on several grounds. The norm group(s) are very large (including a large norm group for Black children), and there are a large number of published studies (over 100 as of 1998) that attest to various properties and uses of the scale. The RCMAS is easy to use, has strong face validity, and can be recommended as part of a battery for assessing internalizing problems with children. However, given the more marginal stability of the three RCMAS subscales as opposed to the total score, it is recommended that the total score be used for most assessment purposes, and that subscale scores be interpreted with caution when they are used.

only use as a part of a battery [handwritten margin note]

Reynolds Child Depression Scale. The Reynolds Child Depression Scale (RCDS; W. M. Reynolds, 1989) is a self-report measure of depressive symptomatology for children in grades 3 through 6 (age 8–12). It contains 30 items that are responded to in a 4-point format ("almost never" to "all the time"). The 30 items were primarily developed based on depressive symptomatology from the *DSM–III*. Some of these items are phrased to represent the presence of depressive symptoms (e.g., "I feel I am no good"), whereas others are phrased to reflect the absence of such symptoms (e.g., "I feel like playing with other kids"). The items are written at about a second-grade level, and are administered orally to children in grades 3 and 4, and to older children who have reading problems. Scoring of the self-report protocol is accomplished through an easy-to-use overlay key that assigns values from 1 to 4 for each item, with higher scores reflecting item endorsement in the direction of depressive symptoms. A mail-in scoring service is also available through the publisher.

Items based on DSM-III symptomatology [handwritten margin note]

The RCDS was standardized on a group of over 1,600 children from the midwestern and western United States. Technical information provided in the test manual indicates that the instrument has acceptable to excellent psychometric properties. Internal consistency of total score is .90 for the entire normative sample, with similar levels reported by grade, gender, and ethnic group breakdowns. Test–retest reliability estimates are reported at .82 at 2-week intervals, and from .81 to .92 at 4-week intervals. A variety of information on the validity of the RCDS is presented in the test manual, including six correlational studies of the RCDS and CDI and four studies correlating the RCDS with self-report measures of anxiety and self-esteem. A few other convergent construct validity studies have also appeared in the professional literature in recent years. Factor analytic research indicates the presence of a reasonably strong five factor structure, although separate factor scores are not obtained in normal scoring of the RCDS. Interpretation of RCDS total scores is based on raw score to percentile score conversions, and critical raw score values. The raw score value of 74 is considered to be the critical value for "clinical" level scores, and evidence presented in the test manual suggests that scores at this level have a high "hit rate" for identifying children who meet other criteria for depressive symptomatology.

The manual for the RCDS is exceptionally well written and documented, the research data presented therein are impressive, and the instrument has a great deal of face validity. It appears to be an excellent self-report instrument for assessing depressive symptomatology with elementary-age children, and it should be very useful for both research and clinical purposes.

Reynolds Adolescent Depression Scale. The Reynolds Adolescent Depression Scale (RADS; W. M. Reynolds, 1986) is a self-report measure of depressive symptomatology for adolescents from age 13 to 18. It is a companion instrument to the RCDS (the

RADS was actually the first of the two instruments to be developed), and it is very similar in structure and format to the RCDS. Like the RCDS, the RADS contains 30 items that are responded to in a 4-point format ("almost never" to "all the time") that were developed to coincide with depressive symptomatology from the *DSM–III*. The majority of items on the RADS are the same as RCDS items, though some are written to reflect adolescent concerns and adolescent appropriate language, and there are a handful of items that are specific to each scale. The RADS can be administered either individually or with groups, and the items appear to be written at a low enough reading level so that even most adolescents with reading problems should be able to understand them. Three forms of the RADS are available; a hand-scored version, an optical scanning version, and a mail-in version for scoring large group administrations.

The RADS was standardized on a group of over 2,400 adolescents from a variety of U.S. geographical regions, and descriptive statistics are reported in the test manual for over 7,000 adolescents in addition to the standardization population. Technical information provided in the test manual indicates that the instrument has acceptable to excellent psychometric properties. Internal consistency for the total sample is reported at .92, with similar high levels reported by grade, gender, and additional sample breakdowns. Test–retest reliability estimates are reported at .80 at 6-week intervals, .79 at 3-month intervals, and .63 at 1 year. Adequate validity information is presented in the RADS test manual, and additional validity evidence has accrued through subsequent published studies using the RADS. The manual and several of these additional studies have shown convergent validity evidence for the RADS through correlational comparisons with other measures of depression and related internalizing symptoms. Correlational studies have also reported where the RADS was compared with various adolescent self-esteem measures, with results showing a moderate to strong inverse relation between RADS depression scores and self-concept scores.

Like the RCDS, factor analytic research on the RADS indicates the presence of a five-factor structure, although separate factor scores are not obtained in normal scoring of the RCDS. Reynolds suggested that interpretation of factor scores should be done in terms of the first four factors, as the fifth factor only contains two items, and these items load sufficiently on Factor 1. Interpretation of RCDS total scores is based on raw score to percentile score conversions, and critical raw score values. The raw score value of 77 is considered to be the critical value for "clinical" level scores, and evidence presented in the test manual suggests that scores at this level have a high "hit rate" for identifying adolescents who meet other criteria for depressive symptomatology. For example, one study reported in the manual found that RADS scores at the cutoff level of 77 correctly classified 82% of adolescent subjects who had been formally diagnosed as being depressed. *RADS should be used in lieu of BDI*

Like the RCDS, the manual for the RADS is exceptionally well written and documented, the research data presented therein are impressive, and the instrument has a great deal of face validity and usability. It is recommended that the RADS be used in lieu of the Beck Depression Inventory (an adult measure that is often used with adolescents) as a self-report screening measure for adolescent clients. The RADS items are more specifically and logically related to adolescent concerns, the size of the adolescent standardization group is impressive, and the documentation of research evidence specific to adolescent populations is substantial and growing. The RADS represents an excellent addition to the adolescent self-report instrumentation, and it is gaining wide clinical and research acceptance.

better for adolescents than BDI

State–Trait Anxiety Inventory for Children. The State–Trait Anxiety Inventory for Children (STAIC; Speilberger, 1973) is a self-report assessment of trait anxiety and state anxiety for children from age 9 to 12. It was developed as a downward extension of the State–Trait Anxiety Inventory (Speilberger, Gorsuch, & Luchene, 1970), a self-report measure for adolescents and adults. The STAIC consists of two separate scales with 20 items each: one to assess state anxiety (how anxious the child feels at the time the inventory is being completed) and one to assess trait anxiety (how anxious the child feels in general). The two scales can be administered separately or together. The STAIC may be administered individually or in groups, and typically requires about 10 minutes for each scale. Like the CDI, each item of the STAIC requires the subject to choose one of three statements that best describe how they feel. The items are scored 1, 2, or 3 points, with the higher score reflecting the statement indicating stronger symptoms of anxiety. Some of the STAIC items are reverse worded and keyed to control for the presence of acquiescent response sets.

The differentiation between state and trait anxiety is based on theoretical underpinnings previously postulated by Speilberger (1966, 1972). Children who are trait anxious will tend to respond to a variety of situations as if they are threatening, whereas children who score high on the state anxiety scale but low on the trait anxiety scale are thought to feel anxious due to a specific situation or event. Previous reviews of the STAIC (e.g., R. P. Martin, 1988) have considered the theoretical orientation of the instrument to be a definite advantage.

Normative data for both scales of the STAIC are from 1,554 subjects in the fourth, fifth, and sixth grades in the state of Florida. The norm sample includes a large percentage (approximately 35%) of African American subjects. The test manual includes normative data for the total sample, and for gender and grade level breakdowns. STAIC raw scores may be converted to T-score and percentiles using tables provided in the manual.

Psychometric properties of the STAIC, as reported in the test manual and subsequent research literature, have generally been adequate to good. Internal consistency coefficients for both scales have generally been reported to be in the .80s range. Consistent with the theoretical underpinnings of the STAIC, test–retest reliability coefficients reported in the manual are higher for the trait anxiety scale (.65 to .71) than for the state anxiety scale (.31 to .41) at 6-week intervals. Several studies have assessed the convergent validity of the STAIC through obtaining correlations with other internalizing self-report instruments (e.g., Hodges, 1990a; Rhone, 1986). Interestingly, some of the validation studies reported in the test manual found significant negative relations between trait anxiety and measures of academic achievement, such as the California Achievement Test. More recent studies have found the STAIC to be valid in identifying child psychiatric patients (Hodges, 1990a), and in differentiating anxiety levels among public school students with varying degrees of academic achievement problems (Rhone, 1986).

Overall, the STAIC has many qualities to recommend its use. The division of state and trait types of anxiety scales is interesting and useful from a theoretical standpoint, and a number of studies validated the differential measurement properties of the two scales. Previous reviews of the STAIC (e.g., R. P. Martin, 1988) have noted that the two major weaknesses of the instrument were a shortage of psychometric validation studies and a geographically limited normative population. The first weakness is now less of a problem, as scores of studies have been published (over 150 by 1998) that used the STAIC as a primary measure. The second weakness continues to be a problem.

Not only is the norm sample limited to one state, but the norms are now approximately 20 years old. A current and nationally representative standardization of the STAIC would be of great use in increasing the confidence of obtained test scores, and in ensuring the continued use of the test, which is deserved.

[handwritten: depression instru. are better than anxiety instrum.]

Concluding Comments on Internalizing Symptoms Self-Report Measures. To conclude this section on self-report assessment of internalizing symptoms, it is important to recognize that self-report instruments designed to measure anxiety and depression have shown varying degrees of effectiveness in actually classifying children with internalizing disorders, despite the otherwise generally good psychometric properties of these measures. In general, it is fair to say that classification studies have shown instruments for depression to be more effective than instruments for anxiety in differentiating among youth with the disorder in question. In commenting on this assessment problem regarding self-report measures of childhood anxiety, Silverman and Ginsburg (1998) stated that "despite the advantages of children's self-rating scales . . . groups defined as anxious via these rating scales are not necessarily defined this way via diagnoses. . . . Specifically, it is not clear that these scales can differentiate children with anxiety disorders from children with other types of disorders" (p. 254). As was suggested earlier in the discussion of positive and negative affectivity, perhaps the critical problem in this regard is that most self-report scales may actually be assessing global negative affectivity rather than a specific internalizing disorder. Remember that negative affectivity appears to be related to both anxiety and depression, whereas the absence of positive affectivity appears to be related only to depression. Perhaps a newer generation of self-report measures that take into consideration the differential effects of both positive and negative affectivity (such as the Internalizing Symptoms Scale for Children) will ultimately be helpful in solving some of the diagnostic problems presented by internalizing disorders.

[handwritten: problem of scales measuring global rather than specific]

Self-Report Instruments for Assessing Multidimensional Self-Concept

[handwritten: - 3 most used measures]

As a conclusion to this section on methods for assessing internalizing disorders, an overview of three of the most widely used self-report instruments for measuring self-concept is provided. In the earlier discussion of self-concept, it was made clear that the definitional focus for self-concept in this chapter would be a multidimensional, as opposed to a unidimensional model. Thus, the following overview precludes any of the several instruments designed to assess the latter view of the construct. The empirically demonstrated nature of self-concept necessarily precludes any assessment methods that rely on observations or perceptions of persons other than the subject. And within the realm of self-report, the preferred assessment method is objective self-report tests rather than interviews, as no structured or standardized interview methods have yet been developed to systematically assess self-concept. The self-report instruments presented in this section include Bracken's (1992) Multidimensional Self-Concept Scale and Harter's (1985a, 1985b, 1988) Child and Adolescent Self-Perception Profiles. It should also be noted that a pictorial self-concept test has been developed by Harter (Harter & Pike, 1984) for use with very young children, but this instrument is reviewed in chapter 13 (Assessing Young Children) rather than the present chapter.

Multidimensional Self-Concept Scale. The Multidimensional Self-concept Scale (MSCS; Bracken, 1992) is one of the more recent additions to the growing body of self-report instruments for assessing self-concept in a multidimensional fashion. The

MSCS was developed for use by children and adolescents in grades 5 through 12, and includes 150 items. These items are rated by examinees on a Likert-type response scale, with 4 points ranging from "Strongly Agree" to "Strongly Disagree." The construction of MSCS items and overall scale structure were theoretically driven, based on a view of self-concept as being "a behavioral construct, not a part of a larger cognitive self-system" (Bracken & Howell, 1991, p. 323). The items are divided into six subscales of 25 items each, based on Bracken's multidimensional factors and global self-concept theory. These subscales include Affect, Social, Physical, Competence, Academic, and Family, and a score is also produced for Global Self-Concept. For each of the seven possible score areas, raw scores are converted to standard scores with a mean of 100 and standard deviation of 15. Tables for *T*-score conversions, percentile scores, and self-concept classifications are provided in the MSCS manual.

The MSCS was normed on a group of 2,501 students in grades 5 through 12 in the United States, with adequate representation given to each U.S. geographical region. Strong internal consistency reliabilities are reported for the six subscales (.85 to .90) and the total score (.98). The MSCS has also been found to have strong stability over time, with subscale reliability coefficients ranging from .73 to .81 and a total score coefficient of .90 at 4-week retest intervals. Although the MSCS is a relatively recent instrument, a body of external published empirical evidence is beginning to accumulate that has shown moderate to strong relations between the MSCS and other multidimensional and unidimensional self-construct instruments, as well as convergent and discriminant support for the construct of multidimensional self-concept as measured by the MSCS. The MSCS manual is very well written and documented, the instrument is easy to use, and it appears to be a potentially useful and well-designed self-report instrument.

Self-Perception Profile for Children.   The Self-perception Profile for Children (SPPC; Harter, 1985b) is a self-report instrument designed to assess multidimensional self-concept with children from age 8 to 15. The SPPC includes 36 pairs of statements that reflect opposing views of particular aspects of self-concept (e.g., "Some kids wish their body was *different*, BUT Other kids *like* their body the way it is"). Examinees are asked to first choose which statement in the pair is most like them, and after they have made this initial choice, they are then asked to determine whether the statement they have chosen is *really true* or *sort of true* for them. Each test item is scored using a 4-point scale, with 1 reflecting the lowest and 4 reflecting the highest self-concept rating.

The 36 SPPC items are divided into six dimensions: scholastic competence, social acceptance, athletic competence, physical appearance, behavioral conduct, and global self-worth. Unlike the MSCS, the global self-worth scale is not a summation of the other subscales, but is comprised of six statements that reflect how subjects feel about themselves in an overall sense. Scoring the SPPC is done by determining the raw score mean value for each of the six dimensions, and then comparing these scores with means and standard deviations of grade- and gender-specific score breakdowns from the normative group, as well as plotting the mean scores on a pupil profile form where score levels are seen to be in either the low, medium, or high range. Higher mean scores for each scale indicate higher perceptions of self-worth. The SPPC also includes two corollary instruments: a rating scale for teachers and an *importance* rating scale for subjects. The teacher rating scale provides a basis for comparing a child's responses against an objective rating, whereas the importance rating allows the examiner to determine if any discrepancies exist between the child's self-perception ratings and the importance of those ratings to their overall self-esteem. For example, a low score on athletic competence may or may not be cause for concern, depending on how important athletic competence is for the child.

The SPPC was normed on four samples of children (1,543 total) from Colorado in grades 3 through 8. Tables of mean scores and standard deviations from the norm group are presented in the test manual based on gender and grade level breakdowns. Internal consistency reliabilities on the SPPC range from .80 to .90 across a number of samples, and test–retest correlations across subscales have been found to range from .40 to .65 at 1-month to 1-year intervals (Harter, 1990). The factor structure of the SPPC appears to be sound, with items loading well into their respective factors and the six scales having only moderate intercorrelations. Significant gender effects in self-concept are reported in the SPPC manual, with the most systematic effects indicating that boys see themselves as significantly more athletically competent than girls, and girls see themselves as significantly better behaved than boys. Some additional significant gender effects were found in the areas of global self-worth and physical appearance, but these effects were not consistent across grade levels. An interesting finding in this regard is that, at the elementary level, there are no significant differences between boys' and girls' scores on these two dimensions. But, at the middle school level, boys' scores in both areas are significantly higher than girls' scores.

The SPPC is a unique and innovative instrument, and can be recommended on several grounds. However, there are a number of weaknesses that warrant using it with caution. It is unfortunate that the SPPC norm group was taken from only one state, thus reducing the confidence with which score interpretations can be generalized. Although the accumulated research evidence regarding the SPPC is substantial (over 75 studies by 1998), a large national norm sample would be extremely useful, as would raw score to standard score and percentile conversion tables. The SPPC is not commercially published at the present time, but can be obtained from Susan Harter at the University of Denver Department of Psychology.

Self-Perception Profile for Adolescents. Harter's (1988) Self-perception Profile for Adolescents (SPPA) is a 45-item self-report instrument that is very similar in design to the SPPC. The items and scales use the same type of rating and scoring format as the SPPC, and thus, only the SPPA characteristics that differ from those of the SPPC are discussed in this section.

The items in the SPPA are mostly similar to those in the SPPC, but are worded specifically for use by teenage subjects (e.g., "Some teenagers wish their physical appearance was different, BUT Other teenagers like their physical appearance the way it is"). In addition to the rewording of items from the SPPC, more items were added to the SPPA to reflect specific concerns of teenagers, such as job competence, close friendship, and romantic appeal. These three areas of concern appear as additional subscales on the SPPA, and thus, the SPPA has a total of nine subscales instead of the six that are found on the SPPC. Like the SPPC, the SPPA includes an importance rating scale for examinees, and a teacher's rating scale for assessing actual student behavior (e.g., "This individual is good looking OR This individual is not that good looking").

The SPPA was normed on a group of 651 students in grades 8 through 11, from four samples in the state of Colorado. For each of the three grade levels, separate norms are provided for males and females. Internal consistency reliability of the SPPA is reported to range from .74 to .91. The factor structure of the SPPA appears to be adequate, and the generally moderate intercorrelations among the nine subscales suggest a basis for a multidimensional construction of self-concept. Like the SPPC, the SPPA has good face validity and offers an innovative and comprehensive method of assessing adolescent concept. A reasonable amount of external research evidence regarding this instrument has accumulated at this point in time. Unfortunately, the SPPA is limited by the lack of a large nationwide norm sample, scant technical information in the manual, and some difficulties in obtaining it (must be ordered through the University of Denver Department of Psychology; see the appendix for details).

LINKING ASSESSMENT TO INTERVENTION

In comparison with externalizing problems, the domain of internalizing problems is more difficult to establish a solid link between assessment and intervention. One of the major reasons this link has been rather tenuous has to do with the very nature of internalizing problems. Given that these types of problems often involve subjective individual perceptions and states, there are not as likely to be tangible and directly observable behaviors to consider for intervention. For example, if a comprehensive assessment reveals that children feel excessive sadness and have an extremely low opinion of themselves, then a clinician should know that these children need some attention. However, this type of assessment information does not necessarily give obvious clues regarding what kind of attention would be best in ameliorating these symptoms. In contrast, comprehensive assessment data regarding externalizing problems often provide direct cues regarding what is needed, because the problem behaviors are overt and easily defined as problems.

This difficult state of affairs regarding linking assessment to treatment does not mean that effective treatment for internalizing disorders is not a possibility. On the contrary, recent reviews in this area have shown that although the number of controlled treatment studies are relatively few, there are indeed several potentially effective interventions for a variety of internalizing problems of children and adolescents (e.g., Hops & Lewinsohn, 1995; Mash & Barkley, 1989; Schwartz et al., 1998; Silverman & Ginsburg, 1998).

The treatment approaches that are likely to be utilized by a given clinician might guide their choice of assessment methods to some extent, but assessment of internalizing problems appears to be more strongly linked to the processes of description and classification as opposed to intervention. Although intervention decisions should not be made in isolation from assessment data, most assessment data for internalizing problems will describe rather than prescribe. It will be a great challenge for the current generation of professionals to develop strongly linked methods of assessment and intervention for internalizing problems.

CONCLUSIONS

In contrast to externalizing problems, the domain of internalizing problems includes *overcontrolled* and *inner-directed* characteristics, and is generally thought of as consisting of emotional rather than behavioral problems. The major areas within the internalizing domain are generally considered to be depression, anxiety, social withdrawal, and somatic problems. Specific classification paradigms, prevalence estimates, and division of symptoms have been more difficult to achieve with internalizing disorders than externalizing disorders, partly because of the more covert nature of internalizing symptoms, and partly because the research in this area has lagged behind in comparison with the research focused on the externalizing domain.

Although internalizing disorders of childhood may not have as negative long-term implications for later life adjustment as do externalizing disorders, they do pose serious problems for the children and their families who suffer from them. Not only do internalizing disorders create substantial barriers to present adjustment and success, but they may persist for several years in some cases. Also, recent research is increasingly indicating that internalizing disorders in childhood are not as benign as once thought; they appear to be associated with various negative outcomes later in life, particularly if they are left untreated.

One of the more recent developments in understanding internalizing disorders has been the articulation of the theory of positive and negative affectivity. These differing aspects of mood states appear to contribute to the development and diagnosis of specific internalizing disorders. For example, persons who are depressed tend to have high levels of negative affectivity and low levels of positive affectivity, whereas persons who are anxious tend to have high levels of negative affectivity but normal levels of positive affectivity. Thus, positive and negative affectivity may be useful in future paradigms of these disorders. Presently, only one widely accessible assessment instrument (the Internalizing Symptoms Scale for Children) has been developed specifically to assist in identifying patterns of affectivity within the broad internalizing domain of problems.

An inverse relation exists between internalizing problems, particularly depression and self-concept. That is, poor self-esteem or poor perceived self-competence is often an attribute or product of internalizing disorders. Therefore, assessment of internalizing problems should also take into account the possibility of self-concept assessment. The most sophisticated current self-concept theories are multidimensional in nature, meaning that they view global self-concept as something more complex than a simple summation of a person's self-concept in specific areas.

Assessment of internalizing problems is uniquely suited for self-report methods, including clinical interviews and the use of self-report instruments. Increasingly, experts in this area are considering obtaining the self-report of a referred child or adolescent with internalizing problems to be an essential part of the overall assessment design. Clinical interviewing, whether unstructured or highly structured, provides an excellent means of assessing perceptions of internalizing problems, as do the many technically sound self-report instruments that have been developed in this area. Behavioral observation of internalizing problems is difficult because so many internalizing symptoms are not easily observed through external means. However, there are certain situations in which direct observation may be helpful. Behavior rating scales suffer from some of the same drawbacks as direct observation as a means for assessing internalizing problems, but they are typically considered to be an important part of the overall assessment design, and recent improvements in this area have been encouraging. Sociometric assessment of internalizing problems also has similar limitations related to external observation of internalizing characteristics, but there have been some impressive developments in this area as well.

Although there are numerous intervention strategies that have proven to be effective in treating internalizing problems, it is still quite difficult to directly link assessment results to intervention planning in this area. Assessment results may guide planning to some extent, but will probably be more useful for description and classification purposes.

However, clinicians should be encouraged by recent findings regarding the potential efficacy of psychological treatments for depression, anxiety, and related internalizing problems.

REVIEW AND APPLICATION QUESTIONS

1. This chapter states repeatedly that internalizing disorders are more difficult than externalizing disorders to identify, empirically classify, and count. Beyond the obvious explanation that internalizing disorders are harder to observe through objective means than externalizing disorders, what are some other possible explanations for these difficulties?

2. Compare Quay's (1986a) behavioral dimensions approach to classifying internalizing disorders with the *DSM–IV* diagnostic categories relevant to internalizing disorders. What do the large differences between the two approaches to classification imply about the current state of classification?

3. What are the major differences between depression as a symptom, depression as a syndrome, and depression as a disorder?

4. What is known regarding persistence and long-term implications of internalizing disorders?

5. What are some assessment issues to be considered, and what is known regarding differences between parent report and child self-report of internalizing symptoms of children and adolescents?

6. If you had to choose between conducting a clinical interview or using an objective self-report instrument with a child or youth who had significant internalizing symptoms, which would you choose, and why?

7. Characterize the state of the art regarding child and adolescent self-report instruments for internalizing problems as compared to any other general category of problems. Related to this issue, what are some of the problems that still exist with internalizing self-report measures?

8. Perhaps paradoxically, assessment of externalization problems is more easily linked to intervention planning than is assessment of internalizing problems, yet the interventions for internalizing problems appear to probably be more effective than those for externalizing problems. What are some reasons for this state of affairs?

CASE STUDY: JENNIFER H.

Background Information

Jennifer H. is a 15-year-old girl who is a 10th-grade student at a small high school in a rural/small town area. She lives with her mother, a community college instructor, and an 11-year-old brother. Jennifer's parents are divorced and her father lives in a distant city, rarely seeing her more than two times per year. Jennifer participated in an intake interview and initial screening assessment at a community psychology clinic. The referral was made by Jennifer's mother, Mrs. H. Although Jennifer was initially reluctant to participate in the intake interview/assessment, she became very cooperative and good rapport was established between her and the intake interviewer. Jennifer agreed to go the clinic at the urging of her mother, who was concerned that her daughter was "very depressed and doesn't understand her feelings."

Basic information obtained from the intake forms was obtained from both Mrs. H. and Jennifer. Mrs. H. noted that Jennifer often cries for no apparent reason, has low self-esteem, and feels as though she has to be perfect; but she also goes through occasional periods where she has plenty of energy and sleeps very little. Mrs. H. noted that Jennifer has sometimes made statements such as "it would be easier if I were dead," but has made no suicidal attempts of definitive threats. She is concerned that her daughter "is too thin and has unhealthy eating habits." Jennifer reported on the intake forms that she gets "real down" at times, and occasionally "gets hyper." She noted that "sometimes I sleep too much and sometimes I don't sleep at all." Jennifer reports being worried about a wide variety of things, such as her school grades, whether her friends are "on my side or not," and her looks (she reports feeling "ugly"). She also says that she has frequent headaches and stomachaches, and that "I get dizzy and feel like fainting sometimes." At school, Jennifer receives good to excellent grades (3.8 G.P.A. for the past 2 years), is in some advanced courses, and is active in student government and a dance team. Mrs. H. reports that Jennifer is popular, well liked by other students, but "is always anxious about keeping her friends."

Assessment Data

The initial intake assessment on Jennifer included a behavior rating scale completed by Mrs. H., three self-report tests completed by Jennifer, and interviews with Jennifer and Mrs. H., both together and individually.

Behavior Rating Scales. Before the initial intake interview, Jennifer's mother rated her using the Child Behavior Checklist. This was the only external rating scale completed for this assessment. Jennifer also completed the CBCL Youth Self-Report, and both sets of scores are listed in Table 10.6.

Self-Report Instruments. In addition to the Youth Self-Report, Jennifer completed the Revised Children's Manifest Anxiety Scale (RCMAS) and the Reynolds Adolescent Depression Scale (RADS).

RADS: raw score = 85; 93rd percentile for girls; "critical items" endorsed: (20) "I feel I am no good," (26) "I feel worried."

TABLE 10.6
Child Behavior Checklist Scores

Cross-Informant Scores	Jennifer's Self-Report (YSR)	Mother's Report (CBCL)
Aggressive Behavior	50	51
Anxious/Depressed	68	79
Attention Problems	65	57
Delinquent Behavior	50	50
Social Problems	58	50
Somatic Complaints	78	70
Thought Problems	68	63
Withdrawn	59	57
INTERNALIZING PROBLEMS	72	73
EXTERNALIZING PROBLEMS	49	49
TOTAL PROBLEMS	66	64

RCMAS: Total Anxiety: raw score = 19, 92nd percentile, *T*-score = 64; Physiological Anxiety: raw score = 6, 91st percentile; Worry/Oversensitivity: raw score = 8, 77th percentile; Social Concerns/Concentration: raw score = 5, 90th percentile; Lie Scale: raw score = 0, 13th percentile.

Interview. Interviews were conducted with both Jennifer and Mrs. H., together and individually. The interview format was slightly structured, following a standardized intake clinic form. A variety of developmental and background information was obtained during the interviews, but the major perceived or presenting problems, from both Jennifer's and Mrs. H.'s viewpoints, are listed in the following table:

Jennifer's Perspective	*Mrs. H.'s Perspective*
I get too hyper	J. doesn't understand her feelings
My friends let me down	J. is too hard on herself
I might not get into a good college	J. is too thin
I feel unattractive	J. has poor eating habits
I have a harder time doing things than most kids my age	J. is depressed
I do bad things	J. thinks she has to be perfect
I have headaches and stomachaches	J. doesn't want to talk about things with Mrs. H.
Something is wrong with my body	J. tries to do too much
Other kids are out to get me	I expect too much out of J.
Mom's rules are unfair	I don't spend enough time with J.
Mom worries too much about me	
Mom doesn't trust me	

Questions to Consider

1. The assessment data presented for this case are from an intake process, and should be considered preliminary screening data. What other information regarding Jennifer would be useful, and what assessment tools or methods would best provide this information?

2. An important concept noted in this chapter is that of *comorbidity* of internalizing problems, or the fact that various internalizing problems often occur in combination. The self-report screening of Jennifer focused for the most part on possible depression and anxiety. Which, if any, of the following characteristics that often relate to internalizing problems should be pursued in greater detail: somatic problems, social isolation, specific fears or phobias, self-concept problems, eating disorders?

3. Assume that Jennifer has only one of the following two types of disorders: a depressive disorder or an anxiety disorder. Taking only the information that was obtained from Jennifer's intake assessment, attempt to make a differential classification of the major problem. What additional information would be needed to make a formal differential diagnosis?

4. Compare the information obtained from Jennifer and the information obtained from Mrs. H. What are the major points of convergence and the major points of disagreement?

5. Based on the information provided in this scenario, make a general statement about the severity of Jennifer's internalizing problems.

CHAPTER

11

ASSESSMENT OF OTHER BEHAVIORAL, SOCIAL, AND EMOTIONAL PROBLEMS

Throughout this book, various behavioral, social, and emotional problems of children and adolescents have frequently been discussed in terms of their place within the two broad dimensions of externalizing and internalizing psychopathology or disorders. This broad-band taxonomic division has become a standard paradigm among researchers who investigate developmental psychopathology, and has been supported by substantial empirical evidence (e.g., Achenbach, 1998; Cicchetti & Toth, 1991; Quay, 1986a). However, not all childhood behavioral or emotional problems fit neatly within this model. Some disorders—as evidenced by the Social Problems, Thought Problems, and Attention Problems cross-informant syndromes in Achenbach's empirically based classification system—are considered to be *mixed disorders*. Within these syndrome scales, some items may load into the externalizing domain, other items may load into the internalizing domain, and some items may not load specifically into either of the two broad-band domains. Additionally, some severe problems, such as psychotic disorders and pervasive developmental disorders, occur with such low frequency in the general child population that it is difficult to justify even including relevant items for them in general screening instruments, and large-scale epidemiologic studies usually identify so few cases that it is difficult to accurately ascertain their appropriate classification dimensions.

This chapter deals with several of these problems and disorders that either do not fit neatly within the externalizing–internalizing dichotomy, or that occur very infrequently in general child populations. For lack of a better descriptive term, these are referred to as "other behavioral social and emotional problems" in this chapter. Because the major emphasis of this text is on assessment and classification of the more common externalizing and internalizing problems, the issues and disorders discussed here are not examined in substantial depth. Rather, this chapter is intended to provide a brief general overview for understanding and assessment of the lower base rate and more diagnostically nebulous problems that may be occasionally encountered by school psychologists, clinical child psychologists, and related professionals, particularly those working in generalist educational and mental health settings. Psychologists who work in pediatric, psychiatric, or highly specialized education settings will certainly encounter some of these problems more frequently than the generalist, and will likely have developed a more comprehensive network of assessment, diagnostic, and intervention aids. School and clinical child psychologists (and related mental health professionals) who are more generalist in nature will likely need to develop a network of contacts among their more specialized colleagues for the purpose of consultation and referral when some of these other problems are encountered.

The format of this chapter differs somewhat from others on assessment of externalizing (chap. 9) and internalizing disorders (chap. 10). It begins with discussions of the two major approaches to classification, and how they treat the various types of problems in question. Because of the wide variety of characteristics and assessment needs of the various problems and disorders covered here, each problem area is then covered separately, including pervasive developmental disorders, the schizoid disorders, tic disorders (specifically, Tourette's Disorder), psychotic disorders, and eating disorders. Rather than including separate discussions of the major methods of assessment, as is the case in chapters 9 and 10, details on assessment of specific problems and disorders covered herein (quite limited in some cases) are presented adjacent to the general descriptions of these problems. The chapter concludes with brief discussions regarding future directions in this area, and some ideas for linking assessment to intervention. An illustrative case study is also included.

CLASSIFICATION AND TAXONOMY

From the very beginnings of psychology as a scientific discipline in the late 1800s, definition and classification of the most low frequency and severe behavioral, social, and emotional problems has been a continuing problem. Because these disorders are relatively rare, and because some of the classification categories have a fair amount of common or overlapping characteristics, the research base for classification and taxonomy in this area has lagged. Until about the 1960s, it was common for the generic term *childhood psychoses* to be used in the classification of all severe childhood disorders, though a number of other labels were previously used with some regularity, including *dementia precocissma, dementia infantilis, childhood schizophrenia, infantile autism, autistic psychopathy, symbiotic psychosis*, and *atypical child* (Howlin & Yule, 1990). Because the term *childhood psychoses* has no precise meaning, it is seldom used today, and most current classification paradigms are connected to the *DSM* system.

Behavioral Dimensions Classification

As mentioned previously, empirical efforts at establishing a reliable classification taxonomy of severe and other low-frequency behavioral disorders have been plagued by problems stemming from very small sample sizes and overlapping behavioral and emotional characteristics. One of the earlier efforts at developing a statistical taxonomy of the broad category of "childhood psychoses" was a study by Prior, Boulton, Gajzago, and Perry (1975), who used an analysis of 162 cases that ultimately led to a division into two categories: one subgroup with early onset and autisticlike features and the other with a later onset of symptoms and less debilitating impairment in social relationships. This interesting study was never replicated, but the general idea of two similar divisions has caught on to some extent in the professional literature (Cantor, 1987; Howlin & Yule, 1990).

An interesting effort at establishing a behavioral dimensions taxonomy for severe behavioral disorders was Quay's (1986a) analysis of 61 multivariate statistical studies describing facets of child psychopathology. Although Quay noted that "the problems associated with describing childhood psychosis have not readily yielded to clarification by multivariate statistical analysis" (p. 16), his effort resulted in an interesting organization with two types of syndromes that are relevant to this chapter. One of these syndromes was labeled *Schizoid-Unresponsive*, with the most frequently identified behaviors being refusal to talk, social withdrawal, extreme timidity, a cold and unresponsive disposition, and an aloof behavioral picture referred to as "cold and unresponsive." The second of these two syndromes was labeled *Psychotic Disorder*, with the few key behavioral features identified, including incoherent and repetitive speech, bizarre behavior, auditory and visual hallucinations, and a group of odd characteristics referred to as "strange ideas, behaviors" (p. 16). These two syndromes are listed with their characteristic behavioral symptoms in Table 11.1. Again, it is important to recognize that this taxonomy effort was fraught with methodological difficulties and should be considered a preliminary or experimental effort, but it is a promising look at what future efforts at multivariate analysis might reveal.

DSM Classification

Over the years, the *DSM* classification system has evolved substantially. With regard to classification categories for some of the more severe and lower base rate childhood disorders, changes over time have been particularly noticeable. Such continuing evolution and change provides evidence that the field of developmental psychopathology has evolved rapidly, and understanding of specific problems and disorders is likewise evolving.

DSM–IV includes several general classification categories, some with numerous specific diagnostic categories, that involve the "other" problems and disorders discussed here. So, the general categories from *DSM–IV* that are pertinent to this chapter include pervasive developmental disorders, tic disorders, schizophrenia and other psychotic disorders, eating disorders, and to a very limited extent, personality disorders. These general categories, with their more relevant specific diagnostic categories, are presented in Table 11.2. The "Not Otherwise Specified" classifications under the general catego-

TABLE 11.1

Major Behavioral Characteristics of Two Types of Severe Behavioral
Syndromes Identified Through Quay's (1986a) Analysis

Schizoid-Unresponsive	*Psychotic Disorder*
Refusal to talk	Incoherent speech
Socially withdrawn	Repetitive speech
Shy, timid, bashful	Acts bizarre, odd, peculiar
Cold and unresponsive	Visual hallucinations
Lack of interest	Auditory hallucinations
Sad affect	Has strange ideas, behavior
Stares blankly	
Confused	
Secretive behavior	
Prefers to be alone	

TABLE 11.2
Some Major Diagnostic Areas and Categories from *DSM–IV* that Constitute
Severe, Low Base Rate, or Less Differentiated Types of Behavioral,
Social, and Emotional Disorders Among Children and Youth

Pervasive Developmental Disorders
    Autistic Disorder
    Rett's Disorder
    Childhood Disintegrative Disorder
    Asperger's Disorder
    Pervasive Developmental Disorder, Not Otherwise Specified

Tic Disorders
    Tourette's Disorder
    *(other tic disorders that are not directly related to behavioral-emotional concerns of children
        and youth are also listed)*

Schizophrenia and Other Psychotic Disorders
    (numerous types and subtypes of schizophrenia and other disorders are also listed)

Eating Disorders
    Anorexia Nervosa
    Bulimia Nervosa
    Eating Disorder, Not Otherwise Specified

ries are not included, nor are the many diagnostic categories for psychotic disorders or personality disorders, many of which are not relevant to children and adolescents. It is important to consider that there are additional general and specific categories within the *DSM* system that are at times associated with behavioral or emotional disorders of children, such as Mental Retardation, Substance-Related Disorders, Elimination Disorders, and Impulse Control Disorders. Readers who desire a more detailed description of any of these categories that are beyond the scope of this book should refer to *DSM–IV* or specific books on psychopathology classification, or developmental psychopathology.

PERVASIVE DEVELOPMENTAL DISORDERS

Pervasive developmental disorders constitute some of the most debilitating psychological conditions seen in children. *DSM–IV* states that "pervasive developmental disorders are characterized by severe and pervasive impairment in several areas of development: reciprocal social interaction skills, communication skills, or the presence of stereotyped behavior, interests, and activities" (APA, 1994, p. 65). Thus, this general category of disorders is not exclusively focused on the domain of behavioral, social, and emotional problems—the focus of this text. However, because the deficits and associated problems of social behavior can be so severe and debilitating, and will certainly require an extensive system of supports and intervention, the pervasive developmental disorders are included in this chapter. This section provides an overview of these disorders, as well as specific information regarding assessment. Because Autistic Disorder is the only one of these several disorders that has consistently been included in various editions of the *DSM*, and because so much more is known about this disorder in comparison with the others, it is presented in much more detail in this section.

TABLE 11.3
Some Major Characteristics and Associated Features of
Four Primary Pervasive Developmental Disorders

Autistic Disorder
   Onset before age 3 years
   Markedly impaired communication and social interaction
   Markedly restricted repetitive stereotyped behavior
   Prevalence of 2 to 5 cases per 10,000
   More common among males than females
   Often associated with mental retardation
Rett's Disorder
   Onset before age 4 years
   Decreased head growth after normal growth for first 5–48 months
   Stereotyped behavior and loss of hand skills at 5–30 months
   Loss of social engagement skills
   Decrease in gait/trunk motor coordination
   Impaired language and psychomotor ability
   Very rare
   Reported to only occur among females
   Associated with severe/profound mental retardation
Childhood Disintegrative Disorder
   Onset between age 2 and 10
   Loss of acquired skills after normal growth up to age 2
   Abnormal social interaction skills
   Impaired language ability
   Stereotypic and restricted behavior, activities, interests
   Very rare
   Appears to be more common among males
   Associated with severe mental retardation
Asperger's Disorder
   Onset during preschool years
   Impaired social interaction
   Restricted stereotyped behavior, interests, activities
   Appears to be more common among males

Rett's Disorder, Childhood Disintegrative Disorder, and Asperger's Disorder were added to the *DSM–IV*, but were not included in *DSM–III–R*. Substantially less knowledge has accumulated regarding these disorders, which tend to have many features in common with autism, and the minor treatment they receive is a reflection of this fact. In addition to the discussion of each of these disorders, their major characteristics and associated features are summarized in Table 11.3.

Description

Autistic Disorder.   Leo Kanner, a pioneer in the study of what is now called Autistic Disorder, first described 11 children in 1943 who fit this general diagnostic picture. He noted that their fundamental disorder was the "inability to relate themselves in the ordinary way to people and situations from the beginning of life," and that a characteristic of this disorder is an aloneness that "disregards, ignores, shuts out anything that comes to the child from the outside" (Kanner, 1943, p. 43). This syndrome was labeled by Kanner as "early infantile autism," because it was noted that the tendency to display these characteristics seemed inborn and present from birth. Howlin and Rutter (1987) noted that although there have been a number of changes since 1943 in the way that this disorder is conceptualized, Kanner's general description of autism is still fundamentally accurate.

Based on the *DSM–IV* diagnostic criteria (see Table 11.4) and a consensus of the current thinking about this disorder, the major characteristics of Autistic Disorder include severe impairment in reciprocal social interaction, severe impairment in verbal and nonverbal communication as well as imaginative activity, and a severely restricted repertoire of activities and interests. Specific characteristics that are commonly seen in autistic children are somewhat varied, but a common general pattern is often observed. In terms of severely impaired social relationships, individuals with Autistic Disorder usually appear to be socially aloof and detached; they may fail to make eye contact, have a noticeably flat affect, shrink from physical contact, and often seem to relate to other persons as objects or conglomerations of parts rather than as people (Ornitz, 1989; Schreibman & Charlop-Christy, 1998). In terms of the specific disorders of communication, individuals with Autistic Disorder may not engage in speech, or they may speak in a peculiar manner, such as using a robotic monotone voice, displaying an odd vocal rhythm and meter, or repeating words and phrases in a stereotypical manner (Howlin & Yule, 1990; Schreibman & Charlop-Christy, 1998). Additionally, individuals with Autistic Disorder often lack or fail to grasp the pragmatics of interpersonal communication, possibly due to an inability to interpret the facial

TABLE 11.4
Diagnostic Criteria for Autistic Disorder from the *DSM–IV*

C. A total of six (or more) items from (1), (2), and (3), with at least two from (1) and one each from (2) and (3):
  1. qualitative impairment in social interaction, as manifested by at least two of the following:
    a. marked impairment in the use of multiple nonverbal behaviors such as eye-to-eye gaze, facial expression, body postures, and gestures to regulate social interaction
    b. failure to develop peer relationships appropriate to developmental level
    c. a lack of spontaneous seeking to share enjoyment, interests, or achievements with other people (e.g., by a lack of showing, bringing, or pointing out objects of interest)
    d. lack of social or emotional reciprocity
  2. qualitative impairments in communication as manifested by at least one of the following:
    a. delay in, or total lack of, the development of spoken language (not accompanied by an attempt to compensate through alternative modes of communication such as gesture or mime)
    b. in individuals with adequate speech, marked impairment in the ability to initiate or sustain a conversation with others
    c. stereotyped and repetitive use of language or idiosyncratic language
    d. lack of varied, spontaneous make-believe play or social imitative play appropriate to the developmental level
  3. restricted repetitive and stereotyped patterns of behavior, interests, and activities, as manifested by at least one of the following:
    a. encompassing preoccupation with one or more stereotyped and restricted patterns of interest that is abnormal either in intensity or focus
    b. apparently inflexible adherence to specific, nonfunctional routines or rituals
    c. stereotyped and repetitive motor mannerisms (e.g., hand or finger flapping or twisting, or complex whole-body movements)
    d. persistent preoccupation with parts of objects
D. Delays or abnormal functioning in at least one of the following areas, with onset prior to age 3 years: (1) social interaction, (2) language as used in social communication, or (3) symbolic or imaginative play.
E. The disturbance is not better accounted for by Rett's Disorder or Childhood Disintegrative Disorder.

Note. From *Diagnostic and Statistical Manual of Mental Disorders* (4th ed.). Copyright © 1994, American Psychiatric Association. Reprinted by permission of the American Psychiatric Association.

expression, intonation, and gestures of others (Prior & Werry, 1986). The severely restricted repertoire of activities and interests that is part of the disorder is characterized by stereotyped body movements (spinning, twisting, head banging, flipping the hands), a peculiar preoccupation with parts of objects (e.g., doorknobs, on–off switches), and exhibition of great distress when routines or insignificant parts of the environment are changed. Behaviors that are part of this third characteristic often take the form of obsession with routine and objects, such as a child repetitively dumping a pile of sticks on the floor and then lining them up in a particular manner.

Aside from the three major features of Autistic Disorder, there are some other interesting correlates to consider. IQ scores of individuals with Autistic Disorder are sometimes in the normal range or higher, but this is not the norm; the majority of individuals with Autistic Disorder consistently test out in the moderate to severely mentally retarded range (Prior & Werry, 1986). Autistic Disorder may often bring with it problems of sensory integration and perception (Wing, 1969) and poor psychomotor development (Fulkerson & Freeman, 1980). And obviously, because the combination of social impairment and low intellectual ability are usually part of the picture, persons with Autistic Disorder almost always have difficulty learning new materials or tasks.

The best current estimates indicate that between 2 and 5 of every 10,000 children meet the *DSM–IV* criteria for Autistic Disorder. This disorder has been found to occur at least three times more frequently in males than in females, with most studies showing a 3:1 or 4:1 ratio. In the vast majority of cases, the pervasive developmental disorders have an onset before age 3. The *DSM–IV* states by definition that onset of Autistic Disorder is before age 3.

Kanner's (1943) early writings on autism considered that there was a strong probability that the disorder had a constitutional or biological origin. However, during this same seminal period of discovery, Kanner and others noted that parents of children with autism often showed a tendency toward emotional insulation, aloofness, or detachment toward the child. Thus, the notion was born and perpetuated by prominent writers (e.g., Bettelheim, 1967; O'Gorman, 1970) that autism may be due to abnormal family functioning. The problem with these theories was that they usually failed to take into account the reciprocal effect of parent–child interactions, and placed too much weight on parent behaviors. The social learning approach would indicate that although parents of children with Autistic Disorder might respond at times in a manner that could be interpreted as emotionally detached, the characteristics of the child may have a great deal of influence on eliciting these behaviors. Despite this line of thinking, which was popular until about the 1970s, research efforts have failed to support the notion that Autistic Disorder is caused by abnormal parenting or family functioning (Howlin & Yule, 1990).

Although there is no conclusive evidence on the specific causes of Autistic Disorder at the present time, current thinking suggests that genetic and other biochemical influences are probably the most direct etiologic factors. Howlin and Yule (1990) reviewed a number of studies addressing concordance rates for autistic symptoms and concluded that "all these findings indicate the presence of important genetic influences" (p. 375).

The best evidence from follow-up studies of children with Autistic Disorder indicates that although some improvements may occur over time (particularly with intense early intervention efforts), many if not most individuals with the disorder will continue to exhibit characteristic problem symptoms over the course of their life. Howlin and Yule (1990) noted that individuals with Autistic Disorder who have the greatest chance of achieving social independence and making satisfactory adjustment are those few with high IQ scores and reasonably good language skills, and that "total social independence is gained by only a very small minority of autistic individuals" (p. 376). Thus, although a select few children with Autistic Disorder may completely overcome their disability, the long-term implications of the disorder are severe, and most will require a high degree of personal, social, and occupational support throughout life.

Rett's Disorder. The most "essential feature of Rett's Disorder is the development of specific deficits following a period of normal functioning after birth" (APA, 1994, p. 71). These deficits include deceleration of head growth between the ages of 5 and 48 months, loss of previously acquired hand skills between 5 and 30 months, loss of social engagement early in the course of the disorder, poor motor coordination, and severe impairments in expressive and receptive language development (a major defining characteristic) coupled with severe psychomotor retardation. This is a very rare disorder, and has been reported only in females. Exact prevalence estimates are unknown, but Rett's Disorder appears to occur much less frequently than Autistic Disorder. In most cases, affected individuals will make some modest developmental gains, but the various difficulties they encounter tend to remain throughout their life span.

Asperger's Disorder. "The essential features of Asperger's Disorder are severe and sustained impairment in social interaction and the development of restricted, repetitive patterns of behavior, interests, and activities" (APA, 1994, p. 75). These problems must result in clinically significant impairment in important areas of functioning. Although these major defining characteristics of Asperger's Disorder bear some resemblance to some of the characteristics of Autistic Disorder, the major difference between the two is that Asperger's Disorder does not include significant delays in language development and functioning. Also, Asperger's is characterized by the lack of clinically significant delays in cognitive development, self-help skills, and nonsocial adaptive behaviors. Information regarding prevalence of Asperger's Disorder is extremely limited, but it is thought to appear more commonly in males. It appears to have a later onset than Autistic Disorder. Perhaps the most critical feature of Asperger's Disorder is the significant difficulties in social interaction. *DSM–IV* states that "individuals with the condition may have problems with empathy and modulation of social interaction" (APA, 1994, p. 76). Asperger's Disorder appears to follow a continuous developmental course, almost always throughout the life span. It is interesting to note that this disorder bears some similarity to the major characteristics of the schizoid-unresponsive behavioral dimension shown in Table 11.1. In fact, this disorder was named after Hans Asperger, who, according to Wolf (1989), was the first person to discuss the so-called schizoid disorders in the 1940s. These disorders are currently identified as separate diagnostic categories in *DSM–IV*, but also have some similarity to Schizoid and Schizotypal Personality Disorders, which might also be diagnosed in older adolescents at times. This general class of schizoid disorders is discussed later in the chapter.

Childhood Disintegrative Disorder. This pervasive developmental disorder is characterized by marked regression in several areas of functioning, after a period of 2 or more years of apparent normal development. With this disorder, the child will show a substantial loss of functioning in two or more of the following areas: expressive or receptive language, social skills or adaptive behavior, bowl or bladder control, play, or motor skills. Children who develop Childhood Disintegrative Disorder typically exhibit some of the social, communication, and behavior features associated with autism. It is usually accompanied with severe mental retardation. Again, prevalence data for this disorder are very limited. However, it does appear to be very rare (occurring much less frequently than Autistic Disorder), and is probably more common among males. The duration of the disorder is lifelong in the majority of cases.

Assessment

Assessment of the various pervasive developmental disorders will necessarily rely heavily on direct behavioral observation, clinical interviews with parents, caretakers, and teachers, and in some instances, specialized behavior rating scales. In addition to behavioral and psychological assessment data, it is crucial to recognize that separate medical assessments of children with serious developmental disorders should also be conducted by qualified medical specialists. Direct interviews with the affected child, self-report instruments, and sociometric techniques are typically not relevant or useful for this class of problems. Most of the general purpose behavior rating scales discussed in chapter 4 will be somewhat useful for initial screening of pervasive developmental disorder symptoms. However, these general purpose rating scales rarely contain more than a small handful of items that are directly relevant to the low-frequency problem behaviors that occur with pervasive developmental disorders.

Several behavioral observation coding systems, behavior rating scales, and structured interview schedules have been developed specifically for use in assessment of autism, and several have been widely documented through research efforts. A sampling of these instruments is discussed in some detail in this section. No specific instruments or techniques specific to Rett's Disorder, Asperger's Disorder, or Childhood Disintegrative Disorder have been reported in the literature at this point in time. Clinicians and researchers assessing such problem areas may find the autism-specific instruments to be somewhat useful, but will also need to rely heavily on observation and interviews with caregivers to make specific diagnostic decisions.

Autism Diagnostic Observation Schedule. The Autism Diagnostic Observation Schedule (ADOS; Lord et al., 1989) is a standardized protocol for observation of the social and communicative behavior that is typically associated with autism in children. The ADOS differs from most other standardized observation schedules in that it is interactive, requiring the observer to engage with the target child as an experimenter/participant on several standardized tasks designed to yield a better qualitative analysis of autistic behaviors than would be possible through simple observation and coding. The ADOS does not focus as much on specific autistic-type behaviors as some other observation schedules, but was designed to "facilitate observation of social and communicative features specific to autism rather than those accounted for or exacerbated by severe mental retardation" (Lord et al., 1989, p. 187). Thus, through its interactive nature, emphasis on examiner behavior, and qualitative focus, the ADOS allows for assessment of some of the crucial features of autism that may distinguish the disorder from other severe developmental disorders.

The ADOS consists of eight tasks that are presented to the subject by the observer within a 20- to 30-minute time frame. Two sets of materials are required for most tasks (a puzzle or pegboard and a set of familiar and unusual miniature figures), and the content and specific demands of these tasks can vary according to the age and developmental level of the subject. The eight tasks include construction, unstructured presentation of toys, drawing, demonstration, a poster task, a book task, conversation, and socioemotional questions. Within these tasks, 11 strands of target behaviors are coded, and general ratings are made following the interaction/observation according to a 3-point qualitative severity scale, in four different areas: reciprocal social interaction, communication/language, stereotyped/restricted behaviors, and mood and nonspecific abnormal behaviors. Reliability and validity data presented by the authors of the ADOS are encouraging, and have demonstrated that the observation has adequate interrater and test–retest reliability, as well as discriminant validity between autistic subjects and subjects with and without other types of developmental disabilities. Although the ADOS is still new and experimental, it appears to be an observational method that may potentially provide a rich array of information on the qualitative aspects of autism.

Autism Diagnostic Interview. The Autism Diagnostic Interview (ADI; Le Couteur et al., 1989) is a standardized structured interview schedule designed to assess the critical characteristics of Autistic Disorder and to differentiate pervasive developmental disorders from other developmental disorders such as mental retardation. The ADI was developed for use by highly trained clinicians in conducting interviews with the principal caregiver(s) of individuals who are at least 5 years old, with a mental age of at least 2 years. The ADI is considered to be an *investigator-based* rather than a *respondent-based* interview, as it requires the interviewer to be familiar with the conceptual distinctions of pervasive developmental disorders and to actively structure the interview probes by providing examples and getting the interviewees to provide highly detailed qualitative information rather than simple yes/no responses.

The basic interviewing task is to obtain detailed descriptions of the actual behavior of the target subject in three general areas: reciprocal social interaction; communication and language; and repetitive, restricted, and stereotyped behaviors. The caregiver descriptions are scored according to a scale ranging from 0 to 3, where a score of 0 indicates the specified behavior is not present and 3 indicates that the behavior is present to a severe degree. Individual item scores are converted into three area scores and a total score, based on a scoring algorithm that was devised using the World Health Organization's *ICD–10* diagnostic criteria for autism. The actual length of time required for the interview will vary according to the skill of the examiner and the amount of information provided by the caregiver, but the developers of the ADI note that test interviews conducted during initial research tended to last 2 to 3 hours.

Reliability and validity research reported by the authors of the ADI are indicative of strong psychometric properties. The ADI item, area, and total scores have been shown to have good reliability (generally in the .70 range), based on agreement between raters from an experiment with 32 videotaped interviews that were scored by four independent raters. The ADI area scores, total scores, and most individual item scores have been shown to differentiate between autistic and mentally retarded target subjects to a significant degree, which indicates that the instrument is sensitive to qualitative differences in developmental problem patterns. The ADI item scores and many of the individual items were also found to have high sensitivity and specificity properties in differentially diagnosing autism and mental retardation. Thus, it should be assumed that the ADI would differentiate between autism and the milder developmental disorders (such as developmental delays and routine learning disabilities) quite easily.

In sum, though there are very few standardized interviews for autism, the ADI represents a very strong though preliminary step in this area. It should be seriously considered by researchers conducting epidemiological studies, and by clinicians who desire a structured method of obtaining information on pervasive developmental problems from caregivers. Proper use of the ADI requires both intensive training of interviewers and a considerable amount of time in actually administering the interview, so potential users should consider these constraints.

Behavior Observation Scale. The Behavior Observation Scale (BOS; Freeman, Ritvo, Guthrie, Schroth, & Ball, 1978; Freeman & Schroth, 1984) is a standardized observation procedure designed to provide an objective basis for measuring the behavioral characteristics of Autistic Disorder and more general features of autism in children. It is an experimental system, and is designed to be used under specific conditions. The most current version of the BOS includes a checklist of 35 behaviors that are intended to differentiate autistic from mentally retarded and normal children. The observation procedure occurs by observing the target child for 27 minutes (9 intervals of 3 minutes each) behind a two-way mirror. The first and last intervals serve as data baselines, and the child is presented with various stimuli during the first part of the remaining seven intervals. Each of the BOS checklist items are scored from 0 to 3 based on the frequency of the observed behaviors. The ultimate goal for the advancement of the BOS is to establish behavioral norms for normal, retarded, and autistic children and different stages of development. Although it is considered to be in the research and development phase, there is some evidence that the BOS is able to discriminate the three conditions based on objective observational criteria (Freeman & Schroth, 1984; Freeman, Schroth, Ritvo, Guthrie, & Wake, 1980). Thus, this observational system may be of interest to researchers and clinicians who work extensively with children who exhibit characteristics of pervasive developmental disorders.

Childhood Autism Rating Scale. The Childhood Autism Rating Scale (CARS; Schopler, Reichler, & Renner, 1988) is a brief (15-item) behavior rating scale designed to identify children with Autistic Disorder, and to distinguish them from individuals with other types of developmental disorders. It was designed to be completed by professionals who work with children in educational, medical, or mental health settings, and can be used with children age 2 and older. The items of the CARS are rated according to a 7-point scale with a continuum of anchor points ranging from *within normal limits* to *severely abnormal*. The item content of the CARS is based on a broad view of autism (not just Autistic Disorder) from multiple diagnostic systems, including the *DSM*. The ratings may be based on a direct observation of child behavior within a given setting, a review of other relevant assessment data, or impressions of observations over time. After the child has been rated on each item, a total score is obtained, and these scores are classified according to the categories of nonautistic, mild to moderate autism, or severe autism. Although the CARS is not a norm-referenced test in the traditional sense, the total score classifications are based on over 1,500 cases over a several-year period.

Data reported in the CARS manual and in several externally published studies (e.g., Dawson, Hill, Spencer, Galpert, & Watson, 1990; Lord & Schopler, 1989; Ozonoff, Pennington, & Rogers, 1990; Sponheim, 1996) indicate that the CARS has strong reliability and is valid for several purposes. Internal consistency reliability has been reported at .94, median interrater reliability has been found to be in the .70 range, and 1-year test–retest reliability is reported to be .88. Strong correlations have been found in comparing CARS scores to subjective clinical ratings of autistic behavior, and the scale has been shown to produce similar results when completed by professionals from different disciplines who evaluate the same child.

Although there are several published rating scales available for use in assessing the characteristics of autism, the CARS was selected for this chapter because of its long tradition, sound technical properties, ease of use, and wide availability. If the CARS is not the best rating scale for assessing autism currently available, then it is surely one of the best. Clinicians who are faced with the task of assessing a child who exhibits some or many of the characteristics of autism will find the CARS to be a useful addition to their assessment design.

THE SCHIZOID DISORDERS

Description

As previously discussed, Quay's (1986a) exploratory attempt at developing a multivariate behavioral dimensions taxonomy for severe behavior disorders identified a classification category he labeled as *Schizoid-Unresponsive* (see Table 11.1). The exact meaning of the term *schizoid*, which was first coined by Hans Asperger in the 1940s, is not precise. However, it is generally thought of as indicating "schizophrenic-like" (but not quite schizophrenic) symptoms. The term *unresponsive* was used by Quay to indicate not only detached and aloof peer relationships, but a general pattern of alienation and social withdrawal. These terms describe a cluster of behavioral, social, and emotional problems that have some things in common with autism and schizophrenia, but are generally more subtle and less blatant. Wolf (1989) noted that a perplexing number of terms have been used to describe the so-called schizoid disorders over the years, which has not helped to clarify the confusion that generally exists regarding them.

Children and adolescents who exhibit the characteristics found in the Schizoid-Unresponsive category may not clearly meet the diagnostic criteria for Autistic Disorder, Psychotic Disorders, or Asperger's Disorder, but are likely to exhibit the following core characteristics: solitariness, impaired empathy and emotional detachment, increased sensitivity (to external stimuli), a rigid mental set, and an odd or unusual way of communicating (Wolf, 1989).

Quay (1986a) suggested that the Schizoid-Unresponsive dimension may be the extreme of the personality style commonly referred to as introversion. As discussed previously, this Schizoid-Unresponsive dimension bears some similarity to the characteristics of Asperger's Disorder. It may also be a counterpart of the *DSM–IV* Axis II categories of Schizoid Personality Disorder and Schizotypal Personality Disorder. These two personality disorders are typified by various degrees and manifestations of social withdrawal, unresponsiveness, and peculiar or odd thought and behavior patterns. It would be highly unusual to diagnose a child with a personality disorder, but it is certainly possible by late adolescence.

DSM–IV states that the essential feature of Schizoid Personality Disorder "is a pervasive pattern of detachment from social relationships and a restricted range of expression of emotions in interpersonal settings" (APA, 1994, p. 641). Individuals who fit this diagnostic picture do not desire or enjoy close social relationships, including familial relationships. They exhibit a highly restricted range of emotional behavior, and come across to others as being cold and aloof. Schizotypal Personality Disorder is described as "a pervasive pattern of social and interpersonal deficits marked by acute discomfort with, and reduced capacity for, close relationships, as well as by cognitive or perceptual distortions and eccentricities of behavior" (APA, 1994, p. 645). Although there is some common ground in the symptoms of these two personality disorders, there is a clear line of demarcation for differential diagnosis: Schizoid Personality Disorder does not include peculiarities of thought, behavior, and speech, whereas Schizotypal Personality Disorder is not so much characterized by the extreme voluntary social detachment of the former disorder.

Very little is known about the prevalence of these disorders in the general population. The *DSM–IV* states that the prevalence of both conditions (and Asperger's Disorder) is low, but provides no objective data. Thus, although it can be assumed that these disorders will be rare in the child and adolescent population, there is no benchmark to go by for determining how often they can be expected. Part of the problem in conducting an epidemiological study in this area is that it is difficult to define the boundaries between normal variations of personality and psychopathology (Wolf, 1989). Because so little is known about prevalence, the gender distribution of these disorders is quite speculative at this point in time. One of the few clinical studies of the schizoid disorders (Wolf & Chick, 1980) found a gender ratio of 3.3 males for every 1 female, but the investigators warned that this ratio may, to some extent, have been a referral artifact.

The essential features of these disorders will most likely be present during early childhood, but differential diagnosis at this stage is difficult, given the overlapping symptoms that exist between them and several of the developmental disorders. Thus, onset of the schizoid disorders tends to be most clear and well defined in middle childhood (Wolf, 1989).

There is no clear evidence at the present time as to the etiology of the schizoid disorders, but some interesting speculations have been offered. One prominent etiological theory contends that a genetic link between the schizoid disorders and schizophrenia should be considered, as about half of individuals with schizophrenia displayed schizoid characteristics prior to the onset of psychosis, children of schizophrenics often exhibit schizoidlike characteristics, and parents of children with the schizoid disorders often exhibit similar behaviors (Blueler, 1978; Erlenmeyer-Kimling, Kestenbaum, Bird, & Hildoff, 1984; Wolf, 1989). Another theory is based on evidence that children who are at the highest risk for developing schizoid disorders may have suffered substantial neglect during early and middle childhood (Lieberz, 1989).

Based on Wolf and Chick's (1980) 10-year follow-up study of schizoid children, there is evidence that the essential features of the schizoid disorders carry on into adult life. Further evidence from Wolf's (1989) follow-up research with this cohort indicated that the intellectual ability of individuals with the disorder may be a critical variable in the quality of their social adaptation over time. "Our tentative impression is that the more gifted people are now less solitary, some having married, but their basic personality characteristics remain distinct. On the other hand, some of the less able and withdrawn people, while often working satisfactorily, remain single and excessively dependent on their families" (p. 223). Aside from this information, very little is known about the long-term implications of the schizoid disorders. It is probably prudent to assume that children and adolescents who exhibit these characteristics to the point where their social and personal judgment is severely impaired will continue these struggles to some extent during their adult life.

Assessment

Assessment of the broad constellation of problems subsumed under the Schizoid-Unresponsive behavioral dimension is a difficult challenge. The confusion in terminology, overlapping symptoms among at least three *DSM–IV* categories, and lack of substantial prevalence data all combine to create a situation where there is very little standard practice for assessment. Direct observation of behavior and general behavior rating scales will likely be useful in identifying patterns of severe social disengagement and peculiar thought or behavior patterns. The Child Behavior Checklist, in particular, has several items pertinent to these areas. Clinical interviewing will likely be very helpful, not only in understanding the self-perceptions of the child, but in allowing the clinician to observe social behavior of the client under standardized conditions. For youth who have sufficient cognitive maturity and reading ability (e.g., at least a sixth-grade level), certain adolescent self-report instruments may be very helpful in screening for schizoidlike characteristics. Specifically, the MMPI–A and MACI are recommended in this regard. Although neither one of these instruments contains specific scales developed to identify patterns of responding associated with the Schizoid-Unresponsive dimensions, it is possible that certain profile configurations or more than one scale may be helpful in generating or verifying hypotheses regarding these problems.

TIC DISORDERS (TOURETTE'S DISORDER)

By definition, tic disorders are disorders of movement. A tic is defined as "a sudden, rapid, recurrent, nonrhythmic, stereotyped motor movement or vocalization" (APA, 1994, p. 100). These disorders tend to feel irresistible to the affected person, but can be suppressed for varying periods of time. All types of tics may be worsened by stress. Most tic disorders are not considered to be behavioral, social, or emotional problems, but rather, neurological problems. However, one specific tic disorder, Tourette's Disorder, is noteworthy in this regard because it is often accompanied by behavioral and social adjustment difficulties, and often co-occurs with disorders in these areas.

Description

Tourette's Disorder is characterized by *multiple motor tics*. The motor tics often involve the head, and may also involve other parts of the body such as the torso and limbs. Eye tics such as blinking, eye rolling, or wide eye opening are a common first motor tic symptom (Sallee & Spratt, 1998). The vocal tics that accompany Tourette's Disorder may include a variety of words and sounds, such as clicking noises, grunts, yelps, barks, sniffs, snorts, or coughs. One specific vocal tic that Tourette's has been associated with is *Coprolalia*, which involves the seeming uncontrollable uttering of obscenities. This unusual tic has inaccurately become associated among the public and some professionals as a hallmark characteristic, perhaps because it is such an unusual and attention-getting activity. However, in reality, only a small percentage of individuals with Tourette's (perhaps less than 10%, according to Sallee & Spratt, 1998) exhibit Coprolalia.

The median age of first onset for Tourette's Disorder is 7 years, and by definition, onset is always before age 18. The symptoms of this disorder are often misunderstood or attributed to other problems. Therefore, accurate diagnosis is often not made for 5 to 12 years after its initial onset (Golden & Hood, 1982). Prevalence of Tourette's Disorder has been estimated at 4 to 5 individuals per 10,000 (APA, 1994), and this disorder is up to three times more common in males than in females. Although the duration of Tourette's is usually lifelong, it is common for the frequency, severity, and variability of symptoms to diminish during adolescence and early adulthood. In some cases, the symptoms will disappear entirely (Sallee & Spratt, 1998). Etiology of Tourette's Disorder is not specifically understood at this point in time, but is widely assumed to be genetic in origin (APA, 1994).

Perhaps the most relevant aspect of Tourette's Disorder for this book is that it is frequently accompanied by co-occurring behavioral disorders and problems. According to the *DSM–IV*, obsessive-compulsive behavior is the most common associated feature. Other common co-occurring symptoms include hyperactivity, distractibility, impulsivity, social discomfort, shame, extreme self-consciousness, and depression. As a result, it is not unusual for individuals with Tourette's to experience problems in academic, social, or occupational functioning. Sallee and Spratt (1998) noted that the incidence of Obsessive-Compulsive Disorder is in the 50% range for individuals diagnosed with Tourette's, and that "even in very mild cases of (the disorder), the incidence of ADHD is seven- to eightfold greater than that in the general population" (p. 339). The major defining characteristics and related features of Tourette's Disorder are summarized in Table 11.5.

Assessment

Assessment and accurate diagnosis of Tourette's Disorder can be a very difficult proposition, because some of the co-occurring symptoms may lead the clinician down the wrong path, and because the core tic symptoms tend to be very transient. In fact, specific tic symptoms of Tourette's may not be directly observed through behavioral observation or in a clinical interview situation in the majority of cases (Sallee & Spratt, 1998). Because of these difficulties, direct behavioral observation will often be challenging, and sometimes uninformative. General problem behavior rating scales may be useful for initial screening purposes, but typically do not include enough specificity for accurate assessment of Tourette's symptoms.

It is critical that assessment of children suspected of having Tourette's Disorder involve extensive clinical interviewing with the referred child or adolescent and their parent(s). The interview should include an extensive developmental history, family history, and questions regarding specific and associated behavioral problems across various situations and settings. A referral for neurological or related medical exami-

TABLE 11.5
Major Characteristics and Associated Features of Tourette's Disorder

Multiple motor tics, often involving the head, upper body, and limbs
Vocal tics, which may vary considerably from person to person in presentation
Tics are chronic, occurring nearly daily in some form
Marked disturbance or impairment in adjustment and functioning
Onset before age 18, with median onset at age 7
1.5 to 3 times more prevalent in males than in females
Frequently accompanied by symptoms associated with ADHD and Obsessive-Compulsive Disorder, with
    high rates of co-occurrence among these disorders
Frequently accompanied by social discomfort, self-consciousness, shame, and depressed mood
Frequently misdiagnosed or confused with other disorders
Frequently not diagnosed for several years after initial onset

nation of children suspected of having Tourette's Disorder may be helpful or even necessary, but it should be understood that "results of the neurological exam of patients with primary (Tourette's Disorder) are usually unremarkable with no focal or lateralizing signs" (Sallee & Spratt, 1998, p. 343).

Some assessment instruments specific to evaluation of Tourette's Disorder have been developed and reported in the literature. The Tourette's Syndrome Questionnaire (Jagger, Prusoff, D. J. Cohen, Kidd, Carbonari, & John, 1982) is an interview instrument designed to obtain historical information regarding the development of tic symptoms and associated features of Tourette's. The Tourette's Syndrome Symptom Checklist (D. J. Cohen, Leckman, & Shaywitz, 1984) is a rating scale designed to be used on a daily and weekly basis to evaluate the presence and disruptiveness of major Tourette's characteristics. The Yale Global Tic Severity Scale (Leckman et al., 1989) is a semistructured interview instrument designed to provide an evaluation of the number, frequency, intensity, complexity, and interference of various Tourette's symptoms. These instruments are not of the commercially published, nationally norm-referenced variety, and the various citations in the research literature should be consulted for more information regarding their appropriate uses.

SCHIZOPHRENIA AND OTHER PSYCHOTIC DISORDERS

The *DSM–IV* diagnostic categories presented in Table 11.2 indicate that there are numerous classification categories of schizophrenia and related psychotic disorders. However, these categories have been developed almost exclusively based on research and clinical efforts with adults, and are thus not generally descriptive of psychotic disorders that occur among children and early adolescents. In fact, *DSM–IV* states that schizophrenia, the hallmark psychotic disorder, usually emerges between "the late teens and the mid 30s, with onset prior to adolescence rare" (APA, 1994, p. 281). However, it has also been noted that schizophrenia and related psychotic disorders do occur earlier in adolescence and childhood (as young as age 5 or 6, according to *DSM–IV*), although the prevalence rates are substantially lower than the .2% to 2% rates reported for adults. This section provides some general descriptive information on psychotic disorders of childhood and early adolescence, as well as recommendations and guidelines for conducting effective assessments of such youth.

Description

The term *psychosis* does not have an exact or universal meaning, but is generally used to indicate a break with reality, or a severe impairment of an individual's sense of reality and ability to perceive things and function as most other persons do. The terms *childhood psychosis* and *childhood schizophrenia* were used earlier in this century to also indicate what is now referred to as Autistic Disorder, but the modern common understanding of these terms generally preclude autism. A defining feature of psychotic disorders is that the advent of the disorder causes a lowering or impairment of functioning from a previous level. Although Autistic Disorder is now considered to be a developmental disorder, where the feature characteristics involve severe limitations in the normal course of development, schizophrenia normally occurs after the early childhood developmental period, and brings with it a loss of functioning.

The major diagnostic picture of schizophrenia includes the following symptoms: delusions of thought, prominent and lasting hallucinations, incoherence or a marked loosening of associations, catatonic behavior (severe restriction of motor activity that sometimes alternates with wild hyperactivity), and flat or grossly inappropriate affect. The delusions of thought in schizophrenia are typically bizarre and implausible, and hallucinations are characteristically pronounced, such as hearing voices for long periods of time. Along with these severe disturbances of perception, thought, and affect, a severe decline in personal and social functioning typically occurs, which might include significantly poor personal hygiene, inability to function effectively at school or work, and a severe impairment in social relationships. Using the *DSM* system, these characteristic symptoms must be present on a continuous basis for a period of at least 6 months in order to make a diagnosis. Individuals with schizophrenia tend to display markedly peculiar behavior, such as talking to themselves in public, collecting garbage, and hoarding food or items that appear to be of little value. Schizophrenia is often accompanied by very strange beliefs or magical thinking not in line with the cultural standard; afflicted persons might believe that their behavior is being controlled by another person or force, or that they have the power of clairvoyance. Some of the characteristics of schizophrenia can be brought on by other conditions, such as severe affective disorders or the use of psychoactive substances. However, a true diagnosis of schizophrenia implies that the symptoms are pervasive and long lasting, and not brought on by a temporary biochemical or affective change. Although the *DSM–IV* criteria are the best working guidelines for schizophrenia currently available, it is important to consider that they may not always describe accurately the development of the disorder during childhood. In fact, Cantor (1987, 1989) noted that the *DSM* symptoms may not always be the most prominent features of schizophrenia that develops during childhood, and the childhood diagnostic picture is often complicated and clouded. Tolbert (1996) noted that when psychotic disorders are manifest in children, they are frequently accompanied by symptoms that are not always seen in adults. Some of these hallmark characteristics of childhood psychosis are presented in Table 11.6.

Because the trademark *DSM* symptoms of schizophrenia are rare before puberty, accurate prevalence estimates with children have been very difficult to determine. Although few large epidemiological studies have been conducted with children, a

TABLE 11.6
Behavioral, Emotional, and Cognitive Symptoms Associated
with Schizophrenia and Related Psychotic Disorders in Children

Severe speech problems
Difficulty distinguishing between dreams and reality
Hallucinations (visual and auditory)
Vivid and often bizarre ideas and thoughts
Confused thinking
Diminished interest in normal activities
Severe moodiness
Odd or peculiar behavior
Lack of inhibition
Believes that someone is "out to get" him or her
Behaves like a much younger child
Severe fears or anxiety
Confuses television programs with reality
Significant peer problems; difficulty making and keeping friends

frequently quoted prevalence figure has been 4 or 5 cases per 10,000 children (Cantor, 1989). However, reviews of more recent evidence indicate that the prevalence figure may actually be lower, closer to 1 in 10,000 children, and that only .1% to 1% of all cases of schizophrenia are manifest before age 10, and only 4% before age 15 (Tolbert, 1996). With adults and older adolescents, schizophrenia tends to occur in similar numbers with males and females. However, it is interesting to note that with the preadolescent population (up to about age 14), the equal gender balance does not hold true. Cantor (1989) stated that the general agreement for a sex ratio for childhood psychosis is 4 or 5 males per 1 female.

The cause of schizophrenia has been a controversial topic for centuries, where explanations of etiology have run the gamut ranging from demon possession to a weak constitution to poor parenting. In recent years, a plethora of research has strongly suggested that schizophrenia has a biochemical basis. The neurotransmitter dopamine has been implicated as a critical variable, as drugs that block dopamine receptor sites tend to be highly effective at controlling the more severe symptoms of schizophrenia, such as delusions and hallucinations. Family studies and investigations of adoption conducted in the United States and Europe over the past several decades have provided additional evidence for a genetic explanation of schizophrenia, as the degree of genetic relatedness to an individual with schizophrenia is a strong factor in predicting the occurrence of the disorder (Gottesman, 1991). For example, in cases where one individual in a set of twins develops schizophrenia, the probability is almost four times greater that the other twin will develop the disorder when the twins are identical rather than fraternal. Although biochemical-genetic factors are certainly prominent in explaining etiology, behavioral and environmental factors are likely to interact with the person variables to increase or decrease the likelihood of schizophrenia; if two individuals have an equal biochemical/genetic predisposition for developing the disorder, then the individual with a dramatically higher level of psychosocial distress may be more likely to ultimately exhibit the symptoms.

Prognosis for children and adolescents who develop schizophrenia is somewhat variable, and appears to hinge on such factors as age level, severity of symptoms, and family history. Tolbert (1996) stated that prognosis is poorest when the onset of the disorder occurs before age 10 to 14, and in youth where there is a family history of psychotic disorders, and only about 25% of patients with adolescent-onset schizophrenia achieve a partial remission of symptoms. There appears to be wide variability in how schizophrenia affects individuals over the life span, and the availability of social support, medical care, and mental health services may be critical factors in how debilitating the disorder becomes to the individual.

Assessment

Children and adolescents with schizophrenia and other psychotic disorders typically experience characteristic private or internal events (such as various disorders of thought and sensation) and also exhibit characteristic overt and easily observed behaviors (such as psychomotor agitation or retardation, highly unusual verbal behavior, and wildly inappropriate social behavior). Thus, the assessment design for these youth must be carefully planned and must include techniques and instruments designed to evaluate both overt and covert symptoms. In addition to the behavioral-psychological types of assessment covered in this text, it is important to recognize that assessment of children and adolescents with schizophrenia and other psychotic disorders should also include appropriate medical assessment data, such as a physical examination, neurologic examination, and laboratory studies (Tolbert, 1996).

Behavioral Observation. Behavioral observation will generally prove to be valuable in assessing children and adolescents with psychotic disorders. Effective observational systems for this purpose will require that the observation domain is carefully defined, and appropriate coding strategies are used. However, there are some specific problems with behavioral observation assessment that should be considered. Many of the characteristic problem behaviors in this domain are not overt or blatant, and they may thus be difficult to adequately assess with direct behavioral observation. For example, hallucinations, delusions, odd thought processes, and a desire to avoid other persons may be extremely difficult to observe unless they are also accompanied by overt behavioral signals such as language, psychomotor agitation with explanatory language signs, or obvious social withdrawal. Thus, to design an effective observational system for assessing the characteristics of psychotic disorders, clinicians must necessarily focus on the disorders' more overt aspects, operationally define them so that they can be observed and coded without question, and defer the assessment of the more internal or covert characteristics of the disorders to other methods (i.e., interviews, self-report, or rating scales completed by individuals who have observed the child over a long period of time).

Behavior Rating Scales. Some of the general problem behavior rating scales reviewed in chapter 4 may be very helpful as screening tools. Specifically, the Child Behavior Checklist and Revised Behavior Problem Checklist both appear useful for initial screening of childhood psychotic disorders. The CBCL includes the Thought Problems cross-informant scale, which contains items pertinent to hallucinations, sensory distortions, and bizarre behaviors. The RBPCL contains a subscale labeled Psychotic Behavior (PB) that includes items regarding reality/fantasy distortions, peculiar or bizarre behavior and thought, and incoherent speech. The RBPCL manual indicates that some of the principal correlates of this scale include *DSM* psychotic diagnoses. Both of these instruments have been demonstrated to show sensitivity in discriminating among youth with psychotic disorders and youth with other types of disorders.

The *Symptom Scale* is an example of a rating scale (or checklist) designed specifically for use in assessing the symptoms of schizophrenia in children and young adolescents (Cantor, 1987, 1989; Cantor, Pearce, Pezzot-Pearce, & Evans, 1981). This instrument consists of 18 checklist-style descriptors that were found through a review of the literature to be associated with schizophrenia in children and youth. Examples of these descriptors include "constricted affect," "perseveration," "inappropriate affect," "anxiety," "loose associations," "grimacing," and "incoherence." Each of 54 schizophrenic children and youth in a study were rated by two clinical psychologists for the presence or absence of these 18 symptoms. The population was broken into three age groups: preschool ($n = 25$), latency ($n = 15$), and adolescent ($n = 14$). Most of the symptoms were found to be present in more than 50% of the subjects in each group, and a few of the symptoms were found to be present in more than 50% of the subjects in one or two groups, but three symptoms (clang associations, echolalia, and neologisms) were found to be present in less than 50% of the subjects in all three groups, indicating that they had relatively poor diagnostic validity. Although the Symptom Scale was not designed to be a norm-referenced diagnostic test, it may be useful in research or in validating behavioral characteristics of schizophrenia obtained from multiple assessment data. It is not commercially published and must be obtained by researching the references listed at the beginning of this section.

Clinical Interviews.   Most of the interview methods discussed in chapter 5 can be utilized to some extent in assessing psychotic disorders. The specific choice of technique will vary depending on the presenting problems exhibited by the referred child/adolescent clients, their age level, language capability, and social maturity, and the availability and cooperation of a parent or primary caregiver. The parent/caregiver behavioral interview will be critically important if the child or adolescent client is not capable of engaging in a traditional interview, or if the referral necessitates the immediate development of a behavioral intervention plan. Traditional unstructured types of interviews with the child or adolescent client may be of limited use in these cases, but may provide some additional insights in cases where psychotic features are emerging. Virtually any of the structured interview schedules reviewed elsewhere in this book (e.g., K–SADS, DICA–R, DISC, etc.) are potentially useful in assessing youth with psychotic disorders. These structured interview schedules all include at least some items that are relevant to the severe behavioral and emotional disorders, and include scoring algorithms that are designed to generate hypotheses about the existence of Axis I and Axis II disorders from the *DSM*.

An example of the utility of one of these structured interviews in assessing and diagnosing psychotic disorders is demonstrated from research conducted by Haley, Fine, and Marriage (1988), who compared DISC interview data from both psychotic and nonpsychotic depressed adolescent inpatients. In this case, several strands of the DISC interview data were found to discriminate between the two groups, as the psychotic group subjects were more likely to have a history of sexual abuse, to have more serious depression, and to have more symptoms of hypomanic behavior than the nonpsychotic group subjects. Other research lending support to the use of structured interviews for assessing the severe disorders comes from an epidemiological study conducted by P. Cohen, O'Connor, Lewis, Velez, and Noemi (1987), who found that the DISC and K–SADS both provided moderate to moderately high accuracy estimates of the prevalence of various *DSM* disorders.

A potential caution in conducting interviews for the assessment of psychotic symptoms involves making inquiries about low frequency and bizarre symptoms such as delusions, hallucinations, thought problems, and severe obsessive-compulsive behaviors. The clinician must word their questions about these areas most carefully, and gauge the responses of both children and their parents with caution. Research by Breslau (1987) has helped to verify the notion that both referred children and their parents may misunderstand structured interview questions about psychotic behavior and related characteristics, and may thus provide answers that lead to high false-positive errors. This research found that subjects often misunderstand the intent of these types of questions, and when appropriate follow-up questioning is introduced, many of the positive responses to questions are recoded as negative responses. For example, children might respond positively to a question such as "do you ever see things that no one else can see," when they are thinking about seeing unique shapes in cloud formations or wallpaper designs rather than any visual hallucinations. Thus, when questioning about "the bizarre," it is extremely important to follow up on affirmative responses and to obtain specific examples.

Sociometric Techniques. Although sociometric techniques tend to be difficult to implement for basic clinical assessment of specific children and adolescents, they have been demonstrated to be quite effective in identifying youth with psychotic disorders, and thus may be of interest to researchers. Of the 20 studies cited by McConnell and Odom (1986) to provide evidence of the predictive validity of sociometrics, 3 were specifically designed to test sociometric assessment with schizophrenic or similar severity populations (Bower, Shelhamer, & Daily, 1960; Kohn & Clausen, 1955; Pritchard & P. Graham, 1966). These and other studies have proven that sociometric techniques that are specifically designed and implemented for assessing and predicting psychotic disorders can be quite effective.

Self-Report Instruments. Depending on the type and severity of presenting symptoms, self-report instruments will range in usefulness from not useful at all to highly useful in assessing children and youth with psychotic disorders. In cases of severe and active psychotic behavior, the most serious manifestations of these problems will usually make the self-reflective tasks involved in a self-report instrument impossible. However, for emerging, less active, or residual cases of schizophrenia, self-report instruments may be of some use. Some of the items and cross-informant scales of the Youth Self-Report appear to have some utility in the assessment of psychotic symptoms. The Thought Problems scale of the YSR appears to be potentially useful in this regard, containing some items that are highly congruent with some of the characteristics of psychotic behavior, such as hoarding behavior, sensory distortions, and disordered thought processes. As discussed in chapter 7, the YSR should be used cautiously, as it contains no controls to detect manipulation or faking, and some research has suggested that it may not effectively discriminate groups of children and adolescents with severe psychopathology (e.g., Bird et al., 1991; Thurber & Snow, 1990). Another important consideration in using the YSR is that unusual responses on some of the items on the Thought Problems and Withdrawn scales should be followed-up with additional questioning—they are not always indicative of psychopathology. For example, it is not uncommon for adolescent respondents to endorse an item such as "I hear things that nobody else seems to be able to hear" when they are simply thinking of something as benign as a favorite song continually repeating in their mind, or to endorse an item such as "I store up things I don't need" to indicate a normal activity like collecting stickers or baseball cards.

The MMPI is probably the best documented and validated self-report instrument for use in assessing some of the characteristics of psychotic behavior with adolescents. As indicated in chapter 7, the original MMPI was known to produce high false-positive error rates in screening for severe psychopathology with adolescents. However, the use of special norms and interpretive techniques with the MMPI may greatly increase the predictive validity of test scores, and the introduction of the MMPI–A was a major positive step in self-report technology for use with adolescents. The best guidebooks for using the MMPI and MMPI–A in assessing adolescent psychopathology are those by Archer (1987, 1992, 1996), which go beyond a simple "cookbook" approach to test interpretation and address the critical issues of adolescent development and psychopathology vis-à-vis their performance on self-report tests. Archer noted that although some MMPI/MMPI–A scales (most notably Scale 8, Schizophrenia) will produce high false-positive rates for detecting severe psychopathology with adolescents when used in isolation, screening and classification accuracy for the severe disorders can be greatly improved through carefully interpreting code types and understanding the meaning of absolute score levels on individual scales. For example, extremely high *T*-scores on Scale 8 (Schizophrenia) usually are not indicative of psychotic behavior, but commonly are reflective of intense, acute situational distress. However, extreme elevations (*T*-scores of 75 or higher) on Scale 6 (Paranoia) typically identify persons with a psychotic degree of paranoid symptomatology, such as paranoid schizophrenia and individuals manifesting paranoid states. Certain 2-point code types may also be indicative of the types of serious psychopathology associated with psychotic behavior, most notably 6-8/8-6 (Paranoia-Schizophrenia), 8-9/9-8 (Schizophrenia-Hypomania), and 4-8/8-4 (Psychopathic Deviate-Schizophrenia). It is interesting to note that the MMPI–A manual contains correlates of the various scales for both the normative and clinical samples, and some interesting differences between the two groups are found on items from several scales, including 4, 6, and 8. Because the MMPI–A is essentially a new instrument, additional research will be needed to verify for certain if the diagnostic features of the MMPI for adolescents with psychotic disorders translate to the MMPI–A.

EATING DISORDERS

The essential feature of eating disorders is severe disturbances in eating behavior. Anorexia Nervosa and Bulimia Nervosa, the two most common types of eating disorders and the focus of this section, are not considered to be problems that first exist during infancy and childhood. Rather, they both typically have a late adolescent or early adult onset. However, school-based clinicians (particularly those working with secondary school populations) and community-based clinicians who work extensively with adolescents often find these disorders to exist in alarming numbers among their clientele, and to cause significant problems for many youth and their families. These disorders are therefore included within this chapter. Both of these disorders appear to occur disproportionately in females (about 90% of all cases), and among Caucasians, are substantially more likely to be observed in the Western industrialized nations than in other parts of the world, and to have increased substantially in prevalence since about the 1950s and 1960s (Williamson, Bentz, & Rabalais, 1998). In its section on eating disorders, the *DSM–IV* includes a diagnostic code for Eating Disorder Not Otherwise Specified, for cases in which there are serious eating disorder symptoms, but the criteria for Anorexia Nervosa or Bulimia Nervosa are not fully met. The major characteristics and associated features of these latter two disorders are summarized in Table 11.7.

Some experts (e.g., W. M. Reynolds, 1992a, 1992b) have included eating disorders under the general domain of internalizing problems. However, behavioral dimensions approaches to classifying child and adolescent psychopathology have not consistently identified a separate eating disorders sector within the internalizing domain, even though they do have many characteristics in common, such as covert maladaptive behaviors, diminished self-esteem, and mood disturbances. Therefore, this topic is addressed in this chapter rather than in chapter 10.

There are other types of eating and feeding disturbances—namely, Pica, Rumination Disorder, and Feeding Disorder of Infancy or Early Childhood—that are considered to be first evident in infancy or early childhood. Nevertheless, these problems are not covered in this text because they have an extremely low base rate, and tend to be

TABLE 11.7
Major Characteristics and Associated Features of the Primary Eating Disorders

Anorexia Nervosa
  Refusal to maintain a minimally normal body weight (85% or less of normal weight for height/age)
  Significant disturbance in self-perception of shape/size of body
  Resulting menstrual irregularities
  Includes food restricting and binge eating/purging subtypes
  Often co-occurs with depression, obsessive-compulsive disorder, and personality disorders
  .5% to 1% prevalence in Western industrialized nations
  May result in menstrual problems, heart problems, biochemical imbalances
  5% to 10% long-term mortality rate
Bulimia Nervosa
  Binge eating episodes
  Inappropriate compensatory strategies
  Self-evaluation excessively influenced by perceptions of body shape/weight
  Individuals are usually within normal weight range
  Often accompanied by excessive shame and depressed mood
  Often co-occurs with mood disorders, substance abuse problems, and anxiety symptoms
  1% to 3% prevalence in Western industrialized nations
  May result in dental problems and biochemical imbalances
Both Disorders
  Mainly prevalent in Western industrialized nations
  Mainly prevalent among females (90% of all cases)
  More prevalent among Caucasians than other racial/ethnic groups
  Typical onset in late adolescence or early adulthood

dealt with in more specialized settings and by highly focused professionals, such as in children's medical centers by pediatric psychologists. Therefore, readers who desire more details on these problems should consult more specialized texts or the pediatric/pediatric psychology literature.

Description

Anorexia Nervosa. "The essential features of Anorexia Nervosa are that the individual refuses to maintain a minimally normal body weight, is intensely afraid of gaining weight, and exhibits a significant disturbance in the perception of the shape or size of his or her body" (APA, 1994, p. 539). Failure to maintain minimally normal body weight is operationally defined as 85% of the expected normal body weight for that individual's height and age. The *DSM–IV* describes two subtypes of Anorexia Nervosa: a restricting subtype, where the individual maintains low body weight essentially through self-starvation, and a binge eating/purging subtype, which is characterized by episodes of keeping the body weight excessively low through episodes of binge eating followed by purging behavior (e.g., self-induced vomiting or the abuse of laxatives).

Anorexia Nervosa often co-occurs with depressive disorders, obsessive-compulsive characteristics, and personality disorders (Williamson et al., 1998). Prevalence studies among adolescent and early adult females have indicated that .5% to 1% of that population within the United States meet full criteria for Anorexia Nervosa, and there are many other individuals who exhibit symptoms but do not meet the full criteria threshold. Theories of etiology have focused on possible biologic underpinnings, psychosocial explanations, and sociocultural pressures for thinness, particularly among females. According to the *DSM–IV*, the mean age of onset for Anorexia Nervosa is 17 years, with possible bimodal peaks at age 14 and 18. Therefore, clinicians working with youth as young as middle school or junior high school age should become familiar with the disorder. In addition to the often co-occurring psychological problems, there are serious physical effects of Anorexia Nervosa, including heart problems, fluid and electrolyte imbalances, and even death.

Bulimia Nervosa. "The essential features of Bulimia Nervosa are binge eating and inappropriate compensatory methods to prevent weight gain" (APA, 1994, p. 545). Additionally, individuals with this disorder tend to evaluate themselves excessively by their own perceptions of body shape and weight. For a diagnosis of Bulimia Nervosa to occur, the binge eating and maladaptive compensatory behaviors must happen on average at least two times a week for 3 months. By definition, binge eating occurs in a circumscribed period of time wherein the individual consumes a substantially larger amount of food (often sweet high-calorie foods such as desserts) than is normal. These episodes of binge eating are often characterized by a frenzied psychological state, a feeling of being out of control, and sometimes, even a dissociative sensation. Binge eating episodes are often brought on by depressed mood states, interpersonal problems, or extreme hunger that is a result of dietary restraint. The most common inappropriate methods to prevent weight gain in Bulimia include self-induced vomiting, and abuse of laxatives and diuretics. Excessive exercise is also a common compensatory strategy. *DSM–IV* lists two subtypes of Bulimia Nervosa: a Purging Type (in which the person regularly engages in self-induced vomiting or similar strategies) and a Nonpurging Type (in which other types of compensatory behaviors, such as excessive exercise or fasting are used).

In contrast to the physical size of individuals with Anorexia Nervosa, individuals with Bulimia Nervosa tend to be within normal weight ranges, although it is not uncommon for them to be slightly overweight or slightly underweight. The prevalence of this disorder among individuals living in industrialized nations has been estimated to range from 1% to 3%, with a typical onset during late adolescence or early adulthood. Etiologic theories of Bulimia are the same as those referred to for Anorexia Nervosa (Williamson et al., 1998). Depressed mood states and feelings of extreme shame often follow an episode of binge eating, and it has also been demonstrated that individuals with Bulimia Nervosa have an increased incidence of mood disorders and substance abuse and dependence than individuals in the general population. Frequent purging episodes may lead to fluid and electrolyte imbalances, metabolic problems, permanent damage to the teeth through erosion of dental enamel, and noticeably enlarged salivary glands.

Assessment

Assessment of both Anorexia and Bulimia Nervosa is typically difficult through direct behavioral observation and informant-based behavior rating scales, because the major behavioral characteristics of both disorders tend to be covert or done in secret (i.e., binge eating, self-induced vomiting), and because other major characteristics tend to involve self-perceptions. However, two important aspects of Anorexia Nervosa may be externally observable at times by individuals who are close to the affected person, namely, food restriction and excessive weight loss. The most effective and widely used methods of assessment for these eating disorders are clinical interviewing and self-report instruments. Clinical interviewing should focus not only on the core aspects of the maladaptive eating and compensatory behaviors, but on possible coexisting psychosocial problems, such as depression, anxiety, distorted thinking patterns, and obsessive-compulsive characteristics.

The most widely used self-report instrument in this area is the Eating Disorders Inventory–2 (Garner, 1991). This instrument is designed for use with individuals age 12 and older. It includes 91 forced choice items (rated on a 6-point scale) regarding various core and ancillary characteristics of eating disorders, as well as a four-page symptom checklist. Raw scores are converted to 11 empirically derived subscales, which are based on a large normative sample. Various comparison norms (e.g., high school students, college students) are also provided in the test manual. The Eating Disorders Inventory–2 is a revision of the original Eating Disorders Inventory. Combined, the two instruments are clearly the most widely researched self-report instruments for assessing eating disorders, with over 100 published studies using them in some way. The psychometric properties, including the diagnostic validity of the instrument, are demonstrated in the test manual and in several of the numerous published studies.

Because of the physical problems that may accompany eating disorders, "a complete medical exam is recommended for all persons with an eating disorder" (Williamson et al., 1998, p. 300). In addition, direct measurement of daily caloric intake and eating diaries are frequent strategies in treating eating disorders.

LINKING ASSESSMENT TO INTERVENTION

Virtually all of the types of information obtained in assessing pervasive developmental disorders, schizoid disorders, tic disorders, psychotic disorders, and eating disorders of children and adolescents that are discussed in this chapter have direct utility for diagnostic purposes. However, whether or not the assessment data are useful in intervention planning and implementation for these problems depends to a great extent on the specifics of the assessment data, the problem, and the type of intervention needed.

The most widely utilized and documented interventions for the pervasive developmental disorders (specifically autism) at the present time are behavioral in nature, and tend to focus on altering either behavioral deficits (i.e., lack of communication and poor eye contact) or behavioral excesses (i.e., stereotypical behaviors such as echolalia and spinning) that tend to compound the social consequences of the disorder. Kauffman (1989) noted that early and intensive behavioral interventions are especially critical for successful treatment of the pervasive developmental disorders, and the prognosis for future adjustment is much better when early interventions are successfully employed. Most of the assessment methods for gauging the characteristics of Autistic Disorder and its related counterparts that have been described in this chapter are quite useful in pinpointing specific behavioral excesses and deficits that are cause for concern. Beyond that, whether or not the assessment data will be of additional use in determining specific targets for intervention will depend on how *functional* they are. By definition, functional assessment data are those pieces of information that help to identify the antecedents, consequences, and frequency or intensity of occurrence of specific target behaviors. Assessment data obtained from behavioral observation and behavioral interviews with parents or caretakers is particularly likely to be of functional use.

The schizoid disorders are notoriously difficult to effectively treat (Butcher, 1990). Part of the problem in linking assessment data to interventions in an effective manner in these cases is that the individuals involved are often very resistant to treatment, particularly when the treatment involves establishing a trusting relationship with a therapist in a 1:1 intervention setting. Self-report data from structured interviews and self-report tests may be useful in diagnosis, but difficult to convert to an intervention plan with the schizoid disorders. Behavioral assessment data from observations, rating scales, and behavioral interviews with parents or caregivers are potentially useful in pinpointing target behaviors for intervention, and in some cases, for determining potential sources of reinforcement available within the immediate environment. Part of the clinical picture that is usually seen with the schizoid disorders is extremely poor social skills and peer rejection. In this regard, there is some hope that structured social skills training conducted in group settings might be an effective approach, although generalizing social skills training effects across settings and time is difficult and takes specific planning (Merrell & Gimpel, 1998). If a child or adolescent client exhibits schizoid-like characteristics with severe social deficits and poor relationships, then the assessment design could benefit from the inclusion of a specific social skills appraisal (see chap. 12), which might help in identifying distinctive clusters of social skills deficits.

Children with Tourette's Disorder often benefit from psychopharmacology interventions that reduce tic behaviors and often tend to ameliorate some of the related attentional problems as well. Therefore, the assessment data that lead to appropriate diagnosis of Tourette's may simply provide the basis for making a medical referral. However, a comprehensive assessment of the child will often identify related or co-occurring problems, such as attentional problems, mood disturbances, social problems, and obsessive-compulsive symptoms. Therefore, a thorough assessment will often result in the identification of specific psychosocial problems that should be the focus of appropriate intervention planning.

Linking assessment to intervention planning in cases of schizophrenic or other psychotic disorders can be a complex challenge. Kauffman (1989) stated that behavioral interventions have been highly successful with psychotic children in a number of research situations, but the results of these projects have not always provided direct and practical treatment implications for classroom teachers. Thus, functional assessment data from observations or behavioral interviews might provide a basis for modifying the child's immediate environment to remediate specific behavioral excesses or deficits, but implementing these interventions outside of a highly controlled environment may be challenging. Smith and Belcher (1985) noted that such individuals often require considerable training in basic life skills such as grooming, hygiene, and community living. For identifying specific areas for these life skills interventions, the use of behavior rating scales may also prove to be useful. In most cases, effective management of psychotic disorders may involve medical referral and the possible use of neuroleptic (antipsychotic) medications. Medical referral and intervention is especially critical in cases where the child or adolescent client is experiencing full-blown psychotic symptoms such as hallucinations and delusions, or when there is an increased probability for them doing harm to themselves or others. Rating scales, interviews, observations, and in some cases, self-report tests may all be useful for identifying the overt symptoms of schizophrenia that warrant intervention. Because children with psychotic disorders (and pervasive developmental disorders) usually exhibit behaviors that are so blatantly maladaptive and different from those of their normal peers, the *template matching strategy* discussed by Shapiro (1996) may be useful in linking assessment to intervention. This strategy involves systematic comparison of the behavior of the troubled individual with behavior of well-adjusted youth, identifying the discrepancies between the two, and then using the "normal" behavior as a template for targeting intervention.

Assessment of eating disorders must necessarily rely heavily on extensive clinical interviewing and self-report instruments, because many of the core characteristics of these disorders may not be easily detectable through external methods of objective assessment. The various information obtained through assessment may be useful in selecting related areas to target for intervention. That is, the core targets for intervention will always be the maladaptive eating behaviors themselves, but there may need to be ancillary intervention targets, such as depression, distorted thinking patterns, obsessive-compulsive characteristics, and various other maladaptive behaviors and cognitions. Self-report instruments and clinical interviews may be very helpful in identifying the appropriate ancillary targets, and perhaps in determining how to best approach the core eating disorder symptoms with particular individuals.

CONCLUSIONS

Not all forms of child and adolescent psychopathology fit neatly within the broad externalizing and internalizing domains that have been so well documented in the research literature. Some types of behavioral, social, and emotional problems are considered to be "mixed," given that the major characteristics may load into either or both of the major broad-band domains. Other types of problems do contain characteristics specific to either of the two major domains, and instead, stand alone in taxonomy to some extent. Additionally, some forms of child and adolescent psychopathology have such an extremely low base rate of prevalence that it is difficult to account for enough cases in large etiologic studies to make broad-band classification possible or desirable.

This chapter provides descriptive information and brief comments on assessment methodology for several of these "other" domains of problems, including pervasive developmental disorders, the so-called schizoid disorders, Tourette's Disorder (a specific tic disorder that often has social-emotional overlays), schizophrenia and other manifestations of childhood psychosis, and the major eating disorders. Development of an adequate classification taxonomy for all of these disorders has been an ongoing problem. The behavioral dimensions approach to classifying severe childhood psychopathology (as illustrated by Quay's taxonomy system) has resulted in two clusters or subdomains of problems. The *DSM* approach to classification of severe problems appears to be in a continual state of flux, at least in part because of the low base rate for occurrence of many of the problems under consideration. Unfortunately, many of the *DSM* diagnostic categories are based on adult models of psychopathology (particularly in the case of schizophrenia and other psychotic disorders), even though there is evidence that childhood and early adolescent manifestations of these severe problems differ markedly from adulthood manifestations in many cases.

Pervasive developmental disorders constitute a class of severe problems that are first evident during infancy and childhood. Autistic Disorder is the best-known manifestation of the pervasive developmental disorders. It is manifest by age 3, and is typified by severe impairment in communication and social interaction skills, as well as by the occurrence of stereotyped and markedly restrictive behaviors, activities, and interests. Three recent additions to the *DSM* pervasive developmental disorder include Rett's Disorder, Childhood Disintegrative Disorder, and Asperger's Disorder. These three disorders are very rare in comparison to autism, and little is known regarding prevalence and etiology. Many of the essential features of these other pervasive developmental disorders include symptoms similar to those found in Autistic Disorder, but with specific and peculiar manifestations. Assessment of pervasive developmental disorders typically must rely heavily on direct behavioral observation, behavior rating scales, and clinical interviews with parents and teachers. Several widely researched instruments of these types have been developed for assessing autism.

The so-called schizoid disorders have been in and out of the *DSM* throughout various editions, but have been verified through behavioral dimensions research, and have been of continual interest to researchers, particularly in parts of Europe. The schizoid disorders are characterized in general by extreme deficits in social interaction skills and by extreme difficulty in developing and maintaining close human relationships. Schizoid and Schizoptypal Personality Disorders from the *DSM–IV* appear to be close parallels to the schizoid symptoms identified through behavioral dimensions research with children, even though these two personality disorders are not typically appropriate for childhood diagnoses. The addition of Asperger's Disorder to *DSM–IV* appears to be a step in verifying the continuing existence of the schizoid disorders, given the similarity in essential features. In some respects, Asperger's Disorder appears to be a childhood parallel to Schizoid and Schizoptypal Personality Disorder, much the way Conduct Disorder is a childhood parallel to Antisocial Personality Disorder. Assessment of the schizoid disorders is a difficult proposition, with few or no domain-specific instruments available. It appears that a broad assessment design is appropriate for assessment, which would include self-report measures such as the MMPI–A and Youth Self-Report with adolescent clients who have adequate reading skills.

Tourette's Disorder is a specific type of tic disorder characterized by multiple and frequent motor and vocal tics, and that often includes social-emotional problems. In fact, Tourette's Disorder co-occurs with Attention Deficit Hyperactivity and Obsessive-Compulsive Disorders in a surprisingly large percentage of cases, and it is often misunderstood, misinterpreted, and misdiagnosed. This disorder usually occurs in early to middle childhood, and fortunately, it is often characterized by an abating or lessening of symptoms by late adolescence or early adulthood. Assessment of Tourette's Disorder among children is best accomplished through a comprehensive assessment design that relies heavily on clinical interviewing of parents and the child in question. Some research interviews and rating scales have been developed specifically for use in assessing Tourette's Disorder. A particular assessment problem in this area is differential diagnosis and dual diagnosis, given the frequent co-occurence of other disorders.

Schizophrenia and other psychotic disorders rarely occur before midadolescence, with the first onset usually occurring in late adolescence or early adulthood. However, psychotic episodes have been reported with children between age 10 and 14, and as young as age 5 or 6. The manifestation of psychotic symptoms among these younger clients typically differs in important ways from the typical adult-oriented classification criteria of the *DSM–IV*. Effective assessment of psychotic behavior in children and youth requires a variable approach, depending on the age and developmental level of the youth in question. Each of the major assessment methods may prove to be useful or even essential for assessment and classification of psychotic disorders with specific clients, including self-report measures such as the MMPI–A with high-functioning adolescents.

Although eating disorders have sometimes been lumped together with the broad band of internalizing psychopathology, and indeed do share some important characteristics and correlates, behavioral dimensions analyses have not consistently placed them as a subcategory of this area, so they are covered in this chapter rather than in chapter 10. The two major eating disorders of interest for this chapter include Anorexia Nervosa and Bulimia Nervosa, both of which occur primarily among Caucasian females in Western industrialized nations, and are characterized by substantial disturbances in eating behavior. The major diagnostic distinction between the two disorders is that Anorexia involves refusal to maintain a reasonably normal body weight, either through caloric restriction or a combination of food restriction and purging. Bulimia, on the other hand, tends to occur among individuals with normal body weight, and involves binge eating accompanied by inappropriate compensatory strategies, such as self-induced vomiting. Both disorders involve distortions in self-perceptions regarding body shape and size, tend to co-occur with mood disorders and other problems, and may have serious, or even lethal, consequences. Assessment of eating disorders through external objective means is difficult. Therefore, assessment must necessarily rely on extensive clinical interviews and self-report instruments, such as the Eating Disorders Inventory–2.

Linkage of these various "other" disorders to effective intervention strategies varies considerably across categories in terms of how easy and effective it is. For the pervasive developmental disorders, functional assessment strategies are critical because intervention tends to be very behavioral in nature, and requires identification of antecedent–behavior–consequence relations. Linking the assessment of the schizoid disorders to intervention is potentially very problematic, because of the often-difficult-to-treat nature of these problems. Obviously, assessment of social skills will be essential, and may assist in planning social skills training interventions. Less is known regarding linkage of Tourette's Disorder to intervention, other than the necessity of making an appropriate diagnosis, and the strong possibility of referring for medication intervention coupled with appropriate social-emotional support. Assessment of childhood psychotic disorders is very difficult to link effectively to intervention, which usually requires a combination of medication and structured behavioral programming. However, for higher functioning adolescents, the MMPI and MMPI–A may provide some empirically developed templates for selection of treatment strategies. Treatment of eating disorders tends to be eclectic, using a variety of behavioral and psychosocial strategies. Assessment of these disorders will probably be best linked to intervention through identification of the key problems, which will then be targeted for intervention.

REVIEW AND APPLICATION QUESTIONS

1. What are the most likely reasons why the "other" behavioral, social, and emotional problems discussed in this chapter do not fit neatly within the major domains of internalizing and externalizing psychopathology?

2. *DSM–IV* lists four specific types of pervasive developmental disorders. Three of these disorders (all but Autistic Disorder) were added to the *DSM* only in the most recent edition. Make an argument for these other three disorders (Rett's, Childhood Disintegrative, and Asperger's) being either separate disorders or just variations of autism.

3. In assessing a child with a pervasive developmental disorder, what practices can be implemented to make the assessment as "functional" as possible in providing information useful for intervention planning.

4. Examine the characteristics of the schizoid disorders vis-à-vis the information on social skills assessment presented in chapter 12. How could an assessment be designed to maximize the usefulness of the obtained information in addressing the most notable social-interpersonal deficits through intervention?

5. What are some of the major cautions that should be considered for interpreting parent and teacher general purpose problem behavior rating scales that have been completed on a child who may possibly have Tourette's Disorder?

6. In making a differential diagnosis with an elementary-age child who may have either a pervasive developmental disorder or psychotic disorder, what would be the key discriminating features to consider in making a diagnostic decision, and how could the assessment be best designed to be useful in this decision?

7. Individuals with eating disorders are often very secretive regarding their maladaptive eating behaviors. Because effective assessment of these problems must necessarily rely heavily on clinical interviewing and self-report instruments, how can these assessments be best used so that the important problems and characterizations are not minimized or ignored?

8. This chapter states that the MMPI or MMPI–A may be useful not only in assessing many adolescents with schizoid disorders and psychotic disorders, but in helping to plan intervention strategies. Referring to chapter 7 for reference as needed, on what empirical basis can these instruments be helpful in differential diagnosis and intervention planning?

CASE STUDY: CARLOS F.

This case involves the difficult problem of ruling in or ruling out a diagnosis of Autistic Disorder with a young child who has severe developmental delays and related developmental problems. To use this particular case study most effectively, it is recommended that readers review the section on pervasive developmental disorders (and the summary in Table 11.3) in this chapter and also review the complete diagnostic criteria for Autistic Disorder from *DSM–IV* (Table 11.4).

Background Information

Carlos F., a 3-year-old boy (44 months), lives with his parents, fraternal twin brother, and 17-year-old sister in a large city. Carlos' father works as a computer programmer, and Carlos' mother is a homemaker. Information from his special education file indicates that with the exception of he and his twin brother being delivered by cesarean section and Carlos having the umbilical chord wrapped around his neck, there were no prenatal or birth abnormalities. However, developmental problems were noted early on with Carlos, and he was placed in a special education preschool at age 2. The I.E.P. goals from Carlos' first preschool were extremely basic, with such goal statements as "will respond to sounds" and "will make eye contact." Copies of several evaluations of Carlos by medical specialists were found in his file, with no specific medical pathology identified. At the time of the assessment, Carlos was placed in a special education preschool four afternoons per week, also receiving direct related services at home from a communication disorders specialist because of speech and language delays. His current I.E.P. goals involve increasing attending, social, and toileting skills (Carlos is partially toilet trained), implementing a total communication program with three basic signs (head nods and shakes for eat, drink, and move), following one-concept commands, and improving his vocal imitation. The reason for the assessment referral was to conduct a screening to evaluate the possibility of Carlos having Autistic Disorder. The special education preschool staff were doubtful that autism was an appropriate diagnosis for Carlos, but indicated he had many "autistic-like behaviors." Carlos' mother was thoroughly convinced that her son was autistic after reading volumes of literature on autism from the local public library.

Assessment Data

Previous Assessment Data. Carlos' file contains results of three assessment procedures conducted by various professionals within 2 months prior to the current assessment. Scores from the Vineland Adaptive Behavior Scales, Classroom Edition (completed by Carlos' preschool teacher) indicated that Carlos has significant deficits in adaptive behavior, as evidenced by domain standard scores on the Vineland scales (based on a mean of 100 and standard deviation of 15) as follows: Communication 52, Daily Living Skills 62, Socialization 53, Motor Skills 63, Adaptive Behavior Composite 53, all of which are in the "low" adaptive level. A psychologist attempted to conduct an intellectual assessment of Carlos using the Stanford–Binet Intelligence Scale, fourth edition, but was unable to get Carlos to comply with the test tasks enough to render a valid score. However, using an informal observation and interaction procedure with various objects aimed at eliciting specific developmental skills, the psychologist provided a "very rough estimate" of Carlos' current intellectual functioning as being somewhere between 12 and 24 months, or at about 30% to 50% of his chronological age level of 44 months. An assessment report by a speech-language pathologist, who evaluated Carlos using the Developmental Communication Curriculum Inventory 1 month prior to the current evaluation, indicated that Carlos was functioning at the 0- to 12-month level in overall communication abilities, with no skills observed at the 18- to 36- and 30+-month levels. It was also noted that Carlos' receptive skills appeared to be greater than his expressive communication skills.

Behavior Rating Scales. Carlos was rated by the examiner using the Child Autism Rating Scale (CARS). The ratings on this 15-item scale were made at the end of the assessment session, after the examiner had observed in Carlos' preschool classroom for over 2 hours, and had taken the opportunity to interview Carlos' teacher and Carlos' mother in detail. The obtained score from the CARS was in a borderline region between the nonautistic level and the mild/moderate autism level. The total score was actually in the nonautistic range, but was within two points of being at the mild/moderate autism level.

Interview. Carlos' mother and teacher were interviewed at length regarding his developmental skills and behavior problems, using a combination of unstructured problem behavior identification and developmental history interviews. Extensive information was obtained during these interviews, but the key points from each interview are summarized as follows, with a breakdown of positive behavioral skills and devel-opmental-behavioral problems:

Interview with Carlos' Mother	Interview with Carlos' Teacher
Positive Behavioral Skills	*Positive Behavioral Skills*
Seems very aware of what is going on in the home	Seems very attached to his mother
Has "good" receptive language skills (up to 40 words)	Responds positively to two children
Seeks comfort when he is upset	Can match same-color blocks
Understands feelings of other family members	Is "mostly" toilet trained
	Gets a drink by himself
	Can feed himself
	Has improved in the last 5 months
Developmental-Behavioral Problems	*Developmental-Behavioral Problems*
Does not play appropriately with other children	Seldom makes eye contact
Constantly engages in imitation	Extremely noncompliant
Very noncompliant	Bangs head on floor when frustrated
Becomes upset when daily routine changes	Occasionally bites when frustrated
Very little expressive language	Uses almost no verbal language
Engages in severe tantrum behavior when upset	Engages in repetitive and stereotypic play with various objects

Behavioral Observations.   Carlos was observed for a period of approximately 2 hours in the preschool setting, during a variety of activities. Both interval recording and event recording observation methods were utilized. Carlos was observed to isolate himself socially and not seek out activities with peers, though he did smile at two different peers who approached him and talked to him, and smiled at the observer several times during the observation period. Carlos did appear to relate to other people as more than objects, and demonstrated a strong attachment to his mother when she arrived to pick him up at the end of the school day, by smiling and running toward her. Carlos produced various incomprehensible vocalizations throughout the observa-tion period (whining, babbling, etc.), but occasionally produced a totally articulate word at an appropriate time (e.g., "please"). He engaged in occasional self-stimulatory behavior, such as banging his head on the floor, pulling his pants down, and spitting water from the drinking fountain. It was noted that Carlos became very stimulated by certain objects that he selected and obviously preferred, such as a can of wooden sticks, which he constantly poured out and put back in the can. He was also observed engaging in some maladaptive behaviors such as trying to eat glue, shred paper, and attempting to put scissors in his mouth. During a 30-minute observation period using partial interval recording with 20-second intervals, Carlos was on-task during 14% of the intervals, while social comparison peers were on-task during 72% of the intervals.

Questions to Consider

1. Is the information from this screening sufficient to determine whether or not Carlos has Autistic Disorder or a related pervasive developmental disorder? If it is not sufficient, list other types and specific kinds of assessment data that would help provide more definitive information.

2. In terms of conducting a differential diagnosis (Autistic Disorder or another pervasive developmental disorder), which condition seems to be most appropriate,

based only on the information provided in this case study, and on the diagnostic criteria discussed in the section on pervasive developmental disorders. Note that a generic category referred to as Pervasive Developmental Disorder, Not Otherwise Specified, is also referenced in *DSM–IV* but not specifically discussed in this chapter.

3. Are there other dimensions or specific classification categories of disorders that should be considered as possibilities in Carlos' case? If so, list them and indicate what type of additional information would be needed to rule in or rule out these disorders.

4. Develop some basic intervention goals for Carlos, linking the assessment data provided in this case study to the intervention goals as directly as possible.

5. Is there any additional developmental history or medical information on Carlos that would be useful in answering questions 1 through 3? If so, what specific kinds of developmental history or medical information would be useful?

12

ASSESSMENT OF SOCIAL SKILLS AND PEER RELATIONSHIPS

Since about the 1970s, there has been a tremendous amount of interest and activity related to assessing social skills of children and adolescents, and in attempting to use these assessment data to develop and implement social skills training interventions (Merrell & Gimpel, 1998). School and clinical child psychologists, special educators, and professionals from related fields who work with children and adolescents will certainly encounter numerous assessment and intervention questions that require a sound knowledge of the overall construct of social skills, as well as effective methods of assessing these skills.

This chapter is designed to provide the reader with the prerequisite background knowledge needed to appropriately conceptualize various aspects of social skills of children and adolescents, conduct effective assessments, and use the obtained assessment information to develop sound intervention recommendations. The chapter begins with an overview of the broad construct of social competence, and some of three major areas that are hypothesized to comprise it. A new theoretical model for conceptualizing the relational components of social competence, social skills, and peer relationships is then proposed. Recent research regarding development of a classification taxonomy for child and adolescent social skills is discussed, as is the research base regarding the importance and long-term implications of social skills and peer relationships. Next, specific methods for assessing various aspects of social skills and peer relationships are presented, particularly as they relate to the five direct and objective assessment methods emphasized in this book. The chapter ends with a discussion of "best practices" in using assessment data to develop effective interventions.

SOCIAL COMPETENCE: A COMPLEX CONSTRUCT

The terms *social skills* and *social competence* are often used interchangeably, but in reality, they each indicate something that is somewhat similar but distinct from the other term. Most expert definitions regard social competence as a broader construct that is

social competence

actually superordinate to and inclusive of social skills (see Merrell & Gimpel, 1998, for a comprehensive review of theoretical definitions). Social competence has been conceptualized as a complex, multidimensional construct that consists of a variety of behavioral and cognitive characteristics, as well as various aspects of emotional adjustment, which are useful and necessary in developing adequate social relationships and obtaining desirable social outcomes. Social competence transcends the divisions of internalizing and externalizing behaviors, which are discussed at length in chapters 9 and 10. Interestingly, peer relationship problems and deficits in social skills have been shown to be a component of both the internalizing and externalizing domain (Merrell, 1993b; Merrell & Gimpel, 1998).

Gresham (1986) conceptualized the broad domain of social competence as being comprised of three more narrow subdomains: *adaptive behavior, social skills,* and *peer acceptance.* Gresham's model, though arguable, is very useful because of the delineation of social competence into distinct areas. These three component areas of social competence from Gresham's model are briefly discussed in the following sections.

3 domains of social compt.

Adaptive Behavior — *developmental + cultural contexts*

Perhaps the most widely cited definition of adaptive behavior during the past two decades is that it is "the effectiveness or degree with which the individual meets the standards of personal independence and social responsibility" (Grossman, 1983, p. 1). Adaptive behavior is assumed to be a developmental construct, in that expectations for independent and responsible behavior vary based on mental and chronological age (American Association on Mental Retardation, 1992; Reschly, 1990). It is also important to consider that adaptive behavior must be viewed within cultural and environmental contexts, given that expectations and demands for independence and responsibility also vary based on the specific culture or subculture in which the individual resides (Reschly, 1990).

Assessment of adaptive behavior is a critical aspect of the classification of developmental delays and mental retardation. The most recent definition of mental retardation from the American Association on Mental Retardation (AAMR) prominently includes the construct of adaptive behavior (or adaptive skills) (AAMR, 1992). In practice, the measurement of adaptive behavior includes assessing functional living skills, which tend to require a qualitatively different evaluation approach and are essential for individuals with pervasive intellectual disabilities and developmental disorders. Because these particular populations and assessment methods differ somewhat from those focused on in this book, this chapter does not cover adaptive behavior assessment per se, but will focus specifically on the other two aspects of social competence, namely, social skills and peer relationships. Readers desiring a more comprehensive treatment of assessing the broader construct of adaptive behavior are referred to several other excellent sources, including AAMR (1992), Kamphaus (1987), and Reschly (1990, 1991).

Social Skills

Social skills have been explained and defined in a number of ways, including cognitive, behavioral, and ecological definitions (Merrell et al., 1992). Certainly, there is no single or unitary definition of social skills that has been agreed on by most experts in the field. In fact, in a recent comprehensive review of theories and definitions of social

[handwritten top margin: social skills = specific behaviors that lead to desirable outcomes]

skills, Merrell and Gimpel (1998) found 15 different expert definitions! For the purposes of this chapter, a good working definition of social skills is that they are specific behaviors, which, when initiated, lead to desirable social outcomes for the person initiating them. From a behavioral standpoint, initiation of social skills increases the probability of reinforcement and decreases the probability of punishment or extinction based on a person's social behavior (Gresham & Reschly, 1987a). For children and adolescents, examples of behavioral classes representing social skills include academic and task-related competence, cooperation with peers, reinforcement of peers' behavior, and social initiation behaviors.

Peer Relationships

[handwritten: 3]

Although peer acceptance (referred to hereafter by a more generic label, *peer relationships*) was proposed by Gresham (1986) as the third overall component or domain of social competence, it is often considered to be a *result*, or *product*, of a person's social skills. This view of peer relationships is reasonable, given that social reputation and the quality of social relationships are in great measure a result of how effectively individuals interact socially with peers (Landau & Milich, 1990; Oden & Asher, 1977). Positive peer relationships are associated with peer acceptance, whereas negative peer relationships are linked with peer rejection.

[handwritten: + peer relat → acceptance]
[handwritten: − peer relat → rejection]

Another Way of Looking at Relationships Among Constructs

[handwritten left margin: hierarchy of constructs ↓ social compt, adap behav + peer accept.]

Gresham's (1986) model of social competence (also outlined in Gresham, 1981b, and Gresham & Reschly, 1987a) has been useful because it proposes a hierarchical structure for the interrelated constructs of social competence, adaptive behavior, and peer acceptance or peer relationships. This model provides a means of identifying component parts of a larger construct, each with unique and important contributions to the superordinate construct. However, as mentioned previously, the specific direction of relations in this model is arguable. Numerous studies conducted during the 1980s and 1990s have shed additional light on the relations among the constructs discussed in this section. Given the overall yield of research in this area, a different series of relations among the constructs of social competence, adaptive behavior, social skills, and peer relationships is more likely than what was proposed by Gresham and colleagues.

Perhaps the most significant difference of opinion in this area regards the hierarchical relation of social competence and adaptive behavior. Whereas Gresham proposed that social competence was the superordinate construct that subsumed adaptive behavior, it is proposed here that the opposite direction of relation is more appropriate and substantiated. In other words, adaptive behavior should be viewed as the overarching superordinate construct, of which social competence is one specific subordinate construct (along with other constructs such as communication competency, motor skills, etc.). This is a more modern view of adaptive behavior, a construct that has taken on significant importance in recent years. In fact, the most recent definition and discussion of mental retardation from the American Association on Mental Retardation (1992) views social competence or social functioning as one component part of the broader construct of adaptive behavior. This view is also supported through empirically derived factor structures of adaptive behavior assessment instruments such

[handwritten bottom margin: MR def - soc comp = one part of adapt. behav]

as the Scales of Independent Behavior (Bruininks, Woodcock, Weatherman, & Hill, 1984) and other adaptive behavior scales (Harrison, 1987).

Regarding the relation between social competence and social skills, this chapter concurs with the Gresham model, which is widely supported by researchers who focus their work in the area of children's social skills. That is, social competence is a broader superordinate construct that includes social skills in a subordinate position. This line of reasoning is illustrated clearly in a widely cited article by McFall (1982), who proposed that social competence is a *summary,* or *evaluative,* term based on conclusions or judgments regarding how adequately an individual performs social tasks. Social skills, on the other hand, are specific social behaviors a person must perform to be judged as competent on a given task. This operational definition of social skills was outlined earlier in the chapter.

As was pointed out earlier in this chapter, peer acceptance or peer relationships is a product or outcome of social skills rather than a separate component of adaptive behavior that is parallel with social skills. In essence, peer relationships are determined by the quality and quantity of a person's social skills. However, the relation between peer relationships and social skills is probably more complex than being reduced to a simple existence–outcome formula. There is good evidence that the relation between peer relationships and social skills is also somewhat *reciprocal* in nature, or that the two constructs mutually influence each other. In other words, although the existence or nonexistence of social skills will result in the outcome of good or poor peer relationships, the quality of an individual's peer relationships is also likely to influence the future development of social skills by enhancing or decreasing opportunities for future observation and modeling of social skills. *Peer relations + Soc. Skills = recipro-cal*

To recap this proposed model for understanding the relation among the four constructs that have been explored, adaptive behavior is viewed as the most broad and superordinate construct in the scheme. Social competence, an evaluative or summary term reflecting judgment regarding the overall quality of an individual's social performance, is a construct that is circumscribed within the broader construct of adaptive behavior. Social skills can be characterized as one of several important behavioral components that lead to social competence. Social skills, in turn, result in the quality of relationships individuals have with their peers. Therefore, peer relationships should be viewed as a product or outcome of social skills, as well as something that will reciprocally affect the development of social skills in the future. A graphic outline of this proposed model of relations among social constructs is presented in Fig. 12.1.

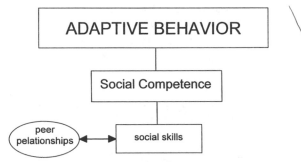

FIG. 12.1. Outline of a proposed theoretical model of the relations among the constructs of adaptive behavior, social competence, social skills, and peer relationships.

DIMENSIONS OF SOCIAL SKILLS

As research and clinical applications regarding children's social skills have increased in importance and volume during the past two decades, it is curious that relatively little work has been done related to identifying the specific underlying dimensions of social skills. Unlike the area of child psychopathology, where there have been numerous empirical efforts aimed at developing and improving classification taxonomies, there has been almost no attention paid to developing a parallel taxonomy for social skills of children and adolescents. Perhaps one of the obstacles to such efforts is that the fields of child psychiatry and psychology have traditionally been pathology oriented, or focused on understanding behavior in terms of a medical model of disease and dysfunction.

To counter this lack of attention to such a potentially important endeavor, Caldarella and Merrell (1997) sought to develop an empirical taxonomy of child and adolescent social skills by employing a similar methodology to that used by Quay (1986a) in developing his widely influential empirical taxonomy for child emotional and behavioral disorders discussed in some detail earlier in chapter 2. A brief overview of this social skills meta-analysis review is presented in this section. For more detail on the methodology or results of this investigation, the reader is referred to the full report.

Following an extensive literature search and study elimination process, a total of 21 studies that utilized multivariate approaches to classifying social skills with over 22,000 children and adolescents were included. The review and synthesis of these studies was accomplished by examining the name of each social skill factor derived in the studies, as well as the underlying behaviors subsumed by the factor (the approach used by Quay, 1986a). For example, items comprising a factor labeled "Peer Interaction" were examined to ensure that the majority of the items (at least 50%) were directly related to peers. If so, that factor would be grouped with other "peer-related" factors under a common dimension. The most common social skill dimensions, those identified as occurring in one third or more of the studies, were then identified. This method was used to eliminate outliers as well as to study specific findings. Using this methodology, five primary dimensions of child and adolescent social skills were identified. These dimensions are labeled and briefly described in Table 12.1.

Following the identification phase, the five dimensions presented in Table 12.1 were more closely examined to determine the most common social skills associated with each. This next step was accomplished by first listing the specific social skill components constituting each of the factors that comprised the dimension. For example, all of the items comprising the first Peer Relationships factor were listed. Individual items of the next Peer Relationships factor were then listed, with similar items being grouped together. This process was carried out for all five of the most common dimensions. Similar social skills were then grouped together to determine the principle behavioral characteristics (those occurring in one third or more of the studies) associated with each dimension. These principle social skills were then rank ordered (based on frequency) as they appear in Table 12.1.

The *Peer Relationships* dimension occurred in 11 (52.38%) of the studies. This dimension appears to be dominated by social skills reflecting children who are positive with their peers. Such skills as complimenting or praising others, offering help or assistance, and inviting others to play or interact appear to describe this dimension well. The *Self-Management* dimension also occurred in 11 studies. This dimension reflects a child who might be labeled by others as emotionally well adjusted. This dimension also reflects children or youth who are able to control their temper, follow rules and limits, compromise with others, and receive criticism well. The *Academic*

Social skill
Dimensions

TABLE 12.1
The Five Most Common Dimensions of Social Skills Developed
from a Review and Analysis by Caldarella and Merrell (1997)

Names of the Most Common Social Skill Dimensions (in descending order of frequency)	Frequency (number of studies)	Percentage of Studies
Peer Relationships	11	52.38%
Social interaction, prosocial, interpersonal, peer preferred social behavior, empathy, social participation, sociability-leadership, peer reinforcement, general, peer sociability		
Self-Management	11	52.38%
Self-control/social convention, social independence, social competence, social responsibility, rules, frustration tolerance		
Academic	10	47.62%
School adjustment, respect for social rules at school, task orientation, academic responsibility, classroom compliance, good student		
Compliance	8	38.09%
Social cooperation, competence, cooperation-compliance		
Assertion	7	33.33%
Assertive social skills, social initiation, social activator, gutsy		

Skills dimension occurred in 10 (47.62%) of the studies reviewed. This dimension is dominated by social skills reflecting children or youth who might be called an independent and productive worker by their teacher. Such skills as accomplishing tasks or assignments independently, completing individual seatwork/assignments, and carrying out teacher directions all appear to describe this dimension well. The *Compliance* dimension occurred in 8 (38.09%) of the studies reviewed. The picture that emerges here is children who essentially get along with others by following rules and expectations, appropriately using free time, and sharing things. Essentially, this dimension involves complying with appropriate requests made by others. The *Assertion* dimension occurred in 7 (33.33%) of the studies reviewed. This dimension is dominated by social skills that reflect a child or youth who might be called "outgoing" or "extroverted" by others. Such skills as initiating conversations with others, acknowledging compliments, and inviting others to interact all appear to describe this dimension well.

These five most common dimensions of child and adolescent social skills have a strong base of empirical support, being derived in more than one third of the studies reviewed, with two derived in over half the studies. To date, no other research has been located with such an extensive review of empirically derived social skill dimensions of children and adolescents. Indeed, this review could be said to be breaking new ground by applying the influential research method used by Quay (1986a), which combines aspects of both meta-analysis and qualitative review, to an area of critical importance, child and adolescent positive social behaviors.

Based on the frequency with which these dimensions of social skills have been identified over the past 20 years of research, practitioners and researchers should consider focusing on these areas for assessment and intervention. Many of the social skills subsumed by these dimensions have already been incorporated into validated assessment and intervention strategies (see Walker, Colvin, & Ramsey, 1995). What this study provides is further empirical support for the five essential social skills dimensions comprising the taxonomy. Gesten (1976) noted that competencies in clients must be identified and reinforced to maximize (treatment and research) outcomes. Perhaps this review and the resulting taxonomy will help to identify appropriate behaviors to reinforce, as well as to balance the scales between assessing for both positive and negative behaviors in children and adolescents.

IMPORTANCE OF SOCIAL SKILLS

A growing body of literature in the fields of child development, education, and psychology collectively points to the conclusion that the development of adequate social skills and peer relationships during childhood has important and far-reaching ramifications. It has been established that development of appropriate social skills is an important foundation for adequate peer relationships (Asher & Taylor, 1981). There is also evidence that childhood social skills and consequent peer relationships have a significant impact on academic success during the school years (Walker & Hops, 1976). In reviewing the literature on peer relationships, Hartup (1983) demonstrated that the ability to relate effectively to others provides an essential contribution to the progress and development of the child.

Given that adequate social skills and peer relationships are an important foundation for various types of success in life, it stands to reason that inadequate development in these areas is related to a variety of negative outcomes. A classic and frequently cited investigation by Cowen et al. (1973) involving an 11- to 13-year follow-up study of third-grade students provides convincing evidence that early peer relationship problems are strong predictors of mental health problems later in life. These researchers found that "peer judgment (using a negative peer nomination procedure) was, by far, the most sensitive predictor of later psychiatric difficulty" (p. 438). Other frequently cited studies have indicated that inadequate social skills and poor peer relationships during childhood may lead to a variety of other problems later in life, such as juvenile delinquency, school dropout, being fired from jobs, conduct-related discharge from military service, chronic unemployment and underemployment, and psychiatric hospitalizations (Loeber, 1985a; Parker & Asher, 1987; Roff, 1963; Roff & Sells, 1968; Roff, Sells, & Golden, 1972).

As the literature on the social, emotional, and behavioral characteristics of children with disabilities continues to grow, it has become increasingly clear that these children are at significantly heightened risk for developing social skills deficits and experiencing peer rejection (e.g., Merrell & Gimpel, 1998). Students identified as learning disabled have been found to experience high rates of social rejection by other children (Bryan, 1974; Cartledge, Frew, & Zacharias, 1985; Sater & French, 1989), to be rated by teachers as having poor interpersonal behavior (Gresham & Reschly, 1986), and to exhibit maladaptive social behaviors in instructional settings (Epstein, Cullinan, & Lloyd, 1986; McKinney & Feagans, 1984; McKinney, McClure, & Feagans, 1982). Students identified as mentally retarded have been found to exhibit deficits in adaptive-social competencies (Gresham & Reschly, 1987b), experience high rates of peer rejection (Gresham, 1981b), and receive inadequate amounts of social support (Park, Tappe, Carmeto, & Gaylord-Ross, 1990). Likewise, students identified as having behavior disorders have been found to be readily discriminated from nonhandicapped students by their maladaptive social-emotional behaviors (Merrell et al., 1992; Stumme, Gresham, & Scott, 1982; Vaughn, 1987), and experience significant rates of social rejection by other children (Hollinger, 1987). Therefore, clinicians who work with children with disabilities and other at-risk children should be especially aware of the social problems these children face, and keep up-to-date on appropriate methods of assessment of both positive and negative social behavior.

METHODS OF ASSESSING SOCIAL SKILLS

- Direct Behav obserV -Self report
-Sociometrics
- Interview

Each of the five major assessment methods covered within this book can be used in assessing social skills and peer relationships. By contrast, projective-expressive techniques, the sixth assessment method covered in this book, may provide some clues for hypothesis building regarding social skills and peer relationships of children, but also requires a tremendous amount of inference and follow-up with one of the five more direct methods of assessment. Direct behavioral observation and behavior rating scales have been used most frequently for assessing social skills and peer relationships in educational and clinical settings. Sociometric approaches have also been frequently employed in research on social skills and peer relationships, but are more limited in terms of day-to-day clinical use. Interview methods hold some promise for assessing social skills and peer relationships, but are most commonly used for other purposes. The use of self-reports in assessing social competence is a relatively new endeavor, but it does show some promise, based on what has been accomplished with the self-report component of the Social Skills Rating System. The use of each of these five assessment direct and objective methods in evaluating social competence is discussed in this section.

Direct Behavioral Observation

Many of the general behavioral observation techniques presented in chapter 3 are highly relevant for assessing social skills and peer relationships. In discussing behavioral observation as a method of assessing social skills, Elliott and Gresham (1987) stated that "analyzing children's behavior in natural settings . . . is the most ecologically valid method of assessing children's social skills" (p. 96). For the clinician or investigator who is serious about conducting valid assessments of child and adolescent social behaviors, mastering the basic methods of observational measurement from chapter 3 is a must.

Several other sources have provided reviews of methods for assessing child and adolescent social behavior through direct behavioral observation (e.g., Asher & Hymel, 1981; Gresham, 1981a; Hops & Greenwood, 1981), but for this chapter, it is useful to look at three examples of how behavioral observation techniques have been used for this purpose in recent published investigations. The first example is an analogue observation system, whereas the second and third examples are both interval-based coding systems for use in naturalistic settings. *Examples of Beh. Obs. techniques in practice:*

(BAT)

Behavioral Assertiveness Test. Originally developed by Eisler, Hersen, and Miller (1973) for use in assessing assertiveness behavior with adults and adolescents, the Behavioral Assertiveness Test (BAT) was later revised by Bornstein, A. S. Bellack, and Herson (1977) for use with children. This observation system has been successfully used in intervention studies where social skills training interventions were implemented with both aggressive and withdrawn children. The BAT utilizes an analogue situation that requires children to role-play in as many as 48 situations that elicit both assertive and nonassertive responses. The analogue situations are videotaped for later coding by observers. The BAT coding system includes 10 targeted behavioral categories,

analogue role plays # situations req assert + nonassert

plus an overall social skills rating. Several clinical outcomes studies (e.g., Bornstein et al., 1977; Bornstein, A. S. Bellack, & Herson, 1980) have demonstrated that the BAT has strong construct validity and robust psychometric properties. Although the BAT was originally designed for use in either inpatient or outpatient clinical settings, it could also be used in school-based assessment, although it is not designed for naturalistic observation in the classroom. The BAT should probably be viewed as more of a research tool than a clinical instrument for everyday use. Nevertheless, it is highly adaptable for use with various target problems, populations, and age groups (e.g., Garrison & Jenkins, 1986; Ollendick, Meador, & Villanis, 1986). Thus, the BAT appears to be widely adaptable and potentially useful for clinical assessment in the hands of an astute practitioner. *BAT is best for RESEARCH (vs. everyday use)*

Peer Social Behavior Code. The Peer Social Behavior Code is the third and final stage or gate of Walker and Severson's (1992) Systematic Screening for Behavior Disorders (SSBD), the multiple gating screening system for use with children in grades 1 through 6 that was discussed in chapter 2. Because the assessment method conducted at each successive gate results in a narrowing down of the population using increasingly intensive procedures, by the time the population has been narrowed following the direct observational process (the third gate), it should consist of children who are truly at-risk for social behavior problems, including social skills deficits. The Peer Social Behavior Code observation system consists of a series of 10-second intervals. The actual number of intervals used in an observation is variable depending on the situation. The recording forms each include spaces for 40 different intervals. Observations are always conducted during free-play situations (e.g., on recess), and a typical observation period might last 15 minutes.

Five different recording categories are included in the Peer Social Behavior Code: Social Engagement (SE), Participation (P), Parallel Play (PLP), Alone (A), and No Codeable Response (N). Behavior in the first two categories may be coded as either positive (+) or negative (−). Behavior in the PLP and A categories is coded by simply checking the appropriate box. No Codeable Response is coded with a check when the child is out of view, and with a dot when the child is interacting with an adult rather than a peer. Following the observation, the observational data is transferred from the recording forms (see Fig. 12.2) to an observational summary sheet (see Fig. 12.3). The number of intervals recorded are entered for each category, and then the percentage of time spent for each category is calculated by dividing the total number of intervals in the session into the intervals recorded under different categories and multiplying by 100. The SSBD manual contains thorough directions for interpreting Peer Social Behavior Code observation data using the normative tables provided. Extensive research went into the development of the Peer Social Behavior Code, and the validity evidence and technical properties reported in the manual and in other sources is impressive. An excellent observer training tape is provided as part of the SSBD kit, which also includes an audio timing tape for accurately using the 10-second intervals. The Peer Social Behavior is an exemplary interval-based coding procedure for direct observation of child social behavior, and may also serve as a model for constructing similar coding systems for more specific purposes.

Target/Peer Interaction Code. Several related studies of the development of anti-social behavior in boys (e.g., Shinn, Ramsey, Walker, Steiber, & O'Neil, 1987; Walker, Shinn, O'Neil, & Ramsey, 1987; Walker, Steiber, & O'Neil, 1990; Walker, Steiber, Ramsey, & O'Neil, 1993) used a variety of assessment methods, including direct

Systematic Screening for Behavior Disorders
PEER SOCIAL BEHAVIOR RECORDING FORM

Student Name _____ Teacher Name _____

School _____ Grade _____ Observer _____

Reliability Observer _____ Date _____ Time Start _____

Time Stop _____ Length of Session _____

Interval Number	+ - SE	+ - P	✓ PLP	✓ A	• ✓ N	Interval Number	+ - SE	+ - P	✓ PLP	✓ A	• ✓ N
0-1						21					
2						22					
3						23					
4						24					
5						25					
6						26					
7						27					
8						28					
9						29					
10						30					
11						31					
12						32					
13						33					
14						34					
15						35					
16						36					
17						37					
18						38					
19						39					
20						40					

FIG. 12.2. Peer Social Behavior Recording Form. From *Systematic Screening for Behavior Disorders* (2nd. ed.), by H. M. Walker & H. H. Severson, 1992, Longmont, CO: Sopris West. Copyright © 1992 by Sopris West. Reprinted with permission.

observation, to assess both positive and negative social behaviors. Of specific interest for this chapter is the use of an observational code for recording the social behavior of children in playground settings, the Target/Peer Interaction Code (TPIC). This direct observation coding system was developed by the researchers in these studies to help answer specific research questions. Because it is empirically sound and practical, and because it was developed for use in a commonly accessible naturalistic setting (school playgrounds), it may be of interest to both researchers and clinicians.

The TPIC requires coding of both the target subject and interacting peers social behaviors during continuous 10-second intervals. Although a complete description of the TPIC codes is beyond the scope of this chapter, certain aspects of the coding structure are of unique interest for assessing social skills and peer relationships. One of the

Systematic Screening for Behavior Disorders
PEER SOCIAL BEHAVIOR
OBSERVATION SUMMARY SHEET

Student Name _____

School _____ Grade _____

Dates Observed _____ and _____

Session #1   Session #2

	Number of Intervals*	Observation #1**	Number of Intervals*	Observation #2**	Average of 1 and 2
1. Social Engagement (SE)	_____	_____%	_____	_____%	_____%
2. Participation (P)	_____	_____%	_____	_____%	_____%
3. Parallel Play (PLP)	_____	_____%	_____	_____%	_____%
4. Alone (A)	_____	_____%	_____	_____%	_____%
5. No Codeable Response (N)	_____	_____%	_____	_____%	_____%
6. Social Interaction (SI)	_____	_____%	_____	_____%	_____%
7. Negative Interaction (NI)	_____	_____%	_____	_____%	_____%
8. Positive Interaction (PI)	_____	_____%	_____	_____%	_____%
9. Total Positive Behavior	_____	_____%	_____	_____%	_____%
10. Total Negative Behavior	_____	_____%	_____	_____%	_____%

* Enter the number of intervals recorded for each category.

** Enter the percentage of time spent for each category by dividing the total number of intervals that you observed during the observation session into the intervals recorded under different categories and multiplying by 100.

FIG. 12.3. Peer Social Behavior Observation Summary Sheet. From *Systematic Screening for Behavior Disorders* (2nd. ed.), by H. M. Walker & H. H. Severson, 1992, Longmont, CO: Sopris West. Copyright © 1992 by Sopris West. Reprinted with permission.

observational areas is *target subject interactive behavior,* which includes the behavioral classes of verbal behavior and physical contact. Within these response classes, behaviors are recorded as being positive or negative, and initiated or noninitiated. Another observational category of interest is *peer interactive behavior,* which includes verbal and physical interactive behavior directed at the target child by their peers, which is coded in much the same way as was described in the previous category of target subject interactive behavior. Additionally, under the peer interactive behavior category, target subjects' responses to the peer behaviors are coded according to whether they ignored, complied with, or appropriately resisted negative requests from peers.

Although each of the four studies cited in this section on the TPIC varied somewhat in overall methodology and findings, some generalized results were found to be consistent. Direct observations conducted using the TPIC were extremely effective at discriminating antisocial subjects and at-risk and normal control subjects, and certain components of the observational data were found to correlate significantly with teacher ratings of social skills. Interestingly, classroom observations of academic engaged time were also found to correlate significantly with teacher ratings of social competence, in some cases to a higher extent than the playground social-behavioral observations did.

Academic Engaged time and Teach. ratings of social competence

Comments on Direct Observation of Child Social Behavior. These examples of using the Behavioral Assertiveness Test, Peer Social Behavior Code, and Target Peer Interaction Code illustrate how direct behavioral observation can be used in effectively assessing social skills and peer relationships of children and adolescents. Such observations may be effectively conducted in both naturalistic and analogue settings. Obviously, many variations are possible in deciding which social behaviors to observe and which observational methods to employ. In using behavioral observation techniques to assess social skills and peer relationships, two specific observational validity issues seem to be particularly important—defining the observation domain and obtaining social comparison data (see chap. 3 for more details). In defining which social behaviors to observe and how to code them, clinicians and investigators would do well to base their targeted behaviors and codes on what is known about the domains of social skills and peer relationships, and to define each class of behavior within the domains somewhat narrowly, to increase the specificity of the observation. Obtaining social comparison data is especially important for observations within these domains, because it allows the observer to make inferences about whether or not the observed child's social skills and peer relationships are effective or deficient.

Behavior Rating Scales

Until the mid-1980s, the vast majority of behavior rating scales were developed to either be omnibus measures of problem behavior, or to assess specific dimensions of problem behavior, such as hyperactivity. Very few, if any, widely available rating scales were specifically designed for assessing children's social skills. Within the past several years there has been a strong surge of interest in school-based assessment of social skills, and providing training to children with social skills deficits. This increased interest has stimulated the development of several social skills rating scales that have good standardization characteristics and psychometric properties, and that are commercially available. Three of these rating scales or systems are detailed here. All three instruments meet the criteria of having large, nationwide standardization samples, good psychometric properties, and being readily available (i.e., commercially produced and marketed). Additionally, the Preschool and Kindergarten Behavior Scales (PKBS; Merrell, 1994b), a rating scale designed specifically for use with the early childhood/preschool population of youngsters, is reviewed in chapter 13 (Assessing Young Children).

Walker–McConnell Scales of Social Competence and School Adjustment. The Walker–McConnell Scales of Social Competence and School Adjustment (SSCSA; Walker & McConnell, 1995a, 1995b) are social skills rating scales for teachers and other school-based professionals. Two versions of the scale are available: an elementary version for use with students in grades K through 6, and an adolescent version for use with students in grades 7 through 12. The elementary version contains 43 positively worded items that reflect adaptive social-behavioral competencies within the school environment. The items are rated using a 5-point scale ranging from 1 = "never occurs" to 5 = "frequently occurs." The scale yields standard scores on three subscales (M = 10, SD = 3) as well as a total score (M = 100, SD = 15), which is a composite of the three subscales. Subscale 1 (Teacher-Preferred Social Behavior) includes 16 items that measure peer-related social behaviors that are highly valued by teachers and reflect their concerns for empathy, sensitivity, self-restraint, and cooperative, socially mature peer relationships (e.g., "Is considerate of the feelings of others," and "Is sensitive to the needs of others"). Subscale 2 (Peer-Preferred Social Behavior) includes 17 items that measure peer-related social behaviors highly valued by other children, and reflect peer values that involve social relationships, dynamics, and skills in free-play settings (e.g., "Spends recess and free time interacting with peers," and "Invites peers to play or share activities"). Subscale 3 (School Adjustment Behavior) includes 10 items reflecting social-behavior competencies that are especially important in academic instructional settings, such as having good work and study habits, following academic instructions, and behaving in ways conducive to classroom management (e.g., "Attends to assigned tasks," and "Displays independent study skills").

The adolescent version of the scale is very similar to the elementary version, in that it was designed as an upward extension of it. The adolescent version includes the 43 items from the elementary version (with nine of the scale items having been revised to better reflect adolescent behavioral content) plus an additional 10 items designed to measure *self-related* social adjustment based on content from an adolescent social skills training curriculum (Walker, Todis, Holmes, & Horton, 1988). The factor structure of the adolescent version includes the same three factors found on the elementary version, plus a fourth subscale containing six items that is labeled as the Empathy subscale. This fourth factor includes items designed to measure sensitivity and awareness in peer relationships, such as "Listens while others are speaking," and "Is considerate of the feelings of others." The adolescent version of the scale uses the same rating format and scoring system as the elementary version, and the four subscale scores are summed into a total score.

Extensive information on the standardization data and psychometric properties of the two versions of the SSCSA are reported in the scale manual. The scales were standardized on groups of approximately 2,000 students representing all four U.S. geographical regions. Studies undertaken during the development of the scales that are cited in the scale manual indicate adequate to excellent psychometric properties.

Reliability of the scales was established using test–retest (e.g., .88 to .92 correlations over a 3-week period with 323 subjects), internal consistency (e.g., alpha coefficients ranging from .95 to .97), and interrater (e.g., a .53 correlation between teachers' and aides' ratings on the total score in a day treatment facility) procedures. Validity of the scales was assessed using a variety of procedures. Sensitivity of the scales to theory-based group differences was established in studies that found the SSCSA to differentiate among groups of students who would be expected to differ behaviorally (behavior disordered and normal, antisocial and normal, behaviorally at-risk and normal, and those with and without learning problems). Criterion-related validity was demonstrated by finding significant correlations between the SSCSA and a number of criterion variables, including other rating scales, sociometric ratings, academic achievement measures, and a systematic behavioral screening procedure. Construct validity of the scales were demonstrated by, among other procedures, finding strong correlations between evaluative comments of subjects by their peers and teacher ratings on the scales, and by finding low social skills ratings to be strongly associated with the emergence of antisocial behavior in a longitudinal study of at-risk boys (Walker et al., 1987; Walker, Steiber, & O'Neil, 1990; Walker et al., 1993).

A number of other psychometric validation studies are reported in the test manuals that substantiate the reliability and validity of the scales. Subsequent investigations have found the SSCSA to correlate highly with other behavioral rating scales (Merrell, 1989b) and to accurately discriminate groups of students referred for learning problems from average students (Merrell et al., 1992; Merrell & Shinn, 1990). The six-item

Empathy subscale from the adolescent version of the SSCSA has been found to discriminate between a group of antisocial subjects with a record of arrests, and an at-risk control group (Walker, Steiber, & Eisert, 1991). The factor structure of the SSCSA scales has been shown to be robust.

Both versions of the SSCSA are brief, easy to use, and contain items that are highly relevant for assessing social skills in educational settings. The research base behind the scales is exemplary. Because neither version of the SSCSA was designed to measure problem behaviors, these instruments should be supplemented with an appropriate problem behavior assessment if warranted by the referral issues.

The measure is not designed to measure problem behaviors

School Social Behavior Scales. The School Social Behavior Scales (SSBS; Merrell, 1993a) is a school-based social behavior rating scale for use by teachers and other school personnel in assessing social competence and antisocial problem behaviors of students in grades K through 12. It includes two separate scales (presented in Figs. 12.4 and 12.5, respectively) with a total of 65 items that describe both positive and negative social behaviors that commonly occur in educational settings. Items are rated using a 5-point scale that ranges from 1 = "never" to 5 = "frequently." Each of the two scales of the SSBS yields a total score using a raw-to-standard-score conversion with a mean of 100 and standard deviation of 15. The two scales each have three subscales, with scores reported as four different *Social Functioning Levels*, including "High Functioning," "Average," "Moderate Problem," and "Significant Problem."

Scales + sub scales

Scale A, Social Competence, includes 32 items that describe adaptive, prosocial behavioral competencies as they commonly occur in educational settings. Subscale A1 (Interpersonal Skills) includes 14 items measuring social skills that are important in establishing positive relationships with and gaining social acceptance from peers (e.g., "Offers help to other students when needed," and "Interacts with a wide variety of peers"). Subscale A2 (Self-Management Skills) includes 10 items measuring social skills relating to self-restraint, cooperation, and compliance with the demands of school rules and expectations (e.g., "Responds appropriately when corrected by teacher," and "Shows self-restraint"). Subscale A3 (Academic Skills) consists of eight items relating to competent performance and engagement on academic tasks (e.g., "Completes individual seatwork without being prompted," and "Completes assigned activities on time").

A = comp
B = Anti-social

Scale B, Antisocial Behavior, includes 33 items that describe problematic behaviors that are either other-directed in nature, or are likely to lead to negative social consequences such as peer rejection or strained relationships with the teacher. Subscale B1 (Hostile-Irritable) consists of 14 items that describe behaviors considered to be self-centered, annoying, and likely to lead to peer rejection (e.g., "Will not share with other students," and "Argues and quarrels with other students"). Subscale B2 (Anti-social-Aggressive) consists of 10 behavioral descriptors relating to overt violation of school rules and intimidation or harm to others (e.g., "Gets into fights," and "Takes things that are not his/hers"). Subscale B3 (Disruptive-Demanding) includes 9 items that reflect behaviors likely to disrupt ongoing school activities and place excessive and inappropriate demands on others (e.g., "Is overly demanding of teacher's attention," and "Is difficult to control").

A number of studies and procedures are reported in the SSBS manual and subsequent published studies concerning the psychometric properties and validity of the instrument. The scales were standardized on a group of 1,856 K–12 students from the United States, with each of the four U.S. geographical regions represented in the standardization process. The percentage of special education students in various classification

Scale A
Social Competence

	Never	Sometimes		Frequently	Scoring Key		
1. Cooperates with other students in a variety of situations	1	2	3	4	5		
2. Appropriately transitions between classroom activities	1	2	3	4	5		
3. Completes individual seatwork without being prompted	1	2	3	4	5		
4. Offers help to other students when needed	1	2	3	4	5		
5. Effectively participates in group discussions and activities	1	2	3	4	5		
6. Understands other students' problems and needs	1	2	3	4	5		
7. Remains calm when problems arise	1	2	3	4	5		
8. Listens to and carries out directions from teacher	1	2	3	4	5		
9. Invites other students to participate in activities	1	2	3	4	5		
10. Asks for clarification of instructions in an appropriate manner	1	2	3	4	5		
11. Has skills or abilities that are admired by peers	1	2	3	4	5		
12. Is accepting of other students	1	2	3	4	5		
13. Accomplishes assignments and other tasks independently	1	2	3	4	5		
14. Completes assigned activities on time	1	2	3	4	5		
15. Will compromise with peers when appropriate	1	2	3	4	5		
16. Follows classroom rules	1	2	3	4	5		
17. Behaves appropriately in a variety of school settings	1	2	3	4	5		
18. Appropriately asks for assistance as needed	1	2	3	4	5		
19. Interacts with a wide variety of peers	1	2	3	4	5		
20. Produces work of acceptable quality for his/her ability level	1	2	3	4	5		
21. Is skillful at initiating or joining conversations with peers	1	2	3	4	5		
22. Is sensitive to feelings of other students	1	2	3	4	5		
23. Responds appropriately when corrected by teacher	1	2	3	4	5		
24. Controls temper when angry	1	2	3	4	5		
25. Appropriately enters ongoing activities with peers	1	2	3	4	5		
26. Has good leadership skills	1	2	3	4	5		
27. Adjusts to different behavioral expectations across school settings	1	2	3	4	5		
28. Compliments others' attributes or accomplishments	1	2	3	4	5		
29. Is appropriately assertive when he/she needs to be	1	2	3	4	5		
30. Is sought out by peers to join activities	1	2	3	4	5		
31. Shows self-restraint	1	2	3	4	5		
32. Is "looked up to" or respected by peers	1	2	3	4	5		
					Totals		
					A1	A2	A3

2

FIG. 12.4. Scale A (social competence) of the School Social Behavior Scales. From *School Social Behavior Scales*, by K. W. Merrell, 1993, Austin, TX: PRO-ED. Copyright © 1993 by PRO-ED. Reprinted with permission.

SSBS

Scale B
Antisocial Behavior

		Never		Sometimes		Frequently	Scoring Key B1	B2	B3
1.	Blames other students for problems	1	2	3	4	5			
2.	Takes things that are not his/hers	1	2	3	4	5			
3.	Defies teacher or other school personnel	1	2	3	4	5			
4.	Cheats on schoolwork or in games	1	2	3	4	5			
5.	Gets into fights	1	2	3	4	5			
6.	Lies to the teacher or other school personnel	1	2	3	4	5			
7.	Teases and makes fun of other students	1	2	3	4	5			
8.	Is disrespectful or "sassy"	1	2	3	4	5			
9.	Is easily provoked; has a short fuse	1	2	3	4	5			
10.	Ignores teacher or other school personnel	1	2	3	4	5			
11.	Acts as if he/she is better than others	1	2	3	4	5			
12.	Destroys or damages school property	1	2	3	4	5			
13.	Will not share with other students	1	2	3	4	5			
14.	Has temper outbursts or tantrums	1	2	3	4	5			
15.	Disregards feelings and needs of other students	1	2	3	4	5			
16.	Is overly demanding of teacher's attention	1	2	3	4	5			
17.	Threatens other students; is verbally aggressive	1	2	3	4	5			
18.	Swears or uses obscene language	1	2	3	4	5			
19.	Is physically aggressive	1	2	3	4	5			
20.	Insults peers	1	2	3	4	5			
21.	Whines and complains	1	2	3	4	5			
22.	Argues and quarrels with peers	1	2	3	4	5			
23.	Is difficult to control	1	2	3	4	5			
24.	Bothers and annoys other students	1	2	3	4	5			
25.	Gets in trouble at school	1	2	3	4	5			
26.	Disrupts ongoing activities	1	2	3	4	5			
27.	Is boastful; brags	1	2	3	4	5			
28.	Cannot be depended on	1	2	3	4	5			
29.	Is cruel to other students	1	2	3	4	5			
30.	Acts impulsively or without thinking	1	2	3	4	5			
31.	Unproductive; achieves very little	1	2	3	4	5			
32.	Is easily irritated	1	2	3	4	5			
33.	Demands help from other students	1	2	3	4	5			
						Totals			
							B1	B2	B3

3

FIG. 12.5. Scale B (antisocial behavior) of the School Social Behavior Scales. From *School Social Behavior Scales*, by K. W. Merrell, 1993, Austin, TX: PRO-ED. Copyright © 1993 by PRO-ED. Reprinted with permission.

categories in the standardization group very closely approximates the national percentages of these figures. Various reliability procedures reported in the SSBS manual indicate the scales have good to excellent stability and consistency. Internal consistency and split-half reliability coefficients range from .91 to .98. Test–retest reliability at 3-week intervals is reported at .76 to .83 for the Social Competence scores, and .60 to .73 for the Antisocial Behavior scores. Interrater reliability between resource room teachers and paraprofessional aides ranges from .72 to .83 for the Social Competence scores, and .53 to .71 for the Antisocial Behavior scores.

Validity of the scales has been demonstrated in several ways. Moderate to high correlations between the SSBS and five other behavior rating scales (including the 39-item version of the Child Behavior Checklist Conners Teacher Rating Scale, the Teacher Report Form, the Waksman Social Skills Rating Scale, and the adolescent version of the Walker–McConnell Scale of Social Competence and School Adjustment) indicates that the scale has strong convergent and discriminant construct validity (Emerson, Crowley, & Merrell, 1994). Other findings indicate the scales can adequately discriminate between gifted and nongifted children (Merrell & Gill, 1994), students with disabilities and regular education students (Merrell, 1993b; Merrell, Sanders, & Popinga, 1993), and between behavior disordered and other special education students (Merrell, 1992). The factor structure of the two scales is strong, with all items having a factor loading into their respective subscale of .40 or greater, and no items being duplicated across subscales (Merrell, 1993b).

The SSBS is a practical and easy-to-use school-based rating scale that provides norm-referenced data on both positive social skills and antisocial problem behavior. It has satisfactory to good psychometric properties, is easy to use, and the items and structure are highly relevant to the types of behavioral issues encountered by school-based professionals. The SSBS has been positively reviewed in the professional literature (Demaray et al., 1995; Kreisler, Mangione, & Landau, 1997). It should be noted that the Antisocial Behavior scale of the SSBS is designed specifically to measure behavior problems that are directly social in nature, or that would have an immediate impact on strained relationships with peers and teachers. The scale was not designed to measure overcontrolled or internalizing behavior problems such as those associated with depression and anxiety, nor was it designed to measure behavior problems associated with attention deficit hyperactivity disorder. If these type of problem behaviors are a significant issue on an assessment case, the assessment should be bolstered by the addition of an appropriate measure designed specifically for these behaviors.

Social Skills Rating System—Parent and Teacher Forms. The Social Skills Rating System (SSRS; Gresham & Elliott, 1990) is a multicomponent social skills rating system focusing on behaviors that affect parent–child relationships, teacher–student relationships, and peer acceptance. The system includes separate rating scales for teachers and parents, as well as a self-report form for students, which is described later in this chapter. Each component of the system can be used alone or in conjunction with the other forms. Separate instruments and norms are provided for each of three developmental groups, which include preschool level (age 3–5), elementary level (grades K–6), and secondary level (grades 7–12). Because there is considerable overlap among the different rating forms of the SSRS, an overview of only the elementary level teacher rating form is provided in this chapter as an example (the preschool forms are reviewed in chap. 13).

The elementary level teacher rating form of the SSRS consists of 57 items divided over three scales: Social Skills, Problem Behaviors, and Academic Competence. For

Social Skills and Problem Behaviors items, teachers respond to descriptions using a 3-point response format based on how often a given behavior occurs (0 = never, 1 = sometimes, and 2 = very often). On the Social Skills items, teachers are also asked to rate how important a skill is (on a 3-point scale) to success in the classroom. The importance rating is not used to calculate ratings for each scale but is used for planning interventions. On the Academic Competence scale, teachers rate students as compared to other students on a 5-point scale. Scale raw scores are converted to standard scores ($M = 100$, $SD = 15$) and percentile ranks. Subscale raw scores are converted to estimates of functional ability called *Behavior Levels*.

The Social Skills scale consists of 30 items used to rate social skills in the areas of teacher and peer relationships. This scale contains three subscales, including Cooperation, Assertion, and Self-Control. The Cooperation subscale identifies compliance behaviors that are important for success in classrooms (e.g., "Finishes class assignments on time" and "Uses time appropriately while waiting for help"). The Assertion subscale includes initiating behaviors that involve making and maintaining friendships and responding to actions of others (e.g., "Invites others to join in activities" and "Appropriately questions rules that may be unfair"). The Self-Control subscale includes responses that occur in conflict situations like turn-taking and peer criticism (e.g., "Cooperates with peers without prompting" and "Responds appropriately to teasing by peers").

The Problem Behaviors scale consists of 18 items that reflect behaviors that might interfere with social skills performance. The items are divided into three subscales, including Externalizing Problems, Internalizing Problems, and Hyperactivity. The Externalizing Problems subscale items reflect inappropriate behaviors that indicate verbal and physical aggression toward others and a lack of temper control (e.g., "Threatens or bullies others" and "Has temper tantrums"). The subscale Internalizing Problems includes behaviors that indicate anxiety, sadness, and poor self-esteem (e.g., "Shows anxiety about being with a group of children" and "Likes to be alone"). The Hyperactivity subscale includes activities that involve excessive movement and impulsive actions (e.g., "Disturbs ongoing activities" and "Acts impulsively").

The third scale, Academic Competence, includes nine items that reflect academic functioning, such as performance in specific academic areas, student's motivation level, general cognitive functioning, and parental support (e.g., "In terms of grade level expectations, this child's skills in reading are:" and "The child's overall motivation to succeed academically is:"). Behavior is rated on a 5-point scale that corresponds to percentages, ranging from 1 = lowest 10% to 5 = highest 10%.

The SSRS was standardized on a national sample of more than 4,000 children representing all four U.S. geographical regions. The demographic information is difficult to interpret because the manual does not provide a clear normative breakdown based on the different test forms. However, given the overall large number of subjects who were rated in the SSRS national standardization, it is assumed that the norms for each rating form in the system at the elementary and secondary levels were developed using a sufficient number of cases.

The overall psychometric properties obtained during scale development ranged from adequate to excellent. For the teacher scale, reliability was measured using internal consistency, (i.e., alpha coefficients ranged from .74 to .95), interrater, and test–retest (i.e., .75 to .93 correlations across the three scales) procedures. Criterion-related and construct validity were established by finding significant correlations between the SSRS and other rating scales. Subscale dimensions were determined through factor analyses of each scale. Items that met a criterion of a .30 or greater factor loading were considered to load on a given factor.

The SSRS has the distinct strength of consisting of an integrated system of instruments for use by teachers, parents, and students, which is its major advantage (Demaray et al., 1995). It is the only rating scale system out of the three reviewed in this chapter that, in addition to providing a school-based assessment, includes a parent rating form for assessing social skills. The manual is very well written, and the rating instruments are easily understood and used. The sections of the instruments that measure social skills are very comprehensive and useful. The sections measuring problem behaviors and academic competence are quite brief, and should be considered as short screening sections to be used in conjunction with more appropriate measures of behavioral/emotional problems, when indicated.

SSRS is the only that includes parent rating scale!

Interviewing Techniques

By their very nature, social skills and peer relationships are difficult at best to assess through interviewing techniques. The essence of these constructs are the behavioral skills a child or adolescent uses to initiate and maintain social communication, and the quality and nature of their resulting relationships with peers. Thus, in attempting to obtain high-quality information about a client's social skills or peer relationships within the context of an interview, the clinician is in the position of having to rely on subjective and difficult-to-verify reports from the child or adolescent clients, or on interview information obtained from parents or other informants. Elliott and Gresham (1987) noted that although behavioral interviews may be the most frequently used assessment method in the initial stages of intervention, they have not been investigated systematically as a social skills assessment technique.

At the present time, there are no widely available structured or semistructured interview schedules that have been developed primarily for the assessment of social skills and peer relationships. Accordingly, the use of less structured techniques is the only alternative for those wishing to assess social skills and peer relationships through the medium of an interview. Although this method may not be as desirable or direct as behavior rating scales or sociometric approaches, a good clinician may still find it useful in obtaining information on a client's social skills and peer relationships.

Within the context of interviewing a child or adolescent client, there are several points and techniques that will facilitate the process of obtaining good data on the client's social skills or peer relationships. One of the first points to consider is that when children are experiencing strained peer relationships or rejection, their report may be colored by lack of insight, defensiveness, or hurt. The younger the subjects, the more likely it is that the interview information may be influenced by these factors. As Boggs and Eyberg (1990) noted, children may not accurately or completely describe the events in their environment due to limited verbal skills or compliance with self-censoring rules they have learned. Clinicians who are experienced in interviewing children known to be experiencing severe rejection by peers often find that when the subject is asked to report on the amount and quality of their peer relationships, most will report having several friends, getting along with them well, and when asked to "name names" will even provide a detailed list of their "best friends." Clinicians conducting interviews in this manner need to use caution in corroborating the client's report with more objective data, and are advised to conduct the interview in a structured, detailed manner, in order to increase the objectivity of the results.

when interviewing children about relations.

they'll often list "best friends"

The use of role playing within a child or adolescent interview, when combined with a careful observation of the client's behavior, can provide some potentially useful information on their level of social skills. Given a carefully structured analogue situation, the clinician may be able to obtain a direct observation within the interview session of such important social skills as eye contact, entering into a conversation, dealing with peer pressure or harassment, requesting help, and giving or receiving a compliment. The process of social skills observation during role playing is relatively easy—the interviewer simply needs to set up the format and expectations, and then observes the client functioning within their designated role. For example, the clinician might say something like this: "Let's pretend that I am a kid at your school who you might want to become friends with. I am going to act like I am sitting down in the cafeteria eating my lunch, and I want you to come up to me and start talking with me about anything you want. Okay? Let's give it a try now." Engaging in a role-playing situation such as this may alert the interviewer to any potential social skills deficits the children or adolescent clients have that may be negatively affecting their peer relationships. The type of information obtained through this process not only can provide good assessment data, but can be helpful in establishing an appropriate intervention following the assessment. Behavioral role-playing techniques such as the example just provided may be considered to be a merger between interviewing and direct behavioral observation, because they use some traditional components of each method. Gresham (1986) noted that behavioral role-playing interview techniques have several advantages for assessment, particularly when the interview setting is tightly controlled and simulated to be similar to the natural environment in which the child's normal social interactions occur. In this regard, it is critical to consider that behavioral generalization and meaningful results are more likely to occur if the role-playing situation is constructed to parallel the real environment (Stokes & Baer, 1977).

When conducting an interview with a parent of a child or adolescent client, useful social skills and peer relationship information may be obtained by carefully structuring the interview questions, and by providing the parent with specific guidelines on how to respond to questions. Remember that the behavior of the interviewer may have a significant impact on the responses of the client during the interview (Gross, 1984). Because the goal of the interview in this instance is to obtain specific information on the social skills and peer relationships of the child, it will be helpful for the interviewer to provide specific prompts to the parent to increase the quality of the interview data. The following scenario illustrates how an interviewer can maximize the quality of the information they obtain by carefully structuring questions and prompts:

Interviewer: Tell me about how Jamie gets along with other children.
Parent: Not very well.
Interviewer: Can you tell me some more about that?
Parent: Jamie doesn't have many friends. . . . When she does have another child over to the house to play, they usually don't want to come back again because they get mad at her.
Interviewer: Could you tell me specifically what kind of things the other kids seem to get mad at Jamie about?
Parent: Usually, when they are playing with toys or a book or something, Jamie won't share with them. . . . She wants to dominate everything, and gets upset when they have something that belongs to her. She wants to take toys and things that they bring over and use them the whole time.

Interviewer: So Jamie has a difficult time sharing with others and doing what they
                 want to do. . . . This seems to be a real problem for her in making
                 friends.
Parent: Yeah, it's a real problem all right. . . . If she could see the other kid's
                 point of view, give-in a little bit, and not be so jealous of her things,
                 I think she could have a lot more friends to play with.

This interchange shows how the interviewer, by going from the general to the specific,
and by providing the parent with express prompts, is able to pinpoint specific types
of social skills and peer interaction problems. The parent interview can vary anywhere
between being very open-ended and being highly structured; the specific level of
structure ought to depend on the purpose of the interview. However, if the goal is to
obtain useful information on the social skills and peer relationships of the child, a
higher degree of structure and prompting seems to be the most useful.

Sociometric Approaches

Sociometric approaches constitute a potentially useful method for assessing social skills
and peer relationships, particularly when used for screening or research purposes.
Virtually any of the sociometric approaches covered in chapter 6 can be easily adapted
to directly assess different aspects of peer relationships, which is their main purpose
and use. Actual social skills tend be assessed less directly with sociometric approaches
than do peer relationships. However, because peer relationships are closely linked with
social skills (Hartup, 1978), sociometric assessment should hold a great deal of heuristic
interest for conducting social skills assessments as well. Because the general methods,
techniques, and properties of sociometric approaches were mapped out in detail in
chapter 6, this section focuses on a few issues and applications of sociometric assessment
for measuring social skills and peer relationships, rather than on duplicating the general
information presented elsewhere.

Some discussion on the nature of the relation between the two constructs of interest
for this chapter—social skills and peer relationships—may be useful at this point.
Perhaps the best way of conceptualizing this relation is to look at it as being reciprocal
in nature. On one hand, peer relationships are seen as being an outcome of social
skills, in that the greater degree of adaptive social competency a person possesses, the
greater their ability to develop positive and fulfilling relationships with other persons
(Gresham & Reschly, 1987a). On the other hand, it has also been demonstrated that
to some extent peer relationships are a *determinant* of social skills, in that the social
learning process involved in peer relationships contributes significantly to the development of social skills (Hartup, 1978, 1983). Thus, the relation between these two
subdomains of social competence is complex, and is best described as being mutually
influential or reciprocal. Figure 12.1 demonstrates this theorized relation between the
two constructs. In one sense, peer relationships may be considered an outcome of
social skills, but in another sense, the constructs are mutually reciprocal in nature.

In preparing to conduct an assessment of social skills or peer relationships using
any of the sociometric approaches covered in chapter 6, the clinician or investigator
must consider two different aspects of the assessment to make the assessment as useful
as possible. The first area to be considered is which general technique to use. Based
on Connolly's (1983) review, the choice of sociometric approaches at the general level
is between using a peer nomination procedure and a peer rating procedure. Peer

nomination procedures have been the traditional method of choice in sociometrics, but peer rating procedures may also be a useful alternative. The main difference between the two general types of procedures is that peer nominations tend to produce a measure of popularity, whereas peer ratings tend to produce a measure of average "likability" (Connolly, 1983). Although these two procedures seem to tap similar constructs, there is an important difference, which is illustrated by the example of a child who through peer ratings receives an average rating, but is not positively or negatively nominated by any other children in the peer nomination procedure. Is this a typical child, or a socially neglected child? It depends on which procedure is used and how it is interpreted. Of course, a good compromise would be to use both types of sociometric approaches in the assessment if possible, which should strengthen the generalizability of the results. When practical considerations keep clinicians from using both types of procedures in an assessment, it is important to carefully define the intended goal or outcome for the assessment, and to accordingly select the general type of procedure to be used. *Use both techniques when possible*

→ The second aspect to be considered is what specific procedure to use within the selected general method. Two needs will guide this decision. The first need to consider is the capability level of the subjects. When assessing younger or lower performing subjects, it is necessary to select a procedure that will not require any extensive reading or writing. In such a case, McAndless and Marshall's (1957) picture board adaptation of the peer nomination procedure would be a good choice, as would the simplified pictorial rating scale procedure for peer ratings (Asher et al., 1979). The other need that will guide the decision regarding the specific procedure to use is the aspect of peer relationships or social skills that are to be measured. In this regard, it is sufficient to say that the face validity of the procedures under consideration (as well as formal validity properties) should be carefully evaluated against the specific assessment needs, and then the choice should be made accordingly. *Consider: capability of subj + face validity*

In sum, the use of sociometric approaches is a time-honored and empirically validated method of assessing peer relationships that also will have indirect validity in assessing social skills. Virtually any of the general methods and specific procedures covered in chapter 6, with proper selection and modification, may be of great use to the clinician or investigator in assessing these specific aspects of behavioral, social, and emotional problems.

Assessment With Self-Reports

Very little has been done on this

At the present time, very little has been done in the area of developing a self-report assessment instrument for measuring social competence with children or adolescents. Perhaps one of the problems with developing effective self-report measures of social skills and peer relationships is that children with deficits in these areas may not be very reliable judges of their own behavior. Only two widely available and technically sound self-report forms for assessing child and adolescent social skills and interpersonal relationships could be identified. Although these two instruments represent a small number compared to what is available for self-report assessment of other areas, their development represents a significant advance from what was available only a decade ago, which was essentially nothing. These two self-report instruments are reviewed here. *children are not very good judges of themselves*

AIR *Assessment of Interpersonal Relations.* The Assessment of Interpersonal Relations (AIR; Bracken, 1993) is an instrument designed to assess the quality of interpersonal relationships from the child's perspective. Theoretically, the AIR is based on the same multidimensional model of psychosocial adjustment as the Multidimensional Self-Concept Scale (Bracken, 1992), and both instruments were normed using the same standardization population. The AIR may be used with children and adolescents between age 9 and 19. It includes a total of 105 self-report items on three separate 35-item scales that assess perceptions of the quality of relationships with parents ("I like to spend time with my . . ."), peers ("I am treated fairly by my . . ."), and teachers ("I am really understood by my . . ."), respectively. Thus, the AIR appears to be not only a measure of peer-related social adjustment, but parent- and teacher-related forms of adjustment as well. Subjects respond to each item by indicating whether they Strongly Agree (SA), Agree (A), Disagree (D), or Strongly Disagree (SD). According to the test author, the AIR takes about 20 minutes to complete. For the parent section, separate responses are recorded for perceptions regarding the subject's mother and father. For the peer rating section, separate responses are recorded for general perceptions regarding peers by gender. Raw scores in each area are converted to norm-referenced standard scores. Given the response breakdowns, the completed profile of scale scores includes separate scores for perceptions of interpersonal relationships in the following six domains: Mother, Father, Male Peers, Female Peers, Teachers, and a Total Relationship Index.

The AIR manual provides ample details regarding scale construction methods, psychometric properties, and other relevant research findings. The AIR was standardized on a sample of 2,501 children in grades 5 through 12 from various communities nationwide. Internal consistency and test–retest reliability (2-week intervals) of the AIR is exceptionally high, with coefficients in the .90s for all scale scores. AIR scores have been shown to differentiate children based on age groupings, gender, and clinical status. Discriminant construct validity was established by finding weak to moderate correlations with the Multidimensional Self-Concept Scale, an instrument purported to measure a somewhat different underlying construct, but that may be nevertheless weakly to moderately associated with interpersonal relationships.

In sum, the AIR seems to hold substantial promise as a self-report measure for assessing perceptions of interpersonal relationships, a key correlate of social skills in children and adolescents. The content validity and reported technical characteristics appear to be solid. However, some cautions and limitations are also apparent. Missing from the AIR manual are any convergent validity data regarding the correlation between AIR scores and other interpersonal relationship measures (i.e., parent or teacher report, direct observation, etc.). Demonstration of at least modest relations between the AIR and other measures of interpersonal relations/social skills is a crucial need that must be met before complete confidence in the AIR is warranted. Another limitation is that this instrument cannot be used with younger children (below grade 5), as the reading level and standardization sample were clearly aimed at the intermediate to secondary school population. Despite these limitations and cautions, the AIR appears to be a substantial improvement in several respects over the earlier generation of self-report measures designed to assess children's perceptions of their own social skills. Future research with the AIR may provide answers to some of the questions that have been raised.

The Social Skills Rating System—Student Forms. As part of the larger, integrated Social Skills Rating System described earlier in this chapter, there are two different self-report forms for a child or adolescent to use in assessing their own social skills.

The Student Form–Elementary Level is designed to be used by children in grades 3 through 6, and includes 34 items rated on a 3-point scale (0 = Never, 1 = Sometimes, 2 = Very Often). The elementary form includes four subscales (Cooperation, Assertion, Self-Control, and Empathy) where the raw scores are converted to Behavior Levels, and a total score, which is converted to a standard score (based on a mean of 100 and standard deviation of 15) and percentile ranking based on same gender norms. Three examples of items on the elementary form include "I make friends easily," "I do my homework on time," and "I ask classmates to join in an activity or game."

The Student Form–Secondary Level is designed to be completed by students in grades 7 through 12. It includes 39 items rated by the student according to two sets of rating. The first set of ratings is a "How Often" rating, where the student rates how often each item is true for them. Like the elementary student version, the "How Often" rating on the secondary student form is done according to the criteria of 0 = Never, 1 = Sometimes, and 2 = Very Often. The second set of ratings is a "How Important" rating, where the student rates how important the specific behavior is in their relationship with others. This second set of ratings is also on a 0 to 2 scale, where 0 = Not Important, 1 = Important, and 2 = Critical. The inclusion of the importance ratings allows for a comparison on specific rating items for any discrepancies between the way a behavioral item was rated and how important it is to that student. For example, if students rate "never" on Item 1, "I make friends easily," yet their importance rating is "critical," then this discrepancy suggests that the students' perceived difficulty in making friends is particularly painful for them. The secondary student form includes the same four-subscale breakdown, and the same raw score to converted standard score system. The items on the secondary student form are in some cases different than those of the elementary form, allowing for a rating of social skills that are particularly important to adolescents. Examples of some of the unique types of items on the secondary student form include "I am confident on dates," "I end fights with my parents calmly," and "I give compliments to members of the opposite sex."

The psychometric properties of the two student forms reported in the SSRS manual do not appear to be as strong as those of the parent and teacher rating forms, but are still generally in the adequate to acceptable range, particularly when considering that the student forms are designed to be used as part of a multirating system rather than by themselves. Internal consistency alpha coefficients for the student scales range from .51 to .77 for the subscale scores, and are at .83 for the total scores. Reported test–retest reliability coefficients for the students forms (at 4-week intervals) ranged from .52 to .68 on the elementary form, but are not reported for the secondary form. Concurrent validity of the elementary student form was assessed through correlations with the Piers–Harris Children's Self-Concept Scale, and the obtained coefficients ranged from −.02 to .43. It should be recognized that these modest concurrent validity coefficients probably have a great deal to do with the fact that self-concept and self-ratings of social skills are two different constructs—at the time the SSRS was developed, there was simply no other self-report measure of social skills with which comparisons could be made.

Like the other components of the SSRS, the two student forms have the distinct advantage of being part of an integrated social skills assessment structure, and having been developed using a large, nationwide sample of subjects. They should be a useful adjunct to the teacher and parent rating forms in assessing social skills, and will be able to provide a good deal of social validity to the process of assessing social skills and peer relationships by obtaining the student's own perspective.

⭐ LINKING ASSESSMENT TO INTERVENTION

This chapter defines the construct of social competence, illustrates its importance, and overviews various methods and instruments for assessing social skills and peer relationships. Although each of the five assessment areas covered have some relevance for measuring social competence, behavioral observation, behavior rating scales, and sociometric approaches are particularly useful, and have been widely reported in the research literature. Some summary information on the standardized assessment instruments covered is presented in Table 12.2.

It is obvious that assessing social competence has a great deal of importance for making classification and intervention decisions, but the specific link between social competence assessment data and effective social competence interventions is sometimes vague. This chapter concludes with two suggestions for increasing the treatment validity of social skills assessment. *Suggestions for treatment validity*

The first suggestion is that recommended treatments should match identified problems. Over the course of several years as a school psychologist, program administrator, university educator of school psychologists, and clinical supervisor, I have read assessment reports where certain social skills deficits and peer relationship problems were identified, and the resulting recommendation from the clinician was that "social skills training should be provided." This generic type of treatment recommendation is somewhat akin to a physician diagnosing bronchial pneumonia in a patient, and then

Trt should match the identified problems

TABLE 12.2
Summary of the Standardized Assessment Instruments
for Measuring Social Skills and Peer Relationships

Name of Instrument	Type	Rater	Number of Items	Grade Range
Walker–McConnell Scales of Social Competence and School Adjustment (Walker & McConnell, 1995a, 1995b)	Behavior Rating Scale	School Personnel	43 on elementary version, 53 on adolescent version	K–6 and 7–12
Social Skills Rating System–Parent and Teacher Forms (Gresham & Elliott, 1990)	Behavior Rating Scale	School Personnel and Parents	Range of 38 through 42 at different levels	Pre-K to 12
School Social Behavior Scales (Merrell, 1993b)	Behavior Rating Scale	School Personnel	65 (32 Social Competence, 33 Antisocial Behavior)	K–12
Assessment of Interpersonal Relations (Bracken, 1993)	Self-Report	Students	105 in three different areas of 35 each (peers, parents, teachers)	9–19
Social Skills Rating System–Student Forms (Gresham & Elliott, 1990)	Self-Report	Students	34 for elementary, 39 for secondary	3–6 and 7–12

recommending that the client needs "medical care"; neither recommendation is particularly helpful in developing an effective treatment. One of the consistent findings over several years of research on effective interventions for children and adolescents with behavioral and emotional problems is that the closer the treatment matches the problem, the more chance the intervention has of being successful (Peacock Hill Working Group, 1991). Assumably, an effective assessment of social skills and peer relationships may result in identifying some very specific aspects of the child or adolescent's behavior that need some attention. A best practice is to identify the specific skills deficits or behavioral excesses that exist, and to recommend interventions for those areas, rather than a generic treatment regimen that may or may not address the problems that have been identified. This method of using assessment results to inform or guide intervention is very similar to the *Keystone Behavior Strategy* for academic skills interventions that has been discussed by Shapiro (1996). This strategy is essentially based on the notion that assessment information may be linked to intervention planning through assisting in identification of the primary problems at hand, which are then specifically targeted for treatment.

The second suggestion, which is aimed specifically at school-based practitioners, is that individual education plan goals can be developed by modifying rating scale items. One of the advantages of using rating scales is that the descriptions they contain are usually concise, well thought-out, and specific in nature. As such, social skills rating scale items are often amenable to being developed into good intervention goal statements with a minimum amount of modification. For example, if a boy named Stefen consistently received "never" ratings on Item 4 ("Offers help to other students when needed") and Item 19 ("Interacts with a wide variety of peers") on the *Interpersonal Skills* subscale of the School Social Behavior Scales, then these items could be reworded into general goal statements as follows:

1. Stefen will increase his level of providing help to other students when it is appropriately needed.
2. Stefen will increase his number of interactions with other students in the classroom and on the playground.

Of course, specific behavioral objectives would need to be developed following the statement of the general goals.

These two examples illustrate how clinicians may develop intervention recommendations using the actual data obtained during the assessment. Research on interventions for social skills deficits and peer relationship problems has been increasingly reported in the professional literature during the past two decades, allowing some generalizations about their effectiveness. In general, social skills training interventions have frequently been shown to be effective but still modest in terms of the amount of change they typically produce (Merrell & Gimpel, 1998). However, there are still numerous difficulties in producing generalization across settings or maintenance over time with these changes. Two of the key aspects of promoting generalization and maintenance with social skills training include making the training setting and situation as similar to the naturalistic setting as is possible, and involving parents and teachers in helping to promote practice opportunities for the new skills that are learned (Merrell & Gimpel, 1998). Consequently, any steps that can be taken to make the assessment of social skills and peer relationships ecologically valid, and to base intervention recommendations on specific assessment findings, are especially important.

CONCLUSIONS

The terms *social competence* and *social skills* are often used interchangeably, but in reality are considered to be separate but related constructs. Social competence is considered to be a summary term reflecting the judgment of the overall quality of an individual's social adjustment, whereas social skills are specific behaviors that lead to peer relationships and social competence. Gresham (1986) proposed a model wherein social competence is considered to be the superordinate theoretical construct, and social skills, adaptive behavior, and peer relationships are considered to be subordinate constructs. However, based on recent evidence and informed by the most recent definition of mental retardation from the AAMR, a new theoretical model of the relation among these constructs is proposed. In this model, adaptive behavior is considered to be the inclusive superordinate construct, with social competence and social skills comprising sequentially smaller links into adaptive behavior, and peer relationships being considered a product or outcome of social skills as well as a mutually reciprocal agent that may influence the development of social skills.

Surprisingly little attention has been paid to the development of a classification taxonomy for child and adolescent social skills that is parallel to the several classification systems that have been developed for child and adolescent psychopathology. This lack of attention to a potentially important area was the stimulus for recent research, wherein a classification taxonomy for child and adolescent social skills was developed following an extensive review and analysis of multivariate studies of dimensions of social behavior. Using this methodology, five primary dimensions of social skills were identified, including Peer Relationships, Self-Management, Academic Skills, Compliance, and Assertion. This new classification taxonomy may have implications for development of new assessment measures and treatment protocols.

A large body of research, some considered to be classic, has been generated regarding the importance and long-term outcomes of social skills and peer relationships. Essentially, development of solid social skills early in life provides a foundation for later personal, social, academic, and occupational adjustment, and is linked to a number of positive outcomes in life. Conversely, social skills deficits and peer relationship problems early in life is part of a pathway that may lead to a variety of negative outcomes, such as mental health problems, conduct-related discharge from military service, antisocial behavior and incarceration, and unemployment or underemployment. These striking outcomes underscore the importance of early detection of children who have social skills problems, so that appropriate interventions may be implemented.

Direct behavioral observation is one of the most empirically validated methods for assessing child and adolescent social behavior. The Behavioral Assertiveness Test, Peer Social Behavior Code, and Target/Peer Interaction Code are all examples of observational coding systems that are specifically relevant for assessing social skills. Clinicians and researchers can easily adapt various types of observational coding systems to target the crucial social skills behaviors they seek to assess.

Behavior rating scales are increasingly being used as a means of assessing social skills, and there have been some impressive developments in this area in recent years. The Walker–McConnell Scales of Social Competence and School Adjustment, School Social Behavior Scales, and Social Skills Rating System are examples of modern applications of rating scale technology to child and adolescent social skills assessment.

Interviewing is an assessment method that has been less frequently reported for assessing social skills, but does seem to hold some promise in this regard. Specifically, behavioral role playing during interviews may help to facilitate an analogue type of assessment of social skills of a child or adolescent client. If behavioral role playing is utilized during an interview, it is critical that it should be designed to be as similar as is possible to the naturalistic setting that is being emulated.

Sociometric approaches to assessing child and adolescent social skills and peer relationships have been in use for several decades. Most of the sociometric techniques described in chapter 6 have some potential uses for social skills assessment. In conducting sociometric techniques for this purpose, it is important to recognize the overall goal for assessment and to plan accordingly. Peer nominations may provide a very different kind of information than peer ratings, for example. Sociometric assessment is probably better suited for research purposes and screening than for individual assessment, because of practical considerations.

Self-report instruments have only recently begun to be used on a large scale for assessing child and adolescent social skills. One of the possible reasons why self-report assessment lags behind other types of assessment in this regard is that individuals with social skills deficits may not be highly reliable reporters of their own social behavior. Two recently developed self-report measures, the Assessment of Interpersonal Relations and self-report forms of the Social Skills Rating System, are promising developments in self-report assessment of social skills.

Social skills assessment data, if used carefully, may provide important information with which intervention planning may be informed. It is preferable to use assessment data to target specific areas for social skills training (the Keystone Behavior Strategy) rather than identifying deficits and simply recommending generic social skills training. Items from social skills rating scales are potentially useful for rewording into IEP goal statements. Based on the yield of research from social skills training interventions, assessment information may be helpful to the extent that it helps to identify important intervention targets and environments, and to serve in progress monitoring of interventions.

REVIEW AND APPLICATION QUESTIONS

1. What is the difference between social competence and social skills? What types of practical assessment techniques are used to assess both of these constructs?

2. Describe how peer relationships may be a product or outcome of social skills as well as a reciprocal influence for the future development of social skills.

3. In what ways might the development of a classification taxonomy for child and adolescent social skills be potentially useful for social skills assessment and treatment?

4. Using the Peer Social Behavior Code as a guide, describe how this playground-based observational system could be used as a model for developing a *classroom-based* social behavior observation system.

5. What are some of the considerations and specific practices that should be used to make behavioral role playing an affective means of social skills assessment during interviews?

6. In comparing the SSCSA, SSBS, and SSRS, what advantages and disadvantages for social skills assessment does each instrument have?

7. Why is it important to carefully plan the purpose of assessment prior to choosing between peer nomination and peer rating techniques for assessing peer relationships?

8. What are some possible barriers to using self-report instruments for assessing child and adolescent social skills?

ASSESSMENT OF
YOUNG CHILDREN

Commenting on the state of the art in assessing young children, Malcom (1993) stated that "a request to assess a child who has not reached school age often strikes fear in the hearts of psychoeducational diagnosticians" (p. 113). This statement may not be true for all clinicians, but it goes right to the center of the issue: There are substantial challenges in assessing young children. In commenting on some of these challenges, Bracken (1987, 1994) noted that the technical adequacy of assessment measures for preschool-age children tends to lag behind that of measures for school-age children. With regard to social-emotional assessment technology for young children, the lag in technical adequacy appears to be even more pronounced (Merrell, 1996a). The specific difficulties in conducting effective social-emotional assessments with young children are many and varied, but can be summed up in general as follows:

1. In relation to what is available for use with school-age children and adolescents, there is substantially less assessment instrumentation and specifically developed methods for assessing social and emotional behavior of young children.

2. The technical adequacy (standardization samples, reliability, validity) of many of the social-emotional assessment instruments available for young children is less than desirable, and in general, their technical adequacy is not as strong as what is typically seen with instruments for school-age children and adolescents.

3. Social and emotional behavior is exceptionally variable among young children, making it quite difficult to determine a standard normative perspective.

4. Social and emotional behavior of young children tends to be influenced tremendously by contexts and settings, which often results in undermining the confidence of social-emotional assessment results obtained in specific situations at specific points in time.

5. Some of the standard methods of social-emotional assessment (i.e., interviews and self-report tests) used with children and adolescents are extremely difficult, and in some cases impossible to implement adequately with young children.

Despite these and other challenges inherent in assessing the social and emotional behavior of young children, there have been some encouraging recent developments in this area. There is also an increasing need for school psychologists, clinical child psychologists, and early childhood special education diagnosticians to provide services to young children and their families, including comprehensive assessment services (Merrell, 1996a). Thus, this chapter fills a particularly important purpose as a resource for social-emotional assessment of young children. Many of the other chapters are quite relevant to this topic, but only this chapter is designed specifically to address assessment of young children.

Some definition of what is meant by the terms *young children* and *early childhood* as they are used herein is useful. There is no universally agreed-on definition of these terms. However, the focus of this chapter is for the most part on what is considered the preschool age range, which is typically age 3 through 5. It makes sense to focus on this age range because these are the young children who are the most likely to be in various settings where assessment referrals may be generated, such as developmental preschools, Head Start programs, child find clinics, and so on. There are some areas within this chapter where the age focus extends down to the infant or toddler years, or up to as high as the kindergarten or first-grade level, but the preschool-age focus (age 3–5) is clearly the target.

This chapter begins with a review of a recently developed diagnostic classification system for behavioral and emotional problems of young children. The largest section is devoted to specific applications of the five major methods of assessment with young children, presented in the same order in which they appear in the chapters found in Part II of this book. An innovative multiple gating system for screening behavioral and emotional disorders of young children is also presented and discussed. Finally, recommended best practices for effective social-emotional assessment of young children are presented.

AN ALTERNATIVE DIAGNOSTIC CLASSIFICATION SYSTEM

In chapter 2, diagnostic classification systems for behavioral and emotional disorders are presented, with a primary focus on the *DSM–IV* and the behavioral dimensions approach to classification. One of the limitations of the *DSM* system is the limited utility or inappropriateness of many of the classification categories for use with young children, particularly those who are in the early stages of the preschool age range and younger. For example, regarding Attention Deficit Hyperactivity Disorder, one of the most common childhood diagnoses, *DSM–IV* states that "it is especially difficult to establish this diagnosis in children younger than age 4 or 5 years because their characteristic behavior is much more variable than that of older children" (APA, 1994, p. 81). Regarding Conduct Disorder, another common diagnostic category, *DSM–IV* states that "the onset of Conduct Disorder may occur as early as age 5–6 years, but is usually in late childhood or early adolescence" (p. 89). These statements are both correct, and the truth of the matter is that the younger the child, the more difficult and tenuous the diagnosis. Despite this state of affairs, clinicians who work frequently with young children and their families may still desire to have at their disposal a diagnostic nomenclature appropriate for young children for the same purposes that these systems are used with older children and adolescents.

As a response to this void in diagnostic classification methodology for young children, a new experimental diagnostic classification was developed in 1994 by Zero to Three/National Center for Clinical Infant Programs, an interdisciplinary organization for leadership in infant development and early childhood mental health. This system is titled *Diagnostic Classification: 0–3*, and subtitled *Diagnostic Classification of Mental Health and Developmental Disorders of Infancy and Early Childhood*. As these names indicate, the age range focus is clearly on infancy and early childhood. Because the authoring committee stated that "*Diagnostic Classification: 0–3* is intended to complement existing approaches" (Zero to Three, 1994, p. 15), this system should be viewed as a supplement to the *DSM–IV*, ICD 9/10, and behavioral dimensions approaches. It is still too early to tell how this system will be received in the child mental health professions, but it clearly is a comprehensive and well-designed system that appears to offer many advantages and is certainly worth some discussion in this chapter.

Diagnostic Classification: 0–3 uses a multiaxial system for classification that is quite reminiscent of *DSM–IV*. The following axes, which are identified in more detail in Table 13.1, comprise the diagnostic framework:

Axis I: Primary Classification

Axis II: Relationship Classification

Axis III: Physical Neurological, Developmental, and Mental Health Disorders or Conditions

Axis IV: Psychosocial Stress

Axis V: Functional Emotional Developmental Level

The primary diagnosis (Axis I) is designed to reflect the most prominent feature of the disorder. The relationship disorder classification (Axis II) is designed to assist in understanding the quality of the parent–child relationship, which sometimes may be an important aspect of the overall presenting problem. Axis III's medical and developmental disorders and conditions are used to note mental health or developmental diagnoses that have been made using other systems, such as *DSM–IV, ICD 9/10*, or specific classifications used by speech-language pathologists, occupational therapists, physical therapists, and special educators. Psychosocial stressors (Axis IV) are simply a method of listing various forms and severity of psychosocial stress that appear to be influencing factors in childhood disorders. The functional emotional developmental level (Axis V) is used to denote or estimate age-expected functional developmental level. Rather than using a numerical scale for this purpose, Axis V utilizes seven categories, which are noted if they are appropriate to a particular case. For example, *mutual engagement* is noted if the infant or child demonstrates the ability for joint emotional involvement, as indicated by looks, gestures, smiles, and so on. Another example is the category of *representational elaboration*, which is noted if the infant or child demonstrates "ability to elaborate a number of ideas in present play and symbolic communication, that go beyond basic needs and deal with more complex wishes or feelings" (Zero to Three, 1994, p. 65). Additionally, *Diagnostic Classification: 0–3* provides in an appendix a Parent–Infant Relationship Global Assessment Scale, which is used to assess the quality of the infant–parent relationship. Specific descriptive anchor points are provided in 10-point increments ranging from 10 (grossly impaired) to 90 (well adapted).

Only time will tell whether or not *Diagnostic Classification: 0–3* becomes widely accepted and utilized. However, it appears to offer several distinct advantages for clinicians who

TABLE 13.1

Multiaxial Organization of the *Diagnostic Classification: 0–3*

Axis I: Primary Diagnosis
  100. Traumatic Stress Disorder
  200. Disorders of Affect
  201. Anxiety Disorders of Infancy and Early Childhood
  202. Mood Disorder: Prolonged Bereavement/Grief Reaction
  203. Mood Disorder: Depression of Infancy and Early Childhood
  204. Mixed Disorder of Emotional Expressiveness
  205. Childhood Gender Identity Disorder
  206. Reactive Attachment Deprivation/Maltreatment Disorder
  300. Adjustment Disorder
  400. Regulatory Disorders
  401. Type I: Hypersensitive
  402. Type II: Under-reactive
  403. Type III: Motor Processing
  404. Type IV: Other
  500. Sleep Behavior Disorder
  600. Eating Behavior Disorder
  700. Disorders of Relating and Communicating
Axis II: Relationship Disorder Classification
  901. Overinvolved
  902. Underinvolved
  903. Anxious/Tense
  904. Angry/Hostile
  905. Mixed
  906. Abusive (verbally, physically, or sexually abusive)
Axis III: Medical and Developmental Disorders and Conditions
Axis IV: Psychosocial Stressors
Axis V: Functional Emotional Developmental Level

work frequently with young children and infants, is comprehensive and well designed, and is certainly worthy of consideration by the professional community.

METHODS FOR ASSESSING YOUNG CHILDREN

With varying degrees of modification and effectiveness, each of the five major methods of assessment can be used to evaluate social and emotional behavior of young children. At the present time, the most technically adequate methods of assessment in this domain are direct behavioral observation and behavior rating scales. Both of these methods include a variety of empirically validated procedures, systems, and instruments designed specifically for use with young children. Assuming that appropriate modifications are made, sociometric assessment methods can be very effective choices for use with young children, especially for screening and research purposes. Clinical interviewing has long been a popular method of assessing young children, but as is demonstrated in this section, requires special care and caution with young children. Objective self-report assessment is the least validated and available method for assessing young children, although some interesting innovations have occurred in this area. This section includes comments, recommendations, and reviews of specific techniques and instruments for social-emotional assessment of young children. It concludes with a description of an innovative and comprehensive new multiple gating program for screening young children for behavioral and emotional disorders.

Direct Behavioral Observation

One of the most commonly used methods of assessing the social-emotional behavior of young children in naturalistic settings is systematic behavioral observation (Lehr, Ysseldyke, & Thurlow, 1987). It has been noted that direct observation of preschool-age children in natural settings is a preferred strategy because it directly measures the behavior of interest, does not impose artificial test room demands that young children are known to be highly reactive to, and provides data that are less likely to be distorted by the expectations and biases of parents and caretakers (Doll & Elliott, 1994). Given the obvious advantages of direct behavioral observation with young children, coupled with the fact that some other methods of assessment will prove to be extremely questionable with this age group, each of the general methods and coding procedures of behavioral observation described in chapter 3 are recommended for use with young children.

In addition to the general threats to reliability and validity of observational data described in chapter 3, direct observation of preschool-age children may require some special precautions to ensure an adequate representativeness of the child's behavior. Because the social-emotional behavior of preschool-age children can change very suddenly in response to situational variables (Wittmer & Honig, 1994), and because their developmental level and progress may strongly influence the content of observed behavior (P. Graham, 1980), it is commonly accepted that special care must be taken to attempt to conduct multiple observations in several settings. Obviously, the issue of behavioral inconsistency with young children, as well as the practical difficulty of conducting multiple observations, poses some serious challenges to clinicians and researchers. One of the issues in this domain that is not fully understood yet is how many observational data should be collected when assessing young children. One of the few studies attempting to answer this question was conducted by Doll and Elliott (1994), who investigated the degree to which observations consistently described the characteristic social behaviors of 24 preschool-age children who were each observed nine times in free-play settings. By comparing partial and complete observational records, these researchers demonstrated that at least five observations were required to adequately represent the children's social behavior! It is unclear how much these results should generalize to routine assessment practice, but the implication is clear: To obtain consistent and representative social observational data with young children, clinicians must be prepared to conduct several different observations across short to moderate periods of time. Thus, clinicians and researchers who are relying heavily on single observations of young children to make inferences about their behavior may be in a precarious position.

An Example: The ESP Social Behavior Observations. Because direct behavioral observation systems tend to not be norm referenced in the same manner as behavior rating scales, and because observational systems are usually developed and modified by researchers and clinicians for specific purposes and settings, there are very few commercially produced observation systems available for general use with young children. One exception to this generalization is the Social Behavior Observations from the Early Screening Project (ESP; Walker, Severson, & Feil, 1995). The entire ESP system is described later in this chapter, but it is useful to focus more closely on its Social Behavior Observations component in this section to provide a specific example of a practical systematic behavioral observation system designed for use with young children. The ESP observations are designed to assess children's social behavior in free-play or unstructured activities, with a more specific purpose being measurement of social adjustments and interactions with peers and adults. This system used a duration coding procedure wherein the observer uses a stopwatch to assist in recording the total amount of time that a child is engaged in a particular category of social, antisocial (negative social engagement, disobeying rules), or nonsocial behavior (tantrumming, solitary play). The resulting duration of time in these categories is then calculated into a percentage of total time of the observation (which should be at least 10 minutes). Categories and examples of antisocial and nonsocial behavior are presented in Table 13.2. The ESP kit includes a comprehensive videotape and stopwatch for use in observer training. Normative comparison data for antisocial/nonsocial behavior are presented in the ESP manual, and provide ranges of percentages of engagement for specific groups. For example, with girls, engagement in antisocial/nonsocial behavior from 37% to 45% of the time places them in the *At-Risk* group, whereas the ranges of 46% to 54% and 55% or more place them in the *High Risk* and *Extreme Risk* groups, respectively. The Social Observations are designed to be an optional part of the broader ESP screening process. However, because normative data are available, and because the system has been comprehensively tested and possesses good technical properties, it seems appropriate for researchers or clinicians to use Social Observations separately from the system for specific purposes as needed.

Behavior Rating Scales

Only a decade or two ago, there were very few behavior rating scales designed for use with young children, most of them were not widely available, and few were developed with national norm samples and possessed adequate technical properties and a solid research base. Within the past few years there have been substantial new developments in this arena, and there are now several widely available and technically sophisticated behavior rating scales designed exclusively for use with young children. This section provides an overview of four such commercially published instruments that appear to be among the most widely researched and adequately developed of what is currently available for use with young children.

> **Behavior Assessment System for Children.** The Behavior Assessment System for Children (BASC; C. R. Reynolds & Kamphaus, 1992) is a comprehensive system for assessing personality and behavior of children and adolescents, and includes parent

TABLE 13.2
Categories and Examples of Antisocial and Nonsocial Behavior
from the Social Observations of the Early Screening Project

1. *A Negative Reciprocal Interchange, Either Verbal or Physical*
   Negative Verbal Behavior
   name calling, bossy commands or statements, statements of rejection, possessive statements, accusations, highly critical or uncomplimentary statements, aggressive threats, pestering taunts, demanding or quarrelsome behavior
   Negative Physical Behavior
   rough or harmful bodily contact, rough, painful, or irritating contact with objects or materials
2. *Disobeying Established Classroom Rules*
3. *Tantrumming*
   yelling, kicking, and/or sulking following a negative social interaction
4. *Solitary Play*
   not playing within 3 feet of another child, not exchanging social signals

and teacher rating scales, self-report forms, a structured observation form, and a developmental history interview form. The parent and teacher rating scales of the BASC were reviewed in general in chapter 4, and the self-report forms were reviewed in chapter 7. Included in the BASC rating scales are parent and teacher rating scales for use with children from age 4 to 5, which were not discussed specifically in the previous chapters.

The teacher rating scale for age 4 to 5 (TRS–P) includes 109 items that are rated according to four dimensions: *never, sometimes, often,* and *almost always.* The parent rating scale for age 4 to 5 (PRS–P) designed and used similarly to the TRS–P, includes 131 items. The items on both forms represent a broad range of positive and negative behavior of various types. These instruments have a complex and sophisticated structure that includes the following empirically derived composites (listed first) and scales (listed in parentheses following the corresponding composite): Externalizing Problems (aggression, hyperactivity), Internalizing Problems (anxiety, depression, somatization), School Problems (attention problems), Other Problems (atypicality, withdrawal), Adaptive Skills (adaptability, social skills), as well as a Behavioral Symptoms Index, which is a combination of scales that reflect the overall level of problem behavior. Raw scores in these areas are converted to *T*-scores and percentile ranks. Additionally, the BASC rating forms provide a means of evaluating excessively negative response patterns and critical items.

Although the overall national norm samples for the BASC are quite large and well stratified, the specific norm samples obtained for the preschool versions of the rating scale are quite modest, and could be best described as marginally adequate. The TRS–P norms are based on teacher ratings of 333 children from age 4 to 5, whereas the PRS–P norms are based on parent ratings of 309 children from age 4 to 5. As stated in previous chapters, the BASC manual is extensively documented, well written, and details substantial reliability and validity evidence. Internal consistency reliabilities for the TRS–P and PRS–P are in the median .70 range for the scale scores, and in the .80 to .90 range for the composite scores. Short-term test–retest reliability for the preschool forms is high, with a median value of .85. Interrater reliability between parents for the preschool form is reported, and spans the .30 to .50 ranges. Convergent construct validity for PRS–P is demonstrated in the manual through significant correlations with the Child Behavior Checklist and Personality Inventory for Children, although no similar studies were conducted for the TRS–P. Construct validity of the BASC rating scales is further demonstrated in the manual through showing sensitivity to differences among various clinical groups, although it is unclear how much the preschool forms were represented in these studies. Although the BASC manual is extensively detailed, there has been very little additional research published documenting the validity of the system for use with young children. One additional published study (McNamara, Holman, & Riegel, 1994) evaluated the usefulness of the BASC in determining the mental health needs of a Head Start population, and provides some additional supporting construct validity evidence.

In sum, the rating scale components of the BASC that are designed specifically for use with young children, namely the TRS–P and PRS–P, appear to be an excellent addition to the available rating scale instrumentation for this age group. The scales are very well constructed, comprehensive, and appear to have very good technical properties. The only possible negative comment regarding the TRS–P and PRS–P is the modest size of the normative samples. If these instruments were introduced as separate tests rather than as part of the larger BASC system, it is likely that the modest norm samples would be a frequent criticism. However, based on the overall strength of the BASC system, there is certainly enough supporting evidence to justify recommending the rating scales designed for assessment of young children.

Child Behavior Checklist. The Child Behavior Checklist (CBCL) and the related Teacher's Report Form (TRF), described in detail in chapter 4 and mentioned in numerous places in other chapters, have some obvious merit for assessing young children. The normative age range of the CBCL extends from 4 to 18 years, whereas the normative age range of the TRF extends from 5 to 18 years. Given the lower extensions of these age ranges, both instruments can be used with children at the kindergarten level, and the CBCL can also be used with older preschool-age children as well as many children in Head Start programs. Because the combination of these two instruments comprise the most widely researched behavior rating scale system ever available, and because their technical properties are known to be good, it is sufficient to state they are both useful and recommended for assessing young children at the lower extensions of the normative age ranges.

Despite the many advantages of these two measures, it is important to recognize an important common limitation concerning assessment of young children. Both instruments include a relatively wide age span, and the items were not devised to be specific to the unique aspects of the early childhood developmental period. Achenbach, the author of the CBCL and TRF, understood this limitation, and subsequently produced similar instruments designed specifically for use with young children, namely the Child Behavior Checklist for Ages 2–3 (CBCL/2–3; Achenbach, 1992) and the Caregiver–Teacher Report Form for Ages 2–5 (C–TRF/2–5; Achenbach, 1997). These two instruments are reviewed here and readers are referred to chapter 4 for more information on the CBCL and TRF.

The CBCL/2–3 is designed to obtain parent ratings of child behavior using 99 problem items. Of these items, 59 have counterparts on the CBCL/4–18 and the remaining items were constructed to be specific to the early childhood developmental period. Like the counterpart instruments in the CBCL system, the CBCL/2–3 items are rated using a 3-point scale, ranging from 0 = Not True to 2 = Very True or Often True. The individual items of this measure are added in various combinations into empirically derived clinical syndrome scores (subscales), broad-band scores (internalizing and externalizing), and a total problems score. Four of the six syndrome scales (Aggressive Behavior, Anxious/Depressed, Somatic Complaints, Withdrawn) have similar counterparts in the cross-informant CBCL system, whereas the other two syndrome scales (Sleep Problems, Destructive Behavior) are specific to the early childhood items and are only found on this measure. Like the rest of the system, raw scores on the CBCL/2–3 are converted to *T*-scores and percentile ranks. Both hand scoring and computer scoring programs are available. The computer scoring program takes less time and has the advantage of calculating agreement indices (referred to as *Q* correlations) between two parents who have rated the same child.

The normative group for the CBCL/2–3 consists of 368 nonreferred children, which should be considered a modest sample size. However, an additional 178 children were used in the construction of the syndrome scales, and the normative sample is well stratified by region, socioeconomic status, and urban–rural residence. Mixed gender norms are used. The manual for the CBCL/2–3 provides adequate documentation of the technical properties of the test, which are generally quite good. Additional published research on the CBCL/2–3 has provided validity evidence in such areas as cross-cultural uses (Auerbach, Yirmiya, & Kamel, 1996; Leadbeater & Bishop, 1994), gender differences (van den Oord, Koot, Boosma, & Verhulst, 1995), relations between child problem ratings and maternal depression, social support and stress (Leadbeater & Bishop, 1994), and group differences between children in and outside of day-care situations (Caruso, 1994).

The CBCL/2–3 is a much-needed downward extension of the 4 to 18 age range version of the instrument, and is particularly important because many of the items were developed specifically for the lower registers of the early childhood age range. The size of the norm sample is relatively modest, although the methods of stratification bolster the confidence in it. The body of supporting literature is growing, and this instrument can be recommended for assessing young children. It has the particular advantage of being one of the few behavior rating scales that extends down to include 2-year-old children.

The C–TRF/2–5 was designed to be a downward extension of the TRF, and is designed for use by preschool and Head Start teachers, day-care center personnel, and in the case of some 5-year-old children, kindergarten teachers. This instrument includes 99 problem items, and contains seven clinical syndrome scales, as well as the same broad-band and total score configurations as the other instruments in the CBCL system. It also utilizes the same raw score to T-score and percentile rank scoring system, with both hand-scored and computer-scored profiles available. The norm group for the C–TRF/2–5 includes 1,075 children who were rated by teachers or child-care providers. This is a robust sample size for a limited age range, and has the additional advantage of being well stratified. A guide for the test is available and provides information on development, reliability, validity, and applications. Because this instrument is so new, no externally published literature on it is yet available, and the guide is much more restricted in scope, length, and technical information and evidence than the manual for the CBCL/2–3. However, the C–TRF/2–5 does appear to be a very promising instrument, and it is assumed that the research base and published literature for it will grow substantially in the next few years. It can be recommended for use with the only caveat being that there is only minimal supporting technical information available at the present time.

Preschool and Kindergarten Behavior Scales. The Preschool and Kindergarten Behavior Scales (PKBS; Merrell, 1994b) is a 76-item behavior rating scale designed to measure typical problem behaviors and social skills of children from age 3 to 6. This instrument may be completed by teachers, parents, day-care providers, or others who are familiar with a child's behavior. The items are generic enough so that a common rating form is used across different informants and settings. The PKBS was developed with a national normative sample of 2,855 children from 16 states representing each of the four U.S. geographical regions, and roughly comparable to the general U.S. population in terms of ethnicity, gender, and socioeconomic status.

Rather than being a downward extension of an existing rating scale designed for use with older children, the PKBS and its items were designed specifically for the unique social/behavioral aspects of the early childhood/preschool developmental period, and systematic item development and content validation procedures were employed. In other words, the initial PKBS item pool was developed following a systematic and comprehensive review of clinical and research literature describing the social, behavioral, and emotional problems of young children, particularly how these problems are manifested in preschool and kindergarten-age children.

The items on the PKBS comprise two separate scales, each designed to measure a separate domain: a 34-item Social Skills scale, and a 42-item Problem Behavior scale. Each of these two scales includes an empirically derived subscale structure. The Social Skills scale includes the following subscales: Social Cooperation (12 items describing cooperative and self-restraint behaviors), Social Interaction (11 items reflective of social initiation behaviors), and Social Independence (11 items reflecting behaviors which are important in gaining independence within the peer group). The Problem Behavior scale includes two broad-band subscales, Internalizing Problems and Externalizing Problems. Consistent with the theoretical and empirical breakdown of the externalizing/internalizing problem dichotomy (see Cicchetti & Toth, 1991), the former broad-band scale includes 27 items describing undercontrolled behavioral problems such as aggression, overactivity, and coercive antisocial behaviors, whereas the latter broad-band scale includes 15 items describing overcontrolled emotional/behavioral problems such as social withdrawal, somatic problems, anxiety, and behaviors consistent with depressive symptomatology. The Internalizing Problems broad-band scale includes two narrow-band scales (Social Withdrawal and Anxiety/Somatic Problems), whereas the Externalizing Problems broad-band scale includes three narrow-band scales (Self-Centered/Explosive, Attention Problems/Overactive, and Antisocial/Aggressive). The two scales of the PKBS are presented in Fig. 13.1.

Technical data reported in the PKBS test manual and in other published sources provide evidence for adequate to excellent psychometric properties. Test–retest reliability estimates for the Social Skills and Problem Behavior total scores at 3-month intervals were found to be .69 and .78, respectively. Child ratings by preschool teachers and teacher aides for the respective total scores have been shown to correlate at .48 and .59. Internal consistency reliability estimates for the Social Skills and Problems Behavior total scores were respectively found to be .96 and .97. Content validity of the PKBS has been demonstrated through the documentation of item development procedures and through moderate to high correlations between individual items and total scale scores. Discriminant convergent construct validity has been demonstrated by examining relations between the PKBS and four other established preschool behavior rating scales, namely, the Matson Evaluation of Social Skills with Young Children, the Conners Teacher Rating Scale, the School Social Behavior Scales, and the Social Skills Rating System (Merrell, 1995a). Construct validity has been shown through analysis of intrascale relationships, factor analytic findings with structural equation modeling (Merrell, 1996b), and documentation of sensitivity to various group differences (Holland & Merrell, 1998; Jentzsch & Merrell, 1996; Merrell, 1995b; Merrell & Holland, 1997; Merrell & Wolfe, 1998).

Reviews of the PKBS in the professional literature have been quite positive (Bracken, Keith, & Walker, 1994; Riccio, 1995), and the PKBS has the advantage of being easy to use and well documented. In sum, the PKBS appears to be useful as a general problem behavior and social skills assessment tool for use with young children, particularly those exhibiting typical types of behavioral problems in typical types of settings such as Head Start programs, and preschool or kindergarten classrooms. For assessing children with severe low frequency behavior problems, such as might be exhibited by children in psychiatric treatment centers, instruments such as the Child Behavior Checklist may be more appropriate.

Social Skills Rating System. The Social Skills Rating System (SSRS; Gresham & Elliott, 1990), which was reviewed in chapter 11, is a comprehensive social skills assessment system for children and adolescents. Included in the SSRS system are teacher

Scale A
Social Skills

	Never	Rarely	Sometimes	Often	Scoring Key		
1. Works or plays independently	0	1	2	3			
2. Is cooperative	0	1	2	3			
3. Smiles and laughs with other children	0	1	2	3			
4. Plays with several different children	0	1	2	3			
5. Tries to understand another child's behavior ("Why are you crying?")	0	1	2	3			
6. Is accepted and liked by other children	0	1	2	3			
7. Follows instructions from adults	0	1	2	3			
8. Attempts new tasks before asking for help	0	1	2	3			
9. Makes friends easily	0	1	2	3			
10. Shows self-control	0	1	2	3			
11. Is invited by other children to play	0	1	2	3			
12. Uses free time in an acceptable way	0	1	2	3			
13. Is able to separate from parent without extreme distress	0	1	2	3			
14. Participates in family or classroom discussions	0	1	2	3			
15. Asks for help from adults when needed	0	1	2	3			
16. Sits and listens when stories are being read	0	1	2	3			
17. Stands up for other children's rights ("That's his!")	0	1	2	3			
18. Adapts well to different environments	0	1	2	3			
19. Has skills or abilities that are admired by peers	0	1	2	3			
20. Comforts other children who are upset	0	1	2	3			
21. Invites other children to play	0	1	2	3			
22. Cleans up his/her messes when asked	0	1	2	3			
23. Follows rules	0	1	2	3			
24. Seeks comfort from an adult when hurt	0	1	2	3			
25. Shares toys and other belongings	0	1	2	3			
26. Stands up for his/her rights	0	1	2	3			
27. Apologizes for accidental behavior that may upset others	0	1	2	3			
28. Gives in or compromises with peers when appropriate	0	1	2	3			
29. Accepts decisions made by adults	0	1	2	3			
30. Takes turns with toys and other objects	0	1	2	3			
31. Is confident in social situations	0	1	2	3			
32. Responds appropriately when corrected	0	1	?	3			
33. Is sensitive to adult problems ("Are you sad?")	0	1	2	3			
34. Shows affection for other children	0	1	2	3			
				Totals			
					A1	A2	A3

2

FIG. 13.1. Social Skills and Problem Behavior Scales of the Preschool and Kindergarten Behavior Scales. From *Preschool and Kindergarten Behavior Scale*, by K. W. Merrell, 1994, Austin, TX: Pro-Ed. Copyright © 1994 by Pro-Ed. Reprinted with permission.

P K B S

Scale B
Problem Behavior

		Never	Rarely	Sometimes	Often	Scoring Key
1.	Acts impulsively without thinking	0	1	2	3	
2.	Becomes sick when upset or afraid	0	1	2	3	
3.	Teases or makes fun of other children	0	1	2	3	
4.	Does not respond to affection from others	0	1	2	3	
5.	Clings to parent or caregiver	0	1	2	3	
6.	Makes noises that annoy others	0	1	2	3	
7.	Has temper outbursts or tantrums	0	1	2	3	
8.	Wants all the attention	0	1	2	3	
9.	Is anxious or tense	0	1	2	3	
10.	Will not share	0	1	2	3	
11.	Is physically aggressive (hits, kicks, pushes)	0	1	2	3	
12.	Avoids playing with other children	0	1	2	3	
13.	Yells or screams when angry	0	1	2	3	
14.	Takes things away from other children	0	1	2	3	
15.	Has difficulty concentrating or staying on task	0	1	2	3	
16.	Disobeys rules	0	1	2	3	
17.	Has problems making friends	0	1	2	3	
18.	Is afraid or fearful	0	1	2	3	
19.	Must have his/her own way	0	1	2	3	
20.	Is overly active; unable to sit still	0	1	2	3	
21.	Seeks revenge against others	0	1	2	3	
22.	Defies parent, teacher, or caregiver	0	1	2	3	
23.	Complains of aches, pain, or sickness	0	1	2	3	
24.	Resists going to preschool or day care	0	1	2	3	
25.	Is restless and "fidgety"	0	1	2	3	
26.	Calls people names	0	1	2	3	
27.	Is difficult to comfort when upset	0	1	2	3	
28.	Withdraws from the company of others	0	1	2	3	
29.	Bullies or intimidates other children	0	1	2	3	
30.	Seems unhappy or depressed	0	1	2	3	
31.	Has unpredictable behavior	0	1	2	3	
32.	Is jealous of other children	0	1	2	3	
33.	Acts younger than his/her age	0	1	2	3	
34.	Destroys things that belong to others	0	1	2	3	
35.	Is moody or temperamental	0	1	2	3	
36.	Is overly sensitive to criticism or scolding	0	1	2	3	
37.	Whines or complains	0	1	2	3	
38.	Gets taken advantage of by other children	0	1	2	3	
39.	Disrupts ongoing activities	0	1	2	3	
40.	Tells lies	0	1	2	3	
41.	Is easily provoked; has a "short fuse"	0	1	2	3	
42.	Bothers and annoys other children	0	1	2	3	
					Totals	B1 B2 B3 B4 B5

3

FIG. 13.1. *(Continued)*

and parent preschool level rating forms for use with children from age 3 to 5. Because these preschool level forms are highly relevant to the topic of social-emotional assessment of young children, and because they were not specifically reviewed in chapter 11, they are reviewed here.

The two SSRS preschool level forms are quite similar to each other, and contain many common items. The teacher form includes 30 social skills items that are rated on a 3-point scale based on how often the behaviors occur, as well as how important they are for success in the particular setting. It also includes a brief 10-item problem behavior screen. The parent form includes 39 social skills items and 10 problem behavior items, which are rated in the same manner as described for the teacher form. The main difference in content between the two forms involves the specificity of items across the home and preschool settings. For example, the teacher form includes an item stating "Appropriately questions rules that may be unfair," whereas the related item on the parent form states "Appropriately questions *household rules* that may be unfair" (italics added). Given that these two forms are part of the general SSRS rating scale system, they were developed as downward extensions of the elementary and secondary parent and teacher rating forms, with minor item revisions, deletions, and additions to make them appropriate for use with young children. Like the other rating forms in the SSRS system, raw scores on the preschool level forms are converted to behavior levels, standard scores, and percentile ranks. Also, like the other versions of the SSRS, the preschool level forms include empirically derived Cooperation, Assertion, and Self-Control subscales within the social skills area, as well as Internalizing and Externalizing areas within the problem behavior screening items.

Although the SSRS manual provides extensive technical data regarding the psychometric properties and research for the various components of the system, very little of it is specific to the preschool level versions. It appears that most of the research efforts for the development of the SSRS went into the various elementary and secondary forms, with the preschool forms being added as an afterthought. Factor analyses and normative data for the SSRS preschool forms were based on only 212 ratings for the teacher form, and 193 ratings for the parent form, and the geographic, racial, and socioeconomic stratification of the preschool form norms is difficult if not impossible to determine from the tables provided in the manual (which often do not have a separate column for the preschool forms). Coefficient alpha reliabilities for the subscales of the preschool forms range from the upper .50 to lower .90 levels, with total social skills score reliabilities in the low .90 range and total problem behavior score reliabilities in the .70 (parent) to .80 (teacher) range. Test–retest reliability data for the preschool forms are not reported in the SSRS manual. Cross-informant correlations between parent and teacher ratings of 193 preschool-age children were reported, and resulted in a coefficient of .25 for the total social skills score, which is at the expected level for ratings across different raters and settings (see Achenbach, McConaughy, & Howell, 1987). No correlational comparisons with the SSRS preschool level forms and other behavior rating scales for young children are reported in the manual, nor are any group separation construct validity studies. Some research on the preschool level forms has appeared in the literature since the publication of the SSRS manual. Convergent construct validity of the SSRS preschool version forms has been established by finding significant correlations with the Preschool and Kindergarten Behavior Scales (Merrell, 1995a), and the Behavioral Assessment System for Children (D. P. Flanagan, Alfonso, Primavera, & Povall, 1996). Additionally, cross-cultural validity evidence for the preschool forms of the SSRS has been reported (Elliott, Barnard, & Gresham, 1989; Powless & Elliott, 1993).

In sum, the preschool level forms of the SSRS appear to be potentially useful in the assessment of social skills of young children, and have the definite advantage of being part of the excellent and comprehensive SSRS system, which is very well designed and easy to use. However, the lack of supporting reliability and (and to some extent, validity) evidence for the preschool forms is somewhat troubling. Perhaps an even larger concern is the small number of ratings on which the norms for the parent and teacher preschool forms were based (193 and 212, respectively). Given that the SSRS has become widely used and positively reviewed (e.g., Demaray et al., 1995), the preschool forms of the test obviously have some merit. However, it would be a tremendous addition to the field if the SSRS authors would increase the normative samples and research base for the preschool level forms in subsequent revisions to the system.

Interviewing Techniques

In chapter 5, there is some discussion of specific challenges, developmental issues, and recommendations regarding interviewing preschool and primary-age children. The purpose of this section is to provide additional insights and suggestions regarding conducting interviews with young children. Perhaps the first issue that should be addressed in this area is the question "how useful is it to interview young children?" The answer to this question really depends on the purpose of the interview. It is well known that interviews with young children where the intended purpose is to gather specific recollections of past events is problematic, to say the least. This problem becomes a particularly thorny issue when interviewing young children who may have been sexually abused, when the purpose of the interview is to gather evidence to document whether or not abuse occurred, and to potentially begin to identify a perpetrator (e.g., Boat & Everson, 1988; Coolbear, 1992). Therefore, if the purpose of assessment is to obtain very specific historically accurate information regarding events in a young child's life, direct interviews with the child may be a poor choice of methods. However, there are many other legitimate purposes for conducting individual interviews with young children, and the clinical interview has a long and credible history to this end.

It is important to recognize that children's competence in verbal communication gradually increases with age, and preschool-age children will certainly tend to be less competent in this area than school-age children. However, this fact does not mean that young children cannot be assessed effectively in an interview situation. J. N. Hughes and Baker (1990) noted that, in recent years, researchers have demonstrated that some of the supposed cognitive limitations of young children that were documented through Piagetian tasks are "artifacts of the way they (the children) are questioned" (p. 30). It is therefore critical to consider and remember that the skill and sensitivity of the interviewer will usually be the key determinant in whether or not an interview yields useful results. Hughes and Baker also noted that in interviewing young children, adult interviewers often err in attempting to assume too much control in the conversation, usually by asking too many questions, or by asking questions that are primarily forced choice or closed-ended.

Given the current state of what is known regarding the cognitive and social developmental characteristics of young children, several techniques can be recommended to enhance the quality of clinical interviews. J. N. Hughes and Baker (1990) recommended that interviewers should use a combination of open-ended and direct questions, not attempt to assume too much control over the conversation, gain familiarity with the child's experience and use this understanding in developing questions, reduce the complexity of interview stimuli to the greatest extent possible, and reduce the complexity of the child's responses by allowing them to communicate with props or manipulatives at times.

Regarding open-ended versus direct (closed-ended) questions, even open-ended questions can be misused with young children. A particular problem is referred to as *leading questions*, or asking a seemingly open-ended question in a manner that slants the content of the response. For example, asking a child a question like "tell me about what happens when your dad gets angry" in the absence of strong evidence to suggest this is even an issue will likely result in a response that confirms that dad is truly an angry person. Young children tend to want to please adults, and providing the kind of statements that they think an adult wants is one way of doing it. In terms of the issue of control over the conversation, clinicians should balance the natural tendency of children to move in and out of a specific topic with their own need to obtain information. A mental reminder prior to the interview—that it is okay to have the interview seem directionless as times—may help in this regard. The other suggestions made by Hughes and Baker are fairly self-explanatory.

An additional consideration for interviewing young children involves the difficulty many young children have in separating from their parent(s). If an interviewer prematurely requests that children separate from their parent and go into the interview room, then the result is likely to be a poor interview, and possibly crying children. A technique that works well for many clinicians in working with young children is to invite both the child and parent into the clinic room or office together first, and invite them to first engage in a nonthreatening activity, like drawing pictures on a white board or playing with a toy. After the child begins to show signs of feeling comfortable and secure, the clinician can then matter of factly ask the parent to go into the other room to fill out forms, or engage in some similar activity. If the child then becomes upset, some empathy and gentle reassurance will usually help calm them. Statements such as "it's okay to feel scared when your mom is gone, but she will be back soon," as well as behaviors such as physically getting down to the child's level and engaging in a fun activity with them will also help in this regard.

In sum, although clinical interviews with young children do possess inherent challenges, these challenges can usually be overcome with additional care and caution. Assuming the interview is only one part of a comprehensive assessment design, it can provide invaluable insights and information, even under less than ideal circumstances.

Sociometric Approaches

Each of the four general sociometric assessment methods illustrated in chapter 6 (peer nomination, peer rating, sociometric ranking, alternative procedures) have been adapted and used with preschool-age children. Despite their frequency of use with young children, these methods have been shown to have somewhat inconsistent psychometric properties and usefulness with this age group. Such findings, when considered in conjunction with some of the unique social development aspects of early childhood, have resulted in questions and cautions regarding the use of sociometric methods with young children (e.g., Connolly, 1983; Hymel, 1983). Despite some legitimate concerns regarding these cautions, sociometrics can be reliably and effectively used with preschool- and kindergarten-age children. This section (in addition to the material presented in chap. 6) comments on some issues in using sociometrics with young children.

It is useful to understand the basis of concerns regarding the effective use of sociometrics with young children. In a comprehensive review on this topic, Hymel

(1983) concluded that, with regard to reliability, the data are less encouraging with children younger than age 4. Hymel also noted that there was a paucity of predictive validity evidence (as opposed to concurrent validity evidence) for sociometric measures obtained with preschool populations. Bullock, Ironsmith, and Poteat (1988) also reviewed the literature on sociometric assessment with young children, finding mixed evidence regarding the stability of measurement over time. Given these findings, why would the sociometric ratings of young children be less stable than those of older children? Perhaps the best answer to this question is that the constructs of friendship and peer popularity are probably less stable with young children. Bullock et al. concluded that younger children's friendships tend to fluctuate more than those of older children. Related to this conclusion is a consistent finding that peer nominations and peer ratings tend to have more similarity with preschool-age children than with elementary-age children, indicating that in comparison to school-age children, younger children do not differentiate as much between being best friends with another child and simply liking them. Any parent of young children can personally attest to these two findings. Preschool-age children may be quite likely to state that a child who they have played with at preschool on one or two occasions is their "best friend," but fail to even mention them only a few months later if asked to name their best friends.

Despite the sometimes amorphous quality that young children's social relationships have, and the resulting lowered temporal consistency with certain types of sociometric procedures, there is still much to be said for using them with this age group. Simple adaptations of basic sociometric methods, such as the use of picture sociometrics for peer nominations, and the additional use of happy, sad, and neutral face drawings to serve as anchor points for peer rating procedures (see Asher et al., 1979), can make sociometric procedures very useful with young children. Although some experts (i.e., Hymel, 1983) have recommended that rating scales should be used instead of nomination procedures with young children, others (i.e., Poteat, Ironsmith, & Bullock, 1986) have argued convincingly that with proper modifications, the two methods may both be reliable. Therefore, the sociometric method of choice by a particular researcher or clinician in assessing young children should be based on the particular questions that need to be answered, and the particular characteristics of the children being assessed. Although there is still more to be learned regarding effective use of sociometrics with young children, they can be recommended. The evidence is clear that negative nominations or ratings are associated with negative behavior, and positive nominations or ratings are associated with positive behavior. It is this demonstrated strong relation between assessment results and actual behavior that continues to advocate for the use of sociometrics, and their use with young children should be no exception.

Self-Report Tests

For obvious reasons, self-report tests are extremely difficult to use with young children, and for the most part are of very questionable utility. As explained in chapter 7, objective self-report tests typically require three prerequisite abilities: the ability to read and understand test items, the cognitive maturity or sophistication to make specific incremental judgments in responding to test items, and the ability to correctly translate these judgments into the marking of the appropriate answer. Several self-report tests designed for social-emotional assessment of elementary-age children do allow for the examiner to read the items and mark the chosen responses for those children who have difficulty reading, which might lead to the belief that they are appropriate for preschool- and kindergarten-age children. This belief is almost always wrong. Even allowing for the examiner to read the test items to the child and to mark their answer forms for them does not solve the more fundamental problem of cognitive maturity or sophistication. The vast majority of preschool- and kindergarten-age children simply do not possess the cognitive ability to make appropriate judgments on self-report tests of social emotional functioning. In fact, most young children lack the intrapersonal insight regarding social and emotional functioning to even adequately understand the concepts they would be asked to evaluate in the majority of self-report tests. Therefore, it is best to assume that researchers and clinicians must rely on other means for assessing the social-emotional behavior of young children, with particular emphases on behavior rating scales, direct behavioral observation, and where appropriate, sociometric approaches.

Despite the limitations of self-report methods for assessing social-emotional status of young children, there is one ingenious self-report instrument that has been developed specifically to overcome the limitations that most self-report tests have for young children, and that has been empirically validated over time. This instrument is reviewed here as an example of one of the very best (and perhaps the only) self-report tests currently available for social-emotional assessment of young children.

The Pictorial Scale of Perceived Competence and Acceptance for Young Children.

The Pictorial Scale of Perceived Competence and Acceptance for Young Children (Harter & Pike, 1980, 1984) is a unique self-report test designed to evaluate the general self-concept and social acceptance of young children, according to their own perceptions. Unlike the vast majority of self-report social-emotional assessment instruments for children, this instrument does not require that the child subject either read or make detailed response discriminations. Rather, the examiner leads them through the items with a series of picture plates and the child is asked to make simple discriminations among paired items by pointing at the picture or symbol that is most like them.

Separate gender picture plates (one depicting male characters and the other depicting female characters) are used at two different developmental levels: one for preschool- and kindergarten-age children, and the other for children in first or second grade. The picture plates for the two different age levels are relatively similar but for some items depict children in activities that are developmentally appropriate at that specific level. For example, the preschool and kindergarten level plates show children working on puzzles, and the parallel item for the first- and second-grade version shows children working on number problems at school. There are 24 items in this test. The manner in which the items are presented to the child first involves the examiner showing them a plate with two opposing pictures on it, and then asking a simple question about it. For example, all children are shown a plate where one picture shows a child who appears to be sad, and the other picture shows a child who appears to be happy. The examiner asks "This girl (or boy) is usually kind of sad (points to the first picture), and this girl (or boy) is usually kind of happy (points to the second picture). Now I want you to tell me which of these boys/girls is most like you?" The child then responds by pointing to the picture within the pair that they select as being most like them. Then the examiner asks the child *how much* the selected picture is like them, and the child responds by pointing to a large or small circle located directly below the picture. For example, if the child had originally pointed to the picture of the child who was usually sad as being most like them, then the examiner would say "are you always sad?" (points to the large circle), or, "are you usually sad?" (points to small circle).

A value of 1 to 4 points is given for each item response, keyed so that the lowest value always indicates the lowest level of perceived competence or acceptance, whereas the highest value always indicates the highest level. Items are clustered into four subscales: Cognitive Competence, Physical Acceptance, Peer Acceptance, and Maternal Acceptance. The scales are scored by calculating a mean value for the items within that scale, and then identifying the general level indicated by that value. For example, if a child received a mean score of 3.83 on Cognitive Competence, then this score would be interpreted as a very high level of perceived self-competence in the cognitive domain, whereas a score of 1.2 would be considered a very low level. Scores for this test are typically interpreted in a criterion-referenced rather than norm-referenced manner.

Although the test manual provides no technical data on the uses and properties of this instrument, several publications over the past two decades have provided evidence that it is a potentially useful instrument for use with young children. For example, significant relations have been shown between this test and measures of academic readiness (Anderson & Adams, 1985), self-perception items have been found to correspond with actual criterion behaviors and teacher ratings (Jongmans, Demetre, Dubowitz, & Henderson, 1996; Priel, Assor, & Orr, 1990), and interesting relations between test scores and differences in the way that boys and girls tend to respond to other stimuli have been found (Harter & Chao, 1992). Additionally, the psychometric properties (i.e., basic reliability and validity) of this test have been shown to be acceptable (e.g., Holguin & Sherrill, 1990; Cadieux, 1996). Although the normative research base and psychometric properties of the Pictorial Scale of Perceived Competence and Acceptance for Young Children are not as strong and extensive as those available for many self-report instruments designed for use with older children and adolescents, this is virtually the only self-report instrument for young children that has been widely researched, and it must be considered that social-emotional behavior is typically a less stable trait in young children. As such, this instrument is particularly valuable as a research tool. Clinical use of the test with young children can be recommended, providing that it is done as part of a comprehensive battery, and that hypotheses generated through evaluating scale scores are supported through other means.

THE EARLY SCREENING PROJECT: A MULTIPLE GATING PROCEDURE FOR YOUNG CHILDREN

In addition to the instruments and procedures for social-emotional assessment of young children within the five general domains of assessment emphasized in this book, an additional assessment system is worthy of discussion in this chapter. The Early Screening Project (ESP; Walker et al., 1995) is an innovative new system designed to assist in screening preschool-age children (age 3–5) who are at high risk for developing significant emotional or behavioral disorders. Rather than being comprised of one specific method of assessment, the ESP is based on a *multiple gating methodology* (see chap. 2) and consists of three stages (or "gates") of assessment, which are successively refined and selective. An outline of the ESP multiple gating system is presented in Fig. 13.2. The ESP assesses both the frequency and intensity of social-emotional

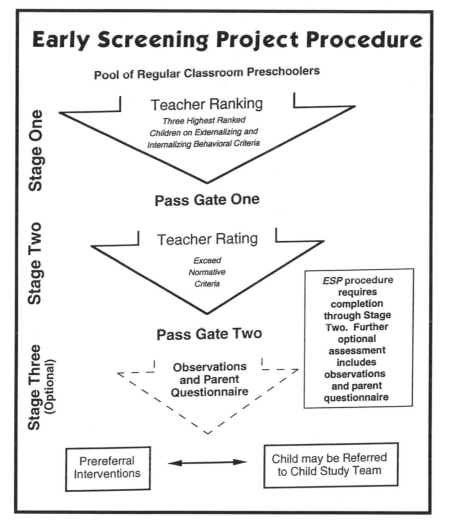

FIG. 13.2. A diagram of the multiple gating stages of the Early Screening Project. From *Early Screening Project*, by H. M. Walker, H. H. Severson, and E. G. Feil, 1995, Longmont, CO: Sopris West. Copyright © 1995 by Sopris West. Reprinted with permission.

problems, and was developed to provide an empirically sound and cost-effective method of screening to aid in the early detection and remediation of social-emotional problems of young children. This screening system is a downward extension of the Systematic Screening for Behavior Disorders, which was discussed in chapter 2.

The first two stages in the ESP rely on the judgment of teachers. Stage 1 involves a teacher nomination and rank ordering process to identify the children in the class who exhibit the highest rates of internalizing and externalizing problems. Six children from the classroom are selected to pass through the Stage 1 gate on to Stage 2: three "internalizers" and three "externalizers." Stage 2 consists of the preschool teacher completing a set of five brief behavior rating scales on each of the six children. Those children who are rated as having high frequency and intensity of problem social-emotional behaviors in the Stage 2 ratings are then passed on to Stage 3, which consists of parent questionnaires and direct behavioral observations of the children by a trained observer. Children identified as having problem behavior excesses and/or social competence deficits during Stage 3 are considered to be good candidates for prereferral interventions or a formal referral and assessment.

The ESP national norm sample is large and diverse, consisting of 2,853 children from age 3 to 6 who were enrolled in a variety of typical and specialized preschool educational programs. The technical adequacy of the ESP has been solidly researched. Median interrater reliability coefficients are in the .70 range, and median test–retest coefficients at medium length intervals are also in the .70 range. The ESP manual and subsequent published studies have documented various forms of test validity, based on correlations with specific assessment instruments and estimation of classification accuracy, among other procedures. The ESP has been empirically demonstrated to result in relatively low false-positive and false-negative error rates in identification (Feil & Becker, 1993; Sinclair, Del'Homme, & Gonzales, 1993), and to have strong construct validity when compared to other methods of assessment and when researched for accuracy of classification results (Jentzsch & Merrell, 1996). The intriguing aspect of this procedure is that it systematically allows for an entire group of children to be screened at a relatively low cost in terms of professional time and training. The implications of the ESP for early treatment are strong. Although the full implementation of this system is time intensive, it appears to be an excellent and ultimately cost-effective way to identify and assess from larger populations young children with significant emotional and behavior problems.

BEST PRACTICES

As has been demonstrated throughout this chapter, social-emotional assessment of young children can be conducted using any or all of the five major assessment methods. However, to be done effectively with young children, such assessment must be conducted with particular precautions, modifications of design, extra care, and special sensitivity. At this point, it is important to emphasize particular recommendations for social-emotional assessment with young children that have an important bearing on both research and practice.

One of the major recommendations for assessment of young children is that it is essential to include parents in the assessment process to the greatest extent possible. Although including parents is an important consideration in assessing children and adolescents of any age group, it is especially crucial where young children are concerned. As has already been discussed, situational specificity of behavior is a particularly salient issue with young children. Therefore, obtaining the parent(s) report and normative perspective from the home setting may help to clarify discrepancies in social-emotional behavior across settings. Involvement of parents of young children is also particularly important because they may not yet be experienced in dealing with professionals from educational and mental health systems. Parents dealing with such systems for the first time may feel intimidated by professional terminology and knowledge, unsure of the processes that they will encounter, and genuinely scared of what may be ahead for their child. In sum, they may need extra attention and reassurance.

Another recommended best practice for social-emotional assessment with young children is to use extra caution in the diagnosis/classification process, and to avoid "overpathologizing" children. As is demonstrated throughout Part II of this book, many

DSM–IV diagnostic categories for psychiatric disorders are simply not appropriate for young children. Furthermore, making classification decisions regarding diagnostic categories that may be appropriate for young children is often extremely difficult, because the way that behavioral problems are exhibited by them often differs markedly from that of older children. Given these diagnostic/classification concerns as well as other related concerns, it is especially important for clinicians to use extra caution and conservatism in making decisions that may have a lasting impact. Approaching referral issues from a functional and disconfirmatory perspective may be helpful in this regard. Approach the referral from the standpoint of clarifying a possible problem and identifying what may be done to solve the problem. Do not automatically assume that psychopathology exists.

A final practice to consider in social-emotional assessment of young children is effectively linking such assessment results to intervention strategies. With older children and adolescents there is typically a greater availability of empirically validated assessment and intervention technologies. Practitioners who work with young children are faced not only with fewer technically sound assessment methods and instruments, but possibly more difficulty in selecting appropriate intervention strategies. Assessment that takes into consideration the important elements that will be needed to develop effective intervention has been referred to as *intervention-based assessment* (Barnett, Bell, Stone, Gilkey, & J. Smith, 1997). In this regard, Flugum and Reschly (1994) identified six quality indicators related to successful interventions: behavioral definition of the problem, direct measurement of the targeted behavior in the natural setting, detailed intervention plan, intervention integrity, graphing of intervention results, and comparison of postintervention performance with baseline data. It is recommended that the link to intervention with young children will be enhanced by selecting methods, instruments, and an overall assessment design that will allow for as much eventual intervention integrity as possible. Without a doubt, most of these characteristics could be used as benchmarks on which to develop and judge the efficacy of a planned assessment.

CONCLUSIONS

School psychologists, clinical child psychologists, special education diagnosticians, and other child-serving professionals are increasingly being asked to provide comprehensive services to young children, including social-emotional assessments. Unfortunately, the state of assessment technology designed specifically for the unique needs of this age group lags behind what is available for use with older children and adolescents. An additional problem is that many clinicians have received minimal or no formal training in assessing young children, which requires special knowledge, care, and sensitivity to do effectively. Despite the problems and challenges involved in social-emotional assessment of young children, there have been numerous improvements and new developments in this area in recent years.

Traditional diagnostic classification systems for emotional and behavioral disorders of childhood (e.g., the *DSM–IV*) are often of limited use with young children. A new alternative diagnostic classification system designed specifically for use with young children, the *Diagnostic Classification: 0–3*, has been developed to supplement the more traditional systems. This new system uses a multiaxial classification format that is somewhat similar to that of *DSM–IV*, but is designed to take into account the specific ways in which behavioral and emotional problems are manifest by very young children. This system is also unique because of its strong focus on the quality of the relationship of the children and their parent.

Each of the five major assessment methods that are the focus of this book can be used with varying degrees with young children, assuming that certain modifications or precautions are taken into consideration. Direct behavioral observation has a long history of use for assessing social and emotional behavior of young children, and offers the advantage of empirical assessment within naturalistic settings. However, recent research has indicated that the social behavior or young children is highly variable, and multiple observations of behavior may be needed to provide a reliable assessment. Developers of behavior rating scales for children historically have ignored the special characteristics and needs of young children, but this situation is changing. Recently developed rating scales such as the Behavioral Assessment System for Children, Child Behavior Checklist for Ages 2–3, Caregiver–Teacher Report Form for Ages 2–5, Preschool and Kindergarten Behavior Scales, and Social Skills Rating System have helped to move rating scale technology for use with young children to increasingly higher standards of technical adequacy and usability.

Clinical interviewing of young children has been an extremely popular method of assessment, albeit one fraught with obstacles. Although even the best clinicians who employ interview methods with young children may have difficulty obtaining consistent or highly objective information, interviews can be used effectively for various purposes. With proper modifications and precautions, interviews can help clinicians better understand and gain rapport with the child, and may serve as a valuable component of comprehensive assessment design. Although the research on using sociometric assessment approaches with young children has yielded mixed results, there is convincing evidence that such techniques may be very useful and predictive of future behavior, particularly when appropriate modifications are made, such as using photographs of children and alternative picture-based response formats. Self-report methods of social-emotional assessment are for the most part virtually impossible to implement with young children, because they require the ability to read and make cognitive differentiations that are simply beyond the capabilities of almost all children younger than about second grade. One exception to the dearth of appropriate self-report assessment instruments for young children is the Pictorial Scale of Perceived Competence and Acceptance for Young Children, a unique instrument that utilizes pictorial item stimuli and response formats to evaluate how young children feel regarding their social acceptance and self-efficacy.

Combining the elements of several different assessment methods, the Early Screening Project (ESP) is an innovative multiple gating assessment system that has been proven useful as a child-find technique for screening emotional and behavioral disorders of young children. The ESP may be used in its entirety for comprehensive screening of populations of young children, or its various components, such as the social behavior observations, may be used with other methods as part of an comprehensive assessment design.

For optimum effectiveness, certain practices should be incorporated into social-emotional assessment of young children, without regard to the type of design or methodology that is employed in the assessment. Among these practices and modifications, full participation and partnerships with parents, caution with respect to "pathologizing" child behavior, and developing effective linkages to interventions are especially recommended.

REVIEW AND APPLICATION QUESTIONS

1. What are some of the major difficulties in conducting adequate social-emotional assessments with young children?

2. How does the Zero to Three diagnostic classification system for young children compare to the major classification systems discussed in chapter 2?

3. What is known regarding the reliability of behavior of young children over time? How does this knowledge translate into practice in terms of conducting direct behavioral observations?

4. Four nationally normed behavior rating scales for use with young children were reviewed. In what circumstances or for what types of referral problems would each of these instruments be best used?

5. Given that interviewing with young children is problematic at best, what can be done to minimize the problems and enhance the validity of the interview?

6. What are some explanations for the lower reliability over time of sociometric procedures with young children in comparison with school-age children? Does this lower reliability necessarily reduce validity of sociometric procedures with younger children?

7. Describe the various "gates," or stages, in the Early Screening Project. For what purposes is this system best used?

8. What are some specific practices in assessment of young children that may be helpful to avoid "overpathologizing" them?

ASSESSMENT AND
CULTURAL DIVERSITY

The general topic of psychological and educational assessment and cultural diversity has received a great deal of professional and public attention during the past three decades. Some well-known court cases in the 1970s and 1980s, most notably *Larry P. v. Riles* and *Diana v. State Board of Education* (both in California) and *Guadalupe v. Tempe Elementary School District* (Arizona), placed the issue of cultural validity of standardized assessment instruments in the forefront, and resulted in legal constraints on special education assessment practices with racial/ethnic minority youth. More recently, a widespread flurry of professional and public attention accompanied Hernstein and Murray's (1994) *The Bell Curve: Intelligence and Class Structure in American Life*, a volume addressing the issue of racial/ethnic differences and possible bias on IQ and achievement tests. These few examples among many provide some evidence that the issue of cultural diversity in assessment has been viewed as a serious concern.

However, professional, public, and legal attention on this topic has been focused almost exclusively within the domain of cognitive assessment, as stated in chapter 1. By comparison, very little serious attention has been paid to the issue of cultural diversity and behavioral, social, and emotional assessment; and most of this attention has been on assessment with adults rather than children. For whatever reason, the assessment establishment and the public have accepted much of the reasoning on behavioral, social, and emotional assessment across cultures rather uncritically. This statement should not be implied to mean that there are no critics of these practices. On the contrary, a handful of writers have decried the current state of affairs regarding assessment and cultural diversity, including the social-emotional domain. For example, Dana (1996), a noted writer and scholar in the area of multicultural applications of psychological assessment, stated:

> With few exceptions the psychological tests used in the United States have been designed by Europeans or North Americans and embody a Eurocentric world view and derivative psychometric technology. Comparisons among ranked individuals or groups expose human differences within a format of psychological judgment using Anglo American normative standards. Standard tests of intelligence, personality, and psychopathology are often as-

sumed to be genuine *etics*, or *culture-general* in application. In fact, most of these tests are *culture-specific* or *emic* measures designed for Anglo Americans, but have been construed as imposed etic measures, or pseudo etics, because the equivalence with different cultural groups has not been demonstrated. (p. 477, italics added)

This strong and unequivocal statement raises many concerns regarding assessment practices with children and youth of diverse cultural backgrounds. Statements such as this one also raise many questions, such as:

- Should it be assumed that standardized norm-referenced tests based on representative normative samples that approximate the general U.S. population are not appropriate for use with individuals from racial or ethnic minority groups?
- Is the use of local norms more appropriate than the use of national representative norms for assessment of minority children and youth who live in areas where their own racial/ethnic group is the majority?
- Are standardized norm-referenced assessment procedures more biased than qualitative or unstructured assessment procedures, such as projective techniques and unstructured interviews, for members of racial/ethnic minority groups?
- Are the assumptions regarding test bias that are based on intellectual and academic achievement measures appropriately inferred for measures of behavioral, social, and emotional functioning?

These are difficult questions, and as is demonstrated throughout this chapter, the answers are equally difficult, and in many cases equivocal or even impossible to fully answer given the relative paucity of empirical evidence in this area. This final chapter is an attempt to explore issues of cultural diversity within the framework of behavioral, social, and emotional assessment of children and adolescents. At present, this topic involves questions and issues that simply have not been sufficiently addressed and answered in most cases. Therefore, this chapter is an attempt to break some new ground and to raise awareness regarding some thorny assessment issues that may take several more years of empirical study to be adequately addressed. In comparison with the voluminous evidence and opinion that has accumulated regarding cultural diversity within the framework of intellectual/academic assessment, relatively little is known in this area regarding personality or behavior assessment (Hood & Johnson, 1997). Added to this problem is a widely held assumption that, in general, knowledge regarding assessment of children tends to lag behind in comparison with the empirical evidence regarding adult-focused assessment practices.

The body of this chapter begins with a discussion of test and assessment bias in professional practice, and the role that organizational standards play in shaping multicultural assessment practices. Next, some concepts related to acculturation and racial/cultural identity development are presented, including theorized stages of identity development. With some cautions in place regarding potential problems that result from overemphasizing between-group differences (e.g., stereotyping and divisiveness between groups), some general demographic information and psychosocial characteristics of the major racial/ethnic groups in the United States is presented. Special considerations for culturally competent assessment of social-emotional behavior within each of the major assessment methods are then reviewed, with an emphasis on the known problems and solutions regarding each method. The chapter ends with the presentation of 11 recommendations for culturally competent assessment practice.

TEST AND ASSESSMENT BIAS IN PROFESSIONAL PRACTICE

This section focuses on some specific aspects of assessment theory and practice that are highly related to the area of cultural diversity. These include theory of test and assessment bias, examination of current professional standards related to culturally appropriate assessment practices, and an overview of current practices and future directions in this area among professionals.

Test and Assessment Bias

The terms *test bias* and *assessment bias* have been used in various ways in the professional literature. Some discussions of these concepts refer to them in terms of inappropriate *uses* of assessment instruments, whereas other discussions couch definitions of bias in terms of the *properties* of the instrument or procedure. In reality, both situations may cause bias. Although there is no universal definition of test or assessment bias, a psychological or educational assessment instrument or procedure is considered to be biased if it "differentiates between members of various groups on basis other than the characteristic being measured" (F. G. Brown, 1983, p. 224). In operational terms, such bias is said to exist if "its content, procedures or use result in a systematic advantage or disadvantage to members of certain groups over other groups and if the basis of this differentiation is irrelevant to the test purpose" (F. G. Brown, 1983, p. 224). Thus, behavioral, social, or emotional assessment instruments or procedures would be considered biased if their use resulted in *systematic improper* diagnosis, classification, or service provision for a specific group of children (i.e., based on race/ethnicity).

Because most discussions of test or assessment bias are usually in relation to cognitive tests (i.e., IQ and academic achievement tests), many of the traditional methods of demonstrating that a test is acceptably unbiased may be problematic when assessment of social-emotional behavior is considered. There are some major differences between cognitive and social-emotional tests that make across-the-board methodological comparisons difficult. For example, virtually all cognitive tests have a correct, or "right," answer, are scored in a dichotomous manner (yes/no, correct/incorrect), and result in distributions of scores that closely approximate a normally distributed bell-shaped curve. Conversely, standardized instruments designed to assess social-emotional behavior almost never have a "right" answer, and often are scored along a gradient, such as a 4-point scale. And unlike cognitive tests, distributions of scores of social-emotional instruments are seldom (if ever) normal, but tend to be skewed toward a lack of symptomatology in the normal population.

Viewing assessment bias as a yes/no or all-or-nothing proposition is a result of faulty reasoning. In fact, because assessment bias may include the properties of an instrument as well as the manner in which it is used, it would be incorrect to state unequivocally that a specific assessment tool was absolutely free of any biasing characteristics. Even if the internal properties of an instrument, such as the items, score norms, and factor structure were demonstrated to be equivalent for various racial/ethnic groups, the instrument could still be used in a manner that may be inappropriate for individuals with particular types of background characteristics. Therefore, the goal for valid assessment of children's social-emotional behavior should be to implement it in a culturally appropriate manner, and to reduce threats of assessment bias.

Professional Ethics and Culturally Appropriate Assessment

During the past two decades, there has been increased emphasis within the ethical codes and standards of professional organizations regarding cultural diversity, cultural differences, and cultural appropriateness of assessment materials. These various ethical standards tend to serve as minimal guidelines. That is, they provide some general statements regarding expectations for appropriate professional practice, but they usually do not go beyond that level of specificity. Thus, the most influential professional organizations that represent individuals who are involved with psychological and educational assessment have demonstrated an interest in advocating for culturally appropriate assessment practices, but have in most cases not prescribed specific models or best practices.

The *Ethical Principles of Psychologists and Code of Conduct* of the American Psychological Association (APA, 1992) were last revised in 1992. The 1992 revision was considered to be a fairly substantial change from the previously existing version in terms of increased relevance to culturally sensitive practice. For example, General Principle D: Respect for People's Rights and Dignity, includes statements regarding valuing human diversity and cultural differences, although it is not specific to assessment practices. Ethical Standard 1.10 involves nondiscrimination, and states that in their work, psychologists do not engage in unfair discriminatory practices based on a variety of human differences, including (among other things) race, ethnicity, and national origin. Most specifically, Ethical Standard 2.04 states that "psychologists attempt to identify situations in which particular . . . assessment techniques or norms may not be applicable or may require adjustment in administration or interpretation because of factors such as an individual's gender, race, ethnicity, national origin, sexual orientation, disability, language, or socioeconomic status." According to Dana (1994), there are other areas of the 1992 code that also have relevance for culturally sensitive assessment practice, such as statements regarding use of clients' first language, culture-specific service delivery styles, and recognition of non-Anglo belief systems.

The *Standards for the Provision of School Psychological Services* of the National Association of School Psychologists, which were last updated in 1997 (NASP, 1997), include several specific standards related to culturally appropriate assessment practice. Standard area 3.5, titled *Non-Biased Assessment and Program Planning*, is most specific in this regard. Perhaps the most relevant specific standards are 3.5.3.1 through 3.5.3.3, which state:

3.5.3.1: Assessment procedures and program recommendations are chosen to maximize the student's opportunities to be successful in the general culture, while respecting the student's ethnic background.

3.5.3.2: Multifaceted assessment batteries are used which include a focus on the student's strengths.

3.5.3.3: Communications are held and assessments are conducted in the client's dominant spoken language or alternative communication system. All student information is interpreted in the context of the student's socio-cultural background and the setting in which she/he is functioning.

The jointly produced *Standards for Educational and Psychological Testing* (1985), a combined effort of the American Educational Research Association, American Psychological Association, and National Council on Measurement in Education, is a highly influential document among educational and psychological testing experts. Like the ethical codes of APA and NASP, the *Standards* include specific statements regarding culturally appropriate methods of administering and interpreting standardized assessment instruments. However, unlike the two ethical codes, the *Standards* include specific details regarding instrument development, and two of these are very specific to cultural diversity:

> When selecting the type and content of items for tests and inventories, test developers should consider the content and type in relation to cultural backgrounds and prior experiences of the variety of ethnic, cultural, age, and gender groups represented in the intended population of test takers. (Standard 3.5, *Standards*, 1985, p. 26)

> When previous research indicates the need for studies of item or test performance differences for a particular kind of test for members of age, ethnic, cultural, and gender groups in the population of test takers, such studies should be conducted as soon as is feasible. Such research should be designed to detect and eliminate aspects of test design, content, or format that might bias test scores for particular groups. (Standard 3.10, *Standards*, 1985, p. 27)

In sum, various professional organizations and associations that have interests in psychological and educational assessment have made cultural aspects of assessment specific targets of their standards in recent years, to varying degrees of specificity. Although some of the changes that have been evidenced in the various revisions of these codes in recent years have indeed focused more attention on cultural sensitivity issues, some writers (e.g., Dana, 1994) have argued that the changes have not gone far enough, and that the standards still avoid areas that remain controversial. In reality, these guidelines only provide a framework for professionals, and do not detail highly specific suggestions for professional practice. It is anticipated that future revisions to these and similar standards will include an increased focus on issues of cultural diversity, including applications in assessment.

Professional Practice

According to Dana (1995), there are three major deficiencies in standard psychological assessment practice that result in culturally inappropriate assessment. These deficiencies include *test construction*, *test administration*, and *interpretation*. In Dana's view, test construction may lead to cultural bias because development of traditional assessment instruments has been based on a psychometric paradigm that may result in culture-specific tests that are only appropriate for individuals within a European-American cultural context. Essentially, these types of development practices may create a "one size fits all" assessment instrument that simply is not appropriate for many individuals. In addition, traditional methods of standardized test administration tend to be impersonal, and may cause individuals who are not comfortable with the examiner or situation to respond in ways that do not reflect their true characteristics. And, traditional methods of test interpretation that are rigid and based on culturocentric views of human behavior may result in "overpathologization" of individuals who are not part of the dominant culture, or in other words, characterize them as being "more disturbed than in fact they are" (Dana, 1995, p. 63). It is obvious that to the extent these problems exist, they clearly violate the spirit and letter of the various professional standards that have been established regarding culturally appropriate assessment. It is also clear that although change in this area has been slow to emerge, it will certainly continue, perhaps with increased speed.

The future of culturally appropriate assessment, according to Dana, will be development, administration, and interpretation procedures that expand the concept of individual differences to include gender and culture. This future will be in the direction of *social constructivism*, or constructing specific methods of assessment and interpretation that are flexible and appropriate within a given context for a given individual. The relationship between examiner and subject will take on a new importance in such an assessment model. In recent years, new models for conceptualizing and implementing assessment in a culturally appropriate manner consistent with Dana's recommendations have been explored. An example of one such model is *responsive assessment*, as advocated by Henning-Stout (1994). Responsive assessment is perhaps best characterized as a way of implementing assessment rather than a type of assessment. The traditional mystique surrounding formal psychological testing and the authority position of the professional conducting the assessment is supplanted by a broader view of assessment as a *process*. In this process, the examiner works with the client and other individuals who have an interest in the outcome of the assessment (i.e., parents, teachers) to design and implement an assessment that is authentic, culturally acceptable, and appropriately focused on the issues of concern. The participants in this process are referred to as *stakeholders*, reflecting the more egalitarian nature of the relationships of those involved, and emphasizing accountability of the examiner. It is certain that other models for implementing psychological and educational assessment in a culturally appropriate manner will continue to emerge during the next decade, and that the sociocultural aspects of assessment will play a role of increasing importance.

ACCULTURATION AND IDENTITY DEVELOPMENT

When dealing with the issue of cultural diversity and educational/mental health service delivery, it is crucial to understand that among individuals of all racial/ethnic minority groups, there is wide variation in terms of their orientation toward the traditional characteristics of their racial/ethnic group, assimilation into the majority culture, and their own racial/ethnic identity. *Acculturation* is defined as "a process of cultural change that occurs in individuals when two cultures meet; it leads the individuals to adopt elements of another culture, such as values and social behaviors" (Sattler, 1998, p. 264). When an individual who is a member of a minority group begins to examine and understand the differences between their group and the majority group, the process of acculturation is inevitable. However, the outcome of this process varies widely. The actual process of acculturation "may involve several stages, including initial joy, relief, and idealization of the new culture; disillusionment associated with the adjustment; and gradual acceptance of the good and bad aspects of the new culture" (Sattler, 1998, p. 264). It should be noted that although acculturation is most often association to racial/ethnic group identity, it is not necessarily limited to this domain. For example, individuals who are members of an obscure religious group that is viewed with disdain by the dominant culture may go through a similar process, as may individuals who do not have a heterosexual orientation.

Factors That Influence Acculturation

According to Kumabe, Nishida, and Hepworth (1985), there are several factors that may influence whether or not individuals from racial/ethnic minority groups maintain or depart from the traditional cultural practices of their group, or allow these traditional practices to coexist with new practices adopted from the majority group. The seven primary factors within this model include history of migration experience (i.e., whether it was freely chosen or coerced), distance from the country of origin and indigenous culture, place of residence and socioeconomic status, type of neighborhood in the resettlement country (i.e., whether there are others close by who share the same racial/ethnic ties), closeness of ties with immediate and extended family, and uniqueness of language and customs from the homeland. Thus, whether an individual from a racial/ethnic minority group maintains strong cultural ties to that group may depend on several important variables, and clinicians cannot presume to understand the degree of acculturation or cultural assimilation without first attempting to investigate it.

Determining Acculturation and Cultural Orientation

In conducting psychological assessments with children, youth, and their families, there may be times when it is essential to determine, as accurately as possible, their level of acculturation and cultural orientation. In some cases, such information may have a direct bearing on how valid the assessment results may be considered. In other cases, acculturation information will be essential for translating assessment data into culturally appropriate intervention plans. Unfortunately, there is no universal method of determining acculturation or cultural orientation. Dana (1993, 1995) reviewed several instruments or research tools that have been developed for determining acculturation or cultural orientation of individuals from specific racial/ethnic minority groups. These instruments often provide information on both the traditional culture and the level of acquisition of values of the dominant society. However, these tools have primarily been developed for use with adults and older adolescents. In most cases, it is unclear how effectively they might be used with children and youth, although it is reasonable to assume they could be at least adapted to provide a general framework.

In the absence of specific child-oriented standardized tools for determining acculturation and cultural orientation of youths from various racial/ethnic minority groups, there are other practices to be considered. Simple information gathering prior to the assessment is one possibility. The examiner could carefully consult existing records and question teachers, parents, and other referral sources regarding such issues as language proficiency and preference, typical social behavior, involvement and participation in customs of the traditional culture, and apparent comfort with adults from other racial/ethnic groups. Another possibility is to attempt to ascertain this information directly from the child or adolescent client during the process of assessment. Admittedly, this latter possibility will be very difficult in some cases. A racial/ethnic minority youth who is primarily oriented toward their traditional culture may not be comfortable with an examiner who is a member of the majority group, and in the absence of a strong relationship of trust that has been formed between the professional and the client, the obtained data are clearly suspect (Dana, 1993, 1995, 1996). Therefore, special care and perhaps extra time should be devoted to the process of building trust, forming rapport, and generally establishing familiarity between the persons who are of strongly differing cultural backgrounds if useful assessment data are to be gathered. Readers are referred to the previous three references by Dana for more information regarding the process of determining acculturation and obtaining valid assessment data with diverse groups of clients.

Racial/Cultural Identity Development

As stated previously, individuals' level of acculturation in their traditional culture is likely to depend on many factors, and the general level of acculturation is likely to have an important bearing on how effective traditional methods of assessment will

TABLE 14.1
Stages of Minority Racial/Cultural Development, Based on Previous Work
by Atkinson, Morten, and D. W. Sue (1989), and D. W. Sue and D. Sue (1990)

Stage	Characteristics
1. Conformity	Depreciating attitude toward self and others of same minority group; discriminatory attitude toward other minority groups; appreciating attitude toward dominant group.
2. Dissonance	Conflict between depreciating and appreciating attitudes toward self, others of same minority group, other minority groups, and dominant group.
3. Resistance and Immersion	Appreciating attitude toward self and others of same minority group; conflict between empathetic and culturocentric feelings toward other minority groups; depreciating attitude toward dominant group.
4. Introspection	Concern with basis of self-appreciation and unequivocal nature of appreciation toward others of same minority group; concern with culturocentric views toward members of other minority groups; concern with basis of depreciation of dominant group.
5. Integrative Awareness	Appreciating attitude toward self, others of same minority group, and other minority groups; selective appreciation for dominant group.

be with these individuals. Related to these concepts is the idea of racial or cultural identity development. In this sense, identity is defined as a sense of belonging to a racial/ethnic group, and how this sense of belonging influences behavior, thought, and affect. D. W. Sue and D. Sue (1990) articulated the emerging evidence and recent thought regarding racial/cultural identity development among minority group members. Based on a wide variety of research and writing in this area, a general consensus has emerged that such identity development tends to follow a distinct set of stages. These include *conformity* (Stage 1), *dissonance* (Stage 2), *resistance and immersion* (Stage 3), *introspection* (Stage 4), and *integrative awareness* (Stage 5). These stages are discussed briefly in this section, and are presented in summary form in Table 14.1.

Stage 1: Conformity. During Stage 1, individuals accept and value the characteristics of the dominant culture as being the norm, and prefer these values over the traditional values espoused by their own group. In fact, individuals at this stage of development take on a self-depreciating attitude, often viewing their own group with disdain. According to D. W. Sue and D. Sue (1990), the conformity stage "represents, perhaps, the most damning indictment of White racism" (p. 96). Individuals at this stage may be immersed in self-hatred, suffer from low self-esteem, and uncritically adopt the values and views of the dominant culture.

Stage 2: Dissonance. During Stage 2, individuals begin to feel discomfort or dissonance regarding some of the beliefs they have adopted. For example, "A Hispanic individual who may feel ashamed of his cultural upbringing may encounter another Hispanic who seems proud of his/her cultural heritage" (D. W. Sue & D. Sue, 1990, p. 101). This tends to be a gradual process. Conflict begins to emerge between self- and group-deprecation and appreciation. Individuals may also begin to have doubts regarding their uncritical valuation and acceptance of the dominant culture.

Stage 3: Resistance and Immersion. In Stage 3, individuals reject the values and views of the dominant culture, and begin to immerse themselves in the minority views of their own culture. At this point, the attitude toward the majority group becomes negative and depreciating, whereas attitudes toward those of other minority groups begin to become conflicted between feelings of culturocentrism and shared empathy for their differing minority experience. According to D. W. Sue and D. Sue (1990), the three most common feelings that characterize this stage are guilt, shame, and anger. The anger may be directed outwardly with great force to combat racism and oppression.

Stage 4: Introspection.   As individuals move into Stage 4, they may begin to question the basis and nature of their unequivocal appreciation and acceptance of their own group values, and the basis for the unanimous rejection of the majority group. Attitudes toward other minorities may reflect concern with ethnocentrism as a basis for forming judgments. As D. W. Sue and D. Sue (1990) put it, "The resistance and immersion stage tends to be a reaction against the dominant culture and is not proactive in allowing the individual to use all energies to discover who or what he or she is" (p. 104). Thus, the need for more realistic self-definition and discovery emerges.

Stage 5: Integrative Awareness.   Individuals who move into Stage 5 have resolved many of their previous conflicts. They now have adopted an attitude that focuses on self-appreciation, group-appreciation, appreciation of other minority groups, as well as selective appreciation of the dominant culture. Their own culture is no longer viewed as necessarily being in conflict with the dominant culture. "There is now the belief that there are acceptable and unacceptable aspects in all cultures, and that it is very important for the person to be able to examine and accept or reject those aspects of a culture that are not seen as desirable" (D. W. Sue & D. Sue, 1990, p. 106).

This stage theory of racial/cultural identity, as discussed by D. W. Sue and D. Sue (1990) and others (e.g., Atkinson, Morten, & D. W. Sue, 1989), has a couple of highly relevant implications for working with children and youth. First, like most social-emotional stage theories of development, not all individuals progress neatly through the various stages, and some individuals never proceed past a given stage. And second, it appears to be linked to some extent to both cognitive and social-emotional development. It would be highly unlikely or impossible for children or adolescents to have moved through all of the stages, because of their limited life experiences and their developing capabilities. It should be recognized that individuals from the dominant culture may also develop racial/cultural attitudes through a similar process, although the characteristics of each stage will differ from those presented herein. Essentially, a majority person who moves through these stages of identity development will progress from a highly ethnocentric worldview to the development of a nonracist identity. An example of a poignant personal account of how an individual may move through the various stages of racial/cultural identity development is found in *The Autobiography of Malcolm X* (Haley, 1996), which vividly tells the story of how a historically prominent Black man moved from an attitude of self-hatred to militant anger to eventual acceptance of the limitations of his previous views shortly before his own violent death.

PROBLEMS WITH CATEGORIES AND GROUP EMPHASIS

One of the major issues in regard to understanding appropriate assessment practices for individuals from specific cultural backgrounds (i.e., similar race/ethnicity) is the development and use of appropriate language and schemas (categories) to describe groups of people. Regarding race and ethnicity, the specific focus of this chapter, there is no single definition of these terms that is generally agreed on, and it is common for researchers and practitioners to refer to ethnicity, culture, and race in an interchangeable manner when identifying and categorizing individuals by these background characteristics (Okazaki & S. Sue, 1995). The term *race* is usually used to imply some observable physical characteristic that is common to a group, such as skin and eye color, hair type, facial features, and so forth. On the other hand, *ethnicity* is commonly used to describe characteristics that may be less externally observable. This term usually refers to a common group cultural history, such as language, country of origin, or religion.

The terms *race* and *ethnicity* have both been constantly under fire in recent years, and at times can be very politically charged. For example, regional allotment of federal government funds is affected by changes in racial category distribution, and district realignment for voting purposes may also be affected (Okazaki & S. Sue, 1995). However, many Americans do not neatly fit into simple categories. For example, professional golfer Tiger Woods referred to himself as "Cablinasian," to reflect his diverse racial/ethnic heritage. During preliminary planning for the national census for the year 2000, the U.S. Bureau of the Census briefly considered the possibility of creating a new "multiracial" category to add to the existing traditional categories, an idea that created tremendous controversy (e.g., Eddings, 1997), and that was ultimately rejected (although it was later determined that individuals could check more than one racial category to describe themselves, and that the category of "Asian or Pacific Islander" would be separated into two distinct categories).

In this chapter, the hybrid term *race/ethnicity* is used to describe the major focus on cultural diversity. However, it must be understood that this term, like all the other categories and labels used to describe groups of people, is imperfect and potentially problematic. For example, take the case of two American children, one who traces his ancestry to Vietnam (his family emigrated to the United States in the 1980s), and the other who traces her ancestry to Japan (her family emigrated to the United States in the 1920s). The U.S. Bureau of the Census would currently classify both of these children as "Asian or Pacific Islander," and a professional research study in which they participated might refer to them in the written report both as "Asian American" participants. However, the cultural characteristics they share in common may be truly minimal, and in some respects, they might each share more background characteristics with individuals from other groups than with each other.

A related problem in this area is that emphasizing specific group membership tends to place a strong emphasis on differences among persons from various racial/ethnic groups, and may in some cases unduly overemphasize such differences. There is certainly an understandable rationale for the practice of describing or trying to understand individuals based on their racial/ethnic background characteristics, because this practice is based on the assumption that "such shared cultural-psychological characteristics are related to personality or psychopathology" (Okazaki & S. Sue, 1995, p. 368). However, it is easy for this type of grouping emphasis to ultimately distort a simple truth regarding human behavior: With very few exceptions, variation within groups is always greater than variation between groups. For example, assume that a norm-referenced self-report test of personality and behavior problems for adolescents, when scrutinized statistically, shows evidence that racial/ethnic group X tends to have higher scores than racial/ethnic group Y on a subscale measuring *emotional distress*. Also assume that these differences are small but still significantly different from a statistical standpoint. A focus on the score differences between the two groups might lead to the assumption that members of group X tend to be in continual emotional turmoil and that, perhaps, this is a defining characteristic of group X. Conversely, a critic of norm-referenced testing might argue that the self-report instrument is not appropriate for (or even biased against) members of group X. Both assumptions could easily mask the truth of the matter: There is substantially more variation in self-reported emotional distress among persons within each group than there is between the two groups. In sum, it appears that although emphasis on and sensitivity to differences in racial/ethnic groups is necessary and important, too much emphasis may result in distortion of fairly small differences among groups, and ultimately lead to stereotyping based on group membership (D. W. Sue & D. Sue, 1990).

MAJOR RACIAL/ETHNIC GROUPS IN THE UNITED STATES: AN OVERVIEW

With the cautions in place regarding the impact of acculturation and moderator variables on racial/ethnic identity, as well as the potential problems and controversies regarding emphasis on shared group identity and characteristics, this section provides some basic information regarding the major racial/ethnic groups in the United States, as they are typically defined. This information includes a focus on population characteristics, including specific issues that may be highly relevant to behavioral, social, and emotional assessment of children and youth.

When considering this information, it is important to recognize that the population distribution statistics for children differ somewhat from the statistics for adults or the general population. For example, the 1990 U.S. census reported that of all children under age 18, 67% were White, non-Hispanic. However, 75.6% of the total population of the United States (all ages combined) was listed in this manner (U.S. Bureau of the Census, 1993a–c, 1997), a difference of about 10%. These estimates indicate that the child and adolescent population in the United States is more racially/ethnically diverse than the adult population, reflecting such factors as a younger mean age for several racial/ethnic minority groups, as well as higher birthrates and emigration patterns in some instances.

Another fact to consider in the interpretation of basic information presented on racial/ethnic groups is that the U.S. demographic makeup is changing rapidly. Population estimates for the near future predict increasing racial/ethnic diversity, and a gradual but continuous diminishment of the percentage of Americans who are in the current racial/ethnic majority group. Whereas the most recent population estimates show that about three fourths of all Americans are White, non-Hispanic, this percentage is expected to shrink to a slight majority (barely over half) by the year 2050 (Rosenblatt, 1996). Embedded in this estimate is the projection that Hispanics will become the largest racial/ethnic minority group in the nation by about 2010 (surpassing African Americans, the current largest minority group), and will comprise nearly one quarter of the entire U.S. population by the year 2050. Thus, it is important to consider the dynamic nature of the American population. In every region of the nation, the population will reflect increasing racial/ethnic diversity as the next few decades emerge. In border states such as California, Arizona, Texas, and Florida, these changes are already making a dramatic impact.

A final note before beginning the information on each specific racial/ethnic group: First, this is a very limited overview that necessarily focuses on only a few key characteristics and at the same time ignores other important characteristics. Readers desiring a more in-depth description of specific racial/ethnic group characteristics should refer to other sources. And, second, although it has been stated explicitly and implied previously in this chapter, it is worth repeating: Psychological charactcristics associated with specific groups are generalities based on group research. They do not apply to all members, or even necessarily a majority of members, of particular groups.

African Americans

African Americans (or Black Americans) include those individuals in the United States who trace their ancestry to the continent of Africa, specifically to native African groups of dark skin color (e.g., as opposed to White South Africans who trace their African ancestry to European colonists). The 1990 U.S. census reported that 12.3% of the general population was African American, which was the largest racial/ethnic minority group. This percentage is expected to increase to 16.2% by 2050, although it is not expected to constitute the largest racial/ethnic minority population at that time because the Hispanic population is expected to grow at a substantially faster rate (Aponte & Crouch, 1995). The majority of African Americans live in the Southeastern U.S. region (53%), followed by the Midwest (19%), Northeast (15%), and West (9%) (U.S. Bureau of the Census, 1997).

Although African Americans may include recent immigrants from the African continent who have left their native nations by choice for various personal, political, or economic reasons (or the descendants of individuals who did likewise), this situation is not the most typical. By far, this category includes a majority of individuals whose ancestors were removed from their African homelands through coercive and violent means, primarily by Europeans, through what has been referred to as the *African Diaspora*: the slave trade that flourished in the colonies and states (as well as other parts of the Western hemisphere) from the 1600s through the mid-1800s. Thus, the collective identity and experience of most African Americans is intertwined with the most divisive and wrenching issue in the nation's history. Indeed, for many Americans, the continuing problem of race relations is primarily viewed as a White/Black issue, owing to the tremendous and continuing ramifications from the nation's past, including the history of institutionalized racism.

Some of the major behavioral, social, and emotional considerations regarding African American youth have been discussed by Rivers and Morrow (1995), and by Sattler (1998). One important charactcristic is the emphasis and prestige placed on strong verbal and language skills, especially assertive and emotionally expressive communication. Many Black children and adolescents speak a variation of standard English that has been referred to as *Black English*, or *Ebonics*, which may be used to varying degrees and in various situations, depending on the acculturation of the individual and their connection to the majority culture. Some basic examples of Black English include the use of "do" instead of the standard English use of "does," omitting "is" and "are" from sentences, and reversing the /s/ and /k/ sounds that appear in that order in Standard English usage, such as pronouncing the word "ask" as "/aks/." Although the uninitiated interviewer from another culture may mistakenly view the use of Black English as an indication of poor language development, in reality, it is a complex linguistic system that has its roots in the oral language traditions of West African languages. In terms of affect, "Black [youth] typically are described as expressive, lively, and extroverted" (Sattler, 1998, p. 283). African American youth have been shown to have similar levels of positive self-concept as White youth, but may value such attributes as verbal skills, assertion, and athletic ability at a higher level. Regarding family life, African American families are more likely than White families to be headed by a female, but typical family structures are likely to be similar among the groups. A significant issue for many Black youth is the low value often placed on success and achievement in the school setting by their peers. Because many Black youth, particularly those who live in poverty in inner-city areas, may feel alienated from the educational system and believe it is futile for them to try to succeed in it, a peer backlash is sometimes focused against those Black youth who are high achieving students (Pearson, 1994). Interpersonally, Black adolescents are known for forming close associations with same-sex peers. Such close associations may provide a stronger sense of social identity, but can also result in pressure to participate in antisocial activities (i.e., through gang membership) in areas where such groups are common. Although the history of institutionalized racism, cultural appropriation, and lack of opportunities many African Americans have experienced has produced a strong resiliency in some, it has resulted in numerous problems for many Black youth: high dropout rates from school; pressure for participation in gang activities; feelings of rage, futility, and hopelessness; and, particularly among young Black males, heightened probabilities for death through homicide and overrepresentation in the criminal justice system.

Asian Americans

Asian Americans comprise a rapidly growing racial/ethnic minority population in the United States. The U.S. Bureau of the Census has historically included Asian Americans within the category Asian and Pacific Islander, although this category is slated to be divided into two separate categories for the 2000 census. In the 1990 census, 3.0% of the U.S. population fit into this category. The absolute numbers and relative percentages of Asian Americans are expected to grow during the next several decades, and this group is expected to comprise 10.7% of the general U.S. population by the year 2050 (Aponte & Crouch, 1995), primarily because of continual emigration to the United States from Asian and Pacific Rim nations. The largest concentrations of Asian Americans are in the West and Pacific Northwest regions of the United States.

Asian Americans constitute an extremely diverse group. Most individuals within this general category trace their ancestral heritage to China, Japan, Korea, the Philippines, and several Southeast Asian nations, such as Laos, Cambodia, and Vietnam. D. Sue and S. Sue (1987) noted that there are at least 29 distinct subgroups of Asian Americans, each with differing languages, customs, religions, levels of acculturation, and historical reasons for emigration to the United States. Some of these subgroups are recent arrivals to the United States, whereas others have been in the nation for several generations (Aponte & Crouch, 1995). Many Asian Americans are faced with special problems such as English language competency. It is interesting to note that there is a bimodal distribution of wealth among Asian Americans, with some having achieved great economic success and a large proportion (primarily those of Southeast Asian descent) living at the economic poverty level (U.S. General Accounting Office, 1990). This notion is attested to by the fact that in the 1990 census, Asian Americans had the highest median family income of any racial/ethnic group, including Whites, but had a higher percentage of families and individuals living at or below the poverty level than Whites. As a group, Asian Americans tend to do well on standardized educational achievement tests, particularly in mathematics and the physical sciences, and they tend to be proportionately overrepresented at prestigious institutions of higher education, such as the University of California at Berkeley and the Massachussetts Institute of Technology. However, there is also a substantial percentage of Asian Americans who do not enjoy such notable educational success because of poverty, discrimination, and significant language barriers (Sattler, 1998).

Although Asian Americans constitute a truly diverse group, there are certain psychosocial characteristics that tend to be associated with the larger group, perhaps because of some common experiences and the heritage of an "eastern" worldview. One notable characteristic among Asian Americans is respect for the customs and traditions of their forebears and extended family. Asian Americans tend to be more socially and politically conservative than members of other racial/ethnic minority groups, often resisting change, stressing a high achievement orientation, and avoiding offending others. They are often perceived by members of other racial/ethnic groups as emotionally restrained because they may not demonstrate emotion in overt ways. Asian cultures tend to encourage interdependency and a group orientation, and to discourage individualism and an autonomous orientation. Asian American youth may experience conflicts regarding opposing pressures of assimilation into mainstream American culture and maintaining traditional family and cultural expectations. Many of these youth feel pressure to conform to stereotypes of being a "model minority," high educational achievers, and focused on mathematics and the physical sciences. Although there is little scientific research in this area, Asian American youth may be especially vulnerable to depression, based on the fact that the incidence of suicide among this group is higher than in the general population (Rivers & Morrow, 1995). It is interesting to note that suicide rates of Asian Americans are highest among recent immigrants, and are perhaps related to the stresses of acculturation and assimilation. It has been noted that Asian Americans tend to underutilize mental health services (D. W. Sue & D. Sue, 1990), and may be very uncomfortable with mental health service systems based on a Eurocentric tradition.

Hispanic Americans

The U.S. Bureau of the Census does not include Hispanic as a racial category. It is considered to be a category of ethnicity that primarily reflects descendence from Spanish-speaking countries in South and Central America and the Caribbean, Mexico, and the Southwestern United States (Aponte & Crouch, 1995). In some cases, Hispanic Americans may speak French or Portuguese. Obviously, this is a diverse racial/ethnic group. Most Hispanic Americans define themselves as White in the census racial category, but a sizable proportion define themselves as Black. Hispanic Americans presently constitute the second largest and fastest growing ethnic minority group in the United States, comprising 9.0% of the total population in the 1990 census, and projected to comprise 21.1% of the total population by 2050, when it will likely be the largest ethnic minority group (Aponte & Crouch, 1995). The largest percentage of Hispanic Americans live in the West (45%), followed by the South (30%), Northeast (17%), and Midwest (8%) (U.S. Bureau of the Census, 1993b). The highest concentrations of Hispanic Americans are in three states: California, Texas, and Florida.

Although Hispanics constitute a somewhat eclectic and diverse ethnic group, the majority of this group (over 60%) are of Mexican ancestry. Perhaps the most significant unifying background characteristic among all Hispanics is the historical (or present) connection to the Spanish language, and ultimately, from Spanish (and Portuguese) exploration and colonization in the Western hemisphere. Another significant historical commonality among Hispanic people is the influence of the Roman Catholic religion. Lee and Richardson (cited in Sattler, 1998, p. 291) stated that "Hispanic culture developed as a result of the fusion of Spanish culture (brought to the Americas by missionaries and conquistadors) with American Indian and African (the result of the slave trade) cultures." Indeed, the culture reflected in this ethnic heritage is eclectic. Historically, the nuclear and extended family, and the dominance of fathers and other males, along with a submissive and home-centered role for females, has played an important role in shaping Hispanic cultural characteristics (Rivers & Morrow, 1995). Group identity appears to be more important to most Hispanics than to most Whites, with the extended family taking priority over the individual in many cases. According to Sattler (1998), Hispanic Americans tend to place a high value on human relationships, identify strongly with their families, and feel comfortable with open displays of affection and emotion.

Because Hispanic American youth are a heterogeneous group, the characteristics that should be especially considered form a behavioral, social, or emotional perspective are varied. One characteristic that will be important for a sizable number of Hispanic American youth is language. Youth whose families have recently emigrated to the United States may speak only or primarily Spanish. Thus, non-Spanish-speaking educators and clinicians who work with them will be faced with a significant challenge, even if an interpreter is available. Children with this type of language background who are placed in schools where there is little support for their primary language (i.e., where there are no bilingual or English-as-a-second-language programs) will certainly feel frustrated, and will likely suffer academic problems as they struggle to immerse themselves in a new culture and acquire a new language—particularly if English is not spoken in their homes. Many children in this situation would naturally want to withdraw from an environment that is so unsupportive of their specific communication needs. A related issue for some Hispanic American youth may be acculturation stress, or difficulties that emerge when trying to assimilate into the dominant culture while still trying to honor the traditions and expectations of their families.

Sattler (1998) noted another potential problem regarding school adjustment of some Hispanic American youth. Traditional Hispanic Americans may be more tolerant of deviant behavior than the majority of Anglo Americans, and may prefer to solve behavioral or emotional problems within a family or extended group context. Thus, there is the possibility of resistence to treatment recommendations that emanate from an Anglo perspective. Also according to Sattler, the more traditional Hispanic families may have a mistrust for special education programs because they may feel such programs are inappropriate for their child, who may receive special treatment or sympathy for a disability. Instead, parents in this situation may want practical answers to their questions, such as wanting to know how long it will take for the child to overcome the disability. Regarding suicide among Hispanic youth, it has been noted that the suicide rate for this group is about one half of what it is for White, non-Hispanic persons (Rivers & Morrow, 1995). People with a traditional Hispanic orientation may underutilize mental health services, but when involved with such services, may feel more comfortable with a very practical, solution-focused approach to service delivery.

Native Americans

Native Americans include those individuals who trace their ancestry to the aboriginal inhabitants of the North American continent (i.e., those who lived in North America prior to European migration). The U.S. Bureau of the Census category for this group also includes the terms *Eskimo* and *Aleut*. Native Americans comprise a broad category of people, including hundreds of federally recognized tribal groups and several tribal nations. This is the smallest racial/ethnic group within the United States, comprising less than 1% of the general population of the nation. Although there are many federally recognized tribes (over 500), only a few have substantial populations. The 1990 census lists only seven tribes that have more than 50,000 members, including (beginning with the largest group) Cherokee, Navajo, Chippewa, Sioux, Choctaw, Pueblo, and Apache (U.S. Bureau of the Census, 1993c). Although population predictions for the next half century project that Native Americans will still be the smallest racial/ethnic minority group in the United States by 2050, the absolute numbers will increase, as will the relative percentage of the population, from the current .08% to 1.2% by 2050 (Aponte & Crouch, 1995).

Although Native Americans are a diverse people in many respects, certain similar hallmark characteristics have been associated with the various tribal groups. The common ethnic background that ties Native Americans together is considered to be a product of shared historical experiences, political ideologies, and worldviews, rather than cultural similarities (Aponte & Crouch, 1995), because there are many differing tribal languages and cultural customs. A major defining shared historical experience among Native Americans is oppression by the U.S. government (as an instrument of the broader American citizenry) through appropriation of their ancestral homelands, forced relocation of their ancestors to reservation areas, and continual violation of treaties. Beginning with the first permanent European settlements on the East Coast and ending with the Atlantic to Pacific borders produced through the "manifest destiny" of the dominant culture, the percentage of Native Americans as a proportion of the general population steadily declined for many years. A shared experience of many Native Americans is poverty, with more than one in four living at the poverty level in the 1990 census. Family structures of Native Americans tend to include a broad extended family rather than a primary emphasis on the nuclear family. Like Asian Americans, traditional Native Americans place a stronger respect for older individuals, some of whom may hold particularly venerated positions of respect as tribal Elders. And unlike the traditions of most European cultures, traditional Native Americans foster a belief in harmony with, rather than mastery over, nature. For many Native Americans, cultural religious beliefs (as opposed to formally theocratic religions) are a highly important aspect of their worldview, with traditional religions emphasizing a reverence for the forces of nature, mysticism, spirituality, and mythology. Almost half of all Native Americans live in the West, with another third living in the South. The remaining population is spread throughout the Midwest and Northeast. About 35% of Native Americans live on reservations or tribal lands or villages.

Certain psychosocial characteristics have been associated with Native Americans, and may be especially true of those who are more traditional as opposed to assimilated within the majority culture. Understanding some of these characteristics may be essential for conducting effective assessments of Native American children and youth. Traditional Native American parents are much more likely than Anglos to use noncoercive and noninterfering methods of parenting (i.e., letting children develop freely), which may be interpreted wrongly by professionals who are not familiar with the culture. Although individuality is respected among traditional Native Americans, there is clearly more of a group orientation as opposed to an individualistic orientation, and modesty and humility are valued characteristics. Thus, traditional Native American children may be uncomfortable being recognized for individual achievements, and instead may prefer to bring honor to the larger group. Traditional Native Americans tend to have a less rigid, more flexible view of time than most other racial/ethnic groups, viewing it in terms of natural processes and internal feelings rather than a mechanical clock time. Alcohol and drug abuse is a serious problem among Native American youth, particularly in high poverty reservation areas, as is hopelessness and suicide (Rivers & Morrow, 1995). In fact, Native American youth have the highest suicide rate of any racial/ethnic group, which is almost twice as high as that of Whites, the second most suicide-prone group (Sattler, 1998). Clinicians who work with Native American youth should carefully consider these possible issues, and should become educated regarding the specific cultural practices and expectations associated with the specific tribal groups whom they serve. Again, it is also important to recognize that there are tremendously varying degrees of acculturation among Native Americans, and the traditional patterns expressed in this section do not reflect the characteristics of a substantial number of Native Americans.

Some General Characteristics of the Majority Culture

Many, and perhaps most, discussions of cultural diversity in the education and mental health fields do not address cultural characteristics of the White majority group, and instead focus only on characteristics of racial/ethnic minority groups. The implied assumptions regarding this type of approach are that readers are already familiar with the essential facts and characteristics of the majority group, or that such information is not pertinent to becoming a culturally competent practitioner. But, such an approach is fallacious, and simply leads to further perpetuation of incorrect notions regarding cultural diversity. One problem with not including the majority White group in discussions of professional practice and cultural diversity is that it perpetuates a notion that the current Caucasian/White majority culture within the United States is the normative or typical standard rather than a cultural variant. In reality, whereas Caucasians currently constitute nearly three fourths of the population in the United States, they do not constitute a majority of the world's overall population. And, even within the United States, the proportion of non-Hispanic Whites is expected to diminish steadily to become a bare majority (only slightly over 50%) by the year 2050 (Aponte & Crouch, 1995). Thus, the time has come for individuals of all racial/ethnic/cultural groups in the United States, including those Caucasians of European ancestry, to realize that they represent just one part of the diverse American cultural landscape. Another problem with majority-omitting discussions on diversity is that it may foster a belief among members of the current majority culture that they are not ethnic, do not have a distinct culture, and that only groups who are variant from this normative perspective should be discussed in examinations of diversity. Again, such conscious omissions will only foster further ethnocentrism by members of the majority group, and this issue is important to a brief discussion in this section.

One of the problems in defining and discussing the White racial/ethnic majority in the United States is that so many terms are applied to it, and the terminology is at times misleading. For example, the U.S. Bureau of the Census uses the category *White, non-Hispanic* to classify the current majority group, but other terms that are commonly applied include *Caucasian* (a racial classification used by anthropologists and ethnobiologists), *European American*, and *Anglo*, as well as a host of lesser known terms. In reality, most discussion of the White racial group within the United States is focused on those individuals who trace their descendence to European nations. Obviously, there is substantial variation in culture and ethnicity among a group so broadly defined.

Descendents of the first permanent European settlers to North America several hundred years ago may feel that they have little in common with modern-day immigrants from Russia or Lithuania, other than the color of their skin. Moreover, many individuals in the United States whom the census bureau considers to be White, have a cultural background that varies dramatically from that of a stereotypical White Anglo-Saxon Protestant (such as individuals who trace their ancestral heritage to the Arabic and primarily Muslim nations of the Middle East).

Although the people of various European/Caucasian ethnic and cultural groups are generally referred to as comprising a monolithic majority group, not all groups who fit within this constellation have historically been treated this way. For example, Irish immigrants to the United States in the mid-1800s were the objects of substantial discrimination and hostility, as were later immigrants from eastern and southern Europe. In fact, immigrants to the United States from almost all parts of the world and at almost all points in time have faced hostility from the dominant culture. In reality though, White or European American immigrants to the United States, though they may face substantial challenges, have had an easier time fitting in within the dominant culture than have Asian Americans, African Americans, Hispanics, and Native Americans, because of such issues as skin color and historically shared cultural heritage.

With all the caveats in place, there are certain psychosocial or cultural characteristics that tend to be considered uniquely European in nature, and that have been used to describe the White majority group in the United States. Individuals in this group, though they may be diverse, tend share a Western worldview and value system (G. Corey et al., 1993). Some major characteristics of this worldview include an emphasis on individualism and fulfillment of individual needs, a nuclear family structure, competitiveness, an orientation toward the future, assertiveness, independence, emphasis on youth, nonconformity and individual freedom, mastery over the environment, and individual responsibility. Persons who hold this value system often go to great lengths to try to gain control over their circumstances and destiny, and may not be able to relate well to persons whose worldview and value system emphasize fate, or who believe that individual efforts will have little influence on the outcome of a situation. Whites of European ancestry are much less likely than Asian Americans and Native Americans to defer personal decisions to the views and needs of the extended family group or elders, and instead tend to focus on self-fulfillment as a means of achieving satisfaction or happiness. As is true in the case of all racial/ethnic groups discussed in this chapter, these characteristics may differentiate the group from other groups, but there is likely to be more substantial variation in these areas among individuals within the dominant culture. White readers of this text who question whether the characteristics presented herein are representative of them should carefully consider how essential it is not to stereotype individuals from other racial/ethnic groups, but to use the available information on cultural generalities as a basis for understanding rather than labeling the individual.

ASSESSMENT METHODS AND CULTURAL DIVERSITY: SPECIAL CONSIDERATIONS

This section includes separate discussions of the six methods of assessment presented in this book, and particularly, what is known regarding the multicultural applications of each method. Each method is associated with certain problems for culturally competent assessment, although substantial progress has been made with some of these methods.

Behavioral Observation

Because there is such a wide variation in potential techniques for direct behavioral observation, the cultural validity of these techniques presumably may also vary widely. The primary advantages of behavioral observation as an assessment method, as detailed in chapter 3, include the potential of strong experimental validation and replicability, the wide flexibility, and the strong potential ecological validity of assessing behavior within the context of behavior–environment relations. If the assessor appropriately takes into account the cultural background characteristics of an individual child in designing the observational coding system and interpreting the obtained data, then direct behavioral observation may be an excellent choice for culturally appropriate assessment of social-emotional behavior.

However, there are numerous potential threats to the validity of direct behavioral observation that may have a significant impact on the cultural appropriateness of this method. Of the potential threats to validity of behavioral observations discussed in chapter 3, the following threats have specific ramifications for culturally appropriate assessment: *lack of social comparison data*, *observer reactivity*, and *situational specificity of behavior*. Regarding the social comparison problem, failure to appropriately compare the observed behavior of a target child to that of their peers may result in interpretations that are not based on a normative perspective, and deviancy of behavior may be under- or overestimated. When observing a child or youth who is a member of a racial/ethnic minority group within a given environment, social comparisons of behavior should be made with other children of their group as well as children who are in the dominant group. Such inclusiveness in defining the social comparison targets may help to discriminate between maladaptive behavior and behavior that simply differs from the norm. In regards to observer reactivity, if the person conducting the observation stands out in some obvious way from the students in the classroom, it is more likely that the students will react behaviorally to the presence of the observer, and that the observational data may be distorted. For example, if African American observers went into a classroom in a tribal school on the Navajo reservation in Arizona to collect data, they would most likely stand out significantly to the children, simply because of the children's lack of experience with African Americans. Likewise, a White observer entering a school with primarily African American students and teachers may evoke a similar reaction. To minimize the effects of such reactivity, observers in such situations should plan extra time for a settling-in and adjustment period prior to beginning the formal observation. With regard to the situational specificity of behavior phenomenon, observers should carefully consider that children who are in a substantial racial/ethnic minority situation in classroom or clinic observation settings may behave differently in those environments than they would in more familiar and comfortable environments. The culturally valid behavioral assessment will include observational data from a variety of normal environments to the greatest extent possible.

Although these cautions and recommendations are based on sound theory and make good sense, it is important to recognize that there is actually very little empirical evidence regarding the effects of race/ethnicity or other cultural variables on the validity of direct behavioral observation. The few studies that have been conducted in this area (e.g., Lethermon, Williamson, Moody, Granberry, Lemanek, & Bodiford, 1984; Lethermon, Williamson, Moody, & Wozniak, 1986; Turner, Beidel, Hersen, & Bellack, 1984) have indicated that, in certain situations, there may be an interaction between the race/ethnicity condition of the observer and the target subjects, and in some circumstances, this interaction may result in biased observational data. However, it has also been stated that *appropriate training* of observers may reduce such bias (Lethermon et al., 1986). Therefore, the recommendations regarding appropriate training and support of observers provided in chapter 3 appear to have special relevance to the topic of culturally valid assessment practices.

Behavior Rating Scales

Because behavior rating scales typically are standardized norm-referenced assessment tools, their validity for use with diverse cultural groups for which they are intended may be ascertained to some extent through the information available in the test manual. In other words, the developers of such instruments should follow specific procedures for item development and accumulation of validity evidence if they desire to make a claim that the instrument is valid for use across groups with differing characteristics along some major demographic domain. For example, the *Standards for Educational and Psychological Testing* (1985) recommended that test developers should carefully examine the appropriateness of the item content for intended target groups, that groups for which the test is intended should be adequately represented in normative samples, and in certain cases, that research regarding similarity or differences among specific groups should be demonstrated. Therefore, it is recommended that potential users of behavior rating scales and other standardized norm-referenced social-emotional behavior instruments should carefully scrutinize the contents of the technical manual before deciding to use the instrument with racial/ethnic minority youth.

One of the ongoing debates (for which there is actually very little empirical evidence) regarding culturally appropriate uses of standardized norm-referenced instruments, such as behavior rating scales, concerns the desirable proportion of representativeness of various racial/ethnic groups within the norm group, and whether local norms are better than national norms. The standard practice in educational and psychological test development in recent years has been to ensure that the norm sample of the instrument, to the greatest extent possible, parallels the characteristics of the general population for which it is intended. In other words, a test developer who intends the completed instrument to be used generally with children and youth in the United States should attempt to develop a norm sample that closely parallels the racial/ethnic, gender, and socioeconomic status characteristics of the general population from the most recent census. In reality, this practice, though laudable, does not necessarily demonstrate a priori cultural validity, and some experts have criticized the practice because minority groups still comprise a small percentage of the norm sample against which their scores are to be compared. For example, based on the 1990 census, less than 1% of the population in the United States (.8% to be exact) are Native Americans. Using the standard practice of instrument development, representation of Native Americans in about 1% of the norm sample for the test should thus satisfy the general standard of equivalency. However, 1% is still a very small proportion, even when it represents the general percentage of a specific subgroup within a general group. Some arguments have been proposed that small representation, even if it is in proportion to the percentage of the group within the total population, might be presumed to result in test bias (e.g., Harrington, 1988).

So, what can be made of the two opposing arguments regarding proportionality in norming? The scant evidence that is available on normative representation within standardized tests may indicate that proportional representation, or even minority overrepresentation within the norm group, may actually have very little impact on the ability of the test to predict behavior or performance in a valid manner, as long as adequate sampling procedures are used in the construction of the norm group, and the content of the test items is relatively free of cultural bias to begin with (Fan, Wilson, & Kapes, 1996). The Fan et al. study used varying proportions (0%, 5%, 10%, 30%, and 60%) of differing ethnic groups (White, African American, Hispanic, Asian American) in a tightly controlled standardization experiment, and found that there was no systematic bias against any of the groups when they were in the not-represented or underrepresented conditions. Fan et al. referred to the notion of proportional or overrepresentation of racial/ethnic minority groups as a best practice as the "standardization fallacy." It should be noted that this interesting study did not specifically target assessment of social-emotional behavior, and a replication using this performance domain would certainly be useful. However, it is one of the few tightly controlled studies to address the issue of representation of specific racial/ethnic groups within standardization groups. Based on the results of this study, it appears that the most important aspects of developing assessment instruments that have wide cultural applicability and validity are the actual content development procedures (to eliminate biasing items) and the use of good sampling methods for construction of the norm group. Other instrument development procedures may also be useful for demonstrating appropriateness with differing racial/ethnic groups, such as conducting specific comparisons with subsamples of various racial/ethnic groups regarding such characteristics as mean score equivalency, internal consistency properties, and factor structure.

Relatively few studies have been conducted regarding culturally appropriate development and use of behavior rating scales across diverse racial/ethnic groups. In reporting research on a national normative sample for the Child Behavior Checklist, Achenbach and Edelbrock (1979, 1981) noted that the effects of race/ethnicity were minimal if socioeconomic status was used as a controlling covariant. Similar results were found with the normative samples of the School Social Behavior Scales (Merrell, 1993a, 1993b) and the Preschool and Kindergarten Behavior Scales (Merrell, 1994b, 1996b). In other words, differences in levels of problem behavior scores across racial/ethnic groups may actually be more strongly associated with variables such as family income and education level than with race/ethnicity. Therefore, developers of behavior rating scales and other standardized assessment instruments should ensure appropriate stratification based on geographical representation and socioeconomic status. Although the actual effects of proportion representation or under- or overrepresentation of various racial/ethnic groups within general norm samples are still somewhat unclear, test developers would also be wise to ensure that the various groups receive adequate representation in the standardization sample.

Clinical Interviewing

The area of clinical interviewing is especially important when considering cultural diversity and social-emotional assessment. Interviewing may involve some of the strongest potential barriers to effective cross-cultural assessment, but is also perhaps the most modifiable and flexible social-emotional assessment method, thus offering great promise for clinicians who acquire the skills for culturally sensitive interviewing (J. N. Hughes & Baker, 1990; Sattler, 1998).

Surprisingly little attention has been given to the topic of making clinical interviews with children more culturally appropriate. Nevertheless, it is clear that attention to this area is needed. In commenting on culturally competent assessment practices in the United States, Dana (1996) noted that the traditional information-gathering styles of many White assessment professionals may pose substantial obstacles for effective assessment:

> Anglo American assessors have been influenced by medical model service-delivery requirements for compliance with a matter-of-fact, somewhat impersonal style that puts business first and discourages a more personal relationship during the service delivery or later. As a result, many Anglo American assessors expect clients to have an immediate task orientation including cooperation and responsiveness to the test materials. . . . However, most traditional persons cannot respond comfortably to assessment tasks if the assessor uses a social etiquette that is uncomfortable, intrusive, frustrating, or alienating. (p. 475)

Certainly, conducting clinical interviews in this manner with any children will be a problem, but it may be substantially more problematic if the child is a member of a racial/ethnic minority group and has a traditional orientation. So, given what is known regarding traditional clinical interviewing practices and cultural differences among the U.S. population, what should be done to encounter this problem?

Perhaps the most cohesive and detailed suggestions for culturally competent interviewing of ethnic minority children (particularly those children who are traditional rather than bicultural or marginal in their acculturation) to date have been offered by Sattler (1998). These suggestions include the following nine recommendations detailed in Table 14.2.

Learn About the Interviewee's Culture.   This would include efforts by the interviewer directed at learning about such factors as family ethnic identification, cultural patterns related to parenting practices, specific family attitudes regarding childrearing, education and occupational background of the parents, and the ethnic community with which they may identify themselves. Attempts to learn about the culture should be tempered with the realization that information may only be partially correct. "Recognize your ignorance about some details of the family's culture. . . . If you are not a member of the ethnic group, you may be viewed as a stranger" (p. 313). It is also recommended that interviewers be frank with the family regarding the lack of knowledge they may have regarding the family's cultural background.

Learn About the Interviewee's Language.   Interviewers should determine the preferred language of the interviewee and their family, as well as the extent of their familiarity with English. This background information will be essential in determining if an interpreter is needed for the interview, assuming there is not another potential interviewer who speaks the language of the family.

Establish Rapport.   The larger the cultural background differences between the interviewer and the client (and their family), the more time may be needed to establish adequate rapport. Sattler recommended that the interviewer should "make every effort to encourage the child's and family's motivation and interest" and "take the time to enlist the child's and family's cooperation" (p. 315). Diplomacy, tact, and respect will be crucial characteristics of attempts to establish good rapport.

Identify Stereotypes.   This process is focused on an inward examination by interviewers regarding their own preconceived notions, prejudices, and stereotypes they may have regarding the racial/ethnic group of the child and their family. There should

TABLE 14.2
Nine Recommendations by Sattler (1998) for Effective
Interviewing of Racial/Ethnic Minority Children and Their Families

Recommendation	Comments
Learn about the interviewee's culture	Active efforts to learn about such cultural issues as ethnic identification, traditional practices and customs, attitudes toward childrearing and education.
Learn about the interviewee's language	Should occur before the interview. If the child/family is not comfortable speaking the language of the interviewer, arrangements should be made for a different interviewer or an interpreter.
Establish rapport	Encouragement of the child/family's participation, interest, and cooperation. Use diplomacy, tact, and avoid being disrespectful.
Identify stereotypes	Inward examination by interviewers regarding their own beliefs, prejudices, and stereotypes regarding the racial/ethnic group of the child/family. Consider that these expectations may not be accurate.
Promote clear communication	Avoid use of jargon, slang, technical language, and statements with double meanings. Use courtesy and respect in communications. If needed, modify the interview format.
Identify family needs	Determine material, physical, and psychosocial needs of child and family, and consider community resources to meet these needs. May be especially important for recent immigrants or families living in poverty.
Identify attitudes toward health and illness	What are beliefs regarding illness, healing, traditional rituals and religious customs? What drugs and folk remedies is child using?
Recognize the extent of acculturation	Determine level of acculturation within traditional group, and assimilation into dominant group. For recent immigrants, determine level of functioning prior to leaving homeland, and level of acculturation stress.
Accept the interviewee's perspectives	Active efforts by interviewer to accept beliefs and attitudes they may not share, coupled with recognition that problems may not be due to minority status.

be no immediate assumptions that the family is traditionally acculturated into the known cultural characteristics of their racial/ethnic group. "Ask them about these matters as needed" (p. 315).

Promote Clear Communication. If the child and their family are not bicultural or well assimilated into the culture of the interviewer, then specific attempts should be made to ensure that communication is enhanced. Avoidance of technical jargon, slang expressions, unusual idioms, or statements with dual meanings may be necessary. If these ethnic group differences begin to hamper the interview, then the interviewer should actively try to monitor their behavior and use other approaches. "Be flexible, and use innovative interviewing strategies tailored to the needs to the family's ethnic group" (p. 316).

Identify Family Needs. Particularly if the child and their family are recent immigrants to the United States, or if they live in poverty, the interviewer should attempt to ascertain whether there are obvious material, physical, or psychosocial needs they are wanting, and what can be done to connect them with appropriate community resources.

Identify Attitudes Toward Health and Illness.   If the child and their family are traditionally oriented to their ethnic culture, they may have concepts of illness, healing, rituals, and religious beliefs that are unfamiliar to the interviewer and most persons within the public school system. In making active attempts to learn about their attitudes and beliefs in this area, the interviewer should try to understand the child and family's expectations regarding professional treatment, and also ascertain what prescription drugs, over-the-counter drugs, folk remedies, and illicit drugs the child may be taking.

Recognize the Extent of Acculturation.   As has been stated many times throughout this chapter, there is tremendous variation among individuals and families regarding how acculturated they are within their racial/ethnic culture, as well as their knowledge and orientation to the dominant culture. If the child and family are recent immigrants to the United States, then it is recommended that the interviewer attempt to assess their level of functioning prior to leaving their homeland, and determine how they are coping with the stresses associated with the process of acculturation.

Accept the Interviewee's Perspectives.   The interviewer should make a substantial effort to accept the cultural perspectives of the interviewee and their family. This is an ideal rather than a technique, and in some cases, may be difficult to achieve. In fact, this process may be the most difficult aspect of culturally competent assessment and intervention. It involves the willingness of interviewers to accept perspectives they may not share, or with which they may even feel uncomfortable. At the same time, efforts need to be made to achieve a balance between understanding any behavioral, social, and emotional problems within the cultural context, and also avoiding attributing all individual and family problems to their cultural background and minority group status.

Any competent assessment professional who sincerely attempts to implement these nine suggestions will surely find that their cultural sensitivity in clinical interviewing is enhanced. However, in some cases, these efforts will not be enough to achieve the desired goal. Willingness to conduct more than one interview may also be necessary, and honesty and reliability in communication will likely enhance the trust between interviewer and client. Ultimately, "improved intercultural communication will ultimately depend on changes in the socio political system. Until our society eliminates racism and discrimination, there will always be vestiges of suspicion and mistrust between people of different ethnicities" (p. 317).

Sociometric Techniques

Although sociometric techniques are most likely to be used as assessment tools for research purposes rather than for everyday clinical practice, there is a small but coherent body of evidence indicating that they may be associated with strong racial/ethnic effects. Therefore, any professional contemplating the use of sociometrics with a diverse group of children should consider this issue carefully. The primary consistent finding in this area is that similarity provides a basis for peer nominations and ratings. This issue is discussed in chapter 7 with respect to gender similarity, which has been shown in scores of studies to influence sociometric results of friendship patterns. In other words, boys are more likely to rate or nominate other boys using positive criteria, and girls are more likely to select other girls in this manner. A smaller but also compelling collection of research in this area has also emerged regarding race/ethnicity as a sociometric prediction variable.

A study by Singleton and Asher (1977) explored social interaction patterns among Black and White third-grade students in integrated schools. In this study, race (as well as sex) was found to be a significant determinant of positive sociometric ratings for play and work. In other words, Black children were substantially more likely to select other Black children as the persons with whom they would most like to play or work, and White children were equally likely to select White children in this regard. This study, which was conducted shortly after the initiation of court-mandated school integration in many areas of the United States, was timely, but did not explore the issue in more detail. The generalities of Singleton and Asher's study were replicated in a later study by Clark and Drewry (1985), who found the same type of racial/ethnic preferences using a more controlled methodology.

More recent sociometric investigations have verified the notion that similarity, whether it be in gender, race/ethnicity, socioeconomic status, or social behavior patterns, provides a strong basis for friendships (Kupersmidt, DeRosier, & Patterson, 1995). However, some of these studies have pushed the issue further, and have provided some more specific answers to the question of racial/ethnic similarity in sociometric assessment. Kistner, Metzler, Gatlin, and Risi (1993) examined peer preferences and perceptions among African American and White children in classrooms where there were clear majority patterns (i.e., classrooms where there was a dominance of African American children and classrooms where there was a dominance of White children). Their findings put a somewhat different twist on the issue of similarity in sociometric assessment, showing that being in a minority situation, regardless of racial/ethnic group, was associated with higher rates of peer rejection for girls, but not for boys. Another interesting finding from this study was that peer preferences may be influenced by cultural dominance. In other words, a child who is in the racial/ethnic minority in a given classroom (regardless of race) is likely to rate children of the dominant group more positively than they would if they were in the majority and the members of the other group were in the minority. Another study that found an interesting race/ethnicity and gender interaction effect in sociometric assessment was conducted by Kistner and Gatlin (1989). These researchers studied both positive and negative nominations of White and Black children, both with and without learning disabilities (most did not). Predictably, there was a racial/ethnic (and gender) effect for positive nominations, where children were more likely to identify as friends those children with whom they felt they had the most similarity. However, effects for negative nominations were also identified. Children of both racial/ethnic groups were more likely to reject children of the opposite gender and racial/ethnic group.

These studies all have a common theme, showing that race/ethnicity is likely to be a significant factor not only in friendship patterns, but in patterns of peer rejection. Therefore, for researchers or clinicians using sociometric techniques, there is an obvious practical implication. Children whose racial/ethnic group comprises a small percentage of the overall classroom may be overidentified as socially neglected or rejected, and faulty interpretations might potentially be reached if these cultural variables are not considered fully. It would be advisable to include a sociometric of racial/ethnic minority youth only within the context of a comprehensive assessment design that overcomes the limitations of reliance on one method.

Self-Report Instruments

In comparison with most areas of behavioral, social, and emotional assessment, a relatively larger body of evidence has accumulated regarding the use of self-report instruments with ethnic minority populations. Because there has been very little research and development work with child populations and self-report assessment until the past decade, most of what is known regarding multicultural applications in this area has come from research with adults. However, the accumulated knowledge and thinking from the adult population can be used as a basis for developing some general guidelines for assessment practices with children and youth. In general, self-report assessment is an area in which tremendous caution should be used for the selection, administration, and interpretation of assessment instruments with members of racial/ethnic minority groups.

The most widely used self-report instrument in existence is clearly the MMPI, and by implication, its various successors (the MMPI–2 and MMPI–A). Several reviews of the use of the MMPI with members of racial/ethnic minority groups (e.g., Dana, 1993, 1995; Greene, 1987; Hoffman, Dana, & Bolton, 1987) have indicated that there are clear patterns of profile differences with these groups as compared to the general instrument norms. Specifically, research has shown that members of racial/ethnic minority groups, regardless of their clinical status, are somewhat more likely than members of the dominant culture in the United States to respond to MMPI items in ways that may result in elevated scores on some of the validity and clinical scales. Dana (1995) noted that African Americans are likely to receive high scores on Scales F, 6, and 8 as a process of becoming Afrocentric; Hispanic Americans tend to exhibit similar patterns of score elevations on these scales as a result of traditional cultural orientation; and, Native Americans are more likely than majority group members to show elevations on Scales F, 4, and 8, regardless of their diagnostic status. Less is known regarding use of the MMPI with Asian Americans, although some studies have shown that they are likely to receive elevated clinical profiles in comparison with the majority-dominated standardization group (J. R. Graham, 1990).

Given that there is no a priori reason to believe that members of racial/ethnic minority groups should respond to a broad-band self-report measure, such as the MMPI, in ways that show more psychopathology than exists among the majority culture, the history of such differences raises serious questions and concerns. Because virtually all of the cross-cultural MMPI research has been with populations who responded to the MMPI or MMPI–2 rather than the MMPI–A, there is additional reason for caution when using this test with racial/ethnic minority youth. Dana (1995) suggested that the MMPI "should be used only when the assessee has been demonstrated to be comparable to the standardization population on demographic variables, including world view as measured by moderator variables, and speaks English as a first language" (p. 66). In other words, use of the MMPI (and presumably the MMPI–A) with racial/ethnic minority clients who are traditional in their orientation is not recommended. Although the MMPI–A norms are more racially/ethnically diverse than the norms for the original MMPI, very little is known regarding specific patterns of response profiles among racial/ethnic minority youth, and it is prudent to assume that caution is warranted.

It should be recognized that the MMPI is a relatively unique type of self-report measure, using empirical criterion keying in the construction of the subscales, using items that are not particularly specific to behavioral, social, or emotional problems (e.g., "I believe in law enforcement," "I like collecting flowers and growing houseplants," or "I would like to be a nurse"), and employing a forced-choice true/false response format. It may be possible that there are some peculiarities associated with the format and structure of the MMPI that make it particularly prone to the racial/ethnic bias in terms of the profile patterns produced.

Aside from the implications of research on the MMPI, relatively little is known regarding cross-cultural applications of self-report assessment, but some new evidence with the newer generation self-report instruments for children and youth is beginning to emerge. Two recent studies using the Internalizing Symptoms Scale for Children (discussed in chap. 10) demonstrated that this instrument produces levels of total and subscale scores with African American children (Sanders, 1996) and Native American youth (M. S. Williams, 1997) that are comparable to those of the general normative sample, even with minority children who are from low socioeconomic status homes. Information in the technical manual for the Personality Inventory for Youth (discussed in chap. 7) indicates that the overall score levels and profile patterns of racial/ethnic minority subsamples tend to be similar to those of the general norm population. And, some of the research on narrow-band self-report instruments, such as the Children's Depression Inventory and Revised Children's Manifest Anxiety Scale (both discussed in chap. 10), has included very large samples of racial/ethnic minority youth, and has not shown any substantial biasing effects for race/ethnicity. These studies, as well as a few similar studies with other self-report measures, are more encouraging from a cultural validity perspective than the cross-cultural research with the MMPI, and provide some hope that future efforts might definitively show that the new generation of child and adolescent self-report measures are appropriate for use with children from varying racial/ethnic backgrounds.

Projective-Expressive Techniques

The general category of projective-expressive assessment techniques, including thematic approaches, drawing techniques, and sentence completion tasks, as discussed in chapter 8, continues to be widely used for social-emotional assessment of children and youth. Although the use of these techniques for diagnostic purposes remains a hotbed of controversy, and the associated limitations and problems have been convincingly documented, they are widely used for cross-cultural applications. In fact, a comprehensive review of the professional journal articles available on CD-ROM databases, such as PSYCH LIT using the keywords projective testing, will quickly reveal that projective-expressive techniques are widely used in research and clinical applications of child assessment throughout the world.

Despite their worldwide popularity, less is known regarding appropriate cross-cultural applications of projective techniques among members of racial/ethnic minority groups in the United States, particularly where children are concerned. There are also differing perspectives and arguments regarding the appropriateness of traditional projective-expressive techniques in American cross-cultural applications. For example, Hood and Johnson (1997) argued that "projective techniques are personality instruments that *undoubtedly* have less value as assessment tools for minority clients" (p. 309, italics added), because they are based on upper-middle-class majority group perspectives. On the other hand, Dana (1993, 1995) took the stance that drawing, thematic, sentence completion, story-telling, and other projective-expressive techniques have considerable promise as assessment tools with members of racial/ethnic minority groups, and provided numerous references for culture-specific applications of such techniques. However, Dana's generally supportive statements regarding cross-cultural applications of projectives are tempered with his numerous other comments criticizing the Eurocentric theoretical bases on which most of the interpretation systems are built (particularly psychodynamic theory) as not being relevant for interpretation of the products produced in projective-expressive assessment by members of cultural minority groups, particularly those who are traditional in their acculturation. Instead, Dana suggested that such techniques be adapted specifically for use with particular racial/ethnic groups through using a *constructivist* approach to understanding their own cultural norms and values. For example, rather than using the traditional Thematic Apperception Test with Native Americans, he suggested it might be more appropriate to use "tribe-specific picture stimulus cards," and for appropriate interpretation of the responses, "assessors should be familiar with the history, customs, ethnography, fiction, and published life histories of individuals for any tribe whose members are assessed using picture story techniques" (Dana, 1995, p. 67). He made similar suggestions to adapt other projective-expressive techniques for use with racial/ethnic minority group members, such as using human figure drawings in a general manner, but to avoid existing scoring systems, and to use sentence completion tasks developed in the native language of the client.

Projective-expressive techniques have some merit for cross-cultural assessment of children and youth, because they are nonthreatening, because they may offer a glimpse of the worldview of the client, and because they may provide a basis for relationship and trust enhancement between the evaluator and the child—something that may be especially challenging when strong cultural differences are present. However, the primary use of projectives for this purpose should be focused on observing and building a relationship with the child, and not on making diagnostic inferences using the traditional interpretation techniques. For example, traditional psychodynamic-based interpretation of drawing techniques often postulate that drawings of trees devoid of leaves may indicate emotional barrenness, and smoke rising out of chimneys of houses may indicate turmoil or conflict within the home. As questionable (if not naive) as such interpretation paradigms are in general, they may be particularly offensive when applied cross-culturally. Would it be unusual for a traditional Navajo youth whose family lives in a hogan, and whose primary heat source is wood fuel, to draw smoke arising from the dwelling? It may be reasonable to assert that projective-expressive techniques have some potentially useful cross-cultural applications, but that extra precautions should be in place for such use to avoid inappropriate and culturally offensive interpretation and overpathologization.

RECOMMENDATIONS FOR CULTURALLY COMPETENT ASSESSMENT

This chapter on assessment and cultural diversity has included a wide variety of topic areas, discussions of problems in current assessment practices, and suggestions for specific types of culturally competent social-emotional assessment practices. Emphasis on cultural diversity within educational and psychological assessment is a relatively recent major focus, and this important topic has been neglected to a great extent in the past. Therefore, it should be understood that much of current empirical knowledge and practical applications of this knowledge is provisional. Much of what is currently known and done regarding multicultural applications of assessment is not well documented, and this area seems to be undergoing constant change. It seems likely that

TABLE 14.3
General Recommendations for Culturally Competent Practice in
Behavioral, Social, and Emotional Assessment of Children and Youth

---

Obtain sufficient background information prior to planning and conducting assessment.

Cultural background information should include estimates of acculturation and comfort with the majority language and dominant culture.

Use a comprehensive assessment design (multimethod, multisource, multisetting) to overcome the culturally limiting factors of any one method.

Examine potential new standardized instruments for evidence of multicultural applications.

Remain flexible in the design and implementation of the assessment, making innovations and modifications as needed.

When in doubt, consult.

Strive for honesty and open communication regarding cultural issues with the client and their family.

Present feedback on assessment results within a culturally acceptable framework.

Strive for sensitization to and awareness of within-group and between-group cultural differences.

Research and development work in assessment should emphasize general multicultural applications as well as specialized techniques for specific populations.

Educators and mental health professionals should introspectively examine their own cultural background, values, beliefs, and ethnocultural assumptions.

---

there will be important developments in this area in the near future, including substantial experimental innovation.

In conclusion, the yield of information regarding best practices or practical applications for culturally competent behavioral social and emotional assessment of children and youth can be summarized in the following 11 points (also listed for additional reference in Table 14.3):

1. Assessment professionals should obtain as much information as possible regarding the cultural background characteristics and orientation of the child or adolescent to be assessed, prior to conducting the assessment, and use this information in developing a tentative plan for the assessment. This issue is particularly important when the examiner is part of the majority culture and the client is not.

2. Cultural background information regarding children and youth to be assessed (and their families) should always include some appropriate estimation of their approximate level of acculturation, and their comfort with the majority language and dominant culture.

3. Use of a comprehensive assessment design such as the multimethod, multisource, multisetting model presented in chapter 1 will help to create an ecologically valid and culturally appropriate social-emotional assessment. The cultural limitations of any one type of method, instrument, or technique can be curbed through the use of such a broad-based design.

4. In their selection of standardized assessment instruments (i.e., behavior rating scales, structured interviews, and self-report instruments), culturally competent professionals will carefully examine the technical manuals for evidence of appropriate multicultural applications, in addition to the characteristics (e.g., reliability and validity) that are traditionally valued.

5. Flexibility should be a key component of culturally appropriate assessment practice. If a given instrument or technique that was administered as part of the original assessment design proves to be obviously inappropriate for a given client, it should be abandoned or discarded. If assessment methods or techniques that were not part

of the original design appear to be valuable in a given situation, they should be adopted.

6. The professional adage "when in doubt, consult" should be particularly adhered to when moving into the realm of cross-cultural or multicultural assessment and intervention services. If interviewers do not know the right answer or direction in a given situation, they should not be afraid to consult with someone else they trust.

7. Honesty and open communication with clients (and their families) who are from different ethnocultural backgrounds than their own is especially important. If examiners are unsure about a particular custom, belief, or issue that they think may be part of their client's worldview, then they should respectfully and appropriately ask about it.

8. Assessment results feedback should be presented within a culturally acceptable framework (i.e., aimed toward the specific beliefs of the child's family regarding health, illness, and treatment), so that they will be more likely to be used to develop appropriate intervention plans.

9. Sensitization to and awareness of multicultural within-group and between-group differences can help to create a greater awareness of cultural differences, and may ultimately lead to more culturally appropriate assessments.

10. Researchers and other developers of assessment instruments should attempt to the greatest extent possible to make new methods, techniques, and instruments as culturally general as possible, and to develop and validate specialized techniques that are designed to meet the needs of unusually specific cultural situations.

11. If they have not previously or recently done so, psychologists and educators of all backgrounds are urged to examine their own values, beliefs, ethnocultural background and assumptions, and general worldview. This type of introspective self-examination will likely lead to greater awareness of the strengths and barriers that a person's background brings to assessment and treatment situations.

CONCLUSIONS

The topic of cultural diversity within psychological and educational assessment has received increasing professional and public attention during the past two to three decades. This increased emphasis has been spurred on primarily by legal decisions and well-known public controversies regarding IQ and educational aptitude testing, but also by a changing consciousness within American culture regarding the importance of culture and race/ethnicity in public and private life. There is an increasing consensus among assessment experts and policymakers that current assessment practices have not gone far enough in promoting equity and utility across various ethnocultural groups.

Test bias, or *assessment bias*, are terms that reflect both the properties and uses of assessment instruments and methods. An instrument or technique is considered to have an unacceptable level of bias when it results in one group being systematically disadvantaged, or shows group differences based on characteristics other than what are purported to be measured. Although the area of behavioral, social, and emotional assessment has not been scrutinized or criticized in this regard as much as cognitive ability testing, bias in assessment is still a major concern. Organizations representing professionals who are concerned with psychological and educational assessment have developed various codes and standards for appropriate practice and ethical behavior.

In recent years, some of these standards have been revised to include a greater emphasis on cultural validity of practices, although some have argued that these changes have not gone far enough. There appear to be several problems with the current state of affairs regarding multicultural applications or assessing social-emotional behavior, and recent efforts have been directed at developing new models and paradigms for culturally appropriate assessment practice.

Acculturation is defined as a process of individual change that occurs when two cultures meet. This process varies widely among individuals and groups, and includes such factors as retention of traditions and customs of the native culture and adoption of new customs and values that are part of the new culture. The process of acculturation can be very stressful for members of racial/ethnic minority groups, and the actual types of stresses and outcomes vary as a function of the particular circumstances. Although specific instruments have been developed for determining the level of acculturation of members of particular minority groups, most of these instruments have been aimed at adults rather than youth. The process of determining level of acculturation may involve such factors as language preferences, adherence to tradition customs, and level of comfort with the new culture. It has been proposed that members of various racial/ethnic groups, including members of the dominant group, may go through various stages of racial/cultural development. Understanding these stages and the process of movement between stages can help professionals better understand the unique characteristics of their clients.

Although increased emphasis on the characteristics of various racial/ethnocultural groups has many potential benefits, there are also some possible problems. One negative outcome may be stereotyping of individuals from specific groups based on a few facts known about general characteristics of that group. It is critical to recognize that within-group differences are almost always greater than between-group differences, and that each racial/ethnocultural group contains individuals of widely varying characteristics. In addition to inaccurate stereotyping, another possible ramification is polarization and divisiveness among various groups.

The 1990 U.S. census indicated that about three fourths of the general population are members of the White/Caucasian majority group, with the following other major racial/ethnic groups, in order of current size: African Americans, Hispanic Americans, Asian Americans, and Native Americans. In reality, the population of children is more diverse than the general population, including only about a two thirds proportion of the majority group. All demographic projections point to the fact that the White/Caucasian majority group will continue to shrink, and will comprise a bare majority (slightly over 50%) of the general population by 2050. By this time, Hispanic Americans are projected to become the largest racial/ethnic minority group, followed by African Americans, Asian Americans, and Native Americans. However, all racial/ethnic minority groups are projected to increase in terms of their absolute numbers of percentages within the general population during this time frame. Each of the five major racial/ethnic groups is diverse in its own right, but has been associated with specific psychosocial characteristics that may hold true for many group members. Clinicians should become aware of these general characteristics, but at the same time recognize that there is wide variation among individuals within groups.

Each of the six assessment methods emphasized in this volume have specific difficulties regarding multicultural applications, but there have been some encouraging developments for culturally competent assessment with each of these methods. Clinicians and researchers should become aware of the problems and limitations associated with multicultural applications of each method, and develop assessment plans accordingly.

Certain recommended best practices for assessing social-emotional behavior within a culturally competent framework have been provided to form the basis of clinical and research practices. These recommendations include obtaining sufficient cultural background information on clients prior to the assessment, using a comprehensive assessment model, selecting instruments and procedures based on their demonstrated multicultural applications, remaining flexible and innovative in the implementation of the assessment, consulting with colleagues as needed, striving for honest communication with clients and their families, presenting assessment results feedback within a culturally acceptable framework, striving for sensitivity to within-group and between-group differences, developing new techniques that will be effective cross-culturally and for specific cultural applications, and introspectively examining one's own belief and value system.

REVIEW AND APPLICATION QUESTIONS

1. Operationally define the term *test bias* (or *assessment bias*) as it relates to behavioral, social, and emotional assessment.

2. Characterize the current status of professional standards and ethical codes for culturally competence assessment. In your view, are the current standards adequate?

3. What have been the major criticisms of current professional practices in educational and psychological assessment with regard to cultural diversity?

4. Focusing on cultural diversity and assessment practices inevitably leads to a focus on some of the notable characteristics of specific racial/ethnic groups and subgroups within the larger groups. What are some of the potential problems that may occur from making generalizations regarding specific groups?

5. Characterize the projected demographic trends in racial/ethnic diversity in the United States between the years 2000 and 2050.

6. For each of the six general methods of assessment covered in this chapter, what are some of the major advantages and problems for multicultural applications?

7. Operationally define the term *acculturation*.

8. Regarding the proposed stages of racial/cultural identity development, what are some of the similarities and differences in the progression through stages for members of racial/ethnic minority groups as opposed to members of the majority culture?

Appendix:
Sources for Published
Assessment Instruments

This appendix includes source information for published assessment instruments and systems discussed in the text. The names of these instruments are listed in alphabetical order, with the name and address (and in some cases, phone number) of the publisher or source. These listings were current at the time this book was prepared, but there is no guarantee that they will remain current over time. Publishers sometimes merge or choose to discontinue certain products. These listings are only for published instruments. In the case of assessment instruments discussed in the text that are reported in the professional literature but not externally published or marketed, readers should consult the appropriate listing in the reference section.

ASSESSMENT OF INTERPERSONAL RELATIONS
PRO-ED
8700 Shoal Creek Blvd.
Austin, TX 78757-6897
512/ 451-3246
800/ 897-3202

ATTENTION DEFICIT DISORDERS EVALUATION SCALES
Hawthorne Educational Services
800 Gray Oak Drive
Columbia, MO 65201
314/ 874-1710

BEHAVIOR ASSESSMENT SYSTEM FOR CHILDREN
(*comprehensive assessment system including parent and teacher rating forms, self-rating forms, developmental history interview form, and behavior observation form*)
American Guidance Service
4201 Woodland Road
Circle Pines, MN 55014-1796
800/ 328-2560

BRACKEN MULTIDIMENSIONAL SELF-CONCEPT SCALE
PRO-ED
8700 Shoal Creek Boulevard
Austin, TX 78735
512/ 451-3246
800/ 897-3202

CHILD AUTISM RATING SCALE
Western Psychological Services
12031 Wilshire Boulevard
Los Angeles, CA 90025-1251

CHILD BEHAVIOR CHECKLIST
(*including Child Behavior Checklist for ages 2/3, Child Behavior Checklist for ages 4–18, and Child Behavior Checklist, Direct Observation Form*)
University Associates in Psychiatry
1 South Prospect Street
Burlington, VT 05401-3456
802/ 656-8313

CHILDREN'S APPERCEPTION TEST
C.P.S., Inc.
P.O. Box 83
Larchmont, NY 10538

CHILDREN'S DEPRESSION INVENTORY
Multi-Health Systems, Inc.
908 Niagara Falls Boulevard
North Tonowanda, NY 14120-2060
800/ 456-3003

CONNERS RATING SCALES/CONNERS RATING SCALES–REVISED
(*comprehensive assessment systems including various teacher and parent report forms, and self-report forms*)
Multi-Health Systems, Inc.
908 Niagara Falls Boulevard
North Tonowanda, NY 14120-2060
800/ 456-3003

DIAGNOSTIC INTERVIEW SCHEDULE FOR CHILDREN
Division of Child and Adolescent Psychiatry
New York State Psychiatric Institute
722 West 168th Street
New York, NY 10032

DRAW-A-PERSON SCREENING PROCEDURE FOR EMOTIONAL DISTURBANCE
PRO-ED
8700 Shoal Creek Blvd.
Austin, TX 78757-6897
512/ 451-3246
800/ 897-3202

EARLY SCREENING PROJECT
(*early childhood multiple gating screening and assessment system*)
Sopris West
1140 Boston Avenue
Longmont, CO 80501
800/547-6747

EATING DISORDERS INVENTORY
Psychological Assessment Resources
P.O. Box 998
Odessa, FL 33556-9901
800/ 331-8378

INTERNALIZING SYMPTOMS SCALE FOR CHILDREN
PRO-ED
8700 Shoal Creek Blvd.
Austin, TX 78757-6897
512/ 451-3246
800/ 897-3202

JESNESS INVENTORY
Multi-Health Systems, Inc.
908 Niagara Falls Boulevard
North Tonowanda, NY 14120-2060
800/ 456-3003

KINETIC DRAWING SYSTEM FOR FAMILY AND SCHOOL
Western Psychological Services
12031 Wilshire Boulevard
Los Angeles, CA 90025

MILLON ADOLESCENT CLINICAL INVENTORY
MILLON ADOLESCENT PERSONALITY INVENTORY
National Computer Systems
Professional Assessment Services
P.O. Box 1416
Minneapolis, MN 55440
800/ 627-7271

MINNESOTA MULTIPHASIC PERSONALITY INVENTORY–ADOLESCENT
National Computer Systems
Professional Assessment Services
P.O. Box 1416
Minneapolis, MN 55440
800/ 627-7271

PERSONALITY INVENTORY FOR YOUTH
Western Psychological Services
12031 Wilshire Boulevard
Los Angeles, CA 90025-1251

PICTORIAL SCALE OF PERCEIVED COMPETENCE AND ACCEPTANCE
FOR YOUNG CHILDREN
Susan Harter, Ph.D.
University of Denver
Department of Psychology
2155 South Race Street
Denver, CO 80208-020
303/ 871-2041

PRESCHOOL AND KINDERGARTEN BEHAVIOR SCALES
PRO-ED
8700 Shoal Creek Blvd.
Austin, TX 78757-6897
512/ 451-3246
800/ 897-3202

REVISED CHILDREN'S MANIFEST ANXIETY SCALE
Western Psychological Services
12031 Wilshire Boulevard
Los Angeles, CA 90025

REVISED BEHAVIOR PROBLEM CHECKLIST
Psychological Assessment Resources
P.O. Box 998
Odessa, FL 33556-9901
800/ 331-8378

REYNOLDS ADOLESCENT DEPRESSION SCALE
REYNOLDS CHILD DEPRESSION SCALE
Psychological Assessment Resources
P.O. Box 998
Odessa, FL 33556
800/ 331-8378

ROBERTS APPERCEPTION TEST FOR CHILDREN
Western Psychological Services
12031 Wilshire Boulevard
Los Angeles, CA 90025

SELF-PERCEPTION PROFILE FOR CHILDREN
SELF-PERCEPTION PROFILE FOR ADOLESCENTS
Susan Harter, Ph.D.
University of Denver
Department of Psychology
2155 South Race Street
Denver, CO 80208-020
303/ 871-2041

SCHOOL SOCIAL BEHAVIOR SCALES
PRO-ED
8700 Shoal Creek Blvd.

Austin, TX 78757-6897
512/ 451-3246
800/ 897-3202

SOCIAL SKILLS RATING SYSTEM
(*comprehensive social skills rating system, including parent, teacher, and self-report forms*)
American Guidance Service
Publishers Building
Circle Pines, MN 55014-1796
800/ 328-2560

STATE-TRAIT ANXIETY INVENTORY FOR CHILDREN
Consulting Psychologists Press
P.O. Box 10096
Palo Alto, CA 94303
800/ 624-1765

SYSTEMATIC SCREENING FOR BEHAVIOR DISORDERS
(*multiple gating screening and assessment system*)
Sopris West
1140 Boston Avenue
Longmont, CO 80501
800/547-6747

TEACHER'S REPORT FORM
(*TRF for ages 6–18, and C–TRF for ages 2–5*)
University Associates in Psychiatry
1 South Prospect Street
Burlington, VT 05401-3456
802/ 656-8313

THEMATIC APPERCEPTION TEST
Harvard University Press
79 Gasden Street
Cambridge, MA 02138

WALKER–MCCONNELL SCALES OF SOCIAL COMPETENCE
AND SCHOOL ADJUSTMENT
Singular Publishing Group
401 West "A" Street, Suite 325
San Diego, CA 92101-7904
800/521-8545

YOUTH SELF-REPORT
University Associates in Psychiatry
1 South Prospect Street
Burlington, VT 05401-3456
802/ 656-8313

REFERENCES

Achenbach, T. M. (1966). The classification of children's psychiatric symptoms: A factor analytic study. *Psychological Monographs, 80* (Whole no. 615).

Achenbach, T. M. (1978). The Child Behavior profile I: Boys age 6–11. *Journal of Consulting and Clinical Psychology, 46,* 478–488.

Achenbach, T. M. (1982a). Assessment and taxonomy of children's behavior disorders. In B. B. Lahey & A. E. Kazdin (Eds.), *Advances in child clinical psychology* (Vol. 5). New York: Plenum.

Achenbach, T. M. (1982b). *Developmental psychopathology* (2nd ed.). New York: Wiley.

Achenbach, T. M. (1985). *Assessment and taxonomy of child and adolescent psychopathology.* Newbury Park, CA: Sage.

Achenbach, T. M. (1986). *Child behavior checklist—direct observation form* (rev. ed.). Burlington, VT: University Associates in Psychiatry.

Achenbach, T. M. (1991a). *Manual for the Child Behavior Checklist and 1991 profile.* Burlington, VT: University of Vermont.

Achenbach, T. M. (1991b). *Manual for the Teacher's Report Form and 1991 profile.* Burlington, VT: University of Vermont.

Achenbach, T. M. (1991c). *Manual for the Youth Self-Report and 1991 profile.* Burlington, VT: University of Vermont.

Achenbach, T. M. (1992). *Manual for the Child Behavior Checklist/2–3 and 1992 Profile.* Burlington, VT: University of Vermont.

Achenbach, T. M. (1997). *Guide for the Caregiver–Teacher Report Form for Ages 2–5.* Burlington, VT: University of Vermont.

Achenbach, T. M. (1998). Diagnosis, assessment, taxonomy, and case formulations. In T. H. Ollendick & M. Hersen (Eds.), *Handbook of child psychopathology* (3rd ed., pp. 63–87). New York: Plenum.

Achenbach, T. M., & Edelbrock, C. S. (1979). The Child Behavior Profile II: Boys aged 6–12 and girls aged 6–11 and 12–16. *Journal of Consulting and Clinical Psychology, 47,* 223–233.

Achenbach, T. M., & Edelbrock, C. S. (1981). Behavior problems and competencies reported by parents of normal and disturbed children aged 14 through 16. *Monographs of the Society for Research in Child Development, 46* (1, Serial No. 188).

Achenbach, T. M., & Edelbrock, C. S. (1983). Taxonomic issues in child psychopathology. In T. H. Ollendick & M. Herson (Eds.), *Handbook of child psychopathology.* New York: Plenum.

Achenbach, T. M., & McConaughy, S. H. (1992). Taxonomy of internalizing disorders of childhood and adolescence. In W. M. Reynolds (Ed.), *Internalizing disorders of children and adolescents* (pp. 19–60). New York: Wiley.

Achenbach, T. M., & Edelbrock, C. S. (1984). Psychopathology of childhood. *Annual Review of Psychology, 35,* 227–256.

Achenbach, T. M., McConaughy, S. H., & Howell, C. T. (1987). Child/adolescent behavioral and emotional problems: Implications of cross-informant correlations for situational specificity. *Psychological Bulletin, 101,* 213–232.

Ackerson, F. (1942). *Children's behavior problems.* Chicago: University of Chicago Press.

Adams, C. D., McCarthy, M., & Kelly, M. (1995). Adolescent versions of the Home and School Situations Questionnaires: Initial psychometric properties. *Journal of Clinical Child Psychology, 24,* 377–385.

Alberto, P. A., & Troutman, A. C. (1990). *Applied behavior analysis for teachers* (3rd ed.). Columbus, OH: Merrill.

Alessi, G. J. (1988). Direct observation methods for emotional/behavior problems. In E. S. Shapiro & T. R. Kratochwill (Eds.), *Behavioral assessment in schools: Conceptual foundations and practical applications* (pp. 14–75). New York: Guilford.

Alessi, G. J., & Kaye, J. H. (1983). *Behavior assessment for school psychologists.* Kent, OH: National Association of School Psychologists.

Altepeter, T. S., & Breen, M. J. (1989). The Home Situations Questionnaire (HSQ) and the School Situations Questionnaire (SSQ): Normative data and an evaluation of psychometric properties. *Journal of Psychoeducational Assessment, 7,* 312–322.

American Association on Mental Retardation (1992). *Mental retardation: Definition, classification, and systems of support* (9th ed.). Washington, DC: Author.

American Psychiatric Association (1987). *Diagnostic and statistical manual of mental disorders* (rev. 3rd ed.). Washington, DC: Author.

American Psychiatric Association (1994). *Diagnostic and statistical manual of mental disorders* (4th ed.). Washington, DC: Author.

American Psychological Association (1992). *Ethical principles of psychologists and code of conduct.* Washington, DC: Author.

Anastasi, A. (1988). *Psychological testing* (6th ed.). New York: Macmillan.

Anastasi, A., & Urbina, S. (1997). *Psychological testing* (7th ed.). Upper Saddle River, NJ: Prentice-Hall.

Anderson, P. L., & Adams, P. J. (1985). The relationship of 5-year olds' academic readiness and perceptions of competence and acceptance. *Journal of Educational Research, 79,* 114–118.

Aponte, J. F., & Crouch, R. T. (1995). The changing ethnic profile of the United States. In J. F. Aponte, R. Y. Rivers, & J. Wohl (Eds.), *Psychological interventions and cultural diversity* (pp. 1–18). Boston: Allyn & Bacon.

Appel, K. (1931). Drawings by children as aids to personality studies. *American Journal of Orthopsychiatry, 1,* 129–144.

Aragona, J. A., & Eyberg, S. M. (1981). Neglected children: Mother's report of child behavior problems and observed verbal behavior. *Child Development, 52,* 596–602.

Archer, R. P. (1987). *Using the MMPI with adolescents.* Hillsdale, NJ: Lawrence Erlbaum Associates.

Archer, R. P. (1988, August). *Interpreting the adolescent MMPI.* Paper presented at the meeting of the American Psychological Association, Atlanta, GA.

Archer, R. P. (1992). *MMPI–A: Assessing adolescent psychopathology.* Hillsdale, NJ: Lawrence Erlbaum Associates.

Archer, R. P. (1996). *MMPI–A: Assessing adolescent psychopathology* (2nd ed.). Mahwah, NJ: Lawrence Erlbaum Associates.

Archer, R. P. (1997). Future directions for the MMPI–A: Research and clinical issues. *Journal of Personality Assessment, 68,* 95–109.

Archer, R. P., & Gordon, R. A. (1988). MMPI and Rorschach indices of schizophrenic and depressive diagnoses among adolescent inpatients. *Journal of Personality Assessment, 52,* 707–721.

Arkes, H. R. (1981). Impediments to accurate clinical judgment and possible ways to minimize their impact. *Journal of Consulting and Clinical Psychology, 49,* 323–330.

Asher, S. R. (1990). Recent advances in the study of peer rejection. In S. R. Asher & J. D. Coie (Eds.), *Peer rejection in childhood* (pp. 3–14). New York: Cambridge University Press.

Asher, S. R., & Hymel, S. (1981). Children's social competence in peer relations: Sociometric and behavioral assessment. In J. D. Wine & M. D. Smye (Eds.), *Social competence* (pp. 125–157). New York: Guilford.

Asher, S. R., & Parker, J. G. (1989). Significance of peer relationship problems in childhood. In B. H. Schneider, G. Attili, J. Nadel, & R. P. Weissberg (Eds.), *Social competence in developmental perspective* (pp. 5–23). Boston: Kluwer Academic.

Asher, S. R., & Renshaw, P. D. (1981). Children without friends: Social knowledge and skill training. In S. R. Asher & J. M. Gottman (Eds.), *The development of children's friendships* (pp. 273–296). New York: Cambridge University Press.

Asher, S. R., Singleton, L. C., Tinsley, B. R., & Hymel, S. (1979). The reliability of a rating sociometric method with preschool children. *Developmental Psychology, 15,* 443–444.

Asher, S. R., & Taylor, A. R. (1981). The social outcomes of mainstreaming: Sociometric assessment and beyond. *Exceptional Children Quarterly, 1,* 13–30.

Atkinson, D. R., Morten, G., & Sue, D. W. (1989). A minority identity development model. In D. R. Atkinson, G. Morten, & D. W. Sue (Eds.), *Counseling American minorities* (pp. 35–52). Dubuque, IA: Brown.

Auerbach, J. G., Yirmiya, N., & Kamel, F. (1996). Behavior problems in Israeli Jewish and Palestinian preschool children. *Journal of Clinical Child Psychology, 25,* 398–405.

Baer, D. M. (1982). Applied behavior analysis. In G. T. Wilson & C. M. Franks (Eds.), *Contemporary behavior therapy: Conceptual and empirical foundations* (pp. 277–309). New York: Guilford.

Baer, D. M., Wolf, M. M., & Risley, T. R. (1968). Some current dimensions of applied behavior analysis. *Journal of Applied Behavior Analysis, 1,* 91–97.

Ball, J. C. (1962). *Social deviancy and adolescent personality.* Lexington, KY: University of Kentucky Press.

Bandura, A. (1977). *Social learning theory.* Englewood Cliffs, NJ: Prentice-Hall.

Bandura, A. (1978). The self system in reciprocal determinism. *American Psychologist, 33,* 344–358.

Bandura, A. (1986). *Social foundations of thought and action.* Englewood Cliffs, NJ: Prentice-Hall.

Barkley, R. A. (1981). *Hyperactive children: A handbook for diagnosis and treatment.* New York: Guilford.

Barkley, R. A. (1990). Attention deficit disorders. In M. L. Lewis & S. M. Miller (Eds.), *Handbook of developmental psychopathology* (pp. 65–75). New York: Plenum.

Barkley, R. A. (1997a). Behavioral inhibition, sustained attention, and executive functions: Constructing a unifying theory of ADHD. *Psychological Bulletin, 121,* 65–94.

Barkley, R. A. (1997b). *ADHD and the nature of self-control.* New York: Guilford.

Barkley, R. A., & Biederman, J. (1997). Toward a broader definition of the age-of-onset criterion for attention-deficit hyperactivity disorder. *Journal of the American Academy of Child and Adolescent Psychiatry, 36,* 1204–1210.

Barkley, R. A., & Edelbrock, C. S. (1987). Assessing situational variation in children's behavior problems: The Home and School Situations Questionnaires. In R. Prinz (Ed.), *Advances in behavioral assessment of children and families* (Vol. 3, pp. 157–176). Greenwich, CT: JAI.

Barkley, R. A., Karlsson, J., & Pollard, S. (1985). Effects of age on the mother–child interactions of ADD–H and normal boys. *Journal of Abnormal Child Psychology, 13,* 631–638.

Barnes, E. (1892). A study of children's drawings. *Pedagogical Seminary, 2,* 455–463.

Barnett, D. W., Bell, S. H., Stone, C. M., Gilkey, C. M., & Smith, J. J. (1997, August). *Defining intervention-based multifactored preschool assessment.* Paper presented at the meeting of the American Psychological Association, Chicago.

Barnett, D. W., & Zucker, K. B. (1990). *The personal and social assessment of children.* Boston: Allyn & Bacon.

Barrios, B. A., & Hartmann, D. P. (1988). Fears and anxieties. In E. J. Mash & L. G. Terdal (Eds.), *Behavioral assessment of childhood disorders* (2nd ed., pp. 196–262). New York: Guilford.

Barton, E. J., & Ascione, F. R. (1984). Direct observation. In T. H. Ollendick & M. Herson (Eds.), *Child behavioral assessment: Principles and procedures* (pp. 166–194). New York: Pergamon.

Baughman, E. E., & Dahlstrom, W. G. (1968). *A psychological study in the rural south.* New York: Academic Press.

Befera, M., & Barkley, R. A. (1985). Hyperactive and normal girls and boys: Mother–child interactions, parent psychiatric status, and child psychopathology. *Journal of Child Psychology and Psychiatry, 26,* 439–452.

Bellak, L. (1975). *The T.A.T., C.A.T., and S.A.T. in clinical use* (3rd ed.). New York: Grune & Stratton.

Bellak, L., & Bellak, S. (1949). *The Children's Apperception Test.* New York: C.P.S.

Belter, R. W., Foster, K. Y., & Imm, P. S. (1996). Convergent validity of select scales of the MMPI and the Achenbach Child Behavior Checklist–Youth Self-Report. *Psychological Reports, 79 (3, pt. 2),* 1091–1100.

Ben-Porath, Y. S. (1996). *Case studies for interpreting the MMPI–A.* Minneapolis: University of Minnesota Press.

Bender, L. (1938). *A visual-motor gestalt test and its clinical use: Research monograph No. 3.* New York: American Orthopsychiatric Association.

Bender, L. (1946). *Bender Motor-Gestalt Test: Cards and manual of instructions.* New York: American Orthopsychiatric Association.

Berg, I. A. (1967). The deviation hypothesis: A broad statement of its assumptions and postulates. In I. A. Berg (Ed.), *Response set in personality assessment* (pp. 146–190). Chicago: Aldine.

Berg, L., Butler, A., Hullin, R., Smith, R., & Tyrer, S. (1978). Features of children taken to juvenile court for failure to attend school. *Psychological Medicine, 9,* 477–453.

Berman, A. L., & Jobes, D. A. (1991). *Adolescent suicide: Assessment and intervention.* Washington, DC: American Psychological Association.

Bersoff, D. N. (1982a). The legal regulation of school psychology. In C. Reynolds & T. Gutkin (Eds.), *The handbook of school psychology* (pp. 1043–1074). New York: Wiley.

Bersoff, D. N. (1982b). *Larry P.* and *PASE*: Judicial report cards on the validity of individual intelligence testing. In T. Kratochwill (Ed.), *Advances in school psychology* (Vol. 2, pp. 61–95). Hillsdale, NJ: Lawrence Erlbaum Associates.

Bettelheim, B. (1967). *The empty fortress: Infantile autism and the birth of the self.* New York: The Free Press.

Bierman, K. L. (1983). Cognitive development and clinical interviews with children. In B. Lahey & A. E. Kazdin (Eds.), *Advances in clinical child psychology* (Vol. 6, pp. 217–250). New York: Plenum.

Biederman, J., Faraone, S. V., Milberger, S., & Jetton, J. G. (1996). Is childhood oppositional defiant disorder a precursor to adolescent conduct disorder? Findings from a 4-year follow-up study of children with ADHD. *Journal of the American Academy of Child and Adolescent Psychiatry, 35,* 1193–1204.

Bird, H. R., Gould, M. S., Rubio-Stipec, M., & Staghezza, B. M. (1991). Screening for childhood psychopathology in the community using the Child Behavior Checklist. *Journal of the American Academy of Child and Adolescent Psychiatry, 30,* 116–123.

Bloom, B. S. (1976). *Human characteristics and school learning.* New York: McGraw-Hill.

Blueler, M. (1978). *The schizophrenic disorders.* New Haven, CT: Yale University Press.

Blumberg, S. H., & Izard, C. E. (1986). Discriminating patterns of emotions in 10- and 11- year-old children's anxiety and depression. *Journal of Personality and Social Psychology, 51,* 852–857.

Boat, B. W., & Everson, M. D. (1988). Interviewing young children with anatomical dolls. *Child Welfare, 67,* 337–352.

Boggs, S. R., & Eyberg, S. (1990). Interview techniques and establishing rapport. In L. M. LaGreca (Ed.), *Through the eyes of the child* (pp. 85–108). Boston: Allyn & Bacon.

Boggs, S. R., Eyberg, S., & Reynolds, L. A. (1990). Concurrent validity of the Eyberg Child Behavior Inventory. *Journal of Clinical Child Psychology, 19,* 75–78.

Bonney, M. E. (1943). The relative stability of social, intellectual, and academic status in grades 2 to 4, and the inter-relationships between these various forms of growth. *Journal of Educational Psychology, 34,* 88–102.

Bornstein, M. R., Bellack, A. S., & Herson, M. (1977). Social-skills training for unassertive children: A multiple-baseline analysis. *Journal of Applied Behavior Analysis, 10,* 183–195.

Bornstein, M. R., Bellack, A. S., & Herson, M. (1980). Social skills training for highly aggressive children in an inpatient psychiatric setting. *Behavior Modification, 4,* 173–186.

Bower, E. (1969). *Early identification of emotionally handicapped children in school* (2nd ed.). Springfield, IL: Thomas.

Bower, E. (1981). *Early identification of emotionally handicapped children in school* (3rd ed.). Springfield, IL: Thomas.

Bower, E. M. (1982). Defining emotional disturbance: Public policy and research. *Psychology in the Schools, 19,* 55–60.

Bower, E. M., Shalhamer, T. A., & Daily, J. M. (1960). School characteristics of male adolescents who later become schizophrenics. *American Journal of Orthopsychiatry, 30,* 712–729.

Bowlby, J. (1973). *Attachment and loss: Vol. 2. Separation.* New York: Basic Books.

Boyle, M. H., Offord, D. R., Racine, Y., & Sanford, M. (1993). Evaluation of the Diagnostic Interview for Children and Adolescents for use in general population samples. *Journal of Abnormal Child Psychology, 21,* 663–661.

Bracken, B. A. (1987). Limitations of preschool instruments and standards for minimal levels of technical adequacy. *Journal of Psychoeducational Assessment, 4,* 313–326.

Bracken, B. A. (1992). *The Multidimensional Self-concept Scale.* Austin, TX: PRO-ED.

Bracken, B. A. (1993). *Assessment of Interpersonal Relations.* Austin, TX: PRO-ED.

Bracken, B. A. (1994). Advocating for effective preschool assessment practices: A comment on Bagnato and Neisworth. *School Psychology Quarterly, 9,* 103–108.

Bracken, B. A., & Howell, K. K. (1991). Multidimensional self concept validation: A three-instrument investigation. *Journal of Psychoeducational Assessment, 9,* 319–328.

Bracken, B. A., Keith, L. K., & Walker, K. C. (1994). Assessment of preschool behavior and social-emotional functioning: A review of 13 third-party instruments. *Assessment in Rehabilitation and Exceptionality, 1,* 259–346.

Breen, M. J., & Altepeter, T. S. (1991). Factor structures of the Home Situations Questionnaire and the School Situations Questionnaire. *Journal of Pediatric Psychology, 16,* 59–67.

Breslau, N. (1987). Inquiring about the bizzare: False positives in Diagnostic Interview Schedule for Children (DISC) ascertainment of obsessions, compulsions, and psychotic symptoms. *Journal of the American Academy of Child and Adolescent Psychiatry, 26,* 639–644.

Bricceti, K. A. (1994). Emotional indicators of deaf children on the Draw-A-Person test. *American Annals of the Deaf, 139,* 500–505.

Brock, S. E., & Sandoval, J. (1997). Suicidal ideation and behaviors. In G. C. Bear, K. M. Minke, & A. Thomas (Eds.), *Children's Needs II: Development, problems, and alternatives* (pp. 361–374). Washington, DC: National Association of School Psychologists.

Brown, F. G. (1983). *Principles of educational and psychological testing* (3rd ed.). New York: Holt, Rinehart, & Winston.

Brown, R. T., & Hammill, D. D. (1983). *Behavior Rating Profile*. Austin, TX: PRO-ED.

Bruininks, R., Woodcock, R. W., Weatherman, R. F., & Hill, B. K. (1984). *Scales of Independent Behavior.* Allen, TX: DLM Teaching Resources.

Bryan, T. (1974). Peer popularity of learning disabled children. *Journal of Learning Disabilities, 7,* 261–268.

Bullock, M. J., Ironsmith, M., & Poteat, G. M. (1988). Sociometric techniques with young children: A review of psychometrics and classification schemes. *School Psychology Review, 17,* 289–303.

Burisch, M. (1984). Approaches to personality inventory construction: A comparison of merits. *American Psychologist, 38,* 214–227.

Burks, H. F. (1977). *Burks' Behavior Rating Scales.* Los Angeles: Western Psychological Services.

Burns, G. L., & Patterson, D. R. (1991). Factor structure of the Eyberg Child Behavior Inventory: Unidimensional or multidimensional measure of disruptive behavior? *Journal of Clinical Child Psychology, 20,* 439–444.

Burns, G. L., Patterson, D. R., & Nussbaum, B. R. (1991). Disruptive behaviors in an outpatient pediatric population: Additional standardization data on the Eyberg Child Behavior Inventory. *Psychological Assessment, 3,* 202–207.

Burns, R. (1982). Self-growth in families: *Kinetic Family Drawings (K-F-D) research and application.* New York: Brunner/Mazel.

Burns, R., & Kaufman, S. (1970). Kinetic Family Drawings (K-F-D): *An introduction to understanding children through kinetic drawings.* New York: Brunner/Mazel.

Burns, R., & Kaufman, S. (1972). *Actions, styles, and symbols in Kinetic Family Drawings (K-F-D): An interpretive manual.* New York: Brunner/Mazel.

Butcher, J. N. (1979). *New developments in the use of the MMPI.* Minneapolis: University of Minnesota Press.

Butcher, J. N. (1990). *The MMPI–2 in psychological treatment.* New York: Oxford University Press.

Butcher, J. N. (1992). *Essentials of MMPI–2 and MMPI–A interpretation.* Minneapolis: University of Minnesota Press.

Cadieux, A. (1996). Psychometric properties of a pictorial self-concept scale among young learning disabled boys. *Psychology in the Schools, 33,* 221–229.

Caldarella, P., & Merrell, K. W. (1997). Common dimensions of social skills of children and adolescents: A taxonomy of positive behaviors. *School Psychology Review, 26,* 265–279.

Campbell, S. B. (1991). Active and aggressive preschoolers. In D. Cicchetti & S. L. Toth (Eds.), *Internalizing and externalizing expressions of dysfunction* (pp. 57–89). Hillsdale, NJ: Lawrence Erlbaum Associates.

Campbell, S. B., & Steinert, Y. (1978). Comparison of rating scale of child psychopathology in clinic and nonclinic samples. *Journal of Consulting and Clinical Psychology, 46,* 358–359.

Campbell, S. B., & Werry, J. S. (1986). Attention deficit disorder (hyperactivity). In H. C. Quay & J. S. Werry (Eds.), *Psychopathological disorders of childhood* (3rd ed., pp. 111–155). New York: Wiley.

Cantor, S. (1987). *Childhood schizophrenia.* New York: Guilford.

Cantor, S. (1989). Schizophrenia. In C. G. Last & M. Herson (Eds.), *Handbook of childhood psychiatric diagnosis* (pp. 279–298). New York: Wiley.

Cantor, S., Pearce, J., Pezzot-Pearce, T., & Evans, J. (1981). The group of hypotonic schizophrenics. *Schizophrenia Bulletin, 7,* 1–11.

Cantwell, D. P. (1990). Depression across the early life span. In M. Lewis & S. M. Miller (Eds.), *Handbook of developmental psychopathology* (pp. 293–309). New York: Plenum.

Cantwell, D. P., & Carlson, G. A. (1981, October). *Factor analysis of a self rating depressive inventory for children: Factor structure and nosological utility.* Paper presented at the annual meeting of the American Academy of Child Psychiatry, Dallas, TX.

Carey, T. C., Finch, A. J., & Carey, M. P. (1991). Relation between differential emotions and depression in emotionally disturbed children and adolescents. *Journal of Consulting and Clinical Psychology, 59,* 594–597.

Carlson, G. A., & Garber, J. (1986). Developmental issues in the classification of depression in children. In M. Rutter, C. E. Izard, & P. B. Read (Eds.), *Depression in young people* (pp. 399–434). New York: Guilford.

Cartledge, G., Frew, T., & Zacharias, J. (1985). Social skills needs of mainstreamed students: Peer and teacher perceptions. *Learning Disability Quarterly, 8,* 132–140.

Caruso, G. A. L. (1994). The prevalence of behavior problems among toddlers in child care. *Early Education and Development, 5,* 27–40.

Cattell, R. B., Eber, W. H., & Tatsuoka, M. M. (1970). *Handbook for the 16 Personality Factor Questionnaire.* Champaign, IL: Institute for Personality and Ability Testing.

Chambers, W., Puig-Antich, J., Hersche, M., Paey, P., Ambrosini, P. J., Tabrizi, M. A., & Davies, M. (1985). The assessment of affective disorders in children and adolescents by semi-structured interview: Test–retest reliability of the K–SADS–P. *Archives of General Psychiatry, 42,* 696–702.

Chandler, L. A., & Johnson, V. J. (1991). *Using projective techniques with children.* Springfield, IL: Thomas.

Chapman, L. J., & Chapman, J. P. (1967). Genesis of popular but erroneous psychodiagnostic observations. *Journal of Abnormal Psychology, 74,* 271–280.

Christenson, S. L. (1990). Review of the Child Behavior Checklist. In J. J. Kramer & J. C. Conoley (Eds.), *The Supplement to the 10th Mental Measurements Yearbook* (pp. 40–41). Lincoln, NE: Buros Institute of Mental Measurements.

Cicchetti, D., & Toth, S. L. (1991). A developmental perspective on internalizing and externalizing disorders. In D. Cicchetti & S. L. Toth (Eds.), *Internalizing and externalizing expressions of dysfunction* (pp. 1–19). Hillsdale, NJ: Lawrence Erlbaum Associates.

Clark, M.. L., & Drewry, D. L. (1985). Similarity and reciprocity in the friendships of elementary school children. *Child Study Journal, 15,* 251–264.

Cohen, D. J., Leckman, J. F., & Shaywitz, B. A. (1984). The Tourette Syndrome and other tics. In D. Schaffer, A. A. Erhardt, & L. Greenhill (Eds.), *The clinical guide to child psychiatry.* New York: The Free Press.

Cohen, M. (1988). The revised Conners Parent Rating Scale: Factor structures with a diversified clinical sample. *Journal of Abnormal Child Psychology, 2,* 187–196.

Cohen, M., & Hynd, G. W. (1986). The Conners Teacher Rating Scale: A different factor structure with special education students. *Psychology in the Schools, 23,* 13–23.

Cohen, P., O'Connor, P., Lewis, S., Velez, C., & Noemi, S. (1987). Comparison of DISC and K–SADS–P interviews of an epidemiological sample of children. *Journal of the American Academy of Child and Adolescent Psychiatry, 26,* 662–667.

Coie, J. D., Belding, M. & Underwood, M. (1988). Aggression and peer rejection in childhood. In B. B. Lahey & A. Kazdin (Eds.), *Advances in clinical child psychology* (Vol. 2, pp. 125–158). New York: Plenum.

Coie, J. D., Dodge, K. A., & Coppotelli, H. (1982). Dimensions and types of social status: A cross-age perspective. *Developmental Psychology, 18,* 557–570.

Cone, J. D. (1978). The behavioral assessment grid (BAG): A conceptual framework and taxonomy. *Behavior Therapy, 9,* 882–888.

Cone, J. D. (1981). Psychometric considerations. In M. Herson & A. S. Bellack (Eds.), *Behavioral assessment: A practical handbook* (pp. 36–68). New York: Pergamon.

Cone, J. D., & Hoier, T. S. (1986). Assessing children: The radical behavioral perspective. In R. Prinz (Ed.), *Advances in behavioral assessment of children and families* (Vol. 2, pp. 1–27). New York: JAI.

Cone, J. E., & Hawkins, R. P. (1977). *Behavioral assessment: New directions in clinical psychology.* New York: Brunner/Mazel.

Conners, C. K. (1969). A teacher rating scale for use in drug studies with children. *American Journal of Psychiatry, 126,* 884–888.

Conners, C. K. (1990). *Conners Rating Scales Manual.* Toronto: Multi-Health Systems.

Conners, C. K. (1997). *Conners Rating Scales–Revised Technical Manual.* Toronto: Multi-Health Systems.

Conners, C. K., & Werry, J. S. (1979). Pharmacotherapy. In H. C. Quay & J. S. Werry (Eds.), *Psychopathological disorders of childhood* (2nd ed.). New York: Wiley.

Connolly, J. A. (1983). A review of sociometric procedures in the assessment of social competencies in children. *Applied Research in Mental Retardation, 4,* 315–327.

Connolly, J., A., & Doyle, A. B. (1981). Assessment of social competence in preschoolers: Teachers versus peers. *Developmental Psychology, 17,* 451–456.

Cook, K. (1991). Integrating Kinetic Family Drawings into Adlerian life-style interviews. *Individual Psychology: Journal of Adlerian Theory, Research, and Practice, 47,* 521–526.

Coolbear, J. (1992). Credibility of young children in sexual abuse cases: Assessment strategies of legal and human service professionals. *Canadian Psychology, 33,* 151–167.

Cooper, J. (1981). *Measurement and analysis of behavioral techniques* (2nd ed.). Columbus, OH: Merrill.

Coopersmith, S. (1981). *Self-esteem Inventories.* Palo Alto, CA: Consulting Psychologists Press.

Corey, G., Corey, M. S., & Callanan, P. (1993). *Issues and ethics in the helping professions* (4th ed.). Pacific Grove, CA: Brooks-Cole.

Cormier, W. H., & Cormier, L. S. (1985). *Interviewing strategies for helpers* (2nd ed.). Pacific Grove, CA: Brooks-Cole.

Costello, A. J. (1989). Developments in child psychiatric epidemiology. *Journal of the American Academy of Child and Adolescent Psychiatry, 28,* 836–841.

Costello, A. J., Edelbrock, C. S., Dulcan, M. K., & Kalas, R. (1984). *Testing of the NIMH Diagnostic Interview Schedule for Children (DISC) in a clinical population* (Contract No. DB-81-0027, final report to the Center for Epidemiological Studies, National Institute of Mental Health). Pittsburgh: University of Pittsburgh Department of Psychiatry.

Council for Children with Behavioral Disorders (1991). New definition of EBD proposed. *Council for Children with Behavioral Disorders Newsletter, February.* Reston, VA: Council for Exceptional Children.

Cowen, E. L., Pederson, A., Babigan, H., Izzo, L. D., & Trost, M. A. (1973). Long-term follow-up of early detected vulnerable children. *Journal of Consulting and Clinical Psychology, 41,* 438–446.

Craig, K. D., & Dobson, K. S. (Eds.) (1995). *Anxiety and depression in adults and children.* Thousand Oaks, CA: Sage.

Cronbach, L. J. (1949). *Essentials of psychological testing.* New York: Harper & Row.

Cronbach, L. J., & Gleser, G. C. (1965). *Psychological tests and personnel decisions.* Urbana: University of Illinois Press.

Crowley, S. L., & Fan, X. (1997). Structural equation modeling: Basic concepts and applications in personality assessment research. *Journal of Personality Assessment, 68,* 508–531.

Crowley, S. L., & Worchel, F. F. (1993). Assessment of childhood depression: Sampling multiple data sources with one instrument. *Journal of Psychoeducational Assessment, 11,* 242–249.

Cummings, J. A. (1980). An evaluation of objective scoring systems for the Kinetic Family Drawings (KFD). *Dissertation Abstracts International, 4*(6-B), 2313.

Cummings, J. A. (1986). Projective drawings. In H. M. Knoff (Ed.), *The assessment of child and adolescent personality* (pp. 199–244). New York: Guilford.

Cunningham, R. (1951). *Understanding group behavior of boys and girls.* New York: Bureau of Publications, Teachers College of Columbia University.

Dalton, J. E. (1996). Juvenile male sex offenders: Mean scores and the BASC self-report of personality. *Psychological Reports, 79*(2), 634.

Dana, R. H. (1993). *Multicultural assessment: Perspectives for professional psychology.* Boston: Allyn & Bacon.

Dana, R. H. (1994). Testing and assessment ethics for all persons: Beginning and agenda. *Professional Psychology Research and Practice, 25,* 349–354.

Dana, R. H. (1995). Impact of the use of standard psychological assessment on the diagnosis and treatment of ethnic minorities. In J. F. Aponte, R. Y. Rivers, & J. Wohl (Eds.), *Psychological interventions and cultural diversity* (pp. 57–72). Boston: Allyn & Bacon.

Dana, R. H. (1996). Culturally competent assessment practice in the United States. *Journal of Personality Assessment, 66,* 472–487.

Danforth, J. S., & DuPaul, G. J. (1996). Interrater reliability of teacher rating scales for children with attention-deficit hyperactivity disorder. *Journal of Psychopathology and Behavioral Assessment, 18,* 227–237.

Davis, J. M., & Sandoval, J. (1991). *Suicidal youth: School-based intervention and prevention.* San Francisco: Jossey-Bass.

Dawson, G., Hill, D., Spencer, A., Galpert, L., & Watson, L. (1990). Affective exchanges between young autistic children and their mothers. *Journal of Abnormal Child Psychology, 18,* 335–345.

Dedrick, R. F. (1997). Testing the structure of the Child Behavior Checklist/4–18 using confirmatory factor analysis. *Educational and Psychological Measurement, 57,* 306–313.

deGroot, A., Koot, H. M., & Verhulst, F. C. (1996). Cross-cultural generalizability of the Youth Self-Report and Teacher's Report Form cross informant syndromes. *Journal of Abnormal Child Psychology, 24,* 651–664.

Demaray, M. K., Ruffalo, S. L., Carlson, J., Brusse, R. T., Olson, A. E., McManus, S. M.., & Leventhal, A. (1995). Social skills assessment: A comparative evaluation of six published rating scales. *School Psychology Review, 24,* 648–671.

DeMers, S. T. (1986). Legal and ethical issues in child and adolescent personality assessment. In H. Knoff (Ed.), *The assessment of child and adolescent personality* (pp. 35–55). New York: Guilford.

Deutsch, C. K., & Kinsbourne, M. (1990). Genetics and biochemistry in attention deficit disorder. In M. Lewis & S. M. Miller (Eds.), *Handbook of developmental psychopathology* (pp. 93–107). New York: Plenum.

Dickson, J. M., Saylor, C. F., & Finch, A. J. (1990). Personality factors, family structure, and sex of drawn figure on the Draw-A-Person Test. *Journal of Personality Assessment, 55,* 362–366.

Dodge, K., Coie, J., & Brakke, N., (1982). Behavior patterns of socially rejected and neglected adolescents: The roles of social approach and aggression. *Journal of Abnormal Child Psychology, 10,* 389–410.

Doll, B., & Elliott, S. N. (1994). Representitiveness of observed preschool social behaviors: How many data are enough? *Journal of Early Intervention, 18,* 227–238.

Drotar, D., Stein, R. K., & Perrin, E. C. (1995). Methodological issues in using the Child Behavior Checklist and its related instruments in clinical child psychology research. *Journal of Clinical Child Psychology, 24,* 184–192.

DuPaul, G. J. (1992). How to assess attention-deficit hyperactivity disorder within school settings. *School Psychology Quarterly, 7,* 61–74.

DuPaul, G. J., & Barkley, R. A. (1992). Situational variability of attentional problems: Psychometric properties of the Revised Home and School Situations Questionnaires. *Journal of Clinical Child Psychology, 21,* 178–188.

DuPaul, G. J., & Stoner, G. (1994). *ADHD in the schools: Assessment and intervention strategies.* New York: Guilford.

Dusek, J. B. (1996). *Adolescent development and behavior* (3rd ed.). Saddle River, NJ: Prentice-Hall.

Dwyer, K. P., & Stanhope, V. (1997). IDEA '97: Synopsis and recommendations. *NASP Communique, 26(1),* handout supplement. Washington, DC: National Association of School Psychologists.

Eddings, J. (1997, July 14). Counting a "new" type of American: The dicey politics of creating a multiracial category in the census. *U.S. News and World Report* [On-line].

Edelbrock, C., & Costello, A. J. (1988). Structured psychiatric interviews for children. In M. Rutter, A. H. Tuma, & I. S. Lann (Eds.), *Assessment and diagnosis in child psychopathology* (pp. 87–112). New York: Guilford.

Edelbrock, C. S., Greenbaum, R., & Conover, N. C. (1985). Reliability and concurrent relations between the teacher version of the Child Behavior Profile and the Conners Revised Teacher Rating Scale. *Journal of Abnormal Child Psychology, 13,* 295–303.

Ehrenworth, N. V., & Archer, R. P. (1985). A comparison of clinical accuracy ratings of interpretive approaches for adolescent MMPI responses. *Journal of Personality Assessment, 49,* 413–421.

Eisenstadt, T. H., McElreath, L. H., Eyberg, S. M., & McNeil, C. B. (1994). Interparent agreement on the Eyberg Child Behavior Inventory. *Child and Family Behavior Therapy, 16,* 21–27.

Eisler, R. M., Miller, P. M., & Herson, M. (1973). Components of assertive behavior. *Journal of Clinical Psychology, 29,* 295–299.

Elliott, S. N., Barnard, J., & Gresham, F. M. (1989). Preschoolers social behavior: Teachers' and parents' assessments. *Journal of Psychoeducational Assessment, 7,* 223–234.

Elliott, S. N., & Busse, R. T. (1990). Review of the Child Behavior Checklist. In J. Kramer & J. C. Conoley (Eds.), *The Supplement to the 10th Mental Measurements Yearbook* (pp. 41–45). Lincoln, NE: Buros Institute of Mental Measurements.

Elliott, S. N., Busse, R. T., & Gresham, F. M. (1993). Behavior rating scales: Issues of use and development. *School Psychology Review, 22,* 313–321.

Elliott, S. N., & Gresham, F. M. (1987). Children's social skills: Assessment and classification practices. *Journal of Counseling and Development, 66,* 96–99.

Emerson, E. N., Crowley, S. L., & Merrell, K. W. (1994). Convergent validity of the School Social Behavior Scales with the Child Behavior Checklist and Teacher's Report Form. *Journal of Psychoeducational Assessment, 12,* 372–380.

Endicott, J., & Spitzer, R. L. (1978). A diagnostic interview: The Schedule for Affective Disorders and Schizophrenia. *Archives of General Psychiatry, 35,* 837–844.

Epps, S. (1985). Best practices in behavioral observation. In A. Thomas & J. Grimes (Eds.), *Best practices in school psychology* (pp. 95–111). Washington, DC: National Association of School Psychologists.

Epstein, M. H., Cullinan, D., & Lloyd, J. W. (1986). Behavior problem patterns among the learning disabled: III. Replication across age and sex. *Learning Disability Quarterly, 9,* 43–54.

Erikson, E. (1963). *Childhood and society.* New York: Norton.

Erlenmeyer-Kimling, L., Kestenbaum, C., Bird, H., & Hildoff, U. (1984). Assessment of the New York High Risk Project subjects in sample A who are now clinically deviant. In N. F. Watt, E. J. Anthony, L. C. Wynne, & J. E. Rolf (Eds.), *Children at high risk of schizophrenia.* Cambridge: Cambridge University Press.

Exner, J. E. , Jr., & Weiner, I. B. (1994). *The Rorschach: A comprehensive system:* Vol. 3. *Assessment of children and adolescents* (2nd ed.). New York: Wiley.

Eyberg, S. M. (1980). Eyberg Child Behavior Inventory. *Journal of Clinical Child Psychology, 9,* 29.

Eyberg, S. M., & Matarazzo, R. G. (1980). Training parents as therapists: A comparison between individual parent–child interaction training and parent group didactic training. *Journal of Clinical Psychology 36,* 492–499.

Eyberg, S. M., & Robinson, E. A. (1982a). Conduct problem behavior: Standardization of a behavior rating scale with adolescents. *Journal of Clinical Child Psychology, 12,* 347–357.

Eyberg, S. M., & Robinson, E. A. (1982b). Parent–child interaction training: Effects on family functioning. *Journal of Clinical Child Psychology, 11,* 130–137.

Eyberg, S. M., & Robinson, E. A. (1983). Dyadic Parent–Child Interaction Coding System: A manual. *Psychological Documents, 13.* (Ms. No. 2582)

Ezpeleta, L., del-la-Osa, N., Domenech, J. M., & Navarro, J. B. (1997). Diagnostic agreement between clinicians and Diagnostic Interview for Children and Adolescents—DICA–R—in an outpatient sample. *Journal of Child Psychology and Psychiatry and Allied Disciplines, 38,* 431–440.

Fan, X., Wilson, V. T., & Kapes, J. T. (1996). Ethnic group representation in test construction samples and test bias: The standardization fallacy revisited. *Educational and Psychological Measurement, 56,* 365–381.

Farrington, D. (1978). The family backgrounds of aggressive youths. In L. A. Hersov, A. L. Berger, & D. Shaffer (Eds.), *Aggression and antisocial behavior in childhood and adolescence* (pp. 73–93). London: Pergamon.

Feil, E. G., & Becker, W. C. (1993). Investigation of a multiple-gated screening system for preschool behavior problems. *Behavioral Disorders, 19,* 44–53.

Feldman, D., Kinnison, L., Jay, R., & Harth, R. (1983). The effects of differential labeling on professional concepts and attitudes towards the emotionally disturbed/behaviorally disordered. *Behavioral Disorders, 8,* 191–198.

Feyh, J. M., & Holmes, C. B. (1994). Use of the Draw-A-Person test with conduct disordered children. *Perceptual and Motor Skills, 78,* 1353–1354.

Finch, A. J., Saylor, C. F., & Edwards, G. L. (1985). Children's Depression Inventory: Sex and grade norms for normal children. *Journal of Consulting and Clinical Psychology, 53,* 424–425.

Fine, G. A. (1981). Friends, impression management, and preadolescent behavior. In S. R. Asher & J. M. Gottman (Eds.), *The development of children's friendships* (pp. 29–52). New York: Cambridge University Press.

Fish, B., & Shapiro, T. (1964). A descriptive typology of children's psychiatric disorders: II. A behavioral classification. In R. L. Jenkins & J. O. Cole (Eds.), *American Psychiatric Association Psychiatric Research Reports #18.* Washington, DC: American Psychiatric Association.

Fisher, P., Wicks, J., Shaffer, D., Piacentini, J., & Lapkin, J. (1992). *National Institute of Mental Health Diagnostic Interview Schedule for Children users' manual.* New York: New York State Psychiatric Institute Division of Child and Adolescent Psychiatry.

Flanagan, D. P., Alfonso, V. C., Primavera, L. H., & Povall, L. (1996). Convergent validity of the BASC and SSRS: Implications for social skills assessment. *Psychology in the Schools, 33,* 13–23.

Flanagan, R. (1995). A review of the Behavior Assessment System for Children (BASC): Assessment consistent with the requirements of the Individuals with Disabilities Education Act (IDEA). *Journal of School Psychology, 33,* 177–186.

Flugum, K. R., & Reschly, D. J. (1994). Pre-referral interventions: Quality indices and outcomes. *Journal of School Psychology, 32,* 1–14.

Forehand, R., & McMahon, R. J. (1981). *Helping the noncompliant child: A clinician's guide to parent training.* New York: Guilford.

Forehand, R., & Peed, S. (1979). Training parents to modify noncompliant behavior of their children. In A. J. Finch & P. C. Kendall (Eds.), *Treatment and research in child psychopathology* (pp. 159–184). New York: Spectrum.

Forehand, R., Peed, S., Roberts, M., McMahon, R., Griest, D., & Humphreys, L. (1978). *Coding manual for scoring mother–child interactions.* Unpublished manuscript, University of Georgia Department of Psychology.

Forness, S. R., & Knitzer, J. (1992). A new proposed definition and terminology to replace "serious emotional disturbance" in the individuals with disabilities education act. *School Psychology Review, 21,* 12–20.

Forster, A. A., Eyeberg, S. M., & Burns, G. L. (1990). Assessing the verbal behavior of conduct problem children during mother–child interactions: A preliminary investigation. *Child and Family Behavior Therapy, 12,* 13–22.

Foster, S. L., Bell-Dolan, D., & Berler, E. S. (1986). Methodological issues in the use of sociometrics for selecting children for social skills research and training. *Advances in Behavioral Assessment of Children and Families, 2,* 227–248.

Frank, L. K. (1939). Projective methods for the study of personality. *Journal of Psychology, 8,* 389–413.

Freeman, B. J., Ritvo, E. R., Guthrie, D., Schroth, P., & Ball, J. (1978). The Behavior Observation Scale for Autism. *Journal of the American Academy of Child Psychiatry, 24,* 290–311.

Freeman, B. J., & Schroth, P. C. (1984). The development of the Behavioral Observation System (BOS) for autism. *Behavioral Assessment, 6,* 177–187.

Freeman, B. J., Schroth, P., Ritvo, E., Guthrie, D., & Wake, L. (1980). The Behavior Observation Scale for Autism (BOS): Initial results of factor analyses. *Journal of Autism and Developmental Disorders, 10,* 343–346.

Frick, P. J. (1998). Conduct disorders. In T. H. Ollendick & M. Hersen (Eds.), *Handbook of child psychopathology* (3rd ed., pp. 213–237). New York: Plenum.

Fuchs, D., & Fuchs, L. S. (1986). Test procedure bias: A meta-analysis of examiner familiarity effects. *Review of Educational Research, 56,* 243–262.

Fulkerson, S. C., & Freeman, W. M. (1980). Perceptual-motor deficiency in autistic children. *Perceptual and motor skills, 50,* 331–336.

Garner, D. M. (1991). *Eating Disorders Inventory–2 manual.* Odessa, FL: Psychological Assessment Resources.

Garrison, S., & Jenkins, J. (1986). Differing perceptions of Black assertiveness as a function of race. *Journal of Multicultural Counseling and Development, 14,* 157–166.

Gelman, R., & Baillageon, R. (1983). A review of some Piagetian concepts. In P. H. Mussen (Ed.), *Carmichael's manual of child psychology* (pp. 167–230). New York: Wiley.

Gesten, E. L. (1976). A health resources inventory: The development of a measure of the personal and social competence of primary-grade children. *Journal of Consulting and Clinical Psychology, 44,* 775–786.

Gettinger, M., & Kratochwill, T. R. (1987). Behavioral assessment. In C. L. Frame & J. L. Matson (Eds.), *Handbook of assessment in childhood psychopathology* (pp. 131–161). New York: Plenum.

Gillberg, I. C., & Gillberg, C. (1983). Three-year follow-up at age 10 of children with minor neurodevelopmental disorders: I. Behavioural problems. *Developmental Medicine and Child Neurology, 25,* 438–449.

Glow, R. A., Glow, P. A., & Rump, E. E. (1982). The stability of child behavior disorders: A 1 year test–retest study of adelaide versions of the Conners Teacher and Parent Rating Scales. *Journal of Abnormal Child Psychology, 10,* 33–60.

Goh, D. S., & Fuller, G. B. (1983). Current practices in the assessment of personality and behavior by school psychologists. *School Psychology Review, 12,* 240–243.

Goldberg, L. R. (1974). Objective diagnostic tests and measures. *Annual Review of Psychology, 25,* 343–366.

Golden, G. S., & Hood, O. J. (1982). Tics and tremors. *Pediatric Clinics of North America, 29,* 95–103.

Goodenough, F. L. (1926). *Measurement of intelligence by drawings.* New York: Harcourt, Brace, & World.

Gottesman, I. I. (1991). *Schizophrenia and genesis: The origins of madness.* New York: Freeman.

Goyette, C. H., Conners, C. K., & Ulrich, R. F. (1978). Normal data on revised Conners Parent and Teachers Rating Scales. *Journal of Abnormal Child Psychology, 6,* 221–236.

Graham, J. R. (1987). *The MMPI: A practical guide* (2nd ed.). New York: Oxford University Press.

Graham, J. R. (1990). *MMPI–2: Assessing personality and psychopathology.* New York: Oxford University Press.

Graham, P. (1980). Epidemiological studies. In H. E. Quay & J. S. Werry (Eds.), *Psychopathological disorders of childhood* (2nd ed., pp. 185–209). New York: Wiley.

Greene, R. L. (1980). *The MMPI: An interpretive manual.* New York: Grune & Stratton.

Greene, R. L. (1987). Ethnicity and MMPI performance: A review. *Journal of Consulting and Clinical Psychology, 55,* 497–512.

Greene, R. L. (1991). *The MMPI–2/MMPI: An interpretive manual.* New York: Grune & Stratton.

Greenwood, C. R., Walker, H. M., Todis, N. M., & Hops, H. (1979). Selecting a cost-effective screening measure for the assessment of preschool social withdrawal. *Journal of Applied Behavior Analysis, 12,* 639–652.

Gregory, R. J. (1996). *Psychological testing: History, principles, and applications* (2nd ed.). Boston: Allyn & Bacon.

Griest, D. L., Forehand, R., Wells, K. C., & McMahon, R. J. (1980). An examination of differences between nonclinic and behavior-problem clinic-referred children and their mothers. *Journal of Abnormal Psychology, 89,* 497–500.

Gresham, F. M. (1981a). Assessment of children's social skills. *Journal of School Psychology, 17,* 120–133.

Gresham, F. M. (1981b). Social skills training with handicapped children: A review. *Review of Educational Research, 51,* 139–176.

Gresham, F. M. (1986). Conceptual issues in the assessment of social competence in children. In P. Strain, M. Guralnick, & H. Walker (Eds.), *Children's social behavior: Development, assessment, and modification* (pp. 143–179). New York: Academic Press.

Gresham, F. M. (1992). Misguided assumptions of the *DSM–III–R*: Implications for school psychological practice. *School Psychology Quarterly, 7,* 79–95.

Gresham, F. M., & Davis, C. J. (1988). Behavioral interviews with parents and teachers. In E. S. Shapiro & T. R. Kratochwill (Eds.), *Behavioral assessment in schools: Conceptual foundations and practical applications* (pp. 455–493). New York: Guilford.

Gresham, F. M., & Elliott, S. N. (1990). *The social skills rating system.* Circle Pines, MN: American Guidance.

Gresham, F. M., & Gansle, K. A. (1992). Misguided assumptions of the *DSM–III–R*: Implications for school psychological practice. *School Psychology Quarterly, 7,* 79–95.

Gresham, F. M., & Reschly, D. J. (1986). Social skills deficits and low peer acceptance of mainstreamed learning disabled children. *Learning Disability Quarterly, 9,* 23–32.

Gresham, F. M., & Reschly, D. J. (1987a). Dimensions of social competence: Method factors in the assessment of adaptive behavior, social skills, and peer acceptance. *Journal of School Psychology, 25,* 367–381.

Gresham, F. M., & Reschly, D. J. (1987b). Issues in the conceptualization, classification and assessment of social skills in the mildly handicapped. In T. Kratochwill (Ed.), *Advances in school psychology* (pp. 203–264). Hillsdale, NJ: Lawrence Erlbaum Associates.

Gresham, F. M., & Stuart, D (1992). Stability of sociometric assessment: Implications for uses as selection and outcome measures in social skills training. *Journal of School Psychology, 30*, 223–231.

Grilo, C. M., Fehon, D. C., Walker, M., & Martino, S. (1996). A comparison of adolescent inpatients with and without substance abuse using the Millon Adolescent Clinical Inventory. *Journal of Youth and Adolescence, 25*, 379–388.

Gronlund, N. E., & Linn, R. L. (1990). *Measurement and evaluation in teaching* (6th ed.). New York: Macmillan.

Gross, A. M. (1984). Behavioral interviewing. In T. H. Ollendick & M. Herson (Eds.), *Child behavior assessment: Principles and practices* (pp. 61–79). New York: Pergamon.

Grossman, H. J. (Ed.). (1983). *Classification in mental retardation.* Washington, DC: American Association on Mental Deficiency.

Hagborg, W. J. (1990). The Revised Behavior Problem Checklist and severely emotionally disturbed adolescents: Relationship to intelligence, achievement, and sociometric ratings. *Journal of Abnormal Child Psychology, 18*, 47–53.

Hagborg, W. J. (1994). Sociometry and educationally handicapped children. *Journal of Group Psychotherapy, Psychodrama, and Sociometry, 47*, 4–14.

Haley, A. (1996). *The autobiography of Malcolm X.* New York: Grove Press.

Haley, G. M., Fine, S., & Marriage, K. (1988). Psychotic features in adolescents with major depression. *Journal of the American Academy of Child and Adolescent Psychiatry, 27*, 498–493.

Hammen, C. (1995). The social context of risk for depression. In K. D. Craig & K. S. Dobson (Eds.), *Anxiety and depression in adults and children* (pp. 82–98). Thousand Oaks, CA: Sage.

Hammer, E. F. (1981). Projective drawings. In A. I. Rabin (Ed.), *Assessment with projective techniques: A concise introduction* (pp. 151–185). New York: Springer.

Handler, L., & Habenicht, D. (1994). The Kinetic Family Drawing technique: A review of the literature. *Journal of Personality Assessment, 62*, 440–464.

Harrington, G. M. (1988). Two forms of minority group test bias as psychometric artifacts with animal models (*Rattus norvegicus*). *Journal of Comparative Psychology, 102*, 400–407.

Harris, A. M., & Reid, J. B. (1981). The consistency of a class of coercive child behaviors across school settings for individual subjects. *Journal of Abnormal Child Psychology, 9*, 219–227.

Harrison, P. L. (1987). Research with adaptive behavior scales. *Journal of Special Education, 21*, 37–68.

Hart, D. H. (1972). *The Hart Sentence Completion Test for Children.* Unpublished manuscript, Educational Support Systems, Inc., Salt Lake City, UT.

Hart, D. H. (1980). *A quantiative scoring system for the Hart Sentence Completion Test for Children.* Unpublished manuscript, Educational Support Systems, Inc., Salt Lake City, UT.

Hart, D. H. (1986). The sentence completion techniques. In H. M. Knoff (Ed.), *The assessment of child and adolescent personality* (pp. 245–272). New York: Guilford.

Hart, D. H., Kehle, T. J., & Davies, M. V. (1983). Effective of sentence completion techniques: A review of the Hart Sentence Completion Test for Children. *School Psychology Review, 12*, 428–434.

Hart, L. R. (1993). Diagnosis of disruptive behavior disorders using the Millon Adolescent Personality Inventory. *Psychological Reports, 73* (3, Pt. 1), 895–914.

Hart, L. R. (1995). MAPI personality correlates of comorbid substance abuse among adolescent psychiatric populations. *Journal of Adolescence, 18*, 657–667.

Harter, S. (1985a). Competence as a dimension of self-evaluation: Toward a comprehensive model of self-worth. In R. Leahy (Ed.), *The development of the self* (pp.   ). New York: Academic Press.

Harter, S. (1985b). *Self-perception Profile for Children.* Denver, CO: University of Denver Department of Psychology.

Harter, S. (1986). Processes underlying the construct, maintenance, and enhancement of the self-concept in children. In J. Suls & A. Greenwald (Eds.), *Psychological perspectives on the self* (Vol. 3, pp. 137–181). Hillsdale, NJ: Lawrence Erlbaum Associates.

Harter, S. (1988). *Self-perception Profile for Adolescents.* Denver, CO: University of Denver Department of Psychology.

Harter, S. (1990). Issues in the assessment of the self-concept of children and adolescents. In A. M. LaGreca (Ed.), *Through the eyes of the child* (pp. 292–325). Boston: Allyn & Bacon.

Harter, S., & Chao, C. (1992). The role of competence in children's creation of imaginary friends. *Merrill-Palmer Quarterly, 38*, 350–363,

Harter, S., & Pike, R. G. (1980). *The Pictorial Scale of Perceived Competence and Acceptance for Young Children.* Denver, CO: University of Denver Department of Psychology.

Harter, S., & Pike, R. (1984). The pictorial perceived competence scale for young children. *Child Development, 55,* 657–692.

Hartup, W. W. (1978). Peer relations and the growth of social competence. In. M. Kent & J. Rolf (Eds.), *Social competence in children.* Hanover, NH: University Press of New England.

Hartup, W. W. (1983). Peer relations. In E. M. Hetherington (Ed.), *Handbook of child psychology: Vol. 4. Socialization, personality, and social development* (pp. 103–198). New York: Wiley.

Hase, H. D., & Goldberg, L. R. (1967). Comparative validity of differing strategies of constructing personality inventory scales. *Psychological Bulletin, 67,* 231–248.

Hathaway, S. R., & Monachesi, E. D. (1963). *Adolescent personality and behavior.* Minneapolis: University of Minnesota Press.

Hayden-Thomson, L., Rubin, K. H., & Hymel, S. (1987). Sex preferences in sociometric choices. *Developmental Psychology, 23,* 558–562.

Haynes, S. N., & Wilson, C. C. (1979). *Behavioral assessment.* San Francisco: Jossey-Bass.

Hayvren, M., & Hymel, S. (1984). Ethical issues in sociometric testing: Impact of sociometric measures on interaction behavior. *Developmental Psychology, 20,* 844–849.

Helsel, W. J., & Matson, J. L. (1984). The assessment of depression in children: The internal structure of the Child Depression Inventory. *Behavior Research and Therapy, 22,* 289–298.

Henning-Stout, M. (1994). *Responsive assessment.* San Francisco: Jossey-Bass.

Hepperlin, C. M., Stewart, G. W., & Rey, J. M. (1990). Extraction of depression scores in adolescents from a general-purpose behaviour checklist. *Journal of Affective Disorders, 18,* 105–112.

Herjanic, B., & Campbell, W. (1977). Differentiating psychiatrically disturbed children on the basis of a structured interview. *Journal of Abnormal Child Psychology, 5,* 127–134.

Herjanic, B., Herjanic, M., Brown, F., & Wheatt, T. (1975). Are children reliable reporters? *Journal of Abnormal Child Psychology, 3,* 41–48.

Herjanic, B., & Reich, W. (1982). Development of a structured psychiatric interview for children: Agreement between child and parent on individual symptoms. *Journal of Abnormal Child Psychology, 10,* 307–324.

Hernstein, R. J., & Murray, C. (1994). *The bell curve: Intelligence and class structure in American life.* New York: The Free Press.

Hesson, K., Bakal, D., & Dobson, K. S. (1993). Legal and ethical issues concerning children's rights of consent. *Canadian Psychology, 34,* 317–328.

Hetherington, E. M., & Martin, B. (1986). Family factors and psychopathology in children. In H. C. Quay & J. S. Werry (Eds.), *Psychopathological disorders of childhood* (3rd ed., pp. 332–390). New York: Wiley.

Hinshaw, S. P. (1987). On the distinction between attentional deficits/hyperactivity and conduct problems/aggression in child psychology. *Psychological Bulletin, 101,* 443–463.

Hinshaw, S. P. (1994). *Attention deficits and hyperactivity in children.* Thousand Oaks, CA: Sage.

Hodges, K. (1987). Assessing children with a clinical research interview: The child assessment schedule. In R. J. Prinz (Ed.), *Advances in behavioral assessment of children and families* (Vol. 3, pp. 203–233). Greenwich, CT: JAI Press.

Hodges, K. (1990a). Depression and anxiety in children: A comparison of self-report questionnaires to clinical interview. *Psychological Assessment, 2,* 376–381.

Hodges, K. (1990b). Parent–child agreement on symptoms assessed via a clinical research interview for children: The Child Assessment Schedule. *Journal of Child Psychology and Psychiatry and Allied Disciplines, 31,* 427–436.

Hodges, K. (1993). Structured interviews for assessing children. *Journal of Child Psychology and Psychiatry and Allied Disciplines, 34,* 49–68.

Hodges, K., Cools, J., & McKnew, D. (1989). Test–retest reliability of a clinical research interview for children: The Child Assessment Schedule. *Psychological Assessment, 1,* 317–322.

Hodges, K., Kline, J., Barbero, G., & Flanery, R. (1985). Depressive symptoms in children with recurrent abdominal pain and in their families. *Journal of Pediatrics, 107,* 622–626.

Hodges, K., Kline, J., Barbero, G., & Woodruff, C. (1985). Anxiety in children with recurrent abdominal pain and their parents. *Psychosomatics, 26,* 859–866.

Hodges, K., Kline, J., Stern, L., Cytryn, L., & McKnew, D. (1982). The development of a child assessment interview for research and clinical use. *Journal of Abnormal Child Psychology, 10,* 173–189.

Hodges, K., McKnew, D. Burbach, D. J., & Roebuck, L. (1987). Diagnostic concordance between the Child Assessment Schedule (CAS) and the Schedule for Affective Disorders and Schizophrenia for school-age children (K–SAD) in an outpatient sample using lay interviewers. *Journal of the American Academy of Child and Adolescent Psychiatry, 26,* 654–661.

Hodges, K., McKnew, D., Cytryn, L., & McKnew, D. (1982). The Child Assessment Schedule (CAS) diagnostic interview: A report on reliability and validity. *Journal of the American Academy of Child Psychiatry, 10,* 173–189.

Hodges, K., & Saunders, W. (1989). Internal consistency of a diagnostic interview for children: The Child Assessment Schedule. *Journal of Abnormal Child Psychology, 17,* 691–701.

Hoffman, T., Dana, R. H., & Bolton, B. (1987). Measured acculturation and the MMPI-168. *Journal of Cross-Cultural Psychology, 16,* 243–256.

Hoier, T. S., & Cone, J. D. (1987). Target selection of social skills for children: The template-matching procedure. *Behavior Modification, 11,* 137–164.

Holland, M. L., & Merrell, K. W. (1998). Social-emotional characteristics of preschool-age children referred for child find screening and assessment: A comparative study. *Research in Developmental Disabilities, 19,* 167–179.

Holguin, O., & Sherrill, C. (1990). The use of a Pictorial Scale of Perceived Competence and Acceptance with learning disabled boys. *Perceptual and Motor Skills, 70* (3, Pt. 2), 1235–1238.

Hollinger, J. D. (1987). Social skills for behaviorally disordered children as preparation for mainstreaming: Theory, practice, and new directions. *Remedial and Special Education, 11,* 139–149.

Hood, A. B., & Johnson, R. W. (1997). *Assessment in counseling* (2nd ed.). Alexandria, VA: American Association for Counseling and Development.

Hops, H., & Greenwood, C. R. (1981). Social skills deficits. In E. J. Mash & L. G. Terdal (Eds.), *Behavioral assessment of childhood disorders* (pp. 347–394). New York: Guilford.

Hops, H., & Lewin, L. (1984). Peer sociometric forms. In T. H. Ollendick & M. Herson (Eds.), *Child Behavioral Assessment* (pp. 124–147). New York: Pergamon.

Hops, H., & Lewinsohn, P. M. (1995). A course for the treatment of depression among adolescents. In K. D. Craig & K. S. Dobson (Eds.), *Anxiety and depression in adults and children* (pp. 230–245). Thousand Oaks, CA: Sage.

Howlin, P., & Rutter, M. (with Berger, M., Hemsley, P., Hersov, L., & Yule, W.). (1987). *Treatment of autistic children.* Chichester, England: Wiley.

Howlin, P., & Yule, W. (1990). Taxonomy of major disorders in childhood. In M. Lewis & S. M. Miller (Eds.), *Handbook of developmental psychopathology* (pp. 371–383). New York: Plenum.

Hughes, H. M., & Haynes, S. N. (1978). Structured laboratory observation in the behavioral assessment of parent–child interactions: A methodological critique. *Behavior Therapy, 9,* 428–477.

Hughes, J. N., & Baker, D. B. (1990). *The clinical child interview.* New York: Guilford.

Hulse, W. (1951). The emotionally disturbed child draws his family. *Quarterly Journal of Child Behavior, 3,* 152–174.

Hulse, W. (1952). Childhood conflict expressed through family drawings. *Journal of Projective Techniques, 16,* 66–79.

Hutton, J. B., Dubes, R., & Muir, S. (1992). Assessment practices of school psychologists: Ten years later. *School Psychology Review, 21,* 271–284.

Hymel, S. (1983). Preschool children's peer relations: Issues in sociometric assessment. *Merrill-Palmer Quarterly, 29,* 237–260.

Hymel, S., & Asher, S. R. (1977, April). *Assessment and training of isolated children's social skills.* Paper presented at the biennial meeting of the Society for Research in Child Development, New Orleans. (ERIC Document Reproduction Service No. ED 136 930)

Iverson, A. M., & Iverson, G. L. (1996). Children's long-term reactions to participating in sociometric assessment. *Psychology in the Schools, 33,* 103–112.

Jacob, S., & Hartshorne, T. (1994). *Ethics and law for school psychologists* (2nd ed.). New York: Wiley.

Jagger, J., Prusoff, B. A., Cohen, D. J., Kidd, K. K., Carbonari, C. M., & John, K. (1982). The epidemiology of Tourette's Syndrome. *Schizophrenia Bulletin, 8,* 267–278.

Janus, M. D., Tolbert, H., Calestro, K., & Toepfer, S. (1996). Clinical accuracy ratings of MMPI approaches for adolescents: Adding 10 years and the MMPI–A. *Journal of Personality Assessment, 67,* 364–383.

Jentzsch, C. E., & Merrell, K. W. (1996). An investigation of the construct validity of the Preschool and Kindergarten Behavior Scales. *Diagnostique, 21*(2), 1–15.

Jersild, A. T., & Holmes, F. B. (1935). Children's fears. *Child Development Monograph, 20.*

Jesness, C. F. (1962). *The Jesness Inventory: Development and validation* (Research Rep. No. 29). Sacramento: California Youth Authority.

Jesness, C. F. (1963). *Redevelopment and validation of the Jesness Inventory* (Research Rep. No. 35). Sacramento: California Youth Authority.

Jesness, C. F. (1965). *The Fricot Ranch study: Outcomes with large vs. small living units in the rehabilitation of delinquents* (Research Rep. No. 47). Sacramento: California Youth Authority.

Jesness, C. F. (1996). *The Jesness Inventory Manual.* North Tonawanda, NY: Multi-Health Systems.

Jesness, C. F., & Wedge, R. F. (1984). Validity of a revised Jesness Inventory I—level classification with delinquents. *Journal of Consulting and Clinical Psychology, 52,* 997–1010.

Johnson, C., Archer, R. P., Sheaffer, C. I., & Miller, D. (1992). Relationships between the MAPI and the MMPI in the assessment of adolescent psychopathology. *Journal of Personality Assessment, 58,* 277–286.

Jolly, J. B., Dyck, M. J., Kramer, T. A., & Wherry, J. N. (1994). Integration of positive and negative affectivity and cognitive content-specificity: Improved discrimination of anxious and depressed symptoms. *Journal of Abnormal Psychology, 103,* 544–552.

Jones, R. R., Reid, J. B., & Patterson, G. R. (1979). Naturalistic observation in clinical assessment. In P. McReynolds (Ed.), *Advances in psychological assessment* (Vol. 3, pp. 42–95). San Francisco: Jossey-Bass.

Jongmans, M., Demetre, J. D., Dubowitz, L., & Henderson, S. E. (1996). How local is the impact of specific learning difficulty on premature children's evaluation of their own competence? *Journal of Child Psychology and Psychiatry and Allied Disciplines, 37,* 563–568.

Kagan, J., Reznick, J. S., & Snidman, N. (1990). The temperamental qualities of inhibition and lack of inhibition. In M. Lewis & S. M. Miller (Eds.), *Handbook of developmental psychopathology* (pp. 219–226). New York: Pergamon.

Kahn, M. W., & McFarland, J. (1973). A demographic and treatment evaluation study of institutionalized juvenile offenders. *Journal of Community Psychology, 1,* 282–284.

Kamphaus, R. W. (1991). Draw-A-Person techniques: Tests in search of a construct. *Journal of School Psychology, 29,* 395–401.

Kane, J. S., & Lawler, E. E. (1978). Methods of peer assessment. *Psychological Bulletin, 85,* 555–586.

Kanner, L. (1943). Autistic disturbances of severe contact. *Nervous Child, 2,* 217–250.

Kaufman, J., Birmaher, B., Brent, D., & Rao, U. (1997). Schedule for Affective Disorders and Schizophrenia for School-Age Children—Present and Lifetime Version (K–SADS–PL): Initial reliability and validity data. *Journal of the American Academy of Child and Adolescent Psychiatry, 36,* 980–988.

Kauffman, J. M. (1989). *Characteristics of behavior disorders of children and youth* (4th ed.). Columbus, OH: Merrill.

Kauffman, J. M., Semmell, M. I., & Agard, J. A. (1974). PRIME: An overview. *Education and Training for the Mentally Retarded, 9,* 107–112.

Kamphaus, R. W. (1987). Conceptual and psychometric issues in the assessment of adaptive behavior. *Journal of Special Education, 21,* 27–35.

Kavan, M. G. (1990). Review of the Children's Depression Inventory. In J. J. Kramer & J. C. Conoley (Eds.), *The Supplement to the 10th Mental Measurements Yearbook* (pp. 46–48). Lincoln, NE: Buros Institute of Mental Measurements.

Kazdin, A. E. (1979). Situational specificity: The two-edged sword of behavioral assessment. *Behavioral Assessment, 1,* 57–75.

Kazdin, A. E. (1981). Behavioral observation. In M. Herson & A. S. Bellack (Eds.), *Behavioral assessment: A practical handbook* (pp. 101–124). New York: Pergamon.

Kazdin, A. E. (1982). *Single-case research designs: Methods for clinical and applied settings.* New York: Oxford University Press.

Kazdin, A. E. (1988). Childhood depression. In E. J. Mash & L. G. Terdal (Eds.), *Behavioral assessment of childhood disorders* (2nd ed., pp. 157–195). New York: Guilford.

Kazdin, A. E. (1995). *Conduct disorders in childhood and adolescence* (2nd ed.). Thousand Oaks, CA: Sage.

Kazdin, A. E., Esveldt-Dawson, K., Unis, A. S., & Rancurello, M. D. (1983). Child and parent evaluations of depression and aggression in psychiatric inpatient children. *Journal of Abnormal Child Psychology, 11,* 401–413.

Kelly, E. J. (1986). *The differential problem sorter: Rationales, procedures, and statistical/clinical values.* Unpublished manuscript, University of Nevada at Las Vegas, Department of Educational Psychology.

Kelly, E. J. (1989). Clarifications of federal eligibility criteria for students identified as "seriously emotionally disturbed" versus exclusion for the "social maladjustment" from C.F.R. part 300.5 (i) (A-E) and (ii). In *Nevada Clarifications.* Las Vegas: University of Nevada-Las Vegas, Department of Special Education.

Keller, H. R. (1986). Behavioral observation approaches to assessment. In. H. Knoff (Ed.), *The assessment of child and adolescent personality* (pp. 353–397). New York: Guilford.

Kent, R. N., & Foster, L. F. (1977). Direct observational procedures: Methodological issues in naturalistic settings. In A. R. Ciminero, K. S. Calhoun, & H. E. Adams (Eds.), *Handbook of behavioral assessment* (pp. 279–328). New York: Wiley.

Kent, R. N., O'Leary, K. D., Diament, C., & Deitz, A. (1974). Expectation biases in observational utility of therapeutic change. *Journal of Consulting and Clinical Psychology, 42,* 774–780.

Kerr, M. M., & Nelson, C. M. (1989). *Strategies for managing behavior problems in the classroom* (2nd ed.). Columbus, OH: Merrill.

Kestenbaum, C. J., & Bird, H. R. (1978). A reliability study of the Mental Health Assessment Form for school-aged children. *Journal of the American Academy of Child Psychiatry, 7,* 338–347.

King, C., & Young, R. D. (1982). Attentional deficits with and without hyperactivity: Peer and teacher perceptions. *Journal of Abnormal Child Psychology, 10,* 483–495.

King, C. A. (1997). Diagnosis and assessment of depression and suicidality using the NIMH Diagnostic Interview Schedule for Children (DISC-2.3). *Journal of Abnormal Child Psychology, 25,* 173–181.

Kistner, J. A., & Gatlin, D. G. (1989). Sociometric differences between learning disabled and nonhandicapped students: Effects of sex and race. *Journal of Educational Psychology, 81,* 118–120.

Kistner, J. A., Metzler, A., Gatlin, D., & Risi, S. (1993). Classroom racial proportions and children's peer relations: Race and gender effects. *Journal of Educational Psychology, 85,* 446–452.

Klein, R. G. (1986). Questioning the clinical usefulness of projective psychological tests for children. *Developmental and Behavioral Pediatrics, 7,* 378–382.

Knoff, H. M. (1986). Identifying and classifying children and adolescents referred for personality assessment: Theories, systems, and issues. In H. M. Knoff (Ed.), *The assessment of child and adolescent personality* (pp. 3–33). New York: Guilford.

Knoff, H. M. (1990) Review of the Children's Depression Inventory. In J. J. Kramer & J. C. Conoley (Eds.), *The supplement to the 10th Mental Measurements Yearbook* (pp. 48–50). Lincoln, NE: Buros Institute of Mental Measurements.

Knoff, H. M., & Prout, H. T. (1985). *The Kinetic drawing system. Family and school.* Los Angeles: Western Psychological Services.

Kohlberg, L. (1969). Stage and sequence: The cognitive-developmental approach to socialization. In D. A. Goslin (Ed.), *Handbook of socialization theory and research.* Chicago: Rand-McNally.

Kohn, M. L., & Clausen, J. A. (1955). Social isolation and schizophrenia. *American Sociological Review, 20,* 265–273.

Kolko, D. J., & Kazdin, A. E. (1993). Emotional/behavioral problems in clinic and nonclinic children: Correspondence among child, parent, and teacher reports. *Journal of Child Psychology and Psychiatry, 34,* 991–1006.

Koppitz, E. M. (1963). *The Bender–Gestalt test for Young Children.* New York: Grune & Stratton.

Kopptiz, E. M. (1968). *Psychological evaluation of children's human figure drawings.* New York: Grune & Stratton.

Koppitz, E. M. (1975). *The Bender–Gestalt Test for Young Children: Vol. 2. Research and applications, 1963–1973.* New York: The Psychological Corporation.

Koppitz, E. M. (1982). Personality assessment in the schools. In C. R. Reynolds & T. B. Gutkin (Eds.), *The handbook of school psychology* (pp. 245–271). New York: Wiley.

Kovacs, M. (1980-81). Rating scales to assess depression in school-aged children. *Acta Paedapsychiatrica, 46,* 305–315.

Kovacs, M. (1982). *The Interview Schedule for Children (ISC).* Unpublished interview schedule, Department of Psychiatry, University of Pittsburgh.

Kovacs, M. (1983). *The Children's Depression Inventory: A self rated depression scale for school-aged youngsters.* Unpublished test manual.

Kovacs, M. (1991). *The Children's Depression Inventory (CDI).* North Tonawanda, NY: Multi-Health Systems.

Kratochwill, T. R. (1982). Advances in behavioral assessment. In C. R. Reynolds & T. B. Gutkin (Eds.), *The handbook of school psychology* (pp. 314–350). New York: Wiley.

Kreisler, T. A., Mangione, C., & Landau, S. (1997). Review of the School Social Behavior Scales. *Journal of Psychoeducational Assessment, 15,* 182–190.

Kumabe, K. T., Nishida, C., & Hepworth, D. H. (1985). *Bridging ethnocultural diversities in social work and health.* Honolulu: University of Hawaii.

Kupersmidt, J. B., DeRosier, M. E., & Patterson, C. P. (1995). Similarity as the basis for children's friendships: The roles of sociometric status, aggressive and withdrawn behavior, academic achievement, and demographic characteristiscs. *Journal of Social and Personal Relationships, 12,* 439–452.

Lachar, D. (1990). *Multidimensional description of child personality: A manual for the Personality Inventory for Children.* Los Angeles: Western Psychological Services.

Lachar, D., & Gruber, C. P. (1995). *Personality Inventory for Youth.* Los Angeles: Western Psychological Services.

Lambert, N., Hartsough, C., & Sandoval, J. (1990). *Manual for the Children's Attention and Adjustment Survey.* Palo Alto, CA: Consulting Psychologists Press.

Landau, S., & Milich, R. (1990). Assessment of children's social status and peer relations. In A. M. LaGreca (Ed.), *Through the eyes of the child* (pp. 259–291). Boston: Allyn & Bacon.

Lanyon, R. I. (1984). Personality assessment. *Annual Review of Psychology, 35,* 667–701.

Lanyon, R. I., & Goodstein, L. D. (1984). *Personality assessment* (2nd ed.). New York: Wiley.

Lanyon, R. I., & Goodstein, L. D. (1997). *Personality assessment* (3rd ed.). New York: Wiley.

Laughlin, F. (1954). *The peer status of sixth and seventh grade children.* New York: Bureau of Publications, Teachers College of Columbia University.

Leadbeater, B. J., & Bishop, S. J. (1994). Predictors of behavior problems in preschool children of inner-city Afro-Americans and Puerto Rican adolescent mothers. *Child Development, 65,* 638–648.

Leckman, J. F., Riddle, M. A., Hardin, M. T., Ort, S. I., Schwartz, K. L., Stevenson, J., & Cohen, D. (1989). The Yale Global Tic Severity Scale: Initial testing of a clinician-rated scale of tic severity. *Journal of the American Academy of Child and Adolescent Psychiatry, 28,* 566–573.

Le Couteur, A., Rutter, M., Lord, C., Rios, P., Robertson, S. Holdgrafer, M., & McClenna, J. (1989). Autism Diagnostic Interview: A standardized investigator-based instrument. *Journal of Autism and Developmental Disorders, 19,* 363–387.

Lefkowitz, M. M., & Tesiny, E. P. (1980). Assessment of childhood depression. *Journal of Consulting and Clinical Psychology, 48,* 43–50.

Lefkowitz, M. M., & Tesiny, E. P. (1985). Depression in children: Prevalence and correlates. *Journal of Consulting and Clinical Psychology, 53,* 647–656.

Lefkowitz, M. M., Tesiny, E. P., & Gordon, N. H. (1980). Childhood depression, family income, and locus of control. *Journal of Nervous and Mental Disease, 168,* 732–735.

Lehr, C. A., Ysseldyke, J. E., & Thurlow, M. L. (1987). Assessment practices in model early childhood education programs. *Psychology in the Schools, 24,* 390–399.

Lethermon, V. I., Williamson, D. A., Moody, S. C., Granberry, S. W., Lemanek, K. L., & Bodiford, C. (1984). Factors affecting the social validity of role-play assessment of children's social skills. *Journal of Behavioral Assessment, 6,* 231–245.

Lethermon, V. I., Williamson, D. A., Moody, S. C., & Wozniak, P. (1986). Racial bias in behavioral assessment of children's social skills. *Journal of Psychopathology and Behavioral Assessment, 8,* 329–337.

Lett, N. J., & Kamphaus, R. W. (1997). Differential validity of the BASC Student Observation System and the BASC Teaching Rating Scale. *Canadian Journal of School Psychology, 13,* 1–14.

Levine, R. J. (1995). Adolescents as research subjects without permission of their parents or guardians: Ethical considerations. *Journal of Adolescent Health, 17,* 287–297.

Lewinsohn, P. (1974). A behavioral approach to depression. In R. Friedman & M. Katz (Eds.), *The psychology of depression: Contemporary theory and research.* Washington, DC: U. S. Government Printing House.

Lewis, M., & Miller, S. M. (Eds.). (1990). *Handbook of developmental psychopathology.* New York: Plenum.

Lieberz, K. (1989). Children at risk for schizoid disorders. *Journal of Personality Disorders, 3,* 329–337.

Links, P. S., Boyle, M. H., & Offord, D. R. (1983). The prevalence of emotional disorders in children. *Journal of Nervous and Mental Disease, 77(2),* 85–91.

Loeber, R. (1985a). Patterns of development of antisocial child behavior. *Annals of child development, 2,* 77–116.

Loeber, R. (1985b, November). The selection of target behaviors for modification in the treatment of conduct disordered children: Caretaker's preferences, key-stone behaviors, and stepping stones. In B. B. Lahey (Chair), *Selection of targets for intervention for children with conduct disorder and ADD\hyperactivity.* Symposium conducted at the meeting of the Association for Advancement of Behavior Therapy, Houston.

Loeber, R., & Dishion, T. J. (1983). Early predictors of male delinquency: A review. *Psychological Bulletin, 94,* 68–99.

Loeber, R., Dishion, T. J., & Patterson, G. R. (1984). Multiple gating: A multistage assessment procedure for identifying youths at risk for delinquency. *Journal of Research in Crime and Delinquency, 21,* 7–32.

Loeber, R., & Schmaling, K. B. (1985). Empirical evidence and covert patterns of antisocial conduct problems. *Journal of Abnormal Child Psychology, 12,* 337–352.

Loevinger, J. (1976). *Ego development.* San Francisco: Jossey-Bass.

Loevinger, J. (1979). Construct validity of the sentence completion test of ego development. *Applied Psychological Measurement, 3,* 281–311.

Loney, J., & Milich, R. (1982). Hyperactivity, inattention, and aggression in clinical practice. In M. Wolrach & D. Routh (Eds.), *Advances in behavioral pediatrics* (Vol. 2, pp. 113–147). Greenwich, CT: JAI.

Lord, C., Rutter, M., Goode, S., Heemsbergen, J., Jordan, H., Mawhood, L., & Schopler, E. (1989). Autism Diagnostic Observation Schedule: A standardized observation of communicative and social behavior. *Journal of Autism and Developmental Disorders, 19,* 185–213.

Lord, C., & Schopler, E. (1989). Stability of assessment results of autistic and non-autistic language-impaired children from preschool years to early school age. *Journal of Child Psychology and Psychiatry and Allied Disciplines, 30,* 575–590.

Lubin, B., Larsen, R. M., & Matarazzo, J. D. (1984). Patterns of psychological test usage in the United States: 1935–1982. *American Psychologist, 39,* 451–455.

Maag, J. W., & Reid, R. (1994). The phenomenology of depression among students with and without learning disabilities: More similar than different. *Learning Disabilities Research and Practice, 9,* 91–103.

Machover, K. (1949). *Personality projection in the drawing of a human figure.* Springfield, IL: Thomas.

Mack, J. (1985). An analysis of state definitions of severely emotionally disturbed children. In Council for Exceptional Children (Ed.), *Policy options report.* Reston, VA: Council for Exceptional Children.

Malcom, K. K. (1993). Developmental assessment: Evaluation of infants and preschoolers. In H. B. Vance (Ed.), *Best practices in assessment for school and clinical settings* (pp. 113–145). Brandon, VT: Clinical Psychology Publishing Company.

Mangold, J. (1982). *A study of expressions of the primary process in children's Kinetic Family Drawings as a function of pre-drawing activity.* Unpublished doctoral dissertation, Indiana State University.

Margalit, M. (1983). Diagnostic application of the Conners Abbreviated Symptom Questionnaire. *Journal of Clinical Child Psychology, 12,* 355–357.

Marks, P. A., Seeman, W., & Haller, D. L. (1974). *The actuarial use of the MMPI with adolescents and adults.* Baltimore: Williams & Wilkins.

Marsh, H. W. (1987). The hierarchical structure of self-concept: An application of hierarchical confirmatory factor analysis. *Journal of Educational Measurement, 24,* 17–39.

Martin, B., & Hoffman, J. A. (1990). Conduct disorders. In M. Lewis & S. M. Miller (Eds.), *Handbook of developmental psychopathology* (pp. 109–118). New York: Plenum.

Martin, R. P. (1983). The ethical issues in the use and interpretation of the Draw-A-Person Test and other similar projective procedures. *The School Psychologist, 38,* 6, 8.

Martin, R. P. (1988). *Assessment of personality and behavior problems.* New York: Guilford.

Martin, R. P., Hooper, S., & Snow, J. (1986). Behavior rating scale approaches to personality assessment in children and adolescents. In H. Knoff (Ed.), *The assessment of child and adolescent personality* (pp. 309–351). New York: Guilford.

Maser, J. D., & Cloninger, C. R. (1990). *Comorbidity of mood and anxiety disorders.* Washington, DC: American Psychiatric Press.

Mash, E. J., & Barkley, R. A. (1989). *Treatment of childhood disorders* (2nd ed.). New York: Guilford.

Masten, A. S., Morrison, P., & Pelligrini, D. S. (1985). A revised class play method of peer assessment. *Developmental Psychology, 21,* 523–533.

Mattison, R. E., Handford, H. A., Kales, H. C., & Goodman, A. L. (1990). Four-year predictive value of the Children's Depression Inventory. *Psychological Assessment, 2,* 169–174.

McAndless, B., & Marshall, H. (1957). A picture sociometric technique for preschool children and its relation to teacher judgments of friendship. *Child Development, 28,* 139–148.

McArther, D. S., & Roberts, G. E. (1982). *Roberts Apperception Test for Children.* Los Angeles: Western Psychological Services.

McCammon, E. P. (1981). Comparison of oral and written forms of the Sentence Completion Test for Ego Development. *Developmental Psychology, 17,* 233–235.

McCarney, S. B. (1989a). *Attention Deficit Disorders Evaluation Scale–Home Version.* Columbia, MO: Hawthorne Educational Services.

McCarney, S. B. (1989b). *Attention Deficit Disorders Evaluation Scale–School Version.* Columbia, MO: Hawthorne Educational Services.

McCarney, S. B. (1995a). *The Behavior Dimensions Scale: Home Version Technical Manual.* Columbia, MO: Hawthorne Educational Services.

McCarney, S. B. (1995b). *The Behavior Dimensions Scale: School Version Technical Manual.* Columbia, MO: Hawthorne Educational Services.

McConaughy, S. H., & Achenbach, T. M. (1990). *Guide for the Semistructured Clinical Interview for Children Aged 6–11.* Burlington, VT: University of Vermont Department of Psychiatry.

McConaughy, S. H., Achenbach, T. M., & Gent, C. L. (1988). Multiaxal empirically based assessment: Parent, teacher, observational, cognitive, and personality correlates of child behavior profile types for 6- to 11-year-old boys. *Journal of Abnormal Child Psychology, 16,* 485–509.

McConnell, S. R., & Odom, S. L. (1986). Sociometrics: Peer-referenced measures and the assessment of social competence. In P. Strain, M. J. Guralnick, & H. M. Walker (Eds.), *Children's social behavior: Development, assessment, and modification* (pp. 215–284). New York: Academic Press.

McFall, R. M. (1982). A review and reformulation of the construct of social skills. *Behavioral Assessment, 4,* 1–33.

McGain, B., & McKinzey, R. K. (1995). The efficacy of a group treatment in sexually abused girls. *Child Abuse and Neglect, 19,* 1157–1169.

McKinney, J. D., & Feagans, L. (1984). Academic and behavioral characteristics of learning disabled children and average achievers: Longitudinal studies. *Learning Disability Quarterly, 7,* 251–264.

McKinney, J. D., McClure, S., & Feagans, L. (1982). Classroom behavior of learning disabled children. *Learning Disability Quarterly, 5,* 45–52.

McMahon, R. J. (1984). Behavioral checklists and rating scales. In T. H. Ollendick & M. Herson (Eds.), *Child behavioral assessment: Principles and practices* (pp. 80–105). New York: Pergamon.

McMahon, R. J., & Forehand, R. (1984). Parent training for the noncompliant child: Treatment outcome, generalization, and adjunctive therapy procedures. In R. F. Dangel & R. A. Polster (Eds.), *Parent training: Foundations of research and practice* (pp. 298–328). New York: Guilford.

McMahon, R. J., & Forehand, R. (1988). Conduct disorders. In E. J. Mash & L. G. Terdal (Eds.), *Behavioral assessment of childhood disorders* (2nd ed., pp. 105–153). New York: Guilford.

McNamara, J. R., Holman, C., & Riegal, T. (1994). A preliminary study of the usefulness of the Behavior Assessment System for Children in the evaluation of mental health needs in a Head Start population. *Psychological Reports, 75* (3, Pt. 1), 1195–1201.

McNamee, G. D. (1989). Language development. In J. Gabarino, & F. M. Stott (Eds.), *What children can tell us* (pp. 67–391). San Francisco: Jossey-Bass.

McReynolds, P. (1986). History of assessment in clinical and educational settings. In R. O. Nelson & S. C. Hayes (Eds.), *Conceptual foundations of behavioral assessment* (pp. 42–80). New York: Guilford.

Meehl, P. E. (1954). *Clinical vs. statistical prediction: A theoretical analysis.* Minneapolis: University of Minnesota Press.

Meichenbaum, D., & Cameron, R. (1982). Cognitive-behavior therapy. In G. T. Wilson & C. M. Franks (Eds.), *Contemporary behavior therapy: Conceptual and empirical foundations* (pp. 310–338). New York: Guilford.

Merenda, P. F. (1996). Review of the BASC: Behavior Assessment System for Children. *Measurement and Evaluation in Counseling and Development, 28,* 229–232.

Merrell, K. W. (1989a). Validity issues in direct behavioral observation: Applications for behavioral assessment in the classroom. *Canadian Journal of School Psychology, 5,* 57–62.

Merrell, K. W. (1989b). Concurrent relationships between two behavioral rating scales for teachers: An examination of self-control, social competence, and school behavioral adjustment. *Psychology in the Schools, 26,* 267–271.

Merrell, K. W. (1990). Teacher ratings of hyperactivity and self-control in learning disabled boys: A comparison with low achieving and average peers. *Psychology in the Schools, 27,* 289–296.

Merrell, K. W. (1992). The utility of the school social behavior scales differentiating students with behavioral disorders from other students with disabilities. *Severe Behavior Disorders of Children and Youth, 15,* 27–34.

Merrell, K. W. (1993a). *School Social Behavior Scales.* Austin, TX: Pro-Ed.

Merrell, K. W. (1993b). Using behavior rating scales to assess social skills and antisocial behavior in school settings: Development of the School Social Behavior scales. *School Psychology Review, 22,* 115–133.

Merrell, K. W. (1994a). *Assessment of behavioral, social, and emotional problems: Direct and objective methods for use with children and adolescents.* White Plains, NY: Longman.

Merrell, K. W. (1994b). *Preschool and Kindergarten Behavior Scales.* Austin, TX: Pro-Ed.

Merrell, K. W. (1995a). Relationships among early childhood behavior rating scales: Convergent and discriminant construct validity of the Preschool and Kindergarten Behavior Scales. *Early Education and Development, 6*(3), 253–264.

Merrell, K. W. (1995b). An investigation of the relationship between social skills and internalizing problems in early childhood: Construct validity of the Preschool and Kindergarten Behavior Scales. *Journal of Psychoeducational Assessment, 13,* 230–240.

Merrell, K. W. (1996a). Social-emotional problems in early childhood: New directions in conceptualization, assessment, and treatment. *Education and Treatment of Children, 19,* 458–473.

Merrell, K. W. (1996b). Assessment of social skills and behavior problems in early childhood: The Preschool and Kindergarten Behavior Scales. *Journal of Early Intervention, 20,* 132–145.

Merrell, K. W., Anderson, K. E., & Michael, K. D. (1997).Convergent validity of the Internalizing Symptoms Scale for Children with three self-report measures of internalizing problems. *Journal of Psychoeducational Assessment, 15,* 56–66.

Merrell, K. W., Crowley, S. L., & Walters, A. S. (1997). Development and factor structure of a self-report measure for assessing internalizing symptoms of elementary-age children. *Psychology in the Schools, 34,* 197–210.

Merrell, K. W., & Dobmeyer, A. C. (1996). An evaluation of self-reported internalizing symptoms of elementary-age children. *Journal of Psychoeducational Assessment, 14,* 196–207.

Merrell, K. W., & Gill, S. J. (1994). Using teacher ratings of social behavior to differentiate gifted from non-gifted students. *Roeper Review, 16*(4), 286–289.

Merrell, K. W., Gill, S. J., McFarland, H., & McFarland, T. (1996). Internalizing symptoms of gifted and non-gifted students: A comparative validity study using the Internalizing Symptoms Scale for Children. *Psychology in the Schools, 33,* 185–191.

Merrell, K. W., & Gimpel, G. A. (1998). *Social skills of children and adolescents: Conceptualization, assessment, treatment.* Mahwah, NJ: Lawrence Erlbaum Associates.

Merrell, K. W., & Holland, M. L. (1997). Social-emotional behavior of preschool-age children with and without developmental delays. *Research in Developmental Disabilities, 18,* 393–405.

Merrell, K. W., Merz, J. N., Johnson, E. R., & Ring, E. N. (1992). Social competence of mildly handicapped and low-achieving students: A comparative study. *School Psychology Review, 21,* 125–137.

Merrell, K. W., Sanders, D. E., & Popinga, M. (1993). Teacher ratings of social behavior as a predictor of special education status: Discriminant validity of the School Social Behavior Scales. *Journal of Psychoeducational Assessment, 11,* 220–231.

Merrell, K. W., & Shinn, M. R. (1990). Critical variables in the learning disabilities identification process. *School Psychology Review, 19,* 74–82.

Merrell, K. W., & Walters, A. S. (1998). *Internalizing Symptoms Scale for Children.* Austin, TX: PRO-ED.

Merrell, K. W., & Wolfe, T. M. (1998). The relationship of teacher-rated social skills deficits and ADHD characteristics among kindergarten-age children. *Psychology in the Schools, 33,* 101–109.

Messick, S. (1965). Personality measurement and the ethics of assessment. *American Psychologist, 35,* 1012–1027.

Michael, K. D., & Merrell, K. W. (1998). Reliability of children's self-reported internalizing symptoms over short to medium length time intervals. *Journal of the American Academy of Child and Adolescent Psychiatry, 37,* 194–201.

Milich, R., & Landau, S. (1984). A comparison of the social status and social behavior of aggressive and aggressive/withdrawn boys. *Journal of Abnormal Child Psychology, 12,* 277–278.

Miller, S. M., Boyer, B. A., & Rodoletz, M. (1990). Anxiety in children. In M. Lewis & S. M. Miller (Eds.), *Handbook of developmental psychopathology* (pp. 191–207). New York: Plenum.

Miller, S. M., Birnbaum, A. & Durbin, D. (1990). Etiologic perspectives on depression in childhood. In M. Lewis & S. M. Miller (Eds.), *Handbook of developmental psychopathology* (pp. 311–325). New York: Plenum.

Millon, T. (1969). *Modern psychopathology: A biosocial approach to maladaptive learning and functioning.* Philadelphia: Saunders.

Millon, T. (1981). *Disorders of personality: DSM–III. Axis II.* New York: Wiley.

Millon, T. (1993). *Millon Adolescent Clinical Inventory.* Minneapolis: National Computer Systems.

Millon, T., Green, C. J., & Meagher, R. B., Jr. (1982). *Millon Adolescent Personality Inventory.* Minneapolis: National Computer Systems.

Mooney, K. C. (1984). The Jesness Inventory. In D. J. Keyser & R. C. Sweetland (Eds.), *Test critiques* (Vol. 1, pp. 381–393). Kansas City, MO: Test Corporation of America.

Moreno, J. L. (1934). *Who shall survive?* Washington, DC: Nervous and Mental Disease Publishing.

Morgan, C. D., & Murray, H. A. (1935). A method for investigating phantasies. The Thematic Apperception Test. *Archives of Neurology and Psychiatry, 34,* 289–306.

Morris, R. J., & Kratochwill, T. R. (1983). *Treating children's fears and phobias: A behavioral approach.* New York: Pergamon.

Mullin, E., Quigley, K., & Glanville, B. (1994). A controlled evaluation of the impact of a parent training programme on child behaviour and mothers' general well-being. *Counseling Psychology Quarterly, 7,* 167–180.

Murray, H. A. (1938). *Explorations in personality.* New York: Oxford University Press.

Murray, H. A. (1943). *Thematic Apperception Test manual.* Cambridge, MA: Harvard University Press.

Murray, T. H. (1995). Commentary on "True Wishes." *Philosophy, Psychiatry, and Psychology, 2,* 311–312.

Naglieri, J., A., LeBuff, P. A., & Pfeiffer, S. I. (1993). *Devereux Behavior Rating Scales, School Form.* Devon, PA: The Devereux Foundation.

Naglieri, J. A., McNeish, T. J., & Bardos, A. N. (1991). *Draw A Person: Screening procedure for emotional disturbance.* Austin, TX: Pro-Ed.

National Association of School Psychologists (1984). *Standards for the provision of school psychological services.* Washington, DC: National Association of School Psychologists.

National Association of School Psychologists (1997). *Standards for the provision of school psychological services.* Washington, DC: National Association of School Psychologists.

Nelson, C. M., Rutherford, R. B., Center, D. B., & Walker, H. M. (1991). Do public schools have an obligation to serve troubled children and youth? *Exceptional Children, 57,* 406–415.

Nelson, R. O., & Hayes, S. C. (Eds.). (1986). *Conceptual foundations of behavioral assessment*. New York: Guilford.

Nezu, A. M. (1993). Identifying and selecting target problems for clinical interventions: A problem-solving model. *Psychological Assessment, 5,* 254–263.

Nuttall, E. V., DeLeon, B., & Valle, M. (1990). Best practices in considering cultural factors. In A. Thomas & J. Grimes (Eds.) *Best practices in school psychology* (Vol. 2, pp. 219–234). Washington, DC: National Association of School Psychologists.

Obrzut, J. E., & Boliek, C. A. (1986). Thematic approaches to personality assessment with children and adolescents. In H. M. Knoff (Ed.), *The assesment of child and adolescent personality* (pp. 173–198). New York: Guilford.

Oden, S. L., & Asher, S. R. (1977). Coaching children in social skills for friendship making. *Child Development, 48,* 496–506.

O'Gorman, G. (1970). *The nature of childhood autism* (2nd ed.). London: Butterworths.

Okazaki, S., & Sue, S. (1995). Methodological issues in assessment research with ethnic minorities. *Psychological Assessment, 7,* 367–375.

Ollendick, T. H., Meador, A. E., & Villanis, C. (1986). Relationship between the Children's Assertiveness Inventory and the Revised Behavioral Assertiveness Test for Children. *Child and Family Behavior Therapy, 8*(3), 27–36.

Olweus, D. (1979). Stability of aggressive reaction patterns in males: A review. *Psychological Bulletin, 86,* 852–875.

Ornitz, E. M. (1989). Autism. In C. G. Last & M. Hersen (Eds.), *Handbook of child psychiatric diagnosis* (pp. 233–278). New York: Wiley.

Orvaschel, H., Puig-Antich, J., Chambers, W., Tabrizi, M. A., & Johnson, R. (1982). Retrospective assessment of prepubertal major depression with the Kiddie–SADS–E. *Journal of the American Academy of Child Psychiatry, 21,* 392–397.

Overholser, J. C., Brinkman, D. C., Lehnert, K. L., & Ricciardi, A. M. (1995). Children's Depression Rating Scale—Revised: Development of a short form. *Journal of Clinical Child Psychology, 24,* 443–452.

Ozonoff, S., Pennington, B. F., & Rogers, J. (1990). Are there emotion perception deficits in young autistic children? *Journal of Child Psychology and Psychiatry, 31,* 341–361.

Paget, K. D., & Reynolds, C. R. (1982, August). *Factorial invariance of the Revised Children's Manifest Anxiety Scale with learning disabled children*. Paper presented at the annual meeting of the American Psychological Association, Washington, DC.

Park, H. S., Tappe, P., Carmeto, R., & Gaylord-Ross, R. (1990). Social support and quality of life for learning disabled and mildly retarded youth in transition. In R. Gaylord-Ross, S. Siegel, H. S. Park, S. Sacks, & L. Goetz (Eds.), *Readings in ecosocial development* (pp. 293–328). San Francisco: Department of Special Education, San Francisco State University.

Parker, J. G., & Asher, S. R. (1987). Peer relations and later personal development: Are low-accepted children "at-risk"? *Psychological Bulletin, 102,* 357–389.

Paternite, C., & Loney, J. (1980). Childhood hyperkinesis: Relationships between symptomatology and home environment. In C. K. Whalen & B. Henker (Eds.), *Hyperactive children: The social ecology of identification and treatment* (pp. 105–141). New York: Academic Press.

Patterson, G. R. (1969). Behavioral techniques based upon social learning: An additional base for developing behavior modification technologies. In C. M. Franks (Ed.), *Behavior therapy: Appraisal and status* (pp. 341–374). New York: McGraw-Hill.

Patterson, G. R. (1976). The aggressive child: Victim and architect of a coercive system. In E. Mash, L. Hammerlynck, & L. Handy (Eds.), *Behavior modification in families: I. Theory and research* (pp. 267–316). New York: Brunner/Mazel.

Patterson, G. R. (1982). *Coercive family process*. Eugene, OR: Castalia.

Patterson, G. R. (1984). The contribution of siblings to training for fighting: Microsocial analysis. In J. Block, D. Olweus, & M. Radke-Yarrow (Eds.), *Developmental of antisocial and prosocial behavior*. New York: Academic Press.

Patterson, G. R., & Bank, L. (1986). Bootstrapping your way in the nomological thicket. *Behavioral Assessment, 8,* 49–73.

Patterson, G. R., & Dishion, T. J. (1985). Contributions of families and peers to delinquency. *Criminology, 23,* 63–79.

Patterson, G. R., Ray, R. S., Shaw, D. A., & Cobb, J. A. (1969). *Manual for coding of family interactions*. New York: Microfiche Publications.

Patterson, G. R., Reid, J., & Dishion, T. (1992). *Antisocial boys*. Eugene, OR: Castalia.

Peach, L., & Reddick, T. L. (1991). Counselors can make a difference in preventing adolescent suicide. *The School Counselor, 39,* 107–110.

Peacock Hill Working Group (1991). Problems and promises in special education and related services for children and youth with emotional or behavioral disorders. *Behavioral Disorders, 16,* 299–313.

Pearson, H. (1994, November 23). The black academic environment. *Wall Street Journal,* p. A14.

Peed, S., Roberts, M., & Forehand, R. (1977). Evaluation of the effectiveness of a standardized parent training program in altering the interaction of mothers and their noncompliant children. *Behavior Modification, 1,* 323–350.

Pekarik, E. Prinz, R., Liebert, D., Weintraub, S., & Neale, J. (1976). The pupil evaluation inventory: A sociometric technique for assessing children's social behavior. *Journal of Abnormal Child Psychology, 4,* 83–97.

Peterson, C. A. (1990). Administration of the Thematic Apperception Test: Contributions of psychoanalytic psychotherapy. *Journal of Contemporary Psychology, 20,* 191–200.

Piaget, J. (1983). Piaget's theory. In P. H. Mussen (Ed.), *Handbook of child psychology* (Vol. 1). New York: Wiley.

Piers, E., & Harris, D. (1969). *The Piers–Harris Self-Concept Scale.* Nashville, TN: Counselor Recordings and Tests.

Piersma, H. L., Pantle, M. L., Smith, A., & Boes, J. (1993). The MAPI as a treatment outcome measure for adolescent inpatients. *Journal of Clinical Psychology, 49,* 709–714.

Pilkington, C. L., & Piersel, W. C. (1991). School phobia: A critical analysis of the separation anxiety theory and an alternative conceptualization. *Psychology in the Schools, 28,* 290–303.

Plomin, R., Nitz, K., & Rowe, D. C. (1990). Behavioral genetics and aggressive behavior in childhood. In M. Lewis & S. M. Miller (Eds.), *Handbook of developmental psychopathology* (pp. 119–133). New York: Plenum.

Poland, S. (1989). *Suicide intervention in the schools.* New York: Guilford.

Pollard, S., Ward, E. M., & Barkley, R. A. (1983). The effects of parent training and Ritalin on the parent–child interactions of hyperactive boys. *Child and Family Behavior Therapy, 5,* 51–69.

Poteat, G. M., Ironsmith, M., & Bullock, M. J. (1986). The classification of preschool children's sociometric status. *Early Childhood Research Quarterly, 1,* 349–360.

Powell, P. M., & Vacha-Haase, T. (1994). What counseling psychologists need to know. *Counseling Psychologist, 22,* 444–453.

Powless, D. L., & Elliott, S. N. (1993). Assessment of social skills of Native American preschoolers: Teacher and parent ratings. *Journal of School Psychology, 31,* 293–307.

Poznanski, E. O., Cook, S. C., & Carroll, B. J. (1979). A depression rating scale for children. *Pediatrics, 64,* 442–450.

Priel, B., Assor, A., & Orr, E. (1990). Self-evaluations of kindergarten children: Innacurate and udifferentiated? *Journal of Genetic Psychology, 151,* 377–394.

Priestley, G., & Pipe, M. E. (1997). Using toys and models in interviews with young children. *Applied Cognitive Psychology, 11,* 69–87.

Prior, M., Boulton, D., Gajzago, C., & Perry, D. (1975). The classification of childhood psychosis by numerical taxonomy. *Journal of Child Psychology and Psychiatry, 16,* 321–330.

Prior, M., & Werry, J. S. (1986). Autism, schizophrenia, and allied disorders. In H. C. Quay & J. S. Werry (Eds.), *Psychopathological disorders of childhood* (3rd ed., pp. 156–210). New York: Wiley.

Pritchard, M., & Graham, P. (1966). An investigation of a group of patients who have attended both the child and adult departments of the same psychiatric hospital. *British Journal of Psychiatry, 112,* 603–612.

Prout, H. T., & Phillips, P. D. (1974). A clinical note: The kinetic school drawing. *Psychology in the Schools, 11,* 303–306.

Pullatz, M., & Dunn, S. E. (1990). The importance of peer relations. In M. Lewis & S. M. Miller (Eds.), *Handbook of developmental psychopathology* (pp. 227–236). New York: Pergamon.

Puig-Antich, J., & Chambers, W. (1978). *The Schedule for Affective Disorders and Schizophrenia for School-Age Children.* New York: New York State Psychiatric Association.

Quay, H. C. (1975). Classification in the treatment of delinquency and antisocial behavior. In N. Hobbs (Ed.), *Issues in the classification of children (Vol. 1).* San Francisco: Jossey-Bass.

Quay, H. C. (1977). Measuring dimensions of deviant behavior: The Behavior Problem Checklist. *Journal of Abnormal Child Psychology, 5,* 277–289.

Quay, H. C. (1986a). Classification. In H. C. Quay & J. S. Werry (Eds.), *Psychopathological disorders of childhood* (3rd ed., pp. 1–34). New York: Wiley.

Quay, H. C. (1986b). Conduct disorders. In H. C. Quay & J. S. Werry (Eds.), *Psychopathological disorders of childhood* (3rd ed., pp. 35–72). New York: Wiley.

Quay, H. C., & Peterson, D. R. (1967). *Manual for the Behavior Problem Checklist.* Coral Gables, FL: Author.

Quay, H. C., & Peterson, D. R. (1987). *Manual for the Revised Behavior Problem Checklist*. Coral Gables, FL: Author.

Quay, H. C., & Peterson, D. R. (1996). *Manual for the Revised Behavior Problem Checklist–PAR version*. Odessa, FL: Psychological Assessment Resources.

Quay, H. C., & Werry, J. S. (1986). *Psychopathological disorders of childhood* (3rd ed.). New York: Wiley.

Rabin, A. I. (1986). *Projective techniques for adolescents and children*. New York: Springer.

Ramsay, R. F., Tanney, B. L., Tierney, R. J., & Lang, W. A. (primary consultants) (1990). *The California helper's handbook for suicide intervention*. Sacramento, CA: California State Department of Mental Health.

Range, L. M., & Cotton, C. R. (1995). Reports of assent and permission in research with children: Illustrations and suggestions. *Ethics and Behavior, 5*, 49–66.

Reep, A. (1994). Comments on functional analysis procedures for school-based behavior problems. *Journal of Applied Behavior Analysis, 27*, 409–411.

Reich, W., & Welner, Z. (1989). *Diagnostic Interview for Children and Adolescents–Revised*. St. Louis: Washington University Division of Child Psychiatry.

Reid, J. B. (1982). Observer training in naturalistic research. In D. P. Hartmann (Ed.), *Using observers to study behavior* (pp. 37–50). San Francisco: Jossey-Bass.

Reid, J. B., Baldwin, D. B., Patterson, G. R., & Dishion, T. J. (1988). Observations in the assessment of childhood disorders. In M. Rutter, A. H. Tuma, & I. S. Lann (Eds.), *Assessment and diagnosis in child psychopathology* (pp. 156–195). New York: Guilford.

Reilley, R. R. (1988). Using the Minnesota Multiphasic Personality Inventory (MMPI) with adolescents. In C. R. Reynolds & R. W. Kamphaus (Eds.), *Handbook of psychological and educational assessment of children* (Vol. 2, pp. 324–342). New York: Guilford.

Reschly, D. J. (1990). Best practices in adaptive behavior. In A. Thomas & J. Grimes (Eds.), *Best practices in school psychology* (Vol. 2, pp. 29–42). Washington, DC: National Association of School Psychologists.

Reschly, D. J. (1991). Mental retardation: Conceptual foundations, definitional criteria, and diagnostic operations. In S. R. Hooper, G. W. Hynd, & R. E. Mattison (Eds.), *Assessment and diagnosis of child and adolescent psychological disorders: Vol. 2. Developmental disorders*. Hillsdale, NJ: Lawrence Erlbaum Associates.

Reynolds, C. R. (1981). Long-term stability of scores on the Revised Children's Manifest Anxiety Scale. *Perceptual and Motor Skills, 53*, 702.

Reynolds, C. R., & Bradley, M. (1983). Emotional stability of intellectually superior children versus nongifted peers as estimated by chronic anxiety levels. *School Psychology Review, 12*, 190–193.

Reynolds, C. R., Bradley, M., & Steele, C. (1980). Preliminary norms and technical data for use of the Revised Children's Manifest Anxiety Scale with kindergarten children. *Psychology in the Schools, 17*, 163–167.

Reynolds, C. R., & Kamphaus, R. W. (1992). *Behavior Assessment System for Children*. Circle Pines, MN: American Guidance.

Reynolds, C. R., & Richmond, B. O. (1985). *Revised Children's Manifest Anxiety scale*. Los Angeles: Western Psychological Services.

Reynolds, C. R., & Paget, K. D. (1981). Factor analysis of the Revised Children's Manifest Anxiety Scale for Blacks, whites, males and females with a national normative sample. *Journal of Consulting and Clinical Psychology, 49*, 352–359.

Reynolds, C. R., & Paget, K. D. (1983). National normative and reliability data for the Children's Manifest Anxiety Scale. *School Psychology Review, 12*, 324–336.

Reynolds, W. M. (1986). *Reynolds Adolescent Depression scale*. Odessa, FL: Psychological Assessment Resources.

Reynolds, W. M. (1989). *Reynolds Child Depression Scale*. Odessa, FL: Psychological Assessment Resources.

Reynolds, W. M. (Ed.). (1992a). *Internalizing disorders in children and adolescents*. New York: Wiley.

Reynolds, W. M. (1992b). The study of internalizing disorders in children and adolescents. In W. M. Reynolds (Ed.), *Internalizing disorders in children and adolescents* (pp. 1–18). New York: Wiley.

Reynolds. W. M. (1992c). Internalizing disorders in children and adolescents: Issues and recommendations for further research. In W. M. Reynolds (Ed.), *Internalizing disorders in children and adolescents* (pp. 311–317). New York: Wiley.

Rhone, L. M. (1986). Measurement of test anxiety among selected Black adolescents: Appropriateness of four anxiety scales. *Journal of School Psychology, 24*, 313–319.

Riccio, C. (1995). Review of the Preschool and Kindergarten Behavior Scales. *Journal of Psychoeducational Assessment, 13*, 194–196.

Rivers, R. Y., & Morrow, C. A. (1995). Understanding and treating ethnic minority youth. In J. F. Aponte, R. Y. Rivers, & J. Wohl (Eds.), *Psychological interventions and cultural diversity* (pp. 164–180). Boston: Allyn & Bacon.

Roback, H. B. (1968). Human figure drawings: Their utility in the clinical psychologists' armamentorium for personality assessment. *Psychological Bulletin, 70,* 1–19.

Roberts, G., Schmitz, K., Pinto, J., Cain, S. (1990). The MMPI and Jesness Inventory as measures of effectiveness on an inpatient conduct disorders treatment unit. *Adolescence, 25,* 989–996.

Robins, L., Helzer, J. E., Croughan, J., & Radcliff, K. S. (1981). National Institute of Health Diagnostic Interview Schedule: Its history, characteristics, and validity. *Archives of General Psychiatry, 38,* 381–389.

Robins, L. N. (1966). *Deviant children grow up.* Baltimore: Williams & Wilkins.

Robins, L. N. (1974). *The Vietnam drug user returns* (Special Action Monograph, Series A, No. 2). Washington, DC: U. S. Government Printing Office.

Robinson, E. A., & Eyeberg, S. (1981). The dyadic parent–child interaction coding system: Standardization and validation. *Journal of Consulting and Clinical Psychology, 49,* 245–250.

Robinson, E. A., Eyberg, S. M., & Ross, A. W. (1980). The standardization of an inventory of child conduct problem behaviors. *Journal of Clinical Child Psychology, 9,* 22–49.

Roff, M. (1961). Childhood social interactions and young adult bad conduct. *Journal of Abnormal Social Psychology, 63,* 333–337.

Roff, M. (1963). Childhood social interactions and young adult psychosis. *Journal of Clinical Psychology, 19,* 152–157.

Roff, M., Sells, B., & Golden, M. (1972). *Social adjustment and personality development in children.* Minneapolis: University of Minnesota Press.

Roff, M., & Sells, S. (1968). Juvenile delinquency in relation to peer acceptance–rejection and sociometric status. *Psychology in the Schools, 5,* 3–18.

Rogers, C. (1951). *Client-centered therapy.* Boston: Houghton-Mifflin.

Rogers, C., Gendlin, E., Kiesler, D., & Truax, C. (1967). *The therapeutic relationship and its impact: A study of psychotherapy with schizophrenics.* Madison: University of Wisconsin Press.

Rogers-Warren, A. K. (1984). Ecobehavioral analysis. *Education and Treatment of Children, 7,* 283–303.

Rosenblatt, R. A. (1996, March 14). Latinos, Asians to lead rise in U.S. population. *Los Angeles Times,* pp. A1, A4.

Rothstein, L. F. (1990). *Special education law.* New York: Longman.

Rotter, J. B., & Rafferty, J. E. (1950). *Manual for the Rotter Incomplete Sentences Blank: College Form.* New York: The Psychological Corporation.

Rutter, M., Graham, P., Chadwick, O.F.D., & Yule, W. (1976). Adolescent turmoil: Fact or fiction? *Journal of Child Psychology, 17,* 35–56.

Sallee, F. R., & Spratt, E. G. (1998). Tics and Tourette's Disorder. In T. H. Ollendick & M. Hersen (Eds.), *Handbook of child psychopathology* (3rd ed., pp. 337–353). New York: Plenum.

Salvia, J., & Hughes, C. (1990). *Curriculum-based assessment: Testing what is taught.* New York: Macmillan.

Salvia, J., & Ysseldyke, J. E. (1995). *Assessment* (6th ed.). Boston: Houghton-Mifflin.

Sanders, D. E. (1996). *The Internalizing Symptoms Scale for Children: A validity study with urban, African-American, seriously emotionally disturbed and regular education students.* Unpublished doctoral dissertation, James Madison University, Harrisonburg, VA.

Sandoval, J. (1981). Format effects in two teacher rating scales of hyperactivity. *Journal of Abnormal Child Psychology, 9,* 203–218.

Sandoval, J., & Echandia, A. (1994). Review of the Behavior Assessment System for Children. *Journal of School Psychology, 32,* 419–425.

Sarbaugh, M. E. (1983). Kinetic Drawing–School (KS–D) technique. *Illinois School Psychologists' Association Monograph Series, 1,* 1–70.

Sartorius, N. (1988). International perspectives of psychiatric classification. *British Journal of Psychiatry, 152* (suppl. 1), 9–14.

Sater, G. M., & French, D. C. (1989). A comparison of the social competencies of learning disabled and low-achieving elementary age children. *Journal of Special Education, 23,* 29–42.

Sattler, J. M. (1988). *Assessment of children* (3rd ed.). San Diego: Jerome M. Sattler, Publisher.

Sattler, J. M. (1998). *Clinical and forensic interviewing of children and families.* San Diego: Jerome M. Sattler, Publisher.

Saywitz, K. J., & Snyder, L. (1996). Narrative elaboration: Test of a new procedure for interviewing children. *Journal of Consulting and Clinical Psychology, 64,* 1347–1357.

Schreibman, L., & Charlop-Christy, M. H. (1998). Autistic disorder. In T. H. Ollendick & M. Hersen (Eds.), *Handbook of child psychopathology* (3rd ed., pp. 157–179). New York: Plenum.

Schwartz, J. A., Gladstone, T. R. G., & Kaslow, N. J. (1998). Depressive disorders. In T. H. Ollendick & M. Hersen (Eds.), *Handbook of childhood psychopathology* (3rd ed., pp. 269–289). New York: Plenum.

Seligman, M. (1974). Learned helplessness and depression. In R. Friedman & M. Katz (Eds.), *The psychology of depression: Contemporary theory and research*. Washington, DC: U. S. Government Printing House.

Serbin, L. A., Lyons, J. A., Marchessault, K., Schwartzman, A. E., & Ledingham, J. E. (1987). Observational validation of a peer nomination technique for identifying aggressive, withdrawn, and aggressive/withdrawn children. *Journal of Consulting and Clinical Psychology, 55*, 109–110.

Shaffer, D., Garland, A., Gould, M., Fisher, P., & Trautman, P. (1988). Preventing teenage suicide: A critical review. *Journal of the American Academy of Child and Adolescent Psychiatry, 27*, 675–687.

Shapiro, E. S. (1996). *Academic skills problems: Direct assessment and intervention* (2nd ed.). New York: Guilford.

Shapiro, E. S., & Cole, C. L. (1994). *Behavior change in the classroom: Self-management interventions*. New York: Guilford.

Shapiro, E. S., & Skinner, C. H. (1990). Best practices in observation and ecological assessment. In A. Thomas & J. Grimes (Eds.), *Best practices in school psychology* (Vol. 2, pp. 507–518). Washington, DC: National Association of School Psychologists.

Shark, M. L., & Handel, P. J. (1977). Reliability and validity of the Jesness Inventory: A caution. *Journal of Consulting and Clinical Psychology, 45*, 692–695.

Shields, J. M., & Johnson, A. (1992). Collision between ethics and law: Consent for treatment with adolescents. *Bulletin of the American Academy of Psychiatry and the Law, 20*, 309–323.

Shinn, M. R., Ramsey, E., Walker, H. M., Steiber, S., & O'Neil, R. E. (1987). Antisocial behavior in school settings: Initial differences in an at-risk and normal population. *Journal of Special Education, 21*, 69–84.

Shivrattan, J. L. (1988). Social interactional training and incarcerated juvenile delinquents. *Canadian Journal of Criminology, 30*, 145–163.

Schopler, E., Reichler, R. J., & Renner, R. R. (1988). *Child Autism Rating Scale*. Los Angeles: Western Psychological Services.

Silverman, W., K., & Ginsburg, G. S. (1998). Anxiety disorders. In T. H. Ollendick & M. Hersen (Eds.), *Handbook of child psychopathology* (3rd ed., pp. 239–268). New York: Plenum.

Sinclair, E., Del'Homme, M., & Gonzalez, M. (1993). Systematic screening for preschool behavior disorders. *Behavioral Disorders, 18*, 177–188.

Singleton, L. C., & Asher, S. R. (1977). Peer preferences and social interaction among third-grade children in an integrated school district. *Journal of Educational Psychology, 69*, 330–336.

Skiba, R. (1992). Qualifications v. logic and data: Excluding conduct disorders from the SED definition. *School Psychology Review, 21*, 23–28.

Skiba, R., Grizzle, K., & Minke, K. M. (1994). Opening the floodgates? The social maladjustment exclusion and state SED prevalence rates. *Journal of School Psychology, 32*, 267–282.

Slenkovitch, J. (1983). *P. L. 94-142 as applied to DSM–II diagnoses: An analysis of DSM–III diagnoses vis-a-vis special education law*. Cuppertino, CA: Kinghorn Press.

Slenkovitch, J. (1992a). Can the language "social maladjustment" in the SED definition be ignored? *School Psychology Review, 21*, 21–22.

Slenkovitch, J. (1992b). Can the language "social maladjustment" in the SED definition be ignored? The final words. *School Psychology Review, 21*, 43–44.

Sloves, R. E., Docherty, E. M., & Schneider, K. C. (1979). A scientific problem-solving model of psychological assessment. *Professional Psychology, 10*, 28–35.

Smetana, J. G. (1990). Morality and conduct disorders. In M. Lewis & S. M. Miller (Eds.), *Handbook of developmental psychopathology* (pp. 157–179). New York: Plenum.

Smith, M. D., & Belcher, R. (1985). Teaching life skills to adults disabled by autism. *Journal of Autism and Developmental Disorders, 15*, 163–175.

Song, L., Singh, J., & Singer, M. (1994). The Youth Self-Report Inventory: A study of its measurement fidelity. *Psychological Assessment, 6*, 236–245.

Speilberger, C. D. (1966). Theory and research on anxiety. In C. D. Speilberger (Ed.), *Anxiety and behavior* (pp. 3–22). New York: Academic Press.

Speilberger, C. D. (1972). Current trends in theory and research on anxiety. In C. D. Speilberger (Ed.), *Anxiety: Current trends in theory and research* (Vol. 1, pp. 3–19). New York: Academic Press.

Speilberger, C. D. (1973). *State-Trait Anxiety Inventory for Children*. Palo Alto, CA: Consulting Psychologists Press.

Speilberger, C. D., Gorsuch, R. L., & Luchene, R. E. (1970). *State-Trait Anxiety Inventory*. Palo Alto, CA: Consulting Psychologists Press.

Spitzer, R. E. (1991). An outsider–insider's view about revising the *DSMs*. *Journal of Abnormal Psychology, 100*, 294–296.

Sponheim, E. (1996). Changing criteria of autistic disorders: A comparison of the *ICD–10* research criteria and *DSM–IV* with *DSM–III–R*, CARS, and ABC. *Journal of Autism and Developmental Disorders, 26*, 513–525.

Sroufe, L. A., & Rutter, M. (1984). The domain of developmental psychopathology. *Child Development, 55,* 17–29.

Standards for educational and psychological testing (1985). Washington, DC: American Psychological Association.

Stark, K. D., Kaslow, N. J., & Laurent, J. (1993). The assessment of depression in children: Are we assessing depression or the broad construct of negative affectivity? *Journal of Emotional and Behavioral Disorders, 1,* 149–154.

Steele, R. G., Forehand, R., Armistead, L., & Brody, G. (1995). Predicting alcohol and drug use in early adulthood: The role of internalizing and externalizing behavior problems in early adolescence. *American Journal of Orthopsychiatry, 65,* 380–388.

Stumme, V. S., Gresham, F. M., & Scott, N. A. (1982). Validity of social behavior assessment in discriminating emotionally disabled and nonhandicapped students. *Journal of Behavioral Assessment, 4,* 327–341.

Stokes, T. F., & Baer, D. M. (1977). An implicit technology of generalization. *Journal of Applied Behavior Analysis, 19,* 349–367.

Stokes, T. F., Baer, D. M., & Jackson, R. L. (1974). Programming among the generalization of a greeting response in four retarded children. *Journal of Applied Behavior Analysis, 7,* 599–610.

Sue, D., & Sue, S. (1987). Cultural factors in the clinical assessment of Asian Americans. *Journal of Consulting and Clinical Psychology, 55,* 479–487.

Sue, D. W., & Sue, D. (1990). *Counseling the culturally different* (2nd ed.). New York: Wiley.

Sulzer-Azaroff, B., & Mayer, G. R. (1991). *Behavior analysis for lasting change.* Fort Worth, TX: Harcourt Brace.

Swallow, S. R., & Segal, Z. V. (1995). Cognitive-behavioral therapy for unipolar depression. In K. D. Craig & K. S. Dobson (Eds.), *Anxiety and depression in adults and children* (pp. 209–229). Thousand Oaks, CA: Sage.

Taba, H., Brady, E. H., Robinson, J. T., & Vickery, W. E. (1951). *Diagnosing human relations needs.* Washington, DC: American Council on Education.

Teglasi, H. (1993). *Clinical use of story telling: Emphasizing the T.A.T. with children and adolescents.* Boston: Allyn & Bacon.

Tellegen, A. (1986). Structures of mood and personality and their relevance to assessing anxiety, with an emphasis on self-report. In A. H. Tuma & J. Maser (Eds.), *Anxiety and the anxiety disorders* (pp. 681–706). Hillsdale, NJ: Lawrence Erlbaum Associates.

Tesiny, E. P., & Lefkowitz, M. M. (1982). Childhood depression: A 6-month follow-up study. *Journal of Consulting and Clinical Psychology, 50,* 778–780.

Tharinger, D., & Stark, K. (1990). A qualitative versus quantitative approach to evaluating the Draw-A-Person and Kinetic Family Drawings: A study of mood- and anxiety-disorder children. *Psychological Assessment, 2,* 365–375.

Thompson, C. L., & Rudolph, L. B. (1992). *Counseling Children* (3rd ed.). Pacific Grove, CA: Brooks/Cole.

Thompson, R. J., Merritt, K. A., Keith, B. R., & Murphy, L. B. (1993). Mother–child agreement on the Child Assessment Schedule with nonreferred children: A research note. *Journal of Child Psychology and Psychiatry and Allied Disciplines, 34,* 813–820.

Thurber, S., & Snow, M. (1990). Assessment of adolescent psychopathology: Comparison of mother and daughter perspectives. *Journal of Clinical Child Psychology, 19,* 249–253.

Todis, B., Severson, H., & Walker, H. M. (1990). The critical events scale: Behavioral profiles of students with externalizing and internalizing behavior disorders. *Behavioral Disorders, 15,* 75–86.

Tolbert, H. A. (1996). Psychoses in children and adolescents: A review. *Journal of Clinical Psychiatry, 57*(Suppl. 3), 4–8.

Trites, R. L., Blouin, A. G., & Laprade, K. (1982). Factor analysis of the Conners Teacher Rating Scale based on a large normative sample. *Journal of Consulting and Clinical Psychology, 50,* 615–623.

Turner, S. M., Beidel, D. C., Hersen, M., & Bellack, A. S. (1984). Effects of race on ratings of social skill. *Journal of Consulting and Clinical Psychology, 52,* 474–475.

U.S. Bureau of the Census (1993a). *We the American . . . children.* Washington, DC: U.S. Department of Commerce

U.S. Bureau of the Census (1993b). *We the American . . . Hispanics.* Washington, DC: U.S. Department of Commerce.

U.S. Bureau of the Census (1993c). *We the . . . first Americans.* Washington, DC: U.S. Department of Commerce.

U.S. Bureau of the Census (1997). *Statistical abstracts of the United States: 1997.* Washington, DC: U.S. Bureau of the Census.

U.S. General Accounting Office (1990). *Asian Americans: A status report* (Rep. No. GAO/HRD-90-36SF). Washington, DC: U.S. General Accounting Office.

Ullman, C. A. (1957). Teachers, peers, and tests as predictors of adjustment. *Journal of Educational Psychology, 48,* 257–267.

van den Oord, E. J. C. G., Koot, H. M., Boosma, D. I., & Verhulst, F. C. (1995). A twin-singleton comparison of problem behavior in 2–3 year olds. *Journal of Child Psychology and Psychiatry and Allied Disciplines, 36,* 449–458.

Vaughn, S. (1987). TLC—Teaching, learning, and caring: Teaching interpersonal problem-solving skills to behaviorally disordered adolescents. *The Pointer, 31,* 25–30.

Veldman, D. J., & Sheffield, J. R. (1979). The scaling of sociometric nominations. *Educational and Psychological Measurement, 39,* 99–106.

Verhulst, F. C., Koot, H. M., & Van-der-Ende, J. (1994). Differential predictive value of parents' and teachers' reports of children's problem behaviors: A longitudinal study. *Journal of Abnormal Child Psychology, 22,* 531–546.

Victor, J. B., & Halverson, C. F. (1976). Behavior problems in elementary school children: A follow-up study. *Journal of Abnormal Child Psychology, 4,* 17–29.

Vollmer, T. R., & Northrup, J. (1996). Some implications of functional analysis for school psychology. *School Psychology Quarterly, 11,* 76–92.

Wahler, R. G. (1975). Some structural aspects of deviant child behavior. *Journal of Applied Behavior Analysis, 8,* 27–42.

Wahler, R. G. (1994). Child conduct problems: Disorders in conduct or social continuity? *Journal of Child and Family Studies, 3,* 143–156.

Wahler, R. G., & Cormier, W. H. (1970). The ecological interview: A first step in out-patient child behavior therapy. *Journal of Behavior Therapy and Experimental Psychiatry, 1,* 279–289.

Wahler, R. G., & Dumas, J. E. (1986). "A chip off the old block": Some interpersonal characteristics of coercive children across generations. In P. S. Strain, M. J. Guralnick, & H. M. Walker (Eds.), *Children's social behavior: Development, assessment, and modification* (pp. 49–91). New York: Academic Press.

Wainwright, A., & MHS Staff (1996). *Conners' Rating Scales: Over 25 years of research—an annotated bibliography.* Toronto: Multi-Health Systems.

Walker, H. M. (1982). Assessment of behavior disorders in school settings: Outcomes, issues, and recommendations. In M. M. Noel & N. G. Haring (Eds.), *Progress or change: Issues in educating the emotionally disturbed: Vol. 1. Identification and program planning* (pp. 11–42). Seattle: University of Washington Press.

Walker, H. M. (1983). Assessment of behavior disorders in the school setting: Issues, problems, and strategies. In M. Noel & N. Haring (Eds.), *Progress or change? Issues in educating the mildly emotionally disturbed.* Washington, DC: PDAS and USOSE Monograph Series.

Walker, H. M., Colvin, G. R., & Ramsey, E. R. (1995). *Antisocial behavior in school settings.* Pacific Grove, CA: Brooks/Cole.

Walker, H. M., & Hops, H. (1976). Increasing academic achievement by reinforcing direct academic performance and/or facilitating nonacademic responses. *Journal of Educational Psychology, 68,* 218–225.

Walker, H. M., & McConnell, S. R. (1995a). *Walker–McConnell Scale of Social Competence and School Adjustment: Adolescent Version.* San Diego, CA: Singular Publishing Group.

Walker, H. M., & McConnell, S. R. (1995b). *Walker–McConnell Scale of Social Competence and School Adjustment: Elementary Version.* San Diego, CA: Singular Publishing Group.

Walker, H. M., & Severson, H. (1992). *Systematic screening for behavior disorders* (2nd ed.). Longmont, CO: Sopris West.

Walker, H. M., Severson, H. H., & Feil, E. G. (1995). *The Early Screening Project: A proven child find process.* Longmont, CO: Sopris West.

Walker, H. M., Severson, H., Stiller, B., Williams, G., Haring, N., Shinn, M., & Todis, B. (1988). Systematic screening of pupils in the elementary age range at risk for behavior disorders: Development and trial testing of a multiple gating model. *Remedial and Special Education, 9,* 8–14.

Walker, H. M., Severson, H., Todis, B., Block-Pedego, A. Williams, G., Haring, N., & Barckley, M. (1990). Systematic screening for behavior disorders (SSBD): Further validation, replication, and normative data. *Remedial and Special Education, 11,* 32–46.

Walker, H. M., Shinn, M. R., O'Neill, R. E., & Ramsey, E. (1987). A longitudinal assessment of the development of antisocial behavior in boys: Rationale, methodology, and first year results. *Remedial and Special Education, 8,* 7–16.

Walker, H. M., Steiber, S., & Eisert, D. (1991). Teacher ratings of adolescent social skills: Psychometric characteristics and factorial replicability. *School Psychology Review, 20,* 301–314.

Walker, H. M., Steiber, S., & O'Neil, R. E. (1990). Middle school behavioral profiles of antisocial and at-risk control boys: Descriptive and predictive outcomes. *Exceptionality, 1,* 61–77.

Walker, H. M., Steiber, S., Ramsey, E., & O'Neil, R. (1993). Fifth grade school adjustment and later arrest rate: A longitudinal study of middle school antisocial boys. *Journal of Child and Family Studies, 2,* 295–315.

Walker, H. M., Todis, B., Holmes, D., & Horton, G. (1988). *The Walker social skills curriculum: The ACCESS program (adolescent curriculum for communication and effective social skills)*. Austin, TX: Pro-Ed.

Walters, A. S., & Merrell, K. W. (1995). Written versus oral Administration of social-emotional self-report tests for children: Does method of execution make a difference? *Psychology in the Schools, 32,* 186–189.

Watkins, C. E., Jr., Campbell, V., & McGregor, P. (1988). Counseling psychologists' uses of the opinions about psychological tests: A contemporary perspective. *The Counseling Psychologist, 16,* 476–486.

Watson, D. (1988). Intraindividual and interindividual analyses of positive and negative affect: Their relation to health complaints and perceived stress, and daily activities. *Journal of Personality and Social Psychology, 54,* 1020–1030.

Watson, D., & Clark, L. A. (1984). Negative affectivity: The disposition to experience aversive emotional states. *Psychological Bulletin, 96,* 465–490.

Watson, D., & Tellegen, A. (1985). Toward a consensual structure of mood. *Psychological Bulletin, 98,* 219–235.

Webster-Stratton, C. (1984). Randomized trial of two parent-training programs for families with conduct disordered children. *Journal of Consulting and Clinical Psychology, 52,* 666–678.

Weinrott, M. R., & Jones, R. R. (1984). Overt versus covert assessment of observer reliability. *Child Development, 55,* 1125–1137.

Weinstein, S. R., Noam, G. G., Grimes, K., & Stone, K. (1990). Convergence of DSM-III diagnoses and self-reported symptoms in child and adolescent inpatients. *Journal of the American Academy of Child and Adolescent Psychiatry, 29,* 627–634.

Weiss, G. (1983). Long-term outcome: Findings, concepts, and practical implications. *Developmental neuropsychiatry.* New York: Guilford.

Weiss, G., Hechtman, L., Perlman, T., Hopkins, J., & Wener, A. (1979). Hyperactive children as young adults: A controlled prospective 10-year follow-up of the psychiatric status of 75 hyperactive children. *Archives of General Psychiatry, 36,* 675–681.

Weiten, W. (1997). *Psychology: Themes and variations* (3rd ed.). Pacific Grove, CA: Brooks-Cole.

Weitz, S. E. (1981). A code for assessing teaching skills of parents of developmentally disabled children. *Journal of Autism and Developmental Disorders, 12,* 13–24.

Werry, J. S. (1986). Biological factors. In H. C. Quay & J. S. Werry (Eds.), *Psychopathological disorders of childhood* (Vol. 3, pp. 294–331). New York: Wiley.

West, D. J., & Farrington, D. P. (1973). *Who becomes delinquent?* London: Heineman.

Whalen, C. K., & Henker, B. (1998). Attention-deficit/hyperactivity disorders. In T. H. Ollendick & M. Hersen (Eds.), *Handbook of child psychopathology* (3rd ed., pp. 181–211). New York: Plenum.

Widiger, T. A. (1985). Review of Millon Adolescent Personality Inventory. In J. V. Mitchell, Jr. (Ed.), *The Ninth Mental Measurements Yearbook* (pp. 979–981). Lincoln, NE: Buros Institute of Mental Measurement.

Widiger, T. A., Frances, A. J., Pincus, H. A., & Davis, W. W. (1991). DSM–IV literature reviews: Rationale, process, and limitations. *Journal of Psychopathology and Behavioral Assessment, 12,* 189–202.

Widiger, T. A., Frances, A. J., Pincus, H A., Davis, W. W., & First, M. B. (1991). Toward an empirical classification for the *DSM–IV. Journal of Abnormal Psychology, 100,* 280–288.

Wiggins, J. S. (1981). Clinical and statistical prediction: Where are we and where do we go from here? *Clinical Psychology Review, 1,* 3–18.

Williams, C. L. (1985). Use of the MMPI with adolescents. In J. N. Butcher & J. R. Graham (Eds.), *Clinical applications of the MMPI* (pp. 37–39). Minneapolis: University of Minnesota, Department of Conferences.

Williams, J. G., Barlow, D. H., & Agras, W. S. (1972). Behavioral assessment of severe depression. *Archives of General Psychiatry, 39,* 1283–1289.

Williams, M. S. (1997). *An investigation of internalizing social-emotional characteristics in a sample of Lakota Sioux children.* Unpublished doctoral dissertation, Utah State University, Logan.

Williamson, D. A., Bentz, B. G., & Rabalais, J. Y. (1998). Eating disorders. In T. H. Ollendick & M. Hersen (Eds.), *Handbook of child psychopathology* (3rd ed., pp. 291–305). New York: Plenum.

Wilson, M. S., & Reschly, D. J. (1996). Assessment in school psychology training and practice. *School Psychology Review, 25,* 9–23.

Wing, L. (1969). The handicap of autistic children: A comparative study. *Journal of Child Psychology and Psychiatry, 10,* 1–40.

Wirt, R. D., Lachar, D., Klinedinst, J. K., & Seat, P. S. (1990). *Personality inventory for children—1990 edition.* Los Angeles: Western Psychological Services.

Wisniewski, J. J., Mulick, J. A., Genshaft, J. L., & Coury, D. L. (1987). Test–retest reliability of the Revised Children's Manifest Anxiety Scale. *Perceptual and Motor Skills, 65,* 67–70.

Wittmer, D. S., & Honig, A. S. (1994). Play, story/song, and eating times in child care: Caregiver responses to toddlers and threes. In H. Goelman (Ed.), *Children's play in child care settings* (pp. 119–147). Albany, NY: State University of New York Press.

Wolf, S. (1989). Schizoid disorders of childhood and adolescence. In C. G. Last & M. Hersen (Eds.), *Handbook of clinical childhood psychiatrict diagnosis* (pp. 209–232). New York: Wiley.

Wolf, S., & Chick, J. (1980). Schizoid personality disorder in childhood: A controlled follow-up study. *Psychological Medicine, 10,* 85–100.

Wolfson, J., Fields, J. H., & Rose, S. A. (1987). Symptoms, temperament, resiliency, and control in anxiety-disordered preschool children. *American Academy of Child and Adolescent Psychiatry, 26,* 16–22.

Worchel, F. F. (1990). Personality assessment. In T. B. Gutkin & C. R. Reynolds (Eds.), *The handbook of school psychology* (2nd ed., pp. 416–430). New York: Wiley.

Worthen, B. R., Borg, W. R, & White, K. R. (1993). *Measurement and evaluation in the schools: A practical guide.* White Plains, NY: Longman.

Wrobel, N. H., & Lachar, D. (1998). Validity of self- and parent-report scales in screening students for behavioral and emotional problems in elementary school. *Psychology in the Schools, 35,* 17–27.

Young, L. L., & Cooper, D. H. (1944). Some factors associated with popularity. *Journal of Educational Psychology, 35,* 513–535.

Zaback, T. P., & Waehler, C. A. (1994). Sex of human figure drawings and sex-role orientation. *Journal of Personality Assessment, 62,* 552–558.

Zangwill, W. M., & Kniskern, J. R. (1982). Comparison of problem families in the clinic and at home. *Behavior Therapy, 13,* 145–152.

Zero to Three (1994). *Diagnostic classification: 0–3. Diagnostic classification of mental health and developmental disorders of infancy and early childhood.* Washington, DC: ZERO TO THREE/National Center for Clinical Infant Programs.

AUTHOR INDEX

Lieberz, K., 287
Links, P. S., 254
Linn, R. L., 77
Lloyd, J. W., 314
Loeber, R., 21, 41, 42, 43, 212, 219, 314
Loevinger, J., 203
Loney, J., 219
Lord, C., 283, 284, 285
Lubin, B., 178, 181, 200
Luchene, R. E., 266
Lyons, J. A., 148

M

Maag, J., W., 92
Machover, K., 187, 188, 189
Mack, J., 34
Malcom, K. K., 337
Mangione, C., 324
Mangold, J., 194
Marchessault, K., 148
Margalit, M., 88
Marks, P. A., 167
Marriage, K., 294
Marsh, H. W., 253
Marshall, H., 146, 329
Martin, B., 218, 220, 221
Martin, R. P., 20, 21, 26, 73, 74, 75, 87, 93, 99,
    155, 158, 159, 200, 205, 266
Martino, S., 165
Maser, J. D., 242
Mash, E. J., 270
Masten, A. S., 146
Matarazzo, J. D., 178, 181, 200
Matarazzo, R. G., 223
Matson, J. L., 261
Mattison, R. E., 262
Mawhood, L., 283
Mayer, G. R., 49, 53, 63
McAndless, B., 146, 329
McArthur, D. S., 184
McCammon, E. P., 201
McCarney, S. B., 77, 225
McCarthy, M., 228
McClenna, J., 284
McClure, S., 314
McConaughy, S. H., 19, 20, 21, 60, 84, 123, 242
McConnell, S. R., 76, 137, 141, 147, 148, 230,
    258, 295, 319
McElreath, L. H., 227
McFall, R. M., 311
McFarland, H., 263
McFarland, J., 234
McFarland, T., 263
McGain, B., 227
McGregor, P., 178, 181
McKinney, J. D., 314
McKinzey, R. K., 227
McKnew, D., 122
McMahon, R. J., 61, 62, 73, 74, 222, 223, 224,
    228, 229, 231
McNamara, J. R., 343
McNamee, G. D., 102
McNeil, C. B., 227
McNeish, T. J., 188, 189, 190, 191

McReynolds, P., 153
Meador, A. E., 316
Meagher, R. B., Jr., 162
Meehl, P., 49
Merenda, P. F., 80
Merrell, K. W., 20, 21, 63, 66, 73, 74, 88, 93, 160,
    174, 178, 225, 244, 262, 263, 300, 308, 309,
    310, 312, 314, 319, 320, 321, 324, 333, 337, 338,
    345, 346, 349, 356, 380
Merritt, K. A., 123
Merz, J. N., 21, 309, 314
Messick, S., 17
Metzler, A., 384
MHS Staff 88
Michael, K. D., 174, 243, 262
Milberger, S., 219
Milich, R., 136, 137, 144, 146, 148, 149, 219
Miller, D., 163
Miller, P. M., 315
Miller, S. M., 245, 247, 248, 255, 257
Millon, T., 162, 164
Minke, K. M., 34
Monachesi, E. D., 167
Moody, S. C., 378, 379
Mooney, K. C., 234
Moreno, J. L., 135, 138
Morgan, C. D., 182
Morris, R. J., 247
Morrison, P., 146
Morrow, C. A., 371, 373, 374, 376
Morten, G., 368
Muir, S., 135
Mulick, J., A.,
Mullin, E., 227
Murphy, L. B., 123, 227
Murray, C., 360
Murray, H. A., 182, 183
Murray, T. H., 15

N

Naglieri, J. A., 77, 188, 189, 190, 191
National Association of School Psychologists, 14, 363
Navarro, J. B., 122
Neale, J., 148
Nelson, C. M., 35, 93
Nelson, R. O., 94, 235
Nezu, A. M., 11
Nishida, C., 365
Nitz, K., 220
Noam, G. G., 174
Noemi, S., 294
Northrup, J., 50
Nussbaum, B. R., 227
Nuttall, E. V., 32

O

O'Connor, P., 294
O'Gorman, G., 281
O'Leary, K. D., 64
O'Neil, R. E., 316, 320
Obrzut, J. E., 182, 183, 185
Oden, S. L., 142, 310

SUBJECT INDEX

A

Acculturation, 365–368
Adaptive behavior, general issues and definitions, 309–311
Affectivity, positive and negative, 252
Analogue observation, 51–52
Applied behavior analysis, 4
Assent doctrine, 15
Assessment Bias, 362
Assessment of Interpersonal Relations, 329–330
Assessment referrals, understanding and clarifying, 9–10
  sources influencing referrals, 9–10
Attention Deficit Disorders Evaluation Scales, 225–226
Autism Diagnostic Interview, 284–285
Autism Diagnostic Observation Schedule, 283–284

B

Behavior Assessment System for Children, 77–81, 160–162, 342–344
Behavior Coding System, 60–61
Behavior Observation Scale, 285
Behavior rating scales, general issues, 72–77, 93–95
  advantages, 74
  for assessing externalizing problems, 224–228
  for assessing internalizing problems, 256–270
  for assessing social skills, 319–326
  for assessing young children, 342–350
  best practices, 93
  and cultural diversity, 379–380
  decision-making, 94–95
  definitions and foundations, 72–74
  measurement and technical issues, 76–77
  problems, 74–76
Behaviorism, 4
Behavior recording techniques, inappropriate, 66
Behavioral Assertiveness Test, 315–316
Behavioral Avoidance Test, 255
Behavioral dimensions approach to classification, 37–40, 212–214, 242, 276–277
Behavioral interviewing, 114–110
Behavioral observation and decision making, 68–69
Behavioral observation, general methods, 50–53
  analogue observation, 51–52
  naturalistic observation, 50–51
  self-monitoring, 52–53
Behavioral observation and cultural diversity, 378–379
Behavioral observation of externalizing problems, 222–224
Behavioral observation of internalizing problems, 254–256
Behavioral observation of social skills, 315–319
Behavioral observation of young children, 341–342
Bender–Gestalt Test, 195–199
Biased expectations in behavioral observation, 67

C

Caregiver-Teacher Report Form for Ages 2–5,
Child Assessment Schedule, 122–123
Child Behavior Checklist, 37–38, 81–85, 344–345
  Direct Observation Form, 60
Childhood Autism Rating Scale, 285–286
Child's Game/Parent's Game, 61–62
Children's Apperception Test, 184
Children's Depression Inventory, 259–262
Children's Depression Rating Scale, 257–258
Class Play (sociometric procedure), 146